TRAVELLERS
Literary Companion

EASTERN & CENTRAL EUROPE

James Naughton

PASSPORT BOOKS
a division of *NTC Publishing Group*
Lincolnwood, Illinois USA

Published by Passport Books
a division of NTC Publishing Group
4255 West Touhy Avenue
Lincolnwood (Chicago), Illinois
60646-1975

ISBN 0-8442-8969-8
Library of Congress Catalog Card Number: on file

First published by In Print Publishing Ltd.
9 Beaufort Terrace
Brighton BN2 2SU, UK

Typeset by MC Typeset
Printed by Bell & Bain, Glasgow

Also available in the Traveller's Literary Companion series:
South and Central America
Africa
Japan
The India Subcontinent
South-east Asia

SERIES FOREWORD

This series of *Traveller's Literary Companions* is the series I have been looking for all my travelling life. Discovering new writers and new countries is one of the greatest pleasures we know, and these books will greatly increase the enjoyment of all who consult them. Each volume is packed with scholarly and entertaining historical, geographical, political and above all literary information. A country lives through its literature, and we have here an illustrated survey not only of a country's own writers, but also of the views of foreigners, explorers, tourists and exiles. The only problem I foresee is that each volume will bring about a compulsive desire to book a ticket on the next flight out.

The writers take us back in the past to each country's cultural origins, and bring us right up to the present with extracts from novels, poems and travel writings published in the 1980s and 1990s. The chapter introductions and the biographical information about the writers are invaluable, and will give any traveller an easy and immediate access to the past and present state of each nation. Conversation with hosts, colleagues or strangers on trains will be greatly assisted. An enormous amount of work has gone into the compiling and annotating of each volume, and the balance of fact and comment seems to me to be expertly judged.

Margaret Drabble

LIST OF MAPS

CONTENTS

CONTRIBUTORS

George Cushing is Emeritus Professor of Hungarian Language and Literature at the School of Slavonic and East European Studies, University of London. He has written widely in both English and Hungarian on Hungarian literature. He has also translated a number of Hungarian classics, including works by Ady, Gárdonyi, Illyés, Móricz and Petőfi.

Dennis Deletant is Reader in Romanian Studies at the School of Slavonic and East European Studies, University of London. He is the author of many articles on Romanian history and culture and has published two manuals on the language. His most recent publication is a study of the Ceauşescu regime.

Celia Hawkesworth is Senior Lecturer in Serbo–Croat at the School of Slavonic and East European Studies, University of London. She teaches the literatures of the Serbo–Croat speaking areas of former Yugoslavia. Her particular interests include contemporary women's writing and translating fiction.

George Malcolm Hyde is Senior Lecturer in English and Comparative Literature at the University of East Anglia. He has spent four years teaching at Polish universities (Lublin and Kraków), and has published numerous essays on Polish literature and translations from Polish literature. His books include *Vladimir Nabokov: America's Russian Novelist* and *D.H. Lawrence and the Art of Translation*. He is currently translating Krzysztof Miklaszewski's memoir of Kantor, and writing a study of Russian Formalism.

James Naughton was born and brought up in Edinburgh and now teaches Czech and Slovak at the University of Oxford (St Edmund Hall). He is the translator from Czech of Bohumil Hrabal's *The Little Town Where Time Stood Still* and Miroslav Holub's *The Jingle Bell Principle*, of lesser known writers in magazine and anthology contributions (such as Alexandra Berková, the poet Sylva Fischerová and neglected Slovak writers Ján Johanides, Dušan Mitana, Rudolf Sloboda and Pavel Vilikovský). He is also the author of the beginner's textbook *Colloquial Czech* and is now writing *Colloquial Slovak*.

Krystyna Stamirowska studied English and Philosophy at the Jagiellonian University, Kraków. She is currently Deputy Director and Head of the Twentieth Century English Literature Section at the Institute of English, Jagiellonian University, where she teaches Modern English Literature. She is author of a critical edition of D.H. Lawrence's *Letters* in Polish translation, of *Representations of Reality in the Post-War English Novel 1957–75*, and of numerous articles on British writers.

Belin Tonchev is an author and translator of poetry, films and prose from and into English. He studied English Philology at the St Kliment Ohridski University of Sofia. He lived in the UK between 1990 and 1992. He has written articles for periodicals in Bulgaria and the UK, and has contributed to the translation of four anthologies of Bulgarian poetry published in the UK. At present, he is proprietor and managing director of BELS & BELIN language centre in Sofia.

Using the Companion

Each country (or area in the case of former Yugoslavia) has its own chapter, subdivided into four sections: (1) a general Introduction to the country and its literature, with supporting historical and cultural background; (2) a Booklist giving details of English versions of works mentioned in the Introduction or extracted; (3) Extracts from writers focusing on particular places or the country in general; (4) Biographies of authors, including those extracted, with a stress on modern writers available in translation.

The **Extracts** are arranged by place, alphabetically, and each has a number to make it easy to locate from elsewhere in the chapter. A quick list of published sources can be found in the **Booklist**, where the Extract numbers are highlighted in bold type. Fuller references are included under 'Acknowledgments and Citations' at the end of the book.

Title dates given in the Introductions and Biographies normally indicate the first editions of the original works (or writing dates for manuscripts, occasionally dates of premières for plays). (In the Booklists such dates are given in square brackets after the title.)

The **symbol** ◊ after an author's name indicates that there is a biographical entry. Where this entry is in another chapter, this is indicated after the symbol, which is then printed in parentheses: eg 'Eminescu (◊ Romania).'

Bold type is used throughout to highlight references to particular places, such as cities and towns, museums, writers' houses, and so on.

There is a general **index** of authors and other significant personal names at the end of the book.

INTRODUCTION

What is Eastern Europe? What is Central Europe? There is no unambivalent answer to this double question. 'Eastern Europe' is clearly perceived as 'not' Western Europe: for several decades the 'Iron Curtain' was the clearly recognized geopolitical border between the two. Another, rather more historical definition might be that of the 'lands between': between Germany and Russia (or the former Soviet Union), south of the Baltic and north of Greece. The latter definition matches quite well the conception of this book, which offers a brief literary–geographical tour through Poland, the Czech Republic, Slovakia, Hungary, Romania, Bulgaria, the lands of former Yugoslavia, and Albania. (Readers will notice another binding factor: the role of the Danube and its tributaries in most of this area.)

That 'Central Europe', which also appears in our title, or 'Mitteleuropa', is hard to measure (where is Europe's eastern border?), but it eloquently insists on the non-peripherality of its (somewhat loosely defined!) area as a kind of crossroads between east and west, north and south; it is most favoured by those people who like to invoke the cultural inheritance of the former Habsburg Monarchy (Austrians, Czechs, Poles . . .). Prague is west of Vienna, and so is Ljubljana in Slovenia . . .

Much of the multilingual area covered by this volume was dominated, for several centuries until 1918, by two great multinational empires: the Habsburg and Ottoman Empires; other parts were ruled by Prussia and Tsarist Russia. In religion the area is traditionally divided between Catholic (and Protestant) Christian to the west and north, and Orthodox Christian to the south and east, with Islam maintaining a presence in the south, from Bosnia to the Black Sea. Most of its languages belong to the Slavonic group, and are closely related: Polish, Czech and Slovak, Bulgarian and Macedonian, Slovene and Serbo–Croat. Others are emphatically different: Romanian (akin to Italian and Latin), Hungarian (distantly related to Finnish), and Albanian (Indo–European, unlike Hungarian, but also very much on its own). Even where languages are closely related, however, the area is full of ethnic disunity, tension and actual conflict (as warfare in former Yugoslavia all too painfully shows). However, the economic, political and, indeed, cultural resemblance created by these countries' experience of Communist regimes is not going to disappear overnight: for better or for worse, this makes the area 'Eastern European' from the point of view of the outside world, particularly 'the West'.

Each of our brief sketches of these countries' literatures, accompanied by some historical background, is followed by a selection of extracts depicting places and environments, combining, we hope, topographical atmosphere with literary interest. Each contributor has taken an independent approach, within this framework, but the result is more or less a survey of Eastern European literature as a whole.

In spite of the fact that the literatures of these countries are comparatively little read in English-speaking countries (except for one or two authors), a surprising quantity of this writing is available in translation: more, at any rate, than most would imagine. (A little test: can you name two authors – on second thoughts, one – from each of the countries covered in this volume?) Occasionally we have supplied our own versions of extracts, but basically this volume seeks to present the variety of what *is*, rather than what is *not*, available in English. A few pieces have also been included from visiting authors (such as Byron, Trollope, Lear and Olivia Manning).

You might like me now to provide you with some pat generalizations about the merits and genius of this assembled bundle of writing: but I'm not really going to try. It's hard to do even for just one of the literatures. For Czech literature one sometimes likes to talk seductively about inimitable qualities of black, whimsical, absurd humour – a kind of plebeian adaptation to imposed regimes, political impotence, and fossilized establishments, but I have my doubts. This picture (even assuming its validity) depends of course on a highly restricted range of authors. A different selection would easily produce a literature swamped in sentimentality, lyricism and mysticism, or full of earnest, moralizing social tracts. The same would doubtless apply to tempting generalizations about the other literatures, upon which I feel even less qualified to speak.

There are of course, as has been said, shared culture-shaping factors. For several decades this century all these countries went through the experience of living under Communist regimes (with great initial enthusiasm on the part of some writers). Several were previously part of a Habsburg culture (whatever exactly that means), while others spent centuries under the Ottoman yoke (a favoured cliché), with cultural isolation, lack of printed books, and low levels of literacy. Frequent lack of political autonomy or statehood, or threats to these, meant that writers were given greater national status than their counterparts generally received in Britain or North America. Writers were looked upon as 'the conscience of the nation', as 'teachers of the nation'; they found themselves expected to cultivate national mythologies and bolster self-esteem.

The merits of an author's work always lie in its particularities, in its detailed individuality, on some level or other. Such qualities are hard enough to convey at all, in any analysis, never mind in the context of broad general surveys. To what extent this volume succeeds in presenting writers' work in an individual way, supplementing description with extracts, it must be up to the reader to judge.

I conclude by thanking, not only my contributors, for their hard work and for putting up with my editing, but also our patient, long-suffering publisher, John Edmondson, without whom this book would never have happened.

James Naughton

Pronunciation Guide

The following rules of thumb should help in producing recognizable versions of names and titles (for those who would like to attempt such a task!).

Vowels

a, e, i (and y), o, u – 'l<u>a</u>, l<u>e</u>t, l<u>i</u>t, l<u>o</u>t, l<u>oo</u>t'.

With acute accents mostly pronounced longer: á, é, í, ó, ú (and ů).

Polish ó 'l<u>oo</u>t'; nasal vowels ą 'av<u>an</u>t, <u>on</u>(g)' and ę '<u>en</u>(g)'.

Czech ě = roughly '<u>ye</u>h'; Slovak ä = e, ô = uo.

Hungarian ü like French t<u>u</u> or German Gl<u>ü</u>ck, ö like German k<u>ö</u>nnen; both lengthened in ű, ő; short a like 'ch<u>a</u>lk'; long é like Scottish n<u>a</u>me, German f<u>e</u>hlen.

Romanian ă short '<u>ag</u>o', î/â lips tenser, more closed; final -i mostly a non-syllabic 'y'.

Albanian ë '<u>ag</u>o' (final -ë may be silent); y somewhat like German d<u>ü</u>nn.

Consonants

('Soft(ened)' means roughly adding a 'y' sound to the consonant.)

c generally '<u>ts</u>etse' (Romanian 'k', but '<u>ch</u>in' in ci-, ce-)
č, cs, cz, ç '<u>ch</u>in'; 'softened' in ć (and Polish ci-)
ch generally like Scottish 'lo<u>ch</u>'
d', Ď '<u>d</u>uty'
dj, đ '<u>j</u>uice'
dh Albanian '<u>th</u>e'
g '<u>g</u>o' generally (Romanian gi-, ge- '<u>g</u>ene')
gy, gj '<u>d</u>uty'
j '<u>y</u>ellow' (Romanian 'plea<u>s</u>ure')
l', lj soft '<u>l</u>urid'
ly Hungarian '<u>y</u>ellow'
ł Polish '<u>w</u>ood'

ĺ   Slovak long (vocalic) l
ň, ń, nj   soft 'o<u>n</u>ion'
q   'kv' (Albanian soft '<u>ch</u>in')
ř   Czech 'Dvo<u>ř</u>ák', between trilled r and 'plea<u>s</u>ure'
rz   Polish 'plea<u>s</u>ure'
ŕ   Slovak long (vocalic) r
s   's' (but Hungarian 'sh')
š, ş, sz   'sh' (but Hungarian sz = 's'); softened in ś (and Polish si-)
sh   Albanian '<u>sh</u>in'
t', Ť   '<u>t</u>une'
ţ   '<u>ts</u>etse'
th   Albanian '<u>th</u>in'
w   'v'
x   Albanian 'foo<u>ds</u>' (otherwise like English)
xh   Albanian 'jam', eg Ho<u>xh</u>a
ž, ż, zs   'plea<u>s</u>ure'; softened in ź (and Polish zi-)
zh   Albanian 'plea<u>s</u>ure'

Cyrillic transcription

Bulgarian, Macedonian and Serbian share the Cyrillic alphabet, used by Orthodox Slavs and related to the Greek. For Serbian and Macedonian we adhere to standard (Yugoslav) Roman transcription, using č, dj, ć, š, ž, as listed above.

Bulgarian is transcribed with ou = 'l<u>oo</u>t', u = roughly 'c<u>u</u>t', ch = '<u>ch</u>in', sh = '<u>sh</u>in', zh = 'plea<u>s</u>ure', and h = 'lo<u>ch</u>' (as in Andrei Danchev *et al*, *An English Dictionary of Names, Spelling and Pronunciation*, Naouka i izkoustvo, Sofia, 1989).

BOOKLIST – General Reading

Child of Europe: A New Anthology of East European Poetry, Michael March, ed, Penguin, London, 1990.

Contemporary East European Poetry: An Anthology, expanded edition, Emery George, ed, Oxford University Press, Oxford and New York, 1993.

Cross Currents: A Yearbook of Central European Culture, Ladislav Matejka, ed, Nos 10–12, Yale University Press, New Haven, CT, and London, 1991–93; Nos 1–9, University of Michigan, Department of Slavic Languages and Literatures, Ann Arbor, MI, 1982–90. (Contains various translations, as well as articles.)

Description of a Struggle: The Picador Book of Contemporary East European Prose, Michael March, ed, Picador, London, 1994.

The Everyman Companion to East European Literature, Robert B. Pynsent and S.I. Kanikova, ed, Dent, London, 1993.

Magris, Claudio, *Danube: A Sentimental Journey from the Source to the Black Sea* [1986], Patrick Creagh, trans (from Italian), Collins Harvill, London, 1990/ Farrar, Straus and Giroux, New York, 1990.

The Penguin Companion to Literature, Vol 2, *European*, Anthony Thorlby, ed, Penguin, London, 1969.

The Poetry of Survival: Post-War Poets of Central and Eastern Europe, Daniel Weissbort, ed, Anvil Press Poetry, London, 1991.

Rothschild, Joseph, *East Central Europe Between the Two World Wars (A History of East Central Europe*, Vol 9), University of Washington Press, Seattle, WA, and London, 1974.

Storm: New Writing from East and West, Joanna Labon, ed, Nos 1–8, now distributed by Carcanet Press, Manchester, 1991–94.

Wandycz, Piotr S., *The Price of Freedom: A History of East Central Europe from the Middle Ages to the Present*, Routledge, London and New York, 1992.

Writers from Eastern Europe, Celia Hawkesworth, ed, Book Trust, London, 1991.

Zeman, Z.A.B., *The Making and Breaking of Communist Europe*, Blackwell, Oxford, 1991.

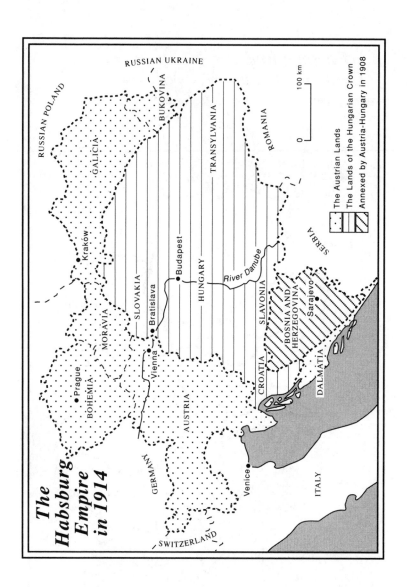

The Habsburg Empire in 1914

RUSSIAN UKRAINE

RUSSIAN POLAND

GALICIA

BUKOVINA

TRANSYLVANIA

ROMANIA

100 km

0

The Austrian Lands

The Lands of the Hungarian Crown

Annexed by Austria-Hungary in 1908

• Kraków

• Budapest

HUNGARY

River Danube

SERBIA

SLOVAKIA

MORAVIA

Bratislava

SLAVONIA

• Prague

BOHEMIA

Vienna

AUSTRIA

CROATIA

BOSNIA AND HERZEGOVINA

• Sarajevo

DALMATIA

GERMANY

• Venice

ITALY

SWITZERLAND

Eastern and Central Europe

ESTONIA
LATVIA
LITHUANIA
BELARUS
Baltic Sea
GERMANY
POLAND
UKRAINE
CZECH REP.
SLOVAKIA
MOLDOVA
AUSTRIA
HUNGARY
SLOVENIA*
ROMANIA
CROATIA*
BOSNIA-HERCEGOVINA*
SERBIA*
ITALY
MONTENEGRO*
Black Sea
BULGARIA
ALBANIA
MACEDONIA*
GREECE
TURKEY
Mediterranean Sea

Heavy borders indicate countries included in this volume.
Asterisk indicates inclusion in the chapter
'The lands of former Yugoslavia'.

0   250 km

POLAND

Krystyna Stamirowska
and George Hyde

'And this familiar landscape associated with the days without thought and without sorrow, this land the charm of which he felt without even looking at it soothed his pain, like the presence of an old friend who sits silent and disregarded by one in some dark hour of life.'
Joseph Conrad, Prince Roman

The eminent poet and critic Donald Davie (who has published distinguished 'free' translations of excerpts from the Polish Romantic poet Adam Mickiewicz) once remarked that a major difference between the USA and Europe is that the USA has geography where Europe has history. He meant that American writing, in its un-usual extensiveness, traces the contours of the body of the Amer-ican continent in a 'frontiersman' way, charting virgin lands that remain to be explored, and places that have no special name or his-torical connotations, but remain to be incorporated into some body of myth. The capacity of the American mind to go on generating such myth is, from this perspective, a sort of compensation for the apparent lack of historical depth that both the continent and the culture arguably still share (when seen from a Eurocentric perspective, of course).

Poland (population about 38.3 million) is an unusually interesting instance of a country which has both geography *and* history in abundance. It has generated rich mythologies out of 'virgin' frontiers which have kept shifting and being redefined, have been lost and recovered (or remembered), only to be lost again; and the mythologies still go on proliferating. Yet the nation that manifests all of this troubled, and troubling, indeterminacy is located at the 'heart of Europe' looking both west and east, with a people intensely sensitive to

1

developments in European history and culture, new and old, and exceptionally well informed about their own history in relation to the larger European and world context.

At the time of writing, Poland's frontiers from the end of the second world war still hold. This historical fact, however, cannot be made to seem either neutral or inevitable, since the once-mighty Soviet Union deliberately pushed Poland westwards to create a more effective buffer against Germany as the war was ending, without any opposition from the Western allies. In doing this, Russia deprived Poland of large areas of its territories, lands that had been saturated in Polish culture since the sixteenth century at least. Of course, Poland's historical claims to Lithuania and parts of the Ukraine may not be as clear-cut as its right to hold that other 'disputed' outpost, Gdańsk (see Extract 2); but there can be no disputing the fact that Wilno (Vilnius) and Lwów (Lvov) were comprehensively Polonized over hundreds of years, and that this situation was brought to an end only with the forceable relocation of the Polish population in the newly Polonized (or once again Polish) Western territories at the end of the second world war.

THEMES OF EXILE, LOSS AND DIASPORA

Thus a town like **Wrocław** (one of those to which Poland has a disputed ethnic claim: in its other guise, as Breslau, it was historically German, though there was a notable Slav presence from earlier times) was resettled with people evicted from the Polish Ukraine (mostly) after the second world war. They brought a special sort of (Polish) energy to the town, which still houses what is left of Jerzy Grotowski's ◊ world-famous Laboratory Theatre. It is for such complex reasons as these, perhaps unparalleled elsewhere in Europe, that the greatest Polish national poet, Adam Mickiewicz ◊, begins his finest work (and surely the most convincing Romantic pseudo-epic in European literature), *Pan Tadeusz*, 1834 (Extract 10) with an encomium not to Poland but to Lithuania: a resounding statement of those themes of exile, memory, and loss which continue to haunt Polish writing to the present day, sometimes as straightforward nostalgia, but often in very remarkable, 'modernistic', transformations. The Nobel Prize-winning poet, novelist, and critic Czesław Miłosz ◊ finds in 'the Lithuanian theme' and all its ramifications a repository of tales both sentimental and sinister (eg in *Dolina Issy* (*The Issa Valley*), 1955, beautifully filmed by Tadeusz Konwicki).

From another angle, Witold Gombrowicz ◊, a difficult, immensely sophisticated writer still neglected and underrated in the Anglo-Saxon world, has found in similar themes rich material for some of the most brilliant and 'abstract' black comedy in post-modern writing. The fact

Adam Mickiewicz

that a traveller can now visit **Wilno (Vilnius)** quite easily is bound to affect the Polish literary perspective on this 'sacred' city; but some other places which, if not equally sacred, were of enormous historical and cultural significance, have literally gone for ever. The Jewish Cemetery in **Drohobycz** (Extract 1), for example, where Bruno Schulz ⟁ is buried, has been built over: and thereby hangs a much longer tale. It is now comparatively easy (but beware of Ukrainean border guards!) for Poles (and the rest of us) to visit **Lwów**, too: but Lwów now has a fairly insignificant Polish population, in terms of numbers, and although the Polish language persists (and there is even some reason to believe that it is growing!) it is not very widespread. This, however, is not the case with Wilno, where there is already, in these post-Communist years, something of an ethnic minorities problem in relation to the substantial Polish population and its language, and status: a problem exacerbated by the chequered and turbulent progress of Lithuanian nationalism.

One might suppose that a preoccupation with the loss of such 'colonies' might have produced a colourful but rather backward-looking literature, similar to much of what comes to us from British India or the Far East, for example; but this is not the case. It is true that *Pan Tadeusz* is essentially a lament for an idealized *szlachta* (gentry) culture, but its melancholy is matched by its sensuous concreteness and sharp satirical spirit; and in this combination of Romantic nostalgia and tougher, more hard-headed elements, the world-view it projects is comparable to the culture of the Anglo-Irish gentry celebrated by W.B. Yeats, which is not exactly marginal. What Mickiewicz's text 'really' records is thus the passing of a moral and social order, with (as in the case of Yeats) a genuine sense of tragedy. In addition, it represents one of the most successful attempts in Romantic verse to draw upon living traditions of folklore, folk narrative, and rural culture – in doing which it is less subjective than Wordsworth, less antiquarian than Scott, and much more 'rooted' than Byron, with all of whom it shares common features.

The work of Mickiewicz still contains, and despite the current victory of 'free market' internationalism will always contain, many powerful rallying-cries for Poles. Productions of his visionary closet-drama *Dziady* (*Forefathers' Eve*), 1823 seem inevitably to coincide with political upheavals. We have not found any confirmation of rumours that the poem *Pan Tadeusz* (for reasons of censorship) was once published in Poland without the opening apostrophe (it should be noted that the opening words of the translated version we have chosen here (Extract 10) – 'my motherland' – are in Polish actually *ojczyzno moja*, 'my fatherland' – an interesting *topos* for Freudians, perhaps!). At least two good complete English versions of *Pan Tadeusz* are easily available; but unfortunately, where *Dziady* is concerned, the English reader has to be content with versions that do not do justice to the original; and there is no version that could possibly be considered actable.

The literary traveller may not feel inclined to go outside Poland in pursuit of Polish places; but something of the wildness, strangeness, and deeper harmonies of Mickiewicz's great poem may still be felt within the territorial limits of present-day Poland in (for example) the **Bieszczady Mountains**, as well as in parts of the **Tatra** (Extracts 13 and 14), or in the **Mazurian Lakes**. The **Vistula**, too, is in some places as atmospheric and archaic as the Niemen. The territory around **Kazimierz Dolny**, for instance, might (if not for the tourists!) be said to have a Lithuanian 'feel' to it – and the Polish–Lithuanian Act of Union (1569) was signed in nearby **Lublin**, a city so far east (or, as a Polish friend corrected, so far to the centre!) that it seems to be off-limits for Poles who do not actually come from the area, despite the extraordinary appeal of the decrepit beauty of its **Old Town** (see Extract 7).

THE POLISH–JEWISH EXPERIENCE

The themes of exile, diaspora, loss, and the 'aesthetics of absence' that accompanies them, make the Polish cultural experience strangely akin to the Jewish, and constitute a significant part of its disturbing modernity (despite the persistent Romantic elements). This will surprise those who have heard only of the animosity between the two races who had lived in such close proximity for so many generations (see Norwid ◊ on the complexity of the relationship, Extract 9). The facts about 'Polish anti-semitism' are, as usual, much more complex than the myths and rumours. Over hundreds of years of history, the two cultures entered into a symbiotic relationship that is evidenced materially in a wide spectrum of the cultural domain, from cuisine to writing and music. Assimilated Jews have made an enormous contribution to Polish literary life. Some very eminent Polish writers turn out, on closer inspection, to have had Jewish blood, or to have been Jews writing under assumed Polish names. What still needs to be assessed, however, is the intellectual formation of the culture of the *shtetl* (Jewish village), which was effectively wiped out by the Nazis. Post-holocaust Jewish history in Poland has been seriously distorted by the sometimes wrong-headed (however heartfelt it may be) urge to make reparations. To turn a synagogue into a rather bleak 'official' sort of museum, and then to feature prominently in it large photographs of SS-men rounding up Jews, as happened in **Kraków**, for instance, is *not* what is needed now. However, the current flood of new publications about Jewish culture, and re-issues of important earlier books as well, bear witness to a profound spiritual change which is very welcome; and the Kraków synagogue-museum has changed utterly.

The literary tourist, even if he or she does not get as far as **Drohobycz**, could do a lot worse than to turn to the pages of Schulz ◊ and of Isaac Bashevis Singer ◊ for an understanding of what the life of Polish Jews, especially in the East, felt like; and our tourist will find in Schulz, for example, some remarkably 'modern' elements, especially in the rich flights of fancy that accompany the tragic/grotesque representation of patriarchy, as well as (*cf* Extract 1) the deep (and maybe irrational!) sense of scepticism about material values, and suspicion of the commercial ethic, which is shared by Jews and Poles alike.

The heir to Schulz (and the rightful heir to Polish Modernism in its more avant-garde manifestations) is the major director, *dramaturg* and theorist Tadeusz Kantor ◊, an artist in many fields who was a product of precisely that uneasy Polish–Jewish symbiosis (but expressed by means of the resources of Kraków Modernism) of which we have spoken. In his case, the ubiquitous small Jewish–Catholic Galician town (which might have had many names!) is called **Wielopole**, and it

Bruno Schulz, self-portrait 1919

was his birthplace. Kantor's work, which incorporates major contributions to the modern stage, painting, sculpture, and aesthetic theory
(via the dynamics of the 'happening') is not represented in this volume
because it has proved impossible to excerpt it adequately. His major
text (or theatrical 'score', as he liked to call such things) about his

birthplace, *Wielopole/Wielopole*, is, however, currently available in an English edition which also prints some relevant theoretical materials.

Kantor obsessively deconstructs and reconstructs his theatrical spaces in a Shakespeare-like *Teatrum Mundi* which seems to contain a whole historical culture within one ever-expanding metaphor. His work reminds us of our opening proposition: that Polish culture is characterized throughout by an all-pervasive anxiety about boundaries and spaces. A great (Dada-like) recycler of materials and artistic modes, a master of 'the empty space', Kantor is also engaged in endless dialogues with the cultural past of a profoundly personal and existential kind. Rewriting is for him a sort of game of existential roulette not unlike Mallarmé's famous 'throw of the dice' (*Un coup de dés*, 1897). He worked with (and presided over) a 'family' of actors and actresses, among whom he played (and subverted) the role of the patriarch, the guardian of history, truth, and art. There is also good reason to link his work with Jewish mystic Hassidism, as expounded by Elie Wiesel and Martin Buber. The only other contemporary Polish theatre so closely associated with a particular place is the **Gardzienice** group (based at the village of Gardzienice, near **Lublin**), which uses folk traditions and rituals as the mainstay of its theatrical 'happenings', which it then feeds back into the life of the community.

Kraków

Kantor, however, lived and worked not in the small town of Wielopole but in **Kraków**. Kraków is the capital of Polish cultural life in the sense that, despite its relative smallness (and even, in some respects, its provincialism), it is the ancient seat of the Polish kings, it was established as a bishopric in the year 1000, and it houses the venerable **Jagiellonian University** (the 'Polish Oxford'): it is therefore deeply imbued with the symbolic values of Polish culture, on to which a lively avant-garde was grafted from the *fin-de-siècle* onwards. With its royal castle, **Wawel**, situated on the river, it is rich in legends which have always appealed to the imagination. From the stories of the founder, Krak, and his daughter Wanda, to those devoted to the resistance to Tartar and German invaders, Kraków's legends have inspired poets and artists. Kings and eminent poets are buried in the **crypt** of the Wawel (Extract 3); minor writers are buried in the **Skałka Church**. Outside this church the Bishop of Kraków, St Stanislas, was killed on the orders of King Bolesław the Bold in 1079, in circumstances strongly reminiscent of the conflict between Henry II and Thomas Becket one hundred years later.

During the Renaissance (a stable period in Poland when the arts flourished), the University and the famous Nowodworski School were

Tadeusz Kantor at the Cricot-2 Theatre in Kraków

centres of learning and artistic life: the Royal Court attracted writers and artists from all over Poland, as well as from many European countries, particularly Italy. During a poetic tournament in 1518 the English poet Coxe made a speech in praise of Kraków, entitled *De Laudibus Celeberrimae Academiae Cracoviensis*. Kraków lost some of its splendour in the eighteenth century, and fell into decline after the loss of independence; yet it never ceased to function as a powerful symbol of national life. It was here that Joseph Conrad ◊ spent his early years on returning from Russia, where he had accompanied his father, Apollo Korzeniowski, into exile. Conrad's father died in May 1869, and was buried in **Rakowice cemetery**, where his grave can still be visited. His funeral turned into a great manifestation of patriotic feelings; his son stayed on until 1873, when he decided to leave Poland for good. His early experience, the fate of his family, the sense of doom, the ethos of sacrifice, profoundly impressed his attitudes and his view of reality. Thirty-seven years later he wrote his short story 'Prince Roman' (Extract 8), bearing witness to the persistence of these experiences; but his sense of Poland's existential predicament is all-pervasive in, for example, *Under Western Eyes*, 1911.

Recognized by UNESCO as one of the twelve major historic sites in the world, and outstandingly beautiful, Kraków is literally layered and textured with history and culture. It is honeycombed with courtyards, cellars, passageways, and attics which are currently changing their shapes and their functions in response to the new commercialism, but which will always preserve living traces of the way the city has functioned, over hundreds of years, to nurture literature and the arts (Kantor's theatre, for instance, was housed in a fine cellar which is still in service as a gallery and theatre; and his archives, in a smaller building which belongs to the Church, are in another such atmospheric cellar, with a fascinating little enclosed space behind it). The Nazi Gauleiter of Kraków, Hans Frank, was captivated by the city, and even ignored the commands of his paymasters by refusing to implement its destruction.

At the turn of the century, when Poland was still partitioned between Austria, Prussia, and Russia, as it had been since the late eighteenth century, certain writers and artists put Kraków and its ancient culture on the Polish map in a new way. The most eminent of these was Stanisław Wyspiański ◊, who was born and spent most of his life here. A poet, painter, and playwright who drew freely on folklore and native legends and (not unlike Yeats) worried inordinately about art's relation to 'the people', Wyspiański found in Kraków the quintessence of Polishness. He embodied this with special vividness in a highly imaginative play called *Wesele* (*The Wedding*), 1901. The leading painter of the period, Jacek Malczewski (1854–1929), says in one of his letters: 'Wyspiański often took me to Wawel, and used to say: this is Poland' – a view which, incidentally, he did not altogether share. Wyspiański designed beautiful stained glass windows in the style of Art Nouveau for the **Franciscan Church**, representing figures of God the Father, St Francis, and St Salomea. Kraków provided the inspiration and the setting for a great number of his poems: *The Legend, Casimir the Great, St Stanislas, Boleslaw the Bold*; and for two of his plays, *Wyzwolenie* (*Liberation*), 1903 (Extract 4) and *Akropolis*, 1904. He devoted much energy to exploring the proper medium, and the proper forum, for a new national (but not necessarily nationalistic) art, which would combine the new aestheticism with traditional Polish cultural values. This was the basis of the powerful cultural and political movement known as 'Young Poland'. One of the numerous testimonies to the *Zeitgeist* of the early twentieth century is the famous coffee house called **Jama Michalikowa** in **Floriańska St**, with original decor which brings to mind the days when poets and artists, the founders of the literary cabaret called *Zielony Balonik* ('The Green Balloon') gathered daily. Much of the satirical verse and song caricatured the excesses of the Young Poland movement.

TATRA MOUNTAINS

Kraków's unique cultural significance in this period spilled over into the nearby **Tatra Mountains**, which ever since the eighteenth century had been the focus of different kinds of revivalist sentiments. **Zakopane** (Extract 14), a popular Tatra resort in modern times, attracted writers and artists who sought there a range of different sensations, from a kind of spiritual (though not always entirely ethereal!) mysticism, to an empathy with the 'earthiness' of the unspoiled peasants, who, they hoped, might be counted on for a renewal of those rather nebulous 'values' long since discarded, and regretted, by the urban intelligentsia. Here again, piety, sentiment, and prophecy, go hand in hand with irony, mockery, and nihilism, in characteristic Polish fashion. Such outstanding beauty spots as **Morskie Oko** ('The Eye of the Sea') can hardly leave a visitor indifferent, but it is perhaps a salutary shock to see what Bielecki's ◊ poem of the same name (Extract 12) makes of this shrine which has long since become a tourist attraction.

Among the dozens of writers who bear witness to the peculiar power of the Tatra, Stanisław Ignacy Witkiewicz ◊, nicknamed 'Witkacy', represented here (Extract 14) in a sardonic mood that anticipates Gombrowicz ◊, was a Modernist of very remarkable talents. Playwright, painter, photographer, aesthetician, and philosopher of art, he was a leading figure of the Polish avant-garde. He was very prolific; his most brilliant plays, *W małym dworku* (*In a Small Manor House*), *Szewcy* (*The Shoemakers*), 1931–34, and *Kurka Wodna* (*The Water Hen*), 1921, anticipate the post-war Theatre of the Absurd of Ionesco, Beckett, and Genet, conveying the drama of the human condition through the grotesque, parody, nightmare and dream. His suicide (on 17 September 1939, the day the Soviets invaded Poland), and the very nature of his *oeuvre*, made it impossible for his works to be published or performed until the 'thaw' in 1956, after which he was recognized as perhaps the most important writer of the pre-war Polish avant-garde, and some of his plays became a part of the theatrical canon.

Witkiewicz's perception of the absurdity of existence, and his unique combination of the absurd and the tragic, seemed strikingly appropriate to the post-war reality of Communist-governed Poland. His plays and novels, generated by first-hand experience of the fall of the Russian Tsars and the Bolshevik revolution (he fought as a lieutenant in the White Army), and on the other hand by his conviction of the terminal decadence of European culture, lent themselves to reworkings and transcodings in sharp response (but cleverly oblique, to outwit the censors) to the ubiquitous Soviet presence during the 1960s and 1970s. Kantor's ◊ extremely bold, free way of dealing with his plays, which, as Kantor himself said, are alternately masterly and fatuous, by (as he said) 'mincing' them, worked exceptionally well. Witkacy's dread of the Bolshevik anthill gave him a cult following in Poland; he is still not well enough known in England.

WARSAW

Warsaw is perhaps the hardest city in Poland to come to terms with, and many tourists (like many Poles), despite its new-found (or restored) 'trendiness', and its beautifully rebuilt **Old Town**, find it unprepossessing, grey, and rather uncomfortable. The reasons for this are not far to seek. The contrasts of which Warsaw seems to be made up, and which strike one instantly on arrival, reflect the city's turbulent history and the post-war role imposed on it by the Soviets as the capital of a satellite state. The huge and hideous **Palace of Culture**, Stalin's unwelcome gift, paid for by the Poles, which greets the new arrival and dominates the city, has become associated with Warsaw almost as much as the venerated symbol of the city's capital status, the 350-year-old **Sigismund (Zygmunt) Column** commemorating king Zygmunt III who moved the capital from Kraków in 1596. These two – the statue of the king holding a cross, and the monumental wedding cake structure totally alien to the Polish style – indicate a basic architectural and cultural incongruity, and epitomize the ironies of Polish history. Warsaw, considered the symbol of national identity and heroic resistance (see Extracts 16 and 17), came also to be associated with the drab architecture of the post-war districts, and buildings modelled on the Soviet style.

The city's history, as recorded by poets and writers generally, reflects the condensed history of the nation. It is here that the conspirators of the 1831 November Uprising met, and planned to kill the Russian Grand Duke Konstantin, events which were dramatized by Juliusz Słowacki ◊ in *Kordian*. It is on the slopes of the **Citadel** that Romuald Traugutt, the last leader of the 1863 Uprising, was hanged, together with four others. The **Royal Castle** was the setting for the four-year parliamentary session (1791 onwards) which passed the first European Constitution (the Constitution of May 3rd). The streets of Warsaw had been the scene of heavy fighting against Russian troops during the Kościuszko Insurrection in 1794. The storming of the **Right Bank** (the Praga district) by General Suvorov, an event known as 'the butchery of Praga', has been commemorated by many poets, most notably Mickiewicz in the famous passage of *Pan Tadeusz* known as 'Jankiel's Concert':

Thousands of ever-louder rumblings could be heard
The rhythm of a march, war, an assault, a siege, shots,
The scream of children, the weeping of mothers. The artful bard
So conveyed the horror of the siege, that the rustics shook,
Calling to mind with tears the sufferings
Of the butchery of Praga, which they knew from song and story

Another district, south of **Żoliborz** (originally 'Joli Bord'), **Wola**, was
the scene of the last tragic battle fought during the 1831 Uprising, led
by the lame General Sowiński, who had lost a leg during the
Napoleonic Wars, and, having refused to surrender, died pierced
through by a Russian bayonet. As Słowacki's ◊ famous poem *Sowiński
on the Fortifications of Wola* suggests, Sowiński wanted his resistance to
be imprinted upon the memory of the nation:

> I must perish . . . on the fortifications
> Defending myself to the death with my sword
> Against the enemies of my fatherland
> Let the city remember . . .
> That on this day there fell on the battlements
> The general – with the wooden leg.

The second world war, which came after a twenty-year period of
independence, brought a re-enactment of the nineteenth century
events of heroic struggle and resistance, this time against the Germans.
The Nazi invasion in September 1939, which inaugurated a five-year
occupation of Poland, followed a particularly bloody course in Warsaw.
It was here that the Resistance, coordinated by the Home Army, was
centred; and the repressions and persecution were of a truly terrible
nature. Round-ups and street executions happened daily, and all the
horrors of war were experienced with particular intensity. It was in
Warsaw that the August 1944 Uprising was organized: it lasted for
nearly two months, while the Red Army on the other side of the
Vistula quietly watched the Polish soldiers and civilians bleeding to
death, and the city, in the end, utterly destroyed. Twenty-two
thousand participants, and one hundred and eighty thousand civilians,
were killed during the Uprising, and eighty per cent of the Left Bank of
Warsaw was destroyed. The younger generation, who had been inspired
by Romantic traditions as well as by their sense of duty to their country,
were decimated, and Poland was bled of some of its best talent.
Krzysztof Kamil Baczyński ◊, one of the young poets killed in the
Uprising, who writes in 'Wiatr' ('The Wind'), 1943,

> I am calling to you, stranger
> Who will dig out the white bones
> Once the fighting is over

> You who will be holding my skeleton
> My country's banner

brings to mind Rupert Brooke, the English poet of the first world war. The final cruel irony was that the fate of the city – and of the whole country – sealed by the Yalta agreements, rendered the heroic struggle and the sacrifice futile. After the defeat of the Nazis, Poland was handed over to the Soviets – and the grim post-war reality gradually prevailed. 'What will be left after we die/Is scrap-iron and the hollow mocking laughter of generations to come' – wrote another poet, Tadeusz Borowski ◊, a survivor, who was soon to commit suicide. Twenty million cubic metres of rubble were the most immediately visible effect of the war in Warsaw: but there were other effects which were more tragic, and far more difficult to deal with.

It was in **Żoliborz** – much of which had been destroyed in the nineteenth century to make space for the Russian-built fortifications (the sinister **Warsaw Citadela**, the place of imprisonments, torture, and executions between 1846 and 1914) – that the **St Stanislas Church** was erected. It now contains the grave of yet another latter-day martyr: Father Jerzy Popiełuszko, killed by security police in October 1984. During the years following the imposition of Martial Law his grave, which was turned into a symbol and a Solidarity shrine, became an indispensable item on any itinerary. Ordinary people came in large numbers, as well as foreign diplomats on official visits to a country governed by a discredited Communist regime: thus joining in a symbolic gesture of solidarity with the oppressed nation. Anna Kamieńska ◊ wrote:

> Does it hurt, to flow down with the blood of the Vistula
> And to choke on slime as on a song
> Be bathed in maternal sobs and tears
> And have a red stole spread on your breast
> Does it hurt – to lie in the heart of Poland
> As on a meadow new-mown for Summer.
> Does it hurt – to nod a last blessing
> On your executioners and butchers.

Nine years later, this church is still very much on the map, though now as part of a very different political landscape, and bearing witness to yet another turning point in history, at which a large-scale transformation of life is taking place. The transition from a Communist-imposed regime to a system of political and economic freedom is far too complex to be described briefly; and its implications involve a profound reassessment of all areas of life, including the roles of nationalism and religion. The new freedoms entail a rapidly changing sense of identity, allegiances, and 'belonging'. They also entail new dangers, unknown to a nation united by the existence of one common and easily identified enemy or threat. Warsaw is now the capital of a very different state striving towards a new identity, and is playing a pivotal role in a different and dynamic new political context. Yet whatever the shape it will assume, and regardless of all the transformations of modes of thinking and of lifestyles, it seems certain that the essential stamp of history is impossible to erase, and it will continue to shape Polish life at the deepest levels, the nature of Polish reality, and Polish national consciousness.

This endless capacity for renewal and adjustment is well expressed by Melchior Wańkowicz ◊, writer, war correspondent, and soldier, who left Poland in 1939, fought on many different fronts, and returned twenty years later from a self-imposed exile in the USA. The title of what is probably his most personal and most profound book, *Ziele na Kraterze* (*Wild Flowers Cover the Crater*), 1951, alludes to the fate of his own family, which epitomizes that of the nation, expressing a belief in the power to survive repeated tragedies and massacres, and to be reborn from the ashes each time like the greenery that grows over the still glowing crater of a volcano.

Between Warsaw and the Baltic

The territory north and north-east of Warsaw, leading towards the Baltic Sea and the eastern border with Lithuania, famous for its remarkable landscape (it includes the **Mazurian Lake District**), is also known for its complex and difficult history, the vicissitudes of which are reflected in the changing place names: Malbork–Marienburg, Lidzbark–Heilsberg, Frombork–Frauenberg, Elbląg–Elbing, Gdańsk–Danzig – to mention only a few.

Poles and Germans have lived here for centuries; the processes of both Polonization and Germanization went on with varying degrees of intensity; and the land changed hands more than once while retaining its essentially heterogeneous identity. The language, culture, and architecture are strongly marked by this dual allegiance. The beautiful **Town Hall** in **Orneta**, for instance, a fine example of the German Gothic style, is surrounded by Polish Baroque houses, and **Wolfschanze** (the 'Wolf's Lair'), Hitler's headquarters in **Kętrzyn**, is only twenty miles away from the cathedral of **Święta Lipka**, one of the most outstanding Baroque churches in Poland. The co-existence of the Polish and German heritages, despite the numerous attempts by propaganda on both sides at various times to unsettle it, remains a striking feature of the character of the whole region.

Among many culturally important and architecturally striking places, two are of special significance: **Frombork** and **Lidzbark**. Frombork was the seat of the Warmian bishopric, established in 1243, and Lidzbark became a residence of the Bishops of Warmia after 1350. It was in Frombork that Copernicus, astronomer and doctor of canon law and of medicine, spent about thirty years of his life as Canon of the Warmian Chapter: the greater part of *De Revolutionibus* was written here, and it was here that he died and was buried. Among the bishops of Warmia, many of whom were eminent scholars, politicians, and writers (eg Marcin Kromer, Jan Dantyszek, and Stanisław Hozjusz), one name is particularly important – that of Ignacy Krasicki ◊, poet and politician, closely connected with the Royal Court in Warsaw, and involved in political reform. Consecrated as Bishop of Warmia in 1766, he moved to Lidzbark (though still a frequent visitor to Warsaw), and this is where most of his poems, fables, and satires were written.

The **Bishop's Palace** in Lidzbark, a Gothic castle with a large Baroque extension which was a centre of the intellectual life of Warmia, was made even more splendid by Krasicki, a patron to musicians and painters, who added numerous precious items to the library and the art collection, built famous gardens, and added a classical extension in the form of an Orangery. With Lidzbark being incorporated into Prussia after the first Partition in 1772, the Bishop's position became increasingly difficult; the fact is reflected in the well known poem by Stanisław Trembecki ◊, who addresses Krasicki, deploring the tragic changes:

> Prince! The branch of the bright house
> To which you return honours greater than those you received,
> You who love your country and are well-loved in return
> Why do we have to seek you outside your native land?

Life, which went on despite political traumas, provided a final paradoxical turn: Krasicki, whose office required visits to Berlin, died in the capital of the hostile power, Russia, in 1801, and his body was brought back 28 years later.

Warmia and **Mazuria**, as well as the adjacent territory including Königsberg (Królewiec, Kaliningrad), were originally inhabited by the Baltic Prussian tribes, which were pagan, and were the object of Polish attempts at conversion and subjugation in the eleventh and twelfth centuries. In 1226, Prince Konrad of Mazovia, who was looking for allies, installed there the Teutonic Order, which had been expelled from Hungary. However, he got more than he bargained for: having obtained (through forgery) the Papal investiture over so-called East Prussia (which included Warmia) in 1234, the Teutonic Knights gained absolute control of the territory, captured by ruthless methods, by the end of the century. The original tribes were now replaced by the

German colonizers, still called Prussians, though ethnically different. The Thirteen Years' War, fought by the Teutonic Knights against Poland, which ended with the Treaty of Toruń (1466), resulted in Warmia, Malbork, and Elbląg, together with the Gdańsk region, now known as Royal Prussia, being incorporated into Poland, while the Teutonic Order state (now called Ducal Prussia) became a fiefdom.

The Polish colonization of these territories intensified from that moment, and the Polish cultural influence grew stronger. This situation continued until after the wars with Sweden (1600–35 and 1655–60) had weakened Poland sufficiently for Ducal Prussia to seek independence, which ultimately led to its incorporation into the Kingdom of Prussia (1701). After the first partition of Poland (1772), Royal Prussia (including Warmia, Malbork, and Elbląg) was officially incorporated into Prussia: a state of affairs which obtained until the first world war. One hundred and twenty years of intense Germanization, and attempts to eradicate Polish identity, were largely successful: a plebiscite organized in 1920, which coincided with the Polish–Soviet War (when Poland struggled to resist the Red Army's advance towards Warsaw, a moment fully exploited by German propaganda) came down in favour of German rule: so that Warmia and Mazuria remained in German hands for another twenty-five years, except for a few small areas along the Vistula.

Yalta deprived Poland of one-fifth of its pre-war territory, but granted it the former East Prussia, except for Königsberg and a large area around it. However, the ratio of Poles to Germans in East Prussia was by this time 1:3, many Germans having fled earlier. As part of the resettlement programme devised by Stalin to perpetuate conflict and hatred, and agreed upon by the allies, Poles from the eastern territories of the pre-war Republic were moved westwards, while the Germans were transferred to Germany. All in all, 16.5 million people were uprooted, leaving many open wounds. In his poem 'The Tree of Life', Klemens Oleksik ◊ writes:

> Swept away by the noise of the front
> people born here
> crouch among the forest trees
> cannot recover
> those who love settlements
> dream of leaving
> will not enclose their yards
> whitewash their houses
> mend pans
> offices determine the degree of kinship
> between those who are abroad

and those who have left their dead behind
buried in small evangelical churchyards.

Now, fifty years on, one can see signs of a new awareness reflected in
writing on both sides of the border: the analysis of the experience of the
present and the past, assessed from the two perspectives, and articulated in the two languages, gives evidence of a new, deeper understanding of both geography and history. As Johannes Bobrowski ◊, a German
writer born in **Tylza** (near Lithuania) into a family of mixed German,
Polish, and Lithuanian extraction, said:

> I come from a family in which the Polish element was mixed with
> the German. I grew up with daily contact with the Lithuanians,
> the Jews, with simple people and small gentry. I remember the
> fact that my genealogy can be traced a thousand years back. I
> therefore have a right – based on my own existence – without
> recourse to imagination – to confront the peoples of the East with
> the Germans – the race to which I belong through my upbringing
> and my language.

BOOKLIST

*The following selection includes the ex-
tracted titles in this chapter as well as
those mentioned in the introduction
which are available in English and other
titles for further reading. In general,
paperback editions are given when possible. The editions cited are not necessarily the only ones available. For most of
the extracted works, the original publisher can be found in 'Acknowledgments and Citations' at the end of the
volume, as can the exact location of the
extracts and the editions from which
they are taken. Extract numbers are
highlighted in bold. Square brackets denote the date of publication of the work
in its original language.*

Andrzejewski, Jerzy, *Ashes and Diamonds* [1948], D. J. Walsh,
trans, Penguin, London, 1965.

(Basis of Andrzej Wajda's film,
1958.)

*Ariadne's Thread: Polish Women
Poets*, Susan Bassnett and Piotr
Kuhiwczak, ed, Forest Books,
London, 1988/Dufour, Chester
Springs, PA, 1988.

Bentchev, Ivan, Eugeniusz Duda,
Dorota Leszczyńska, Michaela
Marek, Reinhold Vetter, *Poland*,
Sebastian Wormell, ed, with an
historical introduction by Man-
fred Alexander, Pallas Guides,
London, 1994.

Bielecki, Adam, 'Morskie Oko', **Extract 12** (G.M. Hyde, trans).

Bobrowski, Johannes and Horst
Bienek, *Selected Poems*, Ruth and
Matthew Mead, trans, Penguin,
London, 1971.

Bobrowski, Johannes, *From the Riv-*

ers, Ruth and Matthew Mead, trans, Anvil, London, 1975.

Bobrowski, Johannes, *Shadow Lands: Selected Poems*, R. and M. Mead, trans, Anvil, London, 1984.

Bobrowski, Johannes, *Baltic Tales: Stories from the Shadowlands*, New Directions, New York, 1994.

Borowski, Tadeusz, *This Way for the Gas, Ladies and Gentlemen and Other Stories* [1948], Barbara Vedder, trans, Penguin, London and New York, 1976.

Buber, Martin, *Hasidism*, New York, 1948.

The Burning Forest: An Anthology of Polish Poetry, Adam Czerniawski, trans and ed, Bloodaxe, Newcastle upon Tyne, 1988/Dufour, Chester Springs, PA, 1988. (From Norwid to the present day.)

Conrad, Joseph, 'Prince Roman' [1911], in *The Informer and Other Stories (The Complete Short Fiction of Joseph Conrad*, Vol 2), Samuel Hynes, ed, William Pickering, London, 1992/Ecco Press, Hopewell, NJ, 1992. **Extract 8.**

Czechowicz, Józef, poems in *Five Centuries of Polish Poetry* (see below).

Czechowicz, Józef, 'The Joys of Winter', **Extract 7** (G.M. Hyde, trans).

Davie, Donald, *The Forests of Lithuania*, adaptations from Adam Mickiewicz, *Pan Tadeusz* [1834], Routledge, London, 1959.

Davies, Norman, *The Heart of Europe*, Oxford University Press, Oxford, 1984.

Drozdowski, Bohdan, *Twentieth Century Polish Theatre*, John Calder, London, 1979.

Dydyński, Krzysztof, *Poland: a Travel Survival Kit*, Lonely Planet, Hawthorn, Victoria, Berkeley, CA, and London, 1993.

Five Centuries of Polish Poetry, 1450– 1950, J. Peterkiewicz and B. Sin-

ger, ed, Oxford University Press, London and New York, 1970/ Greenwood Press, Westport, CT, 1979.

Gombrowicz, Witold, *Ferdydurke* [1937], Eric Mosbacher, trans [from the German], MacGibbon & Kee, London, 1961/Grove Press, New York, 1967.

Gombrowicz, Witold, *Trans-Atlantyk* [1953], Carolyn French and Nina Karsov, trans, Yale University Press, New Haven, CT, 1994.

Gombrowicz, Witold, *Pornografia* [1960], Alastair Hamilton, trans [from the French], Penguin, London, 1991.

Gombrowicz, Witold, *Cosmos* [1965], Eric Mosbacher, trans [from the German], MacGibbon & Kee, London, 1967/Grove Press, New York, 1967.

Gombrowicz, Witold, *Three Novels: Ferdydurke, Pornografia, and Cosmos* [1937, 1960, 1965], Grove Press, New York, 1978.

Grass, Günter, *The Tin Drum* [1959], Ralph Manheim, trans, Picador, London, 1989/Random House, New York, 1962. **Extract 2.**

Grochowiak, Stanislaw, selected poems in *Post-war Polish Poetry* (see below).

Grochowiak, Stanislaw, 'The City', **Extract 16** (G.M. Hyde, trans).

Grotowski, Jerzy, *Towards a Poor Theatre*, Eugenio Barba, ed, Eyre Methuen, London, 1976.

Herbert, Zbigniew, *Selected Poems*, Czesław Miłosz and Peter Dale Scott, trans, Penguin, London, 1968.

Herbert, Zbigniew, *Selected Poems*, John and Bogdana Carpenter, trans, Oxford University Press, London and New York, 1977.

Herbert, Zbigniew, *Report from the Besieged City and Other Poems*, John and Bogdana Carpenter, trans, Oxford University Press, Oxford, 1987/Ecco Press, New

York, 1985.

Herbert, Zbigniew, *Barbarian in the Garden*, Michael March and Jarosław Anders, trans, Carcanet, Manchester, 1985. (Essays.)

Herbert, Zbigniew, *Still Life with a Bridle: Essays and Apocryphas*, John Carpenter and Bogdana Carpenter, trans, Cape, London 1993/Ecco Press, New York, 1993.

Huelle, Paweł, *Who Was David Weiser?* [1987], Antonia Lloyd-Jones, trans, Bloomsbury, London, 1991.

Huelle, Paweł, *Moving House and Other Stories* [1991], Antonia Lloyd-Jones, Bloomsbury, London, 1994.

Jastrun, Mieczysław, 'In the Tatra', **Extract 13** (G.M. Hyde, trans).

Kamieńska, Anna, *Two Darknesses*, Desmond Graham and Tomasz P. Krzeszowski, trans, Flambard Press, Newcastle upon Tyne, 1994.

Kantor, Tadeusz, *Wielopole/ Wielopole*, Mariusz Tchorek and G. M. Hyde, trans, Marion Boyars, London, 1990.

Keneally, Thomas, *Schindler's Ark* [1982], retitled *Schindler's List*, Sceptre, London, 1994/Viking Penguin, New York, 1983. **Extract 15**.

Kochanowski, Jan, *Poems*, Dorothy Prall Rodin, trans, AMS Press, New York, 1978.

Konwicki, Tadeusz, *A Dreambook for Our Time* [1963], David Welsh, trans, Penguin, London, 1976/ MIT Press, Cambridge, MA, 1969.

Konwicki, Tadeusz, *The Anthropos– Spectre–Beast* [1969], George and Audrey Korwin-Rodziszewski, trans, Oxford University Press, Oxford, 1977.

Konwicki, Tadeusz, *The Polish Complex* [1977], Richard Lourie, trans, Viking Penguin, New York, 1984.

Konwicki, Tadeusz, *A Minor Apocalypse* [1979], Richard Lourie, trans, Faber and Faber, London, 1983/Vintage Books, New York, 1984.

Krasicki, Ignacy, selected poems in B. Carpenter, ed, *Monumenta Polonica*, Ann Arbor, MI, 1989, and *Five Centuries of Polish Poetry* (see above).

Krasicki, Ignacy, *The Adventures of Mr Nicholas Wisdom* [1776], T.H. Hossington, trans, Northwestern University Press, Evanston, IL, 1992.

Lec, Stanisław, *Unkempt Thoughts*, Jacek Gałązka, trans, St Martin's Press, New York, 1962.

Lec, Stanisław, *More Unkempt Thoughts*, Jacek Gałązka, trans, Funk and Wagnell, New York, 1968.

Lem, Stanisław, *Memoirs of a Space Traveller* [1957], Michael Kandel, trans, Secker and Warburg, London, 1982/Harcourt Brace, New York, 1982.

Lem, Stanisław, *Return from the Stars* [1961], B. Marszal and F. Simpson, trans, Secker and Warburg, London, 1980/Harcourt Brace, New York, 1980.

Lem, Stanisław, *Solaris* [1961], Joanna Kilmartin and Steve Cox, trans [from the French], Faber and Faber, London, 1971/ Walker, New York, 1970.

Lem, Stanisław, *A Perfect Vacuum* [1971], Michael Kandel, trans, Secker and Warburg, London/ Harcourt Brace Jovanovich, New York, 1979.

Lipska, Ewa, *Poet? Criminal? Madman?*, Barbara Plebanek with Tony Howard, trans, Forest Books, London, 1991. (Poems.)

Mickiewicz, Adam, *Forefathers* [1823–32], Count Potocki of Montalk, trans, Polish Cultural Foundation, London, 1968.

Mickiewicz, Adam, *Konrad Wallenrod and Other Writings* [1828],

Greenwood, Westport, CT, 1975.

Mickiewicz, Adam, *Konrad Wallenrod; and Grażyna* [1828], Irene Suboczewski, trans, University Press of America, 1989.

Mickiewicz, Adam, *Selected Poems*, C. Mills, ed, W.H. Auden and others, trans, Voyages Press, New York, 1957.

Mickiewicz, Adam, *Pan Tadeusz, or The Last Foray in Lithuania*, [1834], G.R. Noyes, trans, Dent, London, 1930/Dutton, New York, 1930; Kenneth Mackenzie, trans, Dent, London, 1966/Dutton, New York, 1966/Polish Cultural Foundation, London, 1986. **Extract 10** (J. Strzetelski, trans).

Miłosz, Czesław, *The Captive Mind* [1953], Random House, New York, 1981.

Miłosz, Czesław, *The Issa Valley* [1955], Sidgwick and Jackson, London, 1981/Farrar Straus and Giroux, New York, 1982.

Miłosz, Czesław, *Selected Poems*, Seabury, New York, 1973.

Miłosz, Czesław, *Bells in Winter*, author and Lillian Vallee, trans, Carcanet, Manchester, 1980/Ecco Press, New York, 1978.

Miłosz, Czesław, *Selected Poems*, Ecco Press, New York, 1980.

Miłosz, Czesław, *The Separate Notebooks*, Robert Hass and Robert Pinsky, trans, Ecco Press, New York, 1986.

Miłosz, Czesław, *Collected Poems*, 1931–1987, Penguin, London, 1988/Ecco Press, New York, 1988.

Miłosz, Czesław, *The History of Polish Literature*, 2nd ed, University of California Press, Berkeley, CA, 1983. (Extensive bibliography of translations.)

Mrożek, Sławomir, *The Elephant* [1958], Konrad Syrop, trans, Grove Press, New York, 1965/Greenwood, Westport, 1975.

Mrożek, Sławomir, *Six Plays* [1958–62], Nicholas Bethell, trans, Cape, London, 1968/Grove Press, New York, 1967.

Mrożek, Sławomir, *Three Plays*, [1961 etc], Grove Press, New York, 1972.

Mrożek, Sławomir, *Tango* [1964], Ralph Manheim and Teresa Dzieduszycka, trans, Grove Press, New York, 1968.

Norwid, Cyprian Kamil, *Poezje/Poems*, Adam Czerniawski, trans, Kraków, 1986. Also poems in *Five Centuries of Polish Poetry* (see above). See also under Strzetelski, Jerzy.

Nowakowski, Marek, *The Canary and Other Tales of Martial Law* [1982–83], Krystyna Bronkowska, trans, preface by Leszek Kolakowski, Harvill Press, London, 1983.

Polish Romantic Drama, Harold B. Segel, trans, Cornell University Press, Ithaca, NY, and London, 1977. (Mickiewicz, *Forefathers' Eve*, part III; Krasiński, *Undivine Comedy*; Słowacki, *Fantasy*).

Post-War Polish Poetry: An Anthology, Czesław Miłosz, ed, University of California Press, Berkeley, CA, 1983.

Potocki, Jan, *The Saragossa Manuscript: a Collection of Weird Tales*, Elizabeth Abbot, trans, Dedalus, Sawtry, 1989.

Prus, Bolesław, *The Doll* [1890], David Welsh, trans, Hippocrene/Twayne, New York, 1972.

Przyboś, Julian, selected poems in *Polish Post-war Poetry* (see above).

Przyboś, Julian, 'To Wawel', **Extract 3** (G.M. Hyde, trans).

Reymont, Władysław, *The Promised Land* [1899], M. H. Dziewicki, trans, London, 1927. **Extract 5** (G.M. Hyde, trans).

Reymont, Władysław, *The Peasants* [1904–09], Michael H. Dziewicki, trans, Knopf, New

York, 1942, four vols. See also under Strzetelski, Jerzy.

Różewicz, Tadeusz, *The Card Index* [1960] *and Other Plays*, Adam Czerniawski, trans, Calder & Boyars, London, 1969.

Różewicz, Tadeusz, *Faces of Anxiety*, Adam Czerniawski, trans, Rapp and Whiting, London, 1969.

Różewicz, Tadeusz, *Selected Poems*, Adam Czerniawski, trans, Penguin, London, 1976.

Różewicz, Tadeusz, *The Survivor and Other Poems*, Magnus J. Krynski and Robert A. Maguire, Princeton University Press, Princeton, NJ, 1976.

Różewicz, Tadeusz, *Unease*, Victor Contoski, trans, New Rivers Press, St Paul, MN, 1980.

Różewicz, Tadeusz, *Conversation with a Prince and Other Poems*, Adam Czerniawski, trans, Anvil Press, London, 1982.

Salter, Mark, and Gordon McLachlan, *Poland: The Rough Guide*, Rough Guides, London, 1994.

Schulz, Bruno, *The Street of Crocodiles and Sanatorium under the Sign of the Hourglass* ['Cinnamon Shops', 1934; 'Sanatorium', 1937], C. Wieniewska, trans, Picador, London, 1988. **Extract 1** (G.M. Hyde, trans).

Sienkiewicz, Henryk, *Quo Vadis?* [1896], Stanley F. Conrad, trans, Dedalus, Sawtry, 1993/ Hippocrene, New York, 1993.

Singer, Isaac Bashevis, *The Magician of Lublin* [1960], Elaine Gottlieb and Joseph Singer, trans [from the Yiddish], Secker and Warburg, London, 1961/Penguin, London, 1979.

Słowacki, Juliusz, selected poems in *Five Centuries of Polish Poetry* (see above).

Słowacki, Juliusz, *Anhelli* [1838], Dorothea Prall Radin, trans, Allen & Unwin, London, 1930/ Greenwood, Westport CT, 1979.

Słowacki, Juliusz, *Balladyna* [1839], Cambridge Springs, 1960.

Słowacki, Juliusz, *Fantazy* [1866], *in Polish Romantic Drama*, H. B. Segel, ed, Cornell University Press, Ithaca, NY, and London, 1977.

Słowacki, Juliusz, 'A Reassurance', **Extract 17** (G.M. Hyde, trans).

Spoiling Cannibals' Fun: Polish Poetry of the Last Two Decades of Communist Rule, Stanisław Barańczak and Clare Cavanagh, ed, Northwestern University Press, Evanston, IL, 1991.

Strzetelski, Jerzy, *Outline of Polish Literature*, Jagiellonski Uniwersytet, Kraków, 1973. **Extracts 9** (Norwid), **10** (Mickiewicz) and **11** (Reymont).

Szymborska, Wisława, *Sounds, Feelings, Thoughts: Seventy Poems*, Magnus J. Krynski and Robert A. Maguire, trans, Princeton University Press, Princeton, NJ, 1981.

Szymborska, Wisława, *Selected Poems*, Grazina Drabik, Austin Flint, Sharon Olds, trans, in *Quarterly Review of Literature*, Vol 23: Poetry Series 4, Princeton, NJ, 1982.

Szymborska, Wisława, *People on a Bridge*, Adam Czerniawski, trans, Forest Books, London, 1990.

Trembecki, Stanisław, selected poems in *Monumenta Polonica*, B. Carpenter, ed, Ann Arbor, MI, 1989.

Tuwim, Julian, poems in *Five Centuries of Polish Poetry* (see above).

Tuwim, Julian, 'Polish Flowers', **Extract 6** (G.M. Hyde, trans).

Wańkowicz, Melchior, *Three Generations*, Krystyna Cekalska, trans, Canadian–Polish Research Institute in Canada, Toronto, 1973.

Wat, Aleksander, *Mediterranean Poems*, C. Miłosz, trans, Ardis, Ann Arbor, MI, 1977.

Wat, Aleksander, *Lucifer Unem-*

ployed, Lilian Vallee, trans, Northwestern University Press, Evanston, IL, 1990.

Witkiewicz, Stanisław Ignacy, *Beelzebub Sonata: Plays, Essays, Documents* [1925 etc], Daniel Gerould and Jadwiga Kosicka, trans, Performing Arts Journal Publications, New York, 1980.

Witkiewicz, Stanisław Ignacy, *The Madman and the Nun and Other Plays* [1923 etc], Daniel C. Gerould and C. S. Durer, trans, University of Washington Press, Seattle, WA, 1968.

Witkiewicz, Stanisław Ignacy, *Tropical Madness: Four Plays*, Daniel and Eleanor Gerould, trans, Winter House, New York, 1972.

Witkiewicz, Stanisław Ignacy, *The Mother and Other Unsavory Plays* [1924, 1931–34, 1920], Daniel Gerould and C. S. Durer, trans, Applause, New York and London, 1993. (Also includes *The Shoemakers* and *They*.)

Witkiewicz, Stanisław Ignacy, *Insatiability: A Novel in Two Parts* [1930], Louis Iribarne, trans, Quartet Books, London, 1985/ University of Illinois Press, Urbana, IL, 1977.

Witkiewicz, Stanisław Ignacy, *The Witkiewicz Reader*, Daniel Gerould, ed, Northwestern University Press, Evanston, IL, 1992.

Witkiewicz, Stanisław Ignacy, *The Demonism of Zakopane*, **Extract 14** (G.M. Hyde, trans).

Wyspiański, Stanisław, 'Liberation', **Extract 4** (G.M. Hyde, trans).

Wyspiański, Stanisław, *The Wedding* [1901], G. T. Kapolka, trans, Ardis, Ann Arbor, MI, 1990.

Young Poets of a New Poland, Donald Pirie, trans, Forest Books, London, 1993.

Extracts

(1) DROHOBYCZ

Bruno Schulz, *The Street of Crocodiles*

Bruno Schulz is one of the modern Polish writers who have attained an unequivocal international fame. True, his short stories keep reminding you of other people: Proust and Kafka, in particular; but the way his fantasy works, Chagall-like, to unsettle an otherwise very material world of objects and day-to-day activities, and transpose it instantly into an archaic realm of myth, epic, fairy-tale, and folklore, is unparalleled outside of the domain of pure psychosis.

Whereas in the Old Town a nocturnal, hole-and-corner sort of trading was the rule, imbued with its own kinds of solemn ceremoniousness, in this new district an up-to-date, no-nonsense kind of commercialism had sprung up all of a sudden. A certain pseudo-Americanism, grafted on to the mouldy old infrastructures of the town, had erupted into an exuberant, but empty and insipid, vegetation of spurious, wretched pretentiousness. Here you could see cheap, shoddily built tenements, with apologies for facades, adorned with monstrous ornaments made of cracked plaster. Crooked old suburban houses had been fitted with hastily contrived porticos, which closer observation soon unmasked as wretched imitations of the arrangements you might find in big cities. Flawed, opaque, dirty window-panes, breaking up their shadowy reproductions of the street into undulating reflections of light, the unplaned timber of the door-frames, the grey atmosphere of those barren interiors, the dust settling on the high shelves, and along the despoiled, crumbling walls, in webs and shreds, had all left the imprint of the savage Klondike on the shops. Shop gave way to shop, one after the other: tailors' workshops, clothes shops, china shops, chemists', hairdressers. Their great colourless windows bore inscriptions in sloping or semicircular, cursive, artistic gilt letters: CONFISERIE, MANU-CURE, KING OF ENGLAND.

The settled inhabitants of our town kept their distance from this district, which had been colonized by sheer scum, rabble, featureless creatures, two-dimensional beings, real moral trash, a tawdry travesty of humanity of the type engendered by ephemeral milieux of this sort. But on those days when moral values collapsed, during those hours when people succumbed to baser temptations, it would happen that some citizen or other would stray, half-accidentally, into this dubious area. Even the best people were not free, from time to time, from the urge to indulge willingly in degradation, to level out all boundaries and hierarchies, to swim in this meagre swamp of communality, banal intimacy, squalid confusion. This district was the Eldorado of such moral deserters, of people fleeing the banner of their own dignity. Everything turned suspect and ambiguous there, everything invited you, with a knowing wink, a cynically suggestive gesture, or an explicit ogle, to harbour unclean desires, everything released your lower nature from its shackles.

(2) Gdańsk

Günter Grass, *The Tin Drum*

Grass's novel goes back to the roots of German Expressionism to find a literary idiom, grotesque, intense, and fraught with contradictions, in which to evoke the life and times of the Free City of Danzig on the eve of the second world war. The much-acclaimed 'Polish Corridor' established in the aftermath of the first world war was an obvious target for Nazi aggression. Extensively damaged during the Russian advance at the end of the second world war, Danzig, present-day Gdańsk, was lovingly rebuilt in its handsome Hanseatic style, turning it into the tourist attraction and thriving port it is today. It was in the Gdańsk shipyard that the workers' movement which overthrew Communism began under the banner of Solidarity.

When his wound had healed, Alfred Matzerath stayed in Danzig and immediately found work as representative of the Rhenish stationery firm where he had worked before the war. The war had spent itself. Peace treaties that would give ground for more wars were being boggled into shape: the region round the mouth of the Vistula – delimited roughly by a line running from Vogelsang on the Nehrung along the Nogat to Pieckel, down the Vistula to Czattkau, cutting across at right angles as far as Schonfliess, looping round the forest of Saskoschin to Lake Ottomin, leaving Mattern, Ramkau, and my grandmother's Bissau to one side, and returning to the Baltic at Klein-Katz – was proclaimed a free state under League of Nations control. In the city itself Poland was given a free port, the Westerplatte including the munitions depot, the railroad administration, and a post office of its own on the Heveliusplatz.

The postage stamps of the Free City were resplendent with red and gold Hanseatic heraldry, while the Poles sent out their mail marked with scenes from the lives of Casimir and Batory, all in macabre violet.

Jan Bronski opted for Poland and transferred to the Polish Post Office. The gesture seemed spontaneous and was generally interpreted as a reaction to my mother's infidelity. In 1920, when Marszalek Pilsudski defeated the Red Army at Warsaw, a miracle which Vincent Bronski and others like him attributed to the Virgin Mary and the military experts either to General Sikorski or to General Weygand – in that eminently Polish year, my mother became engaged to Matzerath, a citizen of the German Reich. I am inclined to believe that my grandmother Anna was hardly more pleased about it than Jan. Leaving the cellar shop in Troyl, which had meanwhile become rather prosperous, to her daughter, she moved to her brother Vincent's place at Bissau, which was Polish territory, took over the management of the farm with its beet and potato fields as in the pre-Koljaiczek era, left his increasingly grace-ridden brother to his dialogues with the Virgin Queen of Poland, and went back to sitting in four skirts beside autumnal potato-top fires, blinking at the horizon, which was still sectioned by telegraph poles.

(3) KRAKÓW

Julian Przyboś, *To Wawel*

The Wawel Castle in Kraków stands by the Vistula as the seat of the Polish kings and the tombs of great Poles throughout the centuries. Many poets have sung its praises. Like other monuments of Polish culture, however, its survival has often been in doubt; not for nothing does the Polish national anthem begin Jeszcze Polska Nie Zginęła ('Poland has not yet perished').

The tower shone, nearby
as if the radio was already broadcasting from it.
With dread, as if cowering after a cannonade,
and with mounting happiness:
they preserved Krakow intact!

Keeping step with our steps
house after house rises on a pyramid of persistence:
I walk down the street as if unveiling a monument!

Under a tank, or the hoof of an apocalyptic horse
a Knight of the Cross, corpse unarmed to the ironclad's fist;
from the feet of Witold, to the feet of every passer-by
he fell, turned black.
Two swords made huge through the centuries,
turned heavenward, sting the bright air.
Golden tracer bullets light up the first star.

Shining, rattling,
thunder of assault
cannonade – overtopping the city like a mountain:
Wawel stands fast on the clash of arms.

(4) Kraków

Stanisław Wyspiański, *Liberation*

The Polish cultural revival at the turn of the century, inspired by international Jugendstil and in some way compensating for Poland's continuing subjection to foreign powers, tended to reinforce the hermeticism of Polish art, but also produced some startling post-Romantic imagery of great power. Wyspiański was an artist of many parts whose work in the visual domain (eg his resplendent murals and stained glass in the Franciscan Church in Kraków) is perhaps more accessible to non-Poles than his writing.

KONRAD: Theatre of the people, art, Polish art!
We want to adorn it here, to paint it,
to build Poland in this theatre of ours!
Put on the hetman's tunic, the dress of yesteryear
Bring me cloth of gold, sashes, sabres, scimitars,
Peasant costumes, overcoats, money-belts. What a crowd in the
 church!
Let bold colours leap to the eye,
let them strike like the sun. – Sashes, ribbons, decorations!
Let me see them gathered, as in golden times of yore,
All gathered together, the magnate, the peasant, the citizen.
Ye homespun! stand yourselves by the Crucified One.
And ye somewhat further! Hussars, who with count Henryk
At your head, survivors from battle – The banner with Mary.
Grey fustian ones, o artists, dreamers, monks.
All of you! – Bedeck yourselves in ornaments
Ornaments, cloth of gold, festive garments
begin the mental strife and verbal joust –
and thou, o Muse, must set the tone.
MUSE: I am already prepared.

(5) ŁÓDŹ

Władysław Reymont, *The Promised Land*

There are a number of big Polish novels from the turn of the century that merit translation, or reissue; but none more so than The Promised Land. A tale of industrial Łódź, successfully filmed in the 1970s by Andrzej Wajda, it reveals the influence of Fyodor Dostoevsky, a considerable presence in Polish writing despite his own anti-Polish sentiments. Reymont's novel also looks forward to German Expressionist evocations of the industrial city, with its 'mass civilization' versus individual ambition and/or integrity.

Łódź was awakening.

The first screeching factory siren pierced the early morning quiet, and it was followed by others which began bursting out on all sides of the town more and more tumultuously, with their turbulent voices, like a chorus of monstrous cocks, crowing from metal throats their peremptory call to work.

Massive factories, whose long black hulks and slender chimney-necks loomed out of the night, in the mist and rain, were slowly awakening, flames blazing from their fires, exhaling clouds of smoke, beginning to live and bestir themselves in the darkness that still enveloped the earth.

A fine rain, March rain mixed with snow, was falling steadily, trailing over Łódź a heavy, sticky veil of mist. It drummed on the tin roofs and gushed off them straight on to the pavement and on to the black streets full of sticky mud, the bare trees that hugged the long walls and shook with the cold, tossed by the wind which rose somewhere on the saturated fields and tumbled heavily across the mud-soaked streets of the town, shaking the tall fences, testing the strength of the roofs, then falling into the mud, soughing in the branches of the trees, beating them against the window-panes of a small one-storey house, where a light suddenly went on.

Borowiecki woke up and lit a candle, while the alarm-clock started to ring violently, which meant that it was five o'clock . . .

The rain was still drizzling endlessly down, or lashing athwart the windows of the little houses, which in this part of Piotrkowska St were huddled closely together, but were shoved aside, as it were, from time to time, by a massive factory or the splendid residence of a factory-owner . . .

'Will we make a go of it?' said Borowiecki again, fixing the chaos of tenements that loomed out of the darkness with a steady gaze; he stared at the mass of black factories, too, motionless as they were, and filled with a special stoney sort of tranquillity, which began to advance gradually in front of him on all sides, with their huge red walls.

'Morgen!', someone rushing past flung at him, as he stood there.

'Morgen . . .' he said half to himself, as he walked on more slowly.

He was racked by doubts, thousands of thoughts, figures, hypotheses and schemes seethed inside his skull, so that he almost forgot where he was and where he was going.

Thousands of workers, a silent black swarm, began suddenly to creep out of the sidestreets, streets which looked like ditches full of swamp-mud; they issued from the houses that stood right at the edge of the city, like great rubbish heaps. They filled Piotrkowska with the scuffle of their steps, the rattle of their tin lanterns, which glinted in the light, and the knock of their wooden-soled clogs, together with their sleepy muttering and the plash of mud under their feet.

(6) Łódź

Julian Tuwim, *Polish Flowers*

Tuwim's Polish Flowers is a clever long poem of a very individual kind: a sort of literary Art Deco, quirky, self-parodying, bright but delicate. The city paid tribute to here is the Polish Manchester, with a present-day population of over a million, and the kind of social problems you might expect from the demise of Communism (with its full employment) in the capital of the Polish textile industry. The nineteenth-century factory developments have belatedly come to be seen as architecturally of great interest: the problem is how to preserve them. Tuwim responds vividly to the urban bustle of this city in the Prussian partition.

In front of the Grand Hotel in the city of Łódź
With a crash the Parademarsch progresses,
The bearded Landsturm, left front row,
And the jankers file, following the Feldfebel,
With stiff and stubborn hobnailed steps. Drum-roll rattles
Thunder of Prussian drums. And on guard
Watchful on the march like loyal dogs
Docile lieutenants and adjutants:
Red collar, monocle, cane,
Slim like the harsh squeal of the fife:
'The Rhine, the Rhine, the German Rhine'
The distinguished visitor: the Fieldmarshal
(Scarlet-and-grey) Mackensen.
And amidst the crush of silly Łódź folk
A thin young man raves on angrily
Hat over nose, starched collar

His tongue flapping with rage like a regatta
His eyes declaim the Marseillaise
He strikes like a blade at the Prussian ranks
For Łódź, for freedom, for his beloved
With whom he's made a date
In the cafe over the road.

(7) Lublin

Józef Czechowicz, *The Joys of Winter*

Isaac Bashevis Singer ◊ wrote The Magician of Lublin; the poet Czechowicz, who spent much of his best years in Warsaw, here celebrates another version of Lublin's magic. Lublin was a major trading post on the route to the Ukraine, and before the war the majority of its inhabitants were Jews (the great Rabbinical College was here). Until recently, the principal monument to their existence has been Majdanek, the concentration camp on the city's outskirts. Now, at last, some attempts at a proper restitution of Lublin's Jewish heritage are being made.

Mother, Lublin all silvery
reminds me of your fairy-tales
about soaring flying horses
about the wondrous lamp of Aladdin . . .

Churches all in white and spires
in Tartar fur hats bright with sunlight
are like the archangel who guards
the heavenly gates at the end of the world . . .

The castle is a ship; in a storm
it lost its rudder, its sails, its mast.
On the white heights, lifeless,
it rests in the shadow of its bastion.

The sidestreets are streaked with blue,
the alleyways – silver and white.
The embrasures of gateways and windows
have filled up with snow: like flocks of sheep . . .

So much for daytime. And when at night
the great sphere of joy here bursts
and stars climb the sky
– o Mother! how lovely it will be!

(8) POLAND: COUNTRYSIDE

Joseph Conrad, *Prince Roman*

Joseph Conrad (né Korzeniowski), Poland's English novelist, occupies a unique position. Having emigrated as a young man to England (via France), and having been formed much more by the French and the Anglo-American literary traditions than by anything distinctively Polish, Conrad can hardly be located among Polish authors. Nevertheless, some critics have discovered some Polish elements in his work: and this extract from a story written in 1911 bears out writer R.B. Cunninghame Graham's claim that Conrad never lost sight of the sufferings of his native land, a country which he described as 'thinking, breathing, speaking, hoping and suffering in its grave, railed in by a million of bayonets and triple-sealed with the seals of three great empires.'

He would have felt as completely lonely and abandoned as a man in the toils of a cruel nightmare if it had not been for this countryside where he had been born and had spent his happy boyish years. He knew it well – every slight rise crowned with trees among the ploughed fields, every dell concealing a village. The dammed streams made a chain of lakes set in the green meadows. Far away to the north the great Lithuanian forest faced the sun, no higher than a hedge; and to the south, the way to the plains, the vast brown spaces of the earth touched the blue sky.

And this familiar landscape associated with the days without thought and without sorrow, this land the charm of which he felt without even looking at it soothed his pain, like the presence of an old friend who sits silent and disregarded by one in some dark hour of life.

One afternoon, it happened that the Prince after turning his horse's head for home remarked a low dense cloud of dark dust cutting off slantwise a part of the view. He reined in on a knoll and peered. There were slender gleams of steel here and there in that cloud, and it contained moving forms which revealed themselves at last as a long line of peasant carts full of soldiers, moving slowly in double file under the escort of mounted Cossacks.

It was like an immense reptile creeping over the fields; its head dipped out of sight in a slight hollow and its tail went on writhing and growing shorter as though the monster were eating its way slowly into the very heart of the land.

The Prince directed his way through a village lying a little off the track. The roadside inn with its stable, byre and barn under one enormous thatched roof resembled a deformed, hunch-backed, ragged giant, sprawling amongst the small huts of the peasants. The innkeeper, a portly, dignified Jew, clad in a black satin coat reached down to his heels and girt with a red sash, stood at the door stroking his long silvery beard.

(9) POLAND: THE JEWISH THEME

Cyprian Kamil Norwid, *Polish Jews*

Cyprian Kamil Norwid uses the immense resources of his dense Symbolist poetics to explore some of the paradoxes and contradictions of the existence of a very large and very influential national minority on Polish soil and within Polish culture. There is no specific geographical place involved: but that is the point.

You are in Europe, O grave Jewish
People, like a monument broken in the East,
With its shards strewn everywhere,
Each bearing an eternal hieroglyph –
And a Northern man, when he meets you
In his pine wood, guesses the sunshine reflection
Of your Motherland, which somewhere in the blue azure
Like Moses, bathed in the water of the Nile! –
And says 'He is great who was so high
And fell so low, and is silent as you are.'

We are sons of the North, our hair is bright,
We are snow-white clouds of the Eastern story,
Beyond the frontiers of the cabals, directly, from earth
Looking up to the high tabernacle of heaven:
As Hagar's sons – through the country's inner soul
As Sarah's sons – through the father's toil;
Before the others – quite otherwise –
We looked kindly towards you, not at all out of despair:
For if our nobleman quartered a coat of arms with you
The cross was in the middle of the quartering – and it did not lie!

And so now, as history is seemingly *chaos*,
While in fact it is *power* and wide *order*
And so now, for history is like a testament,
Seen to by a cherub from high above –
So again Maccabeus stood on the Warsaw pavement
Together with a Pole not in an ambiguous fright.
– And when richer people in the world
Gave him instead of the crosses for which one dies

The crosses that glitter on the breast, then what? he preferred
To open the defenceless arms like David.

Grave nation, honour to you in those who
Were not afraid of the Mongolian–Circassian storm
And defended Moses' God together with us
With a courageous eye, and naked breast!
Like the elders in history, who signal with their hand to the wild mobs
From high above and shout: 'I have withstood!'
I study your banners, I do not count your men,
For when you were nothingness, I had already sucked milk –
I have known nature longer! – and I shall curse the reins
And you will sit your horse like a shepherd without beasts.

(10) POLAND: THE LITHUANIAN THEME
Adam Mickiewicz, *Pan Tadeusz*

> *The greatest Polish Romantic poet, in his pseudo-epic Pan
> Tadeusz (Pan is the everyday Polish for 'Mr', but in this context
> alludes specifically to a representative of the Polish gentry),
> evokes the 'lost domain' of Polish Lithuania and its simple
> pieties. The topos is echoed by subsequent writers with a
> thousand different tonalities and shades of emphasis.*

Lithuania! my motherland! You are like health:
How much you should be prized only he can learn
Who has lost you. Today I see your beauty in all its loveliness
And describe it for I long for you.
Holy Virgin, who defends the bright Częstochowa
And shines in the Gothic Gate! You who protect
The castle of Nowogródek with its faithful folk
As by miracle you restored me to health as a child
(When by my weeping mother I was offered to your
Protection and I raised my dead eyelid,
And could at once walk to the threshold of thy shrines
To thank God for the life returned to me)
So you will return us, by miracle, to the bosom of our motherland.
Meanwhile carry my yearning soul
To those wooded hills, to those green meadows,
Spread broadly along the sky-blue Niemen,
To those fields painted with various kinds of corn;
Gilt with wheat, silvered over with rye;
Where the amber mustard, the buckwheat white as snow,
Where the clover glows with a girl's blush;

And all is girdled, as with a ribbon, with a green bordering path
Of grass, on which a few pear-trees squat quietly.

(11) POLAND: THE RURAL THEME

Władysław Reymont, *The Peasants*

*Reymont's novel was actually written in Brittany, but evokes
(with a Modernist accent) the timeless way of life of the peasants
of virtually any part of Poland. Like other Polish writers,
Reymont, despite travelling extensively, was drawn back to
subject-matter from his childhood and the village where he was
born. He won the Nobel Prize for literature in 1924.*

The whole world was now plunging into the deep stillness of repose.

The village lights were going out one by one, like eyes that are closed
by slumber.

The moon rolled up the high blue-black sky, sown over with starry
twinkling, and rose higher and higher, flew like a bird that wings its
way athwart the void on silver pinions. The scattered clouds slept,
huddled up into balls of soft white down.

On the earth all wearied creatures lay in quiet sweet sleep. Only here
and there a bird sang exuberant songs, only the waters whispered
something as if drowsily; and the trees bathing in the moonlight stirred
now and again, as if they dreamed of day; sometimes a dog growled, or
the night-jar flapped its wings as it passed by, and low earth-clinging
vapour now began to wrap the fields, but slowly, in the manner of a
tired-out mother.

The sounds of quiet breathing rose from the almost invisible orchards
and from under the almost invisible walls; people slept in the open air,
trusting to the night.

In Boryna's room sleep and tranquillity also prevailed, except for the
sound of the cricket on the hearth, and Jagna's breathing, fluttering
like a butterfly's wings.

It must have been in the small hours of the night, for the first cocks
were already crowing, that Boryna began to move in his bed as if
waking. At the same time the moon struck the window-panes, and
poured on to his face its silver seething torrent of light.

(12) TATRA MOUNTAINS
Adam Bielecki, *Morskie Oko*

The Tatra are so steeped in myth and fantasy that modern writers have had to 'deconstruct' the Tatra legend in various ways to add anything of interest, or to take account of the fact that the mountains are both resort and mystique. Adam Bielecki's witty enumeration of statistics, and snapshots of figures in a landscape, shift the mountain-topos from a Symbolist to a Formalist frame of reference. The subject is Lake Morskie Oko ('The Eye of the Sea').

800 m long.
400 m wide.
Sunny inky depths.

The Youth Hostel is staffed the whole year round.
Photographs.
Petrol Station.
The toughest climbing in the Tatra.

People get out of cars
Admire a pine –
people whose colours are reflected
on the opposite shore.

A score of well-defined paths leads through the peaks
through the high mountain passes
with forests.
Visit The Sea's EYE!

Some lost here their cry of wonderment
which wanders
over gullies and terraces
shattered by waterfalls down surrounding precipices
slapping like waves on wet rock –
and with a wing of snow what's more
echoing rumbling in the green deeps –

This is silence.
It is particularly quiet in the evening
in the roar of the waters
of steam trains locked up in the mountain pines.

Colours thicken
caramelising patches of black, white, and grey.
The rest of the day is melting secretively away from Mount Rysy.
I come to know the gentle lake:
a picture postcard from Morskie Oko.

(13) TATRA MOUNTAINS

Mieczysław Jastrun, *In the Tatra*

The Tatra Mountains, as well as being of the greatest interest to tourists and mountaineers alike, are rich in personal (often Romantic) associations and mythologies for a large number of Polish writers. Close to Kraków, these mountains have func-tioned as a kind of personal space into which urban intellectuals can retreat; Zakopane, the foremost resort, has also been a major cultural centre, especially at the turn of the century.

You call endlessly to me from that great distance
Where we bade farewell, rending space
With the mountain's peaks, where evening lit
A star above us, strewing unrustling shadows from trees.

That night, bundled into a traveller's suitcase
Travels on, dumbly ringing out on the horizon
Snatched back again. We have lived from alm-flowers,
From birch-leaf pennies, from shadows under the ash-tree,

We have lived off landscapes, which you knew how to
Conjure to beat at the window like a cloud,
To vanish from plains and find their winter quarters
In our bodies, like colours in the deep air.

Their gaze, overcome by the mauve of the crocus,
Warmed by the heat of the grass, held the silence
And the peace of the mountains. The night wind, which withered
    among herbs
Broke off with my hand what this letter writes to you.

And today, lapsing back into former times, as into gulfs
The blueness of the day opens up, gaps in the sky,
Again we thrust our hands into the streaming hail,
To clutch the star swallowed up by the mountain

So – from the black tempest of the Tatra – from the middle of winter
We entered the green of Summer, where the shepherd's hut
Threw its shadow in the shape of a star, and we call in
Where for the first time you saw dawn in its rawness.

(14) TATRA MOUNTAINS: ZAKOPANE

Stanisław Ignacy Witkiewicz,
The Demonism of Zakopane

*One of the most original talents in Polish Modernist writing,
Stanisław Ignacy Witkiewicz, grew up in Zakopane among its
rather febrile intelligentsia, the brilliant and wayward son of a
respected art-historian father (who took a serious 'ethnographic'
interest in the mountains). 'Witkacy' (his soubriquet) exercised
his merciless wit at the expense of the affectations of Modernist
art and its Bohemian lifestyles (which were, of course, his own
as well). Even during the Communist period, Zakopane never
lost its air of fashionable intrigue and gossip (which Polish calls
'plotki', or 'little plots').*

At all events, the recent discoveries of Freudian psychoanalysis, that
ultimate sheet anchor for the less dangerous kinds of madmen, are by
no means consoling. 'Was ist doch mit diesen polnischen Frauen?
Zakopane, immer Zakopane' – a famous specialist in hysteria from
Vienna is reputed to have murmured to himself on one occasion.
Which seems to demonstrate that (to borrow Freudian terminology)
the 'Zakopane complex' can never be resolved. Even those who did not
turn into incurable Zakopaneites are forced to admit that the most
significant event of their lives took place right here in Zakopane, or if it
hadn't happened to them, then it might, and it would in any case never
happen to them anywhere else.

Zakopane was once described as the 'spiritual capital of Poland'. I
would call it by quite another name: the place where one particular
kind of narcotic which is distinctively Polish is manufactured, the
psycho-chemical nature of which I will try – arguably for the first time
ever – to subject to a comprehensive analysis. Someone who suffers
from what is called the 'Zakopane problem' becomes unintelligible to
lowland bogtrotters. He loses his old friends, doesn't recognize women
who come from 'over there', as my much missed friend Tadeusz
Szymberski used to call them, and the most beautiful woman becomes
incomprehensible to him in all her sexual being if she happens never to
have been subjected to the Zakopane 'dressage'. What, after all, is the
most savage sort of perversion without a dash of pure Zakopane
eroticism, without a dose or two of the Zakopane mixture?

(15) TYNIEC, NEAR KRAKÓW

Thomas Keneally, *Schindler's Ark*

Keneally's novel, retitled Schindler's List, is one of the numerous best-selling fictionalized accounts of the fate of Polish Jews in the second world war. He researched the story of Kraków Jewry extensively for a book which is half fiction, half documentary. His hero, Oskar Schindler, a Sudeten German, used his powerful position in Kraków to save the lives of Jews who came under his jurisdiction, and earned himself a place on Mount Zion. Stephen Spielberg's 1993 film of the novel attracted both critical acclaim and enormous audiences.

Some people from the big cities – from Warsaw and Łódź with their ghettos and Cracow with Frank's *judenfrei* ambitions – went to the countryside to lose themselves among the peasants. The Rosner brothers settled in the old village of Tyniec on a pretty bend of the Vistula with an old Benedictine Abbey on a limestone cliff above it. It was anonymous enough for the Rosners. It had a few Jewish storekeepers and orthodox artisans with whom nightclub keepers had little to converse about. But the peasants, busy with the tedium of the harvest, were as genial as the Rosners could have hoped, finding musicians in their midst.

They'd come to Tyniec not from Cracow, not from that great marshalling point outside the botanical gardens in Mogilska Street where young SS men pushed people on trucks and called out bland and lying promises about the later delivery of all adequately labelled baggage. They had come in fact from Warsaw, where they had been enjoying an engagement at the Basilisk. They had left the day before the Germans sealed up the Warsaw ghetto. Henry and Leopold and Henry's wife Manci and five-year-old son Olek.

The idea of a south Polish village like Tyniec, not far from their native Cracow, appealed to the Rosner brothers. It offered the option, should conditions improve, of catching a bus into Cracow and finding work. Manci Rosner, an Austrian girl, had brought with her her sewing machine and the Rosners set up a little clothing business in Tyniec. In the evening they played in the taverns and became a sensation in a town like that. Villages welcome and support occasional wonders, even Jewish ones. And the fiddle was, of all instruments, most venerated in Poland.

(16) WARSAW

Stanisław Grochowiak, *The City*

Grochowiak's poem about Warsaw is a poem about other Polish cities as well, and it uses Surrealist devices as a way of communicating the grotesque disruption of all values and realities experienced in the context of the German attempt (the latest of many) to wipe out the identity of the Polish nation. The poem finds a paradoxical way of celebrating Poland's powers of survival, and shows the strength and individuality of avant-garde art in the country; though Grochowiak's work is often called 'Baroque'.

I visited a city. In it – apart from the bombs –
Nothing apart from the bombs
Was there in the city.
When I mention the bombs, dogs lift their heads,
Old folks' ears swing slowly round.

The bombs came suddenly – like rain.
Night so far dense, started turning blue:
White cherry trees bloomed in the orchards. Birds
Flew in the sky like little angels.

And they all left. Not from the building's various floors. But
On bridges made of curtains, in the air simply;
In family circles
In constellations of silver,
Poking from under their flimsy clothing.

For the kindly bombs had brightened up the Park.
The Park had been fashioned into a Carousel
So they all took their seats: on the blazing swans,
On the camel's hump
And the smoke
Struck at their nostrils.

Here, the old keep silent. Dogs hang their heads.
But you have to admit it: a few perky ladies
Ran naked off to the twilight meadows
And that was the end of them. The Gypsies, it seems.

Nights of the bomb! Glow-worm nights,
Your magic flower stood on its slender stem
An eye for its calyx, wound round with the threads

Of bloody fibres –
Like some embroidered coat-of-arms.

From today neither the old nor the dogs will remember
Who plucked that flower and bore it away amid the sparks –
From the city, where all that remained
Was just the raw craters
Like mouths gaping in everlasting wonder.

(17) WARSAW

Juliusz Słowacki, *A Reassurance*

Słowacki's lines celebrate Warsaw's powers of survival in a rather different way, from the angle of the Romantic nationalism of the great rival to Mickiewicz. The landmarks he mentions here (the so-called Zygmunt Column, for instance, and the rebuilt Old Town) are still conspicuous features of the landscape of a city with a complex role in Polish history.

What's treachery to us! – We have our column in Warsaw
Where the voyaging storks sit
Encountering its acanthus crown in the clouds
So solitary-proud it seems, and so high!
Beyond this column, dressed in rainbow-mists,
Stands the trinity of blessed towers of St John's;
Further, a dark street, from which, with an air of greyness,
The Old Town peers out in the blue distance;
Still further off, where the mist is darkening,
The panes of windows, like the green eyes of Kilinski,
From time to time lit up by the light of a lantern,
Like eyes of a silent spectre, risen from the sod.

Biographies and important works

BACZYŃSKI, Krzysztof Kamil (1921–1944). Born in **Warsaw**, Baczyński was perhaps the most gifted poet of his generation. He was killed tragically young in the Warsaw Uprising. He left about five hundred poems, twenty stories, and one play.

Inspired by the Romantic tradition and national awareness, Krzysztof Kamil Baczyński's work reflects the experience of the younger generation doomed by war to accept what they saw as their tragic destiny and patriotic duty.

BIELECKI, Adam (1910–). Bielecki was born in **Borysław**. Connected with the Tatra group of writers, he was Professor of Mathematics at the **Marie Curie University, Lublin**. He published (with some success) two volumes of verse, namely *The Aquarium of the Streets*, 1934, and *Heatwave*, 1934, which introduced some striking new elements into the poetry of the Tatras (Extract 12).

BOBROWSKI, Johannes (1917– 1965). Born in **Tylza**, Lithuania, the German poet Bobrowski was a soldier in the Wehrmacht during the second world war. He was a prisoner of war in Russia, and returned to live in East Germany in 1949. His principal volumes are *Sarmatische Zeit* (*The Sarmatian Age*), 1961 and *Schattenland Ströme* (*Shadowland Streams*), 1962. Bobrowski died in Berlin.

BOROWSKI, Tadeusz (1922–1951). Borowski was born in **Żytomierz**. A poet and short story writer, his main works include the translated short stories of *This Way to the Gas*, 1967, *Pożegnanie z Marią* (*Farewell to Maria*), 1948, and *Kamienny Świat* (*A World of Stone*), 1948. His war stories reveal the mechanisms of the inevitable corruption of the victims as well as the aggressors. He committed suicide in **Warsaw** in 1951.

CONRAD, Joseph (1857–1924). Conrad's family were exiled to Vologda in Russia (he was born in **Berdiczew, Podolia**). After twenty years at sea, he settled in England and became one of the greatest English novelists. There are very few explicitly Polish motifs in his writings (see Extract 8 for an example), though Polish commentators have discovered some

Joseph Conrad

covert Polish themes and values, and his dislike of Russians is very evident in several of his works.

CZECHOWICZ, Józef (1903–1939). Czechowicz, who was born in **Lublin** where he also died, came from poor peasant origins, studied in **Warsaw**, and took up with the Kwadryga group. He was active in Lublin cultural life, though shadowed by suspicions of homosexual activities. His principal volumes include *Kamień* (*Stone*), 1927, *Dzień jak codzień* (*Day Like Any Other*), 1930, *Balada z tamtej strony* (*Ballad from the Other Side*), 1932, and *Stare kamienie* (*Ancient Stones*), with F. Arnsztajnowa). Czechowicz's poetry blends the Arcadian with the apocalyptic. His verse has Symbolist affiliations and draws upon magical and folk-lore elements (Extract 7).

GOMBROWICZ, Witold (1904– 1969). Born in **Małoszyce**, the novel-

ist, essayist and playwright Gombrowicz studied law in **Warsaw** and then
philosophy and economics in Paris.
He left Poland for Argentina in 1939,
where he became one of the most
brilliant 'existential' satirical writers
of his time, reserving his most vitriolic gifts for the pretensions of Polish culture in its more nationalistic
manifestations. His *Dziennik* (*Journals*), first published in Paris in 1957–
66 made him *persona non grata* with
the Communist regime. His novels
include *Ferdydurke*, 1937, *Trans-
Atlantyk* (*Trans-Atlantic*), 1953, *Pornografia* (*Pornography*), 1960 and *Kos-
mos* (*Cosmos*), 1965. He also wrote
some highly original plays. He died in
Vence, France.

GRASS, Günter (1927–). Grass
was born in Danzig (now **Gdańsk**).
During the second world war, he was
drafted into the army from the Hitler
Youth Movement at the age of six-

Günter Grass

teen, was wounded and became a
prisoner of war until 1946. After the
war he lived for a time, among other
places, in Paris, where he wrote *Die
Blechtrommel*, 1959 (*The Tin Drum*,
1962 – Extract 2), a bizarre and
picaresque tale of the life and times of
a dwarf, which draws heavily on
Grass's experiences in Nazi Germany.
The novel was hugely successful in
Germany and in translation in
France, the UK and the USA. It was
filmed in 1979 by the German director Volker Schlöndorff. As well as his
novels, for which he is best known,
Grass has also written plays and several volumes of poetry. He has lived in
Berlin since 1960.

GROCHOWIAK, Stanisław (1934–
1976). Grochowiak was born in **Lesz-
no**. He held numerous posts in publishing houses. He attracted critical
attention with his *Ballada rycerska*
(*Chivalric Ballad*) in 1956. A taste for
the baroque went hand in hand with a
parodic and grotesque talent (Extract
16), and the use of 'unpoetic' language, in such volumes as *Menuet z
pogrzebaczem* (*Minuet with Poker*),
1958, *Rozbieranie do snu* (*Undressing
for Bed*), 1959, *Agresty* (*Gooseberries*),
1963, *Kanon* (*Canon*), 1965, *Nie było
lata* (*Not the Summer*), 1969, etc.

Witold Gombrowicz

GROTOWSKI, Jerzy (1933–). Born in **Rzeszów**, Grotowski, who became a theatre director and theorist, graduated from the Moscow State Institute of Theatre Arts. He devised a highly original theatrical method based on the physical and kinetic resources of the actor's body. Although he staged many classic texts, they were 'deconstructed' according to a logic of physical and mental 'encounters', rather than being represented in accordance with the dominance of the word. His experimentalism took him from the 'poor theatre' which had become associated with his name, to ambitious experiments in combining theatre with therapeutic and quasi-mystical 'happenings'.

HERBERT, Zbigniew (1924–). Born in **Lwów**, Herbert attended a clandestine university during the German occupation and was involved in the Home Army resistance. Lwów was incorporated in the Soviet Union after the war, and Herbert moved to **Kraków**, then **Warsaw**. He studied mainly law and economics, and from 1955 to 1976 he was on the staff of the Warsaw literary review *Twórczość*. His first collection, *Struna światła* (*String of Light*) was published in 1956, and later volumes brought him foreign recognition. A visit to Italy and France produced a volume of essays on the Mediterranean, entitled *Barbarzyńca w ogrodzie* (*Barbarian in the Garden*), 1962. His volume *Pan Cogito* (*Mr Cogito*), 1974 introduced the persona Mr Cogito who played a central role in later work. In the 1970s, Herbert spent time in the West, but he returned to Warsaw after the rise of Solidarity and saw the onset of martial law in December 1981. *Raport z oblężonego miasta* (*Report from a Besieged City*) was pub-

lished in Paris in 1983. Mr Cogito is always divided between opposed values of heritage and actuality, culture and experience; Herbert defends the 'besieged city' of human values. For further reading, see S. Barańczak, *A Fugitive from Utopia*, Harvard University Press, Cambridge, MA, 1987.

JASTRUN, Mieczysław (1903–1983). Jastrun was born in **Korolówka**. He studied languages and philosophy at the **Jagiellonian University**. The lectures he gave on contemporary poetry at **Warsaw University** were published in 1973 under the title *Walka o Poezję* (*Battle for the Word*). His early poetry, in such collections as *Spotkanie w czasie* (*Meeting in Time*), 1929 and *Inna młodość* (*Another Youth*), 1933, is notably reflective and introverted (Extract 13), but in his wartime poems he draws closer to historical subjects and everyday speech. His later work inclines towards large moral themes. He was a distinguished essayist, and translated from German, French, and Russian. He died in **Warsaw**.

KAMIEŃSKA, Anna (1920–1986). A poet and translator, Kamieńska was born in **Krasnystaw**. She graduated in **Warsaw**, and worked as a teacher in **Lublin** and the Lublin area during the war. She was the editor of numerous journals, and published collections entitled *Wychowanie* (*Upbringing*), 1949, *O szczęściu* (*On Happiness*), 1952, *Bicie serca* (*Heartbeat*), 1954, and a succession of other volumes. Essentially a moralist, her work belongs to poetic traditions preoccupied by questions of values, social morality, and human growth and development. She also wrote for children. Kamieńska died in **Warsaw**.

KANTOR, Tadeusz (1915–1990). Born in **Wielopole**, Kantor graduated from the **Kraków Academy of Fine Arts** in 1915. Artist, happening artist, theorist, and theatrical director, Kantor was perhaps the last survivor from the heroic age of artistic Modernism, and one of the greatest theatre artists of our time. Starting from his war-time (underground) theatre, Kantor founded a series of 'theatres', on the basis of his Cricot-2 company, shaped by artistic manifestos (Zero Theatre, Impossible Theatre, Theatre of Death) strongly reminiscent of the heyday of the avant-garde, but strikingly coherent and original. His productions give pride of place to brilliant reworkings of some of Witkiewicz's ◊ best plays and to quasi-autobiographical collages of literary and visual 'texts' mangled by history and ideology. Kantor died in **Kraków**.

KENEALLY, Thomas (1935–). Keneally was born in Sydney, Austra-

Tadeusz Kantor

lia. He prepared for the priesthood, but abandoned this vocation just two weeks before his ordination. He subsequently studied law, became a teacher in Sydney, and a drama lecturer at the University of New England. He has since held various academic posts at US universities and has been prominent in the Australian literary establishment (in 1983 he received the Order of Australia for his services to literature). He has written many novels with widely varying topics and themes, although often based on historical fact. *Schindler's Ark* (Extract 15), retitled *Schindler's List*, was published in 1982 to considerable acclaim and won both the Booker Prize and the LA Times Fiction Prize. The novel tells the dramatic and moving story of a man's struggle to save the lives of a thousand Polish Jews during the implementation of Hitler's Final Solution. In 1993, it was made into a hugely successful and Oscar-winning film by Stephen Spielberg.

KONWICKI, Tadeusz (1926–). Konwicki was born in **Nowa Wilejka**. A novelist and film director, he is a prolific writer with a many-sided talent who has passed through a series of turbulent stages in his development towards becoming one of the most eminent men of letters in Poland today. In his early days as a writer, he was fascinated by the Stalinist aesthetic of socialist realism, and contributed to the genre without a trace of cynicism, as did others of his generation who had fought against fascism. The world of his novels is traumatized by war, loss, and persecution, and redeemed intermittently by extreme gestures of commitment as well as by passionate (and often grotesque and/or erotic) fantasies of deliverance and transcendence. A fine, contemptuous irony and a sharp eye for reported detail combine with a terminal view of human folly. His titles include *Sennik współczesny* (*A Dreambook for Our Time*), 1963, *Kompleks polski* (*The Polish Complex*), 1977, and *Mała apokalipsa* (*Minor Apocalypse*), 1979.

KRASICKI, Ignacy (1735–1801). Born in **Dubiecko**, Krasicki was an outstanding representative of the Polish Enlightenment. A poet, prose writer and playwright, he was educated in **Lvov** and **Warsaw**. He entered the court of Stanisław Augustus, where he drew close to the king. He set up his residence at **Lidzbark**, where he amassed a significant library and collection of paintings, etc. Krasicki took little part in the tempestuous political events of his time. His poetry is characterized by clarity and precision, and a talent for aphorism. He also saw literature as the instrument of social education. A critic of Polish 'Sarmatian' (conservative and nationalistic) attitudes, Krasicki nevertheless resisted superficial (and potentially damaging) projects for the 'Europeanizing' of Polish culture. A master of a wide range of literary forms and kinds, Krasicki was highly regarded in his own time, and his reputation has held up well. He died in Berlin.

MICKIEWICZ, Adam (1798–1855). Mickiewicz was born in **Nowogródek**. Generally considered the greatest Polish poet, he studied in Wilno (present-day **Vilnius**), then taught in Kowno (**Kaunas**) from 1819 to 1823. These Lithuanian experiences exerted a formative influence on his personality and his work. His first volume of verse was published in Wilno in 1822, and reveals both his medievalizing tendency and his empathy with folk verse. He was arrested and imprisoned between 1823 and 1824 for his participation in clandestine revolutionary activities, and shortly afterwards published his *Sonety odeskie* (*Odessan Sonnets*) and his *Sonety krymskie* (*Crimean Sonnets*). A substantial part of his Messianic closet drama *Dziady* also dates from this period. After a sojourn in Russia (1825–29) and Germany, he arrived in Paris in 1832, where he wrote his *Pan Tadeusz* (Extract 10), later lecturing on Slav writers and the Slav idea. Mickiewicz's work has withstood the vagaries of changing literary fashions, and his radical and populist convictions, which inspired revolutionaries in Poland and in other nations, have endured as an inspiration to later writers and political leaders. Mickiewicz died in **Istanbul**.

MIŁOSZ, Czesław (1911–). Miłosz was born in **Szetejnie**. A poet, essayist, translator, and historian of literature, he was active in poetry while still studying law (1929–34). He received the Writers' Union prize in 1934, studied in Paris, and worked for the radio (1936–37). Active in the opposition to the German occupation, after the war he served as cultural attaché in the USA and France. He remained in France in 1951, living by writing. He was invited to lecture at the University of California (Berkeley) in 1960, and settled there in 1961. He was awarded the Nobel Prize for Literature in 1980. His early works, *Poemat o czasie zastygłym* (*Poem of a Frozen Time*), 1933 or the collection entitled *Trzy zimy* (*Three Winters*), 1936, often cited as instances of a kind of artistic 'catastrophism' which incorporates a yearning for Arcadia, also represent his stoical vision of human destiny. After the war, a classicizing bent becomes more evident, so does a use

of poetic masks, and also of deliberate formulae and linguistic constraints. In the late 1940s he discovers an ironic and sarcastic tone. His study of the corruption of literary and political thought in his time, *Zniewolony umysł* (*The Captive Mind*), 1953, became one of the key texts of the rejection of Communism, especially in Poland. Miłosz has also published distinguished essays on literary Modernism, and important translations into Polish of major writers, especially English ones. His *History of Polish Literature*, 1969, 1983, is an exceptionally readable and personal as well as a scholarly work.

NORWID, Cyprian Kamil (1821–1883). Born in **Radzimyn**, Norwid was a poet above all, but an artist of many parts. He left Warsaw for Italy in 1842, and continued to Berlin in 1846 and Paris in 1849, where he became a fully-fledged emigré. Deeply influenced by Polish Romantic writers, Norwid became caught up in their ambition to make writing the instrument of historical change, a process which for his purposes could be articulated, at that historical moment, only in a poetic language full of neologisms and obscure distortions and displacements (Extract 9). In contradistinction to the Romantic affirmation of the individual, Norwid created a shadowy, emergent, 'abstract' persona who had not yet become a historical phenomenon. His works include *Pięć zarysów* (*Five Sketches*), 1847–62, *Rozmowa umarłych* (*Dialogue of the Dead*), 1857, and (between 1865 and 1866) his most celebrated work, the *Vade-mecum*. Norwid had a wide-ranging (if self-taught) knowledge of cultural history which placed him among the forerunners of literary Modernism. He died in Paris.

OLEKSIK, Klemens (1918–). Oleksik was born in **Zwoleń**. He moved to **Olsztyn** in 1957, and writes poetry which is a celebration of the **Mazury** region, as well as an exploration of its history. His collections include *Wiersze* (*Verses*), 1948, *Drzewo życia* (*Timber of Life*), 1961 and *Pięc poematów* (*Five Poems*), 1970.

PRZYBOŚ, Julian (1901–1970). Poet and essayist of peasant origins (born in **Gwoźnica pod Strzyżowem**), after studying in **Kraków** (1920–23) Przyboś worked as a schoolteacher, visiting France between 1937 and 1939, where he explored European art. He was arrested by the Gestapo in 1941; on his release he worked on the land. His early poetry is characterized by an intense response to nature and by romantic kinds of eroticism. His later work is concerned with questions of identity, survival, and memory (Extract 3). He was also a prolific critic. Przyboś died in **Warsaw**.

Julian Przyboś

REYMONT, Władysław Stanisław (1867–1925). Reymont was born in **Kobiele Wielkie**. The Nobel Prize winning author of *Chłopi* (*The Peasants*), 1904–09, combined a naturalistic fascination for reportage with a range of other literary methods, from Impressionism to Expressionism (Extract 11). Influenced by Dostoevsky in the 1890s, Reymont wrote *Ziemia obiecana* (*The Promised Land*), 1899 (Extract 5), as antiurbanist (despite the fascination of the city) as *Chłopi* is rustic. In Brittany (1904–07) he wrote a cycle of novels about the sea, and during the first world war he described the fate of villagers caught up in military offensives. His is one of the broadest and most diverse talents in the Polish fiction of the period.

SCHULZ, Bruno (1892–1942). Born in **Drohobycz**, Schulz worked as an art master at the High School there, and produced graphic work of great distinction, but his claim to immortality rests with two volumes of short stories, *Sklepy cynamonowe* (*Cinnamon Shops*), 1933 and *Sanatorium pod klepsydrą* (*Sanatorium under the Sign of the Hourglass*), 1936. A longer work, a novel about the coming of the Messiah, was lost. This smallish body of work has a distinction altogether disproportionate to its magnitude: Schulz's stories (Extract 1) exude a mystical–erotic atmosphere in which obscure power struggles are fought out among shadowy creatures and objects which keep changing their shapes and their allegiances in a cosmic–natural world that keeps dissolving into dream and myth, only to be brought sharply back to the realities of family life and the growing commercialization of a culture deeply resistant to change.

Władysław Stanisław Reymont

Drawing by Schulz for the cover
of *Cinnamon Shops*

SINGER, Isaac Bashevis (1904–
1991). Singer was born near **Lublin**.
He wrote in Yiddish and was educated
at the **Warsaw Rabbinical Seminary**.
In 1935 he emigrated to New York
and worked as a journalist. His
novels, rich in Yiddish culture and
lore, and with characteristic elements
of the supernatural, have been translated into English with considerable
success, and bear witness to his claim
that although the distinctive Jewish
culture of Central Europe was annihi-
lated in the war, some trace of it
survived as a special kind of spirit
'somewhere in the universe'. He has
only recently been properly received
and assimilated in the country of his
birth. He died in New York.

SŁOWACKI, Juliusz (1809–1849).

Born in **Krzemieniec** and one of the leading Romantic poets (with Mickiewicz), Słowacki left Poland in 1831, spent four years in Switzerland and Italy, travelled to Greece, Egypt, and Palestine, and settled in Paris where he lived for the rest of his life. Słowacki was intensely preoccupied with Polish national and political problems: the experience of the loss of independence and the desire to regain freedom are dominant themes around which his poetic *œuvre* is organized. Słowacki shared the Romantic belief in the importance of poetry and in its role in the shaping of national awareness. His works include numerous poems (Extract 17), among which the most famous are 'Anhelli', 'Beniowski' and 'Krol Duch' ('King-spirit'), and plays which, unlike most Romantic drama, are highly successful in the theatrical sense. *Mazepa* (translated into English), *Maria Stuart*, *Fantasy*, and *Balladyna* have continued to fascinate contemporary Polish directors.

TREMBECKI, Stanisław (1739?–1812). Trembecki was born in **Jastrzębniki**. Connected with the court of King Stanisław August, the poet defended the King's policy, and accompanied him into exile in Russia. His best-known poem, 'Sofiówka' ('Sophia's Park'), is a eulogy written for social celebrity of the day Sofia Potocka. He died in **Tulczyn**.

TUWIM, Julian (1894–1953). Born in **Łódź**, Tuwim studied law and philosophy in **Warsaw**, 1916–18. Leopold Staff translated some of his poems into Esperanto. He was associated with a number of Warsaw cabaret artists. After the German invasion of Poland he began his travels, which took him to New York in 1942, where he became associated with Oskar Lange and took a Leftist view of Polish–Soviet relations. After the war he returned to Poland, where he developed a distinctive strain of urbanism (in a very current language) which maintained contact with Modernist vitalism (Extract 6). He translated extensively from Russian. Tuwim died in **Zakopane**.

WAŃKOWICZ, Melchior (1892–1974). Born in **Kalużyce**, Wańkowicz was a journalist and lawyer who left Poland in 1939, lived in the USA from 1949 to 1958, then returned to Poland. His extended reportages combine facts, reminiscences, and historical narratives in a unique way. His best-known works are *Ziele na kraterze* (*Wild Flowers Cover the Crater*), 1951 and *Bitwa o Monte Cassino* (*The Battle of Monte Cassino*), 1945–47. He died in **Warsaw**.

WITKIEWICZ, Stanisław Ignacy (1885–1939). Witkiewicz was born in

Stanisław Ignacy Witkiewicz, self-portrait, c1910

Warsaw. He commonly called himself 'Witkacy', to distinguish him from his distinguished father (*sic!*). One of the first absurdists in world writing, Witkacy was immensely prolific in the domains of theatrical texts, theory, and visual art. He also wrote some important novels. Hard as it is to know for sure when Witkacy is clowning and when he is being serious – even as a theoretician – there is no denying the trenchancy of his satire (Extract 14) and the fascination of his abstract pieces of aesthetic metaphysics. At least one of his novels, *Nienasycenie* (*Insatiability*), 1930, is a savage – and hilarious – exercise in self-vilification, in which the brutal (and comic) lusts, and the narcotic self-indulgence, of his 'decadent' circle, are set off against the Bolshevik plan to dominate the world, and the universal anodyne of Murti-Bing: as if the dystopian visions of Huxley's *Brave New World* and Orwell's *1984* had been rolled into one. Several of Witkacy's plays are regularly in the repertoire of Polish theatres. He committed suicide on 17 September 1939, the day of the Soviet invasion of Poland.

WYSPIAŃSKI, Stanisław (1869–1907). Born in **Kraków**, where he also died, Wyspiański studied Fine Arts there with Matejko, and became one of the leaders of the Polish Secessionists (the Young Poland movement, with its cult of national revival). The most important of his numerous plays – which resemble those of Yeats – was *Wesele* (*The Wedding*), 1901, in which the curious figure of the *chochol* – the 'straw man' in the shape of one of the cones placed over young trees to protect them from frost – came to be accepted as the symbol of Poland's hidden identity and aspirations. Permeated by Nietzsche's vision of history, Wyspiański's plays spoke of the fate of the people, and its eternal capacity for self-transcendence, figured by the myths of the ancient world which are given a new lease of life (Extract 4). Wyspiański remains one of the most inspiring mouthpieces of a revivified Polish nationalism.

THE CZECH REPUBLIC

James Naughton

> '. . . and I felt that if I did nothing else in this little town but climb to the top of this chimney, that might not be much, but I could live on the strength of that for numbers of years, maybe a whole lifetime.'
> *Bohumil Hrabal,*
> *Cutting It Short*

Now that Czechoslovakia is no more – that somewhat recently devised political entity of 1918 having proved apparently ephemeral – would that we might label this chapter 'Bohemia'. This was the traditional name of the medieval kingdom, a venerable geographical term derived from the Celtic tribe of the Boii, who were associated with this region in Classical times. Bohemia, protruding westward into Germany to its north, west and south, has been the meeting place of Slav speakers and Germans for centuries, surrounded by natural defences of forested hills and mountains (**Krušné Hory** and **Krkonoše** to the north, **Šumava** to the south, **Český Les** to the west). Its main rivers, the **Vltava, Berounka** and **Elbe** (Labe in Czech), join and flow northwards to the Baltic Sea. For centuries it has been intimately linked with its sister province of Moravia to the east, whose Polish border runs north of the **Jeseník** mountains, to the east of which the River **Oder** (Odra) flows north through the **Moravian Gate** and **Ostrava** in former Silesia. Moravia's southern border with Austria roughly follows the course of the eastward-flowing **Thaya** (Dyje), a tributary of the **Morava** River, which flows south to join the **Danube**. The population of today's Czech Republic is something over 10.3 million.

Prague, the capital, dominates Bohemia culturally with over 1.2 million inhabitants, its Gothic and Baroque architecture, its rich musical life, and its abundant literary associations, Czech, German and, to the outside world often above all, Jewish – since for many readers Prague is the city of Kafka ♭. Prague-born playwright-president Václav Havel ♭ illustrates the persisting strong political connotations of literature in this geographically, and arguably culturally *echt*-Central-European capital. Beer culture, another *echt*-Bohemian phenomenon, is led by **Plzeň** (Pilsen) (173 000) in the west and **České Budějovice** (Budweiss) (97 000) in the south with its garrison town associations with Hašek's ♭ *Švejk*, but also many smaller brewing sites, such as **Nymburk**, the basis for the transmogrified reminiscences of Bohumil Hrabal's ♭ *Městečko, kde se zastavil čas*, 1976–78 (*The Little Town Where Time Stood Still*, 1993). Industrial **Liberec** (101 000) and **Ústí nad Labem** lie to the north, to their east smaller **Náchod**, the native 'Kostelec' of Josef Škvorecký's ♭ *Zbabělci*, 1958 (*The Cowards*, 1972) and others of his books. And then there are the western spa-towns of **Karlovy Vary** (Karlsbad) and **Mariánské Lázně** (Marienbad), both visited by many German and Russian writers, including Goethe, Schiller, Gogol, and Turgenev. **Brno** (388 000) is Moravia's main cultural focus (also, incidentally, the birthplace of Milan Kundera ♭), alongside the Moravian university town of **Olomouc** (104 000) and industrial **Ostrava** (327 000).

EARLY HISTORY AND WRITING TO THE 18TH CENTURY

The Slavs are supposed by archaeologists to have arrived in the general area in about the 6th century AD. Both Bohemia and Moravia received their Christianity mainly from the West; the medieval literary influences were thus predominantly Latin and German, but also French and Italian. There was also the linguistically and culturally important mission of Cyril and Methodius to the Moravian prince Mojmír in the 9th century. These two Slav brothers from Salonika are credited with the creation of the Church Slavonic liturgy, which was soon expelled from Moravia, was practised for a while in Bohemia, but which struck permanent root in Bulgaria, the Slav Balkans and Kievan Russia.

Bohemia and Moravia were subsequently ruled, up to the 14th century, by the native Bohemian Přemyslid dynasty, founded, as the story goes, when the nobility could no longer bear to be ruled by a woman, Princess Libuše, who told them to follow her horse, till it led them to her husband-to-be Přemysl, ploughing his field. Had he completed his job before they arrived, many a later disaster in national annals would perhaps never have occurred, and the course of Czech literature might have been quite different – one thinks especially of the nineteenth-century historical novel, so often lamely derivative of the work of Walter Scott, and associated in Czech readers' minds above all with the prolific figure of Alois Jirásek (1851–1930). Jirásek is nevertheless still enjoyed for books such as *Staré pověsti české*, 1894 (*Old*

Czech Legends, 1992), retelling these ancient tales of Libuše, of the eponymous patriarchal tribal leader Czech arriving with his people, Moses-like upon the Mount of Říp in Northern Bohemia, of the Amazon-like Wars of the Maidens, and so on – legends of foundation, prophecy, etc, which began their process of detectable creation, accumulation, and mythopoeic refashioning in medieval Latin works such as Cosmas's *Chronica Boëmorum* of the early 12th century. By this time, Latin had ousted the relatively short-lived presence of Church Slavonic writing, which had co-existed with it for a while, latterly at the eleventh-century **Sázava Monastery**, south of Prague. Its texts include legends of St Wenceslas ('Václav' in modern Czech), that 'Good King Wenceslas' of the 19th-century English carol, murdered in 935 by his brother Boleslav, and soon turned into the national patron saint.

The literary tastes of the medieval Kings, later imperial electors, reflected both the often prominent role of Bohemia as part of that loose conglomerate, the Holy Roman Empire, and the large-scale immigration from Germany beginning in the 13th century, involved in trade, rich silver mines and the foundation of many towns. A number of German poets spent some time in Bohemia under the Přemyslid Kings, and later during the reigns of John of Luxembourg and his son the Emperor Charles IV, a strong patron of the Church and the arts, and founder of Prague University in 1348. Indeed, what is perhaps the outstanding masterpiece of pre-Reformation German prose, *Ackermann aus Böhmen* (*Husbandman from Bohemia*), was composed here by a Bohemian German, Johannes von Tepl (*c*1350–*c*1414), in about 1400.

A continuous tradition of Czech vernacular writing had also established itself, however, from the late 13th century (with earlier manuscript glosses), and this produced a remarkable spectrum of 14th-century writing in Czech, by far the widest of any Slav vernacular literature at that time, ranging from the vigorous 'Dalimil' chronicle and legends of the saints, especially *Život svaté Kateřiny* (*The Life of St Catherine*), to satires, courtly love poems and chivalrous romances, including a long and long-undervalued *Tristram a Izalda* (*Tristan and Isolde*). Drastic, punning medieval humour is represented by texts such as *Mastičkář* (*The Quacksalver*), in which a quack purveys dubious ointments to the Marys of the Easter story who visit Jesus's tomb (an English translation exists, and an idea of some of the other texts can be obtained in A. French's bilingual *Anthology of Czech Poetry* – see Booklist).

Prose of the late 14th and early 15th centuries includes medieval classics such as the *Trojan Chronicle* and *Marco Polo*, the theological prose of Tomáš ze Štítného (*c*1335–*c*1409), and a long, luxuriant and effusive Czech text inspired by the German *Ackermann*, known as

Tkadleček (*The Weaver*), c1407. The work takes the form of a dispute between a Lover (the weaver-of-words) and Misfortune (Death in *Ackermann*), who has deprived him of his mistress (not, as in *Ackermann*, his wife). This period also gave rise, as in England, to the first complete vernacular Czech Bible. It is thought to have been initiated by Charles's court in the 1360s, while, in the reign of his son Wenceslas IV, reformist preachers, the most famous among them Jan Hus (c1371–1415), influenced by the English Wyclif, laid the theological, if not the social, groundwork for the Hussite Wars, which followed the burning of Hus at the stake for heresy at Constance. Apart from all the later national literary and dramatic myth-making centred around Hussitism, for which we ought not to blame him (most of it is anyway inaccessible to the English reader), Hus contributed to the Czech language his clear straightforward register and avoidance of archaisms; his name is also linked with the adoption of diacritic marks in Czech spelling to distinguish different sounds (š for 'sh', č for 'tch', etc).

The years of Hussite conflict with the Church, religious factions and fanaticism, intermingled in a complex way with social resentments (in which anti-German feeling was by no means absent). All this led to a literature dominated by moral didacticism, warlike hymns, and pamphleteering satires. Among these, the Czech prose of Petr Chelčický's (c1390–1460) *Siet viery* (*Net of Faith*), c1440–43, stands out sharply. A pacifist proponent of primitive, biblical Christianity, against the official hierarchy of society, Chelčický was recognized by Tolstoy as a forerunner of his own thinking. Secular Renaissance influences are visible in scholarship, in book printing (which reached Bohemia before 1500), in Latin poets, but are prominent only in a few imaginative authors such as Hynek z Poděbrad (c1450–92), son of King George of Poděbrady, author of erotic verse and a collection of bawdy Boccaccio stories. Another 'unserious' amusing text, *Frantovy práva* (*Franta's Laws*), 1518, from the beer town of **Plzeň**, surviving in only one printed copy, makes up disreputable guild-like rules for everyday life and drinking, and tells uproariously irreverent stories of heaven, hell and foolish husbands.

From 1526 Bohemia saw its first rulers from the Habsburg dynasty, which lasted till 1918. One was that famous patron of the arts, sciences and pseudo-sciences, Rudolf II (Emperor from 1576–1612), whose **Prague** court saw figures like the astronomers Tycho Brahe and Kepler – also the English astrologer and magus John Dee, later depicted in the Bohemian German Gustav Meyrink's ◊ novel *Der Engel vom westlichen Fenster*, 1927 (*The Angel of the West Window*, 1991). Prague also became the home of an Englishwoman and fine Latin poet, Elizabeth Weston (d 1612), who compared her fate to that of Ovid, and married an imperial lawyer. Meyrink's most famous novel, *Der Golem*, 1915 (*The Golem*, 1985 – Extract 16) reminds us again of the long-standing importance of Jewish Prague, both for its history and its culture: the book is based on the Prague legend of the sixteenth-century Rabbi Löw, and his creation of a golem, a clay homunculus with affinities to Frankenstein's monster – as well as to the robots in the 20th-century Czech writer Karel Čapek's ◊ play *RUR* (*Rossum's Universal Robots*), 1920, whose success in translation in the UK and the USA in the 1920s gave the word 'robot' to the English language.

In 16th- and 17th-century Bohemia, like today, translation was already a vital source of literary nourishment: imported authors included Erasmus (*The Praise of Folly*), Petrarch (prose), Luther, many versions of Aesop's fables, and so on; while biblical translation culminated in the Kralice Bible (1579–94) of the Protestant Unity of Brethren. Travel writing was already an active genre: the Czech aristocrat Václav Vratislav z Mitrovic (1576–1635) wrote in 1599 of his part in a diplomatic mission to Turkey, involving imprisonment and the galleys – the work is available in English translation. Descriptions of Elizabethan England taken from the Latin of Zdeněk Brtnický z Valdštejna are available in *The Diary of Baron Waldstein* (see Booklist). The writer saw a play at the London Globe theatre in 1600 – what it was, we do not know. (Shakespeare's sea-coasted 'deserts of Bohemia' in *The Winter's Tale* are clearly coasts of the imagination, just as poverty-stricken artistic and writerly 'Bohemians' later received their epithet from Henry Murger's mid-nineteenth-century *Scènes de la vie de bohème*, the term being earlier associated in France with gypsy vagabonds.) For more fascinating or curious information on Anglo–Czech contacts, consult J. V. Polišenský's *Britain and Czechoslovakia: A Study in Contacts*.

The Winter's Tale was performed at the wedding of Elizabeth, daughter of James I of England, to Frederick of the Palatinate. In 1620, a brief bungled attempt by the Bohemian Estates to install this Protestant ruler Frederick as King was defeated by the Habsburg Ferdinand II just outside Prague, at the famous 'Battle of the White Mountain' (*Bílá hora*). This marked the start of the Thirty Years' War between Protestant and Catholic powers in Europe. For nationalistic Czechs, it marked the onset of a period of national 'Darkness' (*Temno* in Czech), represented as a disaster for the Czech language and its culture. In fact, insofar as there were grave weak points (such as widespread indifference to vernacular culture amongst the nobility), they were there already, and it can just as easily, in fact more easily, be argued that Czech imaginative literature derived new impetus from the re-Catholicization, if not from the political changes.

Following the execution on Prague's **Old Town Square** of twenty-seven prominent rebels, there was large-scale confiscation of rebel landowners' estates, royal powers were enlarged, the official use of German alongside Czech was sanctioned, and the practice of no Christian faith other than Roman Catholicism was permitted. Many members of the higher classes chose emigration instead of conversion. Subsequent decades brought lengthy wars with the Turks, and aggravation of peasant burdens, accompanied by periodic revolts. The weakening in the public status of Czech became most apparent in the 18th century, especially when German letters began to achieve a dramatic resurgence. (The aristocracy often preferred to cultivate French.)

Czech remained the majority language of the populace, however, and the later 17th century saw a considerable flowering of Czech imaginative literature, including skilful sermons and lyrical poetry, inspired by the spiritual values of renewed Roman Catholicism, full of bold emotive effects, playful ornament and daring figures of speech. Similar stylistic traits are also apparent in the most famous 17th-century Protestant writer, Jan Amos Komenský (Comenius) (1592–1670), born near **Uherský Brod** in Moravia, and last Bishop of the Unity of Brethren. In exile from 1628, he was famous in his day throughout Europe for his works on education and the encyclopaedic ordering of human knowledge. In Czech he is remembered above all for his classic work of allegorical fiction *Labyrint světa a ráj srdce*, 1623, 1631 (*The Labyrinth of the World and Paradise of the Heart*, two translations), in which a pilgrim, wishing to see the ways of the world for himself, finds only a monstrous chaotic labyrinth in which people absurdly delude themselves, enslave and mistreat each other; the paradise of the heart is reached only when he returns into himself and the Christ within. The text is full of caustic observations, on marriage, the pretensions of philosophers and academics, and on political power.

On the Catholic side one outstanding poet is the Jesuit missionary Bedřich Bridel (1619–80), whose best known poem 'Co Bůh? Člověk?' ('What is God? Man?'), 1659, is powerful in its mystic use of bold metaphor, oxymoron and natural imagery: 'Thou art the chasm's base, top, / I am the smallest droplet, / Thou art the orb of the sun, / I am its tiniest sparklet, / Thou art the very bloom's blossom, / I am but midday's gossamer, / To Thy dew's dew, new world, / I am a bubble at evening.' Another poet was Adam Michna z Otradovic (c1600–70), organist in **Jindřichův Hradec**, author of religious lyrics set to melodies, combining sensually adroit imagery with colloquial familiarity and domesticity: you can find recordings of his Christmas carols and other music. If subsequent decades, from the later 17th century up to the 1780s, were not exactly abundant in works of coherent literary imagination, it ought perhaps to be emphasized (as it generally is not) that a good deal of printed literature was nevertheless published, in the form of playfully vivacious, vivid and emotive sermons and other devotional prose and verse; there were also popular printed tales and songs, as well as folk plays, puppet theatre, and of course a great amount of orally transmitted folksong, forming the basis for the subsequent standard 19th-century collections by the poet Erben ◊ and, for Moravia, by František Sušil (1804–68). Many fine traditional folksongs and ballads are obtainable in modern recordings. There was even an early 18th-century official Czech newspaper, from 1719, albeit struggling with only a small clientele.

The end of this period (generally known as 'the Baroque', a term more familiar to the English reader in architecture and music) is signalled by a series of radical state initiatives, including the institution, under the Empress Maria Theresa, of universal primary schools, in her Ordinance of 1774. German was taught everywhere, and was required for entering secondary schooling and universities (where it had only recently replaced Latin), but the primary schools also brought about general basic literacy in Czech. Her son Joseph II's decrees enlarging peasant liberties and permitting Protestant worship followed in 1781.

THE 19TH CENTURY

Czech authors of the Revival period and later decades of the nineteenth century both adopted the inherited literary standard and gradually evolved a new educated language by elaborately creating further intellectual, poetic and technical vocabulary to compete with other more powerful and esteemed literatures, such as French, English and, now, their arch-competitor, German. German itself was still trying to escape from its own feelings of inferiority, having entered a period of intellectual and literary resurgence only a few decades before. The Czech literary revival began partly in the works of Enlightenment historians and other scholars, most notably the linguist–grammarian and literary historian Josef Dobrovský (1753–1829). The theatre, in Czech as in German (including opera), was a central plank in later 18th- and in 19th-century literary–cultural activity, and it has remained so more or less ever since. Landmarks include the opening of the **Estates Theatre** in Prague in 1783 with a play by Lessing, the premiere of *Don Giovanni* in the same theatre four years after, and later the opening of the grandiose **National Theatre** in 1883 with Smetana's opera *Libuše*. Viennese German authors initially remained at home with Bohemian themes, at least till that Year of Revolutions, 1848: witness Franz Grillparzer's plays *König Ottokars Glück und Ende*, 1825, and *Libussa*, 1841. From the later eighteenth century onwards Czech plays were also regularly staged.

Czech literature, however, though practised by enthusiasts, busily writing and translating (eg the great Czech lexicographer Josef Jungmann's (1773–1847) version of Milton's *Paradise Lost*) and earnestly attempting to emulate middle-class German culture, nevertheless took a few decades to produce a poet or novelist of clearly European stature. The first, it is generally agreed, came in the shape of the Prague-born amateur actor and Romantic poet Karel Hynek Mácha ◊, especially in his untranslatable masterpiece *Máj*, 1836 (*May*, various translations – Extract 4).

In *Máj* Man is prisoner of enigmatic nature and time, subject to agnostic metaphysical agony; seasonal, cyclical nature may be received as beauty, beautiful illusion, or mockery of human love and ideals. The text plays with musical effects, ironic contrasting of nature and man, and submerged erotic *double-entendres*; it lyrically exploits and simultaneously dismantles the pathetic fallacy, the ascribing of human emotions to nature. (Sentimental misapprehension of Mácha's views on 'love' is removed by inspection of his sexually explicit diary.) Literary-minded travellers may visit '**Mácha's Lake**' (Máchovo jezero) near **Doksy** in northern Bohemia, the stated setting for the poem.

Mácha died young, at the age of 26, while his contemporary, the folksong collector Karel Jaromír Erben ◊ did not publish his slender ballad volume *Kytice* (*Bouquet of National Legends*) until 1853, when he was 42. In these now classic Czech ballads (Extract 1), with their terse, vigorous diction, drawing creatively on oral tradition, but also German literary balladry, Erben presents a rather different, though still in a way Romantic, sensibility, of submission to the mysterious natural order and collective morality, transgression of which brings disaster. The poems portray a dialectic of inseparable pain and joy in human intimacy, fragility of life, possessiveness and conflict in bonds between mother and child, man and woman, the impossibility of being at one with the other. Apparently folk idiom, blending peasant Christianity and magic belief, becomes the terse expression of psychological, philosophical and moral anxiety. Erben's ballads later inspired Dvořák's tone poems *Vodník*, *Polednice*, *Štědrý večer* and *Zlatý kolovrat* (*The Water Sprite*, *The Noonday Witch*, *Christmas Eve*, and *The Golden Spinning Wheel*.)

Imaginative prose acquired classic status in the 1850s in the work of Božena Němcová ◊, immortalized by her fairy tales, her stories, and above all by her novel *Babička*, 1855 (*Granny*, 1962 – Extract 21), whose delightfully fluid language again defies wholly successful translation. Born in Vienna, Němcová grew up in **Ratibořice** (near **Česká Skalice**, east of **Náchod**) where her parents worked for the Countess von Sagan. The valley of the **Úpa**, now known as **Grandmother's Valley** (Babiččino údolí), is the setting for the much-beloved novel (one may visit the Countess's mansion, the cottage called the Old Bleaching Place, the Mill, and so on). Living herself in straitened circumstances, when her husband, an excise official, was disadvantaged after 1848 for his Czech patriotism, Němcová moulded a therapeutic re-creation of her childhood into a literary masterpiece by turns descriptively realistic, idyllic and lyrically tragic – lovingly she records the round of the seasons and traditional observances, the minutiae of daily life, within which disaster (floods, or the illegitimate pregnancy and Ophelia-like madness of the village girl Viktorka) are accommodated in a sense (in some way Erben-like) of human acceptance and harmony. This, and the portrayal of the grandmother's simple, pious morality, seem to act as a kind of spiritual compensation for the social disharmonies of the day and loss of spontaneous faith in older values and traditional communal verities. There are some points of comparison between Němcová and Adalbert Stifter (1805–68), an outstanding German Bohemian author of the time, born in Horní Planá (Oberplan), in the **Šumava** region of southern Bohemia, which he depicts in some of his stories, such as 'Der Waldsteig', 1845 ('The Forest Path', 1994).

Another woman writer, Karolína Světlá (1830–99), explicitly addresses rural inequality and gender conflict, in fiction with convincingly delineated, independent-minded female protagonists – such as in *Vesnický román* (*Village Novel*), 1867, where conflicts of matrimony and desire, incompatible character, age and social disparity collide with material need, religious belief and perception of moral duty. There are translations of her stories 'Hubička' ('A Kiss'), 1871 and 'Nebožka Barbora' ('Poor Dead Barbora'), 1873 – later collected in Světlá's *Kresby z Ještědí* (*Sketches from the Ještěd*), 1880 – in *Selected Czech Tales*, 1925, and *Czech Prose: An Anthology*, 1983.

A number of evocative, democratic-minded, mostly rural stories by Světlá's contemporary Vítězslav Hálek (1835–74) also exist in translation – but another poet, writer of short fiction, and prolific journalist, the Prague-born Jan Neruda ◊, has left a more prominent popular legacy than either with his *Povídky malostranské* (*Tales of the Malá Strana* – Extract 17), 1877. These stories of Prague are strongly redolent of the atmosphere of that old picturesque district of narrow streets and old houses beneath **Prague Castle** (or rather, perhaps one should say, the atmosphere of the district and that of the book blend inextricably in the mind, if one is that way inclined – just as Dickens's London is, and is not, the London of his day). Neruda combines evocative local colour, entertaining language, sharply observed settings, and emotionally charged, yet ironic character portrayal with touches of wry social comment, but also what one often takes to be ambivalent self-projections, in gruff, eccentric figures, the solitary, the bachelor and the beggar, the thwarted lover or the child. Similarly, among his several collections of verse, *Prosté motivy* (*Simple Motifs*), 1883, is a tensely emotive cycle of the seasons expressing the aging, unmarried eros of the poet's love for a young girl.

The Year of Revolutions, 1848, associated with the historian and political leader František Palacký (1798–1876) and the journalist and verse satirist Karel Havlíček Borovský (1821–56), had been followed by the bureaucratic absolutism of the 1850s, suppressing any too radical political expression of Czech nationalism. Subsequent events led in 1867 to the splitting of the Empire into the Dual Monarchy of Austria–Hungary, which caused another dashing of Czech national hopes for internal 'home rule'. Amid the continuing historicist nationalism, but also growing class-warfare of politics in the decades leading up to the first world war, Czech literature developed in manifold directions, as well as in sheer bulk, but classic works also become less easy to identify, perhaps because one or two 'major' figures are more developmentally significant than intrinsically compelling.

This situation is represented in poetry by the astonishingly prolific, at best brilliant, but often merely craftsmanlike, verbose, and repetitive poet Jaroslav Vrchlický (1853–1912). He translated gargantuan slices of Victor Hugo, Dante, Leopardi, Tasso, Baudelaire, Petrarch, Shelley, Whitman, and others. Crucially, he further emancipated Czech verse from folksiness, opened it to more celebratory sensuality, extended its metrical range, and shifted it further towards French and other Romance influences. Readers perhaps remember him mainly for a few wistful, controlled short poems, where emotional pain and a sudden sense of futility, of *vanitas rerum*, corrode formal Parnassian evocations of landscape, of natural and sensory abundance: where, in a way, he self-deconstructs.

Among the finer fiction writers one should name Julius Zeyer (1841–1901), for his sensual, linguistically Romance-like prose, expressing somewhat mystic artistic and erotic passions and ideals, in, for example, his *Tři legendy z krucifixu* (*Three Legends of the Crucifix*), 1895, of which 'Inultus' and 'Samko pták' ('Samko the Bird'), have been translated (see *Review 43*, 1943, and *Czech Prose: An Anthology*, 1983). One should also mention the science-fiction mystery tales of Jakub Arbes (1840–1914).

In the area of *fin-de-siècle* poetry there is the delicately crepuscular, musically alluring but also blackly ironic poet Karel Hlaváček (1874–98), from Prague's working-class **Libeň** district. His best poetry, however inaccessible in English, is in two small collections, *Pozdě k ránu* (*Late Till Morning*), 1896, and *Mstivá kantilena* (*Vengeful Cantilena*), 1898. His erotic and Symbolist graphic art has the benefit of needing no translation, and it is introduced in a recent book on *fin-de-siècle* Czech art by Petr Wittlich. Another figure is the belligerent and balladic social poet Petr Bezruč (1867–1958) from **Opava**. In his monumental *Slezské písně* 1903, 1909 (*Silesian Songs*, 1966) Bezruč stylizes himself as a rough Silesian Czech, protesting against the lot of his Germanized and Polonized fellow underdogs. Often highly admired is the impressive visionary Symbolist flow of cosmic humanitarian mysticism practised by the poet and essayist Otokar Březina (1868–1929), who taught and spent his retirement in **Jaroměřice nad Rokytnou** in Moravia, a place of pilgrimage for initiates.

Moving on into the first world war, one should at least name in passing the somewhat sidelined novelist Karel Matěj Čapek-Chod (1860–1927), whose notable, only in part socially analytical novels, such as *Turbina* (*Turbine*), 1916, and *Antonín Vondrejc*, 1917–18, draw upon a Naturalistic, deterministic (or rather semi-deterministic) psychological outlook, but also incorporate strong fictional grotesquerie. Čapek-Chod combines with rich and playful exuberance wide speech registers from the plebeian to the intellectually and archaizingly formal. Another notable writer was Viktor Dyk (1877–1931), perhaps now best remembered for his disillusionist lyrical novella *Krysař* (*Pied Piper*), 1915.

DURING THE FIRST REPUBLIC

An independent Czechoslovak Republic was established after the first world war under its first president Tomáš Garrigue Masaryk (1850–1937). His own writings on the shape of Czech history, war memoirs, and expositions of his political and philosophical ideas won him a devoted following, though there is dubious matter in his interconnecting of Hussitism with the populist aspects of the Czech national revival, and his emotive combination of Czech plebeian traditions (ie lack of culturally and linguistically Czech aristocracy and upper middle class) and modern ideas of democratic government into a Czech role in the grand scheme of things: a Czech 'meaning of history'. A wicked portrait of a frisky old Masaryk in later years can be found in Bohumil Hrabal's ◊ novel *Obsluhoval jsem anglického krále*, 1973 (*I Served the King of England*, 1989).

Jaroslav Hašek's ◊ *Osudy dobrého vojáka Švejka*, 1921–23 (*The Good Soldier Švejk*, 1974 – Extract 13) is an obvious place to begin a brief survey of post-1918 literature, with its first world war theme and its status as the most widely known Czech-language classic from this period. The war-, army-, church- and state-debunking clever-fool picaresque hero of this baggy long novel, with his endless zany blarney, has won the enormous affection of readers, but also incurred worried reactions from earnest thinkers who have seen the hopelessly evasive, unprincipled, basely materialistic aspects of his behaviour as a bad model – an undesirable image for the Czechs. Is this to miss the point? Fans visit the famous tourist-exploiting Prague hostelry **U kalicha** ('The Chalice') in the street **Na bojišti**. Another shrine is **Lipnice nad Sázavou**, with the house where Hašek spent the last months of his life, and his grave in the churchyard. Švejk's exuberantly omniverous language becomes a lot more pedestrian in translation – but never mind, the basics come across, the sheer exuberance of Hašek's anecdotage.

For most readers, however, the most famous Prague author of this century is without doubt Franz Kafka ◊, who wrote in German (as not everyone seems to know). Born of Jewish parents near the **Old Town Square** in Prague in 1883, Kafka in his work is usually felt to be intimately involved with this city, its labyrinthine streets, its Habsburg-inherited bureacracy, **Prague's** ambivalently rooted Jewish community which faced prejudice from both Germans and Czechs. (Czechs often saw Jews as both Jews and Germans – though during the Republic Prague Jews began to gravitate towards a Czech-language upbringing.) Few of Kafka's works are explicitly set in Prague. One of the exceptions is his early 'Beschreibung eines Kampfes' ('Description of a Struggle') of 1904–05, with, for example, its references to the **river embankment** and **Petřín hill** (Extract 14). Yet readers who know Prague will automatically place his novel *Der Prozess*, 1925 (*The Trial*, 1935 – Extract 15) in some fictional (or even documentary!) relation to this city: the cathedral portrayed is taken as **St Vitus'**, and en route to his demise the hero seems to be taken across the river. More or less fanciful or unwarranted assumptions may also be made about the unspecified settings of *Das Schloss*, 1926 (*The Castle*, 1930) and stories such as 'Das Urteil' ('The Judgment'), 1913, and 'Die Verwandlung' ('The Metamorphosis'), 1915.

But Kafka deals more with fictional externalization of inward experience, its transformation into narrative, apparently empirical fact, than with the documenting of social externals – even if the social externals are among the very objects of the mental estrangement, the typical emotional isolation of his heroes, alienated from family, father, authority, social community, spiritual authenticity. For a particularly strong, poetically expressed advocacy of Kafka's affiliatedness with the local specific culture, and literature in whatever language, of Prague and Bohemia, turn to A.M. Ripellino's book *Praga Magica*, translated from Italian as *Magic Prague*, which even attempts comparisons with Hašek, though Hašek's *Švejk* certainly presents a very different kind of fictional absurdity, perhaps even quite anti-spiritual, as well as cheerily unintellectualizing.

Closer to Kafka in tone and spirit, and perhaps even already showing affiliations, are some (untranslated) stories by Richard Weiner (1884–1937), a Czech Jewish writer and poet from **Písek**, who later lived as a journalist in Paris, close to the Surrealists and avant-garde painters such as the Czech Josef Šíma. Some similarity has also been observed between Kafka and the anxious outsider and refugee anti-heroes of Egon Hostovský (1908–73), a younger Czech novelist of Jewish family, who emigrated to the USA after the 1948 Communist take-over. (Incidentally, Kafka's translator, the poet Edwin Muir, lived in Prague for two periods – experiences described in his *Autobiography*.)

Other Prague-based German writers from the earlier 1900s begin by exploiting a certain common extravagantly expressed, mystic–fantastic, horror–dreamlike vein. Something related had already been long present in Czech writing: for example Václav Rodomil Kramerius's (1792–1861) tale 'Železná košile' ('The Iron Shirt'), 1831, which shares the same literary model as Edgar Allan Poe's 'The Pit and the Pendulum'. Other examples would be Mácha's 'Pout' krkonošská' ('Krkonoše Pilgrimage'), or Julius Zeyer's Paris-set novella *Dům 'U tonoucí hvězdy'* (*The House of the Drowning Star*), 1897, or the mystery stories of Jakub Arbes. Gustav Meyrink's ◊ *Der Golem* (*The Golem*) has been named earlier; we might also mention some texts of Prague-born authors recently made available in the *Dedalus/Ariadne Book of Austrian Fantasy*: Paul Leppin's (1878–1944) *Severins Gang in die Finsternis* (*Severin's Road into Darkness*), 1914, Franz Werfel's (1890–1945) *Spielhof: Eine Fantasie* (*The Playground*), 1920, and Kafka's close friend and biographer Max Brod's (1884–1968) *Die erste Stunde nach dem Tod* (*The First Hour After Death*), 1916. Brod also wrote historical novels, a genre practised with success by another Prague-born mystery writer Leo

---

Notes to map (facing page): *See map on page (xv) for location of Bohemia.* [a]*Just before their train reaches Tábor, Švejk and a railway man set off the alarm and bring it to a standstill. Consequently, Švejk arrives late at Tábor, sits around drinking, misses all the trains to České Budějovice, where he is supposed to be going, and is ordered to go on foot.* [b]*Wandering in a direction which takes him further and further away from his destination, Švejk is helped here by a kindly old woman.* [c]*Here Švejk meets Farmer Melichárek who thinks he has deserted.* [d]*At Putim, Švejk sleeps in a haystack with some good companions. Later in his wanderings, he ends up here again and is arrested as a Russian spy.* [e]*At Štěkeň, Švejk takes up with a talkative tramp.* [f]*The tramp, however, is not as talkative as the shepherd who entertains them here in the Schwarzenberg sheepfold.* [g]*At the end of his adventures in Southern Bohemia, Švejk is escorted to Písek by a corporal and is sent to České Budějovice by train. Source: Jaroslav Hašek,* The Good Soldier Švejk, *Cecil Parrott, trans, Everyman, London, 1993, following pp xlviii-xlix.*

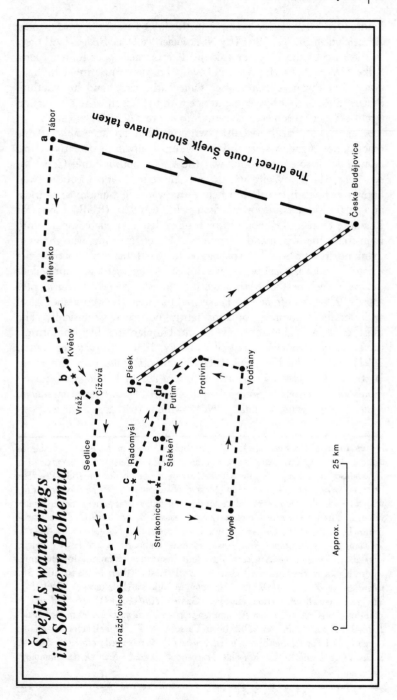

Švejk's wanderings in Southern Bohemia

The direct route Švejk should have taken

Tábor

Milevsko

Květov

Vráž

Čížová

Sedlice

Radomyšl

Horažďovice

Strakonice

Štěkeň

Volyně

Putim

Protivín

Vodňany

Písek

České Budějovice

0   Approx.   25 km

Perutz (1884–1957), for example in the linked stories of *Nachts unter der steinernem Brücke*, 1953 (*By Night under the Stone Bridge*, 1991), set in the time of the Emperor Rudolf. The German poet Rainer Maria Rilke (1875–1926), however, likewise Prague-born, turned his face away from Prague culture, after some early verse, and his youthful Prague tales, so that his acquaintance with the Czech writers Zeyer and Vrchlický becomes merely a curious footnote to literary biography.

A deft, but hardly occultist writer, rather an accessibly affable practitioner of the mystery short-story, especially in its detective form, as well as of science-fiction, was the Czech author Karel Čapek ♢, admirer of H. G. Wells and G. K. Chesterton, who was quite well known in English translation before the war. His humorous, satirical and Expressionist allegorical drama *RUR*, 1920 (RUR stands for Rossum's Universal Robots) turned the Golem and related figures into industrially useful humanoid products of bio-engineering, who threaten mankind and the 'soul'. His play gave the world that word 'robot' (from *robota* – feudal labour) which we now associate with fairly innocuous Japanese machine-tools. His detective stories in *Povídky z jedné a druhé kapsy*, 1929 (*Tales from Two Pockets*, 1962) wear their epistemological and morally exploratory concerns lightly, not to say whimsically. The most readily available of his several anti-Utopian apocalyptical satirical novels of modern society is *Válka s mloky*, 1936 (*War with the Newts*, 1991), in which the newts (like the robots) take over the world (Extract 10). He also wrote an often admired trilogy of novels *Hordubal, Povětroň, Obyčejný život*, 1933–34 (*Three Novels: Hordubal, Meteor, An Ordinary Life*, 1990), which (perhaps a little post-

---

Notes to map (facing page): [a]*His* **birthplace**, *now in Maiselova, beside St Nicholas Church.* [b]*His* **father's shop** *in the early years, Celetná (Zeltnergasse) 12.* [c]*The house* **'U minuty'** *('By the Minute') where the family lived in 1889–96.* [d]*His* **primary school** *(Volksschule) in Masná (Fleischmarkt).* [e]*The* **Gymnasium**, *secondary school in the Kinský Palace; in the same building his father's shop was later situated.* [f]*His residence in* **Celetná (Zeltnergasse) 3**, *1896–1907.* [g]*The* **Karolinum building** *of the University, where Kafka attended law lectures, 1901–06.* [h]*Building of the insurance firm* **Assicurazione Generali**, *where he first briefly worked.* [i]*Building of the* **Workers' Accident Insurance Company for Bohemia** *where Kafka worked from 1908 to 1922.* [j]**Pařížská (then Niklasstraße) 36**, *where the family lived, 1907–13.* [k]*His room in* **Bílkova (Bilekgasse) 10** *(1915).* [l]*His room in* **Dlouhá třída (Langen Gasse) 705/18**, *1915–16.* [m]*House in* **Zlatá ulička** *(Golden Lane or Alchimistengäßchen, Alchemists' Lane) in the Castle, 1916–17.* [n]*Lodging in the* **Schönborn Palace**, *1917.* [o]**Oppelt House**, *on the corner of Old Town Square and Pařížská, where the family lived from 1913. Source: Klaus Wagenbach, Kafka, Rowohlt Taschenbuch Verlag, Reinbek bei Hamburg, 1964, pp 52–53.*

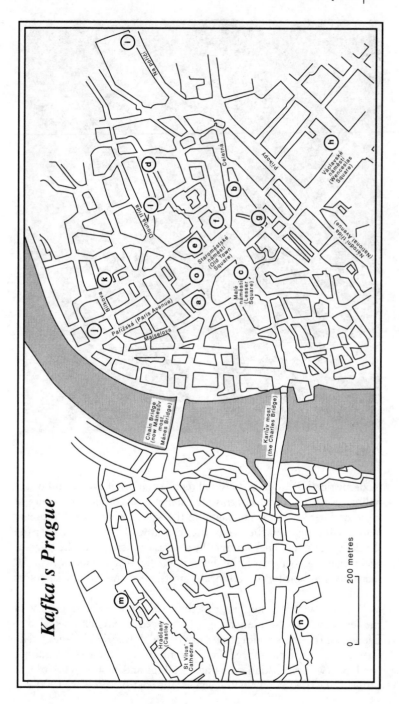

Kafka's Prague

Na poříčí

Celetná

Příkopy

Václavské
Náměstí
(Wenceslas
Square)

Národní třída
(National Avenue)

Dlouhá třída

Staroměstské
náměstí
(Old Town
Square)

Malé
náměstí
(Lesser
Square)

Bílkova

Pařížská (Paris Avenue)

Maiselova

Chain Bridge
(now Mánesův
most,
Mánes Bridge)

Karlův most
(the Charles Bridge)

Hradčany
(Castle)

St Vitus'
Cathedral

200 metres

0

Karel Čapek

modernistically?) examine fictional representation of events and personality, using multiple, contrasting, sometimes conflicting points of
view, and depicting the enigmatic in the (positively viewed) 'ordinary
man'. Dying right on the eve of the second world war, soon after the
shock of Munich, Čapek tends to be seen as emblematic of the tolerant
egalitarian democracy of the First Republic – a democracy which
succumbed militarily, not politically, to the Nazism and Fascism of its
neighbours.

The most visible young poets of the 1920s and 1930s were those of
the left-wing avant-garde, strongly influenced by French poetry since
Baudelaire (the outstanding translator of which was Karel Čapek). The
Czech avant-gardists moved from a primitivist or naivist Vitalism,
combined with Christian-symbolic socialism and Marxist proletarian-
ism – as practised briefly by the adolescent poet Jiří Wolker (1900–24)

– to an associative playfully metaphoric, exoticizing and popular-culture-influenced method called 'Poetism', strongly inspired by the French poet Guillaume Apollinaire, who has a passage about visiting **Prague** in his famous long polythematic poem *Zone* (there is an English version by Samuel Beckett). A later French writer to record his impressions of Prague was Albert Camus (see his *Selected Essays and Notebooks*).

Poetism was posited as modern life's re-creational counterpart to functionalist Constructivism, theorized about especially by the art-and-culture writer Karel Teige (1900–51), and cultivated with huge zest by the poet Vítězslav Nezval ◊, in associative polythematic poems such as *Podivuhodný kouzelník* (*The Amazing Magician*), 1924 and *Akrobat* (*Acrobat*), 1927. Nezval later went through an explicitly Surrealist phase, with which his partly translated topographical collection *Praha s prsty deště* (*Prague with Fingers of Rain*), 1936 (Extract 18), can be regarded as loosely associated. Later he rejected French Surrealist André Breton's doctrine, and returned to a more familiar versifying idiom which was (not merely incidentally, though it also came naturally) more accessible to the Communist comrades. In the post-1948 era this accommodation to politics involved him in a ridiculous and effusive paean of praise to Stalin.

Another prominent Poetist was Jaroslav Seifert ◊, especially in his *Na vlnách TSF* (*On the Waves of Wireless Telegraphy*). Seifert (Extract 19) rejected the Communist Party before the war, outlived nearly all his generation and became a much beloved wistfully affecting grand old poet, winning in the 1980s the Czechs' first Nobel prize for literature.

The poet František Halas ◊, though politically left-wing (and fondly regarded for resonantly patriotic poetry from the time of Munich and 1945) could at times be mistaken for a Catholic poet, so expressively neo-Baroque, quasi-religious, and obsessed with time and nothingness, is the core of his lyric verse (Extract 11). Halas's themes range from the resonantly biblical to the topically political: his 1930 collection *Kohout plaší smrt* (*The Cock Scares Death*) opens with a motto from William Blake's 'Europe': 'Thrice he assayd presumptuous to awake the dead to judgment.' In his poem *Staré ženy*, 1935 (*Old Women*, 1947) quasi-litanical word-play and annulled eroticism address the eternal themes of beauty, women, time and aging.

Another philosophical wrestler with words, the poet Vladimír Holan (1905–80), long outlived him. He is best known in English for his post-war works, both the often teasingly obscure, riddling longer poem *Noc s Hamletem*, 1964 (*A Night with Hamlet*, 1988), and his short, philosophically gnomic lyrical reflections, expressing existential anxiety, and containing submerged Aesopian notes of political protest. Under the Communists, Holan retired to his house in **Kampa Park** beside the Vltava in Prague, and became a paradigmatic Czech poet–recluse.

Next to him lived another of the one-time avant-gardists Jan Werich (1905–80), famous before the war as a double act with Jiří Voskovec (1905–81), who emigrated: as 'V + W', the fast-patter, jazzy song-singing cabaret-satire duo of Prague's 'Osvobozené divadlo' ('Liberated Theatre').

Fiction on the left was most prominently original in the work of Vladislav Vančura (1891–1942), who has, however, proved pretty unexportable with his exuberant verbal acrobatics, full of archaisms and expressive oddities. Nevertheless, his *Rozmarné léto* (*Capricious Summer*), 1926, which opens at a riverside bathing place in a small-town spa, transferred well (with loss of textual complexity) into a charming humorously lyrical film masterpiece by Jiří Menzel in 1968. Likewise, *Markéta Lazarová*, 1931, an avowedly anti-bourgeois, vitalist, epic-reviving, primitive-passion-extolling tale of ancient brigandage, has been effectively filmed (1967, directed by František Vláčil).

Social and social–psychological portrayals in fiction from this period (it is perhaps not too unkind or controversial to say) have left more a series of worthy and tedious attempts than masterpieces, among which Vančura's *Pekař Jan Marhoul* (*Baker Jan Marhoul*), 1924, is atypically imaginative and experimental. Marie Majerová's ◊ left-wing social fiction is more conventionally depictive, though not without documentary qualities: *Siréna*, 1935 (*The Siren*, 1953) (Extract 5) with its **Kladno** industrial setting, and *Havířská balada*, 1938 (*Ballad of a Miner*, 1960) have both been translated.

Place and period are vividly re-created (with past history and present expressivity inextricably combined) by the outstanding historical novelist Jaroslav Durych (1886–1962). Durych's texts display ironic tension between spirituality and sensuality. Though powerful on the Thirty Years' War in his long novel *Bloudění*, 1929 (*Descent of the Idol*, 1935), he is finest in his atmospheric and lyrically skilled short trilogy *Rekviem* (*Requiem*), 1930, three stories set at a time just after the assassination of the ambitious charismatic Bohemian *generalissimo* Valdštejn, or Wallenstein. The first story takes us to **Olomouc**, the second outside **Budějovice**, and the third to **Valdice**, Wallenstein's burial place. (There is still no English version.)

A certain neo-Baroque atmosphere – also found in Halas ◊ and in Nezval's ◊ gloomily apocalyptic use of Surrealist visuals, for example in *Absolutní hrobař* (*Gravedigger of the Absolute*), 1937 – is generally taken to reflect the demise of 1920s optimism, the onset of the Great Depression, and the political crises of the 1930s. The Munich agreement of 1938 led to the dismantling of Czechoslovakia, and the establishment of a Protectorate under Hitler's Germany; the second world war brought obliteration of the Jewish community, and at its end the expulsion of most of the three million Germans from restored Czechoslovakia. An uneasy coalition between Communists and others tipped over into outright Communist rule in February 1948. Much cultural energy was trodden flat or sent underground by the dictates and earnestly myopic heroic didacticism of Socialist Realist doctrines. Many writers of course adapted to cultural dictates, willingly or otherwise, and continued to publish and make a living.

COMMUNIST TAKEOVER, 1948 TO COMMUNIST COLLAPSE, 1989

To some the 'meaning of history' was to bring about the onset of Socialist Utopia, the 'end of history' in fact. History continued, of course. Stalin died in 1953, agriculture was collectivized, public culture remained closely regimented, but the Communist regime inched or lurched its way, heavily implicated in its own (albeit by Soviet standards small-scale) executions and show trials, into the reforms of the 1960s, which then veered into the 'Prague Spring' of 1968 under Alexander Dubček's new-style Communist leadership.

As cultural space widened, Czech writers tried, or perhaps inevitably failed rather, to 'settle accounts' with history. Milan Kundera's ◊ protagonist Ludvík in his first novel *Žert*, 1967 (*The Joke*, 1992 – Extract 8) fails to compensate for past humiliation at the hands of the Party by humiliating people today. History continues to manipulate, to play tricks on the individual. In the stories of *Směšné lásky*, 1963–68, 1970 (*Laughable Loves*, 1975), the protagonists wander entertainingly through sexual labyrinths of inauthenticity and thwarted intentions. History and the individual, love and sex, remain perplexed with one another in all of his later novels.

Josef Škvorecký's ◊ adolescent Danny in his first published novel *Zbabělci*, 1958 (*The Cowards*, 1972) plays jazz, courts girls and gets drawn into uprising activity at the end of the war, taking a bottom-up debunking view of instant heroic monumental history. His novella *Bassaxofon*, 1967 (*The Bass Saxophone*, 1980 – Extract 6) is another apotheosis of jazz, portrayed as a provider of spiritual epiphany. Škvorecký goes on to chronicle his wartime 'Kostelec', alias his north Bohemian home town of **Náchod**, in a whole series of Danny novels. He extends his debunkingly satirical view, in *Mirákl*, 1972 (*The Miracle Game*, 1991) and *Příběh inženýra lidských duší*, 1977 (*The Engineer of Human Souls*, 1986), to the heroes of the Prague Spring itself, and the life of Czech exiles in North America.

The Jewish tradition, community and its fate were scrutinized shortly after the war by Jiří Weil (1900–59) in the novel *Život s hvězdou*, 1949

(*Life with a Star*, 1989); subsequently by Ladislav Fuks (1923–94), in the not unrelated *Pan Theodor Mundstock*, 1963 (*Mr Theodore Mundstock*, 1984) and other books; and also in a number of works by Arnošt Lustig (1926–), including the novel *Dita Saxová*, 1962 (*Dita Saxová*, 1994). Ivan Klíma ◊, who was a boy in **Terezín** concentration camp, produces a gentle love story 'Miriam' out of that setting (Extract 22). In his novel *Láska a smetí*, 1988 (*Love and Garbage*, 1990) and the stories of *Moje zlatá řemesla*, 1990 (*My Golden Trades*, 1992) he will later autobiographically explore, not merely to political effect, the fictional perspectives given to a banned writer post-1968 who takes on otherwise unlikely jobs and occupations.

Another kind of 'reckoning with the present' is to be found in the plays of Václav Havel ◊, technically influenced by Absurdist dramatists such as Ionesco and Beckett. In *Zahradní slavnost* (*The Garden Party*), 1963, *Vyrozumění* (*The Memorandum*), 1965 and *Ztížená možnost soustředění* (*Increased Difficulty of Concentration*), 1968, the playwright and later, from the fall of Communist rule in 1989, President, takes the existential angsts and black comedy of the 'Theatre of the Absurd' and uses them to excoriate a morally and ideologically eroded society. As a leader of Charter 77, formed to monitor Czechoslovakia's behaviour on human rights, its adherence to the Helsinki accords, Havel became a writer for the dissident movement and abroad. In his one-act play *Audience*, 1975, a pseudo-Havel figure faces a boss in **Trutnov brewery**, where Havel briefly worked. Another dramatist, Josef Topol, is a complex, lyrically expressive writer, still unknown to English-speaking theatre-goers, though a translation of one of his plays, *Kočka na kolejích* (*Cat on the Rails*), 1965 has recently been issued.

In recent Czech poetry, apart from the older Holan (and Seifert), English-language readers have particularly taken to the wry, analytically and drily playfully lyrical commentaries of Miroslav Holub ◊, with their own brand of scientific (yet also not un-Absurdist) 'back to basics' mini-narratives (Extract 9).

Another (prose) moralist with his own playful streak is Ludvík Vaculík ◊, whose novel *Sekyra*, 1966 (*The Axe*, 1973 – Extract 3), in its themes of father and son, rural life and urbanizing, industrializing change, seeks to reckon with the recent past, but also just as much with the present (the past's mode of existence).

Bohumil Hrabal's ◊ exuberant works also often address time, the flow of time, presenting an immediacy of temporal flux in cascades of concrete, sensory and sensual detail – this is notable, for example, in his lyrically memorializing and fictionalizing books about his **Nymburk** youth and his parents, *Postřižiny*, 1976 (*Cutting It Short*, 1993 – Extract 7) and *Městečko, kde se zastavil čas*, 1978 (*The Little Town Where Time Stood Still*, 1993). Such concerns are wedded to his particular concept

Ivan Klíma

of *pábitelství*, of palavering inventive play, as a *modus vivendi* amid that 20th-century sense of the absurd, both political, and philosophical, or existential (see the stories in the English volume *The Death of Mr Baltisberger*). His texts often inextricably blend elements of the pub anecdote, popular ramblings and improvisations with something of the inheritance of Surrealism, with juxtaposition and collage of imagery and expressively interlocking details. One of Hrabal's more complex and ambitious longer texts is *Obsluhoval jsem anglického krále*, 1980 (*I Served the King of England*, 1989), which also dismantles the solemn mythologies of Czech history since the 1930s in the story of a young waiter who rises in the world and gets involved with the occupying Nazis.

Another, younger writer, who has some gentle affiliations with Hrabal, and a strong lyric gift, applied to themes of his wartime youth, was Ota Pavel (1930–73), whose main story collections appeared in

Prague in the early 1970s: *Smrt krásných srnců* (*Death of Lovely Roebuck*), 1971, and *Jak jsem potkal ryby* (*How I Encountered Fish*), 1974. Among the various historical novelists, the most effective in giving the genre imaginative and expressive functions (with strong Aesopian references to contemporary conditions) was Jiří Šotola (1924–89) with novels such as *Tovarišstvo Ježíšovo* (*The Society of Jesus*), 1969, *Kuře na rožni* (*Chicken on the Spit*), 1976, about an eighteenth-century puppeteer, and *Svatý na mostě* (*Saint on the Bridge*) 1978, about St John of Nepomuk. Experimental, intellectual prose following in the line of Richard Weiner was practised by Věra Linhartová (1938–), who later moved to Paris. Social mores, the limping Socialist consumer society, careerism, sex and superficiality are powerfully incorporated in energetic, rhythmically seductive textual canvases by Vladimír Páral ◊, in novels such as *Katapult*, 1967 (*Catapult*, 1989 – Extract 2) and *Milenci a vrazi* (*Lovers and Murderers*), 1969; later he moves into science-fiction fantasies, or ostensibly more affirmative depictions of modern society, with notes of hyperbole and parody.

The years after the 1968 Soviet invasion brought internal cultural repression, and serious impoverishment of the domestic publishing scene. Obviously the writing of authors who left for exile, such as Škvorecký, or Kundera, who later did so, was vitally affected by all this, both in its themes and its sensibilities. The 1970s also saw fruitful directions in the work of several non-exile authors: Hrabal, simultaneously accommodating to regime pressures and disobediently circulating typescript texts; Vaculík, Havel and others, who distributed all their writings in typescript samizdat (eg in Edice Petlice, 'Padlock Editions') and abroad. The repression, often too glibly referred to as a cultural desert, affected the reading public at the time (who replaced American light reading with their own, not very exciting domestic equivalents, disguised as morally uplifting social critiques), but in retrospect the 1970s in Czech literature were hardly a desert at all.

The 1980s also began gradually to present, even in official publishing houses (against the grain of the times), a number of younger, in fact rather 'ideologically subversive' names, such as Alexandra Berková (1949–) in prose, or Sylva Fischerová (1963–) in poetry. After 1989 other 'grey area' writers also became more visible, such as two novelists-cum-literary-scholars Daniela Hodrová (1946–) and Vladimír Macura (1945–). Hodrová is notable for perhaps the most complex, accomplished and original of recent Czech novels, a series starting with *Podobojí* (*In Both Kinds*), 1991, and *Kukly* (*Pupae/Masks*), 1991. The novels in part evoke her childhood in the **Olšany–Žižkov** districts of **Prague**, interweaving historical incident and experience into a magic simultaneous whole.

The commercial book market, and the demise of state subsidies, since 1989 has altered the publishing scene beyond recognition, producing a flood of translated entertainment literature, especially American – but native output is continuing to find publishers and, presumably, readers, even if it feels for the time being somewhat drowned by all the rest.

LITERARY LANDMARKS – PRAGUE

Prague is the birthplace of Karel Hynek Mácha, Jan Neruda, Jakub Arbes, Karel Hlaváček, Jaroslav Hašek, Jaroslav Seifert, Václav Havel, and Ivan Klíma; and of the German writers Rainer Maria Rilke, Franz Kafka, Max Brod, Egon Erwin Kisch and Franz Werfel. The following are of course only a few of its many sites with literary associations.

Streets are normally cited without the word *ulice* (street); squares are designated *náměstí*, while *třída* means a larger road, avenue or boulevard; *nábřeží* means embankment, quai. Numbers here are street numbers, not the area number, which houses also display. The German street name is appended, where it might be helpful.

Stare Město (Old Town)

Anenské náměstí: In the late 1950s No 5 was turned into the **Divadlo na zábradlí** (Theatre on the Ballustrade). Here Leon Grossman produced plays such as Jarry's *Ubu Roi*, Beckett's *Waiting for Godot* and a version of Kafka's *The Trial*. Havel worked here in 1960–68. Ladislav Fialka's mime theatre was based here until his death in 1991.

Betlémské náměstí: From 1402 to 1412 the reformer Jan Hus preached here in the austere twin-gabled **Bethlehem Chapel** (reconstructed 1950–52 from remnants).

Celetná (Zeltnergasse): Kafka's father initially had his haberdashery shop at **No 12**, the former Hrzánský Palace. They also lived at **No 2**, Sixtův dům, in 1888–89, and in 1896–1901 at **No 3**, later Prague's only 'Vegetarian Restaurant'.

Karlova, 1: The Klementinum, now the State Library and University Library, with many old books and manuscripts.

Karoliny Světlé, 22: The 19th-century writer Karolina Světlá was born here, and the street is now named after her.

Kožná, 1: This house with a portal featuring two bears is the birthplace of the Bohemian German journalist and writer Egon Erwin Kisch.

Maiselova (Maiselgasse): Adjacent to **St Nicholas' Church** is the site of the house where Franz Kafka was born. The house, except for the Baroque portal, was demolished and replaced at the end of the 19th century, after a fire.

Na příkopě (Graben), 14: A bank building stands on the site of the house where Němcová lived from 1861 till her death in January 1862.

Náměstí Republiky (Republic Square): The splendid Art Nouveau building with its concert hall and cafés, called **Obecní dům (Municipal House)**, has panels by Max Švabinský in the Rieger Hall on the first floor with portraits of national figures, among them Jan Neruda and Božena Němcová.

Národní třída (National Avenue), 2: The **National Theatre** opened in 1881 with a performance of Smetana's opera Libuše. It was swiftly rebuilt after a fire that same year and reopened in 1883. Opposite, at **No 1**, is the **Café Slavia**, a favourite writers' meeting place. **Nos 9 and 11** were the premises of the Union of Czech Writers. Before the second world war the literary café Národní kavárna (The National Café) was situated here. **No 9**, richly stuccoed, was the building of the publishers Topič. On the corner of Perštýn and Národní there once stood the building housing the famous Café Union, where the avant-garde group Devětsil was founded in 1920.

Staroměstské náměstí (Old Town Square, Großer Ring, Altstadter Ring): The square is dominated by the large bronze Monument to Jan Hus, by Ladislav Šaloun, bearing the words 'Truth will prevail'. **No 12** is the Goltz-Kinský Palace, from whose balcony Klement Gottwald proclaimed the Communist coming to power in February 1948. (See also the opening of Milan Kundera's *The Book of Laughter and Forgetting*.) Kafka's father's shop was also later in the Kinský Palace, as was his Gymnasium.

U radnice, 5: The house 'U minuty' ('At the Minute') is not Kafka's birthplace, but the Kafkas lived here in 1889–1896. The exterior is covered with fine sgraffito decorations, executed around 1611, restored in 1919 by Josef Čapek, Karel's brother (and again later).

U starého hřbitova: The famous old **Jewish Cemetery** contains the grave of the legendary Rabbi Jehuda Löw ben Bezalel (c1520–1609), author of important Hassidic writings. Visitors throw bank notes on it, as well as pebbles, hoping that he will grant their wishes. According to tradition he created, from the mud of the Vltava, Yossel the Golem, a humanoid being. A version of the legend was later popularized by Gustav Meyrink in his novel *The Golem* (Extract 16). Prague's old **Jewish quarter** also features in the once popular American novelist Marion Crawford's *The Witch of Prague*, 1882, George Eliot's *The Lifted Veil*, 1859, Trollope's *Nina Balatka*, 1867 (Extract 19), and recently in Bruce Chatwin's *Utz*, 1988.

Železná: The 18th-century **Estates Theatre** building here opened in 1783 with Lessing's play *Emilia Galotti*; four years later it staged the premiere of Mozart's *Don Giovanni*. At **No 9** is the **Carolinum**, part of Charles University, founded in 1348.

Malá Strana, Hradčany, Petřín

Chotkovy sady (Choték Park): At its eastern end stands a fine memorial to the 19th-century writer Julius Zeyer with a grotto, white marble figures and a bronze bust.

Hrad (Prague Castle): Kafka lived briefly here, at **No 22, Zlatá ulička** (Golden Lane, Alchimistengäßchen or Alchemists' Lane). The tiny houses of this now very touristy corner have been dolled up. One of Jan Neruda's stories is set in **St Vitus' Cathedral** (Extract 17), inside the Castle area, and the Cathedral scene in Kafka's *The Trial* is generally read as taking place here (Extract 15). The **Castle** is President Havel's official residence. The place is also associated with the poet Seifert, who lived for a while in the late 1920s and early 1930s in a house, now gone, between the end of Golden Lane and the Daliborka Tower.

Lázeňská, 6: Here, in a house later rebuilt, stayed Peter the Great of Russia in 1698, and in 1833 the French poet Chateaubriand.

Nerudova, 24: At the Cajetan Theatre, sited here in the 1830s, the poet Mácha performed as an amateur actor. Today the street is named after its famous resident Jan Neruda. He lived at **No 47,** 'U dvou slunců' ('House of the Two Suns'). **No 48,** 'U zlaté hvězdy' ('The Golden Star'), is the site of the story about Mr Vorel in Neruda's *Tales of the Malá Strana.*

Petřín (hill and park): Here there is a famous monument to the poet Mácha, and statues of Jan Neruda and Vrchlický. The former was important to the Chilean poet Pablo Neruda (real name Ricardo Reyes) who later wrote in his autobiography, 'I happened upon the name Neruda in a Czech magazine without having the slightest idea that it belonged to a Czech writer . . . As soon as I arrived in Czechoslovakia many years later, I placed a flower at the foot of his bearded statue.'

Říční, 11: A plaque marks the house where Karel and Josef Čapek lived in 1907–23, and where together they wrote *The Insect Play* and Karel wrote *RUR.*

Strahovské nádvoří (Strahov courtyard), 1: A Museum of National Literature was opened in the **Strahov monastery** in 1953. The monastery possesses valuable books and manuscripts, and two magnificent library rooms: the late 17th-century Theological Hall and the late 18th-century Philosophical Hall.

Újezd, 35: Here stood the house 'U bílého orla' ('The White Eagle') where the poet Mácha was born in 1810.

New Town

Hybernská, 15: Here, at the corner of Dlážděná, is the **Café Arco,** once frequented by German-Jewish writers, including Werfel, Brod,

Kafka and Kisch. Karl Kraus satirized the place, writing, '*Es werfelt und brodet und kafkat und kischt*' ('It Werfels and Brods and Kafkas and Kisches').

Ječná, 28: Božena Němcová lived here from 1853 to 1854 and wrote her classic novel *Babička* (*Granny*) – Extract 21.

Jindřišská, 14: Today the head post-office, the first Prague botanic garden was opened here in the 14th century. Petrarch is said to have been a guest of its Italian founder. At **No 17** the house where Rilke was born once stood.

Jungmannova, 11: At the corner of Národní třída is the 1920s Adria Palace, housing the **Laterna Magica** theatre, whose mixed-media illusionist spectacles were first created for the Brussels World Exhibition of 1958 by Alfréd Radok, Josef Svoboda, Miloš Forman and others. Now a tourist attraction, in November 1989 it was the centre for the Civic Forum movement, which took Havel to the presidency.

Jungmannovo náměstí (Jungmann Square): Notable statue of the Revival scholar and writer Josef Jungmann.

Karlovo náměstí (Charles Square): There are statues of Vítězslav Hálek and Karolina Světlá in the gardens. '**Faust's House**', at the south end, is where Edward Kelley practised alchemy in the time of Rudolf. It became a pharmacy in the 18th century, and the legend sprang up that Doctor Faust had been an occupant, till he was carried off by the devil.

Na bojišti, 12: The beer-house '**U kalicha**' ('The Chalice') owes its fame to Hašek's *The Good Soldier Švejk*. Not surprisingly, the place thoroughly exploits the connection.

Na poříčí, 7: Here were the offices of the Workers' Accident Insurance Company for Bohemia, where Kafka worked from 1908 to 1922.

Rašínovo nábřeží, 78: Havel's flat is in an apartment block here designed and owned by his grandfather. The poet Vrchlický lived at **No 76** and **No 72**.

Slovanský ostrov: The famous Slav Congress was held on this island in the river in 1848. There is a memorial to Božena Němcová at the north end.

Školská, 16: The birthplace of Jaroslav Hašek.

Václavské náměstí (Wenceslas Square): The **National Museum** stands at the top of the square, once the Horse Market. In the middle there once stood the wooden Bouda, the first regular Czech-language theatre (1786–1789). **No 19**, now the Polish Cultural Centre, housed the Trieste insurance company Assecurazioni generali, where young Kafka had his first brief job.

Vladislavova, 14: Neruda lived here from 1883, until his death in 1891.

Vyšehrad

Vyšehrad: Writers buried in the cemetery include Jaroslav Vrchlický and Julius Zeyer (in the Slavín section); Božena Němcová 2–77 (tombstone with scenes from *Granny*); Jan Neruda 3–25; Vítězslav Nezval 5–48; Vítězslav Hálek 9–26; Karel Hynek Mácha 10–126, often with candles; and Karel Čapek 12–47. The hill of Vyšehrad was the legendary seat of Princess Libuše, who prophesied Prague's future glories, and married Přemysl the ploughman. Works devoted to her include Grillparzer's drama *Libussa* and Smetana's opera *Libuše*.

Vinohrady, Žižkov

Bratří Čapků, 28–30: The brothers Josef and Karel Čapek lived from 1924 in this street, now named after them.

Nad vodovodem: Franz Kafka's grave is in the modern **Jewish cemetery**, also the ashes of the poet Jiří Orten and the grave of the short-story writer Ota Pavel.

Vinohradská, Olšanské hřbitovy: Writers buried in the Olšany cemeteries include Jan Kollár and Pavel Josef Šafařík (1st civic cemetery); V. M. Kramerius, V. K. Klicpera, Karel Havlíček Borovský (2nd cemetery); Josef Jungmann, F. L. Čelakovský (3rd); Karolína Světlá (4th); Karel J. Erben (5th).

Libeň

Na Korábě: The *fin-de-siècle* poet Karel Hlaváček is buried here in the Libeň cemetery (2nd section, main avenue); he lived at **Podlipného 19** (plaque).

LITERARY LANDMARKS – BOHEMIA AND MORAVIA

The following is, again, a bare, telegraphic selection.

Bohemia

Doksy, 'Mácha's Lake' (Máchovo jezero) and Bezděz: The lake is associated with Mácha's famous poem *May* (*Máj*) – Extract 4. From the village of Doksy a favourite walk of the poet follows an 8 km path to ruined **Bezděz castle** (plaque), which is also a setting for Smetana's opera *The Secret*.

Česká Skalice: Němcová went to school behind the **main square** (statue outside). She was married in the former inn U českého lva (The Golden Lion), now a **museum** to her. She spent her childhood in nearby Ratibořice (see below).

Český Dub: museum to the 19th century writer Karolina Světlá, who wrote on the local Ještěd region.

Dobříš and Strž: The former **Colloredo mansion** in Dobříš, not far from Prague, became a Writers' Union residence from 1945. Not far away, by a small lake, is the finely situated house acquired by Karel Čapek in 1935 at Strž, now a **museum**.

Domažlice: Birthplace of the novelist Karel Matěj Čapek-Chod (**Komenského, 11**) and the philosopher-figure Ladislav Klíma. Němcová lived here for a while, and the poet Vrchlický died here (**náměstí Míru, 125**).

Duchcov (Dux): From 1785 until his death in 1789 Casanova lived here at the **Wallensteins' chateau** and wrote his famous Memoirs. Goethe and Schiller also stayed here.

Františkovy Lázně (Franzensbad): Distinguished visitors to the spa included Herder, Schiller, and Goethe. Němcová also took the cure here.

Horní Planá na Šumavě (Oberplan): This was the birthplace of the German writer Adalbert Stifter (1805–Linz 1868). There is a statue in the **gardens**, and a **memorial room** in the house where he was born.

Hronov, near Náchod: Birthplace of Josef Čapek (1887 – Bergen-Belsen 1945) and the historical novelist Alois Jirásek (1851–Prague 1930), who is buried here. **Memorial room** in the wooden cottage where Jirásek was born.

Husinec, near Prachatice: Birthplace of the reformer Jan Hus (c1371–Constance 1415). There is a small **museum** at **No 36, Prokopovo náměstí.**

Chelčice near Vodňany: Birthplace of the pre-Tolstoyan Christian thinker Petr Chelčický (c1380–c1460). Statue.

Chvatěruby near Kralupy: Castle ruin beloved of the poet Mácha.

Jičín: Birthplace of the Austrian critic and essayist Karl Kraus (1874–Vienna 1936). The town figures in Durych's novel *Bloudění* (*Descent of the Idol*). The partly Renaissance square is dominated by Albrecht von Wallenstein's palace.

Karlovy Vary (Carlsbad): This most famous Bohemian spa was visited by numerous foreign authors, including Schiller, Mickiewicz, Chateaubriand, Gogol, Turgenev, Marx, and Gorky. Between 1785 and 1823, it was regularly visited by Goethe, who wrote many poems here.

Lipnice nad Sázavou: Hašek spent his last months and died here in 1923. He put up at the 'Czech Crown', then in the summer of 1922 he bought a ramshackle house below the castle, but occupied only one room. For the funeral, attended by a few friends, his body weighing over 24 stone had to be taken out through the window. His debtors came and loaded all they could on to a cart. He was buried in the local churchyard. The house has been turned into a small **museum**.

Litoměřice: Associated with the poet Mácha, who briefly worked and was originally buried here. There is a small **museum** at **Máchova ul. 10**, where he died in 1836. In 1938, when the Germans occupied Litoměřice, his tomb was moved to Prague's Vyšehrad cemetery.

Malé Svatoňovice near Úpice: Birthplace of Karel Čapek (1890–Prague 1938). Memorial plaque; statue of the brothers Čapek and **museum**.

Mariánské Lázně (Marienbad): This famous Bohemian spa town was visited by numerous writers, including Gogol, Turgenev, Goncharov, Gorky, Mark Twain, Nietzsche, Ibsen, Bjørnson, and Kipling, but it is especially strongly associated with Goethe, who visited it four times. The **Municipal Museum** in the house 'U zlatého hroznu' ('The Golden Grapes') on (former) Gottwaldovo náměstí, 10, is where Goethe stayed on his last visit in 1823. Here Goethe fell in love with the sixteen-year-old Ulrike von Lewetzow, the muse behind his Marienbad Elegy.

Miletín near Hořice: Birthplace of the poet Erben. Memorial on the square, plaque on the house in **Arnoldova ulice.**

Náchod: Birthplace of Josef Škvorecký, who worked during the war at the local Messerschmitt factory. See his essay 'I Was Born at Náchod', in *Talkin' Moscow Blues*, 1988. In his 'Smiřický' novels the town is thinly disguised as 'Kostelec', and the narrator is cheekily named Daniel Smiřický, after the one-time lords of the castle above the town.

Nymburk: Here in the local brewery Hrabal spent his youth, and his books *Postřižiny* (*Cutting It Short* – Extract 7) and *Městečko, kde se zastavil čas* (*The Little Town Where Time Stood Still*) are based on this setting. The town is also associated with Němcová, who lived here in 1848–50.

Ratibořice: This small place in a valley near Česká Skalice (see above) is the setting of Božena Němcová's classic novel *Babička* (*Granny*) – Extract 21. The valley, now known as **Granny's Valley** (Babiččino údolí), contains features from the book, such as Viktorka's **sluice gate**, the **Old Bleaching Place** (Staré bělidlo), and the **river**. A sandstone group with the Grandmother by Otto Gutfreund stands in front of the **old mill**, while the nearby mansion of **Ratibořice** contains souvenirs of the author's life.

Světlá pod Ještědem: The summer home of Karolina Světlá, 1853–65, and the source of her pen-name. Statue opposite the church.

Teplice: Many writers visited this 19th-century spa, including Goethe, Schopenhauer and Ibsen. The castle has a regional **museum** with rooms devoted to Beethoven and Pushkin.

Terezín (Theresienstadt): In 1940 the Nazis established a prison in the Small Fortress of Terezín and in the following year the whole town was turned into a ghetto housing around 250 000 Jews, of whom about 80 000 were eventually deported to Auschwitz, Treblinka and Majdanek, and many others died of hunger or illness. Several writers have written works based on their experiences, notably the short-story writer Arnošt Lustig. The opening story of My First Loves by Ivan Klíma (Extract 22), is a childhood impression of life in the ghetto. Terezín also appears in the novel A Change of Skin by the Mexican writer Carlos Fuentes, who visited it.

Moravia

Brno: Birthplace of the poet Halas, and contemporary writers Hrabal and Milan Kundera. The town is home to the lively theatre **Divadlo na provázku** (Theatre on a String). The Italian poet Silvio Pellico, imprisoned in the **Špilberk Citadel**, described his experiences in Le mie prigione (My Prisons), 1832.

Fulnek: Komenský taught in the **School of the Brethren** here between 1618 and 1621.

Hranice: Rilke was a pupil at the former military school here in 1890–91.

Ivančice: Jan Blahoslav (1557–71) set up a printing press for the Unity of Brethren in Ivančice, where his New Testament was published in 1564. (Statue in the street **Ve Sboru**.)

Jaroměřice nad Rokytnou: The Symbolist poet Otokar Březina taught here, and died here in 1929. Memorial in house **46/40**, with a plaque.

Jeseník: A plaque in **Tyršova ulice (no 168)** records the visits to this spa of the Russian writer N. V. Gogol in 1845 and 1846.

Kralice, near Náměšt' nad Oslavou: Famous centre of the Unity of Czech Brethren, site of their printing press, which in 1579–94 produced the six-volume Kralice Bible, equivalent in status to the English Authorized Version. **Museum**.

Opava: Birthplace of the Silesian Czech poet Petr Bezruč (1867– Olomouc 1958), who is also buried here. **Museum in Ostrožná ulice 43**.

Prostějov: Birthplace of the German philosopher E. Husserl and the Czech poet Jiří Wolker (room in the local **museum**).

Přerov: Birthplace of the Brethren writer Jan Blahoslav (1523–Mor. Krumlov 1571). Komenský attended the Brethren's school here, and later administered it. Part of the **museum** is devoted to Komenský.

Příbor (Freiberg): Birthplace of Sigmund Freud (1856 – London 1939), whose statue stands by the **post-office**. The modest house of his birth is at **No 117 Zámečnická**, and a small collection of mementoes is in the former **Piarist College**. The composer Janáček was born at nearby **Hukvaldy**, in 1853.

Slavkov, near Brno (Austerlitz): This is the Napoleonic battle site famously described in Tolstoy's novel War and Peace.

Tasov: Birthplace of the unconventional (and untranslated, but interesting) Catholic writer Jakub Deml (1878–Třebíč 1961).

Uherský Brod: There is a **museum** to Komenský in the **castle stables,** and a statue in front. A plaque on **Náměstí Míru** reflects the older view that he was born here.

BOOKLIST

The following selection includes the ex-tracted titles in this chapter as well as those mentioned in the introduction which are available in English and other titles for further reading. In general, paperback editions are given when possible. The editions cited are not necessarily the only ones available. For most of the extracted works, the original publisher can be found in 'Acknowledgments and Citations' at the end of the volume, as can the exact location of the extracts and the editions from which they are taken. Extract numbers are highlighted in bold. Square brackets denote the date of publication of the work in its original language.

Anonymous, *A Sacred Farce from Medieval Bohemia: Mastičkář* [ie *The Quacksalver*], Jarmila F. Veltruský, trans, Horace H. Rackham School of Graduate Studies, University of Michigan, Ann Arbor, MI, 1985.

Anthology of Czech Poetry [bilingual], Alfred French, ed, Department of Slavic Languages and Literatures, University of Michigan, Michigan, Ann Arbor, MI, 1973.

Anthology of Czechoslovak Literature, An, Paul Selver, trans, Kegan Paul, Trench, Trubner and Co, London, 1929.

Arbes, Jakub, 'Newton's Brain' [1877], Jiří Král, trans, in *Clever Tales,* Charlotte E. Porter and Helen A. Clarke, eds, Copeland and Day, Boston, MA, 1897.

Bartušek, Antonín, *The Aztec Calendar and Other Poems* [1970s], Ewald Osers, trans, Anvil, London, 1975.

Berková, Alexandra, two stories from *Book with a Red Jacket* [1986], James Naughton, trans, in *Storm,* Joanna Labon, ed, No 3, London, 1991, and *Description of a Struggle,* 1994 (see below).

Bezruč, Petr, *Silesian Songs* [1903, 1909], Ian Milner, trans, Artia, Prague, 1966.

Brod, Max, 'The First Hour After Death' [1916], Mike Mitchell, trans [from the original German], in the *Dedalus/Ariadne Book of Austrian Fantasy* (see below).

Camus, Albert, *Selected Essays and Notebooks,* Philip Thody, trans, Penguin, London, 1979.

Čapek, Karel and Josef (The Brothers Čapek), *RUR* [1920], and *The Insect Play* [1921], Paul Selver, trans, adapted by Nigel Playfair (*The Insect Play,* also Clifford Bax), Oxford University Press, Oxford, 1991.

Čapek, Karel, *Money and Other Stories* [1921], Francis P. Marchant, Dora Round, E. P. Casey and O. Vočadlo, trans, Hutchinson, London, 1929/Books for Libraries, Freeport, NY, 1970.

Čapek, Karel, *The Absolute at Large* [1922], Macmillan, London, 1927/Garland, New York, 1976.

Čapek, Karel, *Krakatit* [1924], Lawrence Hyde, trans, Geoffrey Blés, London, 1925; Arno Press, New York, 1975; as *An Atomic Phantasy*, Allen and Unwin, London, 1948.

Čapek, Karel, *Letters from England* [1924], Paul Selver, trans, Allen and Unwin, London, 1957/ Arden Library, Darby, PA, 1980.

Čapek, Karel, *The Gardener's Year* [1929], illustrated by Josef Čapek, M. and R. Weatherall, trans, Allen and Unwin, 1966/ University of Wisconsin Press, Madison, WI, 1984.

Čapek, Karel, *Tales from Two Pockets* [1929], Paul Selver, trans, Allen and Unwin, London, 1967/ complete version, Norma Comrada, trans, Catbird, North Haven, CT, 1994.

Čapek, Karel, *Three Novels: Hordubal, Meteor, An Ordinary Life* [1933–34], M. and R. Weatherall, trans, Catbird, Highland Park, NJ, 1990.

Čapek, Karel, *War with the Newts* [1936], Ewald Osers, trans, Picador, London, 1991/Catbird, North Haven, CT, 1990. **Extract 10**.

Čapek, Karel, *The White Plague* [1937], Michael Henry Heim, trans, in *Cross Currents*, Vol 7, University of Michigan, 1988.

Čapek, Karel, *Apocryphal Stories* [1945], Dora Round, trans, Penguin, London 1975/Verry, Mystic, CT, 1965.

Čapek, Karel, *Towards the Radical Center: A Karel Čapek Reader*, Peter Kussi, ed, Catbird Highland Park, NJ, 1990.

Čapek, Karel, *Talks with T.G. Masaryk*, Dora Round, trans, Catbird, North Haven, CT, 1995.

Čech, Svatopluk, 'Hanuman' [1884], Walter W. Strickland, trans, in Walter W. Strickland, *Poems*, B. Westermann, New York, 1929.

Čejka, Jaroslav, Michael Černík and Karel Sýs, *The New Czech Poetry*, Ewald Osers, trans, Bloodaxe Books, Newcastle upon Tyne, 1988. (Establishment poets of the 1980s.)

Chatwin, Bruce, *Utz* [1988], Picador, London, 1989/Viking Penguin, New York, 1989.

Czech Literature Since 1956: A Symposium, William E. Harkins and Paul I. Trensky, eds, Columbia Slavic Studies, New York, 1980.

Czech Modernism: 1900–1945, Jaroslav Anděl *et al*, eds, Museum of Fine Arts, Houston, TX, Bulfinch Press, Little Brown, Boston, Toronto, London, 1989.

Czech Plays, Barbara Day, ed and (in part) trans, Nick Hern Books, London, 1994.

Czech Prose: An Anthology, William Harkins, ed, Michigan Slavic Publications, University of Michigan, Ann Arbor, MI, 1983.

Czech Prose and Verse: a Selection with an Introductory Essay, Robert Pynsent, ed, Athlone, London, 1979. (Introduction in English.)

Dedalus/Ariadne Book of Austrian Fantasy: The Meyrink Years 1890– 1930, Mike Mitchell, trans and ed, Dedalus, Sawtry, and Ariadne, Riverside, CA, 1992.

Czech and Slovak Short Stories, Jeanne W. Němcová, trans, Oxford University Press, London, 1967.

Description of a Struggle: the Picador Book of Contemporary East European Prose, Michael March, ed, Picador, London, 1994. (Hrabal, Kriseová, Berková, Ondřej Neff.)

Devětsil: the Czech Avant-Garde of the 1920s and 30s, Rostislav Švácha, ed, Museum of Modern Art, Oxford, Design Museum, London, 1990.

Durych, Jaroslav, *The Descent of the Idol* [*Bloudění*, 1929], Lynton A. Hudson, trans, Hutchinson, London, 1935/Dutton, New York, 1936.

Eliot, George, *The Lifted Veil* [1859], Virago, London, 1985/Viking Penguin, New York, 1986.

Erben, Karel Jaromír, 'Christmas Eve' [1853], A. French, trans, in *Anthology of Czech Poetry* (see above).

Erben, Karel Jaromír, 'The Willow' and 'The Daughter's Curse' [1853], Paul Selver, trans, in *An Anthology of Czechoslovak Literature* (see above). **Extract 1**.

Erben, Karel Jaromír, 'The Wedding Shirts' [1853], Rev J. Troutbeck, trans [from the German], in Antonín Dvořák, *The Spectre's Bride: a Dramatic Cantata*, Novello, London and New York.

Fischerová, Daniela, *Dog and Wolf* [1979], A. G. Brain, trans, in *Czech Plays* (see above).

Fischerová, Sylva, *The Tremor of Racehorses* [1985–90], Jarmila and Ian Milner, trans, Bloodaxe Books, Newcastle upon Tyne, 1990.

Fischerová, Sylva, poems, James Naughton, trans, in *Field*, No 42, Spring 1990, Oberlin College Press, Oberlin, OH, 1990.

Fischerová, Sylva, poems, Vera Orac, Stuart Friebert and the author, trans; others, James Naughton, trans, in *Prairie Schooner*, Vol 66, No 4, Winter 1992, University of Nebraska Press, Lincoln, NB.

French, Alfred, *The Poets of Prague: Czech Poetry Between the Wars*, Oxford University Press, London, 1969.

French, Alfred, *Czech Writers and Politics, 1945–1969*, East European Quarterly, Boulder, CO, distributed by Columbia University Press, New York, 1982.

Frynta, Emanuel, *Hašek, the Creator of Schweik*, Jean Layton and George Theiner, trans, Artia, Prague, 1965.

Fučík, Julius, *Report from the Gallows* [1945], Stephen Jolly, trans, John Spencer, London, 1957. (Communist wartime martyr.)

Fuks, Ladislav, *Mr Theodore Mundstock* [1963], Iris Urwin, trans, Four Walls Eight Windows, New York, 1991.

Fuks, Ladislav, *The Cremator* [1967], Eva M. Kandler, trans, Marion Boyars, London and New York, 1984.

Goetz-Stankiewicz, Marketa, *The Silenced Theatre: Czech Playwrights without a Stage*, University of Toronto Press, Toronto, 1979.

Good-bye, Samizdat: Twenty Years of Czechoslovak Underground Writing, Marketa Goetz-Stankiewicz, ed, Northwestern University Press, Evanston, IL, 1992.

Gorys, Erhard, *Czechoslovakia*, Pallas Athene, London, 1991.

Gruša, Jiří, *The Questionnaire* [1978], Peter Kussi, trans Blond and Briggs, London, 1982/Vintage, New York, 1983.

Halas, František, *Old Women* [1935], Karel Offer, trans, Editions Poetry, London, 1947.

Halas, František, 'To Prague' [1938], **Extract 11** (J. Naughton, trans).

Halas, František, *Our Lady Božena Němcová* [1940, 1946], Frederick Ost, trans, Handicraft Press, Wellington, New Zealand, 1944.

Halas, František, *František Halas* [poems], Václav J. Sverák, trans, Woodworm Books, Manchester, 1981.

Hálek, Vítězslav, *Hálek's Stories and Evensongs* [1870–74, 1859], Walter W. Strickland, trans, B. Westermann, New York, 1930.

Hanzlík, Josef, *Selected Poems*, Ewald Osers, Jarmila and Ian Milner, trans, Bloodaxe Books, Newcastle upon Tyne, 1993.

Harrison, Tony, *Selected Poems*, Penguin, London and New York, 1987. **Extract 12**.

Hašek, Jaroslav, *The Bachura Scandal and Other Stories and Sketches*, Alan Menhennet, trans, Angel Books, London, 1991/Dufour, Chester Springs, PA, 1992.

Hašek, Jaroslav, *The Good Soldier Švejk and his Fortunes in the World War* [1921–23], Cecil Parrott, trans, Everyman's Library, London, 1993/Knopf, New York, 1993. **Extract 13**.

Hašek, Jaroslav, *The Red Commissar: Including Further Adventures of the Good Soldier Švejk and Other Stories*, Cecil Parrott, trans, Abacus, London, 1983.

Hašek, Jaroslav, *The Tourist Guide*, I. T. Havlů, trans, Artia, Prague, 1961.

Hašek, Jaroslav, *Little Stories by a Great Master*, Doris Kožíšková, trans, Orbis Press Agency, Prague, 1984.

Havel, Václav, *Selected Plays 1963–83*, Vera Blackwell, George Theiner and Jan Novak, trans, Faber and Faber, London and Boston, MA, 1992. (*The Garden Party* [1963], *The Memorandum* [1965], *The Increased Difficulty of Concentration* [1968], *Audience or Conversation* [1975], *Unveiling or Private View* [1975], *Protest* [1978], *Mistake* [1983]).

Havel, Václav, and Pavel Kohout, Pavel Landovský, Jiří Dienstbier, *The Vaněk Plays*, Marketa Goetz-Stankiewicz, ed, University of British Columbia Press, Vancouver, 1987.

Havel, Václav, *Largo Desolato* [1984], English version by Tom Stoppard, Faber and Faber, London, 1987.

Havel, Václav, *Temptation* [1985], George Theiner, trans, Faber and Faber, London, 1988/Grove Atlantic, New York, 1989.

Havel, Václav, *Redevelopment or Slum Clearance* [1987], James

Saunders and Marie Winn, trans, Faber and Faber, London, 1990.

Havel, Václav, *et al*, *Václav Havel or Living in Truth*, Jan Vladislav, ed, Faber and Faber, London, 1987.

Havel, Václav, *Letters to Olga* [1983], Paul Wilson, trans, Faber and Faber, London, 1988.

Havel, Václav, *Tomorrow* [1988], Barbara Day, trans, in *Czech Plays* (see above).

Havel, Václav, *Disturbing the Peace: A Conversation with Karel Hvížďala* [1986], Paul Wilson, trans, Faber and Faber, London, 1990/Knopf, New York, 1990.

Havel, Václav, *Open Letters: Selected Prose, 1965–1990*, Paul Wilson, ed, Faber and Faber, London, 1991/Knopf, New York, 1991.

History of the Czechoslovak Republic, Victor S. Mamatey and Radomír Luža, eds, Princeton University Press, Princeton, NJ, 1973.

Hodrová, Daniela, excerpt from *In Both Species* [1991], Tatiana Firkusny and Veronique Firkusny-Callegari, trans, in *Prairie Schooner*, Vol 66, No 4, Winter 1992, University of Nebraska Press, Lincoln, NB.

Holan, Vladimír, *Selected Poems*, Jarmila and Ian Milner, trans, Penguin, London, 1971.

Holan, Vladimír, *A Night with Hamlet* [1964], Jarmila and Ian Milner, trans, Oasis, London, 1980. Also in *Conductors of the Pit: Major Works by Rimbaud, Vallejo, Césaire, Artaud and Holan*, Clayton Eshleman, Annette Smith and František Galan, trans, Paragon House, New York, 1988.

Holan, Vladimír, *Mirroring: Selected Poems*, C. G. Hanzlicek and Dana Hábová, trans, Wesleyan University Press, Middletown, CT, 1985.

Holub, Miroslav, *Selected Poems*, Ian Milner and George Theiner, trans, Penguin, London, 1967.

Holub, Miroslav, *Sagittal Section: Poems, New and Selected* [1989], Stuart Friebert and Dana Hábová, trans, Oberlin College, Oberlin, OH, 1980.

Holub, Miroslav, *Interferon, or On Theater* [1986], David Young and Dana Hábová, trans, Oberlin College, Oberlin, OH, 1982.

Holub, Miroslav, *Poems Before & After* [1958–86], Ian and Jarmila Milner, Edward Osers and George Theiner, trans, Bloodaxe Books, Newcastle upon Tyne, 1990. **Extract 9** translated by George Theiner.

Holub, Miroslav, *The Dimension of the Present Moment and Other Essays*, David Young, ed, Faber and Faber, London, 1990.

Holub, Miroslav, *Vanishing Lung Syndrome* [1990], David Young and Dana Hábová, trans, Faber and Faber, London, 1990.

Holub, Miroslav, *The Jingle Bell Principle* [1987], James Naughton, trans, Bloodaxe Books, Newcastle upon Tyne, 1992.

Hostovský, Egon, *Seven Times the Leading Man* [1942], Fern Long, trans, Eyre, London, 1945/L. B. Fischer, New York, 1945.

Hostovský, Egon, *Missing* [1956], Ewald Osers, trans, Secker and Warburg, London, 1952/Viking, New York, 1952.

Hostovský, Egon, *The Midnight Patient* [1958], Philip H. Smith, trans, Heinemann, London, 1955/Appleton-Century-Crofts, New York, 1954.

Hostovský, Egon, *The Charity Ball* [1958], Philip H. Smith, trans, Heinemann, Melbourne, 1957/Doubleday, Garden City, NY, 1958.

Hostovský, Egon, *The Plot* [1969], Alice Backer with Bernard Wolfe, trans, Cassell, London, 1961/Doubleday, Garden City, NY, 1961.

Hrabal, Bohumil, *The Death of Mr Baltisberger and Other Stories* [1963–64, 1966], Michael Henry Heim, trans, Abacus, London, 1990.

Hrabal, Bohumil, *Closely Observed Trains* [1965], Edith Pargeter, trans, Abacus, London, 1990/as *Closely Watched Trains*, Northwestern University Press, Evanston, IL, 1990.

Hrabal, Bohumil, and Jiří Menzel, *Closely Observed Trains: a Film (Modern Film Scripts)*, Josef Holzbecher, trans, Lorimer Publishing, London, 1971.

Hrabal, Bohumil, *Cutting It Short* [1976, MS 1970] and *The Little Town Where Time Stood Still* [1978; MS 1973], James Naughton, trans, Abacus, London, 1993/Pantheon, New York, 1993. **Extract 7.**

Hrabal, Bohumil, *I Served the King of England* [1980, MS 1971], Paul Wilson, trans, Picador, London, 1990.

Hrabal, Bohumil, *Too Loud a Solitude* [1980; MS 1976], Michael Henry Heim, trans, André Deutsch, London, 1991.

Interference: The Story of Czechoslovakia in the Words of its Writers, Peter Spafford, ed, New Clarion Press, Cheltenham, 1992.

Jacobs, Michael, *Blue Guide: Czechoslovakia*, A & C Black, London and W. W. Norton, New York, 1992.

Janovic, Vladimír, *The House of the Tragic Poet*, Ewald Osers, trans, Bloodaxe Books, Newcastle upon Tyne, 1988.

Jirásek, Alois, *Gaudeamus Igitur* [1877], Erika Vilímová, trans, Artia, Prague, 1961.

Jirásek, Alois, *Old Czech Legends* [1894], Marie K. Holeček, trans, Forest Books, London and Boston, MA, 1992.

Jirásek, Alois, *Legends of Old Bohemia* [1894], Edith Pargeter, trans, Hamlyn, London, 1963.

Johannes von Tepl (Saaz), *Death and the Ploughman* [c1400], K. W. Maurer, trans, The Euston Press, London, 1947.

Kafka, Franz, *The Complete Novels* (*The Trial, America, The Castle*), Willa and Edwin Muir, trans, Minerva, London, 1992.

Kafka, Franz, *The Complete Short Stories*, Nahum N. Glatzer, ed, Minerva, London, 1994. **Extract 14.**

Kafka, Franz, *Stories 1904–1924*, foreword by Jorge Luis Borges, J. A. Underwood, trans, Cardinal, London, 1990.

Kafka, Franz, *The Trial* [1925], Willa and Edwin Muir, trans, Penguin, London, 1953. **Extract 15.**

Kafka, Franz, *The Trial* [1925], Idris Parry, trans, Penguin, London and New York, 1994.

Kafka, Franz, *The Castle* [1926], Willa and Edwin Muir, trans, Penguin, London, 1957.

Kafka, Franz, *America* [1927], Willa and Edwin Muir, trans, Penguin, London, 1967.

Kafka, Franz, *The Diaries of Franz Kafka 1910–23*, Joseph Kresh and Martin Greenberg with the cooperation of Hannah Arendt, trans, Max Brod, ed, Penguin, London, 1964.

Kafka, Franz, *Letters to Felice*, James Stern and Elizabeth Duckworth, trans, with Elias Canetti, *Kafka's Other Trial*, Penguin, London, 1978.

Kafka, Franz, *Letters to Milena*, Willy Haas, ed, Schocken, New York, 1953.

Kantůrková, Eva, *My Companions in the Bleak House* [1984], Quartet, London and New York, 1989.

Klíma, Ivan, *A Ship Named Hope* [1969]; two novels, Edith Pargeter, trans, Gollancz, London, 1970.

Klíma, Ivan, *Games* [1975], Barbara Day, trans, in *Czech Plays* (see above).

Klíma, Ivan, *A Summer Affair* [1979], Ewald Osers, trans, Penguin, London and New York, 1990.

Klíma, Ivan, *My Merry Mornings* [1979], George Theiner, trans, Readers International, London, 1985.

Klíma, Ivan, *My First Loves* [1985], Edwald Osers, trans, Penguin, London, 1989/W. W. Norton, New York, 1989. **Extract 22.**

Klíma, Ivan, *Judge on Trial* [1986], 'A. G. Brain' (Alice and Gerald Turner), trans, Vintage, London, 1992/Knopf, New York, 1993.

Klíma, Ivan, *Love and Garbage* [1988], Ewald Osers, trans, Penguin, London and New York, 1991.

Klíma, Ivan, *My Golden Trades* [1990], Paul Wilson, trans, Penguin, London and New York, 1993.

Kolář, Jiří, *The End of Words: Selected Works 1947–1970*, Václav Pinkava (poems) and Alexandra Büchler, trans, Institute of Contemporary Arts, London, 1990. (Exhibition catalogue.)

Komenský (Comenius), Jan Amos, *The Labyrinth of the World and the Paradise of the Heart* [1623, 1631], Count Franz H. Lützow, trans, Arno Press, New York, 1971; also, Matthew Spinka, trans, Dept of Slavic Languages and Literatures, University of Michigan, Ann Arbor, MI, 1972.

Kovtun, George J., *Czech and Slovak Literature in English: a Bibliography*, 2nd ed, Library of Congress, Washington, DC, 1988.

Kundera, Milan, *Laughable Loves* [1963–68, 1970], Suzanne Rappaport, trans, Penguin, London, 1975/Viking Penguin, New York, 1988.

Kundera, Milan, *The Joke* [1967], new edition with Michael Henry

Heim's translation revised by the author and Aaron Asher, ed, Faber and Faber, London, 1992/ HarperCollins, New York, 1992. **Extract 8.**

Kundera, Milan, *The Farewell Party* [1979], Peter Kussi, trans, Faber and Faber, London, 1993.

Kundera, Milan, *Life is Elsewhere* [1979], Peter Kussi [with the author], trans, Faber and Faber, London, 1987/Viking Penguin, New York, 1986.

Kundera, Milan, *Jacques and His Master* [1981], Simon Callow, trans [from the French], Faber and Faber, London, 1986/ HarperCollins, New York, 1985.

Kundera, Milan, *The Book of Laughter and Forgetting* [1981], Michael Henry Heim, trans, Faber and Faber, London, 1992/Viking Penguin, New York, 1987.

Kundera, Milan, *The Unbearable Lightness of Being* [1985], Michael Henry Heim, trans, Faber, London, 1985/HarperCollins, New York, 1985.

Kundera, Milan, *The Art of the Novel* [1986], Linda Asher, trans [from the French], Faber and Faber, London, 1988/Grove Press, New York, 1988.

Kundera, Milan, *Immortality* [1990], Peter Kussi, trans, Faber and Faber, London, 1992/HarperCollins, New York, 1992.

Leppin, Paul, *Severin's Journey into the Dark* [1914], Kevin Blahut, trans, Twisted Spoon Press, Prague, 1993.

Leppin, Paul, part of *Severin's Road into Darkness* [1914], Mike Mitchell, trans, in *Dedalus/ Ariadne Book of Austrian Fantasy* (see above).

Linden Tree, The: An Anthology of Czech and Slovak Literature, 1890–1960, Mojmír Otruba and Zdeněk Pešat, ed, Edith Pargeter *et al*, trans, Artia, Prague, 1962.

Linhartová, Věra, 'The Room', from *Space for Distinguishing* [1964], Jeanne W. Němcová, trans, in *Czech and Slovak Short Stories*, Oxford University Press, London, 1967.

Lustig, Arnošt, *Night and Hope* [1958], George Theiner, trans, Quartet, London, 1989/Northwestern University Press, Evanston, IL, 1989.

Lustig, Arnošt, *Diamonds of the Night* [1958], Jeanne Němcová, trans, Quartet, London, 1989/Northwestern University Press, Evanston, IL, 1986.

Lustig, Arnošt, *Dita Saxova* [1962], Jeanne Němcová, trans, Quartet, London, 1994/Northwestern University Press, Evanston, IL, 1993.

Lustig, Arnošt, *A Prayer for Katerina Horovitzova* [1964], Jeanne Němcová, trans, Quartet, London, 1990/Overlook Press, New York, 1987.

Lustig, Arnošt, *Indecent Dreams*, Iris Urwin-Levit, Vera Borkovec and Paul Wilson, trans, Northwestern University Press, Evanston, IL, 1988.

Lustig, Arnošt, *Darkness Casts No Shadow*, Jeanne Němcová, trans, Quartet, London, 1989.

Mácha, Karel Hynek, *May* [1836], Canto 2, Karel Brušák and Stephen Spender, trans, in *Anthology of Czech Poetry* (see above); also William E. Harkins, trans, in *Cross Currents*, Vol 6, 1987; Roderick A. Ginsburg, trans, 1932, privately printed; Hugh Hamilton McGoverne, trans, Orbis, Prague, 1949, Phoenix Press, London, 1949. **Extract 4** translated by James Naughton.

Majerová, Marie, *Ballad of a Miner* [1938], Roberta Finlayson-Samsour, trans, Artia, Prague, 1960.

Majerová, Marie, *The Siren* [1935, rev 1947], Iris Urwin, trans, Artia, Prague, 1953. **Extract 5.**

Masaryk, Tomáš G., *The Spirit of Thomas G. Masaryk 1850–1937: An Anthology*, George J. Kovtun, ed, Macmillan, London, 1990.

Meyrink, Gustav, *The Opal (and Other Stories)* [1913], Maurice Raraty, trans, Dedalus/Ariadne, Sawtry and Riverside, CA, 1995.

Meyrink, Gustav, *The Golem* [1913–14, 1915], Mike Mitchell, trans, Dedalus, Sawtry, 1995/Ariadne Press, Riverside, CA, 1995. **Extract 16**.

Meyrink, Gustav, *The Green Face* [1916], Mike Mitchell, trans, Dedalus, Sawtry, and Ariadne, Riverside, CA, 1992.

Meyrink, Gustav, *Walpurgisnacht* [1917], Mike Mitchell, trans, Dedalus, Sawtry, and Ariadne, Riverside, CA, 1993.

Meyrink, Gustav, *The Angel of the West Window* [1927], Mike Mitchell, trans, Dedalus, Sawtry, and Ariadne, Riverside, CA, 1991.

Modern Czech Poetry: an Anthology, Ewald Osers and J. K. Montgomery, ed and trans, Allen and Unwin for Prague Press, 1945.

Modern Poetry in Translation, 5, *Czech*, Ted Hughes and Daniel Weissbort, eds, Cape Goliard, London, 1969.

Muir, Edwin, *An Autobiography* [1954], The Hogarth Press, London, 1987.

Němcová, Božena, *Granny: Scenes from Country Life* [1855], Edith Pargeter, trans, Artia, Prague, 1962/Greenwood, Westport, CT, 1976. **Extract 21**.

Neruda, Jan, *Tales of the Little Quarter* [ie *Tales of the Malá Strana*, 1877], Edith Pargeter, trans, Heinemann, Melbourne, 1957/Greenwood, Westport, CT, 1976. **Extract 17**.

Neruda, Jan, *Prague Tales* [1877], Michael Henry Heim, trans, Chatto and Windus, London, 1993. (Another version.)

New Writing in Czechoslovakia, George Theiner, ed, Penguin, London, 1969.

Nezval, Vítězslav, poems from *Prague with Fingers of Rain* [1936], Ewald Osers, trans, in *Three Czech Poets: Vítězslav Nezval, Antonín Bartušek, and Josef Hanzlík*, Penguin, London, 1971. **Extract 18**.

Novák Arne, *Czech Literature* [1946], Peter Kussi, trans, William E. Harkins, ed, with a supplement, Michigan Slavic Publications, University of Michigan, Ann Arbor, MI, 1976.

Olbracht, Ivan, *The Bitter and the Sweet* [1937], Iris Urwin, trans, Crown, New York, 1967.

Olbracht, Ivan, *Nikola Šuhaj, Robber* [1933], Robert Finlayson-Samsour, trans, Artia, Prague, 1954.

Orten, Jiří, *Elegie – Elegies*, Lyn Coffin, trans, SVU Press, Washington, DC, 1980.

Otčenášek, Jan, *Romeo and Juliet and the Darkness* [1958], Iris Urwin, trans, Artia, Prague, 1960.

Páral, Vladimír, *Catapult* [1967], William Harkins, trans, Catbird, Highland Park, NJ, 1993. **Extract 2**.

Páral, Vladimír, *The Four Sonyas* [ie *Professional Woman*, 1971], William Harkins, trans, Catbird, North Haven, CT, 1993.

Parrott, Cecil, *The Bad Bohemian; The Life of Jaroslav Hašek*, Bodley Head, London, 1978.

Pavel, Ota, 'A Race Through Prague' from *Death of Fine Roebuck* [1971, this suppressed story: 1990], Paul Wilson, trans, in *Cross Current*, Vol 2, 1983, Dept of Slavic Languages and Literatures, University of Michigan, Ann Arbor, MI.

Perutz, Leo, *By Night under the Stone Bridge* [1953], Eric Mosbacher, trans, Harvill, London, 1991.

Poláček, Karel, *What Ownership's All*

About, P. Kussi, trans, Catbird, North Haven, CT, 1993.

Polišenský, J. V., *Britain and Czechoslovakia: A Study in Contacts*, Orbis, Prague, 1966.

Prairie Schooner, Vol 66, No 4, Winter 1992 ('Czech and Slovak Writing in Translation'), University of Nebraska Press, Lincoln, NB.

Řezáč, Václav, *If the Mirror Break* [*Rozhraní*, 1944], Fern Long, trans, Chilton, Philadelphia, PA, 1959.

Řezáč, Václav, *Dark Corner* [*Černé světlo*, 1940], Iris Urwin, trans, Artia, Prague, 1963.

Rilke, Rainer Maria, *Two Stories of Prague: King Bohush, The Siblings* [1899], Angela Esterhammer, trans, University Press of New England, Hanover and London, 1994.

Rilke, Rainer Maria, *The Selected Poetry of Rainer Maria Rilke* [bilingual], Stephen Mitchell, trans, Picador, London, 1987.

Rilke, Rainer Maria, *The Best of Rilke* [bilingual], Walter Arndt, trans, Dartmouth College, University Press of New England, Hanover and London, 1989.

Ripellino, Angelo Maria, *Magic Prague* [1973], David Newton Marinelli, trans [from Italian], Picador, London, 1995.

Salivarová, Zdena, *Summer in Prague* [*Honzlová*, 1972], Marie Winn, trans, Harvill, London, 1973/ Harper and Row, New York, 1973.

Salivarová, Zdena, *Ashes, Ashes, All Fall Down*, Jan Drábek, trans, Larkwood, 1987.

Seifert, Jaroslav, *The Plague Column* [1977], Ewald Osers, trans, Terra Nova Editions, London and Boston, 1979.

Seifert, Jaroslav, *An Umbrella from Piccadilly* [1979], Ewald Osers, trans, London Magazine Editions, London, 1983.

Seifert, Jaroslav, *The Selected Poetry*, Ewald Osers, trans, George Gibian, ed and trans, André Deutsch, London, 1986. **Extract 20.**

Selected Czech Tales, Marie Busch and Otto Pick, trans, Oxford University Press, London, 1925.

Short, David, *Czechoslovakia (World Bibliographical Series)*, Clio Press, Oxford, 1986.

Škvorecký, Josef, *The Cowards* [1958], Jeanne Němcová, trans, Penguin, London, 1972/Ecco Press, New York, 1980.

Škvorecký, Josef, *The Bass Saxophone* [1967], Káča Poláčková-Henley, trans, Vintage, London, 1994/ Penguin, New York, 1985/Key Porter, Toronto. **Extract 6.**

Škvorecký, Josef, *The Mournful Demeanour of Lieutenant Boruvka* [1966], Rosemary Kavan, Káča Poláčková, and George Theiner, trans, Faber and Faber, London, 1988/W.W. Norton, New York, 1991.

Škvorecký, Josef, *Miss Silver's Past* [ie *The Lion-Cub*, 1969], Peter Kussi, trans, Picador, London, 1980.

Škvorecký, Josef, *The Republic of Whores* [ie *The Tank Battalion*, 1971], Paul Wilson, trans, Faber and Faber, London, 1994.

Škvorecký, Josef, *The Miracle Game* [1972], Paul Wilson, trans, Faber and Faber, London, 1992/Knopf, New York, 1991.

Škvorecký, Josef, *Sins for Father Knox* [1973], Káča Poláčková-Henley, trans, Faber and Faber, London, 1990/W.W. Norton, New York, 1991.

Škvorecký, Josef, *The End of Lieutenant Boruvka* [1975], Paul Wilson, trans, Faber and Faber, London, 1990/W.W. Norton, New York, 1990.

Škvorecký, Josef, *The Swell Season* [1975], Paul Wilson, trans, Vintage, London, 1994.

Škvorecký, Josef, *The Engineer of*

Human Souls [1977], Paul Wilson, trans, Vintage, London, 1994/Ecco Press, New York, 1986.

Škvorecký, Josef, *The Return of Lieutenant Boruvka* [1981], Paul Wilson, trans, Faber and Faber, London, 1990/W.W. Norton, New York, 1991.

Škvorecký, Josef, *Dvořák in Love* [ie *Scherzo Capriccioso*, 1984], Paul Wilson, trans, The Hogarth Press, London, 1989/W.W. Norton, New York, 1988.

Škvorecký, Josef, *All the Bright Young Men and Women: A Personal History of the Czech Cinema*, Michael Schonberg, trans, Peter Martin Associates, Toronto, 1971.

Škvorecký, Josef, *Talkin' Moscow Blues* [essays], Sam Solecki, ed, Faber and Faber, London, 1989.

Solecki, Sam, *Prague Blues: The Fiction of Josef Škvorecký: A Critical Study*, ECW Press, Toronto, 1990.

Součková, Milada, *The Czech Romantics*, Mouton, The Hague, 1958.

Stifter, Adalbert, *Brigitta and Other Tales* [1843–53], Helen Watanabe-O'Kelly, trans, Penguin, London and New York, 1994.

Světlá, Karolína, from *Ještěd Sketches* [1880], 'A Kiss' [1871], M. Busch and O. Pick, trans, in *Selected Czech Tales* (see above), and 'Poor Dead Barbora' [1873], W. E. Harkins, trans, in *Czech Prose: an Anthology* (see above).

Topol, Josef, *Cat on the Rails* [1965], George and Christine Voskovec, trans, in *Czech Plays* (see above).

Trensky, Paul, *Czech Drama Since World War II*, M. E. Sharpe, White Plains, 1978.

Trollope, Anthony, *Nina Balatka* [1867], and *Linda Tressel*, World Classics, Oxford University Press, Oxford, 1991. **Extract 19**.

Tsvetayeva, Marina, *Selected Poems*, David McDuff, trans, 2nd ed, Bloodaxe Books, Newcastle upon Tyne, 1991. ('Poem of the End', set in Prague.)

Vaculík, Ludvík, *The Axe* [1966], Marian Šling, trans, André Deutsch, London, 1973/Northwestern University Press, Evanston, IL, 1992. **Extract 3**.

Vaculík, Ludvík, *The Guinea Pigs* [1977], Káča Poláčková, trans, Northwestern University Press, Evanston, IL, 1986.

Vaculík, Ludvík, *A Cup of Coffee with My Interrogator* [1976–87], George Theiner, trans, Readers International, London, 1987.

Vaculík, Ludvík, excerpts from *A Czech Dreambook* [1983], Michael Henry Heim, trans, in *Cross Currents*, Vol 3.

Vančura, Vladislav, *The End of the Old Times* [1934], Edith Pargeter, trans, Artia, Prague, 1965.

Vratislav z Mitrovic, Václav, *Adventures of Baron Wenceslas Wratislaw of Mitrowitz: What He Saw in the Turkish Metropolis, Constantinople* [1599], A. H. Wratislaw, trans, Bell and Daldy, London, 1862.

Vyskočil, Ivan, 'Jacob's Well' [1960s], R. Kavanová, trans, in *White Stones and Fir Trees* (see below), and 'The Incredible Rise of Albert Uruk' [1960s], G. Theiner, trans, in *New Writing in Czechoslovakia* (see above).

Waldstein, Baron, *The Diary of Baron Waldstein* [c1600], G. W. Groos, trans [from the Latin], Thames and Hudson, London, 1981.

Wallace, William V., *Czechoslovakia*, Ernest Benn, London, 1977.

Weil, Jiří, *Life with a Star* [1949], Rita Klímová with Roslyn Schloss, trans, Collins, London, 1989/Viking Penguin, New York, 1994.

Weil, Jiří, *Mendelssohn Is on the Roof* [1960], Marie Winn, trans, Flamingo, London, 1992/Viking

Penguin, New York, 1992.

Wellek, René, *Essays on Czech Literature*, Mouton, The Hague, 1963.

Werfel, Franz, 'The Playground' [1920], Mike Mitchell, trans [from the original German], in the *Dedalus/Ariadne Book of Austrian Fantasy* (see above).

Werfel, Franz, *The Song of Bernadette* [1941], Ludwig Lewisohn, trans [from the original German], Hamish Hamilton, London, 1942.

White Stones and Fir Trees: an Anthology of Contemporary Slavic Literature, Vasa D. Mihailovich, ed, Bucknell University Press, Lewisburg, PA, 1977.

Wittlich, Petr, *Prague Fin de Siècle* [in English], Flammarion, Paris,

1992.

Wratislaw, A. W., *The Native Literature of Bohemia in the Fourteenth Century*, George Bell and Sons, London, 1878.

The Writing on the Wall: an Anthology of Contemporary Czech Literature, Antonín Liehm and Peter Kussi, ed, Karz-Cohl Publishing, Princeton, NJ, 1983.

Zeman, Z. A. B., *The Masaryks*, I.B. Tauris, London and New York, 1990.

Zeyer, Julius, stories from *Three Legends of the Crucifix* [1895], 'Inultus', Paul Selver, trans, in *Review 43*, No 2, London, 1943; 'Samko the Bird', William E. Harkins, trans, in *Czech Prose* (see above).

Extracts

(1) BOHEMIA

Karel Jaromír Erben, *The Willow*

Erben's ballads have a strong native quality that depends on language, and lore, but little on place. In this extract from 'The Willow', written in 1853, a man consults a wise woman about his wife.

'Tell me, now, with clearness, this:
What is with my bride amiss?

In the evening fresh and bright,
Like a corpse she lies at night.

Naught has sounded, naught has stirred,
Ne'er a trace of breathing heard.

Filled with coldness is her frame,
E'en as if to dust it came.'

'How can she be aught but dead,
Since her life but half is led?

She dwells by day at home with thee,
At night her soul dwells in a tree.

Go to the stream beyond the park,
Thou find'st a willow with shining bark.

A yellow bough the tree doth bear,
The spirit of thy bride is there.'

'I have not espoused my bride,
That with a willow she might abide.

Near to me my bride shall stay,
The willow in the earth decay.'

In his arm the axe he held,
From the root the willow felled.

In the stream amain 'twas cast,
From the depths a murmur passed.

There came murmur, there came a sigh.
As of a mother whose end is nigh.

As of a mother in death's embrace,
Who to her infant turns her face.

(2) Brno

Vladimír Páral, *Catapult*

Jacek Jošt from Ústí nad Labem has acquired various women after placing a personal ad. Mojmíra is one, in his home city of Brno. (Freedom Square = náměstí Svobody; Jakub Square = Jakubské náměstí; the Vegetable Market = Zelný trh.)

By the time they reached the milk bar on Freedom Square they'd added a freckly archeology student from the Low Tatra Mountains, and Mojmíra paid for four strawberry cocktails, 'I got it for my translation!' she cried, crossing the square toward a motorcyclist in leather pants and suspenders, the driver stepped on the gas, drove around the square, and held the door open for them at The Four Ruffians, during the goulash soup a bearded radio technician joined them and all six of them went on to The Noblewomen, at a long table fourteen people were sitting and talking quietly, in their midst, like a priest, the poet Oldřich Mikulášek was stroking the edge of his wineglass, 'We just heard you're celebrating,' a pretty blond on his right told Mojmíra, 'I got it for that Spanish story,' Mojmíra confirmed happily and ordered two bottles of Mikulov Sauvignon, the procession of some eleven people now went to the seafood restaurant on Jakub Square, at their head the motorcyclist in leather pants and in the rear Jacek with Mojmíra and the large black satchel, at a necktie store they were joined by a long-haired unisex creature, 'The fellows at the Slavie said you got paid for that "Executioner's Afternoon" – ' 'Here – ' said Mojmíra, thrusting a crumpled three-crown note into his (her) proffered hand, and (s)he joined the group, from St Jakub's on a gray-haired woman limped along on crutches, 'I got paid today – ' Mojmíra called after her. 'I heard,' the old woman rejoiced, 'For that Alvarez translation!' and she hobbled after them, in the Typos Arcade a fellow in a black waterproof hat was pissing into a grate, 'Vítek,' Mojmíra called after him, 'today – ' 'I heard,' he muttered, and joined the gang, by the portal of the Viceregent's Palace Pavel Vrbka stood with an Admira movie camera around his neck, 'Mojmíra got paid today – ' Jacek called after him, 'I can see,' said Pavel Vrbka, already in formation, and at the M Club there were almost thirty of us.

'Ten days I worked on it like a mule till late at night,' Mojmíra cried, kicking a trashcan down the stairs into the Vegetable Market.

(3) Brumov, Moravia

Ludvík Vaculík, *The Axe*

The setting of this autobiographical novel reflects on life in the area of the author's native Brumov, near Valašské Klobouky, in Moravian Wallachia (Valašsko), near the border with Slovakia.

Ice broke beneath the weir and we could hear the muted flow of water. We stopped by the backwater.

'We'll have to regulate the stream again,' Dad said, and as he spoke, the fish vanished; 'and straighten that path,' and the line of apple trees toppled to the ground; 'and one day, maybe, we'll lay a branch line on the other side to the factory,' he said, and a hideous embankment of slag bulged over the mill-race.

'Many tasks await us,' he frowned, 'and we have many enemies,' he said, and Mother died.

And so we stepped out into the future and simultaneously towards Tarandova. We walked slowly, he continually adjusting his step to mine, which I have always taken to mean that I should keep in step with him. And so we came to the next weir, where I am now standing in the water absorbed in play and in memories of many other happier things than those of which I am now writing. Here the spreading valley resembled a bowl, with strips of woodland weaving down its easy slopes to plunge into the channels of the streams, while the bushes bordering the fields, known in these parts as holts, traced graduated transections. It was to this slanting hill country, now white in the light of the newly risen moon, that Dad pointed.

'Some day we'll put powerful, very powerful tractors, you know, to work here, to plough it right across.'

I believe I said nothing to this, it seemed right to me and it was foolish of me to feel sad.

Suddenly he left the path to cross a snowy field in the direction of the stream, a bit above the weir, a place where the ground sags gently. Pointing to that place he led my eyes along the loop made, evidently, by the stream at some time, which I had never noticed before. At the highest point of the loop, now furrowed by the plough, below the steep bank where the path runs, stood, unaccountably and strangely isolated, a misshapen willow, bent by a pile of stones gathered from the field.

'There, where you see the deep water,' he motioned towards the ground below the willow, where water there was none, 'I used to catch fish there. And what fish!'

'Like what?'

'Like this,' beaming happily, he showed a width three feet with his hands.

I looked towards the willow.

'It's not true any more,' he said casually. We returned slowly to the weir, and suddenly he seemed to me to be weaker and better, not dangerous at all, maybe we had simply been for this walk and nothing else had happened that evening. Suddenly he halted and looked at me in surprise.

'Fifteen years! Fifteen years ago I was in Iran.'

(4) DOKSY, MÁCHOVO JEZERO

Karel Hynek Mácha, *May*

Mácha places the action of the poem, written in 1836, near the small town of Doksy, adjoining the lake now known as Máchovo Jezero, Mácha's Lake. In these lines the poet contemplates the executed Vilém's skull.

Again it was eve – the first in May –
Eve in May – it was love's hour;
The turtle-dove's voice called to love,
Where the pine-grove wafting lay.
Love whispered soft the quiet moss;
The blossoming tree lied love's woe,
The nightingale sang love to the rose,
The rose's was shown by an odorous sigh.
Smooth the lake in shadow'd bushes
Darkly sounded secret pain,
The shore embraced it round and again,
Like brother sister in childish sport.
And round the skull the sunset glow
Laid itself like a garland of roses;
Colouring the bony, white cheek
With its hanging skin beneath the chin.
The wind played through the hollow skull,
As if deep down the dead one laughed.
Here and there a long hair flew
Left to the white skull by time,
And dew drops blushed there beneath,
As if the skull's hollow eyes,
Moved by May's evening beauty,
Glittered there with mournful tears.

And there I sat, till the moon's risen glow
Made both my face and the skull's paler,

And – like a shroud – its widespread white
Stretched far across the vale – the woods – the hills.
At times far off the cuckoo's calls
Still fill the vale, at times an owl laments;
From farms about dogs' barks and howls resound.
The heath is filled with sweet herbs' scent,
Across the mount the virgin's teardrops bloom.
A secret light shines in the lake's great womb;
And glowing fire-flies – like shooting stars –
Make rings about the wheel in flashing play.
At times one landing in the pale white skull,
Flies out a moment later like a falling star.

In my sad gaze two hot tears likewise stood,
Like sparks in the lake, across my cheek they played;
For my fair age also, my fine childhood's age
is now carried far away by times' rude rage.
Far away is its dream, dead as a shadow's shade,
As white towns' images sunk in the lake's lap,
As the last thoughts of the dead,
As their names, the noise of ancient battles,
Age-old northern lights, their extinguished glow,
Wrecked harp's note, torn string's tone,
Vanished age's action, dead star's gleam,
Perished comet's track, dead beloved's feeling,
Forgotten tomb, eternity's fallen dwelling,
Extinguished fire's smoke, molten bell's voice,
Dead swan's song, man's lost paradise,
That is my childhood age.
                                    But today – the time
Of my youth – is, as this poem, May,
Evening May in the womb of the empty rocks;
A light smile on the face, in the heart deep woe.

Do you see the pilgrim, who, down the long meadow,
hastens towards his goal, before the sunset dies?
Never again shall your eyes see this pilgrim,
as he passes behind that rock on the horizon,
never – ah, never! That is my life to come.
Who shall give such a heart what comfort?
Love is without end! – My love deceived!

It is late eve – the first in May –
eve in May – it is love's hour;

the turtle-dove's voice calls to love:
'Hynek! – Vilém!! – Jarmila!!!'

(5) KLADNO

Marie Majerová, *The Siren*

The novel depicts working-class life in the iron-and-steel town of Kladno, a little west of Prague.

The ironworkers' siren flies through the air of Kladno in a powerful arc. Smelters, puddlers, rollers, bessemer men, locksmiths, turners, smithy men and crane-drivers – all the thousands of men in the works are lying in wait for the sound, ready to get the works' gates behind them as soon as the whistle goes.

The ironworkers' wives set their clocks by it, for the siren determines time for them. The ironworkers' children grab the dinner-basket to carry to father, brother or grandad; beef in gravy, dumplings and sauerkraut, pease-pudding and cucumbers, horse-flesh stew – better or poorer food according to the number of mouths to be fed from the breadwinner's dish.

There was nothing mechanical about the trembling sound of the siren once it had left the metal whistle. Over the chimneys and the furnaces, over the soaking pits and the bessemer converters went the sound, like the voice of a panic-striken mob and the roar of a monstrous beast in anguish.

It hoots midday, and men hear it in the workshops; it hoots six o'clock, and the child in its cradle hears it; it hoots morning, noon and night, and women hear it in their kitchens, out in their grey backyards, on their way to the fields or the coal-tip.

But a child intent on a toy can forget everything, and fail to notice even the hooting of the siren. A child sees only itself in the world; he is first, whatever he sees around him. He explores and conquers for himself – that is his heroism; he needs nobody's help.

The siren?

The dreadful din did not upset Molly. Molly ought to have been a boy, she'll always be called a tomboy, and she played boys' games too. She had seen the snow in the ditches turning black, she had felt the March wind growing milder and the sunshine warmer, and so she felt the urgent need of a tipcat. She would have to play and beat all her pals.

For the tipcat Molly found a short stick she could sharpen like a pencil at both ends. For the bat a piece of a broken margarine box would do. The tomboy worked feverishly, her hair falling into her eyes in her enthusiasm. She blew it away impatiently and the whole room seemed to be helping her.

The whole room, a room rented from watchman Janda: two beds, a table under the window, the white-washed stove with its cold black rings, the dresser and the mugs on it with flowers and gold bands (they never used those mugs); shelves in the wall, covered by a calico curtain.

(6) Náchod

Josef Škvorecký, *The Bass Saxophone*

The setting is Škvorecký's home town of Náchod, in north-east Bohemia, turned into a fictional 'Kostelec'.

The girl didn't sing, we did not have time for that. I was only proving that I could handle it; so after an hour we sat down in a room of the hotel (not the room where the bass saxophone player was lying chin up, another one) to eat supper. They brought it up from the hotel kitchen in a big, beaten-up stoneware dish – it was a sort of *eintopf*, turnip ambrosia; everyone got a spoon and so did I, we piled it on plates, we ate; it was a supper like Lothar Kinze's repertoire, but they ate humbly, silently, very modestly; a kind of ritual: I could almost see the interior of some circus trailer, the dirty hands of some skinny cook; for that matter, the room itself might have been a circus trailer, the wallpaper striped pink and baby blue (broad, art nouveau stripes and on the stripes, faded gold butterflies – the entire hotel was like a zoo from the mad dream of an infantile paper hanger), the furniture made of square brass bars, with faded silk cushioning between the bars at the head and foot of the bed. We were sitting around a marble table on brass legs which they had dragged to the middle of the room. 'What about the man next door?' I asked Lothar Kinze. 'Is he your saxophone player?' *Ja*, nodded Lothar Kinze, his hand shaking. A piece of turnip stew fell back into his plate, made a splashing noise, and Kinze did not finish his sentence. 'Isn't that pretty?' said the woman with the big nose. She nodded out of the window, and cleared her throat. Through the round window, Kostelec offered Lothar Kinze and his orchestra a view of its square. It was almost seven o'clock in the evening and a cheerful procession of workers involuntarily transferred to the *Messerschmitt* airplane factory were going past, on their way from the factory after a twelve-hour shift; but that wasn't what was beautiful – what she meant was the church, golden pink, old Gothic, spread out on the square, broader than it was high, settled into breadth like a stone pudding by almost ten centuries of existence, with the wooden shapes of two pudgy moss-covered towers shining green as a forest meadow and above them two red-painted belfries, like two chapels of Our Lady on two green meadow-covered hills, all this rooted in the drop of honey that was the town square, surrounded by lava in the honey and raspberry evening. 'Like where I come from in Spiesgürtelheide,' sighed the woman. '*Mein Vater . . .*' – she turned to her companions who were silently transferring turnips from plate to mouth – 'My father had a butcher shop there, and sausages, a beautiful store on the square.' She sighed. 'It was all pale green tiles, *ja ja, das war vor dem Krieg*, before the war, a long time ago. I was a young girl then.' She sighed.

'And we had the very same church there,' she said, pointing at the pudgy towers that looked like coloured ice-cream ornaments on a well-settled pudding.

(7) NYMBURK
Bohumil Hrabal, *Cutting It Short*

Introduced by the Flaubertian motto 'La Bovary – c'est moi',
Hrabal's novel is set in Nymburk and the local brewery where
the author spent his own childhood. Uncle Pepin and the heroine
(partly Hrabal's mother, but also Hrabal himself) decide to
climb the brewery chimney.

And that which I had dreamed of since my very first day at the brewery, finding the strength to climb up the brewery chimney stack, there it was protruding and rising up before me. I leaned my head back and took hold of the first cramp-iron, the perspective ran back upwards in ever diminishing and diminishing rungs, that sixty-metre chimney from that foreshortened angle resembled an aimed heavy gun, I was allured by the fluttering green leotard which someone had tied to the lightning conductor, and that green leotard, while there was a breeze below, that green leotard fluttered and right through the open window I could hear that green leotard making the din of rattling tin, and I caught hold of the first rung, freed a hand and untied the green bow that bound my hair together, and quickly I went up hand over hand, my legs like coupled axles took on the same rhythm. Halfway up the chimney I felt the first buffet of streaming air, my hair was buoyed up, almost ran ahead of me, suddenly all of me was centred in my loose trailing hair, which spread out and enveloped me like music, several times my hair landed on a rung, I had to watch out and slow down the work of my legs, because I was stepping on my own hair, ah, now if Bod'a had been here, he would have held up my hair for me, he would have been changed to an angel, and in his flight he would have kept watch to see that my hair didn't get caught in the spokes and chain, this chimney climbing of mine was a bit like my bicycle riding. I waited a moment, the wind seemed to have taken it into its head to get a taste of my hair, it lifted and ruffled it so that I had the feeling I was hanging by my hair on a knot tied several rungs above me, then the wind suddenly lulled, my hair untied itself and slowly, like the loosened golden hands on the church clock tower, my hair was falling, as if out of my head a golden peacock spread open wide and then slowly closed its tail. And I used this lull and quickly went up hand over hand, coordinating the motion of my legs with the work of my arms, until I laid my whole hand on the chimney rim, for a moment I recovered my breath like a swimming competitor at the end of a race in the pool, and then I pulled myself up with both arms as if out of the water, cast a leg over the rim, caught hold of the lightning conductor and slowly, as if out of syrup, drew up my other leg. I gathered my hair behind me, sat myself down and tossed my hair over my lap. And suddenly a wind rose and my hair slipped out of my hand, and my golden tresses fluttered out just like last year before the first spring day, my hair flamed out like tendrils of weed in a shallow swift stream, I held on to the lightning conductor with one hand and felt as if I was the goddess of the hunt Diana with a lance, my cheeks burned with rapture and I felt that if I did nothing else in this little town but climb up to the top of this chimney, that might not be much, but I could live on the strength of that for numbers of years, maybe a whole lifetime.

(8) OSTRAVA

Milan Kundera, *The Joke*

As a result of sending his girlfriend Markéta a joke postcard ('Optimism is the opium of the people! A healthy atmosphere stinks of stupidity! Long live Trotsky!') Ludvík is sent on military service to Ostrava in Moravian Silesia.

I had been granted a pass, and still upset over the last one, squandered on Lamp-post, I avoided my fellow soldiers and went off on my own. I climbed aboard an ancient narrow-gauge tram that linked outlying neighbourhoods of Ostrava and let it carry me away. I got off randomly and changed just as randomly to a tram on a different line; the endless outskirts with their curious mixture of factories and nature, fields and garbage dumps, wood and slag heaps, apartment houses and farm-houses, both attracted and disturbed me in a strange way; again I got off the tram, but this time I took a long walk, drinking in the peculiar landscape with something akin to passion and trying to grasp what made it what it was, trying to put into words what gave its multiplicity of disparate elements their unity and order; I walked past an idyllic little house covered with ivy and it occurred to me that it belonged there precisely *because* it was so different from the shabby buildings all around it, from the silhouettes of pit headframes and chimneys and furnaces that served as its backdrop; I walked past low-grade temporary housing and saw a house not too far off, a dirty, gray old house, but with its own garden and iron fence and large weeping willow, a real freak in such surroundings – and yet, I said to myself, it belongs there exactly *because* of this. I was disturbed by all these minor *incompatibilities* not only because they struck me as the common denominator of the surrounding area, but because they provided me with an image of my own fate, my own exile in this city; and of course: the projection of my personal history onto the sheer objectiveness of an entire city offered me a certain relief; I understood that I no more belonged there than did the weeping willow and the little ivy-covered house, than did the short streets leading nowhere, streets lined with houses that seemed to come from a different place; I no more belonged there, in that once pleasantly rustic countryside, than did the hideous temporary housing, and I realized that it was *because* I did not belong there that it was my true place, in this appalling city of incompatibilities, this city whose relentless grip chained together things foreign to each other.

(9) PLZEŇ

Miroslav Holub, *Five Minutes after the Air Raid*

This poem, from Achilles a želva (Achilles and the Tortoise), 1960, relates to Holub's wartime experience of Plzeň (Pilsen). He worked at the railway station, which was badly bombed.

In Pilsen,
twenty-six Station Road,
she climbed to the third floor
up stairs which were all that was left
of the whole house,
she opened her door
full on to the sky,
stood gaping over the edge.

For this was the place
the world ended.

Then
she locked up carefully
lest someone steal
Sirius
or Aldebaran
from her kitchen,
went back downstairs
and settled herself
to wait
for the house to rise again
and for her husband to rise from the ashes
and for her children's hands and feet to be stuck back in place.

In the morning they found her
still as stone,
sparrows pecking her hands.

(10) PRAGUE

Karel Čapek, *War with the Newts*

Written in 1936, not long before Munich, this is one of Čapek's science-fiction apocalypses, parallel in some ways to his earlier play RUR, but lacking its upbeat conclusion. Archers' Island is Střelecký ostrov.

It was a pleasant Sunday afternoon; it was not yet the hour when those lunatics and loafers rush home from their football and similar forms of madness. Prague was empty and quiet; the few people who were strolling along the embankment or over the bridge were in no hurry: they were walking in a decent and dignified manner. They were superior, sensible people who did not jostle in crowds or jeer at fishermen on the river. Papa Povondra again had that good and deep sensation of order.

'What news in the papers?' he asked with paternal severity.

'Nothing much, dad,' the son replied. 'All it says here is that those Newts have worked their way up to Dresden.'

'Well, then the Germans are in the shit,' the old gentleman decided.
[. . .]

Silence reigned over the water. The trees on Archers' Island were already casting long delicate shadows on the surface of the Vltava. From the bridge came the tinkle of trams, and along the embankment strolled nursemaids with prams and conservatively clad people in their Sunday best.

'Dad,' young Povondra breathed in an almost childish voice.
'What is it?'
'Isn't that a catfish?'
'Where?'

From the river, immediately in front of the National Theatre, a large black head was showing above the water, slowly advancing upstream.

'Is it a catfish?' Povondra junior repeated.

The old gentleman dropped his rod. 'That?' he jerked out, pointing a shaking finger. 'That?'

The black head disappeared under the water.

'That was no catfish, Frankie,' the old gentleman said in what did not seem like his normal voice. 'We're going home. This is the end.'

(11) PRAGUE

František Halas, *To Prague*

This poem, well known in the original, is taken from Torso naděje (Torso of Hope), 1938, written in the year which ended disastrously in the ceding of territory to Hitler. The famous equestrian statue of Wenceslas stands at the top of Wenceslas Square.

O ye of little faith Time bone-consuming
gave her beauty only
and the cry from groaning fields illuminated
the stony texts of portals and walls
So will it be always
O ye of little faith
So will it be always

Beyond the gates of our rivers
hard hooves sound
beyond the gates of our rivers
ploughed up with hooves
is the ground
and the dreadful riders of the Apocalypse
wave their banner

Light are the leaves of the laurels
and heavy the fallen ones' shadow

I know I know

Only no fear Only have no fear
such a fugue as never played even Johann Sebastian Bach
we shall play now
when the time comes when the time comes

The horse of bronze the horse of Wenceslas
shook itself yesterday in the night
and the Duke tested his lance
Think of a chorale
O ye of little faith
Think of a chorale

(12) PRAGUE

Tony Harrison,
Prague Spring – on my birthday, 30 April

The poem is set during the poet's period in Prague from 1966–67, when he worked as an English lector.

A silent scream? The madrigal's top note?
Puking his wassail on the listening throng?
Mouthfuls of cumulus, then cobalt throat.
Medusa must have hexed him in mid-song.

The finest vantage point in all of Prague's
this gagging gargoyle's with the stone-locked lute,
leaning over cherries, blow-ups of Karl Marx
the pioneers'll march past and salute.

Tomorrow's May but still a North wind scuffs
the plated surface like a maced cuirass,
lays on, lays off, gets purchase on and roughs
up the Vltava, then makes it glass.

The last snow of this year's late slow thaw
dribbles as spring saliva down his jaw.

(13) Prague

Jaroslav Hašek, *The Good Soldier Švejk*

Here Švejk has come, pushed in a wheelchair, to enlist on the Vltava island known as Střelecký ostrov (Marksmen's Island). On Malá Strana Square (Malostranské náměstí), before the days of the Republic, there was a famous statue of the Austrian Marshal Radetzky.

This German's stock remark was widely famous: 'The whole Czech people are nothing but a pack of malingerers.'

During the ten weeks of his activities, of 11 000 civilians he cleaned out 10 999 malingerers, and he would certainly have got the eleven thousandth by the throat, if it had not happened that just when he shouted 'About turn!' the unfortunate man was carried off by a stroke.

'Take away that malingerer!' said Bautze, when he had ascertained that the man was dead.

And on that memorable day it was Švejk who stood before him. Like the others he was stark naked and chastely hid his nudity behind the crutches on which he supported himself.

'That's really a remarkable fig-leaf,' said Bautze in German. 'There were no fig-leaves like that in paradise.'

'Certified as totally unfit for service on grounds of idiocy,' observed the sergeant-major, looking at the official documents.

'And what else is wrong with you?' asked Bautze.

'Humbly report, sir, I'm a rheumatic, but I will serve His Imperial Majesty to my last drop of blood,' said Švejk modestly. 'I have swollen knees.'

Bautze gave the good soldier Švejk a blood-curdling look and roared out in German: 'You're a malingerer!' Turning to the sergeant-major he said with icy calm: 'Clap the bastard into gaol at once!'

Two soldiers with bayonets took Švejk off to the garrison goal.

'Švejk walked on his crutches and observed with horror that his rheumatism was beginning to disappear.

Mrs Müller was still waiting for Švejk with the bathchair above on the bridge but when she saw him under bayoneted escort she burst into tears and ran away from the bathchair, never to return to it again.

And the good soldier Švejk walked along unassumingly under the escort of the armed protectors of the state.

Their bayonets shone in the light of the sun and at Malá Strana before the monument of Radetzky Švejk turned to the crowd which had followed them and called out:

'To Belgrade! To Belgrade!'

And Marshal Radetzky looked dreamily down from his monument at the good soldier Švejk, as, limping on his old crutches, he slowly disappeared into the distance with his recruit's flowers in his button-hole.

(14) PRAGUE

Franz Kafka, *Description of a Struggle*

At the beginning of this extract from Kafka's early work, Beschreibung eines Kampfes, the narrator, who has fallen over, is reminded by his companion that they meant to go up the Laurenziberg, meaning Petřín hill, across the river.

'Of course,' said I, and got up on my own, but with great pain. I began to sway, and had to look severely at the statue of Karl IV to be sure of my position. However, even this would not have helped me had I not remembered that I was loved by a girl with a black velvet ribbon around her neck, if not passionately, at least faithfully. And it really was kind of the moon to shine on me, too, and out of modesty I was about to place myself under the arch of the tower bridge when it occurred to me that the moon, of course, shone on everything. So I happily spread out my arms in order fully to enjoy the moon. And by making swimming movements with my weary arms it was easy for me to advance without pain or difficulty. To think that I had never tried this before! My head lay in the cool air and it was my right knee that flew best; I praised it by patting it. And I remembered that once upon a time I didn't altogether like an acquaintance, who was probably still walking below me, and the only thing that pleased me about the whole business was that my memory was good enough to remember even a thing like that. But I couldn't afford to do much thinking, for I had to go on swimming to prevent myself from sinking too low. However, to avoid being told later that anyone could swim on the pavement and that it wasn't worth mentioning, I raised myself above the railing by increasing my speed and swam in circles around the statue of every saint I encountered. At the fifth – I was holding myself just above the footpath by imperceptible flappings – my acquaintance gripped my hand. There I stood once more on the pavement and felt a pain in my knee.

'I've always admired,' said my acquaintance, clutching me with one hand and pointing with the other at the statue of St Ludmila, 'I've always admired the hands of this angel here to the left. Just see how delicate they are! Real angel's hands! Have you ever seen anything like them? You haven't, but I have, for this evening I kissed hands – '

(15) PRAGUE

Franz Kafka, *The Trial*

*The setting of the book, and of the chapter 'In the Cathedral'
from which this extract is taken, is not specifically anywhere, but
for those acquainted with Kafka's home city the links are
unmistakable. The Cathedral is based on St Vitus', up on the hill
in the middle of the Castle.*

So the Italian was as sensible as he was discourteous in not coming, for
he would have seen nothing, he would have had to content himself
with scrutinizing a few pictures inch-meal by the light of K.'s pocket-
torch. Curious to see what effect it would have, K. went up to a small
side chapel near by, mounted a few steps to a low balustrade, and
bending over it shone his torch on the altar-piece. The errant light
hovered over it like an intruder. The first thing K. perceived, partly by
guess, was a huge armoured knight on the outermost verge of the
picture. He was leaning on his sword, which was stuck into the bare
ground, bare except for a stray blade of grass or two. He seemed to be
watching attentively some event unfolding itself before his eyes. It was
surprising that he should stand so still without approaching nearer to it.
Perhaps he had been set there to stand guard. K., who had not seen any
pictures for a long time, studied this knight for a good while, although
the greenish light of the torch made his eyes blink. When he played the
torch over the rest of the altar-piece he discovered that it was a
portrayal of Christ being laid in the tomb, quite conventional in style
although a fairly recent painting. He pocketed the torch and returned
again to his seat.

In all likelihood it was now needless to wait any longer for the
Italian, but the rain was probably pouring down outside, and since it
was not so cold in the Cathedral as K. had expected, he decided to
linger there for the present. Quite near him rose the great pulpit, on its
small vaulted canopy two plain golden crucifixes were slanted so that
their shafts crossed at the tip. The outer balustrade and the stonework
connecting it with the supporting columns were wrought all over with
foliage in which little angels were entangled, now vivacious and now
serene. K. went up to the pulpit and examined it from all sides, the
carving of the stonework was delicate and thorough, the deep caverns
of darkness among and behind the foliage looked as if caught and
imprisoned there; K. put his hand into one of them and lightly felt the
contour of the stone, he had never known that this pulpit existed.

(16) PRAGUE

Gustav Meyrink, *The Golem*

This extract from Meyrink's mystic novel of Jewish legend and Prague, written in 1915, takes us in winter from the Old Town Square (Staroměstské náměstí, Altstadter Ring), across the Charles Bridge, and up through the Malá Strana to Hradčany (Hradschin), the Castle and St Vitus' Cathedral.

I made my way through the massive stone arcades of the Old Town Square, past the bronze fountain, its baroque railings covered in icicles, and across the stone bridge with its statues of saints and its monument to St John Nepomuk.

Down below, the river foamed as it pounded the piers of the bridge with waves of loathing.

Half dreaming, my eye caught the monument to St Luitgard: on the hollowed-out sandstone the 'Torments of the Damned' were carved in high relief and the snow was lying thick on the lids of the souls in purgatory and on their manacled hands raised in supplication.

Arches swallowed me up and released me, palaces with arrogant carved portals on which lions' heads bit into bronze rings slowly passed me by.

Here too was snow, snow everywhere. Soft and white as the fur of a gigantic polar bear. Tall, proud windows, their ledges glittering with ice, stared coldly up at the sky. I was astonished to see the air so full of migrating birds. As I climbed the countless granite steps to the Hradschin, each one the width of four bodies laid head to foot, the city with its roofs and gables sank, step by step, from my conscious mind.

Already the twilight was creeping along the rows of houses as I stepped out into the empty square in the middle of which the Cathedral towers up to the heavenly throne. Footsteps, the edges encrusted with ice, led to the side door.

From somewhere in a distant house the soft, musing tones of a harmonium crept out into the stillness of the evening. They were like melancholy tears trickling down into the deserted square.

The well-padded door swung to with a sigh behind me as I entered the Cathedral and stood in the darkness of the side aisle. The nave was filled with the green and blue shimmer of the dying light slanting down through the stained-glass windows onto the pews; at the far end, the altar gleamed at me in a frozen cascade of gold. Showers of sparks came from the bowls of the red glass lamps. The air was musty with the smell of wax and incense.

I leant back in one of the pews. My heart grew strangely calm in this realm where everything stood still. The whole expanse of the Cathedral was filled with a presence that had no heartbeat, with a secret, patient expectation.

Eternal sleep lay over the silver reliquaries.

(17) PRAGUE

Jan Neruda, *St Václav's Mass*

This piece, from Tales of the Malá Strana, 1877, is from a story about a young boy who hides in St Vitus' Cathedral at night, hoping to see the Czech patron saint Wenceslas/Václav.

I saw all those old lords, with their stone eyes, I saw them in the spirit as they led the procession, but, wonderful to relate, I could not imagine their bodies and legs, they remained only busts, yet they moved exactly as if they were walking. Then, perhaps, would come the archbishops who were buried behind there in the Kinský chapel, and after them the silver angels of Saint John, and behind them with the crucifix the silver Saint John himself. After him the bones of Saint Sigmund, only a few bones on a red cushion, but the cushion also would appear to be walking. Then the various knights in armour, and after them the kings and dukes from all the surrounding tombs, some resplendently dressed in garments of faded scarlet, others, George of Poděbrady among them, in white marble. And then, bearing the chalice covered with a silver veil, Saint Václav himself. A tall, youthfully powerful figure. On his head, instead of a biretta, a simple metal helmet; but the coat of mail shielding his body would be covered with a chasuble of gleaming white silk. His chestnut hair flows in rich curls, his face is sublime in kindliness and tranquillity. It was strange that I could conjure up his features quite clearly, the large blue eyes, the cheeks flowering with health, the softly-flowing beard, and yet it was as though this face were composed not of flesh and blood, but of serenely beaming light.

While I had been calling up in my own mind this procession which was to come, I had closed my eyes. Silence, weariness and excited fantasy had their effect – sleep breathed upon me, and my legs gave under me. Quickly I jerked myself upright again, and my startled gaze swept round the vast spaces of the church. Silent and lifeless as before, yet now suddenly this lifelessness had quite a different effect upon me. I felt in an instant how heavy was my weariness, how the cold invaded my body, and suddenly there fell upon me a terror, undefined but all the more shattering for that. I did not know what I feared, yet I was afraid, and my feeble childish mind had no reserves and no refuge.

I crumpled upon the step, and burst into agonised weeping. My tears gushed, my chest was constricted, a loud hiccup burst from my lips, and

I tried in vain to suppress it. As my hiccups grew momentarily more convulsive they echoed painfully through the silence of the church, and the unaccustomed sound increased my terror still more. If only I were not here quite alone in this enormous church! – If only I were not locked in!

Again I uttered a loud gulp, perhaps louder than before, and at that instant, as though in answer, there broke out above me the twittering of birds. Of course, I was not alone here, the sparrows were spending the night with me! I knew their refuge very well – between the beams directly over the tiers of seats. That was where they had found their sacred resting-place, safe even from the incalculable whims of us boys. Every one of us could have thrust in his hand between the beams after them, but none of us ever did.

(18) PRAGUE

Vítězslav Nezval, *Moon over Prague*

Nezval's poem, from Prague with Fingers of Rain, 1936, is playfully illusionistic, with Gothic horror and a touch of Surrealism in the kaleidoscopic imagery.

The decorator is mixing his plaster
He's lit an oil lamp on top of the stepladder
It is the moon
It moves like an acrobat
Wherever it appears it causes panic
It turns black coffee into white
It offers paste jewelry to women's eyes
It changes bedrooms into death chambers
It settles on the piano
It floodlights the Castle theatrically
Today Prague remembers its history
It's the river fête look at that bobbing Chinese lantern
The bells are as brittle as plates
There'll be a grand tourney
White carpets are laid through the city
Buildings have their roles in the great tragedy and all
    belongs to the underworld
The moon enters the tiny garrets
It gleams on the table it is an inkwell
A thousand letters will be written with its ink
And a single poem

The Czech Republic | 111

(19) PRAGUE

Anthony Trollope, *Nina Balatka*

The Kleinseite is the Malá Strana, the bridge is the Charles Bridge over the Vltava (Moldau). The saint is St John of Nepomuk who was thrown into the Vltava and drowned.

Taking the pathway on the other side, she turned her face again towards the Kleinseite, and very slowly crept along under the balustrade of the bridge. This bridge over the Moldau is remarkable in many ways, but it is specially remarkable for the largeness of its proportions. It is very long, taking its spring from the shore a long way before the actual margin of the river; it is of a fine breadth: the side-walks to it are high and massive; and the groups of statues with which it is ornamented, though not in themselves of much value as works of art, have a dignity by means of their immense size which they lend to the causeway, making the whole thing noble, grand, and impressive. And below, the Moldau runs with a fine, silent, dark volume of water, – a very sea of waters when the rains have fallen and the little rivers have been full, though in times of drought great patches of ugly dry land are to be seen in its half-empty bed. At the present moment there were no such patches; and the waters ran by, silent, black, in great volumes, and with unchecked rapid course. It was only by pausing specially to listen to them that the passer-by could hear them as they glided smoothly round the piers of the bridge. Nina did pause and did hear them. They would have been almost less terrible to her, had the sound been rougher and louder.

On she went, very slowly. The moon, she thought, had disappeared altogether before she reached the cross inlaid in the stone on the bridge-side, on which she was accustomed to lay her fingers, in order that she might share somewhat of the saint's power over the river. At that moment, as she came up to it, the night was very dark. She had calculated that by this time the light of the moon would have waned, so that she might climb to the spot which she had marked for herself without observation. She paused, hesitating whether she would put her hand upon the cross. It could not at least do her any harm. It might be that the saint would be angry with her, accusing her of hypocrisy; but what would be the saint's anger for so small a thing amidst the multitudes of charges that would be brought against her? For that which she was going to do now there could be no absolution given. And perhaps the saint might perceive that the deed on her part was not altogether hypocritical – that there was something in it of a true prayer. He might see this, and intervene to save her from the waves. So she put the palm of her little hand full upon the cross, and then kissed it heartily, and after that raised it up again till it rested on the foot of the saint. As she stood there she heard the departing voices of the girls and children singing the last verse of the vesper hymn, as they followed the friar off the causeway of the bridge into the Kleinseite.

(20) PRAGUE

Jaroslav Seifert, *Prague*

This poem, referring to the Emperor Rudolf's court in Prague Castle, with its alchemists and astronomers, is from Seifert's volume Poštovní holub (The Carrier Pigeon), 1929.

Above the elephantine blankets of flower-beds
a Gothic cactus blooms with royal skulls
and in the cavities of melancholy organs,
    in the clusters of tin pipes,
old melodies are rotting.

Cannon-balls like seeds of wars
were scattered by the wind.

Night towers over all
and through the box-trees of evergreen cupolas
the foolish emperor tiptoes away
into the magic gardens of his retorts
and in the halcyon air of rose-red evenings
rings out the tinkle of the glass foliage
as it is touched by the alchemists' fingers
as if by the wind.

The telescopes have gone blind from the horror of the universe
and the fantastic eyes of the astronauts
have been sucked out by death.

And while the Moon was laying eggs in the clouds,
new stars were hatching feverishly like birds
migrating from blacker regions,
singing the songs of human destinies –
but there is no one
who can understand them.

Listen to the fanfares of silence,
on carpets threadbare like ancient shrouds
we are moving towards an invisible future

and His Majesty dust
settles lightly on the abandoned throne.

(21) Ratibořice

Božena Němcová, *Granny*

The local Countess has departed for the winter, as has the children's father, who is one of her employees. Viktorka, a crazed local girl, drowned her illegitimate baby at the weir.

Even in the countryside round the Old Bleaching-Ground it was sad and quiet now. The forest was thinner and lighter; when Viktorka came down from the hill she could be seen at quite a distance moving through the trees. The whole slope had grown yellow, wind and waves carried away drifts of dry leaves God knows where, the treasure of the orchard was stored away indoors. In the garden the only flowers left were asters, marigolds and lion's mouth. The meadow beyond the weir flushed rosy with autumn crocuses, and in the night will-o'-the-wisps danced there. When Granny went out for a walk with the children the boys didn't forget to take with them their paper kites, which they flew from the hilltop. Adelka rushed after them, flourishing on a twig the silken filaments of gossamer, so that they flew bravely in the wind. On the hillside Babbie gathered for Granny the red viburnum berries and aloes she needed for medicines, or picked rose-hips for use in the kitchen, or shook down the rowan berries from which she made strings of corals for Adelka to wear round her throat and wrists.

Granny liked to sit with them on the top of the hill above the manor-house; from there they could see down into the green meadows of the valley, where the flocks from the demesne were at pasture, and as far away as the little town, while the manor-house on its small eminence in the middle of the valley, and the pleasant park which surrounded it, lay at their feet. The green Venetian blinds at the windows were closed, there were no flowers on the balconies, the climbing rose round the white stone railing had faded. Instead of the nobility and their be-laced servants there were workmen tramping about the grounds, covering over with brushwood the flower-beds in which no more rainbow flowers shone, but which cradled the dormant seed of still more beautiful blossoms to delight the eye of the proprietress when she returned to her estate. The rare foreign trees, naked of their green garments now, were bound up in straw; the fountain which had gushed forth such silvery streams was shrouded in boards and moss, and the gold-fish hid themselves at the bottom of the pool, the surface of which, at other times so limpidly clear, was strewn with leaves, pond-weed and green slime.

The children looked down, remembering the day when they had walked through the garden with Hortensia, and eaten refreshments in the salon; they recalled how beautiful everything was there, and thought to themselves: 'I wonder where she is now?' But Granny liked to look out beyond the hillside opposite, over village, preserves, woods, fishponds and forests to Nové Město, to Opočno and Dobruška, where her son lived, and beyond Dobruška into the mountains, where lay a certain small village, and in it so many souls who were dear to her. And if she turned her gaze towards the east, there before her lay the beautiful crescent of the Giant Mountains, from the long hog-back of Hejšovina to the cloud-capped summit of Old Snowy, already covered with snow. Pointing over Hejšovina she would say to the children: 'There I know every path, there in those mountains lies Kladsko, where your mother was born, there are Vambeřice and Varta, there in those parts I spent many happy years.'

(22) Terezín

Ivan Klíma, *Miriam*

This story, from My First Loves, 1985, describes the brief adolescent love of a boy in Terezín, a garrison town in northern Bohemia, Nazi concentration camp in the second world war.

Quietly I got off my palliasse and tiptoed to the window. I knew the view well: the dark crowns of the ancient lime-trees outside the window, the brick gateway with its yawning black emptiness. And the sharp outlines of the ramparts. Cautiously I lifted a corner of the black-out paper and froze: the top of one of the lime-trees was aglow with a blue light. A spectral light, cold and blinding. I stared at it for a moment. I could make out every single leaf, every little glowing twig, and I became aware at the same time that the branches and the leaves were coming together in the shape of a huge, grinning face which gazed at me with flaming eyes.

I felt I was choking and couldn't have cried out even had I dared to do so. I let go of the black paper and the window was once more covered in darkness. For a while I stood there motionless and wrestled with the temptation to lift the paper again and get another glimpse of that face. But I lacked the courage. Besides, what was the point? I could see that face before me, shining through the black-out, flickering over the dark ceiling, dancing in front of my eyes even when I firmly closed my eyelids.

What did it mean? Who did it belong to? Did it hold a message for me? But how would I know whether it was good news or bad?

By morning nothing was left of the joys or the fears of the night before. I went to get my ration of bitter coffee, I gulped down two slices of bread and margarine. I registered with relief that the war had moved on by one night and that the unimaginable peace had therefore drawn another night nearer.

I went behind the metal-shop to play volleyball, and an hour before lunchtime I was already queuing up with my billycan for my own and my brother's eighth-of-a-litre of milk. The line stretched towards a low vaulted room, not unlike the one inhabited by Aunt Sylvia. Inside, behind an iron pail, stood a girl in a white apron. She took the vouchers from the submissive queuers, fished around in the pail with one of the small measures and poured a little of the skimmed liquid into the vessels held out to her.

As I stood before her she looked at me, her gaze rested on my face for a moment, and then she smiled.

Biographies and important works

ČAPEK, Karel (1890–1938). Playwright, translator of French poetry, and writer of fiction, Karel Čapek was born in **Malé Svatoňovice**, near Úpice in the Podkrkonoší (Sub-Krkonoše) region, the son of a doctor. He studied philosophy (including American pragmatism), aesthetics and art history at **Prague**, where he later lived and worked as a journalist, mainly for *Lidové noviny* (*People's News*). The street in the **Vinohrady** district of Prague where he lived from 1924 with his brother Josef (1887 – Bergen Belsen 1945) is now called **Bratří Čapků** ('Brothers Čapek Street'). Travels to Italy, Britain, Spain, Holland and Scandinavia are reflected in several of Karel Čapek's books, such as the whimsical *Anglické listy* (*Letters from England*), 1924. His translations of French verse, collected in *Francouzská poezie nové doby* (*French Poetry of the New Age*), 1920, were crucial for the Czech avant-garde, among them Nezval ◊ and Seifert ◊.

A number of his works were written in collaboration with his brother Josef, including *Ze života hmyzu* (*The Insect Play*), 1921. Other dramas include his anti-Utopian play *RUR* (= Rossum's Universal Robots), 1920, which gave the word 'robot' to the English language; *Věc Makropulos* (*The Makropulos Affair*), 1922, on the subject of longevity, which formed the basis for Janáček's opera; and *Bílá nemoc* (*The White Plague*), 1930. His longer fiction, with related Dystopian, science-fiction elements, includes *Továrna na absolutno* (*Factory of the Absolute*), 1922, *Krakatit*, 1924, and *Válka s mloky* (*War with the Newts*), 1936, in which the world is taken over by the newts, who are analogous to robots (Extract 10). In his loose trilogy *Hordubal, Povětroň, Obyčejný Život* (*Hordubal, Meteor, An Ordinary Life*), 1933–34, Čapek addresses the relativity and elusiveness of truth about individuals, foregrounding the fictionality of narrative and exploiting multiple and alternative viewpoints. Gently lyrical or entertainingly effervescent in their treatment of similar sceptical themes are his short stories – *Trapné povídky* (*Awkward Stories*), 1921, for instance, and the whimsical, ethical and gently epistemological detective stories of *Povídky z jedné a druhé kapsy* (*Tales from Two Pockets*), 1929.

Čapek likes to present amiable quirkiness in ordinary 'little' people, the lovableness of the everyday; he hates absolutism, grandiose Utopias, and mass movements of the Left or Right. There is a **Čapek museum** in the house he acquired in 1935, delightfully situated by a small lake in **Strž**, not far from Dobříš, south of Prague.

ERBEN, Karel Jaromír (1811–1870). Born in **Miletín**, between Hořice and Dvůr Králové in north-east Bohemia, the poet Erben studied at **Prague**, worked for the **Czech Museum** and became archivist of the city of Prague, edited medieval texts, including the works of Hus, and collected Slav folk tales. Influenced by the brothers Grimm, and related thinking in this field, he sought to identify a core of ancient myths in this orally transmitted material. He produced a classic volume of folk songs (*Prostonárodní písně a říkadla*, 1864) and also collected folk tales. His single original poetic volume is *Kytice* (*Garland of National Legends*), 1853, ballads written over a number of years and based on popular beliefs and legends, as well as influenced by German literary ballads and other material (Extract 1). Dvořák composed tone poems inspired by Erben's ballads with the same names: 'Vodník' ('The Water Sprite'), 'Polednice' ('The Noonday Witch'), 'Štědrý večer' ('Christmas Eve') and 'Zlatý kolovrat' ('The Golden Spinning Wheel'). The cantata known as 'The Spectre's Bride' is a setting of Erben's 'Svatební košile' ('The Wedding Shirts'), itself a remodelling of the German poet Bürger's ballad 'Lenore'.

Erben presents a sensibility of submission to the mysterious order of nature ('fate', or divine will) and to community morality, transgression of which courts disaster. Even 'Záhořovo lože' ('Záhoř's Bed'), which began as a response to Mácha's ◊ nihilism, has a legendary, mythic feeling to its Christianity. Underlying the traditional balladic idiom, with its blend of peasant Christianity and magic belief, is a tersely expressed dialectic of inextricable pain and joy in human intimacy, a sense of life's fragility, a harsh depiction of possessiveness and conflict in bonds between mother and child, man and woman, the impossibility of true oneness with the other, expressions of persistent psychological, philosophical, moral and erotic anxiety.

HALAS, František (1901–1949). Born in **Brno**, in Moravia, son of a socialist textile worker, Halas initially worked as a bookseller, and was something of a self-educated man. From 1921 he published in Communist journals; from 1926 he was an editor with the **Prague** publishers Orbis. During the Nazi occupation he lived from 1941 in **Kunštát** in Moravia. After 1945 he was employed at the Ministry of Information, becoming bitterly disillusioned with the Communists after their takeover in February 1948.

His first collection *Sepie* (*Cuttle-Fish/Sepia*), 1927 already blends playful Czech Poetist associative imagery with what would become typical anxious melancholy, self-doubt, erotic anxiety, and sense of futility. In further collections, such as *Kohout plaší smrt* (*The Cock Scares Death*), 1930, with its motto from Blake, *Tvář* (*Face*), 1931, the litanic sequence *Staré ženy* (*Old Women*), 1935, *Dokořán* (*Wide Open*), 1936, and *Ladění* (*Tuning*), 1942, Halas contemplates and exploits the emotive force, magic fascination, yet fragility of language; he confronts, in Baroque-like, quasi-mystically questing, religious–agnostic poems, in clustered metaphors, age-old lyric themes of time, disintegration, nothingness, and death, but also childhood, love, beauty and home. He has other strong poems of committed political and social protest, on the Spanish Civil War, for instance, or, most famously, in resonant imagery and rhetoric, from the time of Munich, in *Torso naděje* (*Torso of Hope*), 1938 (Extract 11).

Immediately after his death, the Stalinist critic Ladislav Štoll excoriated Halas for pessimistic nihilism.

HARRISON, Tony (1937–). Born in Leeds, one of the finer contemporary committed English poets, and also a writer of dramatic verse, Tony Harrison was employed as an English

Tony Harrison

lector in **Prague** in 1966–67. A fruit of this stay is 'Prague Spring' (Extract 12), one of the few effective English poems about Prague, or Bohemia, that this compiler has come across.

HAŠEK, Jaroslav (1883–1923). Born at **No 16, Školská**, in **Prague**, Hašek, the prolific author of *Švejk* and hundreds of stories and sketches, was the son of a schoolteacher who became a bank clerk. He left school early, trained as a pharmacist, went to the **Commercial Academy**, worked briefly at a bank, began writing for magazines and newspapers, and became involved with the anarchists. By 1907 he was under surveillance, and he spent a month in prison for 'incitement to violence against a police officer'. In 1909–10 he was editor of the magazine *Svět zvířat* (*Animal World*), for which he started inventing material. He married in 1910. In 1911 he was briefly in a mental hospital after an assumed attempted suicide from the **Charles Bridge**, and he stood as a candidate for his own invented 'Party of Moderate Progress within the Bounds of the Law'. He was called up in 1915, went to the Galician Front, was decorated, and captured in September by the Russians. He joined up with the Czech legions, wrote nationalist propaganda, but in 1918 switched to the Communists, went teetotal, and became deputy commandant of the town of Bugulma, and later a political Commissar. In 1920 he married a second time, bigamously, in Krasnoyarsk, but he went back home that same year, reverted to his old heavy drinking, and started the final, unfinished version of *Osudy dobrého vojáka Švejka* (*The Good Soldier Švejk and his Fortunes in the World War*), 1921–23. He was overtaken by heart failure in **Lipnice nad Sázavou** at the beginning of 1923.

Hašek published his first book about Švejk, portrayed as a Prague-Žižkov dog-dealer, in 1912. A second version was written in Russia, a period which also produced his Bugulma stories (English versions in *The Red Commissar*). The hero of Hašek's endlessly baggy long novel *The Good Soldier Švejk* (Extract 13) is a war-, army-, church- and state-debunking, picaresque, clever fool (ie not a fool), with endless zany blarney, a figure who has won the enormous affection

Švejk with wheelchair and crutches (by Josef Lada) – see Extract 13

of readers, but also incurred worried reactions from earnest thinkers who have seen his hopelessly evasive, unprincipled, coarsely material behaviour as a bad model, an undesirable image for the Czech nation. Is this to take Švejk too seriously or to miss the point of the book's proto-absurdist debunking collage of a crazy world? Is the book silly and trivial? Answer according to taste and outlook on life.

Fans visit the Prague street **Na Bojišti** (in the New Town) with its famous tourist-exploiting Prague hostelry **U kalicha** ('The Chalice'), which features in Chapter 1. Another shrine is **Lipnice nad Sázavou**, with the house where Hašek spent the last months of his life, and his grave in the churchyard. For the funeral, attended by a few friends, his body, now weighing over twenty-four stone, had to be removed via the window. His debtors came and loaded all they could on to a cart.

Hašek's biography can be read in detailed volumes by Cecil Parrott and Emanuel Frynta.

Opening illustration (by Josef Lada) for *The Good Soldier Švejk*

HAVEL, Václav (1936–). Born in **Prague**, the most famous post-war

Czech playwright, later President, comes from a well-to-do family. His grandfather built the **Lucerna** restaurant and dance-hall building in Prague; his father built villas and a restaurant at **Barrandov** on the edge of Prague, where his uncle founded the Barrandov film studios. Václav Havel was barred from higher education in the early 1950s, trained as a chemistry laboratory assistant, finished secondary school part-time, then studied in 1955–57 at the Economics Faculty of the **Prague Higher Institute of Technology**. After doing his military service in 1957–59, he became a stage hand, first at the **ABC Theatre**, then from 1960 at the **Divadlo Na zábradlí** (Ballustrade Theatre), where he moved up into production. In 1967 he graduated externally from the Drama Faculty of the **Academy of Performing Arts**. He was banned from theatre work in 1969.

In 1974 he had a job working at a brewery in **Trutnov**, but generally he was 'freelance', and involved in samizdat production. In 1977 he was one of the first three spokesmen for Charter 77, formed to monitor Czechoslovakia's observance of the Helsinki accords on human rights. He was held under arrest from January to May, given a suspended sentence, arrested again in January 1978, but released without trial. In 1979 he was sentenced to four and a half years, and was released only in March 1983, after contracting pneumonia. He was arrested again in 1989 for honouring the anniversary of Jan Palach, the student who burnt himself to death on 16 January 1969. In November 1989 he led the Civic Forum movement which harnessed mass popular pressure (in radically altered international circumstances) and toppled the Communist regime. At the end of December he was elected President,

Václav Havel

an office he has held most of the time since, resigning for a while in July 1992 when the split into two countries was imminent.

In his first major play *Zahradní slavnost (The Garden Party)*, 1963, Havel describes the overnight career success of young Hugo Pludek, sent to a garden party run by a Liquidation Office, which he himself later liquidates under the aegis of the rival Inauguration Office, which he then also liquidates, finally becoming boss of a new all-powerful Central Commission for Inauguration and Liquidation. By this time he is unrecognizably depersonalized, the victim of his own linguistic manipulations. Corrupted language is again a central theme in *Vyrozumění (The Memorandum)*, 1965, in which an absurd office has a synthetic language Ptydepe foisted upon it, which functions as an excuse for power play (and, as in the previous work, enjoyable fooling with words and nonsense). Meanwhile the staff get on with more important things like food, sex, drinking parties and split ends. In *Ztížená možnost soustředění (Increased Difficulty of Con-*

centration), 1968, Eduard Huml, a social science writer, has a wife and a mistress, with whom his relations are identical. He procrastinates about breaking with either, lost in a labyrinth of valueless modern life, and dictating endless turgid texts in an action jumbled in its temporal sequence. Researchers enter to study his unique identity by means of Puzuk, a speaking computer. It, like the language Ptydepe, is a kind of a faith-substitute, an ideological shibboleth, a product of mad, dehumanized, misdirected ratiocination in an age of pseudo-scientific collectivism.

Later works include three one-act plays, Audience, 1975, Vernisáž (Private View), 1975, and Protest, 1978, each with a central character Vaněk, parodically based on the author, quizzically facing the slippery slope of moral compromise, and attitudes to dissidents among the more accommodating members of society. The first, a confrontation between a boozy brewer and Vaněk, is based on Havel's time in the **Trutnov brewery**. Other plays include Largo Desolato, 1984, Pokoušení (Temptation), 1985, and Asanace (Redevelopment), 1988. Havel's meditative prison letters to his wife have also been published, as Dopisy Olze (Letters to Olga), 1983, and some of the essays printed in Václav Havel or Living in Truth are sharply analytic – for instance, 'The Power of the Powerless'.

HOLUB, Miroslav (1923–). Born in **Plzeň**, Holub attended its **Classical Gymnasium** and was a railway-station worker till the end of the second world war. In 1946–53 he studied medicine at the **Charles University**, in 1954–71 he worked at the Microbiology Institute of the **Academy of Sciences**, from 1972 at the **Institute for Clinical and Experimental Medi-**

Miroslav Holub

cine. His research field is immunology. From 1951–65 he edited the popular science journal Vesmír (Universe). He has travelled widely abroad, including visits to the USA.

His first collection Denní služba (Day Service), 1958, belongs to the group known as 'poetry of the everyday', a reaction against the pathos of Stalinist versifying. He continued with collections such as Achilles a želva (Achilles and the Tortoise), 1960 (Extract 9), selected poems in Anamnéza (Anamnesis), 1964, Ačkoli (Although), 1969, Beton (Concrete), 1970, and Události (Events), 1971. After a long gap when he was unable to publish his poetry at home, there came Naopak (On the Contrary), 1982, Interferon čili O divadle (Interferon or, On the Theatre), 1986, Sagitální řez (Sagittal Section), 1989, Syndrom mizející plíce (Vanishing Lung Syndrome), 1990, and Ono se letělo (It Flew), 1994, verse and prose devoted to his native city of **Plzeň**.

His intellectually and morally probing, superficially unlyrical poems, often mini-narratives, exploit the vocabulary, idiom and imagery of biology and the other sciences, deriving their original resonance from a sense of continuous analytic engagement, not devoid of irony and humour. He has a sharp exploitation of the rhythms and sounds of Czech that is often somehow overlooked (so that emotive texture tends to be lost in translation, more than the reader imagines). His science and morality essays and mini-essays, published in English in *The Dimension of the Present Moment* and *The Jingle Bell Principle*, broadly share the concerns of his poetry.

The Little Town Where Time Stood Still

Hrabal is a most sophisticated novelist, with a gusting humour and a hushed tenderness of detail' Julian Barnes

Bohumil Hrabal

HRABAL, Bohumil (1914–   ). The connections between Hrabal's fiction, details of his life, and various places are manifold, and much is directly autobiographical. Hrabal was born on 28 March 1914 in **Brno-Židenice**. He lived at first with his grandmother and then, in 1917, when his mother Marie Kiliánová married Francin Hrabal, he went to live with them at the brewery in **Polná**, where a brother, Slávek, was born. After the first world war the family moved to the brewery in **Nymburk**, where his father was appointed manager. In 1924 his uncle Josef (Uncle Pepin) joined them. After secondary school Hrabal began law studies in **Prague**. With the occupation and closure of Czech higher education, he returned to Nymburk, worked in a notary's office, went to commercial school, and began to write poems. From 1942 to 1945 he worked on the railways, including a spell at **Kostomlaty station**, just west of Nymburk. After the war he completed his law studies, worked as an insurance agent, and then as a commercial traveller with the firm H. K. Klofanda.

In 1948, the Communist takeover prevented his first poems from being published, and his father lost his job. From 1949 to 1973 he lived in the **Libeň** district of Prague (**Na hrázi, 24**). He worked at the open-hearth furnaces in the steel town of **Kladno**, but after a bad accident in 1952 he returned to Prague. From 1954 he worked as a wastepaper packer in **Spálená street**. Two of his stories were published in a limited edition as *Hovory lidí* (*People's Conversations*) in 1956, the year he married Eliška Plevová. From 1959 to 1962 he worked backstage at the **S.K. Neumann Theatre**. His first, delayed book was published in 1963, as *Perlička na dně* (*Pearl on the Bottom*), and followed in 1964 by another story volume *Pábitelé* (*The Palaverers*) and a crazily garrulous colourful text, *Taneční hodiny pro starší a pokročilé* (*Dancing Classes for the Older and More Advanced*), based on his Uncle Pepin's unstoppable oral narratives. The novella *Ostře sledované vlaky* (*Closely Observed Trains*), reflecting his time at **Kostomlaty**, appeared in 1965, and was successfully filmed by Jiří Menzel in 1966 (released as *Closely Watched Trains* in the USA).

For some years after the 1968 invasion, publishers could not print him. He bought a house in the **Kersko** woods near Nymburk and began to spend much of his time there, writing *Postřižiny* (*Cutting It Short*), published in 1976 (Extract 7), and its sequel *Městečko, kde se zastavil čas* (*The Little Town Where Time Stood Still*), based on his parents' lives and his own boyhood in **Nymburk**. He also wrote a black-humoured debunking novel of recent Czech history, *Obsluhoval jsem anglického krále* (*I Served the King of England*). It centres on a waiter figure who collaborates during the war. Less controversial books, like *Slavnosti sněženek* (*Celebrations of Snowdrops*), also filmed by Menzel, were published with cuts. Another book, metaphorically exploiting the theme of book-pulping, *Příliš hlučná samota* (*Too Loud a Solitude*), was staged in 1984. From 1982 Hrabal worked on three memoir volumes, narrated as if by his wife, *Svatby v domě* (*Weddings in the House*), *Vita nuova*, and *Proluky* (*Vacant Sites*). His wife died in 1987; in the same year these were published in Toronto. From 1989 Hrabal began to write a series of improvisatory documentary-style texts, presented as letters to an American student April ('Dubenka'). They react to political and personal events, and are collectively titled *Dopisy Dubence* (*Letters to Dubenka*).

KAFKA, Franz (1883–1924). Now Prague's best-known German writer, Franz Kafka was born on 3 July 1883, in a later demolished house U věže ('At the Tower'), just off **Staroměstské náměstí** (the Old Town Square), adjacent to **St Nicholas' Church**.

Later they lived in **Celetná** (Zeltnergasse), and for a time at **No 5, U radnice**, ('By the Town Hall'), in a house near the famous old clock called **U minuty** ('At the Minute').

In 1882 Kafka's father Hermann, a Czech-speaking Jew from Osek near Písek in southern Bohemia, had opened a haberdashery shop in **Celetná street**. Kafka's mother Julie Löwy came from Poděbrady, from a more well-to-do German Jewish family. After elementary school in **Masná** (Fleischmarkt) behind the **Týn Church**, from September 1893 Franz attended the German Gymnasium in the Baroque **Kinský Palace** on the Old Town Square, where his father's shop was now also located. Subsequently he studied law at Prague's **German University**. His first job in 1907 was with the insurance firm Assicurazioni Generali, at **No 19, Wenceslas Square** (more recently the Polish Cultural Centre), and a year later he joined the Workers' Accident Insurance Company for Bohemia, at **No 7, Na poříčí**, where he stayed until he prematurely retired in 1922.

Kafka's earliest preserved work dates from 1904–05, in *Beschreibung eines Kampfes* (*Description of a Struggle* – Extract 14), two excerpts from which were published in 1909 in the Munich journal *Hyperion*. A watershed in his writing came when in one September night he wrote the story 'Das Urteil' (The Judgment', first published in 1913), which he subsequently read to a society at the **Palace Hotel in Panská**, in December 1912. Soon after this Kafka wrote 'Die Verwandlung' ('The Metamorphosis', first published in 1915), the story in which the hero Samsa wakes up and discovers he has turned into a huge bug or insect. He also at that time wrote most of his unfinished novel, now generally known as *Amerika* (*America*, posthumously published in

Franz Kafka

1927). Kafka's relations with his father were fraught, and in all three of these works the father–son theme is an essential element.

Kafka's first attempt at marriage came in 1912–17, when he was twice engaged to Felice Bauer, daughter of a Berlin Jewish businessman. His correspondence to her has been published, as *Letters to Felice*, and his struggle over this relationship has been seen (for example, by Elias Canetti) as partly reflected in his novel *Der Prozess* (*The Trial*, posthumously published in 1925), begun in 1914. In it Josef K., a bank official, is mysteriously arrested on his thirtieth birthday, tries to work out why and what is going on around him, and is finally stabbed by two strange men with a butcher's knife a year later (Extract 15).

In 1914–15 Kafka had to make way for his sister Elli and children at his parents' house in **Mikulášská**; he rented a flat first in **Bílkova**, then in March 1915 in **Dlouhá třída**, and in 1916 he spent some time in a tiny house rented by his sister Ottla in the now very doll's-house-like **Zlatá ulička** (Golden Lane) in the Castle. There he wrote the texts published in *Ein Landarzt* (*A Country Doctor*), 1919. In March 1917 he rented another flat in the **Schönborn Palace** (now the American embassy) in the **Malá Strana**, below Petřín hill. Here one August night in 1917 he first coughed up blood. He spent periods out in the country, attempting to improve his health: in **Siřem** with his sister Ottla, in **Želízy** north of Mělník during which time he met another woman, Julie Vohryzková, in Merano in Italy. His third love affair, in 1920, with his Czech translator Milena Jesenská, ended partly because Milena decided not to leave her husband. Their correspondence shows Kafka's interest in Czech.

In his third, unfinished novel, *Das Schloss* (*The Castle*, posthumously published in 1926), dating from 1922, a surveyor K. comes to a village and vainly attempts to gain admittance to the castle, to which he believes he had been summoned to be given a job. Like the mysteriously guilty one in *The Trial*, the protagonist again faces an inexplicable world.

In 1923 Kafka met the much younger Galician Jew Dora Diamant, his final love, with whom he even set up house for six months in Berlin, but by now his tuberculosis had worsened, and during further treatment in Austria he died in Kierling not far from Vienna on 3 June 1924. Kafka's grave is in the New Jewish Cemetery, in **Prague-Strašnice**.

Much of his work, especially the novels, was published posthumously by his close friend Max Brod. Critical attention, now constituting a veritable Kafka industry, continues to busy itself creating, adjusting and reformulating numerous personal, psychological, social, theological, philosophical and literary textual interpretations. Meanwhile the tourists in Prague happily visit his haunts and purchase their Kafka teeshirts and other Kafkiana.

KLÍMA, Ivan (1931–). Born in **Prague**, the novelist, short-story writer and playwright Ivan Klíma spent three years in **Terezín** concentration camp. He studied Czech literature at the **Charles University** in Prague and became an editor, on the weekly *Květy*, 1956–59, with the publisher Československý spisovatel (Czechoslovak Writer), 1959–63, and from 1964 with *Literární noviny/listy* (*Literary News*), later just *Listy*, banned as a result of the Soviet occupation. In 1969–70 he was visiting professor at the University of Michigan, in Ann Arbor. After returning home he became 'freelance', writing and involved in samizdat production. Apart from his novels he also produced a screenplay for Jiří Trnka's puppet film *Kybernetická babička* (*Cybernetic Grandmother*), 1962, and he has written about Karel Čapek ◊.

Among Klíma's first books was a novel *Hodina ticha* (*Hour of Silence*), 1963, set in Slovakia, reflecting earnest socialist ideals. A volume of stories *Milenci na jednu noc* (*Lovers for One Night*), 1964, followed – often monologues of young people seeking personal fulfilment amid all-embracing banality. The influence of Kafka becomes apparent in works such as his allegorical short novel *Loď jménem Naděje* (*A Ship Called Hope*), 1969, published with *Porota* (*The Jury*). *Milenci na jeden den* (*Lovers for*

One Day), 1970, also uses Kafkaesque and absurdist narrative to express the modern horrors lurking behind the Czech everyday (memory of concentration camps, atmosphere of surveillance and fear). The book was withdrawn and most copies destroyed, in the cultural purge of 'normalization'.

68 Publishers in Toronto eventually issued his next novel *Milostné léto* (*A Summer Affair*), 1979, the story of a married man's quest for fulfilment with a younger woman. Klíma has written of his own 'hopeless desire for a moment which cannot come, which, even if it did come, could not be retained. For a human meeting, for love. One thing has perhaps changed, that I understand perhaps better the vanity of the attempt and the kitschiness of the desire.' In a later novel *Láska a smetí* (*Love and Garbage*), 1988, there is another mistress. The married man, a banned writer, who was also in concentration camp as a boy, and decided to return home from America after the invasion, takes a job (voluntarily) as a street sweeper, and is fascinated by Kafka. A writer's temporary jobs also form the basis of his short-story cycle *Moje zlatá řemesla* (*My Golden Trades*), 1990, which likewise addresses themes of state repression, banality of values, and ecological destruction, an issue for growing alarm in the Czech Republic in the 1970s and 1980s. Another volume of contemporary stories was *Má veselá jitra* (*My Merry Mornings*), 1979, followed by the wistful love stories, including 'Miriam' (Extract 22), of *Moje první lásky* (*My First Loves*), 1985. A more ambitious moral–political novel about the post-war era is *Soudce z milosti* (*Judge on Trial*), 1986. Klíma's play *Hry* (*Games*, première in Vienna, 1975), with its similar figure of a morally compromised judge, uses entertaining black humour to address psychologies of manipulation, victi-

mization and violation; in 1990 it had a fine production at the Gate Theatre in London.

KUNDERA, Milan (1929–). Kundera was born in **Brno**, on 1 April 1929. His father was a musicologist and pupil of Janáček. After leaving the Gymnasium in 1948, by now a young Communist, Milan enrolled at the Arts Faculty of the **Charles University**, Prague. By 1950, however, he had to interrupt his studies for 'saying something I would better have left unsaid', and was expelled from the Party. Subsequently he was admitted to the Film Faculty of the **Academy of Performing Arts** in Prague, where later he taught literature. His study of the Czech novelist Vančura, *Umění románu* (*Art of the Novel*), 1960, dates from this time. (Later he re-used the title for a different collection of essays published in Paris.)

At the Congress of the Writers' Union in June 1967, Kundera delivered a memorable attack on censorship and recurrent Czech provincialism. He lost his job in 1970, and his Party membership (which had been renewed in 1956). For a while after the collapse of the Prague Spring reforms he earned small sums by writing magazine horoscopes, under an assumed name. In 1975 he accepted an invitation from the University of Rennes to be a visiting lecturer, in November 1979 he was shorn of his citizenship, and he settled into a teaching job in Paris.

Some of Kundera's early works have to be regarded as embarrassing juvenilia, especially his early lyric poetry, *Člověk zahrada širá* (*Man a Broad Garden*), 1953, and a verse eulogy to the wartime Communist martyr Julius Fučík, entitled *Poslední máj* (*Last Day of May*), 1955, and revamping bits of the Romantic poet Mácha ◊. His last verse collection, Monology (Monologues), 1957, was shocking in a different way in Czechoslovakia at the time. Sceptical and erotic, it anticipates, if rather more flimsily, his later ironically crafted tales of sexual quests, frustrated intentions and manipulations, amid crumbling social values and banality, collected in Směšné lásky (1963–68, one volume 1970). Kundera also turned to stage plays, his first being a respectable moral drama, Majitelé klíčů (Keepers of the Keys), 1962. It was followed by Ptákovina (Cock-a-Doodle), 1969, an absurdist sex-and-power piece, rejected later by the author, and Jakub a jeho pán/ Jacques et son maître (Jacques and His Master), 1981, based on an admired novel by Diderot.

Kundera completed his first novel Žert (The Joke) in 1965; it was published in 1967 (Extract 8). It tells of a man whose unwise postcard joke to a girlfriend takes him into military labour and misconceived revenge in changed post-Stalinist circumstances; it tells also of love, of music, of personal struggle for value and purpose. A successful film by Jaromil Jireč was based on it in 1969, which the author has approved of. His second novel, Život je jinde (Life is Elsewhere), was completed in 1969, and a French version was published in 1973: one of its themes, represented through the character of a poet, is the dangerous folly of the lyric sensibility. His third novel, Valčík na rozloučenou (The Farewell Party), set in an unnamed Czech spa, appeared in France in 1976, and is one of his most sceptically and fictively playful (like Jacques and His Master). Czech versions of both novels were issued by 68 Publishers in Toronto, in 1979, who also printed Kundera's later books. The next (now moving ever-more into polyphonic interplay of parallel, almost separate, but purposefully choreographed fictional narratives and humorously philosophizing, essayistic writing) was Kniha smíchu a zapomnění (The Book of Laughter and Forgetting, French edition 1979, Czech 1981). Its political side is the myth-making, amnesia and humourless mawkishness of ideological regimes and causes. This was followed by Nesnesitelná lehkost bytí (The Unbearable Lightness of Being, French edition 1984, Czech 1985), which was transformed into a sexy film by Philip Kaufman in 1987 (sex versus love, body and spirit, intellectually discussed, being one of Kundera's favourite subjects). This film completed the process of turning him into a worldwide best-selling Czech author. His next seductive novel (and Kundera writes some of the most seductively crafted Czech prose around) was Nesmrtelnost (Immortality, French edition 1990, Czech, both Toronto and Prague, 1993), the first not to be set, at least partly, in Kundera's native land. His latest published novel is La Lenteur, written in French, 1995.

MÁCHA, Karel Hynek (1810– 1836). Mácha, the magnus parens of the modern Czech lyric, was born in the Malá Strana district of Prague, in the street called Újezd, on the site of today's No 35. The family later moved across the river, to streets near today's náměstí Republiky (Republic Square). He went to the New Town Gymnasium on Příkopy (Graben, named after the one-time moat). His mother came from a family of musicians; his father, a miller's assistant, came to Prague from the country, and later opened a small flour shop on today's Karlovo náměstí (Charles Square), then Dobytčí trh (the Cattle Market), where the family lived, at today's No 34, but the house no longer exists. Here he wrote his most famous poem *Máj* (*May*), 1836.

Mácha's girlfriend, and mother of his short-lived baby son Ludvík, Eleonora ('Lori') Šomková, lived in **Truhlářská street**, at No 11, and Mácha would visit her daily, and help her make little cardboard boxes for medicines and the like. He also attended Czech theatrical performances in the **Estates Theatre** and acted at the Cajetan Theatre in the Malá Strana (it was on **Nerudova, No 24**). With his friends or alone, Mácha loved to take long hikes to ruined castles, rocks and lakes; he travelled on foot to northern Italy and Venice. His reading embraced German Gothic horror stories, Goethe, Shakespeare, Byron and the Polish Mickiewicz (◊ Poland). After studying law in Prague, Mácha found an assistant job in **Litoměřice**, where he tried to establish himself, in order to marry Lori, who was now pregnant. On the eve of his marriage, he fell ill and died, at the age of twenty-six. His remains, buried in Litoměřice, were removed to Prague after the Nazi occupation of the area.

Mácha's first literary attempts were at German verse, but he achieved true originality in Czech, especially in relatively few short poems, including sonnets, and in his lyrical narrative poem *Máj* (*May*), which he published in April 1836 (Extract 4). In it Vilém is executed for killing his father, seducer of his beloved Jarmila, but this is only an ultimately ironized Gothic (and somewhat misleadingly Byronic) skeleton background for lyrically complex, musically compelling expressions of verbal and natural beauty, of man's lost childhood innocence, and irretrievable paradise, of man as prisoner of an unfathomable, apparently, in human terms, aimless universe, of consciousness of enigma-

tic nature and time, of life's sensual beauty and horror, of spiritually envisioned love and its empirical mockery.

Of his prose works, including unfinished attempts at Romantic historical fiction, perhaps the most notable, as well as most often read, are his Poe-like lyrical horror story 'Pout' krkonošská' ('Pilgrimage to the Krkonoše') and the mixed Romantic-realistic story 'Marinka', 1834.

MAJEROVÁ, Marie (1882–1967). The novelist Marie Majerová (penname) came from a working-class family and spent her childhood in the industrial town of **Kladno**, not far from Prague. She worked as a maid in Budapest and a typist in **Prague**. Her first husband was a Social Democrat journalist in Vienna; she studied in Paris, and in 1921 she joined the newly founded Communist Party. From 1920 to 1929 she was an editor for the Communist newspaper *Rudé Právo* (*Red Right*). She was expelled from the Party for indiscipline in 1929, with six other writers who opposed the new Stalinist line (including Vančura, Seifert ◊, and Olbracht), but later returned to the fold. After the war Majerová revamped some of her works, became a much-paraded establishment figure and is regarded as having declined badly as a writer; such was the fate of more than one author during the Stalinist years.

Majerová's first prose included the emanicipatory novel *Panenství* (*Virginity*), 1907, in which a girl is tempted into selling her body to save her fatally ill boyfriend. *Náměstí republiky* (*Place de la République*), 1914, portrays and reflect Majerová's own disillusionment with the life and ideas of anarchists in Paris. Her longer novel *Siréna* (*The Siren*), 1935, is one of the finer specimens of its sort: a panoramic documentary novel depicting several generations in the lives of a working-class **Kladno** family, running from the mid-nineteenth century up to 1918 (Extract 5). Its shorter sequel, *Havířská balada* (*Ballad of a Miner*), 1938, partly using the expressive immediacy of internal monologue, tells the story of a miner in Germany who later returns home to a life of destitution. Both are among the more informative and readable examples of left-wing documentary fiction from this era.

MEYRINK, Gustav (1868–1932). Meyrink was born in Vienna, and died in Bavaria, but his best-known work is set in **Prague**, which he fills with mystery, fantasy and weird atmosphere, using its famous sights of the **old Jewish cemetery**, the **Castle**, and other places wreathed in legend, its labyrinthine old streets and alleyways. 'Other cities, however ancient,' he once wrote, 'seem to me to submit to the power of their inhabitants . . . Prague shapes its inhabitants and moves them like puppets from their first to last breath.' Real name Gustav Meyer, he was the illegitimate son of a Viennese actress and a Württemberg aristocrat. He came to Prague with his mother in 1884, stayed on, and became a banker. He cut a figure as a provocative dandy, liked to shock the bourgeois, apparently suffered a nervous breakdown in 1891, almost committed suicide, read widely on the occult, was involved in theosophy, explored the revelatory powers of the mind, tried hashish, and practised yoga. He married in 1893, and again, after a long liaison, in 1905. In 1902 he was briefly imprisoned, accused, as the story goes, of influencing clients, especially women, through spiritism. Though cleared, his business failed.

Some years later he settled in Bavaria, by Lake Starnberg.

As a writer Meyrink began with grotesque, anti-bourgeois and anti-militarist satirical pieces, recently issued in English as *The Opal (and Other Stories)*. These were followed by his most famous occult fantasy novel *Der Golem* (*The Golem*), 1913, where dreams, visions and reality inextricably merge (Extract 16). Rabbi Löw's clay homunculus, the Golem, is also the narrator's double, in his quest for inner spiritual knowledge. Meyrink's next novel *Das grüne Gesicht* (*The Green Face*), 1916, has an Amsterdam setting. *Walpurgisnacht*, 1917, confronts Prague aristocrats with mob revolution. *Der Weiße Dominikaner* (*The White Dominican*), 1921, is set in Bavaria, but Prague is the main setting again of his last novel, *Der Engel vom westlichen Fenster* (*The Angel of the West Window*), 1927, which features the Rudolfine English magus John Dee.

NĚMCOVÁ, Božena (1820–1862). Born in Vienna, Božena Němcová was brought up in **Ratibořice** in north-east Bohemia. At seventeen, after elementary schooling, she was married to an excise officer Josef Němec, who was many years older than her. When he was posted to **Prague** in 1842 she met the leading writers. Later they moved to the **Chodsko** and **Domažlice** areas, where she collected folk tales and wrote about rural life. Her husband's public involvement in 1848 meant that they were put under suspicion; he went to Hungary, where later he lost his job. She stayed in Prague, with visits to Slovakia between 1851 and 1853, was in conflict with her husband, and one of her sons Hynek died. At the end of 1861 she herself fell seriously ill and she died the following January.

Her fictional masterpiece *Babička* (*Granny*), 1855, arose amid such circumstances, in a desire to escape and create a world of happy recollection and stability (Extract 21). The book opens with the arrival of the grandmother at the family home, introduces a series of local people, up to the countess, in her chateau and its park, contrasting with the rural landscape, and then the narrative goes into the cycle of the rural year, with its many traditional habits and customs. The grandmother of the children provides stability, simple morality, and pious wisdom, and is consulted by all, including the countess. The main heightening of narrative comes from interpolated tales, the most famous that of the girl Viktorka who, seduced by a soldier, drowns her baby and goes mad. Overall, in its placidly flowing sentence rhythms and enumeration of detail, the book is therapeutic, realistic in observation, idyllic, lyrically tragic, but ultimately peaceful. Within the loving observation of the minutiae of daily life, disasters – flooding, or Viktorka's madness – are gently and inexorably erased in a spirit of human acceptance and organic restoration of harmony.

Němcová's fairy tales, which she collected and retold, are widely known to children, and though another novel *Pohorská vesnice* (*Upland Village*), 1856, is less successful, some of her shorter fiction is also read, as is her psychologically telling correspondence. As noted in our introductory essay, her childhood home of **Ratibořice** is a popular place of pilgrimage.

NERUDA, Jan (1834–1891). Born at the later demolished Újezd barracks in **Prague**, where his father, a Napoleonic Wars veteran, ran a canteen, Jan Neruda grew up in Ostruho-vá Street, from 1895 called **Nerudova Street** after him, in the **Malá Strana**. When he was four, his father opened a tobacconist's at **No 47 'U dvou sluncŭ'** ('House of the Two Suns'), with a small back room where they lived. Jan used to sit out on the roof, between the two gables. He attended the local German gymnasium, and from 1850 the Academic Gymnasium, where the headmaster was the dramatist Václav Klicpera, and his fellow pupils included the writer Vítězslav Hálek. In 1855 he enrolled at the Arts Faculty at **Prague**, but also began to work as a reporter for *Tagesbote aus Böhmen*. In 1865 he joined the staff of the Young Czech Party organ *Národní listy* (*The National*), where he spent the rest of his working life. He was involved with the young writer's miscellany *Máj* (*May*) in 1858, named after Mácha's ◊ famous poem. His essay and fiction writing is intimately linked with his journalism, and with his travels: he travelled in France, Germany, the Balkans, to Italy, Constantinople and Egypt (but never to Britain). Neruda had a long courtship with his first girlfriend, in 1862 he was close to the author Karolina Světlá, who was married, he fell in love with a teenage girl who died, and was later very fond of two much younger women, but he never married. His years from 1880 were marked by illness; after a leg accident, he was unable to walk without aid, and he died at his ground-floor flat at **No 44, Vladislavova** street in 1891.

Neruda's first book was a volume of verse, *Hřbitovní kvítí* (*Graveyard Blooms*), 1857, showing the influence of the German poet Heine; this was followed by several more, including *Balady a romance* (*Ballads and Romances*), 1883, with profane and ambivalent treatments of Christian, national historical and socio-political themes, and also the intimate, self-deprecatory love lyrics of the cycle *Prosté motivy* (*Simple Motifs*), 1883. In his most famous volume of stories, *Povídky malostranské* (*Tales of the Malá Strana*), 1877, Neruda mixes emotionally charged, but also ironic, satirical character portrayals, including a number of gruff, eccentric outsiders (the solitary, the bachelor or old maid, the beggar), also thwarted lovers and children, with sharply observed depictions of the local *milieu* (Extract 17). Related volumes of prose include the character sketches and *scènes de la vie* of *Arabesky* (*Arabesques*), 1864, *Různí lidé* (*Various People*), 1871, and *Trhani* (*Navvies*), 1872, which portrays the life of migrant railway workers. He was a socially committed writer, more radical than is perhaps now immediately apparent, writing to his close friend, the writer Karolina Světlá: 'The bread I ate from childhood never belonged to me, always to the grocer, the baker, and as a boy I wondered much at this, until I got used to people reproaching me for living at their expense. Yet my father laboured till his dying day from morn till night, and my mother never healed her caloused hands . . . And then they ask why one does not sing, laughing at the kind of poet one is! Sometimes when I walk in the evening past the houses of the rich, my head full of troubles, my heart full of sorrows, I think I would be quite justified in setting light to their roofs . . .'

NEZVAL, Vítězslav (1900–1958). A leading avant-garde Czech Communist poet of the 1920s and 1930s, Nezval was born in **Biskoupky** in southern Moravia, the son of a teacher. Soon his father moved to another village, **Šemíkovice**, east of Jaroměřice. He attended secondary school in **Třebíč**, studied in **Prague** at the Arts Faculty from 1920, and then lived mostly as a writer. A member of the avant-garde group Devětsil from 1922, a Communist member from 1924, Nezval was a leading practitioner, alongside the theoretical Karel Teige, of that playfully associative 1920s movement known as Poetism, influenced by art trends such as Naivism, Futurism, and Dada, also by Karel Čapek's ◊ translations of French poetry. In 1933 Nezval first travelled abroad, to France and Italy. In 1934 he founded the Czech Surrealist Group, but rejected it in March 1938. The Party was naturally hostile to the Surrealists, who also disapproved of some of Nezval's, in their view, trite though adroit rhymstering. In 1945–51 he occupied a post at the Ministry of Information. He died prematurely in **Prague** in 1958.

His numerous works include several imaginatively associative polythematic poems, influenced by Apollinaire's *Zone*, linking the lyrical gift with life-embracing sensualism and elements of popular entertainment. They include the associatively zany, sensualist, revolution-envisaging reflections of *Podivuhodný kouzelník* (*The Amazing Magician*), 1922, and its more obviously torn, thematic half-sequel *Akrobat* (*The Acrobat*), 1927; another such poem, *Edison*, 1928, is a more conventionally structured, less self-consciously avant-gardist poem about poet and scientist, creativity and the imagination. Nezval has recurrent guilt about the self-absorption and non-usefulness of the poet. He oscillates between revolutionary proclamatory statements and happy epicurean sensualism, with strong proclivities for Gothic horror, morbidity, evocation of childhood, sensory impressionism, eroticism, sheer self-absorption, reminiscence and freely associative play. He produces many whimsical and cheaply seductive poems, seldom unskilful, but also a number of more exploratory, spontaneously semi-automatic texts. *Sbohem a šáteček* (*Goodbye and a Handkerchief*), 1933, is a stream of short travel evocations of France and Italy. *Praha s prsty deště* (*Prague with Fingers of Rain*), 1936, purveys playful kaleidoscopic images with Surrealist affiliations (Extract 18). These are more openly paraded in the (now often comically silly) sexuality of *Žena v množném čísle* (*Women in the Plural*), 1936. A more sober, vivid autobiographical narrative poem is 'Historie šesti prázdných domů' ('History of Six Empty Houses') in *Pět prstů* (*Five Fingers*), 1932. *Absolutní hrobař* (*Gravedigger of the Absolute*), 1937, contains Nezval's most experimental overtly Surrealist poems, along with other more clowning optical riddles and conceits; the Dali- and Arcimboldo-influenced manner of encrusted optical images heaped upon a single figure or scene can make for weirdly fantasmagoric, hallucinatory defamiliarization of the ordinary; reading is retarded and fragmented, within an unusually involved and obscuring syntax; the method is also deployed for weirdly pictorial, monumental, socio-political rhetoric, condemning Franco's Spain.

Nezval also wrote Surrealist-influenced prose, topographical reflections, in *Pražský chodec* (*Prague Pedestrian*), 1938, an amusing Gothic novel *Valérie a týden divů* (*Valerie's Week of Wonders*), 1945, dramas, and *Stalin*, 1949, a ridiculously exaggerated poem of praise, which amounts to self-parody. Nezval achieved a few successful later poems such as 'Moře' ('The Sea'), in *Chrpy a města* (*Cornflowers and Cities*), 1955.

PÁRAL, Vladimír (1932–). One of the leading popular, but also 'serious' novelists from the 1960s, Vladimír Páral was born in **Prague**, son of an officer, but spent his childhood in **Brno**. He completed his studies in 1954 at the College of Chemical Engineering in **Pardubice**. From 1956 he worked in **Ústí nad Labem** as a research worker and patent chemist. He was a freelance writer from 1967 to 1972, then an editor for the North Bohemian Publishing House in **Ústí**. From 1979, he was freelance again.

His first main novels were *Veletrh splněných přání* (*Trade-Fair of Wishes Fulfilled*), 1964, *Soukromá vichřice* (*Private Whirlwind*), 1966, and *Katapult* (*Catapult*), 1967. *Katapult* (Extract 2) tells the story of Jacek Jošt, a married chemist from Ústí who meets another woman on a train between Brno and Prague. By placing a lonely-hearts ad (which Páral himself did), Jošt proceeds to acquire several more women at intervals along the track of his business trips. Like the preceding two novels, *Katapult* energetically, with exuberant, detail-packed, fast-paced, rhythmic prose, depicts the limping socialist version of the consumer society, and the modern quest for happiness, including fulfilment in sex. The hero, or anti-hero seeks to escape, to transcend existential confinement by setting up new lives for himself. He experiences brief epiphanies of bliss, by the sea, in the forest, in re-enacted family intimacy, even in housing-estate life (which Páral perceives with a kind of Jekyll-and-Hyde double vision). Steadily, however, Jošt becomes deluded by escapist hopes of catapulting himself into some dramatic liberation.

In *Milenci a vrazi* (*Lovers and Murderers*), 1969, the Kotex factory becomes a microcosm of an endemic human battleground, of the modern consumerist class-and-career struggle with the eager devil-may-care young 'red' barbarians pushing their way up

Vladimír Páral

into the privileges, possessions and power of their 'blue' elders, who decline into flaccid resignation amidst their hard-won perquisites: their flat, sexual partners, car, country chalet, tourist trips abroad, and so on. This book was not reissued in socialist Czechoslovakia, though others of his were printed in large editions.

Páral's next book was *Profesionální žena* (*Professional Woman*), 1971, which, using parodic exploitation of trivial erotic-fantasy romance, follows the upward mobility of a hotel maid

Sonia. Some of the subsequent novels skate on the thin ice of hyperbolic and parodic comedies of workplace and tower-block Real-Socialism – eg *Radost až do rána* (*Joy Till Morning*), 1975. Others play with science-fiction fantasies – eg *Pokušení A–ZZ* (*A–ZZ of Temptation*), 1982.

His recent English-titled novel *Playgirls I*, 1994, with its nudy back cover, draws a graphically sex-filled satirical entertainment out of life in post-socialist money-making Czecho-land.

SEIFERT, Jaroslav (1901–1986). Born to a working-class family in **Prague's Žižkov** district (one of whose roads was recently named after him), Jaroslav Seifert did not finish secondary school, and became a journalist and professional writer. In the 1920s he was a Communist, but he was expelled with several other writers as a signatory of a letter protesting against Party policy in 1929, and he never returned. At the Writers Congress in 1956, he is remembered for saying: 'May we be truly the conscience of our people. Believe me, I am afraid we have not been that for quite a few years . . . we have not even been the conscience of ourselves . . . If someone else keeps silent about the truth, it can be a tactical manoeuvre. If a writer is silent about the truth, he is lying.' He was briefly head of the Writers' Union after the invasion, in 1969–70, and later a signatory of Charter 77. In 1984 he was the first Czech to be awarded the Nobel Prize for literature, something the regime accommodated itself to with some embarrassment.

He began with proletarian-style verse envisaging revolution but also expressing a straightforward personal sensibility in Město v slzách (City in Tears), 1921. As a member of the avant-garde group Devětsil he adopted the playfulness, exoticism and elements of popular entertainment culture favoured by Czech Poetism. He visited Vienna, Italy and France with Karel Teige in 1924. The trip was followed by Na vlnách TSF (On the Waves of Wireless Telegraphy), 1925, a quintessential product of Poetism, with striking jokey typography, and producing not only amusing verbal jokes and clowning, but also some of Seifert's most metaphorically and sensually effervescent, inventive word conjuring. Seifert later changed the title to Svatební cesta (Honey-

moon). Another significant collection was Poštovní holub (Carrier Pigeon), 1929 (Extract 20). He was also a skilled practitioner of more regular metrical forms, and became established as a lyricist of suggestive texture and neatly crafted, often gently erotic and atmospheric appeal. There is also civic verse reacting to political circumstances and the war. After Píseň o Viktorce (Song of Viktorka), 1950, and Maminka (Mummy), 1954, Seifert shifted away to free verse, in volumes such as Koncert na ostrově (Concert on the Island), 1965, Halleyova kometa (Halley's Comet), 1967, Morový sloup (Plague Column), Cologne 1977, Prague 1981, and Deštník z Piccadilly (An Umbrella from Piccadilly), 1979. Among his last works is the often appealing and informative long volume of reminiscences Všecky krásy světa (All the Beauties of the World), 1981.

Seifert was an unashamed sentimentalist, a poet of women's lovely bodies, of places of attachment, association and beauty, of Prague, of the national past, of gently atmospheric reminiscence, of passing time and old age, of emotive self-communing reflection.

ŠKVORECKÝ, Josef (1924–). Today one of the most celebrated Czech fiction writers, both at home and abroad, Josef Škvorecký was born in the north-east Bohemian town of **Náchod**. After secondary school he was sent to work in the local Messerschmidt factory. In his novels Náchod is thinly disguised as 'Kostelec', and he creates an alter-ego narrator, part fantasy, part reality, called Danny Smiřický, surnamed after the onetime lords of the castle above the town. In 1945–49 Škvorecký studied medicine, then English and Philosophy at the **Charles University, Pra-**

gue, and he became briefly a teacher. In 1951–53 he did his military service. Till 1963 he was a publishing editor with Odeon, with a spell on the magazine *Světová Literatura* (*World Literature*). He then became freelance. In 1969 he emigrated to Canada with his wife, the novelist Zdena Salivarová. They opened what became a successful, long-lived Czech émigré book-producing venture, 68 Publishers, and he started to teach American literature at the University of Toronto. Škvorecký has also translated and written on American fiction.

His first novel *Zbabělci* (*The Cowards*), 1958, a picture, through the eyes of teenager Danny Smiřický, of small-town life, jazz, girls, and muddled resistance in **Náchod** ('Kostelec') at the end of the war, was not published for ten years after it was written. When it was, it was singled out for public attack, to buttress the conservatives' anti-thaw line. As part of an associated clamp-down, Hrabal's ◊ first story volume was blocked, and the younger writer's magazine *Květen* (*May*) was closed. By 1964, however, more relaxed conditions permitted a second edition.

Škvorecký's next volumes included *Legenda Emöke* (*Emöke*), 1963, and *Babylónský příběh a jiné povídky* (*The Babylonian Incident and Other Stories*), 1967. The latter contains the longer *Bassaxofon* (*The Bass Saxophone*), Škvorecký's most lyrical evocation of his wartime jazz theme (Extract 6). *Smutek poručíka Borůvky* (*The Mournful Demeanour of Lieutenant Borůvka*), was the first book in a series of detective stories, later volumes of which were published in Canada. Škvorecký's army service days were reflected in another Danny Smiřický novel, his typically debunking, frivolously comic *Tankový prapor* (*Tank Battalion*), first full edition 1971.

He again uses a detective element in another Danny book, *Mirákl* (*Miracle*), 1972, a large-scale disillusionist, often comic panorama of the social, political and intellectual Czech landscape, from misguided Stalinist idealism and oppression to Prague Spring reformist idealism, with its own illusions, naiveties and foolishness, followed by Soviet invasion. A number of parodies of writers are identifiable. In *Příběh inženýra lidských duší* (*The Engineer of Human Souls*), 1977, Škvorecký returns to his wartime years, but also takes up the theme of Czech emigré life in Canada. By this time Danny is a middle-aged professor of American literature at a Canadian college.

Škvorecký's style mixes clipped sentences and dialogue with more expansive, colourful runs of prose, reflecting perhaps the instrumental exchanges, changing tempos and rhythms of jazz. Jazz with its expression of yearning, its resistance to regimentation, its sense of youthfulness and freedom, and its moments of ecstacy is a strong element in the author's reflections on spiritual values. Danny also pauses sometimes over the atmosphere of religion, with wistful agnosticism. A lot of the time it seems that jazz, and thinking about, going out with (and writing about) pretty girls, will suffice.

TROLLOPE, Anthony (1815–1882). Trollope had been a novelist for twenty years, with fifteen novels to his credit, when he began *Nina Balatka* (Extract 19) shortly after his visit to **Prague** in the autumn of 1865. It was first printed anonymously in *Blackwood's Magazine* in 1866–67. The heroine is a Christian merchant's daughter who falls in love with a Jew, Anton Trendellsohn. Incidentally, the novelist George Eliot also wrote a story based on a visit to Prague, called 'The Lifted Veil', published anonymously, in *Blackwood*'s magazine, in July 1859.

VACULÍK, Ludvík (1926–   ). Born in **Brumov** near Valašské Klobouky, the son of a carpenter, during 1941–46 Ludvík Vaculík worked in the Bat'a shoe factories centred in **Zlín**. He studied politics and journalism in **Prague** at a Party-run college, and was a workers' hostel tutor in 1948–50. After military service he became a journalist–editor, from 1959 he also worked in young people's radio broadcasting. From 1965 he worked, like Ivan Klíma ◊, with *Literární noviny/listy* (*Literary News*), later *Listy*, till it was banned in 1969. During the post-invasion years he became one of the main organizers of samizdat publications.

Vaculík made his reputation with his second, very autobiographical book, *Sekyra* (*The Axe*), 1966, one of the most original of various generation novels dealing with the recent past (Extract 3). In it the son attempts to assimilate his childhood admiration for his father with a wider view of him, seen from an adult perspective, including the father's later career as a keen Stalinist and collectivizer of agriculture. The son has grown up sceptical and he views with dismay the effects of Communist policy on rural life and the countryside. (The novel is an example of ecological worry about industrialism.) Reminiscence of the past and narrative present are mingled, in a text which switches timeframe backward and forward, with humorous, teasing deviousness. This technique also represents, with something of the effect of a mind in action, the shifting and uncertainty of our past memories, their constant re-evaluation within

an uncertain shifting present. Recent personal and collective history is something which one cannot simply 'settle accounts with', and move on away from – one is tied to it by an umbilical chord.

Another novel, *Morčata* (*The Guinea-Pigs*), 1977, has an odd, madly Kafkaesque air about it, including its sense of incompleteness, its pervasive atmosphere of fear or paranoia. It is a mysterious allegorical social fantasmagoria. The hero is employed in a curious **Prague** bank, which is supposed to control circulation of currency. He buys his two sons some guinea-pigs, on which he conducts tormenting experiments. Both guinea-pigs and the bank clerk are enmeshed in circumstances they cannot understand, which make no sense, the hero masters the guinea-pigs, the mysterious social network masters him, and the reader is teased (tormented?) by trying to make sense of the narrative.

From 1975 Vaculík began to write many short personal current-affairs essays, a selection of which have been translated as *A Cup of Coffee with my Interrogator*, 1987. His next book-length work, *Český snář* (*A Czech Dream-Book*), 1983, is also autobiographical. It is a long work in a self-revelatory, though often typically teasing, version of the diary genre, following a year in the author's life, from early 1979 to early 1980. It de-privatizes his adultery and relations with his wife, and furnishes a detailed documentary picture of life in the ghetto that formed around banned writers, samizdat and human-rights protests. His most recent book, *Jak se dělá chlapec* (*How a Boy is Made*), 1993, continues the diary de-privatizing method, with fictional-style shaping, reflecting on his relations with the writer Lenka Procházková and a semi-autobiographical novel she is writing.

SLOVAKIA

James Naughton

'Once an exclusive night-club, the place had passed from private hands into those of the state, after which it had served for a time as a depot for electronic materials. Later it dawned on those in authority that the revolution did not necessarily mean the end of everything . . . so the Manhattan Bar became the Dukla Tavern, after a beauty spot in the Carpathians.'
Ladislav Mňačko,
The Taste of Power

From the tenth century up to 1918, Slovakia was Upper Hungary, the northern part of the kingdom of Hungary. In 1918, at the end of the first world war, it became part of the new state of Czechoslovakia. In 1939, with the collapse of the Czechoslovak Republic after Munich, a client Slovak State was established under German hegemony. In 1945 this territory was returned to Czechoslovakia, minus Sub-Carpathian Ruthenia in the east, attached to the Ukraine by Stalin. From 1968 Socialist Czechoslovakia became a federation (the only main survival of political reforms), but this broke up at the end of 1992 under the pressure of economic, political and national discontents, and an independent Slovak Republic once more came into being (population 5 274 000, 1991 census).

This territory, running north of the Danubian plain of present-day Hungary, has a large majority of Slovaks, speaking a language closely akin to Czech (they can communicate with little trouble). It also has, especially in the south, many Hungarians (about 10%), and there are other significant groups, such as Romany Gipsies and Ukrainians. To the west, Slovakia is demarcated from the Czech Republic by the Biele Karpaty (White Carpathians) and the Morava river. It is divided from Poland in the north by the Tatra and Beskydy mountains. The border with Hungary runs north of the Danube and eastward, first following the river Ipel' (Ipoly), then passing south of Košice and extending almost as far as Uzhgorod in the Ukraine. **Bratislava** in the west, the capital (once called Pressburg) is not far from Vienna, and has a population of about 442 000. The next largest town, at 235 000, is the steel centre of **Košice**, right in the east of Slovakia, with **Prešov** (88 000) to its north. Other urban centres include ancient **Nitra** (90 000), east of Bratislava, **Žilina** (84 000), further north, and nearby **Martin** (Turčiansky Svätý Martin, 58 000), where the cultural institution **Matica Slovenská** was founded in 1863. Moving south again, **Banská Bystrica** (85 000) in central Slovakia was the focus of the major Slovak Uprising against the Nazis in August 1944, an event much mulled over in post-war Slovak prose.

EARLIER LITERATURE UP TO PRE-MODERN TIMES

The history of Slovakia is largely that of Hungary (*qv*). Slav tribes arrived in the area between the 5th and 7th centuries AD. The embryonic state of 'Great Moravia' extended its rule into the territory when, in about 833, Mojmír of Moravia drove Pribina out of Nitra. Western church activity was followed from 863 by the Byzantine missionaries Constantine (Cyril) and Methodius, who introduced a Slavonic liturgy (see chapter on Bulgaria). The arrival in force of Hungarian-speaking Magyars on the Danubian plain soon after 900 led to incorporation in the emerging kingdom of Hungary. From the reign of Stephen I (977–1038), Hungary was firmly in the orbit of the Western Church and Latin culture. The surviving literary texts are in Latin, including the *Legend of Saints Svorad and Benedict*, by Bishop Maurus (died 1070), who celebrated these saints' hermit lives at **Skalka** near Trenčín, north-east of Bratislava.

The lack of any sufficiently large urban centre worked against the creation of a written Slovak in medieval times. Moreover, its closeness to Czech caused the Czech standard to be adopted (alongside Latin, German and Hungarian). Influx of Slovaks into initially German-dominated towns brought some use of Czech for town records. Scholarly connections with Prague University and Czech Hussites had some influence. It was also significant that from the 15th century onward, Bohemia and Hungary began often to share one monarch. In the 16th century literary Czech, through the Czech bible, was reinforced by the spread of Lutheranism into Slovakia.

After the battle of Mohács in 1526, Hungary was mostly occupied by the Turks, and the remnant, not much more than present-day Slovakia, joined the Habsburg domains. Some of the Hungarian nobility took refuge here from Turkish rule, which continued until the later 17th century.

The earliest specimens of Czech vernacular consist of 15th-century town documents and devotional texts (eg the *Žilina Town Book*, the *Spiš Prayers* of 1480). A brief blossoming of Humanist culture occurred with the founding in 1465 of the short-lived Academia Istropolitana in Pressburg/Bratislava under King Matthias Corvinus. (The site, at **Jiráskova 3**, now houses part of the Academy of Performing Arts.) Book printing began in the later 16th century, and Latin Humanism produced a number of authors, such as the poet Martin Rakovský (c1535–79). A number of 16th and 17th century eminent Slovaks were active in the Czech Lands, among them the medical scholar Ján Jessenius (Jesenský). Born 1566, in Wrocław, he taught at Wittenberg and Prague, where he conducted the first public dissection. He was one of those executed on the Old Town Square in 1621, his tongue having first been removed. Another, Vavřinec Benedikti z Nedožer, was author of the first proper Czech grammar (*Grammaticae Bohemicae*, 1603). Also of Slovak birth were two vernacular authors of biblical plays, Pavel Kyrmezer (died Uherský Brod 1589) and Jiří Tesák Mošovský (died Prague 1617). Another author, Jakub Jakobeus (c1591–1645), was a Protestant Czech from Kutná Hora who settled in Prešov after 1620; his verses in *Gentis Slavonicae Lacrumae, Suspiria et Vota*, 1642, lament the horrors of tyranny, Turkish hordes, war, natural calamity and pestilence.

Surviving native literary compositions of the period include ballads (sometimes with Hungarian analogues, see chapter on Hungary) such as Martin Bošňák's 'Song of Murány Castle', 1549, an eyewitness account of the taking of **Murány** by royal troops and execution of its robber baron; also, the 'Song of Sziget' of 1566, describing the Turkish siege of the town, the bravery of its defenders, and the death of their leader Miklós Zrínyi. The love theme is represented by the 'Song of Two Hungarian Lords and the Turkish Emperor's Daughter' ('Siládi and Had'maži'), telling of two captive noblemen in Constantinople. Helped to escape by the Sultan's daughter, who runs away with them, they both fall in love with her. Also, 16th-century love lyrics have been found, recorded in **Liptov** in 1604 by Ján Jób Fanchali, some associated with the Hungarian poet Balassi, if not composed by him.

Religious poets include Ján Silván (c1493–1573) and Eliáš Láni (1570–1618). There is also much hymnography, both Catholic and Protestant. The most famous is the standard Lutheran collection, first published in **Levoča** in 1636, known to all good Protestants as *Tranoscius*, after its compiler and part author, Jiří Třanovský, from Těšín, another of the Protestant exiles who came to Slovakia after the Bohemian Protestant debacle of 1620. Here in Slovakia the Counter-Reformation trod much more lightly, and a significant proportion of the population were able to remain Protestant.

A strong centre of re-Catholicization, and of Baroque writing, was **Trnava** (a short distance north-east of Bratislava), where a Jesuit university was founded in 1635. Sermons, hymns and the like formed the major element in vernacular book production during the 17th and 18th centuries. Meditative devotional verse was practised by authors such as Ondrej Lucae (1596–1673) and Daniel Sinapius Horčička (1640–88). There was also memoir writing, such as *Sors Pilarikiana – Osud Pilárika Štěpána*, 1666, a verse description by the author Štefan Pilárik of his Turkish captivity and release; also Ján Simonides' Latin memoir of Protestant ministers condemned to the Spanish galleys (c1677), or Daniel Krman's *Itinerarium* (1709–11), describing conditions in Poland, Prussia, Lithuania, Belorussia, the Ukraine and Moldavia. (Daniel Krman witnessed the defeat of the Swedes at Poltava in 1709.)

Eighteenth-century love poems, mostly anonymous, include 'Obraz pani krásnej, perem malovaný' ('Picture of a Beautiful Lady, Painted by the Pen'), 1701, written by a law student, Štefan Selecký, in Trnava speech. A particularly long, moralizing cycle (of 17 000 lines) was composed by the Francisan Hugolín Gavlovič, with the title *Valašská škola – mravov stodola* (*Wallachian-Shepherd School – The Garner of Morals*), 1755. One outstanding local-minded scholar was Matej Bel (1684–1749), author of *Noticia Hungariae Novae Historico-Geographica* (*Historical–Geographical Account of Modern Hungary*).

Traditional folksong and balladry abounded. One particularly famous theme was the life and exploits of Juraj Jánošík (1688–1713), a Robin Hood type figure, originally a soldier with Prince Rákóczi's army, who led a bandit group in North-West and Central Slovakia in 1711–13, was captured, imprisoned in **Vranov castle**, near **Liptovský Mikuláš**, and executed on the town square, condemned to be hung from one of his ribs. He became a favourite theme of 19th-century poets, including, for example, Botto ◊.

LATER 18TH CENTURY AND EARLY 19TH CENTURY: NATIONALISM

An incipient scholarly nationalism may be discerned in 18th century writers such as Juraj Papánek or Juraj Sklenár, where the theme starts to develop of the Slovaks as co-creators of the early Moravian state and of medieval Hungary, in which they are seen as playing a civilizing role *vis-à-vis* the Magyar invaders. Texts such as these start to create the basis for the mythology and historicist ideology of future Slovak-language writers.

The reigns of the Emperor Joseph II (1780–90) and his mother Maria Theresa (1740–80) form a watershed which marks the disintegration of the old (roughly feudal) order and the beginnings of a new (later industrial, capitalist) era. One symptom of the modern era, linked crucially with general literacy, was an increasingly dominant tendency to attempt to equate language community with political nation. Hungarian élites began to aspire to achieving a homogeneous, Hungarian-language political nation (initially in opposition to Habsburg ambitions to have German as the dominant élite medium, supplanting Latin). Joseph II, however, was also keen to encourage local vernaculars for lower popular education, and thus central policy simultaneously both Germanized and vernacularized.

Jesuit Czech usage, centred on **Trnava** in the west of Slovakia, was somewhat Slovakized during the 18th century, and this process was taken further by Jozef Ignác Bajza (1754–1836), who introduced his own spelling and local linguistic features into his pioneering Slovak novel *René mládence príhody, a skusenosti* (*The Adventures and Experiences of the Young Man René*), 1783–85. It is a diffuse picaresque narrative with satirical elements: the hero travels in foreign lands, but also in Slovakia (from Vienna to around Trnava), observing the life of the people.

The first systematic codification of a distinct Slovak was the work of the Catholic priest Anton Bernolák (1762–1813), one of a circle at the short-lived Josephinist General Seminary at **Pressburg (Bratislava) Castle**. In 1787, at the age of 25, Bernolák laid down its spelling; his *Grammatica slavica* followed in 1790; his huge six-volume Slovak–Czech–Latin–German–Hungarian Dictionary appeared only posthumously in 1825–27. Its preface notes the advantage gained by the increased ease with which Slovaks would now be able to gain fluency in Hungarian.

Bernolák's Slovak was short-lived. Its first writer was Juraj Fándly, a colleague of Bernolák, popular educator, and one of the founders of the Slovak Learned Society (1792) based at **Trnava**. The Bible was also translated (1829–32), but the outstanding author was another Catholic priest, Ján Hollý (1785–1849), associated in memory especially with the parish of **Madunice** near Piešt'any. He translated Virgil's *Aeneid* (1828), and went on to produce verse epics in classical hexameters, on emotive Slovak–Slav themes such as the Moravian prince Svatopluk (in *Svatopluk*, 1833), or Cyril and Methodius (in *Cyrilo-Metodiáda*, 1835). Hollý is venerated as the founding father of Slovak poetry, and there are strong touches of lyric freshness in his fusion of classical and Slovak idiom, especially in his Theocritan pastoral verse. Bernolák's Slovak failed to be adopted by Protestants, and Trnava also declined culturally after the transfer of its University to Buda in 1777.

The main Protestant centre was Pressburg (**Bratislava**), where a chair of Czecho-Slovak was established in 1803 at the Lutheran

Lyceum. Loyalty to the Czech bible kept the Czech tradition strong. The leading Czech-language poet was Jan Kollár (1793–1852), resident in Budapest, author of a famous sonnet cycle *Slávy dcera (Daughter of Slavia)*, 1824, 1832, in which the poet's beloved Mína becomes daughter of a mythic Slav patron Goddess, and a pilgrimage is conducted through Slav lands and, in Dante-like style, into a Slav paradise and hell. Kollár was a valiant propagator of inter-Slav cultural cooperation, and an important collector of folksong. Another Protestant, Ján Chalupka (1791–1871), minister for many years in **Brezno**, was the first significant dramatist, achieving popularity with his comedy *Kocourkovo*, 1830, a satire of small-town ways, which raises language consciousness, and uses crazily distorted Latinisms and Hungarianisms in a plot revolving around the selection of a new schoolteacher.

THE ŠTÚR GROUP AND THE FOUNDING OF MODERN SLOVAK

By the 1840s, however, a young energetic group of Lutherans led by Ľudovít Štúr (1815–56) became attracted by the idea of a separate Slovak literary language (to which the poet Kollár remained strongly opposed). Instead of Bernolák's Western Slovak, they forged a new standard based on Central dialects, and this is the variety on which the modern language is now based. Štúr's chief partners in this were Jozef Miloslav Hurban and Michal Miloslav Hodža; the decision was formally taken at the vicarage in **Hlboké**, near Senica, north of Bratislava, in 1843.

Štúr started a Slovak-language daily paper in 1845. In 1847 he became a member of the Hungarian Diet, and during the 1848–49 Revolution he participated in the Slav Congress in Prague. Then he took Vienna's side against the Hungarians, organizing military volunteers, in the hope of winning Slovak autonomy. Instead, Vienna's victory inaugurated a period of centralism, and Štúr moved on towards Messianic faith in Tsarist Russia's mission to liberate.

In literature Štúr stressed native originality, influenced by the German writer Herder, and believing the Slavs were destined to give great poetry to human culture. Poetry, for him the highest product of the human spirit, should take folksong as its starting point, not its goal; it should match spirituality with objectivity, espouse high ideals. Štúr died suddenly and prematurely after a hunting accident in 1856, but his Slovak had somehow taken root, though still facing great odds.

Štúr's Slovak had the fortune to find writers, especially poets, who made an immediate impact: of these three poets Janko Kráľ' ◊, Andrej Sládkovič ◊ and Ján Botto ◊ are of primary importance.

Janko Kráľ' has become the most celebrated, both for his lyrics and

L'udovít Štúr

details of his biography. In 1848, he joined a teacher friend in southern Slovakia, rousing the local villagers to overthrow the landowners. Held in **Šahy** and Budapest, after release he later became involved with pro-Habsburg anti-Hungarian volunteers. After the Hungarian defeat, Kráľ' joined government service and virtually stopped writing. His best known poems are ballad-inspired verses, in which folk idiom combines with a central Romantic figure, *divný* Janko, 'strange Janko', a solitary withdrawn hero, alienated from his surroundings, aspiring to soar eagle-like to freedom, but falling into suicidal melancholy (Extract 10).

Another, staunchly optimistic, poet was the Protestant pastor Andrej Sládkovič ◊. His most famous work is the long poem *Marína*, written in lyrical sonnet-like ten-line stanzas, inspired by his unhappy love for a **Banská Štiavnica** burgher's daughter. Where for Kollár erotic and patriotic love are divided, in some sense incommensurate, here they harmonize. Love for Sládkovič is not a mere intoxicating, sensual adventure of youth, it is a divine gift that enables Man to transcend his physical being, a force that enables one to contemplate and embrace truth through beauty, that joins in harmony body and mind, the physical world and the world of the spirit. All this is coloured by a Hegelian vision of progress towards freedom and harmony. Sládkovič's second famous long poem *Detvan*, 1853, celebrates the uplanders of **Detva**, an area beneath Poľana, a vision of unspoilt innocent vigour.

The younger poet Ján Botto is remembered for his allegorical balladic composition *Smrť Jánošíkova* (*The Death of Jánošík*), 1862, revised 1870s, the most famous work on the theme of the executed bandit Jánošik. Throughout the poem there is a tension between fairy-tale-like visions (blended with messianism) and gloomy realism (almost) – a sense that ideals of freedom exist in a world apart from the world of men – there is a chasm between the mythic dreamworld represented by Jánošík and the portrayal of passive Slovak peasants (or ideals and mankind's lot).

The best years for educational and cultural furtherance of the Slovak language cause had been those after the fall of the Bach regime in Vienna. Then Štúr's Slovak was introduced into primary schools, and the first Slovak-language secondary schools were founded, in **Veľká Revúca, Turčiansky Svätý Martin** and **Kláštor pod Znievom** (1862–66). Another milestone was the founding of the cultural institution Matica slovenská in 1863, centred in **Martin**. However, the 1867 Dualist solution removed Hungarian internal policy from Viennese oversight. The Slovak secondary schools were closed in 1874–75, as was Matica slovenská, in 1875 (it reopened only in 1919).

Slovak fiction was ostensibly wholly in the shadow of poetry. One original prose writer however is Ján Kalinčiak ◊, whose masterpiece *Reštavrácia* (*County Elections*), 1860, describes humorously, in a fictional setting, underhand goings-on during a Hungarian county election in the pre-1848 period. The overall tone is humorous, untendentious, almost apolitical – but the lack of reverence amounts to a form of attack on the myth of the Slovak gentry as a force to be reckoned with in the national cause. Kalinčiak uses his material for humorous fiction, as a vehicle for story telling and stylistic virtuosity – with sharp figure painting and flamboyant use of idiom, colourful sayings and proverbs. The whole book may be seen as a display of verbal and narrative technique, just as much as it is a heightened portrayal of gentry types.

The most famous Slovak collector of folk-tales was Pavol Dobšinský (1828–95), and some of the tales from his classic *Prostonárodné slovenské povesti*, 1880–83, have been re-told in English.

FROM REALISM TO SLOVAK MODERNA

During the last three decades of the century the leading poet was Pavol Országh Hviezdoslav ◊, who worked as a lawyer, mostly in **Dolný Kubín**, east of Martin. Poetry was his fulfilment. His most celebrated longer narrative poem is *Hájnikova žena* (*The Gamekeeper's Wife*), 1884–86, the story of a young gamekeeper Michal Čajka and his wife Hanka, who kills her would-be rapist, the morally corrupt aristocrat Artuš Villáni. The centre of the poem is the upland life, the natural life of the forest, and celebration of its freedom. The seasons are portrayed, local scenes and human activities integrated with the life of the forest (fetching of water, tree felling, raspberry picking, stag hunt, the night stars, the woodland torrent like the crashing of chains 'which however does not bind, does not fetter legs, or spirit, does not confine in its circle the spirit which flew like an eagle in between the hills, to sate itself with freedom, and feel that it is spirit'). Hviezdoslav is somewhat of a cosmopolitan (but also patriotic Slovak) Parnassist. Sometimes diction is all: he enriches the poetic language with dialect expressions and neologism, pursuing eloquent texture, even at the cost of textual obscurity. His *Krvavé sonety* (*Sonnets of Blood*), 1919, express bitterness about the madness of the war, which tramples on his struggling optimism; he doubts the future of man, and God's justice; but ends on a note of optimistic longing. Hviezdoslav's contemporary fellow-poet Svetozár Hurban Vajanský (1847–1916), son of the writer and national figure Jozef Miloslav Hurban, was initially a lawyer, then editor of the newspaper *Národné noviny*. He was twice imprisoned for his views. His first collection, *Tatry a more* (*The Tatras and the Sea*), 1879, was stimulated by army service in the Balkans during the occupation of Bosnia-Herzegovina. His writing also includes fiction, such as *Letiace tiene* (*Flying Shadows*), 1883, and *Suchá ratolesť* (*Dry Branch*), 1884. Vajanský expressed the faith that the most able members of the zeman (gentry) class would come round to identifying with the Slovak nation, that the future lay in an alliance between such people and intellectuals of lowly peasant origin. He also believed fervently in the liberation of Slovakia by Russia. While wishing to paint a portrait of contemporary social life, he was more a Romantic idealist. He wrote in 1883, 'There is no real darkness in us; our weaknesses, our oddities, our faults are but flying shadows; above them there rules the silent, eternal brightness of the Ideal . . . Oh, have faith in the Ideal, have faith in its light.' He portrays Slovak middle-class life, creating individuals embodying hope or disintegration: the impoverished, disorientated zeman, the officials dependent for their living on the establishment, the tragic woman driven to insanity, young educated men faithful to their roots and eager to serve the Slovak cause.

Slovak fictional realism reached its peak perhaps in the works of Martin Kukučín ◊, a writer more evocative and empirical than purposefully uplifting in manner. Initially he produced stories dealing especially with the environment typified by his native village, Jasenová, in the Orava region (Extract 4). One of his finest, more than a mere psychological study, is *Neprebudený* (*The Unawakened*), 1886, about a mentally defective gooseherd. His best-known full-scale novel is his Dalmatian work *Dom v stráni* (*House on the Hillside*), 1903–04, an acutely observed picture of Croatian rural life, centred about two lovers from different social classes, who, unromantically, have to part.

The turn of the century also saw a number of women writers make their mark: perhaps the most distinguished was Timrava ◊, pen-name of Božena Slančiková. She does not have the warm sympathy for the village life of Kukučín, and she rejects the sentimental clichés of love, depicts erotic disappointment, and middle-class smugness (Extract 9).

The last years before the first world war are marked by a group known as the 'Slovak Literary Moderna', related to European Symbolism, with often soft-focus, connotative use of visual metaphor, and melancholy ironic, subjectively atmospheric, visual-art-influenced *fin-de-siècle* technique.

The crucial Moderna poet was Ivan Krasko ◊, famous for only two slim collections *Nox et solitudo*, 1909, and *Verše* (*Verses*), 1912. Most of his poetry was written in Bohemia, not far from Prague. Krasko's musically refined, often ostensibly quite simple (but then enigmatic) verse typically expresses moods of loneliness, melancholy, hesitation and pessimism in mistily defined (often erotic) situations slenderly sketched against lyrical, typically autumnal, crepuscular landscapes. Elements of Christianity function as nostalgia, emblems of traditions or collapsed values, more than of faith (Extract 7).

PROSE BETWEEN THE WARS

Another young Moderna poet was Janko Jesenský ◊, whose work straddles the pre-1918 and later periods. His fiction is more characterized by straightforward critical social realism. His major novel is *Demokrati* (*The Democrats*), 1934–37, a humorously and affectionately ironic portrait of hypocritical 'democracy' in practice, of middle-class life, public and private, civil servants, and the petty politicking of the day (Extract 1).

In order to give the Czechoslovak Republic, founded on 28 October 1918, a clear majority nationality, the constitution had erected the concept of a single language, existing in two variants, Czech and Slovak. In practice Slovak became the dominant official language of Slovakia. In **Bratislava** the **Comenius University** was founded in

1919, and a **Slovak National Theatre** opened in 1920. From being a mainly Hungarian and German town Pressburg, now Bratislava, became rapidly more and more Slovak. The cultural centre of gravity now shifted somewhat away from Martin, with its revived Matica slovenská. Czech–Slovak economic and general cultural disparities, however – and failure to tackle Slovak resentments in a situation where Czech élites held many influential positions in education and government, replacing ousted Hungarians – undermined newly forged solidarity, and helped Hitler to induce local politicians to break away after Munich and establish a puppet Slovak State.

Fiction opens up further to the world, both topographically and thematically. Historical writing, grimly analytical of human nature, in a somewhat Zolaesque manner, is practised by the older Jégé (Ladislav Nádaši, 1866–1940), particularly in *Adam Šangala*, 1923, set in the Counter-Reformation. Outward looking, more exotic, technically ambitious writing includes: Ján Hrušovský (1892–1975), with stories of Rome in *Pompiliova Madona* (*Pompilius's Madonna*), 1923, also *Muž s protézou* (*Man with a Prosthesis*), 1925, a first world war novella about a cynical, 'prosthetic-hearted' officer's uprootedness; Tido J. Gašpar (1893–1972), elegant man-about-town, later jailed for Slovak State collaboration, author of ornamentally stylish, erotic, romantically disillusioned stories reflecting his time as a young naval officer; Ivan Horváth (1904–1960), another vitalistic, exotic writer, on Paris, for example, where he was a law student in the 1920s; he was jailed for alleged treason in the 1950s, and posthumously rehabilitated.

Among writers for whom domestic social themes are central, Milo Urban (1904–1982) is especially revered for his novel *Živý bič* (*The Living Scourge*), 1927, regarded as his masterpiece – a panoramic chronicle, full of visionary pathos, of the wartime agonies of a fictional village, transformed from passivity into revolutionary violence. In 1940–45 he edited the main Slovak Fascist daily *Gardista*. His other novels from the 1930s to the 1960s, chronicling Slovakia in the years up to 1945, are less well regarded.

Portrayal of the class struggle, using journalistic, propagandistic Socialist Realism, was the goal of writers such as Peter Jilemnický (1901–49), eg *Pole neorané* (*Unploughed Field*), 1932, and Fraňo Kráľ (1903–55), eg *Cesta zarúbaná* (*Obstructed Road*), 1934.

A more provocatively compelling author, Gejza Vámoš (1901–1956) was the son of a Hungarian Jewish railway official, who studied medicine, practising first in Prague, then in the Slovak spa town of **Piešťany**. Following the short stories of *Editino očko* (*Edita's Eye*), 1925, portraying biological drives and human cruelty, Vámoš's novel *Atomy Boha* (*Atoms of God*), 1928, full of sarcastic commentary, continues his medically inspired semi-autobiographical line. A doctor in a Prague VD clinic infects himself while experimenting; his girlfriend, raped by an infected degenerate, commits suicide with him. In *Odlomená haluz* (*Broken Branch*), 1934, he portrays his own Jewish community from around **Nitra**. In 1939 he left for China and Taiwan, as a Jew, then worked among the poor in Brazil, where he died of beriberi, contracted in the Far East.

Jozef Cíger-Hronský ◊ is one of the very few significant Slovak novelists to have been translated. His narrative method combines depictive realism, focused on rural life, with lyrical expressivity in depicting the symbiosis of man and nature. In *Jozef Mak*, 1933, set in the pre-war era, and depicting the inner world of a lumberjack and railway navvy, Mak is both the apotheosis of ordinary submissiveness and passivity, and of simple natural resilience, the resilience of grass which 'withstands more than anything in the world' (Extract 3).

The end of the 1930s saw the arrival of a trend which has become known as 'lyricized' or 'naturist' prose, and which peaked in the 1940s, during the years of the Slovak State. Instead of analysis of rural change, there is a return from urban chaotic ferment to emotive evocations of elemental freedom in isolation, presenting myths of nature, exploiting modes of folklore and fairy-tale narrative; there is some influence from the French regionalists such as Charles-Ferdinand Ramuz and Jean Giono. The main names are Chrobák, Figuli and Švantner, again little translated.

Dobroslav Chrobák (1907–51) has been called a 'modern traditionalist'. After studying electrical engineering in Prague, he worked in Bratislava radio. Alongside the stories of *Kamarát Jašek* (*Friend Jašek*), 1937, his main work is the skilfully structured and narrated balladic novella-tale *Drak sa vracia* (*Dragon Returns*), 1943. The foundling potter Drak ('Dragon'), object of superstition and irrationally blamed for local misfortunes, overcomes enforced alienation, showing inner moral strength, when, in company with his rival in love, he saves the villagers' herd menaced by burning forest, returning to gain communal acceptance. Margita Figuli (1909–   ), born in **Vyšný Kubín**, began with the short stories of *Pokušenie* (*Temptation*), 1937, their themes generally of love and the sensibilities of young women. Her novella-tale *Tri gaštanové kone* (*Three Chestnut Horses*), 1940, inspired by the upland region of the author's **Orava** home, depicts the victory of pure, honest commercial traveller Peter over ungoverned rich farmer and occasional horse smuggler Ján, who dies under the hooves of his tormented horse, so that Magdaléna, whose hand he had won, may be united with Peter. They go off together to their childhood country. The lyrical atmosphere is heightened by a symbolic trinity of chestnut horses, denoting beauty, fighting manliness and sensuality. Purity wins over evil in an enclosed fictional world with its own laws. Figuli went on to write a monumental biblical historical novel *Babylon*, 1946, portraying the fall and disintegration of the glorious Chaldean empire to Persian conquest. The youngest of this group, František Švantner ◊, was inspired by the highland region of the **upper Hron** dominated by the peaks of **Ďumbier** and **Chopok**, and by tales of fantasy and demonic beings. In *Malka*, 1942, he produced a cycle of eight lyrical–balladic tales of passion and retribution (Extract 6), followed by *Nevesta hôl'* (*Upland Bride*), 1946, a novella which shares the same setting, and themes of death, sensuality, the irrational, and the participation of mythically demonic, primeval nature in human life.

POETRY SINCE THE 1920s

Slovak poetry has been little translated into English, and even less of it well, unfortunately.

Emil Boleslav Lukáč (1900–79), a Lutheran pastor and parliamentary deputy, developed a somewhat neo-Romantic idiom of permanent discontent. He moved from Symbolist-style home-and-abroad meditations in *Dunaj a Seina* (*The Danube and the Seine*), 1925, through tersely agonized erotic and reflective verse in *O láske neláskavej* (*Of Love Unloving*), 1928, and *Križovatky* (*Crossroads*), 1929, then continued into trenchantly castigatory treatment of social and patriotic themes in collections such as *Elixír*, 1934, *Moloch*, 1938, or *Bábel*, 1944. After enforced silence, he was able to publish again from the mid-1960s. Ján Smrek (1898–1982), brought up in **Modra** in a children's home, worked as a journalist and publisher's editor, and founded the Prague-based Slovak literary monthly *Elán* in 1931. From his second collection *Cválajúce dni* (*Galloping Days*), 1925, he became the main Slovak Vitalist poet, and a generally happy-toned, deftly lyrical eroticist, though the second world war altered his carefree note for a while. In his longer composition *Básnik a žena* (*Poet and Woman*), 1923–34, he depicts meetings with a lady over four seasons of the year. Appreciation of his verse is very much a matter of response to lyrical artistry.

Valentín Beniak (1894–1973) came from a large peasant family near **Topoľčany**, and worked later as a civil servant in Bratislava. He is a more original, and also more enigmatic magic spinner of words than either Smrek or Lukáč. Beniak's topics, in collections from 1928 onward, include rural hardship, tradition and beauty; existential disharmony; artistic themes from France and Italy; apocalyptic vision of war. He absorbs influences of Symbolism, Czech Poetism, Surrealism, and folklore. His work has been regarded as culminating in the long sequence *Žofia* (*Sophia*), 1941, continued in *Popolec* (*Ash Wednesday*), 1942. These rehabilitated him poetically from some pro-Slovak-State sentiments. He was able to publish again from the mid-1960s.

Proletarian verse, evoking working-class oppression and the class struggle, would be a misleading label for the more complexly resonant poetry of Ladislav Novomeský (1904–76). A Communist activist belonging to the left-wing group DAV ['Throng'], Novomeský was imprisoned as a 'bourgeois nationalist' in 1952 (rehabilitated, 1962). Early becoming sceptical about poetry's public role, Novomeský produced associative, playful, gently melancholy, reminiscing, generally unpropagandistic social and personal verses from *Nedeľa* (*Sunday*), 1927, and *Romboid*, (*Rhomboid*), 1932, onward, which remind one often of Nezval (◊ Czech Republic) and Czech Poetism. In *Stamodtiaľ a iné* (*From Over There and Others*), 1964, Novomeský recalls his imprisonment for 'bourgeois nationalism' in the Stalinist years, but reaffirms his Socialist faith.

The most admired woman poet from the inter-war period is Maša Haľamová (1908–   ), an effectively simple lyricist; she lived for many years in the **Tatras**.

Slovak Surrealism's main poet was Rudolf Fabry (1915–82), remarkable for startling imagery, as indicated by titles such as *Uťaté ruky* (*Severed Arms*), 1935, *Vodné hodiny piesočné* (*Waterclock Sandglass*), 1938, and *Ja je niekto iný* (*I Is Someone Else*), 1946. Surrealist idiom, rejigged as Slovak '*Nadrealismus*' ('Super-realism'), soon began to be used to express clearly anti-Fascist, socio-political tones.

Central names in post-war Slovak poetry include Miroslav Válek (1927–   ), and Milan Rúfus (1928–   ), both associated from the 1950s with the anti-Stalinist thaw. Younger poets range from Marián Kováčik (1940–   ), long-time editor of the literary journal *Romboid*, to the provocative Taťjana Lehenová (1961–   ). See also the recent anthology *Not Waiting for Miracles*, for other names.

POST-WAR PROSE

If Slovak poets have received inadequate attention from the outside world, Slovak prose is not very much better off. One of the favourite post-war themes has been that of wartime partisans and the events of the significant Slovak Uprising of 1944, which, though major in scope, failed to link up with the Red Army advance and was suppressed, some months before the eventual liberation.

In Slovakia, under the Stalinists, like elsewhere, Socialist Realism became official doctrine, though policy later grew much more accommodating than this statement would suggest. The anti-Stalinist thaw can be regarded as beginning as early as 1954, in Alfonz Bednár's (1914–1989) unrosily depicted 'construction novel' *Sklený vrch* (*Glass Peak*), 1954. Clear-cut hostility to Stalinism, its hypocrisy and corruption, and unvarnished views on the famous Uprising and human violence, certainly arrive with the stories of Bednár's *Hodiny a minúty* (*The Hours and Minutes*), 1956. These two books are obvious landmarks in the emancipation of post-war Slovak fiction. Other notable novels of the era include František Hečko's (1905–1960) *Červené víno* (*Red Wine*), 1948, the chronicle of a wine-growing village, and Rudolf Jašík's (1919–1960) *Námestie svätej Alžbety* (*St Elizabeth's Square*), 1958, a sensitive psychological portrait of love, a wartime town and the fate of Slovak Jews, transported to death camps.

The Communist writer Dominik Tatarka ◊ established anti-Stalinist credentials with *Démon súhlasu* (*The Demon of Conformity*), 1956, 1963, a work preceded by Socialist Realist style novels. After the Soviet invasion of 1968, Tatarka refused to conform, became the leading Slovak dissident figure, and pursued his writing in autobiographical, polythematically diarist, sensualist, 'shockingly' eroticist, meanderingly rhapsodic and playful texts. Another Communist turned anti-Stalinist, the most translated one, was Ladislav Mňačko ◊, who latterly lived in Austria. Mňačko described Stalinist persecutions in his *Oneskorené reportáže* (*Delayed Reportages*), 1964, partly in order to 'document my own guilt in these events.' His novel *Ako chutí moc* (*The Taste of Power*), 1967, traces the life of a leading Communist politician, corrupted by his position (Extract 2).

Some writing of considerable fresh charm and psychological sensitivity is to be found in the teenage novels of Klára Jarunková ◊, one of which has been translated (Extract 5).

Novelists who came to prominence in the 1970s include Vincent Šikula (1936–), whose lyrically rural–plebeian trilogy about the Uprising, *Majstri* (*The Master Carpenters*), 1976–79, has attracted the most critical attention. Another well-regarded writer is Ladislav Ballek (1941–), whose novels evocatively chronicle events in his native Šahy, near the Hungarian border, since 1945; they include *Pomocník* (*The Assistant*), 1977, *Agáty* (*Acacias*), 1981, and *Lesné divadlo* (*Forest Theatre*), 1987.

One of the most original writers is Ján Johanides ◊, who ranges from a sometimes laconic Existentialist-influenced idiom to an often exuberant, syntactically expansive, imaginatively and linguistically rich prose, including a remarkable historical novel *Marek koniar a uhorský pápež* (*Marek, Master of Horse and the Hungarian Pope*), 1983. Alongside biological, genetic, ecological, and morally reflective concerns, and elaborate psychological presentations (which are at the same time self-consciously literary and dream-like), Johanides conducts teasing games of narrative and imagery with multiple and symbolic, even mystic, significances and parallels.

There are very few translations of recent fiction, but individual short stories by Johanides and three other authors, Vilikovský, Sloboda and

Mitana, appear in the recent anthology *Description of a Struggle*. One of the most acute and innovative contemporary writers is Pavel Vilikovský ◊ (Extract 8), also editor of *Romboid*, a leading literary magazine, and a notable translator of English and American fiction. Rudolf Sloboda (1938–) briefly studied, worked as a miner, builder's labourer, and foundry worker, later as an editor and in films. His books include novels and short stories. Dušan Mitana (1946–), who studied film and television, published a first book of short stories, *Psie dni* (*Dog Days*) in 1970, and has several notable volumes to his credit, including the successful novel *Koniec hry* (*End of Game*), 1984. In the same anthology there is also a story by a prominent writer from the significant Hungarian community, Lajos Grendel (1948–). Another young Slovak writer, and now publishing editor, is Martin M. Šimečka (1957–), son of the notable Bratislava-based Czech dissident writer Milan Šimečka, and author of an autobiographical novel reflecting the life of a dissident's child, *Džin*, 1985, 1990, recently translated as *Year of the Frog*, 1993.

The Slovak literary scene was rather less restricted politically than its domestic Czech equivalent in the 1970s and 1980s. It is to be hoped that its current state will not be adversely affected by the present political and economic adjustments, in which public figures, including former Communists, are tempted into chauvinist national gestures.

LITERARY LANDMARKS

Ábelová, near Lučenec: The fiction writer Timrava lived here between 1909 and 1945. She has a statue here, and a memorial room in the former nursery school where she worked.

Bánovce nad Bebravou: Statue of Štúr on the square.

Banská Bystrica: This was the centre of the Slovak National Uprising. Various writers went to school here, including Hurban Vajanský, Kollár, Kukučín, Timrava, and Švantner. The poet Sládkovič was born in **Radvaň**, now part of the town.

Banská Štiavnica: Petőfi (◊ Hungary) and Sládkovič studied here, in the former Lycée. Botto and Kalinčiak were residents of the town. The house of Marína Pišlová, heroine of Sládkovič's poem *Marína*, is here, and her grave is in the cemetery.

Bernolákovo (former Čeklís), near Bratislava: Anton Bernolák worked here as chaplain, in 1787–91 (statue in front of the Catholic vicarage).

Borský Mikuláš, near Senica: The birthplace of the poet Ján Hollý is at **No 181** (memorial room, statue in the garden).

Bratislava (formerly Pressburg): Many writers studied here. **Hrad (Castle):** This housed the General Seminary where Bernolák studied.

Hviezdoslavovo nám.: On the square is a statue of the poet Hviezdoslav; the Slovak National Theatre was built in 1884–86. **Konventná 13 and 15:** Here stands the former Evangelist Lyceum with a plaque commemorating national figures who studied there, including Štúr. **Panenská 19:** Štúr lived and edited his newspaper *Slovenské Národné Noviny* here. At **No 25**, the Hungarian poet Sándor Petőfi once stayed. **Rudnayovo nám.:** This square has a statue and a bust of Bernolák, and a bust of Liszt. **Sad J. Kráľa (Petržalka):** This park on the south bank of the Danube is now named after the poet Janko Kráľ'. His statue is less impressive than that of the Hungarian poet Petőfi (◊ Hungary), a powerful work by János Fadrusz, a leading late-19th-century Hungarian sculptor. **Somolického:** At **No 2** there is the house which belonged to the poet and novelist Janko Jesenský. A museum since 1952, the house has been kept as it was in the writer's lifetime. **Štúrova 5:** House with a plaque commemorating Štúr. **Štúrovo nám. (Štúr Square):** This square has a modern statue of Štúr by T. Bártfay in stone and bronze replacing a destroyed bronze statue of Maria Theresa, executed in 1895–95 by one of the best Hungarian sculptors of last century, János Fadrusz. **Devín:** Situated outside Bratislava, this was a Slav fort. The ruins of the castle picturesquely crown a rocky outcrop above the confluence of the Danube and Morava rivers. It often features in national literature. There is a plaque with a relief of Štúr commemorating a famous excursion of young Slovak nationalist students here in 1836.

Brodzany, near Partizánske: In the castle here, which once belonged to Pushkin's sister-in-law A.N. Goncharova, there are mementos of Pushkin.

Budmerice, near Modra: Various writers have stayed in the castle, belonging to the Slovak Literary Fund, since 1945, including Ivan Krasko, Fraňo Kráľ', and Hečko.

Dobrá Voda, near Trnava: Ján Hollý lived here in 1843–49, where he died at the Catholic vicarage. (Memorial room and grave with bust.)

Dolná Strehová, near Modrý Kameň: The Hungarian poet Imre Madách (1823–64), author of the *Tragedy of Man*, was born here, and there is a museum in his honour. (Grave in the park with a memorial.)

Dolný Kubín: Here lived and died the poet Pavol Országh Hviezdoslav and the novelist Ladislav Nádaši-Jégé. On **Hviezdoslavovo nám. 9** (Hviezdoslav Square) there is the house where Hviezdoslav lived, and at **No 40** the Čaplovič Library containing his Museum. He is buried in the cemetery. Nearby Vyšný Kubín is his birthplace (memorial on the site beside **No 79**).

Hlohovec: Heinrich Heine's mother is buried in the Jewish cemetery. The poet Ján Hollý lived here, 1811–14.

Hybe, near Liptovský Hrádek: In the Catholic church here is buried the great Hungarian poet Bálint Balassi, who fell in battle against the Turks at Esztergom in 1594. The 20th-century writer Chrobák is buried in the cemetery.

Jasenová, near Dolný Kubín: This is the birthplace of the famous short-story writer and novelist Martin Kukučín (at **No 21**), and he was a teacher here. The poet Hviezdoslav went to school here.

Kobeliarovo near Rožňava: Birthplace of the 19th-century Slavonic scholar Pavel Josef Šafařík, memorial room at the Evangelist vicarage.

Komárno: West of the main square, at **No 32 Gábora Steinera**, there is a small museum devoted to the composer Franz Lehár and also to the Hungarian writer Mór Jókai (◊ Hungary), whose romantic historical novels such as *Midst the Wild Carpathians* were popular in the late 19th century. There is also a powerful late-19th-century bronze statue of Jókai, at whose feet wreaths and flowers are still placed.

Krupina: Birthplace of the poet Andrej Sládkovič; house at **Sládkovičova 1**. Memorial room. Statue in Park Míru.

Liptovský Mikuláš: At **Námestie Osloboditel'ov 19** is the birthplace of the Romantic poet Janko Král'. In **Palúdzka** (now part of the town) is the castle of Vranov, where the famous bandit Jánošík was imprisoned. He was condemned and executed in 1713 at the former toll near the present-day concrete bridge.

Lukovištia, near Rimavská Sobota: This was the birthplace in 1876 of the Symbolist poet Ivan Krasko. His house is at **No 2** (plaque), with a statue and tomb in the cemetery (he died in Bratislava).

Madunice, near Hlohovec: The poet Ján Hollý lived here at the Catholic vicarage, in 1813–43; there is a statue in front of the council building.

Martin (Turčiansky Svätý Martin): **Osloboditel'ov 28:** This is the house where the Slovak newspaper *Národnie Noviny* and the literary journal *Slovenské pohl'ady* were edited. The space beneath the lindens in front of the Evangelist church is where the Memorandum Assembly was held in 1861, which called for autonomy. **No 37** is the old building, from 1865, of the cultural organization Matica Slovenská. **National Cemetery:** graves of Martin Kukučín, Svetozár Hurban Vajanský, Ján Kalinčiak, Janko Král', and others.

Modra: On the main square there is a statue of L'udovít Štúr, who lived here from 1850 till his death in 1860. He is buried in the local cemetery.

Mošovce near Turčianske Teplice: This is the birthplace of the 19th-century poet Ján Kollár (plaque on the site, statue on the square, memorial room).

Námestovo: The poet Hviezdoslav worked here as a lawyer in 1879–99 (house at **Hviezdoslavova 24** with a plaque, statue in front of the Catholic church).

Slanica (today beneath the Orava reservoir): This was the birthplace of Anton Bernolák, first codifier of an autonomous literary Slovak. His statue is now on an island with a church.

Nové Zámky: Anton Bernolák lived here till his death in 1813 (statue on the square, tomb in the chapel).

Oravská Polhora, near Námestovo: This spa was often visited by the poet Hviezdoslav. The gamekeeper's house on **Podvršie** with a plaque is the setting for Hviezdoslav's famous poem *Hájnikova žena* (*The Gamekeeper's Wife*), 1886.

Polichno, near Lučenec: Birthplace of Timrava, 1867. She was born at the Evangelist vicarage.

Revúca: The first Slovak Gymnasium was founded here in 1862. It is the setting for Kukučín's novella *Mladé letá* (*Youthful Years*), 1889.

Šahy: Here, in the south of Slovakia, the poet Janko Kráľ' and his friend Ján Rotarides were imprisoned in 1848 (bust of Kráľ').

Terchová, near Žilina: Terchová is famous as the birthplace of one of Slovakia's heroes, the bandit Juraj Jánošík, commemorated by a shining memorial rising on a hill to the south of the village.

Trnava: Following the Battle of Mohács in 1526 the Hungarian archbishopric at Esztergom was moved here, making the town Hungary's main religious centre for over 200 years. In 1635 a Jesuit Academy was founded, later raised to the status of a university, but it moved to Buda in 1777. Here in 1792 Anton Bernolák founded the first Slovak Learned Society.

Uhrovec, near Bánovce nad Bebravou: In the mansion of 1613 where Štúr was born there is now a small museum devoted to the Slovak National Uprising. Another distinguished native of Uhrovec was the Prague Spring politician Alexander Dubček.

Valaská Dubová, near Ružomberok: Here is the inn where the bandit Jánošík was captured in 1713.

Záturčie, near Martin: This is the birthplace of the 19th-century fiction writer Kalinčiak (memorial with bust).

Zlaté Moravce, near Nitra: Janko Kráľ' practised as a lawyer here in 1862–76. At **Janka Kráľa 35** is the house where he lived and died (plaque, memorial in the park).

Zvolen: This was the birthplace of the novelist Jozef Cíger-Hronský. The castle was the residence of the king Matthias Corvinus, and in 1626 the Hungarian poet Bálint Balassi was born in the castle, which now houses an art gallery.

BOOKLIST

The following selection includes the extracted titles in this chapter as well as those mentioned in the introduction which are available in English and other titles for further reading. In general, paperback editions are given when possible. The editions cited are not necessarily the only ones available. For most of the extracted works, the original publisher can be found in 'Acknowledgments and Citations' at the end of the volume, as can the exact location of the extracts and the editions from which they are taken. Extract numbers are highlighted in bold. Square brackets denote the date of publication of the work in its original language.

Anthology of Slovak Poetry, Ivan J. Kramoris, trans, Obrana Press, Scranton, PA, 1947.

Anthology of Slovak Literature, Andrew Cincura, ed, University Hardcovers, Riverside, CA, 1976. **Extracts 6 and 7.**

Anthology of Czechoslovak Literature, Paul Selver, trans, Kegan Paul, Trench, Trubner & Co, London, 1929.

Anthology of Czech Poetry, Alfred French, ed, Czechoslovak Society of Arts and Sciences in America, Ann Arbor, MI, 1973.

Botto, Ján, *The Death of Jánošík* [1862], Ivan J. Kramoris, trans, National News Print, Pittsburgh, PA, 1944.

Brock, Peter, *The Slovak National Awakening*, University of Toronto Press, Toronto, 1976.

Cíger-Hronský, Jozef, *Jozef Mak* [1933], Andrew Cincura, trans, Slavica Publishers, Columbus, OH, 1985. **Extract 3.**

Description of a Struggle: the Picador Book of Contemporary East European Prose, Michael March, ed,

Picador, London, 1994. (James Naughton, trans, stories by Vilikovský, Johanides, Mitana, Sloboda; and Richard Aczel, trans, Hungarian story by Lajos Grendel.) **Extract 8.**

Dobšinský, Pavol, *The Enchanted Castle, and Other Tales and Legends* [1880–83], Ann Macleod, adapted, Hamlyn, London, 1967.

Gorys, Erhard, *Czechoslovakia*, Pallas Guides, Pallas Athene, London, 1991.

History of the Czechoslovak Republic, Victor S. Mamatey and Radomír Luža, eds, Princeton University Press, Princeton, NJ, 1973.

Hviezdoslav, Pavol Országh, *Bloody Sonnets* [1919], Jaroslav Vajda, trans, Obrana Press, Scranton, PA, 1950; also, *A Song of Blood: Krvavé sonety*, Tatran, Bratislava, 1972.

Jacobs, Michael, *Blue Guide: Czechoslovakia*, A & C Black, London, and W. W. Norton, New York, 1992.

Jarunková, Klára, *Don't Cry for Me* [1963], George Theiner, trans, Dent, London, 1971. **Extract 5.**

Jašík, Rudolf, *St Elizabeth's Square* [1958], Margot Schierl, trans, Artia, Prague, 1964.

Jašík, Rudolf, *Dead Soldiers Don't Sing* [1961], Karel Kornel, trans, Artia, Prague, 1963.

Jesenský, Janko, *The Democrats* [1934–37], Jean Rosemary Edwards, trans, Artia, Prague, 1961. **Extract 1.**

Kirschbaum, Joseph M., *Slovak Language and Literature: Essays*, University of Manitoba, Dept of Slavic Studies, Winnipeg, 1975.

Kovtun, George J., *Czech and Slovak Literature in English: a Bibliogra-*

phy, 2 ed, Library of Congress, Washington, DC, 1988.

Kráľ, Janko, 'The Enchanted Maiden in the Váh and Strange Janko', **Extract 10** (J. Naughton, trans).

Kráľ, Janko, *Janko Kráľ 1822–1972*, Jaroslav Vajda, trans, Tatran, Bratislava, 1972.

Krasko, Ivan, 'Vesper Dominicae', Jaroslav J. Vajda, trans, in *Anthology of Slovak Literature*, Andrew Cincura, ed, University Hardcovers, Riverside, CA, 1976. **Extract 7.**

Kukučín, Martin, *Seven Slovak Stories* [c1885–88], Norma Leigh Rudinsky, trans, Slovak Institute, Cleveland, OH, and Rome, 1980. **Extract 4.**

Lettrich, Josef, *History of Modern Slovakia*, Praeger, New York, 1955; Slovak Research and Studies Centre, Toronto, 1985.

The Linden Tree: An Anthology of Czech and Slovak Literature, 1890–1960, Mojmír Otruba and Zdeněk Pešat, eds, Edith Pargeter *et al*, trans, Artia, Prague, 1962.

Mňačko, Ladislav, *Death is Called Engelchen* [1959], George Theiner, trans, Artia, Prague, 1961.

Mňačko, Ladislav, *The Taste of Power* [1967], Paul Stevenson, trans, Weidenfeld and Nicolson, London, 1967. **Extract 2.**

Mňačko, Ladislav, *The Seventh Night* [1970], Panther, London, 1969/ Dutton, New York, 1969.

Modern Slovak Prose: Fiction Since 1954, Robert B. Pynsent, ed, Macmillan, London, 1990.

Modern Slavic Literatures, Vasa Mihailovich, ed, Ungar, New York, 1976. (Slovak critical extracts, Igor Hájek, ed.)

New Writing in Czechoslovakia, George Theiner, ed, Penguin, London, 1969. (Miroslav Válek, Jaroslava Blažková, Ján Johanides.)

Not Waiting for Miracles, James

Sutherland-Smith, Stefania Allen, Viera Sutherland-Smith, trans, M. Peter, Levoča, 1993. (Anthology of modern Slovak poetry.)

Olbracht, Ivan, *The Bitter and the Sweet* [1937], Iris Urwin, trans [from the original Czech], Crown, New York, 1967.

Olbracht, Ivan, *Nikola Šuhaj, Robber* [1933], Robert Finlayson-Samsour, trans [from the original Czech], Artia, Prague, 1954.

Rudinsky, Norma, *Incipient Feminists: Women Writers in the Slovak National Revival*, Slavica Publishers, Columbus, OH, 1991.

Short, David, *Czechoslovakia*, World Bibliographical Series, Clio Press, Oxford, 1986.

Šimečka, Martin M., *The Year of the Frog* [1985–90], Peter Petro, trans, Louisiana State University Press, Baton Rouge, LA, and London, 1993.

Slávik, Juraj, 'One Hundred and Twenty Years of Slovak Literary Language', in *The Czechoslovak Contribution to World Culture*, Miloslav Rechcígl, ed, Mouton, The Hague, 1964.

Šmatlák, Stanislav, *Hviezdoslav: a National and World Poet*, M. Hünnigenová, trans, Obzor-Tatrapress, Bratislava, 1969.

Steiner, Eugen, *The Slovak Dilemma*, Cambridge University Press, Cambridge, 1973.

Števček, Pavol, *Contemporary Slovak Literature*, Oľga Horská, trans, Obzor, Bratislava, 1980.

Švantner, František, 'Malka', Andrew Cincura, trans, *Anthology of Slovak Literature*, Andrew Cincura, ed, University Hardcovers, Riverside, CA, 1976. **Extract 6.**

Tatarka, Dominik, *The Demon of Conformity* [1956, 1963], Peter Petro, trans, abridged text, in *Cross Currents*, Vol 6, 1987, L. Matejka, ed, Department of Slavonic Languages and Literatures, University of Michigan, Ann Arbor, MI.

Timrava (Slančíková, Božena), *That Alluring Land: Slovak Stories by Timrava*, Norma L. Rudinsky, trans, University of Pittsburgh, Pittsburgh, PA, and London, 1992. **Extract 9.**

Válek, Miroslav, poems in *Contemporary East European Poetry: An Anthology*, Emery George, ed, expanded edition, Oxford University Press, New York and Oxford, 1993; also, *Modern Poetry in Translation*, 5, Cape Goliard, London, 1969.

Vilikovský, Pavel, 'Escalation of Feeling', J. Naughton, trans, in *Description of a Struggle: the Picador Book of East European Prose*, Michael March, ed, Picador, London, 1994. **Extract 8.**

Wallace, William V., *Czechoslovakia*, Ernest Benn, London, 1977.

White Stones and Fir Trees: an Anthology of Contemporary Slavic Literature, Vasa D. Mihailovich, ed, Bucknell University Press, Lewisburg, PA, 1977.

Extracts

(1) Bratislava

Janko Jesenský, *The Democrats*

Jesenský's novel from the inter-war years offers a sharp, irreverent portrait of political and middle-class professional life in Slovakia's capital from 1918. (Hainburg, mentioned below, is just over the Danube, in Austria.)

Landík counted eleven other young girls and women in national costume. They stood out against the dark coats of the spectators like coloured flower patches in a black forest. Želka wore a Kyjov costume. The red colour suited her and the short, bouncing skirts revealed more than usual of her lovely legs in their dainty shoes. He went up to her and thanked her warmly for her 'magnificent' help. Želka stuck her tongue out at him, which in the jargon of the young ladies of the town meant: 'I like you.'

Landík felt his position as main organiser of the ceremony. He examined the public and decided that from the administrative point of view nothing more could be desired. Police cavalry and infantry were present, so too were the goatee beard of the ceremonial department, the carefully concealed bald pate of the State security organ, the gold tooth of public law and order and the diffident mien of the foreign travel department.

All that was missing was the Indian king's ship. Time was passing and the longed-for wisp of smoke was still not visible over the Danube. The sun was sinking behind Hainburg, red patches appeared on the golden waves. Slowly a pale twilight spread over the sky and the river darkened. The eyes of small night owls seemed to blink. Little boats with the silhouettes of the rowers were lost to sight, paddle steamers and wharves were swallowed up by the darkness, Hainburg merged into the hillside and its ramparts vanished among the trees. The belt of forest beyond the Danube and the surrounding hills, not long before distant and misty, grew black and loomed nearer. Lights gleamed on the shores and the bridge. The wide windows of the Museum coffee-house cast sheets of light on to the pavement. Specks of light began to emerge from the nearby houses and dance across the water, settling on the steamers and forming chains across the waves, and the powerful headlamps of cars and trams streaked across the clusters of trees.

The Indian king's boat still did not arrive.

(2) Bratislava

Ladislav Mňačko, *The Taste of Power*

Sometime before about 1960 Frank visits an old haunt in Bratislava, still carrying the insignia of its capitalist past.

He turned round and went in. Perhaps Lisa would still be behind the bar?

She was. But the place had come down in the world since he had last been there. Once it had been exclusive, and so had she. Things get old and worn out, and so do people. The upholstery round the walls was threadbare and greasy, and water seeping through the ceiling had made a dirty yellow pattern in the best tradition of abstract art. Frank wondered what sort of marks time had made on Lisa's smooth white body . . .

He did not go straight to the counter, but stood in the middle of the place and looked around him. It was half empty. One or two tarts sat waiting, not too hopefully, for a rich customer to turn up. In a corner, a youth in a leather jacket sat fondling a rather unattractive girl. The gipsy musicians were still there, but they looked much older than when he had last seen them three years ago.

The long side-wall was adorned by what had once been a huge and splendid oil-painting representing the blue sea and, behind it, the towers of Manhattan all in white. (The place had actually been called the Manhattan.) A luxury liner was seen approaching the Statue of Liberty, and on its deck a sun-burnt gentleman with well-chiselled features was paying court to a beautiful lady. The paint alone for this enormous masterpiece must have cost a fortune.

None the less, time had had its way with it. The smoky atmosphere had turned the blue sea to grey and the skyscrapers to a dingy yellow, not unlike the real buildings outside. Here and there the plaster had broken away. The lady's evening gown and the gentleman's white shirt-front had been disfigured by the contents of a glass of red wine which some reveller had hurled against the wall.

Once an exclusive night-club, the place had passed from private hands into those of the state, after which it had served for a time as a depot for electronic materials. Later it dawned on those in authority that the revolution did not necessarily mean the end of everything, that private life had to go on somehow or other, and that wine and spirits were a useful stock-in-trade. So the Manhattan Bar became the Dukla Tavern, after a beauty-spot in the Carpathians.

(3) Hron Valley

Jozef Cíger-Hronský, *Jozef Mak*

Jozef Mak becomes engaged to Jula Petrisková on a walk in the fields outside their village, near the river Hron.

Neither one looked at the other as they spoke for the first time about their coming wedding, and so it was that they became engaged.

A weariness and immense solemnity settled upon the stubble field around them. The violet colchicum flowers with their short stems barely revealed their motley heads and hardly disturbed the great truth the gravelly soil was saying silently: This is what I have borne; I bore as much as I had the strength to produce, but the summer has worn me out. And the firs on the slopes grew a little greyer, though they would not admit it. The scattered oaks turned crimson as if they were ashamed to be among the conifers, for their summer-long parasitism on the other species would soon be revealed when the winter exposed their naked-ness. The wind loitering somewhere above the mountain peaks was not in a prankish mood. It did not carry the foamy summer clouds on its light palm but smeared them in long grey horizontal scribblings across the sky. Pebbles hidden under cover throughout the summer now appeared white everywhere, lying firmly and soberly in the fields and furrows, unable to conceal the paltriness of the harvest. Only the untouched potato fields slightly contrasted the remaining fields, though they too were hurrying to turn yellow, and were covered with dust like everything else. Even the sunlight fell like forced laughter upon the scene.

So Jozef silently betrothed himself for the second time. He did it without noticing the living redness of the dog rose. Nor was he disturbed by the torn-up soil around the future railroad bed. Everything now had the color of red clay, so the embankments of the future railroad seemed perfectly natural.

(4) JASENOVÁ, NEAR DOLNÝ KUBÍN

Martin Kukučín, *At the Community Sheepfold*

This nineteenth-century story gives a town boy's view of a salaš, a mountain sheiling where ewes were pastured, and sheep's cheese (oštiepok) made and smoked in the summer. The original koliba described here is now generally a pseudo-primitive hut where you go and eat charcoal-grilled meat.

After a two-hour hike we walked out through the coniferous forest into an alpine meadow. The dark green forest made a lovely frame for the bright meadow, which was overgrown with short, succulent grass. A beautiful picture: the woods all around like a velvet frame, and within it the meadow forming a green background for the sheep pens and *koliba*. As if the *koliba* wouldn't feel right in the centre of the meadow, it was drawn back into the shade of old fir trees on the edge of the woods. A strange hut! Probably the kind that beavers built above the water. I looked round to see if a beaver might appear. Well, there was no beaver, but in its place a giant stood in front of the *koliba* door. Really a giant, tall man such as you don't see in our region very often.

We went into the *koliba*. It was very difficult to imagine how eight men could find a place here. There was only one bench, with a cushion placed on the end that led into the corner: it was the only luxury, and one which probably the *bača* [head shepherd] alone could allow himself. The *valasi* [other shepherds, 'Wallachians'] didn't have pillows; probably they put a block of wood under their heads. There were no beds either; they had to lie on the ground, which had the advantage that if a fellow fell he wouldn't fall far. Only the *bača* could lie on the bench, but who would envy him? The bench would have been too short even for me; no matter how the *bača* curled up, his legs below the knees would hang onto the ground. The *koliba* also had a side room separated only by a board wall.

'Good day!' I greeted the *bača* politely, and I took off my hat as a proper boy should do in a strange house.

'May the good Lord hear you!' the *bača* answered me.

This was a completely unsuitable answer, obviously, because it would be enough to reply to my greeting with 'Thank you.'

Had I greeted him in the wrong way? It seemed so; my godfather also looked at me strangely and put in: 'This is my godson – he insisted on coming with me, said he'd never been at a *salaš*.'

The *bača* yawned and came toward me. 'Well, just put that mushroom back on your head. You aren't in church here.'

He caught up my hat, which he'd called a mushroom – a pertinent name compared to his own wide-brimmed hat – and pushed it onto my head.

(5) Low Tatras

Klára Jarunková, *Don't Cry for Me*

Olga is on a ski trip in the Low Tatras. Chopok (2024 m) is at the top of the chair lifts south of Liptovský Mikuláš, or north of Brezno. Neighbouring summits are Ďumbier, to its east, Pol'ana to its west.

I went up the ski lift with Uncle Thomas. He was marvellous, doing his best to keep my mind off things by talking all the time, but even so I kept looking round in case that brute in the turtle-neck sweater happened to be anywhere around. But he wasn't. Maybe he sleeps in the daytime and only comes out at night, looking for fresh victims. I bet he does – he was so awful.

Up on the mountaintop the sun was baking hot, as if it were summer. All those university people were there, and they came over to me at once. They'd found a nice sheltered nook and made backrests out of their skis, and invited me to join them. When they saw me hesitate, they invited Aunt Masha and Uncle Thomas too.

It was terrific up there. We stripped off all we could and reclined on our skis, which we propped against the poles, every now and then someone would collapse, skis and all, and we'd laugh our heads off. The sun beat down on us with all its might – you could *see* the heat coming at you in large, misty circles. All the girls stuck bits of paper on top of their noses, and so of course I did too. It was a marvellous day. I'd never seen such whiteness before. The snow was soft and loose at first, but then a thin transparent film of ice formed on it from all that heat. When we were quiet, not making any noise, I heard a soft, strange sound I couldn't identify for a long time. Then I discovered it was the ice melting, little drops of water dripping down into the snow. And something else: the snow gave off a pleasant smell! No, I'm not making this up – it really did smell, only I can't for the life of me say what the smell was like.

(6) Low Tatras
František Švantner, *Malka*

This story is set in Švantner's home region north of Brezno in the upper Hron valley.

After the evening milking, when the sun dropped behind one of the mountains, I put my sheepskin coat on my shoulders, thrust the fife into my sleeve, and hurried down to the Pits. I ran from the sheep farm directly down the steep track around the place where the men of Beňuša used to burn charcoal for the Bystrica foundry. I decided to wait for Malka there. I was not worrying that she would not find me for Michalčík, Malka's employer, used to mow the glade in the Pits; thus she frequently carried her bundle of hay down the glen to the village, and in the mornings and evenings crawled up with the basket to cut some grass for the cows. I thought she would come, 'just so,' to meet me there.

I lay down in the grass in the middle of the glade. My heart throbbed under my shirt like a bird with its feet tied together. Though pounding with a clear, steel-like sound, my heart seemed to be diverted from its regular rhythm by the delightful expectation which held me in its arms. I was imprisoned by a convincing dream, despite my open eyes and clear head. The moon, floating in the sky like a royal sailboat, exerted a magic, hypnotic power over me. The moon opened my soul as Indian summer opens a cracked poppy head. Face to face with the moon, I was unable either to pretend or to hide anything. I mentioned the lyrics flowing into my soul lately from the skylark's song, from the dawns etching into my veins, from young juniper berries bursting with strongest juices, from the cut roots of scrubby mountain-ash, from everything that caused the wild thirst of my body and filled my solitary nights with anxiety, that closed my eyelids and rumpled my hair, that split my burning lips into a passionate gape, that brought the fragrance of polypody saturated with the evening wind and the moisture of moss and the resin of budding pine needles to my nostrils, everything that chanted the moonlit night's psalms about my twenty years of life. I could not wait in silence any longer.

(7) Lukovištia

Ivan Krasko, *Vesper Dominicae*

This poem, from Nox et solitudo, 1909, recalls Krasko's home village, north of Rimavská Sobota, and his mother reading the old Czech prayerbook.

Far, far away there
in the dark mountains
a small white village
leans slightly earthward,
peaceful and quiet.
In it the ancient
sombre appearing
houses are sleeping.
Surely in one there
my care-bent mother
sits solitary
at an old table.
With a hand bony
props up a forehead
furrowed with wrinkles
– shadows of worry
linger upon it:
so I recall it
from early childhood.
There lies her prayerbook
open before her
– its worn hinges,
smooth from the fingers
of my forebears,
glittering dully
in the late twilight –
At the last pages
she keeps on staring
at a notation
stiffly inscribed there:
'The Lord has blessed us
with a son who is . . .'
until her eyes are
sprinkling with tears the
long-yellowed pages . . .
But the old volume
which brought her tears up

will soothe my mother
once again surely:
now she is singing
in a soft thin voice,
'God's Day is ending,
let us now praise him . . .'
– Dusk soon is falling
deeper and deeper
into the small room –
And the peace settles
quietly, slowly
on the grey head
of my dear mother.

(8) PIEŠŤANY

Pavel Vilikovský, *Escalation of Feeling*

Set in the spa town of Piešť any on the river Váh, the short story from which this is taken depicts an encounter between a man and a sixteen-year-old girl in a wheelchair.

'A tree,' he said gaspingly. He touched the bark with his hand. She heard a special crinkling noise, as if the trunk were made of paper. 'This is a tree. And that down there,' he stamped, 'is earth. Grass. Is that clear? Let's get it agreed once and for all. A tree. Don't you believe me? Go on, get a feel of it,' and she scarcely had time to utter a quiet little astonished 'no', before he was holding her in his arms, all at once she was light herself, incredibly, and when, automatically, as a reflex, she put her arms round his neck, she felt him slippery with sweat, 'don't be afraid, eh? A tree. And this here, everywhere, there,' he pointed around him, finally the hand stopped with his finger indicating the other bank of the Váh, and above the tree-tops she saw with abrupt, even painful inward perception the roof of the Hotel Slovan . . . that's where Mum took her, once every Sunday, when she came to visit, 'that's Piešť any. Easy as ABC. And this here, this is love.' She didn't understand him right away, she didn't know what he was talking about, she was just thinking of something else, some words her mother always told her; she tried to remember, in the park in the middle of the flowers there was a statue of Lovers, two rather angular bodies, leaning away from each other, she had just thought to herself, why lovers?; she was thinking of something else, and the movement wasn't even abrupt, there was nothing alarming about it, the body was preparing itself to sit down in the wheelchair. 'This is love.' The words didn't scare her, but suddenly it seemed to her she felt cool air, a breeze on her knees, and realized . . . but that's the sentence, and she felt like when, in the dark, a bat flits past, close above your head: The blanket! Where's the blanket?! 'It's love, and all that various stuff that's talked about, described in that book of yours as well . . . is this.'

(9) SLOVAKIA: RURAL ROMANCE

Timrava, *Battle*

This extract from Timrava's story, written in 1900, portrays a koliba, a hut at shielings where sheep were grazed in the summer. It was also, as we see, a favoured spot for romantic excursions. (Kukučín gives another description in Extract 4).

Evening came to the hilltop meadow where Mr Bukovič had his koliba. The open fire had died down under the large kettle of sheep's milk whey which the old shepherd was stirring with a large and elaborately carved wooden ladle. In a wide circle around the fire, guests were sitting on logs or chunks of wood, their faces red with the heat. The beautiful Mária sat with two of the Beňušovská sisters, and Anča was standing aloof at the side. The new clerk with his big eyes was parading around in front of the women and thinking he was amusing them. Tall and high spirited, he felt only one sorrow in life, the fact that his mustache was so sparse. He had already spent at least seventeen gold pieces on creams and little brushes for it.

Nikodém had come with his fiancée. He sat down by the older men, between Bukovič and Ďuro Bolkin. He was smoking a cigarette, narrowing his eyes as he watched the younger group, not saying a word. Evička, her eyes gleaming with a hidden fear and her cheeks flaked with red, was trying to find a comfortable place. The fire was too hot here, back there it was sultry, and the same over here. Breathing fast, she wiped her perspiring forehead with her palm. She was frightened to look at Mária, but her eyes kept flitting there. What dazzling beauty! No wonder everyone who saw her fell in love with her.

'Why did you bring Eva?' Ďuro Bolkin asked his brother as he watched Evička moving from one place to another, her eyes glittering unnaturally. 'She must be sick?'

Nikodém was deliberately not watching her, and though he felt every move she made he ignored her. He felt comfortably lazy like all the others, and didn't want to disturb the peaceful singing in the warm evening. Maybe if he didn't pay attention she would calm down.

Marta as usual stood modestly behind the others. She was leaning against the cabin so that she didn't have to see Ďuro Bolkin, because she was still angry with him. She was watching and listening to Mária like everyone else, but then, not enjoying anything, she got up to sit alone behind the cabin. The sun had set, and the pond below lying amidst the green fields no longer sparkled blindingly. Now it looked like a large bed sheet spread out on the ground not far away.

(10) VÁH RIVER

Janko Král',
The Enchanted Maiden in the Váh and Strange Janko

This extract is from the best known of the ballad-inspired verses of Král', the nineteenth-century Romantic poet.

Their son is very strange, and never happy,
proud, cruel, wild, and bold to go anywhere;
respecting no-one, befriending no-one,
seeking no love in people, nor fearing anger;
people hate him, he wants to be revenged,
all's one to him: to rot today or tomorrow.
His father beats him like a horse from infancy,
with tears his poor mother scolds him;
but should the very archangel descend from heaven,
Janko would not give way a single step.
He suffers no friendship, keeps himself to himself,
alone he sits on the bank of the Váh:
often when they pass with horses at early dawn,
they see him there, poor fellow, sad.
It's Ascension – the bells' voice calls believers,
they swarm like bees from the villages to church;
old and young kneel down before the Holy Mother
and say their rosaries, sighing before their God.
Who would be so wayward at that holy hour
not to go and serve the saints, the Lord!
But Janko walks by the river Váh all gloomy,
not even dressed in his Sunday best,
in a long black cloak like some raven
he walks down paths, down ditches, this way, that.
Darkness falls. He comes home, sits to supper,
says not a word to his own mother,
not a word to his own sisters, or his uncle,
nor even to his grey-haired father.
All get up from the poor table,
To Almighty God all render thanks,

But he seizes his hat and speaks to no-one,
bangs the door shut and leaves the house.
God knows where he means to go! He goes beneath the willows,
Alone in the field he comes to a ditch:
he leaps that ditch, he stares about him,
and again across the open field sets off.
Across the hills, the valleys, the clouds spread out,
with dark cloaks they cover the silent copses,
between the valleys the green meadows vanish,
till only the peaks seem like some spectres,
like some large-winged, black-feathered birds,
like some great giants standing there on guard.
There's no moon in the sky – and pity the stars –
who knows how long they'll be behind those clouds! –
The field is like one black cotton kerchief
worn by a widow in mourning for her husband,
in which she hides her face in her great grief,
and goes to the dear one's grave to cry at night:
no moon shines upon her, no sun warms her,
she has nothing in the world her own but a hope.

Biographies and important works

BOTTO, Ján (1827–1876). The poet Ján Botto studied at **Levoča**, went to the Polytechnic in Budapest, and became a surveyor. In 1868 he was employed on the construction of the Košice-Bohumín railway line. He is remembered above all for his allegorical balladic composition *Smrt' Jánošíkova* (*The Death of Jánošík*), 1862, revised 1870s. The work opens with twelve brigands (like the 12 apostles, or the 12 counties of Upper Hungary), 'falcons of the Tatras', 'when they light their fire on the Hron hills, in twelve counties white day dawns.' The poem, influenced by the Czech Mácha (◊ Czech Republic) describes Jánošík's capture, when an evil witch betrays his weak spot, Jánošík in jail,

visited by his beloved, Jánošík meditating in jail, Jesus-like, 'the shadow of a cross on his chest, a glow of light on his brow, hands and feet bloody – and a smile on his cheek'. In the procession to execution Jánošík appears like a victor, while the 'people silent as a shade creep about./And the people blind – cannot see in the broad light of morning:/they kill their father, who rouses them from sleep!' He goes to the gallows, the 'altar of freedom'. His death will be a sacrifice for the future. Pardon comes too late, and the people do nothing. Throughout the work there is a tension between fairy-tale-like visions (blended with messianism) and (almost) gloomy realism – a sense that ideals (of freedom, etc) exist in a world apart. There is a chasm between the dreamworld of Jánošík and the poem and passive Slovaks (or mankind). A democratic radicalism flashes through the whole, while recurring undertones of pessimism reflect in part his view of the Slovak situation.

CÍGER-HRONSKÝ, Jozef (1896–1961). A devoted school teacher, who wrote also for children, and later worked for Matica slovenská in **Martin**, Ciger-Hronský is seen as perhaps the outstanding inter-war novelist. His pen-name is taken from the river Hron, which flows through his native **Zvoleň**. He emigrated in 1945, first to Rome, then to Argentina. His narrative method combines depictive realism, focusing on rural life, with lyrical expressivity, depicting the symbiosis of man and nature. His most celebrated work is the novel *Jozef Mak*, 1933, set in the pre-war era, depicting the inner world of an ordinary man, a lumberjack and railway navvy (Extract 3). Mak is a symbol of resignation, the weakened doormat of everyone, constantly knocked down by life: he is taken off into military service, his girlfriend marries his half-brother, who sells half his house. He can neither avoid his former love, nor reach her, his own wife's submissiveness repels more than it attracts; she dies. Jozef Mak is the apotheosis of ordinary man's passivity and submissiveness, but also of simple natural resilience, the resilience of grass which 'withstands more than anything in the world'.

HVIEZDOSLAV, Pavol Országh (1849–1921). Born in **Vyšný Kubín** in Orava county, the poet Hviezdoslav came from a poor zeman (gentry) family. He attended secondary school in Miskolc (for the sake of his Hungarian), where children from Orava often went, to school or to learn a trade; subsequently he moved to **Kežmarok**, then seen as a German town. While at school he wrote Hungarian verse influenced by Petőfi and Arany (◊ Hungary), and also German. He studied law at the academy in **Prešov**, joined a literary circle of Slovak students there, and co-published a miscellany volume *Napred*, 1871, which upset the older generation with its love poetry. He worked as a lawyer for the rest of his life, mostly in **Dolný Kubín**. He travelled little abroad. Poetry was his fulfilment. He married Ilona Nováková in 1876; they had no children, but he adopted his brother's two children (who died in 1915).

Among his longer narrative poems the most celebrated is *Hájnikova žena* (*The Gamekeeper's Wife*), 1884–86 – the story of a young gamekeeper Michal Čajka and his wife Hanka, into whose life steps the morally corrupt aristocrat Artuš Villáni. When Artuš tries to rape Hanka during a deer hunt, she kills him, but Miško takes the blame on himself. He is about to be sentenced, when Hanka, driven insane, rushes into the courtroom and confesses; Hanka later regains her balance of mind and peace returns to the gamekeeper's cottage. The centre of the poem is the upland life, the natural life of the forest, celebration of its freedom. The text begins with a greeting to the mountains, and ends with a farewell to them. The seasons are portrayed, the local scenes and human activities integrated with the life of the forest (fetching of water, tree felling, raspberry picking, stag hunt, the night stars, the woodland torrent like the crashing of chains 'which however does not bind, / does not fetter legs, or spirit, / does not confine in its circle the spirit which / flew like an eagle in between the hills, / to sate itself with freedom, / and feel that it is spirit'). Fundamental is Hviezdoslav's sheer enjoyment of his inventively flowing lyrical expressivity.

In his later narrative poems, *Ežo Vlkolinský*, 1890 and *Gábor Vlkolinský*, 1897–99, Hviezdoslav treats the theme of social relations between gentry and peasants. Among his other works is the five-act tragedy *Herodes a Herodias* (*Herod and Herodias*), 1909. He also translated Pushkin's *Boris Godunov*, Lermontov's *Demon*, Mickiewicz (◊ Poland), Schiller, Goethe, Shakespeare's *Hamlet* and *A Midsummer Night's Dream*; also the Hungarian writer Madách's (◊ Hungary) *The Tragedy of Man*.

Hviezdoslav takes Slovak verse away from reliance on folk idiom. He is somewhat of a cosmopolitan (but patriotic Slovak) Parnassist. His lyrics are largely an expression of his inner life; often they raise a contrast between desires and reality (remaining Romantic in that sense); often there is a despairing, critical attitude to the surrounding society – but also an obstinate optimism, a belief in ideals of justice and equality. He is capable of unaffected, sensitive, verbally rich evocation of the countryside; sometimes diction is all: he enriches the poetic language with dialect expressions and neologism, pursuing eloquent texture, even at the cost of textual obscurity. 'What I give, I give from soul's sincerity: / now thought's blossom, again warm feeling . . . / repugnant to me is what opposes nature, / only truth I honour, her simple countenance!'

His *Krvavé sonety* (*Sonnets of Blood*), written in August and September 1914, published in Prague in 1919, express his bitterness about the madness of the war; he sees it as trampling on his every ideal, on his struggling optimism; he doubts the

future of man, and God's justice. Though he ends on a note of optimistic longing, and later welcomed the independent Republic, he continued to see the impossibility of his desire for human harmony.

JARUNKOVÁ, Klára (1922–). A children's author, from **Červená Skala**, Jarunková worked as a teacher, later in radio, and then as an editor for the satirical magazine *Roháč*. Her novel about a fourteen-year-old adolescent girl *Jediná*, 1963 (translated as *Don't Cry for Me*, 1971 – Extract 5) has a fresh, accessible authenticity of narrative and character psychology.

JESENSKÝ, Janko (1874–1945). Originally a Slovak Moderna writer, whose work straddles the pre-1918 and later periods, Jesenský was born in **Martin** from a zeman (gentry) family, ultimately the same family as the 17th-century physician Jessenius. He studied law. During 1914–18 he

Janko Jesenský

went over to the Czecho-Slovak legions in Russia. Afterwards he occupied senior government positions in Slovakia, and was anti-Fascist during the Slovak State. His first poetry, *Verše* (*Verses*), 1905, brought a personal note of simple, sometimes self-ironic lyricism. His later verse often tends to satire and declarative viewpoint. His fiction is more characterized by straightforwardly critical social realism.

Jesenský's major novel is the two-volume *Demokrati* (*The Democrats*), 1934–37. The first part is a small-town story of the young free-thinking doctor Landík (and his shocking relationship with a maidservant). The second part takes place in **Bratislava**, with the figure of the politician Petrovič in the foreground. The novel is traditional in narrative form, a humorously and affectionately ironic portrait of hypocritical 'democracy' in practice, of middle-class life, public and private, civil servants, politics and the petty politicking of the day. There is a film version (1980, director Jozef Zachar) as well as, unusually, an English translation.

JOHANIDES, Ján (1934–). The distinguished contemporary author Johanides studied art history, and has been a freelance writer since 1969. He was unable to publish for some years in the 1970s. Several books have been translated into Hungarian and German. Johanides ranges from a sometimes laconic Existentialist influenced idiom to an often exuberant, syntactically extended, extensive, imaginatively and linguistically rich prose in books such as *Súkromie* (*Privacy*), 1963, *Podstata kameňolomu* (*Essence of the Quarry*), 1965, *Nepriznané vrany* (*Unacknowledged Crows*), 1978, *Balada o vkladnej knižke* (*Ballad of a Savings Book*), 1979, and the

notable historical novel *Marek koniar a uhorský pápež* (*Marek, Master of Horse and the Hungarian Pope*), 1983. His recent *Holomráz* (*Ground Frost*), 1992, has been translated into German. Alongside biological, genetic, ecological, Existentialist and moral reflective concerns, and elaborate presentations of psychological inwardness (at the same time self-consciously literary, and dream-like), Johanides conducts teasing games with the reader in narrative and imagery with multiple and symbolic, even mystic, significances and parallels. 'Memorial to Don Giovanni', in the recent English anthology *Description of a Struggle*, is a story from his book *Krik drozdov pred spaním* (*Cry of Thrushes Before Sleep*), 1992.

KALINČIAK, Ján (1822–1871). One of finest 19th-century Slovak prose writers, Kalinčiak came from a Protestant pastor's family in **Horné Záturčie**, near Martin and Vrútky. His family moved to **Svätý Ján** in Liptov in 1831, then he went to **Gemer** to improve his Hungarian. A famous election campaign in 1836 in Gemer county provided material for part of his novel *Reštavrácia* (*County Elections*). In 1836 his father took him to **Levoča** to learn German, where national sentiment among pupils had produced Magyar and Slovak factions, and where he also witnessed election campaigning. After three years he was sent to Pressburg (**Bratislava**), where he decided to become a teacher. In 1843 he went to Halle, staying till 1845. In 1846 he was appointed to a post in **Modra**, where the national leader Štúr lived. The first year he taught in Latin, three subsequent years in Hungarian, and eight years in German and Slovak. In 1858 he left Hungary and became head of the Protestant gymnasium in

Těšín, until 1869. He died consumptive, in **Martin**, unmarried.

Best known for his prose fiction, Kalinčiak was also a collector of folk tales, songs, and especially sayings and proverbs, which he wove into his prose, especially his masterpiece *Reštavrácia*, (*County Elections*), 1860. This describes a Hungarian county election campaign in the pre-1848 period – in a fictional setting, based on his own experiences and tales he had heard about the underhand dealing associated with the canvassing for support among the lesser gentry. The scenes are linked by the election campaign and two families battling for power – the Potocký and Bešeňovský families. Material inducements had a strong effect on the poor gentry, who expected feasts and hospitality from the candidates who courted their support. The action provides an excuse for a good number of figure studies of zemans (gentry), with their wit, pride, greed, sense of honour and weaknesses. Nationalism and ideology play hardly any explicit role, with few exceptions – eg a few references to the infiltration of Magyar language and habits, or to outmoded gentry privileges (one side proposes they should be subject to tax). Light-hearted nostalgia is mixed with humour, irony and satire. Kalinčiak uses his material for humorous fiction, as a vehicle for his story telling and stylistic virtuosity – with sharp figure painting and flamboyant use of idiom, colourful sayings and proverbs. The book may be seen as a display of verbal and narrative technique, just as much as it is a humorous satirical portrait of gentry types.

KRÁL', Janko (1822–1876). Born in **Liptovský Mikuláš**, the remarkable Romantic poet Janko Král', later admired by Roman Jakobson, attended the Pressburg (**Bratislava**) Lyceum. Eight poems of his appeared in the first Slovak volume *Nitra II*, 1844. In 1848 he joined a teacher friend in southern Slovakia, rousing the local villagers to overthrow the landowners. Incarcerated in **Šahy** and in Budapest, after release in January 1849, he became involved with the pro-Habsburg, anti-Hungarian volunteers. After the Hungarian defeat, Král' joined government service and virtually stopped writing. Transferred from place to place, he finally lost his job after the 1867 dualist division of the Monarchy, worked later as a lawyer's assistant, and died suddenly, apparently of typhoid fever, in **Zlaté Moravce**. The precise spot of his grave is unknown: the memorials in Zlaté Moravce and **Martin** are symbolic. In 1851 he arranged to marry one Mária Modrány, sister of another poet, by whom he had several children.

His best known poems are ballad-inspired verses, especially 'Zakliata panna vo Váhu a divný Janko' ('The Enchanted Maiden in the Váh and Strange Janko' – Extract 10), 'Zverbovaný' ('Conscripted'), and 'Zabitý' ('Slain'), in which folk idiom combines with a central Romantic figure, *divný* Janko (strange Janko), a solitary withdrawn hero, alienated from his surroundings, aspiring to soar eagle-like to freedom, but falling into suicidal melancholy. The plan of his unfinished torso of a large poetic cycle is disputed; it caustically attacks a world without meaning where man is a slave and a drudge, and envisions its apocalyptic collapse. The cycle ends (depending on your editor) either with a Slav Messianic salvation or a fairy-tale vision of the hero's quest for the golden bird of freedom. In the 1930s Roman Jakobson called Král' a poet who 'in his ruggedly beautiful improvisations brilliantly blurs the boundary between vertiginous delirium and folk song, and is even more ungoverned in his imagination, more spontaneous in his seductive provincialism than Mácha' (◊ Czech Republic). He also sees him as almost a textbook case of the Oedipus complex, given the centrality of the mother-and-son theme in his quite remarkable ballads.

KRASKO, Ivan (1876–1958). Real name Ján Botto. Famous for just two slim collections, *Nox et solitudo* (*Night and Solitude*), 1909 (Extract 7), and *Verše* (*Verses*), 1912, Krasko was born in the village of **Lukovištia**, north of Rimavská Sobota, to a farming family. He took his pen-name from the nearby village of **Kraskovo**. He was schooled at the Hungarian gymnasium in Rimavská Sobota, then at the German gymnasium in Sibiu, and a Romanian school in Braşov (1894–96). After military service, and travel to Russia, he entered the Prague Technical College in 1900, living in Vinohrady and graduating in chemical engineering in 1905. Here he became more acquainted with Czech literature, including Hlaváček (◊ Czech Republic); he had already translated some of the work of the Romanian poet Eminescu (◊ Romania). Krasko was active in the student society Detvan, and also associated with the Masaryk-linked Slovak Hlasists, grouped around the journal *Hlas*, and propagating Czecho-Slovakist views. Most of his poetry was written in Bohemia, not far from Prague. In 1905 he went to work at a sugar refinery in Klobuky, where much of his poetry was written, and in 1912 he became production manager at a chemical factory in Slané. In 1912 at the age of 36 he married Ilona Kňazovičová from Dolný Kubín (Hviezdoslav ◊ was a witness). He spent the war in Poland, Russia and the Italian front, but was released, suffering from a lung ailment, apparently caused by inhaling noxious gases in Slané. From 1918 he was engaged in politics as a member of the Agrarian party. He retired from state service at his own request in 1938. Some influence of the Czech poet Hlaváček, and occasionally Bezruč, is discernible in Krasko, as well as French poetry, but on the whole he was no imitator.

His musically refined, often ostensibly simple (but enigmatic) verse typically expresses moods of loneliness, melancholy, hesitation and pessimism in mistily defined (often erotic) situations slenderly sketched against lyrical, typically autumnal, crepuscular landscapes, both external and simultaneously inner. The poems use recurring emotively symbolic figures: church, cemetery, wayside cross, poplar tree, mist and rain. Elements of Christianity function ambivalently as agony or nostalgia, as emblems of collapsed values, more than of faith. There are also a few poems of louder rhetoric, castigating Slovak passivity, more often translated than his typical poems hinging on subtle blending of musical rhythm and euphony with visual setting and metaphor.

KUKUČÍN, Martin (1860–1928). Real name Dr Matej Bencúr. Born in the small Orava village of **Jasenová**, Kukučín went to secondary school in **Revúca**, and then, when it closed, in **Martin** and **Banská Bystrica**. He trained as a teacher in **Kláštor pod Znievom** (from 1875), and taught in his home village (1878–84). Later he went to study medicine in Prague, where he was a member of the Slovak student group Detvan. After completing his studies (1885–93) he went to Dalmatia, which became his second home, and he worked on the island of

Martin Kukučín

Brač (1894–1907). In 1894 he married. At this time many people from Slovakia were emigrating, and also from Croatia and Dalmatia. Kukučín likewise emigrated, to South America, arriving in Buenos Aires in 1907, but moving on to Santiago in Chile, and finally Punta Arenas. He returned to visit Slovakia, and Croatia, in 1922–25, and subsequently settled in Lipik, in Croatia, where he died.

During his earlier periods in Slovakia and Prague, he produced short stories (Extract 4) and novellas dealing especially with the environment typical of his native village, **Jasenová**, in the Orava region. Among the best of these are 'Ryšavá jalovica' ('The Red Heifer'), 1888, with a sympathetic humorous portrayal of a village shoemaker, hard working, but a weak drunkard, 'Z teplého hniezda' ('Out of the Warm Nest'), 1885, about a son about to leave and study in the city, and, one of his finest, 'Neprebudený' ('The Unawakened'), 1886, about a mentally defective gooseherd, Ondráš Machuľa, who falls in love with a

girl, who teasingly leads him on. He dies in a fire on the day of the girl's wedding to another man. After other short works, such as the autobiographical *Mladé letá* (*Years of Youth*), 1899, about schoolboy love in **Revúca**, he went on to large-scale novels, the first his two-volume Dalmatian novel *Dom v stráni* (*House on the Hillside*), 1903–04, about lovers from different social classes, one from a landowner's family, the other from a simple patriarchal farming family. Unromantically, they have to part. This acutely observed picture of Croatian social circumstances was followed by the five-volume *Mat' volá* (*Mother Calls*), 1926–27, a saga of struggle for livelihood, freedom and moral integrity set among Croatian immigrants in Chile at the turn of the century.

MŇAČKO, Ladislav (1919–94). The most translated Communist writer, later anti-Stalinist, Mňačko spent time in a concentration camp in the second world war. After his semi-documentary account of partisan warfare and SS unit reprisals in *Smrt' sa volá Engelchen* (*Death is Called Engelchen*), 1959, Mňačko went on to describe Stalinist persecutions in *Oneskorené reportáže* (*Delayed Reportages*), 1964, partly in order to 'document my own guilt in these events.' His novel *Ako chutí moc* (*The Taste of Power*), 1967, traces the life of a leading Communist politician, corrupted by his position (Extract 2). In August 1967 he defected to Israel in protest against the official line on the Israeli–Arab conflict, returning only to go after August 1968 into long-term exile in Austria.

SLÁDKOVIČ, Andrej (1820–1872). A Protestant clergyman and leading poet of the Štúr generation (see introductory essay), Sládkovič was born in **Krupina**, in a teacher's family. He studied in **Bratislava** and Halle, living subsequently in the region of **Banská Bystrica**, from 1856 as pastor in **Radvaň**, where he is buried. His year in Halle introduced him to Pushkin, and the philosophy of Hegel. His most famous long poem, *Marína*, 1846, written in sonnet-like ten-line stanzas, is a lyrical meditation on love, beauty and truth, inspired by his unhappy love for a Banská Štiavnica burgher's daughter. The poem portrays Marína singing in her room, getting into her white bed at night, awakening in the morning, longing and meditating, watering flowers in the garden, weaving garlands and catching butterflies, rejecting a rich old suitor and swearing eternal loyalty to her beloved. Subjective erotic, disappointed love and exaltation of sensory beauty are metamorphosed into an imaginative poetic vision. A fairy maiden, a Víla of the river Hron, at first lures him deathward, then raises him up into an ethereal world, but finally he is returned to earth, their love transformed into a driving force of selfless humanitarian love in which both will serve their fellow men. Love for his native country is seen as co-embodied in his love for the Slovak girl Marína. Where for the earlier Jan Kollár, in *Slávy dcera* (*Daughter of Sláva*), erotic and patriotic love are divided, in some sense incommensurate, here they harmonize. Love for Sládkovič is not a mere intoxicating, sensual adventure of youth, it is a divine gift that enables us to transcend our physical being and embrace higher ideals, a force that enables us to contemplate and embrace truth through beauty, that joins in harmony body and mind, the physical world and the world of the spirit. All this is coloured by a Hegelian (but also Christian) vision of progress towards freedom and harmony.

In 1847 Sládkovič married another woman. The following year he finished his second long poem *Detvan* (published only in 1853), a poetic apotheosis of Slovakia and its people, especially the uplanders of the **Detva region**, beneath Pol'ana. The outwardly historical framework (set in the time of Matthias Corvinus) is fairly frankly mythical.

ŠVANTNER, František (1912–1950). A 'naturist' lyrical prose writer, Švantner came from **Bystrá** near Brezno. Inspired by this highland region of the upper Hron dominated by the peaks of **Dumbier** and **Chopok**, and by tales of fantasy and demonic beings, Švantner produced in *Malka*, 1942, a cycle of eight enigmatic lyrical–balladic mystery tales of passion and retribution (Extract 6), followed by *Nevesta hôl'* (*Upland Bride*), 1946, a novella which shares their highland setting, and themes of death, sensuality, the irrational, and the participation of mythically demonic, primeval nature in human life.

TATARKA, Dominik (1913–1989). In the 1970s and 1980s regarded as the main 'dissident' Slovak writer, in early life Tatarka studied French in Prague and at the Sorbonne, and then became a Communist journalist. He later established his anti-Stalinist credentials with *Démon súhlasu* (*The Demon of Conformity*), first published in 1956 in *Kultúrny život* (*Cultural Life*). Earlier, after more experimental beginnings, he produced his own Socialist Realist novels: *Farská republika* (*The Parish Republic*), 1948, about the wartime puppet state, and *Prvý a druhý úder* (*First and Second Blow*),

1950, about a partisan who later builds bridges. During the 'normalization' years after the Soviet invasion of 1968, Tatarka refused to conform, and pursued his writing in autobiographical, polythematically diarist, sensualist, 'shockingly' eroticist, rhapsodic and playful texts, entitled *Písačky* (*Jottings*), continued in his tape-recorded *Navrávačky* (*Tapings*), 1988. These ramblingly repetitive texts are either admired with keen delight, treated with cool politesse, or rejected with withering scorn, depending on one's outlook.

TIMRAVA (1861–1951). Born Božena Slančíková in the village of **Polichno**, north-west of Lučenec, in the south of central Slovakia, Timrava was the daughter of a Lutheran pastor. Timrava lived in the area most of her life. She became a nursery school teacher, from 1919–29, and remained unmarried. Timrava's autobiographical stories and novellas give a woman's version of psychological and social realism. She depicts the peasantry, but also the scattered intelligentsia of clergy, schoolteachers, and minor officials. She is without the warm sympathy for village life of Kukučín ◊, and subverts the sentimental clichés of love (Extract 9). One of her novellas, *Skúsenost'* (*Experience*), 1902, depicts the erotic disappointment of a young woman, supposedly companion, but more maidservant, in the smug household of a middle-class widow related to the greatest Slovak poet, Javor (ie Hviezdoslav ◊). Timrava herself had briefly been such a companion. In *Ťapákovci* (*The Ťapák Family*), 1914, Timrava analyses a poverty-stricken conservative rural family: its men are passive, immobile; one of the women, Il'a, is discontented, a midwife, wanting

Timrava

change, the other, Anča, is a cripple, longing in vain for love.

VILIKOVSKÝ, Pavel (1941–). Son of an eminent Czech medievalist, but living in Slovakia, Pavel Vilikovský has translated authors such as Virginia Woolf, William Faulkner, Malcolm Lowry, Ian McEwan, William Burroughs, and Kurt Vonnegut. He has been co-editor of *Romboid*, the most independent Slovak (and Czechoslovak) literary magazine of the 1970s and 1980s. Much of his fiction has been printed years after it was written. 'Escalation of Feeling' (Extract 8), from his short-story volume of the same title (*Eskalácia citu*, 1989), dates from the 1970s and appears in the English anthology *Description of a Struggle*.

HUNGARY

George Cushing

> 'A mountain chain, pierced through from base to summit – a gorge four miles in length walled in by lofty precipices; between their dizzy heights the giant stream of the Old World – the Danube.'
> Mór Jókai,
> Timar's Two Worlds

Modern Hungary is a compact Central European republic in the Danube Basin, populated overwhelmingly by Hungarian nationals who account for 96.6% of the total population of some 10 400 000. Along the northern frontier run the foothills of the Carpathians; the highest point in Hungary is here, a well-wooded summit 1014 m above sea-level named **Kékes**. **Transdanubia** to the west of the Danube consists mainly of rolling hills and includes the largest lake in the region, **Lake Balaton**, often called 'the Hungarian Sea' and frequently hymned by poets through the ages. In contrast, the south and east of Hungary are flat and featureless, watered by the **Tisza** and its tributaries which join the Danube south of the border with Serbia.

The present boundaries have existed only since 1920. Before that the extensive territories belonging to the Crown of St Stephen included Slovakia to the north, Transylvania to the east, Croatia to the south-west and Burgenland in the west, forming the multinational and multilingual eastern half of the Austro–Hungarian Empire.

HUNGARIAN HISTORY

The history of Hungary is a chequered one. It began at the end of the ninth century AD with the occupation of the Danube Basin by Hungarian-speaking peoples from the East. Christian missionaries soon began work among them, and in 1000 AD Stephen, the first king, was crowned with the blessing of the Pope. From that time onwards

176

Hungary was firmly linked to the Western Christian church and West European culture; her monarchs forged links with Western royal families and adopted legal and constitutional institutions and practices from the same region. But both geographically and historically Hungary has always been exposed to invasion from the East and has felt itself to be on the easternmost flank of Western Christendom. The most devastating early invasion occurred in 1241–42, when the Mongols virtually destroyed the country – an event commemorated by harrowing eye-witness accounts in prose and verse (see below, under 'Hungarian Literature'). A long period of reconstruction and consolidation ensued, culminating in the renaissance splendour of the reign of Matthias Corvinus (1458–90), whose palaces and court were among the most magnificent in Europe. Meanwhile the Ottoman Empire was slowly expanding from the south-east. Although there were numerous skirmishes during the fifteenth century, the decisive battle came at the south Hungarian town of Mohács in 1526, when the Turks routed a large Hungarian army which included the king and both state and church dignitaries.

For the following century and a half, Hungary was effectively divided into three parts. The north and west were ruled from Vienna, the central area, including Buda and most of modern Hungary to the east, became a Turkish province, and Transylvania was an independent princedom under Turkish tutelage. The whole region now became a frontier area as the Turks tried to expand further north. A further complication was the arrival from the north and west of the Reformation; its effects were most marked in the Turkish-occupied areas and can still be seen today: while Transdanubia is largely Catholic, Eastern Hungary is mainly Calvinist, and there is a Lutheran presence along the northern part of the country. Unitarianism, which began in Transylvania, also took root. All four faiths eventually became recognized by the state as 'received religions', giving them an enhanced status which still exists. All have added their characteristics to the culture of Hungary.

After the recapture of Buda in 1686 the Turks gradually withdrew, leaving Hungary depopulated and devastated. The most visible effect of their occupation is the pattern of new settlement in the **Great Plain**, where there are widely separated large towns contrasting sharply with the small and frequently-encountered villages of Transdanubia. The Turkish withdrawal was followed by a brief period of rebellion against the monarchy in Vienna, culminating in the nationwide revolt led by Prince Ferenc Rákóczi II; he went into exile when peace was restored in 1711. The rest of the eighteenth century was a period of reconstruction and consolidation. It is from that date that most churches (of all denominations) in rural Hungary have their origin, as do the larger country houses – hence the preponderance of Baroque architecture there. Moreover, this style lasted through most of the following century. Meanwhile communications improved, and the effects of French enlightenment began to appear throughout Hungary, much to the alarm of both church and state to whom it preached subversion. Paradoxically it was the 'enlightened monarch' Joseph II (1780–90) whose efforts to impose some unity on his multinational domains provoked such resistance in Hungary that the whole culture of the Hungarians changed for ever. Up to then the arts had reflected developments seen elsewhere in Western Europe.

Latin was the language of state and the educated classes; indeed it was only from the 1830s up to 1844 that Hungarian replaced Latin as the official language. Literature also existed in both German and Hungarian. Now, however, the Hungarian language and literature assumed a national importance and became a focus of resistance to Vienna. Henceforward Hungarian literature was viewed as part of the political scene, playing the role of the opposition in a democratic parliament.

During the first half of the nineteenth century, the prime target of the newly invigorated literature was Austrian oppression of Hungary. The revolution of 1848 was fuelled by young writers, whose national importance was firmly established. When the poet Petőfi ◊ declared that it was the poets who were to lead the people to the promised land, he merely expressed a belief that still holds good. Thus subsequent revolutions, including that of 1956, have been preceded by literary ferment.

After Russian intervention had suppressed the revolution, there ensued a short period of harsh Austrian rule. Finally in 1867 a compromise was reached: under a single ruler each country had its own government apart from certain key ministries which were to be common. Deprived of its original opposition role, Hungarian literature appeared to lose its way; but elsewhere the effects of the new agreement were quickly seen. There was a sudden influx of industry and rapid mechanization of agriculture. As rural unemployment spiralled, some of the former land-workers moved to the towns to take unskilled work in the new factories, but the majority emigrated to North America, there to establish the still considerable Hungarian community.

Meanwhile **Budapest**, the centre of industrial activity, grew from a provincial capital into a vast new metropolis with public buildings designed to rival those of Vienna. A new cultural problem soon became evident: hitherto it had been assumed that Hungarian literature and arts were destined for the countryside, but now there was a new urban intelligentsia to provide for. At the same time new young writers, dissatisfied with the traditions of the previous century, began to seek new inspiration from the West. At home their new cause was to reform the social situation: Hungary maintained a well-nigh feudal structure with an ever-widening gap between the few who had both wealth and political power and the millions who lived in penury and had no means of changing their fate.

The first world war saw the collapse of the Austro–Hungarian Empire and a brief flirtation with republicanism and Communism in the dire conditions that ensued. This was quickly followed by the totally unexpected dismemberment of Hungary by the Treaty of Trianon in 1920. Although social reform was still an urgent concern, this new challenge predominated during the inter-war years; it posed both a political and a cultural problem, for efforts to restore the old political boundaries were matched by concern for the future of Hungarian culture in areas where Hungarians now found themselves to be national minorities – and out of every three Hungarian speakers one was now living outside the new boundaries. It is no surprise that the promise of restoration of the old frontiers lured Hungary into the Axis sphere of influence, and some areas were indeed regained briefly from 1938 to the end of the second world war.

For most of that period, Hungary remained relatively unscathed, but the Soviet advance westwards, driving the German forces inexorably into retreat, left the country in ruins, conquered and desperate. After a short-lived period of democracy, during which some of the much-needed social reforms were initiated, Communist rule was imposed and the pattern of events largely decreed by Moscow. True, the social change so often advocated by writers had taken place, but the increasing harshness of the new regime and its determination to harness the arts for its own propaganda and to stamp out opposition led to either silence or sullen conformity.

It was not long, however, before the opposition tradition emerged once again in the events preceding the revolution of 1956 and, just as in 1849, writers were called to account by the succeeding regime. After the initial reprisals ended, a gradual easing of restrictions allowed a degree of freedom. Well-versed in misleading the authorities after centuries of censorship, writers took full advantage of the possibilities offered. Although 'underground' publishing came into existence, it was relatively late and its products were widely circulated. The 32 years of János Kádár's regime certainly left Hungary the 'jolliest barracks in the camp', but at immense economic cost, for foreign loans were used not for much-needed investment in industry but for consumer goods.

The gradual relaxation of central control and the development of private enterprise during the 1980s meant that the transition from Communism to multi-party democracy in Hungary was less of a shock than in some other countries. The effects, however, are likely to cause problems for a long time to come. The previous framework of life, with its known taboos and censorship, its irksome rules and restrictions, has disappeared, but there is nothing yet to take its place. In this confused situation there is no obvious target for literature to make the focus of its traditional opposition.

HUNGARIAN LITERATURE

The history of literature in Hungary is a fragmented mosaic. War, fire and vandalism have destroyed many works that are known to have existed; some writers and their works are known only from references elsewhere. Two main periods can be distinguished: the first extends from the eleventh to the late eighteenth century and the second from then until the present day.

During the earlier period literature in Hungary formed part of the general culture of Western Europe. Latin was the main language until the Reformation; then Hungarian gradually replaced it as the literary language, though Latin remained the language of state until the mid-nineteenth century. Literature also existed in other languages, notably in German.

The second period, that, basically, of modern nationalism, began with the self-conscious elevation of the Hungarian language and its literature to the status of an essential national asset. The result was that the Hungarian language rapidly became culturally predominant and its literature assumed a political role. In criticism, aesthetic quality was subordinated to political relevance as the idea of national literature took root. But there remained a strong urge to keep abreast of contemporary trends in Western Europe; journals duly reported them and translations helped to promote them, though often this led to imitation rather than originality.

During most of its history, Hungarian literature has been subject to censorship, first by the church, then by the state, with varying degrees of severity. Particularly during the modern period, when literature has played an effective opposition role in national politics, writers have developed ways of misleading the censor into a fine art; allegory and satire are common, and readers tend to search between the lines for the message they assume is there. The foreign reader unused to this practice may therefore miss the significance of an apparently unremarkable work. Moreover the writer has a status unknown in the UK, for example, as political commentator and agitator, even as prophet. Literature is therefore important in everyday life; it is taken seriously and often possesses a didactic strain that may alienate the uninitiated foreigner.

Early literature to the Reformation

Whatever culture the Hungarians brought with them into the Danube Basin was quickly submerged beneath the Latin tradition disseminated by the first Christian missionaries. So the earliest literary products were in Latin, normally written anonymously by monks and scribes for either church or state use. These include lives of early Hungarian saints, mainly of the royal household, and some highly coloured chronicles (*gesta*) which are nearer to fiction than to history. A good example of the latter is the spirited *Gesta Ungarorum*, compiled in the twelfth century by an anonymous notary. There were verse-chronicles too; the finest example is the *Planctus destructionis regni Hungariae per Tartaros*, a harrowing account of the Mongol invasion of 1241–42. Some Hungarian texts have also survived from this period; the most notable are a brief Funeral Oration (c1200) and an elegant verse-paraphrase of a Latin Lament of the Virgin Mary (before 1300), whose refined language and style suggest that a Hungarian lyric tradition was already established.

Hungarian priests and scholars received their training mainly in Italian universities, hence the spread of Italian renaissance and Humanist ideas in Hungary. The climax of these came during the reign of Matthias Corvinus (1458–90), in the wide-ranging Latin verse of Janus Pannonius (1434–72). A virtuoso poet, he composed fulsome panegyrics, delicate lyric verse and mischievous epigrams to become one of the foremost Humanist poets in Europe. Hungary also produced a Franciscan anti-Humanist preacher, Pelbart Temesvári (c1450–1504), whose colourful sermons for the ordinary people were disseminated throughout Western Europe. Meanwhile, there was a pressing need for ecclesiastical texts to be translated for the use of clergy and nuns whose Latin knowledge was rudimentary; hence the appearance of some fine Hungarian versions of Latin hymns and liturgical texts that are preserved in codexes of the fifteenth and sixteenth centuries.

The Reformation and Counter-Reformation

The Turks, the Reformation and the printing-press all arrived in Hungary at the same period, a concatenation of events that both stimulated literary activity and isolated writers from each other. The reformers had no urban bases; their work was most effective in the Turkish-occupied parts of Hungary, where they often used portable presses for their publications, including bible-translations, hymnals, psalters, sermons and moral tales. The Protestant translation of the complete Bible (printed in **Vizsoly**, 1570) has had greater influence on literary language and style than any other work. Original hymns began to appear, no longer cloaked in anonymity, and it is interesting to note that some of these earliest writers were women.

Secular works also began to appear in print; these were mainly popular verse-tales, chronicles and histories in Hungarian. The contemporary struggle against the Turks was a common theme, best exemplified in the verse of Sebestyén Tinódi (c1505–56), who witnessed many of the encounters he described so graphically and performed them to his own musical settings. Most of the verse of the period was intended for singing, and the adoption by the Calvinists of the Geneva Psalter was an important stage in the development of Hungarian verse. Poets discovered that the flexibility of the Hungarian language meant it could adapt itself not only to classical metres but also to the demands of French-inspired melodies. The version of the complete psalter by Albert Szenci Molnár (1575–1634), still in use today, has a rare poetic quality that makes the English and Scottish metrical versions appear primitive.

The most remarkable personality of the age was the soldier-poet Bálint Balassi (1554–94), whose works, couched in elegant and exuberant language, ranged from deeply personal penitential verse to passionate love-lyrics and poetry in praise of nature and military life. His technical skill, revealed in complex metres and rhyme-patterns that were often imitated later by poets of lesser inspiration, was unrivalled. His death during the siege of **Esztergom** robbed Hungary of its first major poet.

For most of the seventeenth century Hungary was still waging desultory war with the Turks, and a sense of weariness replaced the feverish activity of the Reformation. This was the age of the Counter-Reformation and the adoption of the Baroque style in literature. Both elements were combined in the prose of Cardinal Péter Pázmány (1570–1637), whose powerful sermons and skilful polemical works were composed in a style both polished and immediately comprehensible – something not always achieved by his contemporaries.

In verse a similar blend of baroque exuberance and technical artistry characterized the narrative poems of István Gyöngyösi (1629–1704). Unusually in Hungarian literature, they were written with the sole purpose of amusing the reader and gained instant popularity, attracting the aristocracy who were not normally drawn to literature in Hungarian. Gyöngyösi's metrical perfection set standards for narrative verse that were still recognized two centuries later.

His contemporary, the soldier-poet Miklós Zrínyi (1620–64), has often attracted criticism for failing to meet these standards, but he was not attempting the same metre despite a superficial resemblance. Nor did he write to amuse; he was a fierce advocate of driving the Turks once and for all from Hungary. He wrote several passionately argued tracts on the subject, but is best known for his rugged epic which describes heroic defiance of the Turks by his kinsman, another Miklós

Zrínyi, at the siege of **Szigetvár** in 1566. Generally known as *Szigeti veszedelem* (*The Peril of Sziget*), it was first published at Vienna in 1651. The author, well versed in European literature, used all the trappings of classical epic to relate a dramatic historical event with a contemporary message.

Meanwhile drama existed chiefly in schools, both Catholic and Protestant, some of which possessed their own theatres and staged didactic and moral dramas based mainly on biblical and classical sources, relieved occasionally by themes from Hungarian history. Public performances outside the schools were virtually non-existent in a land devastated by war and lacking in urban centres.

Entertainment was provided, however, in the increasingly popular verse-tales known as *széphistória* ('fine story'). The term covers a wide variety of narrative verse based on themes derived from sources as diverse as folk-tales and Boccaccio, the classics and historical episodes. There were also love-lyrics with the generic name of *virágének* ('flower-song'), in which the beloved was named after a flower or bird. Both kinds of verse ranged in style from the elegance of Baroque refinement to barrack-room crudity. Aware of the strong disapproval of the church, the authors generally remained anonymous. The publication of such verse continued throughout the following century, when publishers too disguised their whereabouts for fear of reprisals.

Much verse was also circulated in manuscript. This was particularly true of politically dangerous poetry, which flourished during the rebellions against the Habsburgs that followed the expulsion of the Turks in 1686. This large corpus of poetry includes soldiers' songs, eulogies of leaders, exiles' laments and mockery of the foe. Such verse was written by both sides and in various languages. Some of the songs of that turbulent age were revived during later revolutions; the Rákóczi Song of the early eighteenth century is a fine example.

Some of the finest prose in Hungarian can be found in the memoir, a genre which first emerged in the sixteenth century and still remains strong today. The authors are as diverse as their reasons for writing. During the seventeenth and eighteenth centuries the memoir flourished in **Transylvania**, with notable contributions from a prince, János Kemény (1607–62), a chancellor, Miklós Bethlen (1642–1716) and an educated housewife, Kata Bethlen (1700–59).

The eighteenth century

This was a time of comparative peace and stability, with Hungary once more open to Western Europe. The literary scene changed perceptibly. Prose, primarily in translations from German and French, gradually replaced narrative verse as light reading. Some one hundred romances (popular novels) are recorded before 1800. Not surprisingly, the products of the Enlightenment began to filter into the country, causing alarm to both church and state. Censorship was tightened to a degree never exceeded again; the regulations imposed an almost total ban on imaginative writing, with a corps of 'Book Police' (*Bücherpolizei*) to enforce them.

The later 18th century saw renewed interest in the language and its capacity to support literature for a new age, and small groups of writers began to explore these possibilities. Foremost among these was a mainly Vienna court-based group led by György Bessenyei (1747–1811). They published prose, verse and drama based on what they saw as enlightened principles; they also urged the establishment of an Academy to act as a focus for Hungarian culture.

Meanwhile sentimentalism and early Romanticism or 'Sturm und Drang' influences entered Hungary from several sources. Goethe's *Werther* inspired a number of imitations, the best of which was *Fanni hagyományai* (*The Memoirs of Fanni*), 1794, by József Kármán (1769–95). Edward Young's *Night Thoughts*, 1742–45, introduced a wave of sentimentalism in poetry. The continuation of the native Baroque tradition in verse, though mingled with influences as diverse as Pope and Rousseau, led to the rococo, comic and often splendidly vulgar poetry of Mihály Csokonai Vitéz (1773–1805), the most original Hungarian lyric writer since Balassi.

Drama began to emerge from the schools, where performances of Racine and Holberg added variety to the customary fare established by tradition; affluent aristocratic families, like the Esterházys, had their own theatres, and occasional plays were staged in **Pest** from 1784–85, mainly for the delectation of young aristocrats. Goethe, Schiller and Lessing provided their staple diet.

It was the Enlightenment centralizing reforms of the Emperor Joseph II (1741–90) that suddenly changed the course of Hungarian literature. Alarmed by his attempts to unify his multinational empire and to impose German as the language of state and higher education, Hungarian intellectuals began to voice their opposition through their language and literature. From that time onwards, literature in Hungary became overwhelmingly national in character and seriously political in content. Writers were increasingly drawn into the new cultural centre, the twin cities of **Buda** and **Pest**, seat of a re-established university and the most important market in the country.

The nineteenth century to the revolution of 1848

The first organizer of the new literature was the poet and essayist Ferenc Kazinczy (1759–1831), who single-handedly cajoled his contemporaries into using classically elevated language and a polished style to convey their ideas. This implied a break with what he regarded as the

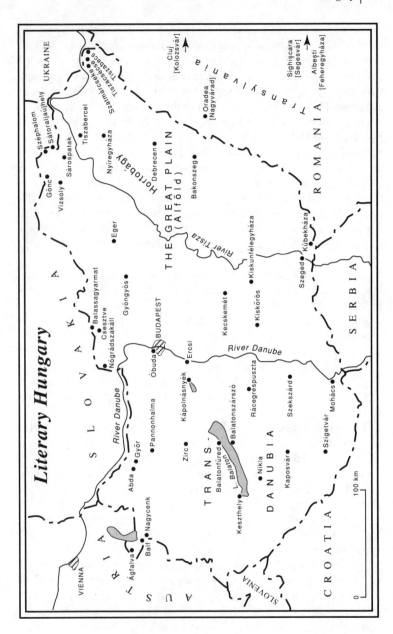

Map: See 'Literary Landmarks' (pp 195–199) for details on each location.

vulgar native tradition as seen in the popular novel and the rococo verse of such poets as Csokonai, and the adoption of what often seemed artificial language full of neologisms. At a time when Romanticism was gaining ground, his classical ideas were at odds with the general mood. The clash between the two was best seen in the verse of Dániel Berzsenyi (1776–1836) – refined in language and classical in form, its content smoulders like a volcano about to erupt. Freer rein was given to Romanticism by Ferenc Kölcsey (1790–1838), author of the Hungarian national anthem (*Himnusz*, 1823), and the first of many writers to play an active role in politics; he became a fine orator. In Hungarian Romanticism the evocation of the nation's past glory and present distress played a major role. This was a time when fear of the possible national extinction of the Hungarians was a recurrent theme, one that has never been far from the surface, even to the present day. Until the last few years before the 1848 revolution there was little optimism for the future in Hungarian writing.

The younger Romantic writers jointly produced an attractive annual *Aurora* (1821–37) under the genial direction of the popular poet and playwright Károly Kisfaludy (1788–1830). Their activity helped considerably to widen interest in literature which till then had been in danger of becoming merely the preserve of an intellectual clique. Also at this time the long-desired Academy of Sciences was founded in **Pest** (1830). Among its aims was the promotion of literature in Hungarian, and it has always kept a close watch on language developments. In 1837 a national theatre was established, also in **Pest**, to promote drama in Hungarian.

These new ventures coincided with increasing demands for political and economic reform. Count István Széchenyi (1791–1860), named 'the greatest Hungarian' by his more radical rival Lajos Kossuth (1802–94), not only wrote powerful treatises on reform, but also helped to finance such projects as the Academy and the regulation of the Danube.

As the demands for change grew stronger, so the pace of literary life increased. *Aurora* gave place to the tri-weekly *Athenaeum* (1837–43), edited by a trio of young writers of whom the poet and dramatist Mihály Vörösmarty ◊ was the most renowned. His skilfully composed expressive lyric poetry was written in language from which he had excised the more grotesque refinements of Kazinczy's age; he was the creator of the modern verse-language. This was also the age of the finest Hungarian classical tragedy. *Bánk bán*, by József Katona (1791–1830), a native of **Kecskemét**, was written in 1814–15 but not staged until after the author's death; in the years preceding the 1848 revolution it became immensely popular for its national sentiments.

Imaginative prose always suffered more than verse at the hands of the censor, so the Romantic novel came late to Hungary. Miklós Jósika (1794–1865), a Transylvanian baron, followed in the footsteps of the Scottish novelist Walter Scott. His *Abafi*, 1836, is a fine example of the genre and opened a new era in Hungarian writing. The novel quickly became an accepted part of the programme of reform, as can be seen in *A falu jegyzője* (*The Village Notary*), 1845, by the statesman József Eötvös (1813–71); it is a comprehensive exposure of contemporary injustices that demanded redress. Eötvös, like Széchenyi and many other reformers, visited Britain to study conditions there and derive inspiration for their plans in Hungary. Meanwhile there was a considerable growth in periodical publications, and with it a corresponding demand for short stories, thus initiating the link between journalism and *belles-lettres* which still exists. The short story as a genre has flourished in Hungary and attracted some of the finest writers.

Into this scene of considerable activity burst Sándor Petőfi ◊, a lyric poet of natural talent for whom the literary norms of an older generation meant nothing. Young and impetuous, he poured all his thoughts and emotions into verse of astonishing variety couched in language which ranges from the high Romantic to the commonplace. He continued the tradition of Csokonai, broken by the efforts of Kazinczy and his followers, and also derived direct inspiration from folk-poetry. This he did not seek to 'elevate' like his predecessors; instead he used folk themes, forms and language in his own work, which promptly gained him widespread popularity. He travelled widely in Hungary, and some of his finest poetry is in praise of the **Great Plain** where he was born (Extract 6). His political stance caused consternation as the inevitable revolution grew nearer; he was fiercely patriotic and anti-Austrian and an unabashed republican. Like many of his friends, he was well-versed in the history of the French Revolution, and when 1848 dawned this was the model to be followed in Hungary, according to the young writers who set it in motion. Petőfi himself perished in the revolutionary events, for the national cause which had for so long dominated the literary scene.

From revolution to the twentieth century

The aftermath of the revolution, the collapse of national aspirations and the imposition of a harsh Austrian rule resulted in a period of soul-searching and rethinking of the role of literature in Hungary. Many writers were in exile or hiding, and there was no place for revolutionary sentiments. Two main trends emerged: one was escapism, and here the most popular and prolific of all Hungarian novelists, Mór (Maurus) Jókai ◊ was pre-eminent (Extract 5). His fertile imagination and readable style endeared him to readers, if not to critics, who found his characterization weak and took him to task for

Mór Jókai, with his second wife Bella

evading national issues, though some of his best historical novels were inspired by Hungarian history and included the 1848 revolution.

This same trend is also evident in the countless imitations of Petőfi's rustic idylls and in the popularity of light drama. The other, more serious, tendency was to draw inspiration and hope from the glories of the past and at the same time to explore the deep reasons for the failure of the national cause. This was seen in the narrative verse of János Arany ◊, notably his *Toldi* trilogy, 1847–79, and his unfinished Hun epic *Buda halála* (*The Death of Buda*), 1864. The mood of the age was also caught by his remarkable psychological ballads which, like all his verse, bear the stamp of a technically accomplished poet. It was Arany who added the stylistic polish to another soul-searching work of this period: *Az ember tragédiája* (*The Tragedy of Man*), 1861, a dramatic poem by Imre Madách (1823–64), the stage version of which has been part of the standard Hungarian repertoire since 1883. In his search for meaning Madách traces the history of mankind from the Creation to the end of the world in a series of scenes depicting the failure of great ideals. He concludes that the purpose of life is to struggle, an affirmation to be explained by his own personal conflicts and the failure of the revolution.

The same concerns emerged in the sombre novels of Zsigmond Kemény ◊ whose historical works examined the interaction of fate, individual motives and human weakness with a psychological insight that is rare in Hungarian literature.

After the conclusion of the so-called 'Compromise' with Austria in 1867, the political target that had inspired so much literature earlier in the century disappeared. The mood of questioning and self-doubt, however, persisted. The situation was not helped by the concentration of so much critical and editorial policy in the hands of one man. Pál Gyulai (1826–1909) firmly advised aspiring writers to follow his own narrow ideals, derived from Vörösmarty, Petőfi and Arany, who to him represented the best form of national and popular literature. He castigated those who, like Jókai, escaped into fantasy or sought inspiration from foreign sources. Hungarian literature towards the end of the century was dominated by frustration, particularly on the part of younger poets who found it almost impossible to express themselves in their own way.

One novelist, however, managed to maintain a more cheerful outlook. Kálmán Mikszáth ◊ loved human eccentricity, which he found abundantly among the decaying nobility and gentry of his native region of northern Hungary, the area round **Balassagyarmat**. His sketches of life there are a blend of ironic humour and criticism.

The age of Nyugat

The rapid growth of **Budapest** and the concentration of new industries there focused attention on the capital. The urban reader was a new phenomenon for whom no provision had been made before, and a spate of short-lived journals attempted to supply his needs. Since there was a large Jewish population, it is no surprise that the two most influential and long-lasting periodicals attracted both readers and writers from that community. A Hét (The Week), 1890–1924, flourished under the brilliant editorship of the poet József Kiss (1843–1921), and provided a forum for contemporary writing and criticism. Modern in outlook and presentation, it catered for a sophisticated readership interested in the wider European scene.

In 1906 the poet Endre Ady ◊ published a volume of 'new songs for new times'. Entitled simply Új versek (New Poems), it was intended to shock; its mixture of patriotic despair, radical politics, eroticism and prophecy, all couched in the language of symbolism, achieved this aim. The literary world was divided between the older generation which deemed him outrageous and unintelligible and the younger, which hailed him as a genius. Ady remains the most controversial poet of the twentieth century, but none can deny his technical skill or the fact that he initiated a much-needed rejuvenation of literature in Hungary. He published most frequently in the second of the important journals of the age, Nyugat (West), 1908–41, which encouraged the aspirations of new writers and opened a window on contemporary developments in Western Europe. Politically radical, it espoused the cause of social reform which occupied an increasing number of writers until the end of the second world war.

There was a wealth of literary talent at this time in Hungary. Most European in outlook was Mihály Babits ◊ whose brilliant and scholarly verse derived much inspiration from Greek and Latin classicism. Dezső Kosztolányi ◊ was a master of polished style and precise language; he was both an accomplished lyric poet and an unrivalled short-story writer, whose prose remains unmatched during the century (Extract 3). Zsigmond Móricz ◊ surveyed contemporary Hungarian society in novels, short stories and reports of rare power, revealing the inhumanity that existed not only between classes but also among members of the same social groups (Extract 7). The aspirations of the lonely and depressed emerge in the delicate but compelling lyric poetry of Gyula Juhász (1883–1937) and Árpád Tóth (1886–1928). Margit Kaffka (1880–1918) portrayed the position of women in contemporary society in both verse and novels of sensitive psychological insight. A very different, but equally important, contribution to the literary scene was the work of Frigyes Karinthy (1887–1938), a keen observer of human folly and a master of satirical humour. His literary parodies offered sharper criticism than did the regular critics of his day. These and many other writers were all attracted to *Nyugat*, whose editorial policy was that only the best writing, of whatever kind, deserved publication in its columns and whose editors were men of remarkable discernment.

Some writers remained unattached to the mainstream *Nyugat* circle. One of the most popular was Ferenc Herczeg (1863–1954), whose conservative tastes and lightness of style appealed particularly to urban readers; his historical novels and dramas gained widespread admiration. Ferenc Molnár ◊ was by far the best-known Hungarian playwright; his witty dramas have been staged all over the world, and his appreciation of stagecraft was a rarity in a country where didactic drama is paramount and the stage is regarded as a pulpit. Another lone writer was Gyula Krúdy ◊, a master of lyrical prose whose novels diffuse an atmosphere of timelessness in which action is subordinate to mood (Extract 1).

Few authors managed to resist the attractions of **Budapest**, which in any case was the centre of publishing, as it still is today. Thus even those who began writing in the provinces where there were some notable cultural centres like **Nagyvárad (Oradea**, Romania) and **Kolozsvár (Cluj**, Romania) usually gravitated to the capital. Among those who resisted this temptation the most notable were Géza Gárdonyi (1863–1922) and Ferenc Móra (1879–1934). Gárdonyi made his home in **Eger** and wrote his finest historical novels there, including *Egri csillagok* (*Stars of Eger*), 1901 (translated as *Eclipse of the Crescent Moon*), still one of the most popular works in Hungary. Móra was the director of the museum in **Szeged**, whose life he describes with sympathetic humour in many of his novels and short stories.

After the shocks that followed the first world war, the short-lived republic and the flirtation with Communism, the dismemberment of the country administered a fearful blow to an already disorientated literature. Nothing like this had been seen since the Turkish occupation. The unity of Hungarian literature had been shattered, and what was formerly regional writing suddenly gained importance as the culture of an ethnic minority in the new states then created. In the larger Hungarian communities in Transylvania, Slovakia and the Banat (Yugoslavia), some fine writing emerged between the two world wars. It was markedly different from that produced in Hungary proper, as was only to be expected from a politically sensitive literature. Most distinctive was that of Transylvania, where the novels of Károly Kós (1883–1977) and Áron Tamási (1887–1966) are outstanding examples of Hungarian writing outside the new borders. Nevertheless the magnetism of Budapest still attracted writers to settle there, as Tamási himself eventually did.

All writing in the new Hungary was overshadowed by the new national cause, the restoration of the pre-war frontiers. In the early confusion of the post-war years, the pamphleteer and novelist Dezső Szabó (1879–1945) caught the mood with his warnings of the death of Hungariandom couched in rhetorical prose of immense pathos. He had a considerable but brief influence on younger writers, though his increasingly racist ideas repelled those who regarded them as dangerously close to the Fascism that was gaining ground in Germany.

The radical tradition continued among writers who were attracted to various avant-garde movements elsewhere in Europe. Lajos Kassák (1887–1967) edited a series of journals devoted to contemporary trends in art and literature. He himself painted in a constructivist idiom as well as writing free verse. Gyula Illyés ◊, later to become one of the most respected of all Hungarian writers, was influenced originally by the avant-garde poetry he encountered in France. He was an outspoken advocate of social reform and had a deep concern for the future of Hungary; few modern writers have surpassed him in precision of language or verse-technique (Extract 14).

By far the most radical poet to emerge after the first world war was Attila József ◊. His urgent demands for social reform, particularly for the urban poor, and his own spiritual turmoil were expressed in a rare blend of savagery and beauty, drawing on the terminology of both Marx and Freud (Extract 2). He fell foul of both the right-wing government and of the Communist party, which expelled him.

A division gradually appeared in Hungarian writing. On the one hand there were the so-called 'populists', who pressed for social reform and backed up their demands with a series of brilliant studies on rural conditions, a form of literary sociography that alarmed the government and caused some of the books to be withdrawn. Their opponents, named 'urbanists', regarded the populists as too narrowly Hungarian; they emphasized the universality of literature and its aesthetic quality, and deplored what they saw as the danger of isolation from West European culture. In a literary world so small and compact, this division had unfortunate consequences: since most of the urbanists were Jewish, there were overtones of anti-semitism in the rift, just at the time when Hungary was being drawn into the orbit of the Axis powers in an attempt to regain her lost territories.

Some writers kept apart from these developments. Babits, now editor of *Nyugat*, strove to maintain European cultural values in a Europe threatened by Fascism. László Németh ◊, who believed in the leading role of the intellectual in society, acted as modern encyclopaedist in his erudite essays, novels and plays which are all didactic. Lőrinc Szabó (1900–57) expressed the suffering of the individual in an age of contradictions in scholarly verse of rare perfection.

The second world war coincided with the death of many of the older distinguished writers and effectively ended a literary era. What continuity there might have been was further interrupted by the death in labour camps and captivity of some of the most talented younger authors, such as the lyric poet Miklós Radnóti ◊, the distinguished essayist Gábor Halász (1901–45), and the novelist Antal Szerb (1901–45).

Literature since 1945

Once again Hungary emerged from a world war defeated and devastated. After a brief period of democracy, welcomed by writers who earlier had pressed for social reform, Communist rule was imposed and policy dictated by Moscow. Literature was to be harnessed to the needs of propaganda and forced to renounce the opposition tradition of the previous century and a half. Writers could either conform or relapse into silence. The history of literature was rewritten to stress the contribution of suitably socialist authors who might act as models for the new age. Some, like Petőfi, Ady and József, were extolled, others tolerated and some condemned. All earlier literature, and particularly that of the twentieth century, was re-edited and in some cases rewritten to conform to the Party's view, with the result that most modern editions of earlier works are defective.

The original literature of the early Communist period with its sycophantic praise of Stalin and local leaders, its glorification of Communism and execration of 'Western imperialism' serves as an awful example of political manipulation of literature. Yet the opposition tradition gradually asserted itself after the death of Stalin and paved the way for the revolution of 1956. The most powerful condemnation of Communism in general was Gyula Illyés's poem *Egy mondat a zsarnokságról* (*One Sentence on Tyranny*), written in 1950 but first published in 1956, but there were numerous other writers whose frustration could no longer be contained. They included the erstwhile Communist Tibor Déry ◊, who with certain other writers suffered imprisonment for his outspokenness after the revolution was crushed. Several writers of note left Hungary after 1956; scattered throughout the world, they contributed to the considerable volume of emigré Hungarian literature that now exists.

The regime of János Kádár (1956–88) gradually relaxed controls on literature but still retained a careful watch over it with a whimsical censorship always ready to pounce. The result was an uneasy compromise; writers themselves had to decide how far they might express their ideas, and this could be more restrictive than overt censorship. There was little room for innovation, but within the bounds of traditional forms some fine writing evolved. Sándor Weöres ◊, whose works included children's rhymes as well as huge metaphysical and cosmic myths, often of oriental inspiration, was a poet of striking intellectual power and technical virtuosity (Extract 10). János Pilinszky ◊ expressed intense personal suffering and spiritual anguish in disturbing verse of stark economy, giving the lie to Adorno's often cited dictum that after Auschwitz there is no poetry (Extract 12). Notable prose works were published by Géza Ottlik ◊ and Miklós Mészöly ◊ (Extract 11). These and many other authors strove to keep Hungarian literature attuned to contemporary European developments, and younger writers educated in the post-war world to derive inspiration from folk-poetry now threw off such limitations.

Experiment and innovation gradually reappeared. The novels and short stories of Péter Nádas ◊ extend the bounds of traditional prose works in their exploration of the emotional world (Extract 9). György Konrád ◊, well known abroad as a dissident writer, turns his intellectual power and linguistic skill to the support of his belief in Central European culture, threatened as it is by alien interference (Extract 8). Péter Esterházy ◊ is a virtuoso linguist who uses his talent to expose the follies of an imposed culture and to question accepted traditions.

Verse has been less inventive, but there are some outstanding examples of traditional genres, such as the tough and demanding verse of Ottó Orbán ◊ (Extract 4) and the savage satirical poetry of the dissident György Petri (1943–   ). There has also been a welcome revival of good drama, from the grotesque plays of István Örkény (1912–76) to the startling dramas of György Spiró (1946–   ), whose *Csirkefej* (*Chicken Head*), 1987, explores the desperate need of the individual for social contact. Historical drama has been used to criticize the social order, notably by the Transylvanian playwrights András Sütő (1937–   ) and Géza Páskándi (1933–   ).

With the collapse of Communism in 1989 and the virtual end of censorship, much soul-searching is taking place. While formerly taboo subjects such as criticism of the former Soviet Union and the fate of the Hungarian minorities in neighbouring countries can now be discussed, as yet there is no clear way ahead for Hungarian literature. The past still casts a long shadow over the present; this is seen particularly in a distrust of intellectuals who are accused of compromising with the previous regime. The idea that it is the poets who are to lead the people to the promised land no longer carries conviction, and indeed the national role of literature is questioned. For the twentieth century has seen the gradual disintegration of a formerly compact, Budapest-centred Hungarian culture. The process began with mass emigration to the USA at the beginning of the century and continued with the dismemberment of Hungary in 1920; later writers escaped from Fascism and Communism, many of them in a further mass emigration after the

János Pilinszky

revolution of 1956. The result is that Hungarian writing is now published in widely separated parts of the world, a totally unforeseen development that poses new and searching questions concerning the function of Hungarian literature in the future.

LITERARY LANDMARKS

(See 'Literary Hungary' map for locations. Statues are listed separately, at the end of this section.)

Abda: Memorial to Radnóti near the site on Road 1 where he was killed in 1944.

Bakonszeg: House, now memorial museum, of György Bessenyei, the eighteenth-century apostle of Enlightenment.

Balatonfüred: Jókai's villa. In the lakeside park, memorials to the Indian poet Rabindranath Tagore and Italian poet Salvatore Quasimodo, who both sought cures at the spa.

Balatonszárszó: Memorial museum to Attila József who committed suicide here.

Balf: Site of the labour camp where the poet and novelist György Sárközi (1899–1945), the novelist Antal Szerb and the essayist Gábor Halász died during the last days of the second world war, with memorials.

Budapest (arranged by districts):

I   **31 Logodi u, 133 Attila u,** and **65b Attila u** – sites of Babits's homes from 1931 until his death in 1941. **12 Tábor u** – Kosztolányi's home from 1917 until his death in 1936.

II   **9 Józsefhegyi u** – home of Illyés from 1941 until his death in 1983. **37 Mártirok u** – home of Móricz from 1937 until his death in 1942.

III   The former Zichy mansion in **Fő tér** (Óbuda) houses the Kassák memorial museum.

V   The Petőfi Literary Museum in the former Károlyi mansion (**16 Károlyi Mihály u**) houses a permanent exhibition of the works and artefacts connected with Petőfi, Ady, József, Radnóti and other writers. It also displays temporary exhibitions on literary themes. **4–6 Veres Pálné u** – Ady memorial museum in the house where he lived from 1917 until his death in 1919.

VII   The **Hungária Coffee House** (9–11 Erzsébet Körút), formerly known as the New York, was a favourite meeting place of the writers of *Nyugat*, who frequently wrote of its life and society. **68 József körút** – birthplace of the dramatist Ferenc Molnár.

VIII **Kerepesi Cemetery** (Fiumei út), burial place of many of the most famous writers including Petőfi, Vörösmarty, Arany, Jókai, Mikszáth, Ady, Kosztolányi, Móricz, Babits, Krúdy, József and Radnóti. **Nemzeti Múzeum** (National Museum, 14–16 Múzeum körút) – traditionally the site where Petőfi recited his National Song at the outbreak of the revolution on 15 March 1848, though there is no evidence to support this. A tablet marks the site.

IX   **3 Gát u** – birthplace of József, with a memorial room. **95 Üllői ut** – home of Móricz between 1906 and 1926.

XII   **Farkasrét Cemetery**, burial place of Margit Kaffka, Árpád Tóth, István Örkény, László Németh and Gyula Illyés, among other writers. **21 Költő u** (Szabadság hegy) – Jókai villa, now the National Conservation Office, with a Jókai memorial exhibition on the ground floor. **48b Városmajor u** – *Nyugat* Literary Museum, with exhibits from the history of this influential journal.

XIII **Margit Island**, named after St Margaret of Hungary who lived in the former Dominican convent here, and is commemorated in works by Géza Gárdonyi, including *Isten rabjai* (*Slaves of God*), 1908, Krúdy and Ady. The island was Krúdy's home from 1918 to 1930.

XIV **Városliget** (City Park), the setting of Molnár's play *Liliom*.

Csesztve: Home of the playwright Imre Madách from 1845 to 1853, now a memorial museum.

Debrecen: Birthplace of Csokonai; the site is at **23 Hatvani u.** The Reformed Church College was where many writers were educated, including Csokonai, Kölcsey, Arany and Móricz.

Eger: The home, now a memorial museum, of Géza Gárdonyi, who is buried in the grounds of the castle. It is also the site of his best-known novel, *Egri csillagok*. The siege he describes is also commemorated in works by the chronicler Tinódi and Vörösmarty.

Ercsi: Burial place of the novelist and reformer József Eötvös. The house in which he spent his childhood contains a small memorial room.

Esztergom: The site of the siege by the Turks in 1594 in which the poet Bálint Balassi perished. Summer residence of Babits, now a memorial museum, famous for the wall on which visitors signed their names.

Hortobágy: The river which gives its name to the region, now a national park, celebrated in verse by Petőfi and many other writers. It is also the scene of Jókai's novel *Sárga rózsa* (*The Yellow Rose*), 1892, which contains some fine descriptions of it.

Kápolnásnyék: Birthplace of Vörösmarty, now a memorial museum, to the south of Road 70.

Kecskemét: Birthplace of the dramatist József Katona, who is also buried here. A memorial marks the spot where he collapsed and died.

Kiskőrös: Birthplace of Petőfi, now a memorial museum.

Kiskunfélegyháza: Birthplace of Ferenc Móra, now a memorial museum. The so-called 'Hattyú house' was the scene of Petőfi's childhood, commemorated by a plaque.

Nagycenk: The seat of the Széchényi family from 1741 and the burial place of Count István Széchenyi the reformer, with a memorial museum.

Nikla: Home of the poet Dániel Berzsenyi from 1804 until his death in 1836. He is buried in the village cemetery.

Nyíregyháza: Birthplace of Krúdy.

Rácegrespuszta: Birthplace of Gyula Illyés, who recalls its life in *Puszták népe* (*People of the Puszta*).

Szatmárcseke: Tomb of Ferenc Kölcsey, the poet and politician, who also wrote the National Anthem here.

Szeged: Birthplace of the poet Gyula Juhász, with a memorial bronze marking the site. He is buried in the central cemetery, also the burial place of Ferenc Móra, who worked in the museum from 1902 until his death in 1934.

Szekszárd: Birthplace of Babits (13 **Babits Mihály u**), now preserved as a memorial museum. Birthplace of the poet János Garay (1812–53), whose poem *Az obsitos* (*The Old Soldier*), 1843, inspired Kodály's comic opera *Háry János*, 1927.

Széphalom: Home of the critic and reformer Ferenc Kazinczy from 1804 till his death in 1831, now the site of his mausoleum. The name *Széphalom* ('Beautiful Hill') was his invention.

Szigetvár: Site of the siege (1566) commemorated in Miklós Zrínyi's epic *Szigeti Veszedelem*, 1651, and the author's own victory over the Turks during the winter campaign of 1664.

Tiszabercel: Birthplace of György Bessenyei (1747).

Tiszacsécse: Birthplace of Móricz, who commemorates the village in *Életem regénye* (*The Novel of My Life*), 1939, and *Ficfás Tiszaháton, ahol gyermek voltam* (*On the Willow-Clad Banks of the Tisza, Where I was a Child*), 1942.

Vizsoly: The first complete Bible in Hungarian was printed in the church here in 1590; its editor, Gáspár Károlyi (Károli), was Calvinist pastor from 1559 to 1591 of the neighbouring village of **Gönc**.

Statues of literary figures

(Only the more important statues are listed. Most large towns possess statues of Petőfi.)

Anonymous (the unknown author of the *Gesta Ungarorum*): Budapest, XIV, Városliget.

János Arany: Budapest VIII, in the garden of the National Museum.

Bálint Balassi: Esztergom, beneath the walls of the fortress.

Dániel Berzsenyi: Kaposvár, Szabadság Park, and Szombathely, in the square named after him.

György Bessenyei: Nyíregyháza, in the square named after him.

Mihály Csokonai Vitéz: Debrecen, Kálvin tér.

József Eötvös: Budapest V, in the square named after him.

Géza Gárdonyi: Győr, Batthyány tér.

Attila József: Budapest V, Kossuth Lajos tér (south of the Parliament building).

József Katona: Kecskemét, in the garden beside the theatre named after him.

Ferenc Kazinczy: Sátoraljaújhely, in the main square.

Károly Kisfaludy: Győr, Köztársaság tér.

Gyula Krúdy: Budapest III, Szentlélek tér (Óbuda).

Kálmán Mikszáth: Budapest VIII, in the square named after him.

Ferenc Móra: Kiskunfélegyháza, Daru u.

Sándor Petőfi: Budapest V, Petőfi tér, the scene of many political demonstrations since it was unveiled in 1882; the anniversary of the 1848 revolution (15 March) is marked by a wreath-laying ceremony here.

István Széchenyi: Balatonfüred.

Rabindranath Tagore: Balatonfüred.

Mihály Vörösmarty: Budapest V, Vörösmarty tér.

Miklós Zrínyi (the poet): Szigetvár, Felszabadulás tér.

BOOKLIST

The following selection includes the extracted titles in this chapter as well as those mentioned in the introduction which are available in English and other titles for further reading. In general, paperback editions are given when possible. The editions cited are not necessarily the only ones available. For most of the extracted works, the original publisher can be found in 'Acknowledgments and Citations' at the end of the volume, as can the exact location of the extracts and the editions from which they are taken. Extract numbers are highlighted in bold. Square brackets denote the date of publication of the work in its original language.

Ady, Endre, The Explosive Country, G. F. Cushing, trans, Corvina, Budapest, 1977.

Ady, Endre, Poems of Endre Ady, Anton N. Nyerges, trans, Hungarian Cultural Foundation, Buffalo, 1969.

Arany, János, The Death of King Buda [1863], W. Kirkconnell, trans, Benjamin Franklin Bibliophile Society, Cleveland, OH, 1936.

Babits, Mihály, The Nightmare [1916], Corvina, Budapest, 1966.

Bodor, Ádám, The Euphrates at Babylon (short stories), Richard Aczel, trans, Polygon, Edinburgh, 1991.

Csoóri, Sándor, Barbarian Prayer: Selected Poems, Corvina, Budapest, 1989.

Czigány, Lóránt, The Oxford History of Hungarian Literature, Clarendon Press, Oxford, revised ed, 1988.

Dent, Bob, Blue Guide: Hungary, A & C Black, London, and W W Norton, New York, 1991.

Déry, Tibor, The Portuguese Princess, Kathleen Szász, trans, Calder and Boyars, London, 1966.

Déry, Tibor, The Giant, Behind the Brick Wall and Love, Kathleen Szász and Ilona Duczyńska, trans, John Calder, London, 1964.

Déry, Tibor, Niki [1956], E. Hyams, trans, Secker and Warburg, London, 1958.

Description of a Struggle: the Picador Book of Contemporary East European Prose, Michael March, ed, Picador, London, 1994. (Péter Nádas, László Márton, Péter Esterházy, Lajos Grendel.)

Eötvös, József, The Village Notary [1845], O. Wenckstern, trans, Longman, London, 1850.

Esterházy, Péter, *The Book of Hrabal* [1990], Judith Sollosy, trans, Quartet, London, 1993.

Esterházy, Péter, *The Glance of Countess Hahn-Hahn (Down the Danube)* [1991], Richard Aczel, trans, Weidenfeld and Nicolson, London, 1994.

Esterházy, Péter, *Helping Verbs of the Heart* [1985], Michael Henry Heim, trans, Quartet, London, 1992/Grove Atlantic, New York, 1990.

Fodor, András, 'A Vízrenéző', **Extract 13** (G. Cushing, trans).

Forty-Four Hungarian Short Stories, Lajos Illés, ed, Corvina, Budapest, 1979.

Füst, Milán, *The Story of My Wife*, Ivan Sanders, trans, Pan/ Jonathan Cape, London, 1990.

Gárdonyi, Géza, *Eclipse of the Crescent Moon* [1901], George F. Cushing, trans, 2nd ed, Corvina, Budapest, 1994.

Hoensch, Jörg K., *A History of Modern Hungary 1867–1986*, Longman, London, 1989.

Hungarian Helicon, Watson Kirkconnell, trans, Széchenyi Society Inc, Calgary, 1985; poems by Sándor Petőfi ('The Alföld', 1844), and Ferenc Juhász ('Village Elegy', 1855). **Extracts 6 and 15**.

Hungarian Quartet, A (Ottlik, Mándy, Mészöly and Esterházy), Mária Kőrösy, ed, Corvina, Budapest, 1991.

Hungarian Short Stories, Corvina, Budapest, 1962.

Hungary, Nelles Guides series, Robertson McCarta/Nelles Verlag, London and Munich, 1991. (Includes new street names, often reverting to names from before 1947.)

Kiss, The: 20th Century Hungarian Short Stories, István Bart, ed, Corvina, Budapest, 1993.

Illyés, Gyula, *Selected Poems*, T. Kabdebo and P. Tabori, trans,

Chatto and Windus, London, 1971.

Illyés, Gyula, *People of the Puszta* [1936], G. F. Cushing, trans, Corvina, Budapest, 1967, 2nd ed, 1979. **Extract 14**.

Jókai, Mór (Maurus), *The Baron's Sons* [1869], P. F. Bicknell, trans, Macqueen, London, 1900.

Jókai, Mór (Maurus), *Timar's Two Worlds* [1873], Mrs Hegan Kennard, trans, William Blackwood & Sons, Edinburgh and London, 1888, 1930. **Extract 5**.

Jókai, Mor (Maurus), *The Yellow Rose* [1892], B. Danford, trans, London, 1909.

Jones, D. Mervyn, *Five Hungarian Writers* (Zrínyi, Mikes, Vörösmarty, Eötvös and Petőfi), Clarendon Press, Oxford, 1966.

József, Attila, *Selected Poems and Texts*, John Bátki, trans, Carcanet, Cheadle Hulme, 1973.

József, Attila, 'Night in the Slums' [1932], Edwin Morgan, trans, as 'Night in the Suburbs' in *The Penguin Book of Socialist Verse*, Alan Bold, ed, Penguin, London, 1970. **Extract 2**.

Juhász, Ferenc, and Weöres, Sándor, *Selected Poems*, Edwin Morgan and David Wevill, trans, Penguin Modern European Poets series, London, 1970/Peter Smith, Magnolia, MA. See also *The Plough and the Pen*.

Juhász, Ferenc, 'Village Elegy', in *Hungarian Helicon*, Watson Kirkconnell, trans, Széchenyi Society, Calgary, 1985. **Extract 15**.

Konrád, György, *A Feast in the Garden* [1989], Marc Goldstein, trans, Faber and Faber, London, 1992/Harcourt Brace, Orlando, FL, 1993.

Konrád, György, *The Loser* [1980], Ivan Sanders, trans, Harcourt Brace Jovanovich, New York, 1982. **Extract 8**.

Konrád, György, *The Case Worker* [1969], Paul Aston, trans,

Hutchinson, London, 1975.
Kosztolányi, Dezső, *Darker Muses* [1922], Clifton R. Fadiman, trans, Corvina, Budapest, 1990.
Kosztolányi, Dezső, *Anna Édes* [1926], George Szirtes, trans, Quartet, London, 1991. **Extract 3.**
Kosztolányi, Dezső, *Skylark* [1924], Richard Aczel, trans, Chatto and Windus, London, 1993.
Krúdy, Gyula, *The Crimson Coach* [1913], Paul Tabori, trans, Corvina, Budapest, 1967. **Extract 1.**
Ma – Today, An Anthology of Contemporary Hungarian Literature, Éva Tóth, ed, Corvina, Budapest, 1987.
Madách, Imre, *The Tragedy of Man* [1861], Iain Macleod, trans, Canongate, Edinburgh, 1993 (latest of several translations).
Mészöly, Miklós, 'Lament for a Mother', in *The Kiss, 20th Century Hungarian Short Stories*, István Bart, ed, Corvina, Budapest, 1993. **Extract 11.**
Mikszáth, Kálmán, *St Peter's Umbrella* [1895], B. W. Worswick, trans, Corvina, Budapest, 1962.
Mikszáth, Kálmán, *The Siege of Beszterce* [1894], Dick Sturgess, trans, Corvina, Budapest, 1982.
Mikszáth, Kálmán, *A Strange Marriage* [1900], G. Farkas, trans, Corvina, Budapest, 1964.
Modern Hungarian Poetry, Miklós Vajda, ed, Columbia University Press, New York, 1977.
Molnár, Ferenc, *The Guardsman* [1910], modern version by Frank Marcus, Eyre Methuen, London, 1978.
Molnár, Ferenc, *Liliom* [1909], B. F. Glazer, trans, 1921, adapted as the musical *Carousel* by Rodgers and Hammerstein, 1956.
Molnár, Ferenc, adapted by P. G. Wodehouse, *The Play's the Thing* [1926], New York, 1927, and in P. G. Wodehouse, *Four Plays*, Methuen, London, 1983.

Molnár, Ferenc, *The Paul Street Boys* [1907], L. Rittenberg, trans, Macy-Masius, New York, 1927.
Molnár, Ferenc, *The Plays of Ferenc Molnár*, Jarrolds, London, 1927.
Móricz, Zsigmond, *Seven Pennies and Other Short Stories* (includes 'Sullen Horse', 1934), George F. Cushing, trans, Corvina, Budapest, 1988. **Extract 7.**
Móricz, Zsigmond, *Be Faithful unto Death* [1920], L. Körösi, trans, Corvina, Budapest, 1962.
Nádas, Péter, 'A Tale about Fire and Knowledge' [1988], Z. Kövecses, trans, in *The New Hungarian Quarterly*, Vol 30, No 116, Budapest, 1989. **Extract 9.** Also excerpts from *Book of Memoirs* in *The New Hungarian Quarterly*, Vol 25, No 95, Budapest, 1984, and in *Storm*, No 1, London, 1991; 'Family Portrait against a Purple Sunset', in *Nothing's Lost*, Budapest, 1988.
Nemes Nagy, Ágnes, *Selected Poems*, Bruce Berlind, trans, International Writing Program, Iowa City, IA, 1980.
Nemes Nagy, Ágnes, *Between: Selected Poems*, Hugh Maxton, trans, Corvina, Budapest, and Dedalus, Dublin, 1988.
Németh, László, *Guilt* [1936], Gyula Gulyás, trans, Peter Owen, London, 1966.
Németh, László, *Revulsion* [1947], Kathleen Szász, trans, Eyre and Spottiswoode, London, 1965.
New Hungarian Drama (Sütő, Páskándi, Csurka, Spiró and Kornis), Eugene Brogyányi, ed, Corvina, Budapest, 1991.
Nothing's Lost, Lajos Illés, ed, Corvina, Budapest, 1988. (Modern short stories.)
Old Hungarian Literary Reader, Tibor Klaniczay, ed, Corvina, Budapest, 1985.
Orbán, Ottó, *The Blood of the Walsungs: Selected Poems*, George Szirtes, ed, Corvina, Budapest,

and Bloodaxe Books, Newcastle, 1993. **Extract 4.**

Ottlik, Géza, *School at the Frontier* [1959], Harcourt, Brace & World, New York, 1966.

Parsons, Nicholas T., *Hungary: A Travellers' Guide*, Christopher Helm, London, 1990. (Contains useful information on sites of literary interest.)

Petőfi, Sándor, translations of selected prose and poetry in Köpeczi, Béla, *Sándor Petőfi, Rebel or Revolutionary?*, Edwin Morgan and G. F. Cushing, trans, Corvina, Budapest, 1974.

Petőfi, Sándor, 'The Alföld', in *Hungarian Helicon*, Watson Kirkconnell, trans, Széchenyi Society Inc, Calgary, 1985. **Extract 6.**

Petri, György, *Night Song of the Personal Shadow*, Clive Wilmer and George Gömöri, trans, Bloodaxe Books, Newcastle-upon-Tyne, 1991.

Plough and the Pen, The: Writings from Hungary, 1930–1956, Ilona Duczyńska and Karl Polányi, eds, foreword by W. H. Auden, McClelland & Steward, London, 1963.

Pilinszky, János, *Selected Poems*, Ted Hughes and János Csokits, trans, Carcanet, Manchester, 1977. Revised and enlarged as *The Desert of Love*, Anvil, London, 1989. **Extract 12.**

Pilinszky, János, *Crater* (*Poems 1974–75*), Peter Jay, trans, Anvil

Press, London, 1978.

Present Continuous, István Bart, ed, Corvina, Budapest, 1985. (Modern short stories.)

Radnóti, Miklós, *Forced March*, Clive Wilmer and George Gömöri, trans, Carcanet, Manchester, 1979.

Radnóti, Miklós, *The Complete Poetry*, Emery George, trans, Ardis, Ann Arbor, MI, 1980.

Saecula Hungariae, Széchenyi Arts Centre, Budapest, 1985. (Twelve small volumes containing writing on Hungarian culture through the ages.)

Tezla, Albert, *Hungarian Authors, A Bibliographical Handbook*, Harvard University Press, Cambridge, MA, 1970.

Tezla, Albert, *Hungarian Literature, An Introductory Bibliography*, Harvard University Press, Cambridge, MA, 1964.

Vas, István, *Through the Smoke: Selected Poems*, Corvina, Budapest, 1989.

Weöres, Sándor, *Eternal Moment: Selected Poems*, Anvil Press, London, 1988.

Weöres, Sándor, 'Still So Many Things' [1980], William Jay Smith, trans, in *Ma – Today, An Anthology of Contemporary Hungarian Literature*, Corvina, Budapest, 1987. **Extract 10.**

Weöres, Sándor, see also Juhász, Ferenc, and Weöres, Sándor, above.

Extracts

(1) BUDA

Gyula Krúdy, *The Crimson Coach*

Krúdy was a master of lyrical prose. His stories have a dreamlike and timeless quality that sets them apart from other modern Hungarian writing. In this extract, 'Matthias' is King Matthias Corvinus (1440–1490), the great Renaissance ruler of Hungary, whose castle dominated Castle Hill, and 'Sigismund' is Sigismund of Luxembourg (1368–1437) who became King of Hungary in 1387.

Mr Rezeda lived in Buda, on Castle Hill, and at night when he walked home he often met the old kings who emerged from the stone wall. Rezeda doffed his hat, well-mannered, to Matthias in his student's cloak or the grim, black-bearded Sigismund and stood, his head bowed, near the bastion until the ghostly figures of the ancient kings, the shadows woven from the mist of autumn night, the silver of the pale moon and the dully-echoing bell-strokes of the historic towers disappeared somewhere along the castle wall. At other times he stopped, listening, in one or other of the deeply slumbering streets, as if he heard from underground, the cellars or arched tunnels under the Castle, the sound of revelry. From deep down it sounded: the voice of the fifes, the clinking of the metal winecups, the wine-sodden singing of the revellers. It was the same sound as the singing of soldiers at night as the rushing train carries them across the plains to the wars. Who knows what old king's stalwarts had remained behind, making merry in the cellar under the Castle; the doors had been locked from outside, the archway of the entrance had collapsed, blocking the exit for ever . . .

Then maids-in-waiting, wrapped in hooded cloaks, slipped past him in the silent night and their steps were as soundless as the graveyard breeze. One or the other had golden heels to her slipper. The cloak touched Mr Rezeda's shoulder, but he never permitted himself the unchivalrous act of spying on the ladies of olden times, haunting the night. The golden-heeled slippers carried their mistresses secretly along the twisting streets of Castle Hill to some ancient house where the knight of past centuries must have been certainly waiting.

Perhaps our melancholy hero took lodgings on Castle Hill so that his midnight walk should differ from those of the young men of Pest. Mr Rezeda loved mysteries and the night.

(2) BUDAPEST

Attila József, *Night in the Slums*

The poet grew up in the slums of Budapest, whose grimness here inspires one of his finest lyric poems (this is not the complete poem).

The workshops stand
like a ruin;
within
the thickest gloom
a plinth for silence to assume.

On the windows of the textile factory
the bright moon now climbs
in a cluster of light,
the moon's soft light
is a thread at the boards of the looms,
and all through the idle night
the darkened machines weave the dreams
of the weaver-girls – the unravelled dreams.

Farther on, iron-works, nut-and-bolt works
and cement works, bounded by a graveyard.
Family vaults alive with echoes.
The factories sleep with their arms over
the sombre secret of their resurrection.
A cat comes poking a paw through the railings.
The superstitious workman catches
a will-o-the-wisp – a flash of
brilliance – the cold
glitter of beetle-backed dynamos.

A train-whistle.

The damp explores the greyness,
probes the leaves of splintered trees,
lays the dust more heavily
along the streets.

(3) BUDAPEST

Dezső Kosztolányi, *Anna Édes*

The author was one of the most elegant stylists in both prose and verse. His novel is set in the Budapest he knew and loved immediately after the first world war. Gerbeaud is still a fashionable pâtisserie, in Vörösmarty Square. Váci utca is the heart of Pest, now a pedestrian shopping street. Crown Prince utca is now Petőfi Sándor Street.

It was a mild, dreamy afternoon, idyllic and fresh, a winter afternoon when one's appetite for life is keener than ever. The town was covered in a coat of crisp snow. Snow had settled on the manes of the lions at the entrance to the Chain Bridge: they looked as though they were wearing white headscarves. Skates jingled in women's hands as they hurried to ice-rinks, sleighbells tinkled. The frost, severe yet healthy, brought a glow to people's faces. Chandeliers sparkled in the Gerbeaud *konditorei* and Váci utca and Crown Prince utca, and all the old nineteenth-century streets of the city centre were aglow with shops and window displays where everything seemed more desirable, more entrancing than ever before: the shoes, the books, the flasks of mineral water arranged on a mossy rock beside a miniature fountain, the jars of quince jelly, the little piles of hazelnuts and walnuts, and the heaps of tasty, still moist Tunisian dates, everything suggesting a distant childhood and memories of presents and Santa Claus. The whole theatrical spectacle was aided and abetted by the sky which changed momently. First it loomed apple green behind Mount Gellért, then it blushed a deep pink over the Royal Palace, then again it melted into a soft ashen grey which was quickly pierced by the tiny powerful winter stars.

(4) BUDAPEST

Ottó Orbán, *Around My Stony Cradle*

Born in Budapest in 1936, Orbán experienced the horror of war and the destruction of his birthplace as a child. War has been a constant theme in his work. He is a versatile and outspoken writer, whose verse ranges from prose-poems to 14-line 'sonnets', of which this is an example. 'Illyés' refers to Gyula Illyés ◊, who lived in Buda. 'Spring of 45' – Budapest was besieged by Russian troops between December 1944 and February 1945, by which time the city was in ruins.

Illyés did not like Budapest –
of course he lived in Budapest at the time,
and not where he said the worthwhile people lived.
For my part, cruising these streets some fifty years
is like living with a woman you don't know,
precisely because you know her all too well . . .
Love has always been adept at contradictions;
I've seen so many towns, I'm dripping with them,
but only one I've seen in ruins; her.
her uncombed hair of grey smoke straggling over her brow,
and under her torn furs the tanks creeping like lice . . .
I'll never forget while I live, how she shook herself, spring of 45,
the small-time whore in her skirt of light. Hope lures
the future to her foul mattress and winks: *You coming, kid?*

(5) THE DANUBE

Mór (Maurus) Jókai, *Timar's Two Worlds*

One of the most widely read Hungarian novels begins with a graphic description of a boat journey up the Danube. The author, Mór Jókai, was the most popular and prolific Hungarian Romantic novelist.

A mountain chain, pierced through from base to summit – a gorge four miles in length walled in by lofty precipices; between their dizzy heights the giant stream of the Old World – the Danube.

We seem to approach a temple built by giants, with rocky pillars, towering columns and wonderful colossi on its lofty frieze, stretching out in a perspective of four miles and, as it winds, discovering new domes with other groups of natural masonry and other wondrous forms. One wall is smooth as polished granite, red and white veins zigzagging across it like mysterious characters in the handwriting of God; in another place the whole face is rusty brown, as if of solid iron; here and there the oblique strata suggest the daring architecture of the Titans. At the next turn we are met by the portal of a Gothic cathedral, with its pointed gables, its clustered basaltic columns; out of the dingy wall shines now and again a golden speck like a glimpse of the Ark of the Covenant – there sulphur blooms, the ore-flower. But living blossoms also deck the crags; from the crevices of the cornice hang green festoons. These are great foliage-trees and pines, whose dark masses are interspersed with frost-flecked garlands of red and gold.

Now and then the mouth of some valley makes a break in the endless dizzy precipices, and allows a peep into a hidden paradise untrodden by man.

Here between two cliffs lies a deep shadow, and into this twilight shines like a fairy world the picture of a sunny vale, with a forest of wild vines, whose small red clusters lend colour to the trees and whose bright leaves weave a carpet below. No human dwelling is visible; a clear stream winds along, from which deer drink fearlessly; then the brook throws its silver ribbon over the edge of the cliff. Thousands pass by the valley, and each one asks himself who lives there.

Then follows another temple more huge and awful than the first; the towering walls drawing closer by three hundred yards and soaring three thousand feet into the sky.

(6) THE GREAT PLAIN
Sándor Petőfi, *The Alföld*

The most famous 19th century lyric poet Sándor Petőfi was a native of the Great Plain, whose beauty he extols in the following lines from this well known poem.

Upwards I mount in ecstasies of thought
Above the earth, to cloud-heights still more near,
And see beneath the image of the plain
From Danube to the Tisza smiling clear.

Tinkling beneath a sky mirage-possessed
Kis-Kunság's fatted herds by hundreds stray;
At noon beside the well's long windlass waits
The double trough to which they make their way.

Stampeding herds of horses, as they run,
Thunder across the wind with trampling hoof,
As lusty herdsmen's whoops resound again
And noisy whips crack out in sharp reproof.

Across the gentle bosom of the farm
Soft breezes hold the swaying wheat enthralled
And crown the pleasant beauty of the scene
With myriad gleams of living emerald.

(7) HORTOBÁGY

Zsigmond Móricz, *Sullen Horse*

*The novelist Zsigmond Móricz was a chronicler of contemporary
Hungarian life. This short story, written in 1934, is set in the
Great Plain at the time of the great annual fair by Hortobágy
Inn. The 'puszta', in Eastern Hungary, is the wide-open space
of the Great Plain.*

The village comes awake too. Now the tiny houses stand there in the
white light of dawn.

The horses are let out. They run between the houses, their numbers
gradually growing, without a single human being to accompany them;
they all know their own route. They are off to the puszta.

Children watch them go. And even from the windows it is only the
children who watch them. The adults go off to harvest and the village
is left to the children.

By morning the puszta is a miraculous world; morning belongs to the
animals. Cows move over the flat ground singly and in groups, then
merge into immense herds. Lambs come along, so do sheep, suddenly
raising their heads on the banks of the little ditch and bleating to the
sky.

A cow on the top of a six-foot mound looks as if it is about to take off
into the heavens.

Hungarian ewes surge forward; their horns are sharp and their long
woolly fleece droops low. They cannot find space for themselves on the
vast puszta and nudge and bump into each other.

Geese fly off cackling and cover the pasture.

Pigs grunt. They dig at the soil.

The puszta comes to life.

Herdsman Sárkány nods to his son who lets out his long whip and
cracks it. The herd of horses circles round at a gallop, rejoicing in its
freedom. The boy once again pulls his hat down over his eyes.

'You've got what it takes to be a horseherd!' his father rebukes him.
'You've got Sárkány blood in you. Your father's a Sárkány, your
grandfather was a Sárkány and all your ancestors were Sárkánys . . .
They're ploughing up the Hortobágy and there are fewer horseherds
. . . Their glory's coming to an end. But there'll always be a place for a
Sárkány on the Hortobágy . . .'

(8) HUNGARY: THE INTELLECTUAL

György Konrád, *The Loser*

*Konrád has been a controversial figure since his first novel A
látogató (The Case Worker), 1969, offended the Communist
authorities at home and won admiration abroad. In The Loser
(literally and more appropriately 'The Accomplice'), he reflects
on the dubious role of the intellectual in modern Central Europe.*

If you extricate yourself from the state culture, writing becomes an
adventure. Pulling out your notebook from its hiding place and making
entries in it amounts to engaging in subversive activity. The words can
be confiscated; they can be turned against you as part of an indictment.
Anarchists lug around bombs in their briefcases – here you just slip your
diary in your bag, and presto you've become an outlaw. A man can
come up to you on the street, flash his badge, and quietly ask to see
what's in the briefcase. The police division in charge of intellectuals
exists to prevent intellectuals from defining themselves. I don't just
look for new hiding places for my notes; I keep censoring them. Facts
can't be recorded, only opinions, and mine alone. A record of events
that includes names, places and other factual information is state
security's favourite reading matter. To make sure I risk only my own
neck, I generalize. The combined strength of the state is sustained by
the combined weight of public inertia – the mere perception of this fact
is considered a guerrilla operation. An honor guard made up of
camouflaged police cars, the excited bustle of several hundred detec-
tives whose only task is to prevent a single study from seeing the light of
day is the state's tribute to independent thought.

The higher the state rises over the social edifice, the more paradigmatic each brick becomes – and the more each built-in being knows
and likes his place in the great wall. If his superiors like him, the brick
is happy; if not, the brick is miserable. Education is an all-
encompassing, cradle-to-grave campaign to make a brick out of
everyone. There are no gray areas; the state culture has a ready-made
statement on just about everything. If you don't want to run up against
taboos, be sure your mind gropes around ever so gingerly. Better yet, do
not have anything in your head that was not put in by the culture – that
way you won't entertain thoughts that might induce you to dissemble.
Do not simply turn *down* the person who asks you to sign a letter of
protest – turn him *in*.

(9) Hungary: Language and Meaning

Péter Nádas, *A Tale about Fire and Knowledge*

Péter Nádas, born in Budapest in 1942, was both photographer and journalist before becoming one of the leading prose-writers in Hungary.

One hot summer night, Hungary was set on fire at all four corners by unknown persons for no apparent reason under unknown circumstances. All we know is that the fire started at Ágfalva in the west, at Tiszabecs in the east, at Nógrádszakáll in the north and at Kübekháza in the south. The stubble and the fields made dry by the drought were burning, and shortly after midnight the fire reached the first houses in the villages. Even the most gentle and innocent of breezes blowing across the borders at Ágfalva from the west, at Tiszabecs from the east, at Nógrádszakáll from the north and at Kübekháza from the south was driving the flames towards the interior of the country. Unaware of all this, Budapest was asleep.

Although it was announced as the seventh item in the morning news that comprehensive fire-drills were being held in the western, eastern, northern and southern counties, from this insignificant news item every Hungarian knew that the event was significant.

Although everybody knew that the news item meant something different from what it meant, everybody pretended not to know what it meant. For example, in the Hungarian language of the time, significant meant insignificant and insignificant meant significant, though these words had not completely lost their original meanings either, and therefore there could be no public agreement as to how to define them. There was merely a tacit agreement to define what non-existent public agreement could not mean.

If the words, through some happy coincidence, might have lost their original meanings, they would have acquired new ones, which however was inconceivable without first making individual knowledge public, without a new public agreement. For this reason, then, almost every word of their language meant something different from what it meant according to their individual knowledge or their common non-knowledge, and they had to try to work out the meanings of words sometimes on the basis of the speaker's position, and sometimes on the basis of the new sense relative to the original. And if a word had apparently lost its meaning, since it could not be understood either on the basis of its sense or the speaker's position, then this impossibility acquired a more profound meaning than if the word had actually meant something. Words with incomprehensible meanings in the language of the Hungarians referred to the deep human community, of which otherwise they were not allowed to think.

(10) HUNGARY: MEMORIES

Sándor Weöres, *Still So Many Things*

Sándor Weöres was a prolific virtuoso poet whose work ranged from children's rhymes to sombre metaphysical verse, often influenced by Near-Eastern mythology and Chinese philosophy.

There are still so many things to be told,
things we have lived, learned, observed;
and the meetings that occurred so many times
and those that took place only once.

Every flower is waiting to be mentioned,
every handful of dust is worthy of note,
but only one of them will fit into the telling,
and of that one fragments only.

When it comes to memories, man is a multimillionaire,
but a pauper when it comes to recording them;
almost everything gets left out of a book
and only bits and pieces, along with the dream, remain.

(11) HUNGARY: PERSECUTION

Miklós Mészöly, *Lament for a Mother*

Mészöly is an innovator and experimenter; his stories are muted and mysterious, and his style is deliberately understated and allusive.

The war ended as usual, with contradictory hopes. And law and order were able to perform their eternal role: while embodying new justice in the law, they did not forget those injustices which, it is customary to believe, protect the new justice. They soon discovered that the husband, with criminal intent, had allowed water to inundate the fertile plain around the town at the time of the spring floods. The court, however hard it tried, could not make anything out of the show-trial, but it served its end anyway. The sluice was his life-work: they charged him with operating it with ill-intent; in vain was he cleared of the charge, he never recovered from it. He brushed any defence aside, but left doors and windows open for death. It took five years for the guest to arrive. His agony lasted for several days, during which the woman became dazed. And like her son on that day long past she became almost incapable of movement, she gazed *fixedly* at what was happening and suddenly lost all her previous competence. A single fly circled over the sick-bed; it did not settle, but hovered like a disabled, hysterical vulture. When death ensued, the woman tore her clothes and had a fit of tears and laughter; she kept insisting that only Borjád and Ózsák-puszta had not been flooded. It was then that she moved from the official flat into the back-kitchen she had been allotted. All the same, the trial had far-reaching effects, and she was unable to find work for a long time. There followed a period when women left in widowhood betray with enigmatic calm that they know immeasurably more than men, and not only about the cradle; when with incredible tenacity they manage to tack together a silhouette out of dearth, a silhouette that is 'unharmed by snow and ice' and has much more to do with the minutely-detailed organization of endurance than with happiness. She had received a balanced inheritance from her ancestors: she was able to combine growing vegetables (and sending the surplus to market) with continuing her music (even taking on a few pupils). It was an event when she succeeded in finding a job washing up in the canteen of a local factory.

(12) HUNGARY: SOLITUDE

János Pilinszky, *As I Was*

Pilinszky, a solitary figure scarred by his wartime experiences, is a poet of rare intensity and spiritual power. The bleakness of his vision is enhanced by his economy of language.

As I was at the start
so, all along, I have remained.
The way I began, so I will go on to the end.
Like the convict who, returning
to his village, goes on being silent.
Speechless he sits in front of his glass of wine.

(13) LAKE BALATON

András Fodor, *A vízrenéző*

The poet, a native of the Balaton region, here commemorates the painter József Egry (1883–1951), whose atmospheric canvases capture the luminous radiance of the lake. The title may be translated as 'The Water-Gazer'.

The silken, pearly-coloured lake
clings to the sickle of the shore
where shimmers on the water's face

the shadow of each mirrored tor.
How pure the air that meets the sky –
the sky the vault of silence there!
And perfume like a gentle mist
floats to the greying upper air.

(14) RÁCEGRES, TRANSDANUBIA

Gyula Illyés, *People of the Puszta*

*Gyula Illyés was one of the leading writers of the century. In
1936 he published this classic survey of the landless peasantry,
based on his own boyhood among them. In Western Hungary,
'puszta' is the name for a conglomeration of farm buildings and
dwellings on a large estate.*

We may well assume that Rácegres, like all the Transdanubian pusztas,
was once a flourishing place. Today it is a warm, cosy little hollow in
the folds of the hills, sheltered from storm and tempest; even figs grow
there. From it rise the sounds of piglets and babies squealing, oxen
lowing and bailiffs grumbling; to the outside world these are the only
signs of life. It is invisible even to the traveller who passes right by it, or
rather flounders above it in the sea of sand which forms the main road
from Simontornya to Sárszentlőrinc, flanked by tall gleditsias. From
outside the puszta is hidden by a thick barrier of leaves which seal it off
as hermetically as the lid of a pot. From the road a steep narrow track
leads down to the puszta.

Running up this same steep narrow track from time to time, I would
peep at the outside world, at my native land, at Europe. The highroad
was already a foreign world, dangerous and forbidden. Once or twice a
week gipsies, tradesmen or wedding-parties would go past. On the other
side the count's pinewoods stretched into the far distance, with the
cattle-pastures in the foreground. Just like the gophers who poked their
curious heads out of the holes down there in the pastures, the bolder
ones even standing on their back legs to see further, I would push my
head out of the security and warmth of the little valley; I would sniff the
air curiously and observe the country round, longing to go ever further
afield. This is how I remember those days . . .

All in all, I came to know the countryside in every detail like the
back of my hand. Came to know it? What did I see in it then? Beautiful
hillsides, single wheatfields that stretched as far as the eye could see,
fields of tall maize like forests where one might get lost for hours before
reaching the far side, thickets of broom and willow by the misty rivers,
and here and there a village or two, to which at first I cautiously gave a

wide berth, like the wild beasts of the field to whom I felt more akin than to human beings.

(15) TRANSDANUBIA

Ferenc Juhász, *Village Elegy*

Born in a Transdanubian village, Ferenc Juhász is a major poet and literary figure; he often derives inspiration from the country-side. This extract is not the complete poem.

On uptorn rushes autumn frosts are grey
on nails and glass, in summer flung away;
a dried-up toad lies stiff, grass-stalks are done;
purple mists roll across the fading sun.

Stone-rose and mallow dally; nests are bare;
statued Saint John smiles in the frosty air;
old bird-filth fouls his fingers and his face,
but his stone-smile still beams with heavenly grace.

The sparrow, crow and gull in mist lament,
girls for the dance on dressing are intent;
young men are courting now tomorrow's bride;
they drink and whoop their nervousness to hide.

Biographies and important works

ADY, Endre (1877–1919). The most controversial Hungarian twentieth-century poet, startled the literary world with his *Új versek* (*New Poems*) in 1906, and continued to rouse passions with subsequent volumes. They contain a heady mixture of erotic passion, radical politics, patriotic despair, love of money, Calvinist theology, apocalyptic visions and Messianic prophecy, all couched in strict metrical forms but wildly exuberant language of which symbolism was the main feature. Conservative critics deemed him unintelligible and traitorous; younger writers hailed him as a genius. Though associated with the journal *Nyugat*, Ady was a lonely figure who castigated Hungary as a cultural backwater and prophesied doom. During the first world war, which appeared to fulfil his dire predictions, he protested vigorously against the inhumanity of the conflict in verse that had now been refined and simplified. Ady's journalism displayed the same passionate language and concerns as his verse. Not surprisingly, he founded no school and remains a unique phenomenon in modern Hungarian literature. His verse is extremely difficult to translate, and only some of the versions in the large collection *Poems of Endre Ady*, 1969, are successful. Some of his prose appears in *The Explosive Country*, 1977.

ARANY, János (1817–1882). With the publication in 1847 of the first part of his trilogy *Toldi*, Arany won both recognition and the friendship of his younger contemporary Petőfi ◊. Arany was essentially an epic poet, scholarly and well versed in the classics; it is therefore no surprise that his hero was a strong man, essentially good, but flawed. His violent temper led him to commit murder, but after various adventures he received a royal pardon. Arany told his story simply, but with colourful imagery and linguistic artistry, features that became typical of his verse, and careful attention to historical accuracy. This was even more true of his projected Hun trilogy, of which he completed only the first part, *Buda halála* (*The Death of King Buda*), 1863. Again this depicted a flawed hero, Attila, who might conquer the world if he could only master himself. Like Kemény ◊, Arany was deeply disturbed by the failure of the 1848 revolution and the loss of Petőfi; he too probed the psychology of human behaviour, with results best seen in his remarkable psychological ballads, written at various times during his life. If Petőfi represented a peak in lyric verse, Arany was his counterpart in epic. All his work was deliberately Hungaro-centred; indeed he scorned

cosmopolitanism. He was also a fine essayist and a brilliant translator of both Aristophanes and Shakespeare.

BABITS, Mihály (1883–1941). Poet, novelist and essayist, Babits was the most scholarly writer of his age. He was rooted in the classics, with a particular love of Greek culture, and had a wide knowledge of European and especially English literature. In his verse he strove to write 'objective lyric', rejecting both personal and national concerns that were typical of Hungarian verse-tradition. A diffident and solitary writer, he was nevertheless driven, by the threat of Fascism to the Europe he loved, to write a powerful confession of faith in human values (*Jónás könyve* – *The Book of Jonah* – 1938, supplemented by *Jónás imája* – *Jonah's Prayer* – 1939). His wide-ranging themes reflect his abiding interest in all facets of contemporary European life and culture, as does his brilliant history of European literature (*Az európai irodalom története*, revised edition, 1936). His novels are experimental, often exploring psychological phenomena: *A gólyakalifa* (*The Stork King*), 1913, translated as *The Nightmare*, 1966, follows the tragedy of a youth who lives a second life in his dreams. Babits was an accomplished translator not only of medieval Latin hymns and erotic verse but also of Dante's *Divine Comedy*. As Editor of *Nyugat* in its last years, which died with him, and penetrating essayist, he exercised a profound and civilizing influence on a whole generation of younger writers, despite attempts by the Communist authorities to play down his role.

DÉRY, Tibor (1894–1977). Novelist, playwright and short-story writer, Déry joined the Hungarian Communist Party in 1919 and as a result spent most of the inter-war period in exile. Although he began to write during those years, it was not until 1947, with the publication of A befejezetlen mondat (The Unfinished Sentence), that he was acclaimed as a good Communist writer; the book describes life in the illegal Party in Hungary in the pre-war period. Déry fell foul of the new régime in 1952 when his novel Felelet (Answer) was condemned as pessimistic, and again in 1956 with his subtle short novel Niki. After the 1956 revolution, which he supported, he was sentenced to nine years' imprisonment but was released in 1960 after international protests. He then became a prolific writer with a wide range of themes, mainly inspired by current events. He also discarded the turgidity of style that had characterized his early works. Other works published in English are The Giant; Behind the Brick Wall and Love and The Portuguese Princess.

in English, including Helping Verbs of the Heart; 'No Title: This Isn't It Either' in the anthology Nothing's Lost, 1988; 'The Transporters', in A Hungarian Quartet, 1991; and The Book of Hrabal.

ESTERHÁZY, Péter (1950–). Novelist, essayist and short-story writer, Esterházy combines linguistic virtuosity with an enquiring mind that leads him constantly to question traditional literary norms and forms and to consider how relevant the accepted commitment of Hungarian literature to national causes is in the modern world. He uses pastiche, allegory, an impish sense of humour and textual and typographical innovations to express his views, and is regarded either as an iconoclast or as a bold innovator. Much of his earlier work was collected in Bevezetés a szépirodalomba (Introduction to Literature), 1986. He is a tireless experimenter with the process of literary communication and a thorn in the flesh to those who seek to enlist literature in a particular cause. Some of his work has appeared

FODOR András (1929–). Poet and essayist, Fodor offers a good example of the writer who triumphs over political pressure and personal concerns to compose poetry of beauty and lasting value, despite the vicissitudes of post-war life in Hungary. Like an artist, he is sensitive to colour and scenery (Extract 13); he also has an ear for music, and this too emerges not only in his often expressed love of Bartók but also in the musicality of his lyric. His technical skill is evident in the variety of his metrical inventions. He stresses the importance of humanity in an often inhumane world in a tone that is gentle but urgent. Fodor has also published a perceptive biography of Attila József ◊ (Szólj költemény, 1971) and two important documents of the Communist period. The first is his diary of encounters with the philosopher and art-historian Lajos Fülep (*Ezer este Fülep Lajossal*, 1986) and the second the account of his life at the Eötvös College in its last days before its closure by the Communist authorities (*A Kollégium*, 1991).

ILLYÉS, Gyula (1902–1983). Illyés was one of the most respected writers of the twentieth century, a lyric poet, novelist, playwright and essayist. Of landless peasant stock, he nevertheless acquired a university education and spent some years in Paris, the effect of which is seen not only in his early love of the avant-garde but also in the crisp clarity of his style in both prose and poetry. He had a passionate concern for both the underprivileged and for the future of his nation. His largely autobiographical *Puszták népe* (*People of the Puszta*), 1936 (Extract 14) became a classic of the populist movement. Illyés had an overriding concern for justice and humanity, and refused to commit himself to the post-war Communist cause, although it

Gyula Illyés

appeared to have achieved some of the reforms he had urged. His famous outburst *Egy mondat a zsarnokságról* (*One Sentence on Tyranny*), written in 1950 and published in 1956, reveals his thoughts on the situation at that time. He voiced his concern for the future of Hungariandom in prose and verse of controlled passion, continuing the tradition of the great nineteenth-century poets and often incurring the wrath of the Communist authorities. In his later years he became a master of the brief epigrammatic verse. He left a rich legacy of beautifully crafted poetry and thought-provoking prose. The publication of his diary notes (*Naplójegyzetek*, 1986–) adds to his fascination. English versions of his verse appear in several anthologies and in *Selected Poems*, 1971.

JÓKAI, Mór (Maurus) (1825–1904). Still the most popular Romantic Hungarian novelist and by far the most prolific writer of his age, Jókai possessed a fertile imagination and a fluent style. He set his plots in the past, present and future and in all parts of the world, with a preference for exotic regions where he could use his undoubted gift for description and dramatic action. His characterization was generally weak, as his critics frequently complained; his male heroes tended to be superhuman and his female characters virtuous and passive. But the public, both at home and abroad, loved him, for he offered a welcome escape from reality in a rapidly changing and confusing world. Some of his novels, however, were related to contemporary events, such as the 1848 revolution, which is recalled in *A kőszívű ember fiai* (*The Baron's Sons*), 1869. One of his best novels, and the one that established his fame abroad, was *Az arany ember*

(*Timar's Two Worlds*), 1873 (Extract 5), whose hero leads a double life and possesses a complexity of character unusual in Jókai. During his long life, Jókai published 202 volumes. His great achievement was to introduce a natural and unaffected style into both narrative and dialogue, thus liberating the Hungarian novel from the stiffness and didacticism that so often afflicted it. His popularity in Britain, where some 27 of his works were published in translation, long outlived him; cheap editions of them were published up to the second world war.

JÓZSEF, Attila (1905–1937). József grew up in the poverty of the **Budapest** slums and was orphaned in youth. Intellectual curiosity, an innate talent for poetry and a good education blended with his realization that he was an outcast in society; this led him to publish verse expressing both his own longing for love and sympathy for the poor (Extract 2). At first he experimented with avant-garde forms of expression, then turned to traditional verse-forms and proved a master of them. He joined the illegal Hungarian Communist Party; some of his poetry of the early 1930s exhibits typical themes and slogans. But if Marx satisfied his desire for social reform, it was Freud, he believed, who could liberate the individual. His attempt to marry the two ideas led to his expulsion from the Party. Driven increasingly into isolation and deep depression, he committed suicide at **Balatonszárszó**, leaving behind a unique corpus of lyric verse that could be savagely powerful or delicate, intensely personal or universal in its appeal. He found beauty in the slums as well as in the countryside – indeed, beauty is one of the hallmarks of his verse. The post-war

Communist regime extolled him as a hero, even rewriting some of his verse to make it more conformist and excluding poems that revealed his desperate search for God. The genuine texts were restored only in 1984 (*József Attila összes versei*, critical edition, Béla Stoll, ed). Selections of József's work have appeared in English anthologies and also in *Selected Poems and Texts*, 1973.

JUHÁSZ, Ferenc (1928–). Poet and editor, Juhász is very much a product of the post-war age. Born in a **Transdanubian** village and educated at one of the short-lived 'people's colleges', he quickly adopted the populism officially urged on would-be writers. His first poems were mediocre but officially acceptable, but he soon abandoned rustic simplicity (Extract 15) for an infinitely more complex idiom to match his fertile imagery in which mythical beasts, lush vegetation and the achievements of modern technology proliferate. His language became increasingly abstruse with its strange compound words, and his

Ferenc Juhász

style altered accordingly. The finest example of this stage, whose English translation won the admiration of W.H. Auden, is 'A szarvassá változott fiú kiáltozása a titkok kapujából' ('The Boy Changed into a Stag Cries Out at the Gate of Secrets') 1956. It draws its inspiration from Bartók's *Cantata Profana*. His later verse has varied between strict verse forms and exuberant prose-poetry. The two meet in a volume dedicated to the memory of his mother, *Föld alatti liliom* (*Lily Beneath the Ground*), 1991, which expresses his belief in 'dense, pure enraptured lyric'. A selection of his earlier verse appeared in *The Plough and the Pen*, edited by Ilona Duczyńska and Karl Polányi, with a foreword by W.H. Auden. Other poems are included in Ferenc Juhász and Sándor Weöres, *Selected Poems*, 1970.

KEMÉNY, Zsigmond (1814–1875). Few writers pondered more deeply or productively on the failure of the 1848 revolution than Kemény. Born into an old Transylvanian family of distinction, he was temperamentally inclined to see tragedy in both national and personal life. The first results of his meditation appeared in two treatises, *Forradalom után* (*After Revolution*), 1850, and *Még egy szó a forradalom után* (*Yet Another Word After the Revolution*), 1851, both concluding that *rapprochement* with Austria was the only sensible course, a highly unpopular idea at the time, but one that Kemény worked for until it was achieved in 1867. His historical novels, set in his homeland of **Transylvania**, are concerned with individual tragedy. Their action is slow and interrupted by long soliloquies in which Kemény displays remarkable psychological insight. His heroes come to grief not through some flaw of character but from external and usually minor mistakes. Kemény was a Calvinist and a fatalist. Unlike many of his contemporaries, he did not believe that virtue was necessarily rewarded or that good invariably triumphed. It is only in modern times that he has gained recognition as a pioneer of the psychological novel. His ponderous style does not make for easy reading. Of his novels *Gyulai Pál* (*Pál Gyulai*), 1847, *A rajongók* (*The Fanatics*), 1858, and *Zord idő* (*Stormy Times*), 1862, show him at his best.

KONRÁD, György (1933–). Novelist and essayist, Konrád studied Hungarian at **Budapest University**, then worked in the guardianship department of a local authority and later in a town-planning institute before becoming a full-time writer. He drew on his experiences at work in the powerful novels *A látogató* (*The Case Worker*), 1969, and *A városalapító* (*The City Founder*), 1977. Both explore the often devastating effect of authoritarian regulations and directives on the lives of those who have to put them into effect as well as on those they are supposed to benefit. Both books aroused a storm of criticism, as did other articles and studies, and Konrád became one of the best-known Hungarian dissidents. A third important novel, *A cinkos* (*The Accomplice*), 1980, was first published in Paris and translated into English (*The Loser*, 1982) before achieving publication in Hungary in 1983 (Extract 8). It is a disturbing reflection on the life of the intellectual in a totalitarian state. It is not surprising that Konrád, who does not conceal his message in coded language or seek to defend his own complicity in the situations he describes, suffered an almost complete ban from legitimate publication in Hungary for a number of years.

KOSZTOLÁNYI, Dezső (1885–1936). Poet, novelist and short-story writer, Kosztolányi was a self-confessed aesthete who cultivated a detached elegance of style, often deceiving readers into believing that he lacked humanity. The most urbane and popular of the writers associated with the journal Nyugat, he revelled in city life and wrote of it with relish and sympathy. His verse is as finely chiselled as his prose, and he was a notable translator from numerous languages. In his most popular verse-cycle A szegény kisgyermek panaszai (Complaints of a Poor Little Child), 1910, he views the world through the eyes of an infant, not mawkishly but with great discrimination and in evocative language. In later years his lyric verse acquired a deeper and more philosophical tone as he battled with cancer. His novels are perceptive studies of human motivation. Nero, a véres költő (Nero, the Bloody Poet), 1922 (translated as Darker Muses), won the admiration of Thomas Mann. Édes Anna (Anna Édes), 1926

DEZSŐ KOSZTOLÁNYI

ANNA ÉDES

TRANSLATED AND WITH
AN INTRODUCTION BY
GEORGE SZIRTES

QUARTET ENCOUNTERS

is a precise account of innocence exploited (Extract 3). Kosztolányi's short stories are among the finest of the genre, with widely ranging themes expressed in polished and colourful language. Also available in English is his short novel Pacsirta (Skylark), 1924.

KRÚDY, Gyula (1878–1933). Novelist and short-story writer, Krúdy was a solitary figure in the Hungarian literary world. He was a prolific writer with a fertile imagination; in all his work atmosphere was more important than action and time was of no consequence. So his best known hero Sinbad, who figured in a large number of his stories published between 1912 and 1917, travels nostalgically to half-remembered places, the scenes of former amorous adventures; Sinbad is ageless and though the setting is usually rural the time may be contemporary or the distant past or a mixture of both (collected edition, Szindbád, 1973). Other favourite themes are the pleasures of city life, and horse-racing and eating in particular. Krúdy revels in fantasy and his prose style heightens it; it is evocative, full of minute descriptions and poetic imagery, sweeping the reader into a dreamlike and colourful world often far removed from everyday concerns. The author himself remains a delighted and mildly ironical observer of the human scene. His novel A vörös postakocsi (The Crimson Coach), 1914, is translated into English (Extract 1). Of his short stories 'Death and the Journalist' appeared in Hungarian Short Stories, 1962, and 'The Last Cigar at the Grey Arab' in the anthology The Kiss, 1993.

MÉSZÖLY, Miklós (1921–). Novelist, playwright and short-story writer

Mészöly achieved fame with his novel *Az atléta halála* (*Death of an Athlete*) in 1966. It is a penetrating study of human behaviour, and pinpointed him as an innovator and experimenter. He continues to write tightly controlled, deliberately muted stories; his style emphasizes his excursions into the grotesque and allegory and his intellectual curiosity. In 1976 his novel *Film*, with its interplay of present and past events, roused Communist critics to fury, an episode that was repeated when it was republished a year later. In a country whose readers invariably search for coded messages in a text, Mészöly is one of the most subtle writers. Examples of his short stories in English anthologies are 'The Falcon', in *Nothing's Lost*, 1988, 'Forgiveness' in *A Hungarian Quartet*, 1991, and 'Lament for a Mother' (Extract 11) in *The Kiss*, 1993.

MIKSZÁTH, Kálmán (1847–1910). Mikszáth remains one of the most popular novelists and short-story writers in Hungary. An eccentric himself (he married his wife twice), he loved human eccentricity and found plentiful examples in his native region of **northern Hungary**, with its mixture of Slovaks and Hungarians in communities where time seemed to stand still and an air of genteel decay persisted. This he portrayed with gentle irony and genuine humour. Many of his stories are little more than anecdotes, of which he was an indefatigable collector, sharpened with lively dialogue. His most popular novel *Szent Péter esernyője* (*St Peter's Umbrella*), 1895, greatly admired by Theodore Roosevelt who visited the author in 1910, illustrates one of Mikszáth's favourite techniques: he introduces two apparently unconnected stories and gradually draws

them together. Several of his books are based on surprising contemporary incidents, such as *Különös házasság* (*A Strange Marriage*), 1900, and *Beszterce ostroma* (*The Siege of Beszterce*), 1895. But he could be sharply critical of contemporary society and politics, as evidenced by *Új Zrínyiász* (*New Zrínyiad*), 1895, in which he resurrects the hero of the Szigetvár siege in the business world of **Budapest**. Mikszáth was a story-teller *par excellence*; rarely did a writer establish a closer relationship with his readers, who are invited to share his obvious delight in his role.

MOLNÁR, Ferenc (Franz) (1878–1952). Molnár has a worldwide reputation as a dramatist, but was also a novelist and short-story writer of distinction. A sharp observer of city life, he was acclaimed in Hungary for his novel *A Pál utcai fiúk* (*The Paul Street Boys*), 1907, an adolescent classic that has been filmed and adapted for the stage. Of his plays *Liliom*, 1909, won greater acclaim as the musical *Carousel*, 1945. P.G. Wodehouse adapted his *Játék a kastélyban*, 1926, as *The Play's the Thing*, 1927; it was also the basis of Tom Stoppard's play *Rough Crossing*, 1985. A *testőr* (*The Guardsman*), 1910, is a frequently staged test of acting ability. His plays in general, though criticized as superficial, reveal a sense of theatre that is rare in Hungary, and may be compared with those of Noël Coward. Like him, Molnár can be sentimental and satirical, and his dialogue is crisp and witty. During the first world war he achieved the remarkable distinction of having his memoirs as a war-correspondent (*Egy haditudósító emlékei*, 1916) published in the *New York Times*. They are a personal record of the suffering he had encountered at the front, and evidence of the sympathy he showed elsewhere for the underprivileged – see *Az éhes város* (*The Hungry City*), 1901. He emigrated to the USA before the threat of Fascism and died in New York. *Plays of Molnár*, 1927, includes a selection of his most popular pieces.

MÓRICZ, Zsigmond (1879–1942). Novelist, short-story writer and dramatist, Móricz was a precise recorder of contemporary Hungarian life. He was educated in various Calvinist colleges and first undertook research into the folklore of his home region of **north-east Hungary**, a task he enjoyed. There he encountered village life in the raw and found ample material for his early stories of rural poverty, tragedy and inhumanity. He won instant acclaim for the short story 'Hét krajcár' ('Seven Pennies'), 1908, and thereafter became associated with the journal *Nyugat* and its writers. His technique, perfected over many years, was to present a scene in graphic but realistic prose, leaving the reader to draw his own conclusions. He offered no solutions to the social problems he described. Gradually he extended his interest from the peasantry and country gentry to the slum-dwellers of **Budapest**, whose life he describes with both sympathy and humour. Another favourite theme is the relationship between man and woman, reflecting his own fragile and tormented marriages. Móricz was also a fine historical novelist, as seen in his trilogy *Erdély* (*Transylvania*), 1922–35. Among works published in English are his novel *Légy jó mindhalálig* (*Be Faithful unto Death*), 1920, and a selection of short stories in *Seven Pennies*, 1988 (Extract 7).

NÁDAS, Péter (1942–). Nádas worked as cameraman and journalist before devoting his life to literature. His earliest short stories, *A biblia* (*The Bible*), 1967, explore his own youth against a background of the personal conflicts and contradictions of Hungarian society after the second world war. He experiments with symbolic, grotesque and mythological elements in detailed and emotionally charged prose, behind which there always lurk surprises. His *Emlékiratok könyve* (*Book of Memoirs*), 1986, is a skilful blend of narrations in a compelling study of historical continuity and memory. He uses a similar technique in his *Évkönyv* (*Almanach*), 1989, a philosophical chronicle blending diary and memoir. Available in English are excerpts from *Book of Memoirs* in *The New Hungarian Quarterly*, Vol XXV, No 95, Budapest, 1984 and in *Storm*, No 1, London, 1991. The short story 'Family Portrait against a Purple Sunset' appears in the anthology *Nothing's Lost*, 1988, and 'A Tale about Fire and Knowledge' (Extract 9) was published in *The New Hungarian Quarterly*, Vol 30, No 116, Budapest, 1989.

NÉMETH, László (1901–1975). Essayist, playwright and novelist, Németh studied medicine and then applied his powerful intellect to the social and political problems of Hungary after the first world war. Combining social philosophy, utopian thought and a belief in the leading role of the intellectual, he saw himself primarily as an educator of the nation. He wrote and edited single-handed the periodical *Tanú* (*Witness*) in 1932–36, an encyclopaedic survey of contemporary culture and philosophy that aroused widespread discussion in Hungary and particularly among the populists. His novels test his theories, often through female heroines, as in *Iszony* (*Revulsion*),

1947. As a dramatist he is unashamedly didactic, often expressing his views through questing but tragic heroes like John Hus (*Husz János*, 1948), Joseph II (*II. József*, 1954) or Galileo (*Galilei*, 1953); these are all products of the post-war age when Németh chose silence rather than submission to Party direction. As well as *Revulsion*, his 1936 novel *Bűn* (*Guilt*) has been translated.

ORBÁN, Ottó (1936–). A versatile poet and translator, Orbán spent his childhood in war-torn **Budapest**. The horror of his experiences and the loss of his Jewish father left scars as ineradicable as those of Pilinszky ◊. He grew up in a state orphanage, where he was encouraged to write as a therapeutic exercise; there he was regarded as a child prodigy, though later he declared that then he did not

Ottó Orbán

know what poetry was. The strict form and rhythm of Kosztolányi's ◊ verse caught his imagination, and he strove to acquire these disciplines. A spectator of the 1956 revolution, he suffered a breakdown in 1957, then married and in 1960 produced the first of many volumes of verse to general acclaim. He also became a notable translator of contemporary poets, including Allen Ginsberg, under whose influence he became known as Hungary's Beat poet, with some justification. This, however, was merely a stage in an ever-widening range of themes and forms. Some of his finest work is seen in his prose-poetry and his so-called 'sonnets' (Extract 4). His is an individual voice, ironic, scathing, tender and tough in turn; sometimes his language is deliberately unpoetic and at other times he administers sudden shocks which suggest that the impishness of the street-urchin still lurks behind his mature work. A selection of his verse in English, edited by George Szirtes, was published in 1993, entitled *The Blood of the Walsungs*.

OTTLIK, Géza (1912–1990). Novelist and short-story writer, Ottlik was a native of Budapest. He quickly gained a reputation for clarity and precision in his work. His output was relatively small but always excellent. His short stories, collected in *Hamisjátékosok* (*Swindlers*), 1941, and *Minden megvan* (*Nothing's Lost*), enlarged edition 1991, are elegant, ironic and paradoxical. His chief claim to fame is his novel *Iskola a határon* (*School at the Frontier*), 1959, a powerful and well constructed fictional investigation of the ways in which the human spirit can survive in a totalitarian society. One of the best novels to appear in Hungary since the second world war,

it is based on life in the military academy at **Kőszeg**.

PETŐFI, Sándor (1823–1849). Petőfi is the most celebrated Hungarian lyric poet. He is commemorated throughout the country with statues, plaques and street-names – not surprisingly, since he travelled widely and always indicated where he had written his verse. With his youthful impetuosity and splendid natural gift for verse he charmed pre-revolution Hungary. He had a formidable range of styles, from the deceptive simplicity of folksong to high Romanticism (Extract 6) and from tender love poetry to impassioned revolutionary propaganda. His technical virtuosity was unrivalled, as was his refusal to countenance the seriousness of the art of poetry. His life can be charted in his verse, for his output was prodigious, laying him open to the charge of superficiality. This, however, is only partly true, for there are sudden flashes of deep insight in some of his most epigrammatic poems as well as in his longer verses. His romantic appeal was only heightened by his disappearance during a skirmish near **Segesvár** (Sighişoara, Transylvania) in the 1848 revolution. The site in the village of **Fehéregyháza** (**Albeşti**, Transylvania) is marked by a memorial and a small museum. One of his greatest achievements was to introduce Hungarian verse to a wider readership than ever before. He had many imitators, but none succeeded in capturing his magic even though they apparently used the same ingredients. Petőfi's poetry first appeared in English during his short lifetime, in 1847, and has frequently been published since then. A selection of both prose and poetry appears in Béla Köpeczi, *Petőfi, Rebel or Revolutionary?*, 1973.

PILINSZKY, János (1921–1981). Poet and essayist, Pilinszky was a devout Catholic. Overwhelmed by the extent of human suffering he encountered in labour camps during his army service in Germany in the last years of the second world war, he could never rid himself of his memories, which form the main theme of his verse. His terse, uncompromising, bleak poetry is both intensely moving and profoundly disturbing (Extract 12). He wrote with difficulty and his output is comparatively small. But his verse is concentrated, deceptively unstructured and intellectually demanding. The unashamedly Christian moral responsibility he felt so deeply made him a unique phenomenon in a country nominally professing Communist ideals; moreover he is unusual in addressing his message not to Hungarians alone but to mankind in general. Technically he was one of the most accomplished post-war poets. Good English versions of his poetry are found in *Selected Poems*, translated by Ted Hughes and János Csokits, 1976 and revised and enlarged as *The Desert of Love*, 1989. *Crater* (*Poems 1974–75*), translated by Peter Jay, appeared in London in 1978.

RADNÓTI, Miklós (1909–1944). A poet of rare sensitivity, Radnóti began to write under the shadow of Fascism, which eventually brought about his death. His early poetry was experimental, mildly erotic and youthfully iconoclastic (*Pogány köszöntő – Pagan Greetings – 1930*). Later he found it easier to express himself in strict traditional verse forms, and in them affirmed with growing intensity his fear of death and longing for love, its antidote. His finest poems are his classically inspired *Eclogues*, a series begun in 1938, in which he examines the fate of the individual in a world turned upside down; the later eclogues include his own experience as a Jew condemned to forced labour, with the prospect of death always present. Radnóti's purity of form, controlled language and moral dignity place these among the best wartime poems in Hungarian. He was shot dead at **Abda**, near **Győr** on the main road to the Austrian frontier, during a forced march that had begun at a prison-camp in Serbia. In his coat-pocket were discovered his last short poignant verses written during his last days alive. There are numerous translations of his work, including *Forced March*, 1979 and *The Complete Poetry*, 1980, the latter with a good introduction.

VÖRÖSMARTY, Mihály (1800–1855). Poet, critic and dramatist, Vörösmarty fulfilled the desire of the young Hungarian Romantics for a historical epic with his *Zalán futása* (*The Flight of Zalán*), 1825. It was a valiant failure, for though it recalled the glorious past in fine verse, Vörösmarty was essentially a lyric poet, and his poem is remembered for its splendid lyrical passages. After a few further short epics, he turned to drama. Only *Csongor és Tünde* (*Csongor and Tünde*), 1831, which pursues the quest for human happiness in scenes involving both human and fairy elements, has stood the test of time. As a lyric poet, however, he represents the peak of Hungarian Romanticism. He blended his personal worries with national concerns in verse of expressive beauty, pervaded by the underlying pessimism that always haunted him. He did not share the general optimism that preceded the 1848 revolution, and when his forebodings proved justified, he was a broken man. His last poems are a terrifying lapse into the nihilism that shadowed his work. Yet his literary achievement was remarkable. In him vivid imagination was matched by a rare intensity of emotion, and reached expression in graceful verse. He refined the poetic language of the day, rejecting the more extreme neologisms imposed on it by the enthusiastic disciples of Kazinczy (see introductory essay), and in so doing created the modern Hungarian poetic language.

WEÖRES, Sándor (1913–1989). Poet and playwright, Weöres combined erudition, versatility and consummate technical skill in his work. His range was enormous: he wrote attractive children's rhymes and nonsense verse as well as sombre metaphysical poetry. He was influenced by such varied sources as ancient Chinese verse, the myth of Gilgamesh, Polynesian legends and Negro mythology as well as numerous European ideas. His serious lyric verse was highly individual and intellectually demanding; its appeal was universal rather than narrowly Hungarian (Extract 10). But he had a sprightly sense of humour too; this was particularly evident in *Psyche*, 1972, a collection of lyric poems purporting to be the work of an early nineteenth-century Hungarian poetess of remarkable talent; Weöres captures the mood of the period and the eccentricities of its language with obvious relish. He also edited a wide-ranging anthology of forgotten Hungarian verse, entitled *Három veréb hat szemmel* (*Three Sparrows with Six Eyes*), second enlarged edition 1982, it serves as a valuable complement and corrective to the accepted corpus of poetry in Hungary. Selections of his work in English appear in Sándor Weöres and Ferenc Juhász, *Selected Poems*, 1970, and in *Eternal Moment*, 1988.

ROMANIA

Dennis Deletant

'The remote wildness of these uncharted places, the sprawling reed-forests waving their bronze tips in the wind, this deep silence dominating the whole area, all makes you think that you are far from the earth, on a deserted planet.'
Alexandru Vlahuţă,
Picturesque Romania

Romania is the twelfth largest country in Europe (area 237 500 square kilometres), with a population of some 23 million. Most of the population speak Romanian, but there is also a significant Hungarian minority of about 2 million. To the north is the former Soviet Union; the River Danube lies to the south (marking the frontier with Bulgaria); to the east is the coastline of the Black Sea; and to the west Hungary and former Yugoslavia. Running from north to south over half-way down the centre of the country, like a backbone, are the **Carpathian** mountains, which then curve sharply westwards to form an arc, encompassing the plateau of **Transylvania**, one of Romania's three provinces. East and south of the Carpathians are the provinces of **Moldavia** and **Wallachia**, the former characterized by rolling hills, the latter largely a flat, undulating plain.

ROMANIAN HISTORY

Modern Romania is largely the product of the Paris Peace Settlement which followed the first world war. Transylvania had been part of the Habsburg Empire and was awarded to Romania in 1920 on the basis that eleven of the province's fifteen countries had a clear Romanian majority. The incorporation of Bessarabia, with its Romanian majority, was also ratified at the same time, but this territory was annexed by the Soviet Union in 1940 and provided the core for the Soviet Republic of Moldavia which declared its independence as Moldova in 1991.

Origins

The history of the area has been extremely turbulent and there are few periods upon which Romanians can look back with national pride. Geography has played a major role. Situated at the crossroads of Europe, the territory has been prey to successive waves of invaders. Its fertile soil and gold deposits attracted peoples such as the Scythians and Thracians. A tribe of the Thracians, the Dacians, settled here and were conquered by the Romans between AD 101 and 106 during the reign of Trajan. The Romans formed a new province, Dacia, and colonized it with settlers from various parts of the empire. According to most Romanian historians, these came in sufficient numbers to Romanize the local population by implanting Latin language and culture, and the resultant Daco–Romanian people are said to be the direct ancestors of the Romanians. After the withdrawal of the Roman legions between 271 and 275, Dacia again became a gateway to the south for invaders from the Russian steppe and Central Europe, the Daco–Romanians retreating to the mountains and preserving their Latin language.

Another view has it that the Romanians are derived from a wider group of Romanized inhabitants of the Balkans living south of the Danube, known as the Vlachs, although today their language, closely related to Latin and Romanian, survives only in pockets in northern Greece and southern Albania. The ancestors of the Vlachs lived under Roman rule for several centuries, whereas the Dacians were subject to the Romans for a little over one hundred and fifty years. A number of historians, especially Hungarian but also Romanian, have suggested that the Romanians in fact derive from Vlachs who migrated north of the Danube in the twelfth and thirteenth centuries. A mixture of the two views is also possible.

The ethnic composition of what is now Romania was enriched by Hungarian rule over Translyvania. The Hungarian crown encouraged Szekler (Hungarian) and German colonists to settle during the twelfth and thirteenth centuries. Today the Hungarian population of Transylvania has grown to about two million, whereas the number of Germans has dwindled to less than 70 000 as a consequence of emigration to Germany.

The development of medieval states south of the Carpathians occurred some two centuries later. An attempt by the King of Hungary to subjugate Wallachia was successfully resisted by Basarab, a leader of Cuman origin, in a battle fought in the district of **Argeş** in 1330. Hungarian expansion also led to the creation of the sister principality to the east, **Moldavia**. The nobleman Dragoş was granted a Hungarian fiefdom near the river Moldova about 1347, but his successor Bogdan rose against the Hungarian king and laid the foundations of an independent principality.

The fortunes of both Wallachia and Moldavia, from the middle of the fifteenth century until their union in 1859, and their final deliverance from Turkish suzerainty in 1881, when they became the kingdom of Romania, were determined by the imperial ambitions of the Ottoman Turks, the Austrian Habsburgs, and the Russian Romanovs. The only Romanian figures of this period who successfully challenged their more powerful neighbours were Stephen the Great of Moldavia (1457–1504) who defeated the Turks in several battles and Michael the Brave (1593–1601) who briefly united all three provinces. Michael's achievement fired the minds of Romanian nationalists in the nineteenth century and his example was partially emulated in 1859 with the union of Moldavia and Wallachia. It was only in return for Romania's entry into the first world war in 1916 on the Allied side that it was awarded Transylvania in the Treaty of Trianon (June 1920); it was also given Bessarabia (basically present-day Moldova, in the former Soviet Union).

Between the wars

The position of Romania in the period between the first and second world wars proved to be of vital strategic interest to the major powers of Europe. The country's oil reserves and cereals, and its location at the crossroads of southeastern Europe, represented a powerful magnet. Thus in the late 1930s control of Romanian oil, invaluable for the German war machine, became the object of German policy. Conversely, the UK and France sought to deny Germany that control. At the same time the Soviet Union, faced with a continental Europe dominated by Germany, made its own accommodation with Nazi expansion by conspiring, under the terms of the Nazi–Soviet Pact of August 1939, in the carving up of Eastern Europe; among the victims of the Pact was Romania from which the Soviet Union amputated the regions of Bessarabia and Northern Bukovina in 1940.

Internally, Romania was a country of major contrasts and contradictions. The legacy of a different historical experience of the Romanians in these constituent lands, coupled with the diverse ethnic mix of the large minority Hungarian, German and Jewish minority populations which they contained, posed major problems of harmonization and consolidation in the enlarged Romanian state, problems which, in the brief interlude of the interwar period, its leaders had little time, capacity and will to address. The failure to solve them, and the Western democracies provided precious little help to this end, was to blight the country's progress towards modernization and the exercise of genuine democratic rule.

There were contrasts in the pattern of economic development. Transylvania had benefited from Austrian and Hungarian investment until 1914, but the rest of the country remained underdeveloped. Although it possessed great natural wealth, with fertile soil and raw materials such as natural gas, lignite, oil, metals, and forests, Romania lacked the industrial capacity to use these resources to the full, and so the country remained predominantly agricultural, with great discrepancies between town and country. In 1930 80% of the population of 18 million lived in villages. In the more backward regions of Bessarabia and Moldavia education and health services were virtually nonexistent. In these conditions the incidence of infant mortality over the whole country reached the highest levels in Eastern Europe.

The greatest contradiction lay between the façade of Western-type political institutions and the actual practice of government. Under the constitution of 1923 the King had the power to dissolve parliament and appoint a new government. That new government then habitually did its best to manipulate the elections to produce a majority in its own favour. (The only elections deemed to have been relatively free of such manipulation were those of 1928.) Institutionalized corruption was matched by personal corruption. Among a ruling elite which looked upon rapacity as proof of dexterity and cunning, corruption of principles was widespread. This élite was helped by the absence of a native economic, as opposed to bureaucratic, middle-class, since most commerce was in the hands of the largely disenfranchised Jews, who were barred from public service.

Although a radical land reform was introduced after the first world war, governments remained subservient to the interests of the banks and prominent industrialists. The depression of the 1930s fostered a decade of instability in which the xenophobia of the impoverished peasantry was exploited by right-wing movements, principally the Iron Guard, and directed against the Jews. The growth in support for the Guard, with its promise of spiritual regeneration and its programme of combatting 'Jewish communism', stemmed from a widespread disillusionment with parliamentary government. A campaign of murders by the Guard and its leader Corneliu Codreanu's refusal to work with the monarch led King Carol II to institute a personal dictatorship in February 1938 and to have Codreanu assassinated in November. At the same time, Romania's geographical position, and her economic survival, forced her into Hitler's arms.

The second world war

'Nothing could put Romania on Germany's side', remarked an official of the Romanian Foreign Ministry to the British minister in Bucharest in March 1940, 'except the conviction that only Germany could keep the Soviets out of Romania'. That conviction formed quickly after the collapse of France in May 1940 and the Soviet Union's seizure of

Bessarabia and Northern Bukovina one month later. The choice for Romania was no longer between Germany and the Anglo–French, but between Germany and the Soviet Union. After the abdication of King Carol, Romania allied itself with Germany, Italy and Japan. Hitler, by offering Romania's new ruler General Ion Antonescu the chance to gain the lost provinces of Bessarabia and Northern Bukovina, found a willing partner in his attack on the Soviet Union in 1941.

Anglo–American air raids on Romania during 1943 and, more importantly, the Soviet advance in early 1944 led Antonescu to seek armistice terms that would guarantee Romania's independence of Soviet authority. However, the advance of Soviet forces persuaded the young King Michael to arrest Antonescu on 23 August 1944.

Soviet control and the rise of Ceauşescu

Stalin lost little time in imposing his will on the country. In March 1945 he forced the King to appoint a 'Popular Front' government in which real power lay with the Communists, supported by the presence of the Red Army, the last divisions of which did not leave the country until 1958. Elections in 1946, now known to have been falsified, presented the Popular Front as having won a major victory. Romania's subjugation was confirmed at the end of December 1947 when King Michael was forced to abdicate.

Under Gheorghe Gheorghiu-Dej, General Secretary of the Communist Party, Romania became one of the Soviet Union's most reliable puppets. In the late 1950s, however, Dej emerged from subservience by resisting pressure to become the granary of COMECON (Council for Mutual Economic Assistance) and by embarking on a policy of rapid industrialization, aimed at enabling Romania to break its dependency on the Soviet Union, and achieve greater economic self-reliance.

The autonomous policies inaugurated by Dej were continued by his successor Nicolae Ceauşescu, who was elected First (later General) Secretary of the Party in March 1965. Romania developed relations with China, was the first country in the Eastern bloc to establish diplomatic relations with West Germany in 1967, and did not break diplomatic ties with Israel after the Six Day War. Ceauşescu's finest hour came on 21 August 1968 when he denounced the Soviet-led Warsaw Pact intervention in Czechoslovakia. Growing recognition of Romania's political usefulness as a thorn in the flesh of the Soviet Union opened a period of increasing Western courtship, exemplified by President Nixon's visit in 1969, Ceauşescu's return visit to the USA in 1970, President Ford's granting of Most Favored Nation status in 1975, and Ceauşescu's repeat visit to the USA in 1978. Three months later he was the guest of Queen Elizabeth II on a state visit to the UK.

Lavish international recognition of Ceauşescu obscured worrying signs in the country's economic performance. In order to provide finance for continuing rapid industrialization Ceauşescu had turned to the West for large-scale loans. Nature also conspired against the regime, in the form of a severe earthquake in 1977, and floods in 1980 and 1981, which disrupted production and reduced exports of food-stuffs, which Ceauşescu now looked to in order to reduce foreign debt. Ceauşescu's image was delivered a shattering blow by his acceptance of conditions from the Western banks; a mark of his anger was his defiant declaration in December 1982 that he would pay off the foreign debt by 1990. To achieve this he introduced a series of austerity measures unparalleled even in the bleak history of Communist regimes. Ration-ing of bread, flour, sugar and milk was introduced in some towns in early 1982, and in 1983 it was extended to most of the country with the exception of the capital. Monthly personal rations were reduced to the point where on the eve of the revolution they were, in some regions of the country, two pounds of sugar, two pounds of flour, a half-pound pack of margarine, and five eggs. At the same time the energy needs of export heavy industry outstripped the country's generating capacity, and drastic energy-saving measures were introduced which included a petrol ration of 30 litres per month for private car owners. Other strictures stipulated a maximum temperature of 14 degrees centigrade in offices (in winter outside temperatures usually drop to well below zero) and limited periods of provision of hot water (normally one day a week in state-owned flats).

On the international stage Ceauşescu's importance was grievously undermined by the accession to power in the Soviet Union of Mikhail Gorbachev in 1985. Ceauşescu's usefulness as a bridge between East and West rapidly evaporated. Furthermore, the reforms to the Com-munist system advocated by Gorbachev were rejected by Ceauşescu, who continued to apply his Stalinist policies in an even more draconian manner by introducing in November 1987 a seven-day working week and reduced domestic heating quotas. In the same month the first major challenge to Ceauşescu was launched by several thousand workers in **Braşov**, the country's second largest city, when they sacked the local Party headquarters in protest at his new measures. The leaders of the protest were rounded up, beaten and jailed as Ceauşescu defiantly refused to make any concessions.

Ceauşescu's programme to complete by the year 2000 the urbaniza-tion or 'systematization' of about half of Romania's 13 000 villages, a plan revived in March 1988, also provoked international criticism. The coercive application of this policy, initially involving the bulldozing at short notice of villagers' private houses and the destruction of their plots of land in order to force them into small blocks of apartments in new 'agro-industrial' complexes, focused attention on the wider issue of

Romania's failure to honour its human rights commitments under the Helsinki process.

Ceauşescu's downfall

The first link in the chain of events which led to Ceauşescu's overthrow was forged by a local protest in the western Transylvanian town of **Timişoara** against the harassment of a Hungarian pastor Laszlo Tokes. On the night of 15 December 1989 members of his flock maintained a vigil outside Tokes's house to prevent him being taken away for questioning by the security police. The following day the vigil turned into a major demonstration when several thousand Romanians joined the Hungarian parishioners and the protesters marched into the town centre chanting 'We want bread!' and 'Down with Ceauşescu!'. They were dispersed by baton-wielding militiamen but no shots were fired, even though Ceauşescu had given orders that the security police and the army should fire on the demonstrators. The demonstrations continued on 17 December but on that afternoon the army did open fire on the crowd. The number of casualties was initially put at several thousand but subsequent investigations put the figure at less than two hundred. On the orders of the Presidents' wife, Elena Ceauşescu, who by then was Vice President in all but name, forty of the dead were transported by lorry to Bucharest and cremated so as to make identification impossible.

On 20 December Ceauşescu made an unrepentant televized address to the nation. Misjudging the public mood he then convened a mass meeting of support on the next morning in **Bucharest**. To his evident amazement his speech was interrupted by cries and heckling. He attempted to placate the crowd by announcing salary increases, but this only angered it further. At the end of his speech large groups of young people remained in the city centre and, encouraged by the mild, unseasonal weather, lingered into the evening. It was at this point that they were fired upon by the army and security police and many were shot dead. On the morning of 22 December large crowds gathered in front of the Central Committee building and when Ceauşescu stepped out onto the balcony to address them stones were thrown. Ceauşescu fled from the rooftop in a helicopter accompanied by his wife, two of his closest allies, and two bodyguards. The Ceauşescus were later captured and taken to the **Târgovişte** military garrison where they were tried and executed on Christmas Day.

Into the vacuum created by Ceauşescu's downfall stepped the Council of the National Salvation Front, a body representing an alliance of reform-minded Communists and prominent dissidents. Ion Iliescu was declared interim President and Petre Roman was appointed Prime Minister. Both men were members of the Communist Party.

Both were given a popular mandate in elections in May when Iliescu won 85% of the vote for the Presidency and Roman's government received 67%. However, a crisis of authority, civil unrest, rising unemployment and currency devaluation soon cast a shadow over the euphoria that had greeted the overthrow of Ceauşescu. In June Iliescu appealed to miners to come to Bucharest to restore order after anti-government demonstrations and for two days the miners terrorized the population of the capital. Their ranks were swollen by members of the *securitate* (Ceauşescu's security police). Iliescu thanked the miners for their actions, attracting condemnation from most Western governments.

Thousands of young Romanians left the country in the summer of 1990, despairing of the prospects for democracy and the rule of law. Soon the social costs of the economic reforms and a press campaign with distinctly anti-semitic tones (Petre Roman is of Jewish background) undermined public support. Once again the miners came to Bucharest in September 1991, this time not to defend the government but to bring it down, precipitating the resignation of Roman and the setting up of a coalition government. Since then, successive governments have cautiously followed a recipe for economic and social reform advocated by the West.

Romanian Literature

Creative literature in Romanian can only be said with conviction to have emerged in the early nineteenth century. Before then Romanian literature was largely an expression of the Byzantine culture, which the Romanians had received in a Slavonic form from their contacts with the Bulgarians and Serbs during the fourteenth century. This literature was largely of religious inspiration and consisted of translations from the Church Slavonic of the Bible, of liturgical books, of the lives of the saints, and of the works of Byzantine theologians. The printing-press in Wallachia and Moldavia was monopolized·by the prelates of the Romanian Orthodox Church until the end of the eighteenth century and the Reformation made virtually no impact there.

The Transylvanian School and Lazăr

The experience of **Transylvania** was different. Here in the 18th century a secular culture, independent of the church, began to emerge. The creation of the Romanian Uniate, or Greek Catholic Church, in 1700 made Western centres of Catholic learning accessible to a small number of Romanians and produced the leading figures in the Şcoala Ardeleană (Transylvanian School). This educated élite brought their fellow countrymen into contact with the 'Enlightenment' and at the same time stimulated the development of a national consciousness by publishing studies which emphasized the Roman origins of the Romanian people.

It was only a short while before the influence of the Transylvanian School percolated south and east of the Carpathians among educated Romanians in Wallachia and Moldavia, ruled since the second decade of the eighteenth century by Phanariot Greeks sent by the Sultan. The dissemination of the historical and linguistic arguments propounded by the School received a major impetus with the introduction of elementary education in Romanian. In **Wallachia** this was the work of Gheorghe Lazăr, himself a Transylvanian by birth and a former professor at the Orthodox Theological Seminary in **Sibiu**. Regarded as a recalcitrant by the authorities in Sibiu, Lazăr was forced to leave his post in 1816, and he made his way to **Braşov**. Here he met the widow of a prominent Bucharest boyar who was looking for a personal tutor for her children, and he was offered the position since alongside his religious training Lazăr had studied geometry and topography. These skills were, in fact, to prove the principal elements in his success.

Lazăr crossed the Carpathians to **Bucharest** in the widow's company and began his scholastic duties in that same year, 1816. Word soon travelled of his skills and competence as a teacher in Romanian and the widow's friends began to send their own children to his private classes. Heliade (see below) tells us that shortly after arriving in Bucharest Lazăr met the poet Iancu Văcărescu who introduced him to the members of the Council for the administration of schools (Eforia). Such schools as there were at the time in Wallachia were conducted in Greek, the principal one being the Academia domnească (The Prince's Academy) in Bucharest. Lazăr took the opportunity of this contact to raise the possibility of opening a school in which Romanian would be the language of instruction. In December 1817 the Council requested the Prince, Ioan Caragea, to sanction the establishment of a Romanian school in which 'philosophical matters and other languages' could be taught. The school's seat was to be in the grounds of the monastery of Saint Sava, and Lazăr was appointed its principal.

His pupils were of differing abilities and backgrounds; some were children of simple artisans who could scarcely read or write, others came from boyar families, finding Lazăr's lessons in technical drawing of more interest and practical use than the rote-learning practices of the Greek Academy in Bucharest. Classes in Latin and French were taught by a fellow Transylvanian, a Hungarian it seems, by the name of Ladislau Erdelyi who translated the first play to be staged in Romanian in Wallachia, Molière's *L'Avare* (*The Miser*) performed by the pupils of St Sava in 1818.

Two years after the collapse of the revolt led by Tudor Vladimirescu in 1821 against Phanariot rule in Wallachia, Lazăr died at his birthplace, **Avrig** in Transylvania, having first allegedly tried to drink himself to death. However, despite its collapse, the Vladimirescu revolt destroyed Turkish confidence in the Greeks and they consequently brought Phanariot rule in the principalities to an end.

Emergence of literature in Romanian

The following year native princes were appointed in Wallachia and Moldavia, under whose auspices the national awareness which Lazăr had fostered now developed. Without Phanariot patronage Greek influence, in education, literature, dress and manners, quickly waned. Romanian aspirations were given eloquent voice and practical application by one of the most enlightened Wallachian boyars of the age, Constantin (Dinicu) Golescu (1777–1830), whose travels in Western Europe between 1824 and 1826 prompted him to write a travelogue highlighting the political, social and cultural backwardness of the principalities. Golescu's account was at once a statement of what the Wallachians were and an expression of what he would like them to be. For him, backwardness was often equated with Phanariot or 'oriental' influences, while advancement was associated with following the example of Western Europe. Here we have a source for the belief, widely held during the mid-nineteenth century among Romanian intellectuals in the principalities, that modernization on the Western model automatically conferred civilization.

As initial steps towards the enlightenment of his people, Golescu proposed the establishment of a system of education in Romanian and the translation of cultivated and technical literature; to set this in motion he proposed the formation of a Literary Society, for which purpose he coopted one of Lazăr's pupils, Ioan Heliade Rădulescu (1802–72).

In 1829, with funds from Golescu, Heliade launched *Curierul Rumânesc* (*The Romanian Courier*), the first Romanian journal to appear in **Wallachia**. In his Romanian grammar of 1828 Heliade advocated the adoption of a phonetic rather than etymological spelling for Romanian, simplifying the use of the Cyrillic alphabet in which Romanian continued to be written in Moldavia and Wallachia, since letters which did not correspond to a Romanian sound were removed. This change can be seen as the first step towards the replacement of the Cyrillic by the Roman alphabet in the two principalities, a reform introduced in Wallachia in 1860 and in Moldavia in 1862.

In 1830 Heliade bought one of the few printing-presses in Wallachia and installed it in his house in **Bucharest**. His ownership of this press, on which not only *Curierul Rumânesc* but also much of Romanian literature, both original and translated, was to appear during the following decade, made him a unique arbiter of literary taste and orthographic reform. As grammarian, translator, editor and publisher, Heliade was the most influential figure in the emergence of a literature in Romanian in this period.

A counterpart in **Moldavia** of Heliade and Lazăr was Gheorghe Asachi (1788–1869). The son of a wealthy Orthodox priest, he was taken by his father to Lemberg (**Lvov**) for his schooling at the age of eight and in 1805 he went to Vienna to study astronomy. Three years later he moved to Rome where archaeology and Italian literature were his prime interests.

In 1812 he settled in the Moldavian capital **Iaşi** and was hired as a teacher of algebra and geometry in Romanian at the Greek Academy. This is believed to be the first instance of public instruction in Romanian in the principality. Another 'first' for Asachi was his staging in Romanian of his own adaptation of the play *Myrtil and Chloe* by Florian and Gessner in 1816 in the house of a boyar in Iaşi. This was the first in a long series of translations made by Asachi which punctuated his work in the educational and publishing fields.

The remarkable similarities between Asachi's career and that of Heliade continued in 1829 with his editing of the first Romanian journal in Moldavia, *Albina Românească* (*The Romanian Bee*). Three years later he set up a printing and lithographic press. Less influential than Heliade in the direction language development was to take, Asachi nevertheless remains as significant a patron of Romanian letters as his Wallachian colleague.

A major contribution to poetry and drama was made by Vasile Alecsandri ◊ who was among the first to use oral literature as an inspiration and who almost single-handedly created a theatre repertoire. After failing to complete a university education in Paris, and a year after his return to Moldavia in 1839, he became one of three directors of a newly created National Theatre. The absence of a Romanian repertory led him to create one and he began with an adaptation of a French farce. He moved from farce to comedy, and then into historical drama. In the 1840s he travelled throughout Moldavia collecting ballads which he published at his own expense and in 'corrected form' in Paris in 1852. His collection not only gave a national image to Romanian verse but also, through translation, introduced it to a European audience.

Barely thirty years later, Romanian verse was to advance from an endearing naivety to a peak of its expressive capability in the hands of Mihai Eminescu ◊. Only one volume of his poetry, *Poesii* (*Poems*), 1883, was published during his lifetime but his allegorical, pessimistic and patriotic verse, exquisitely crafted from a literary language which he himself created, has left a legacy which is the most potent of any

Mihail Eminescu

Romanian writer. His genius lies in his ability to weave his motifs of national history, of folk myth and of disenchantment in love into a grand design, and to express the commonplace in a language of crystalline simplicity yet striking musicality. Eminescu's achievement has made those who have sought to denigrate the influence of the West in Romanian culture and politics at various periods during this century claim him as their symbol, and his obsession with a pristine paradise and anxiety in the face of reality have struck a sympathetic chord in those facing the uncertainty of radical change. Such treatment of him was symptomatic of a culture still struggling to reconcile the impact of Western-inspired modernity with a veneration of indigenous tradition based largely on folk myth.

This debate between the virtues of the indigenous and the external dominated the writings of Titu Maiorescu (1840–1917), the most influential critic of the 19th century. In 1863 he founded the literary society Junimea (Youth) whose journal, *Convorbiri literare* (*Literary Discussions*), set the agenda for a continually recurring debate concerning the direction of Romanian culture. In his studies *O Cercetare Critică asupra Poeziei Române de la 1867* (*O Critical Examination of Romanian Poetry in 1867*) and *In Contra Direcţiei de Astăzi în Cultura Română* (*Against Today's Direction in Romanian Culture*), 1868, Maiorescu advocated a verse based on oral literature and denounced foreign, particularly French, influences. This fear of submergence by foreign influences expressed by Maiorescu also led in the early 1900s to the creation of reviews stressing the importance of national and peasant traditions, the most notable of these being *Sămănătorul* (*The Sower*), which was founded in 1901, and *Viaţa românească* (*Romanian Life*), founded in 1906.

There was no keener observer of perennial Romanian attitudes than Ion Luca Caragiale ♭, an author of plays and short stories, and his observations are uncannily accurate. His period of playwriting opened in 1879 with *O noapte furtunoasă* (*A Stormy Night*), a comedy of lower middle-class life in **Bucharest**, and reached its height with *O scrisoare pierdută* (*A Lost Letter*), 1884, a satire of political intrigue in a provincial town. These comedies show the playwright as a master of comic dialogue. A preoccupation with the macabre pervades a number of his short stories, notably 'O făclie de Paşte' ('An Easter Torch'), 1890, while the supernatural is subtly handled in the tale 'La Hanul lui Mânjoală' ('At Mânjoala's Inn') 1898.

Early 20th century experimentation

At the same time as emphasis was being placed on the indigenous and the typical in Romanian literature, experiments in the poetic exploitation of words were beginning to be made by Tristan Tzara (1896–1953), pseudonym of Sami Rosenstock, born into a Jewish family in **Moineşti** in Moldavia. He made his literary debut in 1912 when he published four poems in the Symbolist mould in *Simbolul* (*The Symbol*), a literary review which he co-founded with Ion Vinea, Emil Isac and Marcel Iancu. There followed a silence of three years. His name reappeared again under a handful of poems in various journals before his departure in the same year, 1915, for Zurich. Unpublished poems in Romanian by Tzara dating from 1914 show that he was breaking with the rhythmic traditions of Romanian verse. In a letter to a friend in 1922 he wrote: 'Already in 1914 I had tried to take away from words their meaning, and to use them in order to give a new global sense to the verse by the tonality and the auditory contrast.' Such poems show how the origins of the Dada movement, founded by Tzara in Zurich in 1916, are to be found in the cultural environment of Bucharest before the first world war.

Tzara's destruction of conventional language by recording words in an arbitrary order of spontaneous thought was accompanied by flights of fancy characterized by black humour and may have been influenced by the prose pieces *Pagini bizare* (*Bizarre Pages*), written by Urmuz (pseudonymn of Demetru Demetrescu-Buzău, 1883–1923), oral versions of which were circulating in Bucharest at the time of Tzara's experiments. One of Urmuz's admirers was Eugène Ionesco (**Slatina** 1912–Paris 1994), the self-imposed Romanian exile, who described him as 'one of the precursors of the universal literary revolt, one of the prophets of the dislocation of social forms, of the thought and language of this world which, today, under our very eyes is disintegrating, as absurd as the heroes of our author.' In so far as spontaneous expression and black humour were instruments in that exploration of the unconscious defined by the French Surrealist André Breton's *Manifeste du surréalisme*, 1924, both Tzara and Urmuz were precursors of Surrealism. A third figure alongside Tzara and Urmuz who merits the loose label of 'avant-garde' is Ilarie Voronca (1903–46), a poet remarkable for his extraordinary imagery.

The most original exponent of the Symbolism which Tzara had soon renounced was George Bacovia (pseudonym of George Vasiliu, 1881–1957). He took his pseudonym from his birthplace where the monotony of provincial life provided the setting for much of his poetry and, perhaps, the trigger for his neurosis. His volumes *Plumb* (*Lead*), 1916, and *Scântei galbene* (*Yellow Sparks*), 1926 are infused with a melancholy and pessimism which are expressed by a repetitive use of stark colour words and phrases. The poet is haunted by damp, decay, rain and snow and these elements constitute Bacovia's universe of putrefaction and gloom. Dusk and night, autumn and winter, grey, black and violet characterize the neurosis of which his use of repetition is symptomatic.

Between the wars

The inter-war period is one of unrivalled intellectual expression in Romania. While the conventions of literary expression were being challenged by the avant-garde, the search for 'national' values remained at the centre of the debate over the nature of Romanian culture opened by Maiorescu in the previous century. Broadly speaking, the debate was conducted between two protagonists, the 'Europeans' and the 'traditionalists'. Representing the former was the literary review *Sburătorul* (*The Winged Spirit*) and its editor Eugen Lovinescu (1881–1943) who advocated the theory of 'synchronism', according to which Romania should modernize by adapting what was best from the West. Opposing this idea were the 'traditionalists', whose most influential mouthpiece was *Gândirea* (*Thought*). Under its second editor, Nichifor Crainic (1889–1972), the review was given the task of promoting an exploration of the native spirit through religious experience and an examination of the spirituality of folklore. Both were elements which, Crainic argued, stood at the core of the Romanian national character. Orthodoxy and tradition became the bywords for *Gândirism*.

Yet not all contributors to *Gândirea* shared Crainic's emphasis on the need to appeal to the teachings of the Orthodox Church to restore the moral rectitude of the Romanians, one which had been perverted by Western influences. Writers such as Lucian Blaga (Extract 6), Adrian Maniu, Ion Pillat (Extract 5) and Cezar Petrescu, while recognizing the debt owed by Orthodoxy to the spiritual and cultural life of the Romanians, were receptive to other sources of inspiration.

In *Poemele Luminii* (*The Poems of Light*), 1919, Blaga ◊ explored the mysterious character of 'light' as a natural agent of the universe, often using the background of myth. For the poet, man lives aspiring to the revelation of mysteries and his existence is the genetic transition towards death: *În marea trecere* (*In the Great Transition*), 1924. As a dramatist, Blaga adapted national myths in *Zamolxe*, 1921, *Meşterul Manole* (*Master Manole*), 1927, as well as universal ones in *Arca lui Noe* (*Noah's Ark*), 1944. In his principal work on the philosophy of culture *Trilogia culturii* (*The Trilogy of Culture*), 1944, Blaga formulated the concept of the 'stylistic matrix', the impression of which is given by the unconscious to everything created by man.

Cezar Petrescu ◊ set out to write 'a chronicle of the 20th century' in which he aimed at portraying the evolution of Romanian society in all of its classes. Behind his novels lies the idea of destiny which acts upon society and is born from a conjunction of historical, geographical and socio-political factors. Writing in 1932 he declared that all of his characters 'seemed predestined to a monotonous decline' and that the age was marked by 'a psychology of failure'. His principal themes are the consequences of *déracinement* in *Calea Victoriei* (*Victory Road*), 1929, the perfidious effects of industrialization in *Comoara regelui Dromichet* (*The Treasure of King Dromichet*), 1931, and the inability of social groups to communicate in *Întunecare* (*Gathering Clouds*), 1927, and *Carlton*, 1942.

Rural Romania provided the setting for a second major novelist of the inter-war period. Liviu Rebreanu ◊ expressed his artistic credo in an article published in 1924: 'Art, like the divine creation, becomes the most wonderful mystery. By creating living people with their own lives, the writer approaches the mystery of eternity. It is not beauty, a human invention, which is of interest in art, but the pulsation of life.' His first novel *Ion*, 1920 (Extract 15), is notable for the cold detachment with which the author allows his central figure, a land-hungry young peasant, to satisfy his inexorable greed for land at any cost.

The reader's sense of inevitability about Ion's premature death in a duel is matched by a similar feeling concerning the hero's destiny in *Pădurea spânzuraţilor* (*The Forest of the Hanged*), 1922, which is based on the fate of the author's brother Emil, a Transylvanian Romanian hanged for attempted desertion from the Austro–Hungarian army in 1917 when faced with fighting his fellow Romanians during the first world war. The novel follows the crisis of conscience of a soldier in whom the bond of national brotherhood proves stronger than his sense of duty to the state. This crisis is presented in terms of the conflict between allegiance to the state, in this case Austria–Hungary, and love of one's people. The dilemma of the protagonist, Apostol Bologa, can be seen in terms of a dialectic between the real and the ideal, the real being his sense of obligation to the state, and the ideal being natural attachment to nation or community.

More regional in character are the novels of Mihail Sadoveanu (1880–1961). A native of **Moldavia**, Sadoveanu excels as a story-teller, displaying a powerful historical imagination based on a detailed knowledge of Moldavia's past. His description and dialogue are enriched with the savour of local Moldavian dialect. *Baltagul* (*The Hatchet*), 1930, is the most enduring of his stories. As one critic observed, it raises the tale of a peasant woman's search for her murdered husband and his murderers to the dignity of a classical tragedy. Sadoveanu describes with a simple directness the lives of the Carpathian shepherds and at the same time unravels a narrative thread that has the compulsive power of an accomplished story of detection as it draws the reader along the trail followed by the widow and her young son.

Equally compulsive are the writings of Mircea Eliade ◊, a novelist and historian of religions who is better known in his latter capacity to most English-speaking readers. An accomplished author of novels and tales of the fantastic, Eliade's early fiction is marked by its autobiographical character and draws heavily on his journal, conceived, as he admitted, as a repository of recollections, observations, and intimate experiences. In *Domnişoara Christina* (*Miss Christina*), 1936, Eliade explored through a horror story the manner in which the supernatural reveals itself in everyday life. *Noaptea de Sânziene* (*Midsummer Night*),

Mihail Sadoveanu

first published in French in 1955 as *La Forêt Interdite* (*The Forbidden Forest*), follows its hero's search to distinguish the sacred and profane in everyday life in terms of fundamental time as opposed to historical time. These concepts are expounded in Eliade's philosophy of myth, expressed in *Le Mythe de l'Éternel Retour* (*The Myth of the Eternal Return*), 1949. A preoccupation with the supernatural (Extract 2) dominates the three novellas, written between 1975 and 1979, which make up the collection *Youth Without Youth*. Here we have illustrated the communion between, on the one hand, Eliade's scholarly investigations into mythical time and space and the role of myth in history, and, on the other, his fiction which serves the same function as myth by creating fresh meanings.

The inter- and post-war years were also spanned by Tudor Arghezi (pseudonym of Ion Theodorescu, 1880–1967), but whereas Eliade chose not to return to Romania after the second world war, Arghezi remained and eventually adapted himself to the cultural requirements of the Communist regime. He was almost fifty before he achieved recognition as a major poet with the publication of *Cuvinte potrivite* (*Fitting Words*), 1927, his first collected volume of poems written over the previous thirty years. The volume caused consternation in literary circles by breaking with conventions of prosody and language; among the poet's innovations were the use of lurid and abrasive metaphor to express a bitterness often bordering on the blasphemous. Many of the poems reflect the anguish of a spirit in search of God and the poet's identification with the land and the peasant.

There was no stronger critic of Arghezi's break with linguistic convention in the late 1920s than Ion Barbu (1895–1961), a poet and mathematician. He made his debut as a poet in 1918, his first collection *După melci* (*After the Snails*), 1921, being largely cast in the Parnassian mould. His compositions between 1920 and 1925 are marked by their Turkish flavour, offering charming cameos of life inspired by the former Ottoman-ruled province of **Dobrogea** on Romania's Black Sea coast. After 1925 his creations are cryptic and hermetic, reflecting a mathematical vision of the world. His collected verse was gathered in the volume *Joc secund* (*Second Play*), 1930, upon which his literary reputation rests, for afterwards he devoted himself entirely to mathematics. His preoccupation with the analogies between poetry and mathematics inspired a verse distinguished by mathematical metaphor, by the symmetrical regularity of stanzas, and yet also by its striking musicality.

The early years under Communism

The proclamation of the People's Republic on 30 December 1947 marked the beginning of an era in which the Communist Party would seek to exploit literature for its own ends. The measure of its success was reflected in the form and content of published literature between 1948 and 1989. What distinguished Communist Romania from most of the other East European countries was the blandness of intellectual dissent. Given the lack of sympathy for Marxism–Leninism among Romanians and its association with the Soviet Union, a traditional enemy, this conformity was striking.

One reason for it was the absence of a focal point of opposition. There were virtually no challenges to the Communist regime's authority from within the Communist party. The Orthodox Church was completely subservient to central authority while the Greek Catholic (Uniate) Church, the only other faith embraced by a large number of Romanians, was outlawed and its leaders jailed. Those intellectuals who were not prepared to conform, such as Blaga and Barbu, were condemned to silence. Blaga ◊ became a symbol of resistance to the blandishments of the Communists. He was removed from his chair at **Cluj University** and spent the years until his death as an archivist. Others less principled, like Arghezi and Sadoveanu, allowed themselves to be manipulated by the regime and were well rewarded. The peasants, who constituted 80% of Romania's population in 1945, were politically emasculated, first through the arrest and imprisonment of the leaders of the National Peasant Party on charges of 'treason' in 1947, and then through the detention of 80 000 of their number for resistance to the programme of forced collectivization of the land initiated in 1949.

Opportunism was the single major explanation for compliance with the Communist regime. The prospect of material gain by accommodation with the authorities proved irresistible to many intellectuals and was recognized by the poet Ana Blandiana ◊ as a blight on Romanian society and culture. The most significant recruit to 'Socialist Realism' was Mihail Sadoveanu, whose *Mitrea Cocor*, 1949, was described by Jack Lindsay as being 'conceived and realized in the perspective opened [by] the revolutionary changes lived through by the author. Following the classic method of Socialist Realism, he gives to his character, the unfortunate orphan Mitrea, the inner qualities of the Romanian peasant: ingenuity, love of work and of justice.'

Failure to conform to the method invited problems with the censor, even for those who enjoyed the favour of the regime. George Călinescu ◊, was unable to publish his novel *Bietul Ioanide* (*Poor Ioanide*), which he had completed in 1949, until four years later (Extract 1). Yet the fact that the novel appeared in 1953 was indicative of an indulgence, manifest after Stalin's death in the same year, towards literature that did not wear the strait-jacket of Socialist Realism.

This was most clearly exemplified in 1955 with the appearance of *Moromeţii* (*The Morometes*) by Marin Preda (1922–80). The novel introduced one of the most convincing characters of post-war Romanian literature, the peasant farmer Ilie Moromete. Set in the inter-war years, the novel is centred on Ilie's relationship with his family and the village community. Scornful of change, indifferent to innovation, Ilie is the champion of the old established order, one validated by time. 'How can you live if you are not left in peace?', he asks himself as he stubbornly but vainly defends a stability that proves to be ephemeral in the face of time, a time which, to use one of the author's aphorisms, 'no longer had patience'. The fragile family relationship of the Morometes is broken when Ilie's sons rebel against his authority and flee to **Bucharest**.

A further sign that aesthetic qualities could triumph over ideological considerations was provided by the publication in 1957 of *Groapa* (*The Pit*) by Eugen Barbu (1924–1994). Its difficult nine-year gestation during which, according to the author, it was revised thirteen times, is explained more by its reception at the hands of some literary critics than by the writer's search for a definitive version. A recrudescence of naturalism was the 'danger' identified with the novel. This charge was founded on Barbu's use of colourful slang in depicting the often insalubrious activities of a community of rogues that inhabited a seedy quarter on the fringes of **Bucharest**. The demolition of this area in 1946 inspired Barbu to recall its world of vagabonds and swindlers. His eye for detail in describing characters and their surroundings, coupled with their bawdy repartee, makes *Groapa* one of the most original creations of the post-war Romanian novel.

Yet at the same time, the writers' principal role as 'engineers of human souls' was reflected in Arghezi's *Cîntare Omului* (*Hymn to Mankind*), 1956, a collection of verse dedicated to man's gradual evolution towards self-discovery and his eventual self-realization in the new socialist order.

Arghezi's alignment with the regime followed a period of silence between 1948 and 1954 which began when he was attacked in the Party daily *Scânteia* (*The Spark*) for 'representing the standard goods of decadent bourgeois art.' Another cycle of verse in harmony with the regime's cultural dictates was *1907*, 1955, devoted to the peasant uprisings of that year.

Recognition of the regime's success in manipulating writers and establishing firm control over them was given by the Soviet choice of Romania as exile for the Hungarian Marxist critic György Lukács after the revolution of 1956.

Distancing from the Soviet Union and reassertion of national culture

The Romanian Communist Party's rejection in 1963 of Khrushchev's plans to give COMECON (Council for Mutual Economic Assistance) a supranational economic planning role marked the beginning of an independent Romanian line in economic and foreign policy. Defiance of the Soviet Union enabled Dej, General Secretary of the Romanian Communist Party, to increase the Party's popularity in Romania. He distanced himself further from his Soviet overlord by reversing the trend of Russianization in Romanian culture and education. The

Russian Institute in Bucharest was closed and Romanian names were restored to main streets in Romania's cities.

These measures signalled an ideological thaw that ushered in the rehabilitation of historical, literary and political figures who were prominent in the nineteenth-century movement for independence. In literature the most significant act of rehabilitation was that of Titu Maiorescu in 1963. As an advocate of art for art's sake, his readmittance into the public arena definitely marked the abandonment by the Party of Socialist Realism as its aesthetic creed. This rejection paved the way for the restoration in 1964 of outstanding writers of the nineteenth century to their respected place in Romanian culture, and for the rehabilitation of a number of twentieth-century authors whose works had been banned because of their association with 'undemocratic forces' or with 'decadent' literary movements, or because they had refused to conform to the principles of Socialist Realism.

Biographies of Eminescu ◊ were republished, poetry by Barbu and Blaga ◊ was republished, and some of Caragiale's ◊ plays were staged for the first time since 1948. The thaw also allowed the Party to claim to have harnessed to it the younger talents which were now allowed to emerge in the wake of this relaxation of rigid ideological control. Among them were Ana Blandiana ◊, Marin Sorescu ◊ (Extract 4) and Nichita Stănescu ◊. They were accompanied in their emergence by the reappearance of an older generation who had written for the desk drawer, including Ion Caraion (1923–86) and Ştefan Augustin Doinaş (1922–). Both groups revitalized Romanian verse by breaking free from the clichés of the 1950s.

It is significant that this relaxation of ideological control resulted not from intellectual pressure but from the changes in the political relationship between Romania and the Soviet Union. The concessions to writers were dispensed by the regime and not exacted from it, and the compliance which had characterized relations between the intelligentsia and the Party continued undisturbed after Nicolae Ceauşescu's election as First Secretary in March 1965. But within the bounds of that compliance a literature of greater thematic diversity surfaced. Marin Preda's *Intrusul (The Intruder)*, 1968, gave a strikingly realistic portrayal of a young man unable to adapt to the new morality of contemporary urban society in which the novelist sees a corruption of traditional values. Notable for its metaphorical colour was Fănuş Neagu's (1932–) *Îngerul a strigat (The Angel Cried Out)*, 1968, an account of one man's vendetta to avenge the murder of his father set against the background of the war and the upheaval of the late 1940s.

The invasion of Czechoslovakia in 1968 brought the Party and writers even closer together. Ceauşescu's denunciation of Warsaw Pact allies in front of a huge crowd in Bucharest caught the public mood exactly and created a wave of support for the Party unequalled before or since. The rally to the Party colours was illustrated by a declaration in *Gazeta literară* signed by twenty-three young writers, including Alexandru Ivasiuc (1933–77), Petre Popescu (1944–), Adrian Păunescu (1943–) and Dumitru Ţepeneag (1944–) which expressed their 'complete agreement with the position of the Party and of the Romanian government, as defined by comrade Ceauşescu', and their undertaking to do 'all in our power to defend our fundamental values, our country, and the peaceful construction of socialism in our country.' The reassessment of the Stalinist era in *F*, 1969, by Dumitru Radu Popescu (1935–) and the critique of contemporary society in *Absenţii* (*The Absent Ones*), 1970, by Augustin Buzura ◊ confirmed writers in their optimism that the Party would tolerate a broader range of themes in creative literature.

Absenţii is aesthetically one of the most accomplished novels of the 1970s. Constructed in the form of a monologue, the novel examines the spiritual crisis of a young doctor, Mihai Bogdan. This crisis is provoked by the corruption and opportunism which Bogdan encounters in the research institute where he works, and by his gradual estrangement from his friend and colleague who has been tainted by these vices. In coming through his crisis Bogdan represents the survival of the individual and the triumph of positive values in a society corrupted by the psychosis of opportunism and deformed by its brutalization.

Ceauşescu's 1970s clampdown and his regime in literature

Any hopes that ideological constraints would continue to be relaxed were rudely shattered by Ceauşescu's 'mini cultural revolution' of July 1971 which virtually constituted a return to the method of Socialist Realism. The 'theses' enunciated by the Romanian leader following a visit to China and North Korea called for 'a more rigorous control . . . to avoid publication of literary works which promote ideas and conceptions harmful to the interests of socialist construction'. Buzura's *Absenţii* was withdrawn from bookshops and intimidation used to isolate those writers who attacked the proposals. These included Nicolae Breban (1934–), Buzura ◊, Paul Goma ◊, Păunescu and Sorescu ◊. In December 1971 a new law was introduced prohibiting the broadcasting or publication abroad of material originating in Romania that might prejudice the interests of the state. Goma and Ţepeneag were disowned by most of their colleagues in the Writers' Union because of their readiness to challenge the Party's cultural dictates and each gradually found himself 'persona non grata' in his own country.

Ţepeneag was deprived of his citizenship in 1975 while in France on the false grounds that he had requested political asylum there. Goma was expelled from the Party in 1973 and four years later was arrested after making public the contents of a letter addressed to Pavel Kohout, one of those involved with Charter 77 in Czechoslovakia, and sending two letters to Ceauşescu denouncing the *securitate* (security police). Goma was allowed to leave Romania with his wife and child on 20 November 1977. The 'Goma affair' represented the sum of Western awareness of Romanian writers' activity during the late 1970s. His treatment by the regime for exposing human rights abuses caught the attention of the Western media, whereas the success of non-conformist writers in overcoming the ideological strictures passed unrecognized.

In 1980 there appeared what was politically the most notable novel of the post-war years in Romania: Marin Preda's *Cel mai iubit dintre pământeni* (*The Most Beloved of the Earth Dwellers*). This testimony of the first fifteen years of Communist power (ie the *pre-Ceauşescu* period) not only challenged some principles of Marxist theory, such as the collectivization of agriculture and the nationalization of all means of production, but targetted the subversion of the law for political ends and the abuses of the *securitate*. The author's graphic description of conditions in forced labour camps conveyed the torment and misery of a society at the mercy of the arbitary use of power. Equally striking was Preda's assessment of the pernicious moral effect that this totalitarian regime had upon its citizens. The perversion of traditional values in a society highjacked by the 'troglodytes' is seen as a concomitant of the country's fate during what Preda's hero terms 'the era of the villains'.

Unlike the novels of his contemporaries, Buzura's *Refugii* (*Places of Refuge*), 1984, was set in Ceauşescu's Romania. Two newly married graduates are assigned posts in different towns, the husband as a teacher in a village called 'The Hump', the wife as a translator in a provincial town factory named 'Solidarity'. The satirical strain in these names is intentional, yet the novel is not satirical but realist. The teacher uses paraffin lamps for light since 'electricity is on for only four hours a day', the policeman is interested only in accumulating fines for petty infractions of the law, the factory managers drink real coffee and enjoy pheasant while the workers' canteen offers clear soup, beans with onion, and semolina with sugar water. The greatest travesty of 'socialist equity' is the local hospital's refusal to receive the old and gravely ill for fear of raising its mortality figures.

For statements on the realities of life under Ceauşescu during the late 1980s, poetry was equally revealing. In a negative sense the activity of Adrian Păunescu was eloquent. The cap of opportunism sat well on the head of this poet since, from being in the vanguard of critics of the 1971 'mini-revolution', he ingratiated himself sufficiently with the Party to be appointed editor-in-chief of the literary weekly *Flacăra* in 1973 and remained until 1985. The reason for his dismissal was a concert of verse and music organized by him in the spring of 1985 at which his exhortation to perform the rites of the season during a temporary blackout was taken too literally. Despite his fall from grace he continued to publish paeans of praise to Ceauşescu in the hope of regaining the President's favour.

One of the bitterest critics of opportunism, Ana Blandiana ◊ soon became a victim of repression. Following publication in the student review *Amfiteatru* in December 1984 of four poems condemning the regime's brutalization of Romanians, she received telephone death threats and was forbidden to publish verse. In the spring of 1985 she was allowed a regular half-column of comment in the literary weekly *România literară* and an anthology of her poetry, excluding her recent work, appeared in April 1989. Only a month earlier the poet Mircea Dinescu (1950–) was placed under house arrest after the publication of an interview in the Parisian daily *Libération* in which he attacked the regime's spiritually degrading treatment of its people. Dinescu shared the experience of Doina Cornea (1926–), lecturer at **Cluj University** who was dismissed from her post in September 1983 for sending a letter critical of the regime to Radio Free Europe and was later placed under house arrest.

Despite the growing paranoia of Ceauşescu, a small group of writers and critics tried to set in motion a spiritual regeneration. Their inspiration was the philosopher Constantin Noica (1909–87), who in the early 1980s attracted a circle of followers from the younger generation of intellectuals. Gabriel Liiceanu's ◊ *Jurnalul de la Păltiniş* (*Păltiniş Diary*), 1983 (Extract 8), records Noica's conversations with his 'pupils', principally Liiceanu and the art critic Andrei Pleşu (1948–), at Noica's mountain retreat of **Păltiniş** between 1977 and 1981. In the sense that Noica, through his conversation, sought the dialectical improvement of his learner, he was a Socratic figure. Liiceanu's choice for the *Jurnal* of the subtitle 'An Educational Model for Humanist Culture' was a reflection of his recognition that the regime in Bucharest had launched itself in the mid-1970s on a cultural offensive that trumpeted what he called 'eastern and native' values while rejecting European ones. By denying external influences, a band of writers and historians, following the lead of the President's brother Ilie Ceauşescu, deformed the Romanians' perception of themselves and their place in history. The *Jurnal* was a plea for normality, and the symbol of that normality was Noica.

In the last five years of Ceauşescu's rule it was the abnormal that became normal. Pleşu, a friend of Dinescu, was dismissed from his post after signing a letter of protest with six critics and writers against Dinescu's expulsion from the Writers' Union. On 5 April 1989 he was sent into internal exile to a museum near **Bacău**, a town some 200 km north-west of Bucharest. A more forceful protest came from Doina

Cornea, who four days later addressed an open letter to the President calling for 'an end to this repressive policy that is more destructive than the economic disaster which you have generated.' This was the sum of reaction to Dinescu's house arrest. In early December Dinescu called on his fellow writers to take a stand against what he called 'Stalinism' in Romania and twenty-one responded by sending open letters to the West urging the authorities to stop persecuting Dinescu and his family. Within a fortnight Ceauşescu had been toppled.

After Ceauşescu – the dilemma of freedom

The overthrow of Ceauşescu and the removal of censorship placed writers in a new situation. They were faced by two considerations. The reading public now had access to a rich, diverse press and mass media. If in the past literature had no competition from newspapers or from television, and it even assumed part of the media's functions, after 1989 the writer had to take cognizance of a new situation. Disciplines such as history, sociology and political science, which were deliberately castrated under Ceauşescu, now developed and reconquered a part of the ground lost to the novel. The public no longer had to read Preda's *Cel mai iubit dintre pământeni* (*The Most Beloved of the Earth Dwellers*) in order to learn about the labour camps of the 1950s.

The second consideration was linked to the means of expression. An Aesopic language characterized a major part of the literature of the Communist era. Novels developed numerous allusive formulae, such as the parable. Poetry had recourse to an entire symbolism stemming from the same strategy of circumlocution and suggestion. In the literature composed after the revolution, reality will no longer need to be encoded in this way.

LITERARY LANDMARKS

In the extensive demolition and reconstruction of Bucharest ordered by Nicolae Ceauşescu, several sites associated with authors disappeared. The **Museum of Romanian Literature** on that part of **Bulevardul Dacia** which was formerly called Strada Fundaţiei contains many items of memorabilia connected with the lives and careers of prominent writers.

Avrig: Memorial museum to Gheorghe Lazăr.

Bran Castle: *Not*, as is often claimed in tourist literature, 'Dracula's Castle'. The original castle, called Dietrichstein after its founder, was built in the 13th century by a Teutonic Knight who had settled at the invitation of King Andrew II of Hungary. The only connection of the castle with Prince Vlad Ţepeş of Wallachia, the alleged inspiration for *Dracula* (Extract 16), was that he may have attacked it in 1460.

Braşov: Schei Church in the Schei district is the site of one of the earliest Romanian printing presses, supervised by the deacon Coresi between 1557 and 1587. The **German School** next to the Black Church was founded by Johannes Honterus (1498–1549), a Saxon who brought the Reformation to Braşov.

Bucharest: Bellu cemetery (on Calea Şerban Vodă) is the burial place of many prominent writers including Eminescu, Caragiale, Rebreanu (Extract 15) and Sadoveanu. The **Capsa restaurant** (Calea Victoriei 63) was the meeting place of Caragiale and his contemporaries. The **George Enescu Museum** (Calea Victoriei 141) was the home of Romanian composer George Enescu (1881–1955).

Ciucea: Home of the Romanian poet Octavian Goga (1881–1938). House belonging to Hungarian poet Endre Ady (1877–1919).

Constanţa: Statue of Ovid in Piaţa Ovidiu. Constanţa grew on the site of Tomis, the port to which Ovid was banished in AD 8 for a 'poem', his *Ars amatoria*, and a 'blunder' (probably relating to a sexual scandal involving the family of the Emperor Augustus). It was at Tomis that the Roman poet wrote his *Epistulae ex Ponto* (*Letters from the Black Sea*) and his poems *Tristia* (*Sorrows*).

Hobniţa: Birthplace of the sculptor Constantin Brâncuşi (1876–1957).

Iaşi: The **Church of Trei Ierarhi** (Three Hierarchs) is the site of one of Moldavia's earliest printing presses (1642). There is a **Mihai Eminescu Museum** in the Copou Park, next to the University. The **National Theatre** on Strada 9 Mai was completed in 1896. There is a **memorial museum** in the house of Ion Creangă, writer in his native Moldavian idiom of short stories based on folklore.

Lancrăm: Family house of Lucian Blaga.

Mirceşti: Museum dedicated to Vasile Alecsandri in the writer's house.

Ipoteşti: House belonging to Eminescu family.

Paşcani: House in which Mihail Sadoveanu was born.

Satu Mare: Strada Cuza Vodă 6 is where the Hungarian poet Sándor Petőfi (◊ Hungary) lived in 1847.

Târgu Jiu: Displayed in **Parcul Jiu** are Brâncuşi's sculptures *Column of Endless Memory*, *Table of Silence*, the *Avenue of Chairs*, and the *Gateway of the Kiss*.

Târlişua: House in which Rebreanu was born.

BOOKLIST

The following selection includes the extracted titles in this chapter as well as those mentioned in the introduction which are available in English and other titles for further reading. In general, paperback editions are given when possible. The editions cited are not necessarily the only ones available. For most of the extracted works, the original publisher can be found in 'Acknowledgments and Citations' at the end of the volume, as can the exact location of the extracts and the editions from which they are taken. Extract numbers are highlighted in bold. Square brackets denote the date of publication of the work in its original language.

Anthology of Contemporary Romanian Poetry, Andrea Deletant and Brenda Walker, eds, Forest Books, London, 1984/Dufour, Chester Springs, PA, 1990.

Anthology of Contemporary Rumanian Poetry, Roy MacGregor-Hastie, ed, Peter Owen, London, 1969/ Dufour, Chester Springs, PA, 1969.

Arghezi, Tudor, Selected Poems, M. Impey and B. Swann, trans, Princeton, NJ, 1976.

Bacovia, George, Plumb: Lead [1916], Peter Jay, trans, Minerva, Bucharest, 1980.

Banus, Maria, Demon in Brackets, Dan Duțescu, trans, Forest Books, London and Boston, MA, 1994.

Blaga, Lucian, Poems of Light [1919], Don Eulert, Stefan Avadanei and Mihail Bogdan, trans, Minerva, Bucharest, 1975.

Blaga, Lucian, The Great Transition, Roy MacGregor-Hastie, trans, Eminescu Publishing House, Bucharest, 1975.

Blaga, Lucian, Poezii/Poems, Michael

Taub, trans, Department of Romance Languages, University of North Carolina, Chapel Hill, NC, 1983.

Blaga, Lucian, At the Court of Yearning: Poems, Ohio State University Press, Columbus, OH, 1989.

Blaga, Lucian, The Chronicle and Song of the Ages, **Extract 6** (D. Deletant, trans).

Blandiana, Ana, Poems (bilingual), Dan Dutescu, trans, Eminescu Publishing House, Bucharest, 1982.

Blandiana, Ana, Don't Be Afraid of Me: Collected Poems, G. Alexe, Detroit, MI, 1985.

Blandiana, Ana, The Hour of Sand: Selected Poems 1969–89, Peter Jay and Anca Cristofovici, trans, Anvil, London, 1990.

Călinescu, George, Poor Ionaide [1953], **Extract 1** (D. Deletant, trans).

Caragiale, I. L., Sketches and Stories, Dacia, Cluj, 1979.

Caragiale, I. L., The Lost Letter and Other Plays [1884 etc], Lawrence & Wishart, London, 1956.

Caraion, Ion, The Error of Being, Marguerite Dorian and Elliott B. Urdang, trans, Forest Books, London and Boston, MA, 1994.

Carlton, Charles M., and Perry, Thomas Amherst, Romanian Poetry in English Translation: An Annotated Bibliography and Census of 249 Poets in English (1740–1989), Suppl. to Miorița, Vol 12, 1988, Rochester, NY, 1989.

Cassian, Nina, Blue Apple, Eva Feiler, trans, Cross Cultural Communications, Merrick, 1982.

Cassian, Nina, Lady of Miracles, Laura Schiff, trans, Cloud Marauder Press, Berkeley, CA, 1983.

Cassian, Nina, *Call Yourself Alive: The Love Poems of Nina Cassian*, Andrea Deletant and Brenda Walker, trans, Forest Books, London, 1988/Dufour, Chester Springs, PA, 1989.

Cassian, Nina, *Life Sentence: Selected Poems*, William Jay Smith, ed, W. W. Norton, New York and Anvil, London, 1990.

Cassian, Nina, *Cheerleader for a Funeral*, Brenda Walker with Nina Cassian, trans, Forest Books, London, 1992.

Cioran, E. M., *The Temptation to Exist* [1956, 1975], Richard Howard, trans [from the French], introduction by Susan Sontag, Quartet, London, 1987/Seaver Books, New York, 1986.

Cioranescu, Alexandre, *Vasile Alecsandri*, Twayne, New York, 1973.

Cioranescu, A., *Ion Barbu*, Twayne, Boston, MA, 1981.

Crăsnaru, Daniela, *Letters from Darkness* [1984, 1987], Fleur Adcock, trans, Oxford University Press, Oxford and New York, 1991.

Cu bilet circular. With a Travel Card, Mircea Zaciu, ed, Dacia, Cluj-Napoca, 1983. (Anthology.)

Deletant, Andrea, and Deletant, Dennis, *Romania, World Bibliographical Series*, Vol 59, Clio Press, Oxford, 1985.

Deletant, Dennis, *Ceauşescu and the Securitate: Coercion and Dissent in Romania, 1965–1989*, Hurst, London, 1995.

Dennis-Jones, Harold, *Where to Go in Romania*, Settle Press, London, 1991. (Does not include new names. Many street names have been changed to eradicate testimony to the Communist regime; in many cases they revert to names in use before 1948.)

Description of a Struggle: the Picador Book of East European Prose, Michael March, ed, Picador, London, 1994. (Mircea Cărtărescu, Ana Blandiana, George Cuşnarencu, Ştefan Agopian.)

Dinescu, Mircea, *Exile on a Peppercorn: The Poetry of Mircea Dinescu*, Forest Books, London and Boston, MA, 1985.

Eliade, Mircea, *Two Tales of the Occult* [1940], Herder and Herder, New York, 1970; as *Two Strange Tales*, Shambhala, Boston, MA, 1986.

Eliade, Mircea, *The Forbidden Forest* [1955 in French, Romanian original 'Midsummer Night' 1971], Notre Dame University Press, Notre Dame, IN, 1978.

Eliade, Mircea and Niculescu, Mihai, *Fantastic Tales* [Eliade, 'Twelve Thousand Head of Cattle' and 'A Great Man', 1961; Mihai Niculescu, 'The Cobbler of Hydra', 1963], Eric Tappe, trans, Forest Books, London, 1990. **Extract 2.**

Eliade, Mircea, *Tales of the Sacred and the Supernatural* ['With the Gipsy Girls', 1963, and 'Les Trois Grâces', 1976], Westminster, PA, 1981.

Eliade, Mircea, *The Old Man and the Bureaucrats* [1968], University of Chicago Press, Chicago, IL, 1988.

Eliade, Mircea, *Youth Without Youth and Other Novellas* [*The Cape, Youth Without Youth*, and *Nineteen Roses*, written 1975–76], Mac Linscott Ricketts, trans, Forest Books, London, 1989/ Ohio State University Press, Ohio, 1988.

Eliade, Mircea, *Patterns of Comparative Religion*, New American Library, New York, 1987.

Eliade, Mircea, *From Primitives to Zen*, Collins, London/Harper and Row, New York, 1977.

Eliade, Mircea, *Zalmoxis, the Vanishing God*, University of Chicago Press, Chicago, IL, 1986.

Eliade, Mircea, *Autobiography, Vol 1:*

Journey East, Journey West: 1907–1947, Vol 2: 1937–1960, Exile's Odyssey, University of Chicago Press, Chicago, IL, 1990.

Eminescu, Mihai, selected poems in Roy MacGregor-Hastie, *The Last Romantic*, Iowa City, 1972.

Eminescu, Mihai, selected poems in *In Celebration of Mihai Eminescu*, Brenda Walker, ed, Forest Books, London, 1989.

Fischer, Mary Ellen, *Nicolae Ceauşescu: A Study in Political Leadership*, Lynne Rienner, Boulder, CO, 1989.

Fischer-Galati, Stephen, *Twentieth-Century Rumania*, 2nd ed, Columbia University Press, New York, 1991.

Georgescu, Vlad, *A History of the Romanians*, Ohio State University Press, Columbus, OH, 1991.

Goma, Paul, *My Childhood at the Gate of Unrest* [1987], Readers International, London and Columbia, LA, 1990.

History and Legend in Romanian Short Stories and Tales, Ana Cartianu, ed, Minerva, Bucharest, 1983.

Hitchins, Keith, *Rumania 1866–1947*, Oxford University Press, Oxford, 1994.

Introduction to Rumanian Literature, Jacob Steinberg, ed, Twayne, New York, 1966. (A prose anthology.)

Iorga, Nicolae, *Romania As It Was Before 1918*, **Extract 12** (D. Deletant, trans).

Liiceanu, Gabriel, *Păltiniş Diary*, **Extract 8** (D. Deletant, trans).

Ludlam, H., *A Biography of Dracula: The Life Story of Bram Stoker*, W. Foulsham, London and New York, 1962; also as *A Biography of Bram Stoker: Creator of Dracula*, New English Library, London, 1977.

Manning, Olivia, *The Balkan Trilogy* (*The Great Fortune, The Spoilt City, Friends and Heroes*) [1960, 1962, 1965], Penguin, London and New York, 1988. **Extract 3.**

Modern Romanian Poetry: An Anthology, Nicholas Catanoy, ed, Mosaic Press, Oakville, Ottawa, 1977.

Pied Poets, The: Contemporary Verse of the Transylvanian and Danube Germans of Romania, Robert Elsie, trans, Forest Books, London and Boston, MA, 1990.

Pillat, Ion, 'Dusk in the Delta', **Extract 5** (D. Deletant, trans).

Rebreanu, Liviu, *The Uprising* [1932], Peter Owen, London, 1964.

Rebreanu, Liviu, *Ion* [1920], Peter Owen, London, 1965. (**Extract 15** – D. Deletant, trans.)

Rebreanu, Liviu, *The Forest of the Hanged* [1922], A. V. Wise, trans, Peter Owen, London, 1967.

Rebreanu, Liviu, *Adam and Eve*, Minerva, Bucharest, 1986.

Romanian Short Stories, Olivia Manning, ed, Oxford University Press, Oxford, 1971.

Romanian Poems: A Bilingual Anthology of Romanian Poetry, Sever Trifu and Dumitru Ciocoi-Pop, eds, Dacia, Cluj-Napoca, 1972.

Rumanian Prose and Verse, E. D. Tappe, ed, Athlone Press, London, 1956.

Sadoveanu, Mihail, *Mitrea Cocor* [1949], Fore Publications, London, 1953.

Sadoveanu, Mihail, *The Hatchet: the Life of Stephen the Great* [1930], Allen and Unwin, London, 1965; East European Monographs (Columbia distr), New York, 1991.

Sebastian, Mihail, *The Accident*, **Extract 9** (D. Deletant, trans).

Silent Voices: An Anthology of Contemporary Romanian Women Poets, Andrea Deletant and Brenda Walker, eds, Forest Books, London, 1986. **Extract 10.**

Sorescu, Marin, *Vlad Dracula the Im-*

paler: A Play [1978], Forest Books, London, 1987.

Sorescu, Marin, The Thirst of the Salt Mountain: a Trilogy of Plays, Forest Books, London and Boston, MA, 1985.

Sorescu, Marin, Selected Poems 1965–1973, Michael Hamburger, trans, Bloodaxe Books, Newcastle upon Tyne, 1983.

Sorescu, Marin, Hands Behind My Back: Selected Poems, Gabriela Dragnea, Stuart Friebert and Adriana Varga, trans, Oberlin College Press, Oberlin, OH, 1991.

Sorescu, Marin, The Biggest Egg in the World, Bloodaxe Books, Newcastle upon Tyne/Dufour, Chester Springs, PA, 1987.

Sorescu, Marin, The Youth of Don Quixote, John F. Deane, trans, Dedalus, Dublin, 1987.

Sorescu, Marin, Let's Talk About the Weather . . . and Other Poems, Forest Books, London and Boston, MA, 1985.

Sorescu, Marin, 'Village Museum', Extract 4 (D. Deletant, trans).

Stănescu, Nichita, The Still Unborn about the Dead, Petru Demetru Popescu and Peter Jay, trans, International Writing Program, University of Iowa, Iowa City, IA, 1974/Anvil, London, 1975.

Stănescu, Nichita, Bas-Relief with Heroes: Selected Poems, 1960–1982, Thomas C. Carlson and Vasile Poenaru, trans, Memphis State University Press, Memphis, TN, 1988.

Stoker, Bram, Dracula [1897], Penguin, London and New York, 1993. Extract 16.

Tartler, Grete, Orient Express, Fleur Adcock, trans, Oxford University Press, Oxford and New York, 1989. Extract 11.

Vlahuţă, Alexandru, Picturesque Romania, Extracts 7 and 13 (D. Deletant, trans).

Wagner, Richard, Exit: A Romanian Story [Ausreiseantrag, 1988], Quintin Hoare, trans, Verso, London and New York, 1990. Extract 14.

Young Poets of a New Romania, Brenda Walker with Michaela Celea Leach, trans, Forest Books, London, 1991.

Extracts

(1) BUCHAREST

George Călinescu, *Poor Ioanide*

*Călinescu began to write Poor Ioanide in 1947 and completed it
in 1949, but was unable to publish it until four years later
because of political censorship. In the extract, 'Mincu' is Ion
Mincu (1852–1912), a Romanian architect who adapted
features of peasant houses such as wooden verandas and arcades
in his buildings.*

Despite its name Tritons' Street has nothing about it to suggest the
ocean or classical mythology. It probably owes its name to a mayor who
was proud of our Latin ancestry since other streets with names from
Classical antiquity (Sirens' St, Cyclops St, Minotaur St, Trajan St,
Virgil St etc) form a poetic family with it. It is a quiet street, lacking in
significant buildings, the road and pavement being made up of large
stones. The houses are of a single storey and in exceptional cases you
find outhouses at the back of courtyards with a low second storey like a
mezzanine. Far from the main roads, in a vast labyrinthine suburb
without anything distinctive in it, the street is difficult to find for an
eye used to landmarks. Nowhere in the vicinity is a square, with a
fountain or a monument. Here and there a whitewashed church, with a
roof of metal plates, appears before the eyes, yet the passing stranger
cannot distinguish it because there are several which are almost
identical in their monotony.

In this relatively recently constructed quarter, whose population
began to expand at the end of the last century, you will not see a single
slum. The residents belong to a middle class which assembled here
without dislocating others, and the dwellings, without aspiring to
luxury, are generally of sufficient comfort, despite being limited in size.
No building belongs to a particular style. Constructed by second-rate
builders or architects, they are of the most varied styles, with imitations
of Mincu, the *Sécession* style (horseshoe-shaped doors, balustrades
covered with enormous stucco leaves which gave them the appearance
of being made of melted shapeless wax), and Cubism with its flat roofs
prone to erosion from rainfall. Generally speaking the courtyards have
small gardens, but since some of the houses are situated on the roadway
and others are set back a little or at the end of courtyards, the streets
have no line and unfortunately the vegetation is not sufficiently
versatile to cover up the empty spaces.

(2) BUCHAREST

Mircea Eliade, *Twelve Thousand Head of Cattle*

The name of Mircea Eliade is probably associated by most English-speaking readers with studies of the history of religions. He was also an outstanding writer of tales of the supernatural – the story from which this extract is taken is an example.

He suddenly quickened his step, enraged, but after reaching the end of the street, stopped abruptly, swore several times and returned almost at a run. Outside No 14 Strada Frumoasei he took off his hat and pressed his whole palm on the bell push. He stayed like that for some time, with his hat in one hand and with the other on the bell, listening to the sound which seemed to return from very far off, coming back to him solitary and sinister from the empty house. He felt the thick drops of sweat gathering on his eyebrows, but he could not bring himself to take his hand off the bell and wipe himself. He was in a fury.

Then, strident and improbable, came the sound of the siren. Gore felt that his legs would sag and raised his glance despairingly. The sky was of a washed-out blue, with a few whitish clouds gliding at random, as if they had not decided which direction to take. 'They're mad! It's past twelve, what's come over them?' he found himself thinking. He began to look for his handkerchief, trembling, and passed it unconsciously over his face. He thought he heard voices in the neighbouring houses, doors banged, and a young woman's shrill scream.

'Ionică!', called the woman. 'Where are you, Ionică?'

Gore stealthily cast glances in all directions, then firmly lowered his chin to his chest and set off up the street at the double. With a last long startled groan the siren faded out. 'Six thousand head of cattle, of the best quality!' Gore found himself thinking. 'I've got the export licence. If only the Treasury gives its approval.' At that moment he saw, stuck on a fence, the familiar notice with an index finger in black paint: *Air Raid Shelter 20 Metres*. He felt the blood pouring into his cheeks again and set off running harder. When he arrived in front of the door and opened it, he heard, very close by, the short whistle of a policeman.

(3) BUCHAREST

Olivia Manning, *The Great Fortune*

The Great Fortune is the first volume of Manning's The Balkan Trilogy. Here Prince Yakimov, a down-at-heel Russian émigré, makes his way through the streets of Bucharest.

The light was failing. He was beginning to doubt his direction when, at a junction of roads, it seemed confirmed by a statue, in boyar's robes, wearing a turban the size of a pumpkin, that pointed him dramatically to the right.

Here the city had come to life again. The pavements were crowded with small men, all much alike in shabby city clothes, each carrying a brief-case. Yakimov recognized them for what they were; minor government officials and poor clerks, a generation struggling out of the peasantry, at work from eight in the morning until eight at night, now hurrying home to supper. In his hunger, he envied them. A tramway car stopped at the kerb. As the crowd pressed past him, he was buffeted mercilessly from side to side, but maintained his course, his head and shoulders rising above the surge with an appearance of unconcern.

He stopped at a window displaying jars of a jam-like substance that held in suspension transparent peaches and apricots. The light shone through them. This golden, sugared fruit, glowing through the chill blue twilight, brought a tear to his eye. He was pushed on roughly by a woman using a shopping basket as a weapon.

He crossed the road junction. Tramway cars, hung with passengers like swarming bees, clanged and shrilled upon him. He reached the other side. Here as he followed a down-sloping road, the crowd thinned and changed. He passed peasants in their country dress of whitish frieze, thin men, lethargic, down-staring, beneath pointed astrakhan caps, and Orthodox Jews with ringlets hanging on either side of greenish, indoor faces.

A wind, blowing up towards Yakimov, brought a rancid odour that settled in his throat like the first intimations of sea-sickness. He began to feel worried. These small shops did not promise the approach of the British Legation.

The street divided into smaller streets. Keeping to the widest of them, Yakimov saw in every window the minutiae of the tailoring trade – horse-hair, buckram, braid, ready-made pockets, clips, waistcoat buckles, cards of buttons, reels of cotton, rolls of lining. Who on earth wanted all this stuff?

(4) BUCHAREST

Marin Sorescu, *Village Museum*

The verse of Marin Sorescu is characterized by its rich vein of irony and humour and is notable for its epigrammatic caricatures of love and death. The inspiration comes from daily life and the tone is prosaic. Here the poet turns his attention to the Village Museum in Bucharest (this is not the complete poem).

Here the most numerous exhibits
are the hovels scooped out of the earth.
After tilling the soil
the peasants went straight into the ground,
to rest.

In the spaces between the hovels
uprisings are inserted:
by figures like
Doja, Horia, Cloşca and
Crişan, Tudor[1] as well,
built this time on the surface
with an amazing sense of architectural
symmetry.

Visitors,
don't touch the poverty and sadness
displayed in the museum.
They are original exhibits
coming from the hand, the soul and the essence of this people
in a moment of stress and spontaneity
which has lasted
2000 years.

---

[1] Gheorghe Doja (?–1514): Szekler peasant who led a peasant uprising in Transylvania in 1514. Horia, Closça and Crişan were also peasant leaders of an uprising in 1784. Tudor Vladimirescu raised a revolt against the rule of the Phanariot Greeks in Wallachia in 1821.

(5) DANUBE DELTA

Ion Pillat, *Dusk in the Delta*

This poem is from the cycle Limpezimi, first published in 1928, and belongs to what has been termed the 'traditionalist' phase of the poetry of Pillat (1891–1945), verse inspired by the Romanian landscape. The Lipovans (second stanza) are descended from a Russian-speaking group of religious dissenters, known as Raskolniki or Old Believers, who were exiled to this southern fringe of the Russian Empire some two or three centuries ago.

As far as the eye can see, the green bank of reeds
ripples in the evening wind with a rustle.
From time to time a clearing reveals
a pool of still water. A crane
rises on the wing
from the reeds, with a heart-rending whine,
or Tatar horses, intrepidly circling,
neigh rebelliously on a ridge.

Dusk envelops the whole delta in gold,
the colour of the towers in a Lipovan village,
but the deep blue is pervaded by
shadows from the floating islands of reeds.

A steamer cleaves the murmuring night,
the waves ever darkening into
the purple gold of the plum
as the five hills rise in the distance.

(6) CENTRAL TRANSYLVANIA

Lucian Blaga, *The Chronicle and Song of the Ages*

This extract is from the autobiography of the childhood and youth of the poet, dramatist, and philosopher Blaga.

My parents' house in Lancrăm, a village situated between the small town of Sebeş Alba and Alba Iulia, was an old and fairly solid structure in comparison with the surrounding houses. We had inherited it from Simion Blaga who had been the village priest until 1870. Facing the lane, on one side and the other of the courtyard, were two little gardens surrounded by pillars of bricks and a fence. One was a flower garden, the other, at the very front of the house, was unplanted: here was a wilting pine, under which I would often gather the yellowish fallen needles which resembled mosquitoes with five long legs. In this same little garden stood a giant chestnut which dominated the whole house with its crown. I imagined that beneath the bark resided a spirit which was linked mysteriously to the destiny of the house and of the family (the chestnut in fact died later in the very year that father died).

Stone steps, worn by feet and smoothed by the rain, rose from the courtyard into the house. Alongside was the entrance to the cellar, to which we gained access down stone slabs. Inside the entrance, and immediately below the opening to the cellar, a colony of toads had made their breeding ground. The front of the house was completely covered by Virginia creeper bearing small berries. Packed in between the house and the barn was a summer kitchen, guarded by a luxuriant mulberry tree, under which we would eat during the summer to the accompaniment of song birds. Inside the house were four rooms in a line, one of which was the 'luxury' room, the one facing the lane (the 'front room' as we also called it). It was a modest sitting room, almost always kept shut and opened only for guests from the city. A stony coldness characterized this room which was furnished in a petit-bourgeois way. I remember two old cupboards of walnut wood, with doors which sparkled like a water fountain, and a Biedermeyer chest of drawers, on top of which there stood a golden clock in a glass dome which played two period Viennese melodies with lively, twinkling sounds when wound up. I would often slip into the front room in order to release the playing mechanism of the clock.

(7) MOLDAVIA

Alexandru Vlahuţă, *Picturesque Romania*

Vlahuţă's enduring travelogue of Romania was first published in 1901. Agapia and Văratec, two convents of nuns, about eight kilometres apart, renowned for the beauty of their situation, are described in the chapter entitled 'In the Neamţ mountains'.

The monastery of Agapia is situated deep in the highlands, nestling in a convergence of valleys. It is protected from the north by a hill called 'The Flower Peak', to the west is a dark wall of forest, while before it stand fir trees which lead you to unexpected clearings with names like 'The bishop's glade', and 'The Mother Superior's glade'. From higher up in the mountain pastures you can see below the Văratec monastery, on the right the spas at Bălţăteşti, on the left the citadel of Neamţ and the town Târgu Neamţ, and before you the wide, unending valley of Moldavia.

The sun lingers on the sheep-fold on the Cruce mountain. From the archimandrite's verandah I rest my eyes on the courtyard of short grass, enclosed by the clean, white, silent monastery cells. From the centre of the yard rises the gleaming 'great church', with interior paintings by our master Grigorescu.[1]

There is a dream-like silence. Suddenly I hear, like a signal, a clear, powerful, musical sound: I look down – in the doorway of the church I see a tiny old nun bearing a light *toaca*[2] at arm's level in her left hand, and in her right a small wooden hammer; she struck the *toaca* once and stopped, as though waiting for the echo of the first beat to cease, and then she moved slowly along the church wall, striking the *toaca*, initially with several heavy, determined, solitary blows, and then gradually the interval between them decreased, until all you could hear was a cascade of brief, soft, staccato-like beats, like the hurried whisper of a prayer. They seemed to fade and return, and again they became more isolated, more pronounced, their lingering echo hanging in the corridors and in the vaulted ceilings, making the whole monastery sing like a violin.

[1] Nicolae Grigorescu (1838–1907) has the greatest claim to be Romania's national artist. His scenes from Romanian peasant life, his portraits of Jews, his landscapes and his depiction of episodes in the War of Independence in 1878, attracted international attention by his one-man exhibition at the Galeries Martinet in Paris in 1886.

[2] *toaca* – a length of flat wood, struck with a small mallet by monks or nuns in order to summon the faithful to prayer.

(8) Pălтiniş, Southern Transylvania

Gabriel Liiceanu, *Păltiniş Diary*

In this diary, Liiceanu records conversations with the philosopher Constantin Noica at Noica's mountain retreat in Păltiniş. Émile Cioran was a French philosophical essayist of Romanian origin who was a student colleague of Noica and who settled in Paris in the mid-1930s.

Tuesday 22 March 1977

Yesterday as we passed through the village of Răşinari where the Cioran family lived, Noica showed me the church near which lay the grave with a white cross of Father Cioran. There was also a second cross, with Relu Cioran's birthday engraved upon the cross. 'Relu comes here every Sunday from Sibiu. He says that he comes to visit his parents' grave but I suspect that he visits his own and has the secret pleasure of crying to himself. His own name on the cross drives him to it.' I remember that

Noica told me of his friendship with Cioran, such as it was, in the train. They studied Philosophy at university at the same time but without meeting each other, because Cioran had a provincial complex and was a recluse. Attendance was not compulsory and the opportunities of meeting or working together on seminars were rare. It was only after they graduated that they met. They both received two month scholarships to study in Geneva from Rădulescu-Pogoneanu, the son of Maiorescu's pupil. They shared a room and Noica, who at that time only knew Kant well, found himself faced by a more rounded cultural universe represented by Cioran [. . .]

Today we started the programme which would mark out the four days here. We meet at breakfast at 8.30, after which Noica takes his ninety minute walk. He then works until 1.30. After lunch he joins me for coffee in my room. He then has a rest for half an hour. He resumes work until 6 pm and between then and 7.30 takes his evening walk. Following the evening meal we step out for a while and then go up to my room where he talks to me about himself and his world.

The subject this evening was his *curriculum vitae*. 'I have no *curriculum vitae*, I just have books. Degree at twenty-three, then a year of mathematics and two as a librarian at the university. I have lived deliberately in reclusion. I refused any involvement in professional life and did so without hypocrisy, even with pleasure.'

(9) THE PRAHOVA VALLEY

Mihail Sebastian, *The Accident*

Sebastian describes the sight of the mountain Postăvarul during winter.

The news ran through the forest like a cry: the clouds are breaking! the mist is clearing!

The morning was grey, visibility low, and the light continually lacked brilliance. The summit of Postăvarul seemed squat under the damp, opaque sky which had descended too far.

Everybody had gathered on the terrace, as though on the bridge of a ship, in order to follow the unexpected return of the sun. When it was clear you could see the whole of the region around Braşov, as far as the Făgăraş mountains. It was like a window of Postăvarul opened onto the plain, a window hidden since the beginning of winter in clouds and through which for a few seconds had appeared that morning the sunlit image of Braşov, only to disappear again.

The people seemed stunned by the over rapid image that had flashed and faded in the distance. The mist settled again on the fir-trees and rocks with its diffuse light, extinguishing the last reflections from the stones.

'Look!', someone shouted.

The skyline had parted and a floating circle of blue light emerged like a ghost-like town from amongst the clouds. Curtains of smoke parted and walls of mist crumbled. A citadel sparkled in the sun, with metal roofs and javelins and shields raised in the light.

It was not Braşov. It was too far to be Braşov, it was too blinding. Cascades of clouds covered it, casting it once again in mist, but a moment later it reappeared elsewhere, like a travelling island, like a fantastic gulf in this ocean of smoke and fog.

Sometimes the images were precise and simple, easily recognisable. Someone was pointing through the clouds to Râşnov or Zizin, to the snaking road towards Bran, the gleaming towers of Zărneşti. But in a split second everything disappeared.

(10) Sibiu

Daniela Crăsnaru, *Transylvanian Town*

Sibiu (Hermannstadt in German) is one of the seven towns said to have been founded by settlers from the archbishopric of Cologne in the early 13th century. The seven towns give the German name Siebenburgen for Transylvania. This poem is included in the anthology Silent Voices – see Booklist.

Do you remember the town where we once went together?
Delirious streets climbing higher,
keyboards of a piano, a sonorous stair.
It happened an eternity ago. Now an era, a year.

It was a medieval town, walled and scholastic.
Climbing of our own free will, two heretics
on a huge stake.
Two handsome heretics, swimming through waters of dusk
through time stopped at the town's gate.

The clock in the tower had no hands, no hours.
Sweet fragrance drifting over everything, oh such aromas.
Do you remember how our bodies and breath drew signs
On the white pages of calendars?

We were there in a time without a name.
Always near evening, almost never near daytime.

It's a year now since we were there, a decade.
Another millenium. Another lifetime.

(11) Sighişoara

Grete Tartler, *Sighişoara 1982*

*Grete Tartler's family is of German ancestry from Transylva-
nia; one of the province's most picturesque towns is itself a
German foundation, Sighişoara (German name Schässburg).*

If you had the insight
as the river has, flowing between
yellow and green houses with chained doors,
breathing out two breaths – the scent
of lime trees and that of damp –
listening to the organ-music of tiles:
    piano (the ones with moss on them)
    forte (the redder ones).
If you had the impulse
as the cannon do, booming
    over ANDREAS RATH, IRONMONGER,
    over the high school, over the volley-ball field,
    over the jasmine and gnomes in the garden.
If you would bring supplies
from the other side of the river!

To be clouded and indifferent as silt!
You have lived many lives here in vain.
The water carves a scar
on the face of the town;
even you have set the gold ring
from your finger under your eyelids now:
a snake painted on the chemist's shop wall –
you read there 'Water Level, 1970'.
But you, so indifferent, don't bring
supplies, although you've been crossing
to and fro across the river for so long.

(12) SINAIA

Nicolae Iorga, *Romania As It Was Before 1918*

Polyhistorian and prominent politician, Iorga wrote with characteristic erudition about the landscape, life and history of his country.

Here, amongst the other trees divested by the cold autumn winds, stands the impassive fir, as resilient as it is slender. Behind are massed the Bucegi mountains, Vârful cu Dor, Jepii, Caraimanul, standing shoulder to shoulder, like a manifestation of the deepest past, of the most indomitable power, and of the loftiest embodiment of grandeur. Their pointed peaks and craggy summits are covered by the snows of an imperial old-age.

Below villas tumble down the foothills, sheltered by the firs and darkened as though by a permanent threat even when the sun's rays play on more prominent peaks. This is Sinaia, with its monastery and royal castle. It is, at the same time, a mountain resort for the wealthy, an industrial town and a village. The monastery is the oldest building. The sanctity of its seclusion, guarded by mountain eagles and lumbering cave bears, was disturbed solely by the cautious step of the highwayman singing his song of liberty and revenge among the firs until Mihai Spătarul Cantacuzino, a Wallachian boyar full of piety and burdened by the abundance of his wealth, had a monastery built here for the forgiveness of his sins, to the glory of God's name, and to help the traveller. He was returning from the monastery of the holy mountain of Arabia, where the Ten Commandments had been handed down, and so he called his foundation Sinai which the local peasants Romanianized to Sinaia. For two centuries this harmonious stone building with beautiful towers echoed with hymns and was imbued with holy incense, while the thick walls of the cells and the corner towers under their black shingle tile roofs gave protection from the enemies in the surrounding wastes: wild animals and men.

(13) SULINA

Alexandru Vlahuţă, *Picturesque Romania*

In this passage Vlahuţă describes the Sulina channel, one of the three arms into which the Danube radiates as it debouches into the Black Sea.

No sooner had the windmills on the hills overlooking Tulcea disappeared from sight than we came upon the third arm of the Danube, branching out from the Sulina channel. The white line of this arm, called 'the Saint George', curves away towards the right and disappears amongst the reed banks. As it rolls its waves over the delta the Danube seems to be trying to hide, to flee the overwhelming power of the sea which draws and summons it from afar with the cry of its breakers. All around, as far as the eye can see, is a marshy plain covered with bullrushes and willow trees. The Sulina arm, dredged and made navigable, is lined with stone embankments and extends like a straight, white waterspout over this boundless, smooth green deserted plain. Here and there you can see on the bank a fishermen's retreat, a deep cave covered with bundles of reeds. A boat with billowing sails appears from time to time on the silvery strip of water like a bird from another world. Wild horses with flowing manes emerge from the thickets, shake their heads, and look at us attentively with a quizzical air of surprise. The remote wildness of these uncharted places, the sprawling reed-forests waving their bronze tips in the wind, this deep silence dominating the whole area, all makes you think that you are far from the earth, on a deserted planet.

(14) TIMIŞOARA

Richard Wagner, *Exit*

Wagner was born near Timişoara, the city in the western part of Romania which became the birthplace of the 1989 Romanian revolution. He emigrated to West Germany in 1987. Exit chronicles the pressures on Wagner which forced him into exile (see biographical entry).

Stirner walked through the park beside the cathedral. It was the only one in the city where the benches, for some unknown reason, were undamaged; benches dating back to the sixties, with broad planks supported by concrete pedestals. Nearby stood more recent benches, iron rods welded together, thin slats on top. In the middle of the park there was a broad avenue. Here stood the monument to the Romanian soldiers who'd fought in the Second World War, or more precisely in the final phase of the war, after the palace revolt of 23 August 1944 when Romania had switched sides. Nobody ever spoke about the first three years of war. Romania on the Eastern Front, as an ally of the Third Reich: that had never existed. That period didn't figure in the history books. Only pensioners would talk about it, as of a bygone youth, a time irretrievably past. Odessa, the Crimea, Stalingrad, what did the young people know about these?

The monument was composed of white marble blocks and stood on a tall plinth: a soldier, with flag raised high and rifle at the ready. The side reliefs showed allegorical scenes: on the left, soldiers fighting in close combat with an invisible enemy; on the right, women with flowers, workers, peasants and children thronging round the victors. Steps led up to a little platform, also of marble, on the front of the monument. On October mornings there'd be children in pioneer uniforms standing on this platform, performing the 'Pioneereid' under their teachers' direction. Patriotic poems would be recited. Songs sung. The children would pledge allegiance to the President and to the Fatherland. A short way off parents would stand, children's jackets in their arms, gazing mutely on. They'd be men and women of Stirner's age. They'd be working an afternoon shift, or else have left work. Just for a moment. At the close of the ceremony, a photographer would arrive who'd previously been standing to one side. He'd scurry up like a wedding photographer.

(15) NORTHERN TRANSYLVANIA

Liviu Rebreanu, *Ion*

Rebreanu's first novel depicts a land-hungry peasant dominated by a primitive egotism. The author sets the novel in the region of the town Sângeorz-Băi. He has renamed some of the localities, although the village of Cârlibaba, and the rivers Someş and Bistriţa can be followed in this opening description.

The main road from Cârlibaba snakes its way along by the Someş river as far as Cluj and even beyond. From it branches off a white road which crosses the river by an old wooden bridge covered by a mouldy shingle roof; this smaller road cuts through the village of Jidoviţa and runs down towards Bistriţa, where it joins the other main road that descends from Bucovina through the Bârgău pass.

Leaving Jidoviţa the road climbs precariously until it makes its way through narrow hill-passes, and then turns on smoothly, sometimes becoming obscured by the young beech-trees in Domneşti woods. It halts a little at Dead Man's Well, where cool water trickles unceasingly from the spring, and then swerves suddenly under Devil's Ravines in order to burst into the village of Pripas hidden in a hollow.

At the edge of the village you are met on the left by a crooked cross with a Christ crucified, a Christ with a weather-beaten face and a wreath of faded flowers dangling from his legs. There is a light breeze and Christ is mournfully creaking his rusty tin body on the worm-eaten wooden cross, blackened by time.

The village seems dead. The sultry heat which hovers in the air weaves a shroud of oppressive silence. Only now and again can you hear the lazy rustle of limp leaves in the trees. A wisp of bluish smoke sluggishly rises from amongst the branches, lurches like a drunken monster and tumbles into the dusty gardens, covering them in an ashen mist.

(16) TRANSYLVANIA

Bram Stoker, *Dracula*

The success of Dracula as one of the most popular horror stories ever written has made Transylvania synonymous with its central figure. Here, Stoker describes Jonathan Harker's journey to Count Dracula's castle. The Bârgău (Borgo in the extract) Pass, traversing the Bârgău Mountains, carries one of the roads linking Transylvania and Bukovina and runs between the towns of Bistriţa and Vatra Dornei.

The excitement of the passengers grew greater; the crazy coach rocked on its great leather springs, and swayed like a boat tossed on a stormy sea. I had to hold on. The road grew more level, and we appeared to fly along. Then the mountains seemed to come nearer to us on each side and to frown down upon us; we were entering the Borgo Pass. One by one several of the passengers offered me gifts, which they pressed upon me with an earnestness which would take no denial; these were certainly of an odd and varied kind, but each was given in simple good faith, with a kindly word, and a blessing, and that strange mixture of fear-meaning movements which I had seen outside the hotel at Bistritz – the sign of the cross and the guard against the evil eye. Then, as we flew along, the driver leaned forward, and on each side the passengers, craning over the edge of the coach, peered eagerly into the darkness. It was evident that something very exciting was either happening or expected, but though I asked each passenger, no one would give me the slightest explanation. This state of excitement kept on for some little time; and at last we saw before us the Pass opening out on the eastern side. There were dark, rolling clouds overhead, and in the air the heavy, oppressive sense of thunder. It seemed as though the mountain range had separated two atmospheres, and that now we had got into the thunderous one. I was now myself looking out for the conveyance which was to take me to the Count. Each moment I expected to see the glare of lamps through the blackness; but all was dark. The only light was the flickering rays of our own lamps, in which steam from our hard-driven horses rose in a white-cloud. We could now see the sandy road lying white before us, but there was on it no sign of a vehicle. The passengers drew back with a sigh of gladness, which seemed to mock my own disappointment. I was already thinking what I had best to do, when the driver, looking at his watch, said to the others something which I could hardly hear, it was spoken so quietly and in so low a tone; I thought it was, 'An hour less than the time'. Then, turning to me, he said in German worse than my own:–

'There is no carriage here'.

Biographies and important works

ALECSANDRI, Vasile (1821–1890). Alecsandri was a dramatist and poet. After studies in Paris (1834–39), he was appointed a director of the newly-founded National Theatre in Iaşi. The absence of a repertory in Romanian led him to become a playwright, and his first efforts in this direction were adaptations of French farces. Using this experience he wrote a number of farces based on contemporary Moldavian society which enjoyed great popular success and which made a theatre in Romanian socially acceptable. In the 1840s, he travelled throughout Moldavia collecting folk ballads which he published in Paris in 1852. The influence of folk poetry is evident in his own early verse but his most successful poems are contained in *Pasteluri* (*Pastels*), 1875, delicate landscapes of the countryside during the four seasons. Since his death his reputation as a poet has declined in the face of charges of banality. There is a fine appraisal of his life and work in Alexandre Cioranescu's *Vasile Alecsandri*.

BLAGA, Lucian (1895–1961). A poet, dramatist and philosopher, Blaga was born in **Lancrăm** in Transylvania (Extract 6). He studied philosophy at Vienna between 1917 and 1920 and took his doctorate there in 1922 with the thesis *Kultur und Erkenntnis* (*Culture and Knowledge*). From 1937 until 1948 he held the Chair of the Philosophy of Culture at **Cluj University**. In 1948 he was dismissed for opposing the educational reforms introduced by the Communist government and spent the years until his death as an archivist. His obsession with 'light' and its mysterious character is the theme of *Poemele luminii* (*The Poems of Light*), 1919. His predilection for what might be called the great cosmic themes is exemplified in *În marea trecere* (*In the Great Transition*), 1924, *Lauda somnului* (*Praise of Sleep*), 1929, and *La curţile dorului* (*At the Court of Longing*), 1938. As a dramatist he adapted national myths in *Zamolxe* (*Zamolxis*), 1921, and *Meşterul Manole* (*Master Manole*), 1927. His works on the philosophy of culture show the influence of Kant and Spengler and are notable for their vast syntheses and hazardous schematization.

BLANDIANA, Ana (1942–). Blandiana's courageous stand against the opportunism and sycophancy which characterized much of literary expression during the 1970s and 1980s has made her one of the most admired public figures in Romania. In September 1990 she played a leading role in setting up the Civic Alliance, a voluntary association with no political affiliation, of student, professional and trade-union organizations, which proved extremely successful in mobilizing anti-government street protests. In her early cycles of poetry, *A treia taină* (*The Third Sacrament*), 1970, and *Octombrie, noiembrie, decembrie* (*October, November, December*), 1972, she is preoccupied with purity, expressed by angels, butterflies, and crystalline waters. She uses this in later collections such as *Ora de nisip* (*The Hour of Sand*), 1983, *Stea de pradă* (*Star of Prey*), 1985, and *Poezii* (*Poems*), 1989, as a weapon with which to confront a corrupt age. Her concern that civilized human values have been perverted stems from a native Transylvanian sense of probity and dedication which has been submerged in contemporary public life by the 'oriental' values of Bucharest. A selection of her poems has been translated and is available in Ana Blandiana, *The Hour of Sand: Selected Poems 1969–89.*

BUZURA, Augustin (1938–). Buzura is a novelist whose work retains its intrinsic power despite having been written under the totalitarian conditions of Ceauşescu's rule. The main themes of his novels are the corruption of Romanian society by the psychosis of opportunism, its degradation by brutalization, and its passivity. Moral integrity and an unflinching adherence to a belief characterize both *Absenţii* (*The Absent Ones*), 1970, and *Orgolii* (*Forms of Pride*), 1977. Romanian passivity grows in the absence of such qualities and is condemned in *Refugii* (*Places of Refuge*), 1984. Despite being raised to a virtue by Romanians, it is interpreted by the author as cowardice. In the postures of conformity and compliance lies an explanation for the degradation of Romanian society under Ceauşescu. How desperate that situation had become for the writer is revealed in *Drumul cenuşii* (*The Road to Ash*), 1989, where the central character, a journalist, is overwhelmed by a sense of futility in his search for an engineer who disappeared after trying to defend miners' rights during the strike in the **Jiu valley** in 1977. Buzura's work also played a didactic role, informing the public about taboo subjects such as the career and fate of Iuliu Maniu, the Peasant Party leader jailed by the Communists in 1947 (*Orgolii*), about the abuses of collectivization (*Feţele tăcerii* – *The Faces of Silence* – 1974), and about the miners' strike in 1977 (*Drumul cenuşii*).

CĂLINESCU, George (1899–1965). One of Romania's most original and prolific literary critics, Călinescu was appointed director of the Institute of Literary History and Folklore in 1949. He began his novel *Bietul Ioanide* (*Poor Ioanide*) in 1947 and completed

George Călinescu

it a year later, but was unable to publish it for four years, because the novel failed to conform to the literary dictates of Socialist Realism, and displayed excessive candidness in its portrayal of different reactions from intellectuals to the rise of right-wing movements in pre-war Romania (Extract 1). His monumental *Istoria literaturii române* (*History of Romanian Literature*), 1941, was banned after the second world war and not republished in Romania until 1982.

CARAGIALE, Ion Luca (1852–1912). A journalist and writer of plays and short stories, Caragiale was born into a family of actors – his childhood and youth were dominated by the theatre. He attended a mime school run by his uncle and at the age of eighteen became a prompter in the National Theatre in **Bucharest**. His period of playwriting opened in 1879 with *O noapte furtunoasă* (*A Stormy Night*), a comedy of lower middle-class life in Bucharest. In 1904 he inherited money and moved with his family to Berlin.

Generally regarded as Romania's most accomplished comic playwright and humorist, and unquestionably its most enduring author, Caragiale encapsulates in his work the typical traits of the Romanian character. As a journalist he perfected a talent for observing the manners and behaviour of his fellow citizens and these observations he incorporated into his comedies. Such is the perennial nature of the attitudes displayed by his characters, and the vivid colloquial quality of his language, that Caragiale's comedies possess a timelessness which ensures their continuing popularity with Romanian audiences. The hallmarks of his comedies are frenzy and agitation; characters often mill around incessantly in unbridled commotion. These features are present in *A Stormy Night*, which is based on the theme of the deceived husband, naively confident in the good faith of his younger assistant who is his wife's lover. The theme is repeated in *O Scrisoare Pierdută* (*A Lost Letter*), 1884, where the lower middle-class triangle of the earlier comedy is replaced by three figures from the upper middle class. Caragiale's last play, *Năpasta* (*Injustice*), 1890, is an unconvincing drama of a peasant woman's revenge for the murder of her husband. A preoccupation with the macabre features in the short story 'O făclie de Paşte' ('An Easter Torch'), 1890, while the supernatural is skilfully handled in 'La Hanul lui Mânjoală' ('At Mânjoală's Inn'), 1898. Translations of these stories are available in *Sketches and Stories* and of the plays in *The Lost Letter and Other Plays*.

CARAGIALE, Matei (1885–1936). Caragiale's short story 'Remember', 1924, is one of the most memorable creations of Romanian literature. Set in the Berlin of the 1900s it recounts the author's chance meeting with an English gentleman Aubrey de Vere. In describing Berlin's art galleries and parks Caragiale produces a hypnotic atmosphere reminiscent of Gerard de Nerval's hallucinatory dreams. The novel *Craii de Curtea Veche* (*The Profligates of the Old Court*), 1929, is unique for its portrayal of a society of aristocratic degenerates who frequented a seedy quarter of **Bucharest**.

CRĂSNARU, Daniela (1950–). Born in the southern Romanian town of **Craiova** in 1950, Daniela Crăsnaru studied English and Romanian at Craiova University, and made her debut as a poet in 1973, the year she graduated. She worked in publishing and has had about a dozen volumes published to date, as well as some children's books. In 1990 she was elected to the Romanian parliament as an independent. Her collections include *Lumină cât umbră* (*Light as Shade*), 1973, *Spaţiul de graţie* (*Space of Grace*), 1976, *Arcaşii orbi* (*The Blind Archers*), 1978, *Crângul hipnotic* (*The Hypnotic Grove*), 1979, *Poezii de dragoste* (*69 Love Poems*), 1982, *Niagara de plumb* (*Niagara of Lead*), 1984, and *Emisferele de Magdeburg* (*The Magdeburg Hemispheres*), 1987. Some English translations appeared in *Silent Voices: An Anthology of Contemporary Romanian Women Poets* (Ex-

Daniela Crăsnaru

tract 10). Several poems from her collection *Niagara de plumb*, translated by Fleur Adcock, appeared (bilingually) in the magazine π (*PI*), a trimestrial poetry review, Vol 9, No 1, May 1990, Special Issue entitled *Freiheit . . . Contemporary Poetry from Middle and Eastern Europe*, Leuvense Schrijversaktie, Louvain, 1990. The volume *Letters from Darkness*, 1991, is also translated by Fleur Adcock – the poems are mainly from *Niagara de plumb* and *Emisferele de Magdeburg*, and from previously concealed and unpublishable texts.

ELIADE, Mircea (1907–1986). Eliade was a novelist and a historian of religions. After graduating in philosophy at **Bucharest** in 1928 he received an offer of a bursary to study in India from the Maharajah of Kassimbazar and began a three-year study of Indian philosophy under the tutelage of Surrendranath Dasgupta, Professor of Philosophy at Calcutta University. On his return to Romania he was appointed Associate Professor in the Faculty of Letters at **Bucharest University**. He was Romanian cultural attaché in London (1940) and in Lisbon (1941–44). After the war he remained in the West, holding positions at various European universities before becoming in 1956 Professor of the History of Religions at Chicago.

In Eliade's fiction the sacred and the mythical often manifest themselves in everyday life. In *Domnişoara Christina* (*Miss Christina*), 1936, he explored by creating a horror story the manner in which the supernatural reveals itself to ordinary people. *Noaptea de Sânziene* (*Midsummer's Night*), first published in French in 1955 as *La Forêt Interdite* (*The Forbidden Forest*), follows its hero's search to distinguish the sacred and profane in terms of fundamental time as opposed to historical time. These concepts are expounded in Eliade's philosophy of myth, expressed in *Le Mythe de l'Éternel Retour* (*The Myth of the Eternal Return*), 1949. A preoccupation with the supernatural dominates the three novellas, written between 1975 and 1979, which make up the collection *Youth Without Youth*.

Eliade's extensive research into the history of religions led to basic works such as *Traité d'histoire des religions*, 1949, *Patterns of Comparative Religion*, 1958, *From Primitives to Zen*, 1967, *Zalmoxis, the Vanishing God*, 1972, and *Histoires des croyances et des idées religieuses*, 1976–81. Selected translations of his fiction can be found in *Two Tales of the Occult*, 1970, *The Forbidden Forest*, 1978, *The Old Man and the Bureaucrats*, 1979, *Youth Without Youth and Other Novellas*, 1988, and *Fantastic Tales*, 1990 (Extract 2). There are two volumes of autobiography – *Autobiography*, Vol 1, 1981 and Vol 2, 1988.

EMINESCU, Mihai (1850–1889). Born in **northern Moldavia**, Eminescu attended German-language elementary and secondary schools in the nearby Austrian-administered town of Czernowitz (Chernovtsy) where he came under the influence of the Romanian nationalist schoolteacher Aron Pumnul. He abandoned his studies following Pumnul's death in 1866 and went on the road with a troupe of actors. Between 1869 and 1874 he attended classes at Vienna and Berlin universities and on his return worked as a librarian. In 1877 he joined a conservative newspaper in **Bucharest** but a frenetic workload brought on a mental collapse in 1883 from which he never recovered.

Only one volume of his verse, *Poesii* (*Poems*), 1883, was published during his lifetime. His vision of the world is characterized by antitheses and contrasting destinies and is derived from his own experience of life. This experience, converted with sincerity into art, permeates his verse. The two poles of the poet's adult life are marked by intense love and disillusionment. They owe their origin to his infatuation with Veronica Micle, a young married woman who never fully reciprocated Eminescu's feelings. The disillusionment caused by this relationship gave him a predilection for Schopenhauer which had been nurtured by his studies at Vienna and Berlin. Yet the expression of detachment and pessimism in his verse does not mean that the poet himself remained aloof and indifferent. His work as a librarian, when he strove avidly to collect as many early Romanian manuscripts as possible, as a proofreader of school textbooks, as a journalist, almost single-handedly keeping one of Bucharest's principal dailies supplied with copy, show a man committed to the cultural and political development of the young Romania. His capacity to live his own life and its problems, and those of his country, at fever pitch is reflected equally in his poetry and his journalism, and both give a unity to his personality. Selections of his poems have appeared in Roy MacGregor-Hastie, *The Last Romantic*, 1972, and in Brenda Walker, *In Celebration of Mihai Eminescu*, 1989.

GOMA, Paul (1935–). Goma was the most outspoken of a handful of Romanian dissidents who expressed themselves publicly during the 1970s. In 1954 he was admitted to the School of Literature and Literary Criticism in **Bucharest**. During a seminar in 1956 he read out part of his novel *Durerile facerii* (*The Pains of Conception*), in which the hero sets out to establish a students' movement similar to that in Hungary. He was promptly arrested and sentenced to two years' imprisonment. On release he was exiled to a village east of Bucharest where he spent four years in compulsory confinement. Unable to resume his studies as an ex-political prisoner he took a number of manual jobs in various towns in southern Transylvania.

Goma's first volume of short stories *In camera de alături* (*In the Room Next Door*) appeared in 1968, shortly before he joined the Communist Party. The manuscript of his first novel *Ostinato*, based on his experiences at the hands of the security police, was submitted for publication in the winter of 1967 but the reader claimed to recognize Elena Ceauşescu in one of the characters and an interdiction was placed on further publication of Goma's writings. All his subsequent novels were published in the West. *Ostinato* appeared in German translation in 1971 and as a result Goma was dismissed from the Party. In April 1977 he was arrested after making public the contents of a letter addressed to Pavel Kohout, one of those involved with Charter 77 in Czechoslovakia, and sending two letters to Ceauşescu denouncing the *securitate*. Goma was allowed to leave Romania with his wife and child on 20 November 1977 and settled in Paris where he wrote a succession of novels drawing on his life in Romania which were published in French.

The principal theme of Goma's writing is the ambiguity of living in a totalitarian state. His novels portray the ever-present duplicity of existence in a society in which the citizen must strike a balance daily between the demands of 'official' life and the attempt to lead an 'unofficial' one. His prison experience in **Gherla** in Transylvania provides the subject of

Gherla, 1976, and *Les Chiens de mort* (*The Dogs of Death*), 1981. The fear, uncertain loyalties and apathy of those whose aid Goma solicited when attempting to overcome the ban placed on his writing is chronicled in detail in *Le Tremblement des hommes* (*The Earthquake Under People*), 1979. *Le Calidor*, 1987, translated in English under the title *My Childhood at the Gate of Unrest*, 1990, centres on Goma's childhood experiences in his native **Bessarabia**.

IORGA, Nicolae (1871–1940). A polyhistorian and man of vast erudition, Nicolae Iorga was an outstanding personality in Romanian affairs during the first four decades of the 20th century, a professor in Bucharest (from 1895), founder of the Institute for the Study of South-Eastern Europe (1913), member of parliament (1907–40), founder of the National Democratic Party (1910), prime minister and foreign minister (1931–32). His political influence made him a target of the Fascist Iron Guard, by whom

Nicolae Iorga

he was murdered in 1940. He is the author of *Geschichte des romänischen Volkes* (*History of the Romanian People*), 1905, *Geschichte des osmanischen Reiches* (*History of the Ottoman Empire*), 1908–12, and other writings (Extract 12).

LIICEANU, Gabriel (1942–). Liiceanu was born in **Râmnicu Vâlcea**. He was educated at the **University of Bucharest**, where he studied philosophy and Classical languages and obtained his doctorate in philosophy in 1965. Among other things, he has been a researcher in philosophy and art history at the Romanian Academy. In 1990, he founded Humanitas Publishing House in Bucharest, of which he is now President. Liiceanu is the author of various books and articles on philosophy (including *Jurnalul de la Păltiniş*, 1981 – Extract 8), has translated numerous Classical works from Ancient Greek and German, and has collaborated on scripts for art documentaries, including two on Émile Cioran (see Extract 8).

MANNING, Olivia (1915–1980). Novelist and journalist, Olivia Manning was born in Portsmouth, the daughter of a naval officer. Marriage to R. D. Smith, a British Council lecturer, took her to **Bucharest** on the eve of the second world war. The couple stayed on in the city until October 1940, when they were evacuated, first to Athens, and then, in 1942, to Cairo. Her experiences and observations of this period form the basis for her best known work, *The Balkan Trilogy* (1960–65), of which *The Great Fortune*, 1960, is the first part (Extract 3), *The Spoilt City*, 1962, the second, and *Friends and Heroes*, 1965, the third.

PETRESCU, Cezar (1892–1961). Petrescu set out to write 'a chronicle of the 20th century' in which he aimed to portray the evolution of Romanian society in all of its classes. In fact, the fate of the intellectual élite is his major preoccupation. Behind his novels lies the idea of destiny which acts upon society and is born from a conjunction of historical, geographical and socio-political factors. His work is dominated by the themes of the consequences of *déracinement* (*Calea Victoriei* – *Victory Road* – 1929); the perfidious effects of industrialization (*Comoara regelui Dromichet* – *The Treasure of King Dromichet* – 1931); and the inability of social groups to communicate (*Întunecare* – *Gathering Clouds* – 1927, and *Carlton*, 1942). His characters are marked by what he called 'a psychology of failure' which he regarded as the feature of Romanian society during the first half of this century.

PILLAT, Ion (1891–1945). Born to a wealthy landowner and a daughter of Ion Brătianu, a former Prime Minister of Romania, Pillat had a privileged upbringing in Paris where he completed his secondary and university education, and on his family's estates in **Wallachia** and **Moldavia**. He turned to poetry in his teens and his early verse is in the Parnassian mould. His best-known volume *Pe Argeş în sus* (*Up Along the Arges*), 1923, is inspired by childhood memories of summer spent on the Wallachian estate. His volume *Limpezimi* (*Clarities*), published in 1928 (Extract 5), also belongs to this 'traditionalist' phase in his work which he defined as 'native, simple, and sentimental.'

REBREANU, Liviu (1885–1944). Rebreanu was born in **northern**

Liviu Rebreanu

Transylvania at a time when the province was part of the Austro–Hungarian Empire. He attended Romanian, German and Hungarian schools and served for a year in the Austro–Hungarian army before moving to **Bucharest**, the capital of the Kingdom of Romania, in 1909 to become a writer. His first novel *Ion*, (Extract 15), is the story of a peasant's ruthless pursuit of land. Ion is depicted with cold detachment as a figure completely dominated by a primitive egotism. The reader's sense of inevitability about Ion's premature death is matched by a similar feeling concerning the hero's destiny in *Pădurea Spânzuraţilor (The Forest of the Hanged)*, 1992, based on the fate of the author's brother Emil, hanged for attempted desertion from the Austro–Hungarian army in 1917 when faced with fighting his fellow Romanians. It follows the crisis of conscience of a soldier in whom the bond of national brotherhood proves stronger than his

sense of duty. *Răscoala (The Uprising)*, 1932, depicts the social pressures leading to the peasant revolt of 1907 and is memorable for its crowd scenes. Rebreanu's three major novels have been translated into English (*The Uprising*, 1964; *Ion*, 1965; *The Forest of the Hanged*, 1967).

SEBASTIAN, Mihail (1907–45). A journalist, essayist, novelist and dramatist, Sebastian was tragically killed in a road traffic accident in **Bucharest**. He is best known to Romania's post-war generation as an accomplished playwright. His *Jocul de-a vacanţa (Let's Play Holidays)*, 1936, *Steaua fără nume (Nameless Star)*, 1944, and *Ultima oră (Stop Press)*, 1945, are still performed on the Romanian stage but few have heard of his novel *Accidentul (The Accident)*, 1940, and even fewer of his remarkable first novel *De două mii de ani (For Two Thousand Years)*, first published in 1934 and reprinted in 1946. The latter is written in the form of a journal which interweaves observation and introspection and produces a kaleidoscopic effect. In the words of one critic, it 'projects a historical moment and a generation's dilemma through the eyes of a Jewish intellectual.' The novel opens with the narrator as a young man in **Bucharest** in the early 1920s, during a wave of anti-Semitic violence in the university. It presents the reader with forebodings of a violent upheaval which were borne out in the pogrom of January 1941 in Bucharest.

SORESCU, Marin (1936–). Poet, dramatist and painter, Sorescu is one of the most original voices of contemporary Romanian literature. His first major volume of *Poeme*, 1965, signalled the poet's belief in nature's ability to overcome adversity, its rich vein of irony and humour bringing him immediate success with both the critics and the public. His subsequent volumes, offering oblique criticism of censorship, secured him an unequalled audience, particularly with the young, among Romanian contemporary poets. However, much of his writing for the theatre fell victim to Ceauşescu's censors. In *Iona* (*Jonah*), 1968, the biblical tale becomes a metaphor for freedom. Jonah cuts himself out of the belly of the whale only to find that it had been swallowed by a larger one, and so the fisherman's predicament is repeated, down to the suggestion that the universe is itself a confined space. Jonah is only able to overcome this paradox by taking his own life. After the play's six-week run in 1969 it was staged only once in Romania during Ceauşescu's lifetime, in 1982, by a group of Latin American drama students. *A treia Ţeapă* (*The Third Stake*), 1978, befell a similar fate. Its portrayal of the multi-faceted Vlad the Impaler's cruelty and indifference to the daily life of his subjects was too topical for the censors and it was staged only for a brief run in the provinces in 1979 and for a two-week season in Bucharest in September 1988. The inspiration for Sorescu's verse (Extract 4) comes from everyday life, the tone prosaic, the mood ironic. The expression of everyday experience is, in the poet's hands, a virtuoso act which triumphs over the constraints of censorship, and will maintain its power.

Selected translations of his plays appear in *The Thirst of the Salt Mountain*, 1985, and *Vlad Dracula the Impaler*, 1987. His poems can be found in *Selected Poems 1965–1973*, 1983, *Let's Talk About the Weather . . . and Other Poems by Marin Sorescu*, 1987, *The Biggest Egg in the World*, 1987,

The Youth of Don Quixote, 1987, and *Hands Behind my Back*, 1991.

STĂNESCU, Nichita (1933–83). Stănescu emerged as one of the most innovative poets of the post-war generation. He won the Poetry Prize of the Romanian Writers' Union in 1964, 1969, 1972 and 1975. He belongs to the tradition of experiment in Romanian literature, challenging our conventional view of the world, inviting us to consider new perspectives, and each perspective is itself multi-faceted. As the poet himself asks: 'Since man has a perspective of the leaf, why shouldn't the leaf have a perspective of man?' His search for a new reality, for a new 'purity of existence' is conducted in the volumes *Sensul iubirii* (*The Sense of Love*), 1960, and *O viziune a sentimentelor* (*A Vision of Feelings*), 1964. It is continued in *Dreptul la timp* (*The Right to Time*), 1965, which introduces his perspective of time; only the future is important because only the future is true. In his *11 elegii* (*11 Elegies*), 1966, Stănescu pursues his search in a dialectical form (one of the elegies is dedicated to Hegel), with the debate alternating between two planes. The essence of language itself becomes the object of his scrutiny as the poet attempts to isolate form from content. This aspiration for an absolute language, one which, in the poet's view, does not need to communicate, only to identify, leads him to *Necuvintele* (*Non-Words*), 1969, and subsequent volumes. The word is only a vehicle for speech. True poetry is only vision, feeling, a transparent glimpse of an absolute which does not require the vehicle of speech. Selections from his sixteen volumes of verse have appeared in *The Still Unborn About the Dead*, 1975, and *Bas-Relief with Heroes*, 1988.

STOKER, Bram (1847–1912). Born in Dublin, Bram Stoker studied at Dublin University, became a civil servant, wrote drama reviews, and was appointed the actor Henry Irving's touring manager. Author of short stories and novels, he was also on the staff of the *Daily Telegraph*. He is mainly remembered now for his story *Dracula*, 1897, told in the form of journals and letters, about the Hungarian vampire Count Dracula (Extract 16). Various film versions now exist, but none outdoes an early version starring Bela Lugosi, issued in 1931. See H. Ludlam, *A Biography of Dracula: The Life Story of Bram Stoker*, 1962.

TARTLER, Grete (1948–). Born in **Bucharest**, into a family of German ancestry from Transylvania, Tartler studied at the **Ciprian Porumbescu Conservatory** (graduated 1972). While teaching the viola at a secondary school, she began to study Arabic and English at **Bucharest University** (graduated 1976). She has published a number of volumes of verse (Poetry Prize of the Writers' Union, 1978) and also translated extensively from classical Arabic literature. Her collections include *Substituiri* (*Substitutions*), 1983, and *Achene zburatoare* (*Winged Seeds*), 1986. Translations of her work appear in the anthology *Silent Voices*, and a volume of her poetry, translated by Fleur Adcock, has been published as *Orient Express*, 1989 (Extract 11).

VLAHUȚA, Alexandru (1858–1919). Journalist, poet, and short-story writer, Vlahuța came to Bucharest from his native **Moldavia** as a young man and earned his living as a journalist. He was one of the founders of the literary review *Sămănătorul* (*The Sower*) which appeared in December 1901 and stressed the importance of national and peasant traditions. His own devotion to his homeland permeated his travelogue of the Romanian provinces, published in 1901 and entitled *România pitorească* (*Picturesque Romania*) – Extracts 7 and 13. Among the ideas propounded by Vlahuța was that the peasants could be educated to a higher level by concerted effort on the part of 'intellectuals and schoolmasters', but he failed to offer a practical means of achieving this.

WAGNER, Richard (1952–). A German-language writer, Richard Wagner was born near **Timișoara**, in the western part of Romania, which, with its mixed population of Romanians, Hungarians, Serbs and Germans, became the birthplace of the recent Romanian revolution. In the early 1970s Wagner joined the 'Aktionsgruppe Banat', which offered a critique of the Ceaușescu regime until it was broken up by the security police. In 1987 he emigrated to West Germany. His novel *Aussreiseantrag*, 1988, has been translated by Quintin Hoare as *Exit, A Romanian Story*, 1990 (Extract 14). *Exit* chronicles the pressures on Wagner which forced him to emigrate. It is a work of disenchantment, written in the style of a documentary, with a series of cameo portraits and situations which, taken together, provide a vivid overall picture of what it was like to live in Ceaușescu's Romania.

BULGARIA

Belin Tonchev

'Now am I truly home. All
round me hills / And
mountain ridges rear; tall
virgin forests / Are rustling;
clear as crystal, foaming
torrents / Go roaring past.
On every side life
thrills. / Humming a song to
soothe me, mother
Nature / Enfolds me lovingly
in her embraces.'
Ivan Vazov,
Near the Rila Monastery

Bulgaria occupies a central position in the Balkans. The name of
the peninsula itself derives from
the Balkan mountain range which
runs through the country like a
backbone. The River Danube
forms the natural border with
Romania to the north, the Black
Sea to the east; Greece and Turkey lie to the south, Macedonia
and Serbia to the west.

Present-day Bulgaria covers
110 994 square km. The relief is
extremely varied. The **Balkan
range** is known to the local
population as Stara Planina,
southern ranges are the Rodopi
(**Rhodope Mountains**), and the
Pirin and **Rila Mountains** (the Rila's highest peak **Mousala** is 2925 m).
The **Danubian plain**, the plain of **Trakia** (Thrace) and the fragrant
Valley of Roses contain the country's most fertile farmland. The
climate is mainly moderately continental and milder on the Black Sea
coast and in the south, with many sunny days in summer. The average
temperature over the year is about 12°C. A considerable part of
Bulgaria's territory is covered by deciduous and coniferous forests.
Animal life includes over 13 000 species, among them bears, roe deer,
boars, rabbits, and a great variety of birds. Bulgaria's energy and
mineral resources are limited, mainly hard and lignite coal, iron and
manganese ore. Chief exports are food, non-ferrous metals, leather
goods, iron, tobacco and textiles. Tourism, mainly on the Black Sea
coast and in the mountains, traditionally attracts Western European
tour operators and travel agencies.

281

Sofia (population over 1 million), in the west, is the capital, and other major cities are **Plovdiv, Rouse, Bourgas** and **Varna**. Bulgaria is a Republic with a single-chamber parliament and a multiparty system. The President is head of state. The population (1993 census) totals 8 473 000, of which 7 272 000 (85.8%) are Bulgarians, 822 000 (9.7%) are Turks, 288 000 (3.4%) are Gypsies, and 91 000 (1.1%) are from other ethnic groups. Bulgaria's Orthodox Church unites 86.2% of the population, and other religious groups include Muslims, Protestants, and Roman Catholics. Bulgarian is the official language. Ethnic groups in Bulgaria are granted linguistic and religious freedom.

BULGARIAN HISTORY

Ancient and medieval Bulgaria

Throughout the centuries Bulgaria was a border land between various civilizations. Thracian traditions were taken over by Slavs, then by Bulgars. One of the first civilizations in Europe flourished here between the Danube, the Aegean Sea, the Black Sea and the River Vardar. The earliest gold artefacts, dating from the 5th millenium BC, were found in **Varna**'s necropolis on the Black Sea coast. Bulgaria is rich in archaeological remains, such as the **Tomb of Kazanluk**, the **Horseman of Madara** bas-relief, the gold treasures of **Vulchitrun** and **Panagy-urishte**, and the silver treasure of **Rogozen**. Thracian religion was polytheistic, and the legend of Orpheus, poet and lute-player, originates from the southern Rhodopes.

The strategic position of Thrace, neighbouring Moesia and Macedonia, attracted the attention of Rome, whose legions conquered Thrace in the 1st century BC. Spartacus, who led a famous popular uprising against Rome, was Thracian by origin. The Romans founded a number of cities in the new provinces. In Serdica (today's **Sofia**) the rotunda of **Sveti Georgi** (St George) from the 4th century AD is the oldest surviving building. 'Sofia' derives from the 5th century church of **Sveta Sophia** (St Sophia).

Following invasions by Huns, Goths and other barbarian tribes, Slavs began to settle in the Balkans in the 4th century AD. Attacks of Bulgars against Byzantium date from the end of the 5th century. In 681 Asparouh, their Khan, allied with the more numerous Slavs, achieved recognition of a Bulgarian state with Pliska (near present-day **Shoumen**) its capital. The rule of Khan Kroum (803–814) made Bulgaria the third power in Europe after Byzantium and the Frankish Empire.

Until the middle of the 9th century the country was basically pagan. Some surviving Bulgarian folk festivals and rituals, for example Koukeri (mummers) and Nestinari (fire-walking), still testify to these ancient traditions.

In 864 Tsar Boris adopted Christianity. Old Bulgarian or 'Church Slavonic' was adopted for liturgical use by the brothers Konstantin (Cyril) and Metodiy (Methodius), who are credited with being the devisers of the alphabet, evidently the Glagolitic alphabet, predecessor of the present Cyrillic. They translated Christian literature and led educational missions in Pannonia and Moravia. Kliment, Naum and Angelariy, disciples of Cyril and Methodius, spread their teachers' spiritual heritage.

The reign of Simeon I (893–927), who twice besieged Constantinople, and defeated the Byzantines at **Aheloi**, coincided with a significant age of Bulgarian letters. His capital was Veliki ('Great') Preslav where literature and art flourished, especially icon-painting in the rich Orthodox tradition. The **Rila Monastery** was founded during that period.

The foundations of the state, however, were undermined by the usual squabbles among the nobility, Byzantine schemes, and by the heresy of Bogomilism which originated here and subsequently spread to Italy and France. In 1014 the Emperor Basil II, later the 'Bulgar-Slayer', is reputed to have blinded 15 000 defeated Bulgarian soldiers, and by 1018 Bulgaria had fallen under Byzantine rule.

Second Bulgarian state

Bulgarian national identity was preserved in the regions of Moesia, Macedonia and Thrace. In 1185 brothers Peter and Asen of **Veliko Turnovo** led a popular uprising as a result of which Bulgaria regained independence, with its centre now the religious capital of Turnovo. This marked the beginning of the second Bulgarian kingdom. Kaloyan, the third brother, became Tsar (1197–1207). He defeated Baldwin of Flanders, Emperor of the Latin Empire. Tsar Ivan Asen II (1218–1241) favoured peace and he balanced between the Latin and the Byzantine Empires. During his reign Bulgaria bordered on three seas – the Aegean, the Adriatic, and the Black Sea.

A number of monasteries were built in this period, among them the monastery of **Kilifarevo**, known as the Theodosius School of Letters, a central Bulgarian and Slav institution of higher learning. The mural paintings in the Church of **Boyana** near Sofia introduced individualism and naturalism into religious paintings in 1259, two generations before Cimabue and Giotto. The miniatures in the Gospel of Tsar Ivan Alexander, now exhibited at the British Museum in London, are also exquisite specimens from this medieval period.

The Ottoman Conquest

In the second half of the 14th century the menace of the Ottoman hordes was looming on the horizon. Veliko Turnovo, defended by Tsar

Ivan Shishman, fell in 1393. Evtimiy, the Bulgarian Patriarch, was exiled and the church was placed under the Constantinople patriarchate. The Vidin feudal Tsardom of Ivan Stratsimir fell in 1396 which marked the beginning of a five-centuries long deviation in Bulgaria's development.

Islam was essentially alien to Bulgarian medieval civilization. The Ottoman rule prevented its natural progress in line with the European Renaissance. Bulgarian patriarchal tradition and Christian Orthodox religion were preserved mainly in the rural areas and monasteries. The Balkan Mountain range, the geographical backbone of the country, proved also to be the backbone of spiritual survival for Bulgaria.

Many of the indigenous population were massacred or driven away in the face of Turkish aggression. Some attempts were made to Islamicize forcefully a few regions in north-east Bulgaria and the central Rhodopes. Small boys were taken from their mothers and brought up as Janissaries. Waves of refugees moved towards Wallachia, Moldavia, and other areas free from Ottoman occupation.

Acts of violence triggered resistance. Numerous rebellions were cruelly suppressed, among them the **Chiprovtsi** uprising in 1688. Bulgarian land lay too close to central Ottoman power and this made organized resistance difficult. Groups of armed Bulgarians, known as Haiduks, sought personal revenge by attacking Turkish local administration and smaller military detachments.

Towards national liberation

Hopes for national liberation were associated with the wars which Europe and specifically Austria, then Russia, led against Turkey. These wars stimulated many mass uprisings but, partly due to the inconsistent policy of the European powers towards the Christian population in the Balkans, they were drowned in blood.

A fresh impetus to national feeling was given by the *History of Slavo–Bulgarians* by Father Paisiy of Hilendar, written in 1762. Neofit (Neophyte) Bozveli, Ilarion Makariopolski, and the Miladinov brothers fought for an autonomous Bulgarian church, free from Greek Orthodox domination. The travel writings of Englishman William Hunter in 1792 testify to a yearning of Bulgarians for national dignity and liberation.

The urge towards national identity in the 18th and 19th centuries revived old traditions in art, literature and crafts. Solid and beautiful homes were built in the towns of **Arbanasi, Kotel, Tryavna, Koprivshtitsa** and **Bansko**, decorated with exquisite woodcarvings and paintings. In 1834 Dobri Zhelyazkov set up the first Bulgarian factory for cloth in **Sliven**. In 1865 the brothers Geshovi established a commercial branch in Manchester, England.

Georgi Stoikov Rakovski (1821–67) conceived the idea of forming a *legia* (legion) of Bulgarian émigré fighters for national liberation. His views clashed with the more peaceful educationalist conceptions of the writer Lyuben Karavelov (1834–79), but ideas in favour of organized struggle prevailed. In 1868 the *chetas* (forces) of Stefan Karadzha (1840–68) and Hadzhi Dimitur (1840–68) fought against numerous Turkish troops, events much detailed in works of literature (Extract 1).

Vasil Levski (1837–73), a much revered leader, advanced the idea for an internal revolutionary organization which, through a network of committees, should start a general uprising relying on Bulgaria's own resources, not help from abroad. Levski did much preparatory work, but was caught by Turkish soldiers and hanged on 19 February 1873 in what is now central Sofia.

Preparation for a general uprising was in full swing at the beginning of 1876. It flared up in April, but failed, and its leaders – Georgi Benkovski, Panayot Volov, Todor Kableshkov, Vasil Petleshkov and Bacho Kiro – met their death. In May 1876 the *cheta* of Hristo Botyov ◊, poet and fighter for national liberation, faced a Turkish army in the Balkan Mountains near the town of **Vratsa**. He died in combat on 2 June 1876. The Turkish atrocities in suppressing the April uprising drew the attention of many European public figures: William Gladstone, Eugene Skyler (US council in Constantinople), George MacGahan (special correspondent of the *Daily News*), Oscar Wilde, William Morris, Victor Hugo, Giuseppe Garibaldi, Fyodor Dostoevsky and Charles Darwin were among those who stood up in defence of the Bulgarian cause.

Liberation and Balkan Wars

Panslavism and the Balkan aspirations of Tsar Alexander II led to the Russo–Turkish War of 1877–78. The battles at the **Shipka Pass** and the town of **Pleven** were turning points. Turkey was defeated and the Treaty of San Stefano was signed, in which Bulgaria was liberated. It was given its former wide territories, stretching from the Danube to the Aegean, from the Black Sea to Ohrid and Skopje. Britain and the Austrian Empire, however, feared expanding Russian influence in the Balkans, and a new treaty was signed at the ensuing Congress in Berlin, which was much less favourable to Bulgaria. The Berlin Treaty confined Bulgaria proper to the area between the Danube and the Balkan range; the area south of this was designated as an autonomous Ottoman province of Eastern Rumelia. Serbia was awarded territory to the west seen as ethnically Bulgarian.

The unification of Bulgaria and the formation of a state government within the smaller territory became primary objectives. Liberals defeated Conservatives at the Constituent Assembly. In 1879 the Constitution of Veliko Turnovo was adopted, based on the democratic Belgian model. Alexander of Battenberg, a German prince, became monarch. Pro-Russian orientation conducted by the church and the army existed side by side with anti-Russian and pro-Western feelings. Bulgaria and Eastern Rumelia were unified in a national uprising declared in **Plovdiv** on 6 September 1885. While the Bulgarian army was tensely awaiting the reaction of the Ottoman government the Serbian Prince Milan surprisingly declared war on Bulgaria, but the Serbian army was defeated at **Slivnitsa** near Sofia and repulsed.

After an attempt to suspend the liberal Constitution, Battenberg was deposed, and Ferdinand of Saxe-Coburg-Gotha, a prince of German and Hungarian origin, became Knyaz in 1887. Stefan Stambolov, Prime Minister and Head of the Liberal Party, expelled Russian spies from Bulgaria and fended off the attempts of Moscow to remove the new ruler.

The country's final independence from the Ottoman Empire was declared in 1908 when Bulgaria was proclaimed a monarchy. Macedonia, however, remained under Ottoman suzerainty. The biggest uprising for Macedonian liberation broke out in 1903. VMRO, the Internal Macedonian Revolutionary Organization, strove to unify the territory with Bulgaria. James Bourchier, Balkan correspondent of the *Times* from 1888, examined the Macedonian question and stood up for the Bulgarian cause. When he died in 1920, he was given solemn burial at **Rila Monastery**.

A Balkan War for the liberation of the Christians of Macedonia and lower Thrace broke out in 1912. Bulgaria, Serbia, Montenegro and Greece joined forces against Turkey. Bulgarian troops came quite close to capturing Istanbul. Large north-western territories were detached from the Ottoman Empire. The allies, however, quarrelled over the division of the spoils, and a Second (Inter-Allied) Balkan War broke out following a secret anti-Bulgarian treaty between Greece and Serbia. Bulgaria's neighbours did not want to allow the creation of a unified greater state in the heart of the Balkans. Fighting against its former allies, joined by Romania, Bulgaria lost Eastern Thrace, Southern Dobroudzha and the greater part of Macedonia.

First world war to 1944

Hoping to regain its lost territories, Bulgaria allied itself with Germany and the Central Powers during the first world war. After defeat, Bulgaria signed the Treaty of Neuilly, which deprived it again of large territories to the west and to the south. Bulgaria was also made to pay substantial reparations. In the course of only six years it had fought three wars in which it had lost territories which it regarded as ethnically

Bulgarian. Tsar Ferdinand abdicated and was succeeded by his son Boris III in 1918.

The Bulgarian Agrarian National Union, headed by Alexander Stamboliyski, emerged as the strongest political party. The Agrarian government tended to marginalize the powers of the Tsar, and to underestimate the urban élite. The Agrarians also clashed with the VMRO, which remained committed to unification with Macedonia. Stamboliyski was assassinated in June 1923 in a bloody *coup d'état*.

The period 1919–23 was also marked by the infiltration of trained Communist agents into the democratic parties, aiming to prepare the ground for a Bolshevik revolution. A string of terrorist acts in Sofia, instigated by Moscow, attempted to destabilize the situation. The Communists inspired a popular uprising after the June *coup*, in September 1923, which cost many lives.

A coalition styled 'Naroden Sgovor' ('Democratic Concord') led by Alexander Tsankov had come to power in the June *coup*, which was followed by a string of political purges in 1925, including government terrorism with hired assassins and Communist terrorism in retaliation. The world economic crisis from the late 1920s affected Bulgaria too. A wave of dictatorial regimes swept across Europe. Tsankov's movement and the 'Zveno' ('Link') political circle of Kimon Georgiev both borrowed elements from Italian Fascism and German Nazism, but the political climate in Bulgaria was oriented more towards authoritarianism than towards outright Fascism. In 1933 the Reichstag in Berlin was set on fire; three Bulgarian Communists, including Georgi Dimitrov, were among the accused. The economic and political situation, with 42 parties existing in the country, went from bad to worse. After another military *coup*, a Zveno government came to power in May 1934. All political parties and movements were banned. Then, after a succession of caretaker governments, Boris III established personal rule.

At the outbreak of the second world war, Boris III declined Hitler's invitations to join the Axis, but later in March 1941, he was forced to consent. Once again Bulgaria hoped to regain its lost territories by supporting Germany. Bulgaria did not send a single soldier to the front, but it served as a military base for German troops. In return, it recovered its territories in Macedonia and Thrace.

Hitler pressed for elimination of the Jews, but Boris III and members of parliament supported by democratic circles as well as the Orthodox Church of Bulgaria and the Writers' Union managed to save the Bulgarian Jews from the gas chambers.

The Comintern sent instructors for subversive actions to Bulgaria in an attempt to provoke Red terror and a Communist revolution. The advance of the Red Army stimulated the partisan resistance movement, which, however, remained relatively small and ineffective.

At the sight of retreating German troops Boris III tried to make a U-turn and achieve peace with Britain and the USA. He died, however, in August 1943, on return from the Führer's headquarters. Sofia was heavily bombed by American and British planes. All attempts to reach national reconciliation with the partisans failed, and as a result a great number of them were killed by government troops. By September 1944 the government of Konstantin Mouraviev had managed to disarm the remaining German troops; it banned Fascist organizations and included the opposition in government structures. But this did not stop Soviet forces from invading Bulgaria on 8 September: a Communist takeover took place on 9 September as a direct result. The bloodbath which Bulgarian Communists staged after 9 September 1944 took on terrible proportions. About 20 000 people were massacred without trial in the autumn of that year. More than 400 000 died in labour camps and prisons in the years after.

After September 1944 Bulgarian troops were sent to the West to fight the Germans. When the Wehrmacht capitulated, Bulgarian soldiers met the 8th British army at the Austrian Alps. Over 34 000 Bulgarian soldiers lost their lives fighting Nazi Germany. This fact, however, had little political effect. Bulgaria remained bound to the sphere of Soviet influence. According to the Paris Treaty of 10 February 1947, Bulgaria was regarded as a defeated ally of Germany. Southern Dobroudzha was the only territory which Bulgaria was allowed to retain.

Communist rule to Communist collapse

Under the Communist regime show trials were staged in 1946 against the opposition leaders Krustyo Pastouhov, Tsveti Ivanov, Dr G. M. Dimitrov and Trifon Kounev, and in 1947 against Nikola Petkov, leader of the banned Bulgarian Agrarian National Union. The monarchy was abolished in 1946, and the democratic Turnovo Constitution of 1878 was suspended in 1947.

When Georgi Dimitrov, the Communist Prime Minister, died in 1949, Vulko Chervenkov came to power. In 1954 Todor Zhivkov became Party leader, and head of state in 1962. Todor Zhivkov made three failed attempts to annex Bulgaria to the Soviet Union as its 16th republic. Bulgaria joined the Warsaw Pact and COMECON (Council for Mutual Economic Assistance). Bulgaria's Communists formed a mock coalition with the Fatherland Front, and with the Agrarian Union, which served only as a cover-up for what was actually a one-party system. Communist rule resulted in massive violations of human rights, including the name-changing campaign against ethnic Turks and the subsequent exodus of 300 000 people to Turkey. Religions of all kinds were stifled.

Industry, after its nationalization in 1947, was developed in Five-Year Plans, with little regard for ecology, mainly using cut-price Soviet ores and oil. Small farmholdings were pooled into ineffective collective farms. Nearly half the population migrated towards the bigger urban centres.

The system sat on people's backs for 45 years, until the thaw at the end of 1989, marked by demonstrations and anti-Communist marches organized by Ecoglasnost and other underground movements. Todor Zhivkov was replaced as Communist Party leader and head of state, and a multi-party political system was introduced in December. The Union of Democratic Forces (UDF), an opposition coalition of 16 parties, was formed. Round table talks on political and economic reform took place, but the UDF spurned an invitation to participate in a coalition government with the Communists.

In April 1990, the Bulgarian Communist Party renamed itself the Bulgarian Socialist Party (BSP), and in democratic elections held in June voters returned it to power. The UDF again refused the offer of a coalition government. President Peter Mladenov resigned in July, following a controversy surrounding a videotape, in which Evgeni Mihailov, a Bulgarian film director, had recorded Mladenov's words: 'The best thing to do is to bring in the tanks.'

The new National Assembly elected Zhelyu Zhelev, leader of the UDF, as President (he was subsequently re-elected in 1991 in the first-ever nationwide democratic presidential elections). The BSP formed a government, but it stayed in office for only two months. A transitional coalition led by Dimitur Popov was formed in December.

The Union of Democratic Forces won the next elections in October 1991, and Filip Dimitrov became Prime Minister. This government survived until the end of 1992 when it was deposed by a no-confidence vote in Parliament. A new government of experts was then formed, led by Lyuben Berov. Although Berov's government declared itself 'committed to mass privatization', it achieved only modest results. The country plunged into one of its deepest recessions, yet again the Communist-led Parliament helped the government to survive six no-confidence votes from the opposition UDF. Parliament passed some openly anti-democratic laws defending the interests of the new economically powerful groups, mostly former Communists. Living standards fell, together with the popularity (a mere 10%) of this Parliament. Lyuben Berov resigned in September 1994 and President Zhelev appointed a caretaker government headed by Reneta Indzhova, whose main task was to prepare new parliamentary elections. They were held in December 1994 and were won by the BSP with a definite majority of votes. An all-socialist government took over at the end of January 1995. Whatever future governments are elected will have to weather

major economic and social challenges to sustain any kind of construc-
tive political continuity.

BULGARIAN LITERATURE

'The Bulgarians were among the first, after the decline of the ancient
world, to found their own state and launch their own culture.' (Emil
Georgiev, *Bulgarian Literature in an All-European Context.*)

Old Bulgarian

The Bulgarian state was founded in 681 and it inherited rich cultural
traditions. The Thracians, an indigenous tribe on Bulgarian land,
served as a model for the Hellenic culture. About 250 words, 500 place
names, and 1000 proper names in modern Bulgarian are of Thracian
origin. The Thracians worshipped nature and they built pagan shrines.
One of these is the surviving **Tomb of Kazanluk**, decorated with
magnificent frescoes.

About 100 inscriptions on columns and tombstones have survived
from the age of the Proto-Bulgars – for example, *Imennik na bulgarskite
hanove (The Names of Bulgarian Khans)*, and *The Horseman of Madara*.

Christianity was adopted as the official religion of Bulgaria in 864.
As noted above, the brothers from the area of Salonika, Kiril (Cyril,
also called Konstantin the Philosopher, 826–869) and Metodiy
(Methodius, 815–885), are credited with the invention of the Glagoli-
tic alphabet which was later reshaped into the Cyrillic, still used today.
The new alphabet accurately reflected the phonetics of Bulgarian
speech. With its help, the two brothers embarked on a religious and
political mission to bring the pagan Slavs and Bulgars into the world of
Christianity. Their chief recorded Slav mission was to Moravia and
Pannonia.

Cyril and Methodius translated liturgical books, sermons and expositions; they wrote original works in defence of the Slavonic script
against accusations of heresy. Kliment, Naum, Sava, Gorazd and
Angelariy, disciples of Cyril and Methodius, launched a Golden Age of
Bulgarian ecclesiastical letters, which played a historic role in winning
over the peoples of the eastern part of Europe to Christian religion and
culture.

Two schools of letters flourished in the Golden Age: the School of
Preslav and the School of Ohrid. Konstantin Preslavski, with *Azbouch-
na molitva (Alphabet Prayer)* and *Ouchitelno evangelie (Didactic Gospel)* –
one of the first collections of the ecclesiastical art of rhetoric – Yoan
Ekzarh, with *Shestodnev (Hexaemeron)*, Chernorizets Hrabur ♭, with *O
pismeneh (On Letters)*, and Tsar Simeon I the Great (864–927) himself,
belonged to the School of Preslav. *On Letters* by Chernorizets Hrabur

Cyril and Methodius

was written in an expressive colloquial style; it is also an ardent defence of the right of Bulgarians to have their own letters and books (Extract 15).

The Palace of Tsar Simeon housed a rich library where numerous clergymen and other illuminated minds spent hours bent over their works. Allegedly Tsar Simeon compiled *Zlatostruy* – a collection of '*slova*' (short sermons) and didactic writings. Bulgarian monasteries (the **Rila Monastery** and the **Bachkovo Monastery**, to mention but two) were at the heart of vigorous literary activities.

The School of Ohrid in south-western Bulgaria was renowned for the works of Kliment Ohridski (840–916) and Naum Ohridski (?–910). Kliment Ohridski trained over 3 500 priests, deacons and teachers, and wrote *Pohvalno slovo za Kiril i Metodiy* (*Eulogies of Cyril and Methodius*).

Fundamental writings relevant to the Christian education of the people were translated into Old Bulgarian.

The Bogomil movement appeared in the middle of the 10th century. Prezviter Kozma wrote *Beseda protiv bogomilite* (*Discourse Against the Bogomil Heresy*). Bogomilism spread throughout Southern Europe under various names.

The period is also marked by a flood of apocrypha – *Adam and Eve, King Solomon, Virgin Mary Visits Hell*, and other encyclopaedic compilations which were quoted in Russia as 'Bulgarian fables'. Folk superstitions and prognostications of the future were also recorded, as well as short stories, medieval novels about miracles and heroic acts, and chronicles about *Genesis* (eg *Istorikiyi* by Konstantin Preslavski).

During the Byzantine occupation in the 11th and 12th centuries, the official Bulgarian literature declined, and a more democratic tradition emerged – legends (*The Legend of Thessaloniki*) and lives of Bulgarian saints (*The Life of Ivan Rilski*), etc.

Medieval writings and pre-modern literature

The Slavonic letters spread to central and eastern Europe – Moravia, Pannonia, Slovakia, Poland, Serbia, Romania and Russia. Against the contemporary European background, Old Bulgarian civilization and, specifically, literature, were innovative and untraditional.

Art and literature continued to flourish in medieval Bulgaria. Yoan Koukouzel, the 'Angel-voiced' Bulgarian composer from the end of the 13th century, revolutionized church singing and notation by including Bulgarian folk motifs and by introducing chromatic scales into his music. The frescos from 1259 in the **Church of Boyana** near Sofia, with their highly humanistic appeal, were early manifestations of the Renaissance spirit in Europe, before Giotto and Cimabue.

Under Tsar Ivan Alexander (1331–71) Bulgaria reached a second peak at the time when the Renaissance in Europe was emerging. The Literary School of Patriarch Evtimiy (1325–1401) and Teodosiy Turnovski (1300–63) appeared in the middle of the 14th century. Patriarch Evtimiy reformed the Bulgarian language by establishing a uniform orthography based on the works of Cyril and Methodius. He is the author of four *Zhitiya* (*Lives*), and four *Pohvalni slova* (*Eulogies*) about Bulgarian saints. Other outstanding figures from the Literary School of Turnovo were Kiprian (1330–1406), Grigoriy Tsamblak (1364–1420) and Konstantin Kostenechki (1380–1443).

Writers and theologians gathered in the Palace of Tsar Ivan Alexander. The monasteries of **Bachkovo, Kilifarevo, Dragalevtsi** and **Athos** were also centres of art and literature. The rock monasteries at the village of **Ivanovo**, and the murals in a number of churches in **Turnovo**, the then capital of Bulgaria, are specimens of art of the highest calibre. *Manasieva Hronika* (*The Chronicle of Constantine Man-asses*), now in the Vatican Library, and *The Gospel of Tsar Ivan Alexander*, now in the British Museum, arouse modern interest with their exquisite miniatures.

At the end of the 14th century, when Bulgaria was conquered by the Ottoman hordes, Christian men of letters believed that it was right to distance themselves from this Islamic civilization. National identity was maintained culturally through the folk tradition. Favourite literary forms were epics about heroic deeds (the epic of *Krali Marko*), sagas which helped to preserve family ties and kinship, fairy tales, ballads with fantastic subjects, love lyrics, riddles, proverbs, and folk rituals associated with Christmas celebrations and wedding ceremonies. Among popular authors who emerged from anonymity were Vladislav Gramatik and Dimitur Kantakouzin; they took up the literary tradition of Patriarch Evtimiy.

Towns – Plovdiv, Sofia, Skopje, Pleven, Rouse and Kyustendil – grew and expanded. The monasteries at **Zograph** and **Athos** were the most significant literary centres in the 16th century, where old Bulgarian books were eagerly transcribed and copied. Pop (Priest) Peyu wrote about the life of Georgi Sofiyski (of Sofia) Novi, a Bulgarian martyred by the Turks for refusing to adopt Islam. Matei Gramatik described the life of Nikola Sofiyski Novi, another martyr for the Christian faith. Clergymen worked as teachers at the early monastic schools. They perpetuated an antiquated literary language as a symbol of the historic past. In the 15th century some Bulgarians founded monasteries in Wallachia and Moldavia, where Old Bulgarian was practised.

In 1519 Yakov Kraikov, the first Bulgarian printer, set up his printing press in Venice: his first book was illustrated with etchings. In 1651 Filip Stanislavov (1610–74) compiled and published in Rome *Abagar*, the first printed Bulgarian book in Cyrillic. All this happened in the face of a tradition blessed by the Turkish authorities, which dictated that Greek, and not Bulgarian, should be the established language in Christian schools and publishing.

The perfection of iconography was reflected in the mural paintings and frescos of churches in **Turnovo, Bachkovo, Nesebur** and **Plovdiv**. The network of monastic schools expanded to include also teachers with secular education. At the beginning of the 18th century, about 270 Bulgarian towns and villages were sources for the dissemination of *damaskins* – compilations of miscellaneous literary works, and apoc-rypha. Yosif Bradati was one of the most popular *damaskin* writers who wrote in a colloquial Bulgarian style. Peter Bogdan (1601–74), Peter Parchevich (1612–74), Hristofor Zhefarovich (?–1753) and Parteniy Pavlovich (1695–1760) were Bulgarian Catholics who wrote patriotic historical works. A number of wealthy Bulgarian merchants and manufacturers tended to call themselves 'Hellenic-voiced Bulgarians', but the general population, especially 'pig-headed' peasants, continued to use their 'vulgar' mother Bulgarian.

National revival

The development of the modern Bulgarian revival was delayed by the centuries-long Turkish domination. In 1762 Paisiy (1722–73), a monk from the Monastery of **Hilendar**, finished his *Istoriya slavyanobolgars-kaya* (*History of Slavo–Bulgarians*), considered as the true beginning of a national revival. His book aimed to boost the morale of his compatriots and to kindle a sense of national identity and pride ('Among all Slavic people the Bulgarians first adopted Christianity, they had powerful Tsars and Patriarchs who conquered much land.'). Paisiy Hilendarski's style is ardent and persuasive. In 1792 there appeared a *Short History of the Slavo–Bulgarian People* by Pop (Priest) Spiridon who also appealed to a sense of national awareness.

In 1806 Sofroniy Vrachanski (1739–1813) published his *Nedelnik*, considered the first book written in a modern Bulgarian literary idiom, and later *Zhitiye i stradaniye greshnago Sofroniya* (*Life and Sufferings of Sinful Sofroniy*), an autobiographical work. Sofroniy's primary objective was to raise the educational level of the Bulgarian people. Yoakim Kurchovski, Kiril Peichinovich and Teodosiy Sinaitski, all of them Sofroniy's followers, went on to mould a literary style based on colloquial idiom. Another pioneering figure was Dr Peter Beron (1800–71), with wide knowledge and varied interests – medicine, society, literature, philosophy, chemistry, physics and mathematics. In 1824 he published his famous *Riben Boukvar* (*Fish Primer*), a textbook named after its printed emblem.

Other prominent literary figures from that period are Konstantin Fotinov (1790–1858), a secular educationalist who published *Lyuboslo-vie* (*Love of Literature*), the first Bulgarian magazine, and Vasil Aprilov

---

Notes to map (facing page): *Places shown include those listed under 'Chitalishta' and highlighted in the chapter as significant centres in the development of Bulgarian literature. Other selected points of interest include:* [a]**Ivan Vazov** *worked as a clerk in these towns in the early part of his life.* [b]**Hristo Botyov** *was killed near here fighting against the Turks in 1876.* [c]*Birthplace of* **Elin Pelin**. [d]*Birthplace of* **Yordan Yovkov** – *its people and life figure prominently in his work.* [e]*Birthplace of* **Dimcho Debelyanov** *(see Extract 6).* [f]*Birthplace of* **Hristo Botyov**. *Also fictionalized by* **Ivan Vazov** *in* Under the Yoke *(see Extract 5).* [g]*Birthplace of* **Konstantin Konstantinov**. [h]*After he left school,* **Peyo Yavorov** *found a job here with the post office.* [i]*See Extract 7.* [j]**Ivan Vazov** *praised the beauty of the mountains around the Rila Monastery (Extract 9).* [k]*Birthplace of* **Ivan Vazov**.

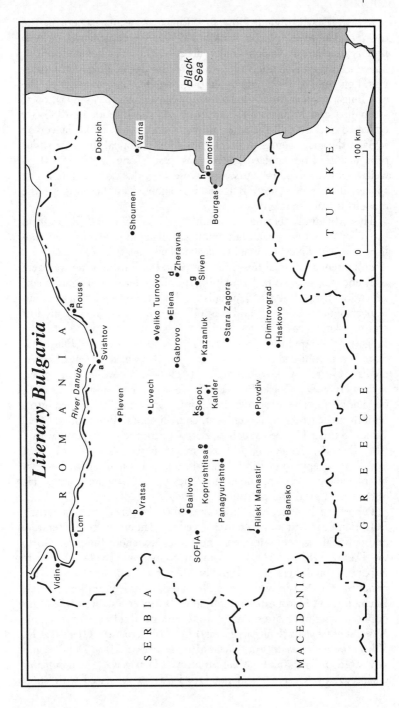

Literary Bulgaria

Black Sea

ROMANIA

River Danube

Lom

TURKEY

GREECE

MACEDONIA

SERBIA

100 km

0

Dobrich

Varna

Pomorie

h

Bourgas

Shoumen

Zheravna

d
Elena

g
Siliven

Veliko Turnovo

a
Rouse

Svishtov

a

Gabrovo

Kazanluk

Stara Zagora

Dimitrovgrad

Haskovo

Pleven

Lovech

k Sopot

f
Kalofer

Plovdiv

e
Koprivshtitsa

i

Panagyurishte

Rilski Manastir

j

Bansko

b Vratsa

c Bailovo

SOFIA

Vidin

(1789–1847) who founded the first Bulgarian secular school in the town of **Gabrovo**. Neofit Rilski (1793–1881) contributed to new literary standards. Naiden Gerov (1823–1900), teacher and writer, introduced the celebration of 24 May as the day of Bulgarian letters. Ivan Bogorov (1820–92) published *Bulgarski Orel* (*Bulgarian Eagle*), the first Bulgarian newspaper. Petko Rachov Slaveikov (1827–1895), poet, journalist, and Minister for Education and the Interior in 1880–81, collected over 18 000 Bulgarian proverbs and words. Petko Slaveikov revived the main genres of literary folklore: historical songs, *yunashki pesni* (songs of heroic deeds), *haidoushki pesni* (songs of Haidouks), as well as ritual songs, milieu songs, prose legends and folk tales. The spoken dialect of eastern Bulgaria was adopted as the basis for the modern literary standard.

The Miladinov brothers – Dimitur (1810–62) and Konstantin (1830–62) – strove for an autonomous Bulgarian church. They published *Bulgarski Narodni Pesni* (*Bulgarian Folk Songs*) in Zagreb.

Enlightened personalities from the period of Bulgarian revival were truly encyclopaedic, often combining the characteristics of churchman, educationalist, folk-lorist, journalist, publicist, and sometimes revolutionary fighter. Lyuben Karavelov (1834–79), writer, poet, journalist and translator, was a master of narrative who was fascinated with the Bulgarian folk tradition. His most famous prose works are *Bulgari Ot Staro Vreme* (*Bulgarians of Olden Times*) and *Maminoto Detentse* (*Mollycoddle*). Georgi Stoikov Rakovski (1821–67), a revolutionary poet, wrote fiery verse; 'Gorski Putnik' ('Traveller in the Forest') is his most popular poem. The name of Hristo Botyov or Botev ◊ has turned into a nationwide legend – he is seen as an embodiment of Bulgarian national values (Extract 1). Poems such as 'Borba' ('Struggle'), 'Moyata molitva' ('My Prayer'), 'Haidouti', and 'Na moeto purvo libe' ('To My First Love') are deeply rooted in folk motifs and colloquial idiom. Some of his melodious poems provided the lyrics for contemporary songs. He also wrote topical and polemical *feuilletons*.

Publishing houses, bookshops and also *chitalishta* – characteristic Bulgarian 'reading rooms', centres for education, art, culture, literature and political disputes – formed a network throughout Bulgaria. Hristo G. Danov (1828–1911) and Dragan Manchov (1834–1908) were important publishers from **Plovdiv**. The founding members of the *chitalishta* at Svishtov, Lom, Shoumen, Bitolya, Prilep, Veles, Bucharest and Constantinople all aimed to meet a rising demand for national reading matter and culture. Original plays, for example *Neshtastna familiya* (*Unhappy Family*) by Vasil Droumev (1841–1901), *Krivorazbranata tsivilizatsiya* (*Civilization Misunderstood*) by Dobri Voinikov (1833–78), and *Mnogostradalna Genoveva* (*Long-suffering Genoveva*) by Krustyo Pishourka (1823–75), were staged with enormous success at such *chitalishta*, a number of which expanded into wider cultural societies.

The art schools of **Tryavna, Debur** and **Samokov** also flourished during this period. Zahariy Zograf (1810–53), an artist and iconographer, painted the murals at the monasteries of **Bachkovo, Rila** and **Troyan**.

A number of Bulgarian students attended famous foreign universities. Many studied at Robert College in Constantinople. French missionaries had also set up a network of 19 schools well before Bulgarian liberation in 1878. About 2 000 French words were adopted into the language about that time. Sunday schools were established in many Bulgarian towns, and Orthodox, Catholic and Protestant religious education expanded, especially after publication of the first vernacular Bible in 1844.

After 1878

The years after Bulgarian national liberation in 1878 witnessed a wider and freer development of the national literature. Writers modelled their works on the best contemporary European authors, and wrote some highly original novels, poems and drama. The general trend was realistic, with strong nationalist overtones, and prose predominated as a genre. Ivan Vazov ◊ is celebrated as the patriarch of modern Bulgarian literature. He was a powerful and prolific author whose name has become synonymous with national liberation, optimism and patriarchal harmony and serenity. He deeply respected the French novelist Victor Hugo whom he called '*mon Maitre et inspirateur*'. *Pod igoto* (*Under the Yoke*), 1888, is Vazov's most famous epic novel, and it has been translated into many European languages (Extract 4 – its first-ever translation was into English).

Another writer from the later 19th century is Konstantin Velichkov (1855–1907), who was educated in France. He wrote travel books and sonnets, and in 1884, together with Ivan Vazov, he compiled *Bulgarska Hristomatiya* (*Bulgarian Chrestomathy*), an encyclopaedic work. Zahari Stoyanov ◊ is famous for his *Zapiski po bulgarskite vustaniya* (*Notes on the Bulgarian Uprisings*), perhaps the most comprehensive work about the 1876 uprising (Extract 7). The prose of Aleko Konstantinov (1863–97) reflects the clash between the ideals of national revival and the corruption of morals in Bulgaria after liberation. His *Bai Ganyu* (*Uncle Ganyu*) is a celebrated book about a vulgar, pragmatic upstart and hypocrite. Is he *homo balcanicus*, or does he blend racial, biological, or cultural features, in a more universal sense? This question still remains open. The author, who called himself with bitter irony '*Shtastlivetsa*' (The Happy Man'), was murdered by someone who dramatically resembled Bai Ganyu, his fictional character. Aleko Konstantinov was also considered a founder of organized tourism in Bulgaria, and he wrote a travel book, *Do Chikago i nazad* (*To Chicago and Back*). Also from that period is Stoyan Mihailovski (1856–1927), educated in France, who combines in a peculiar way religious faith with philosophical nihilism. He wrote works permeated with irony and pessimism, including *Filosoficheski i satiricheski soneti* (*Philosophical and Satirical Sonnets*). Tsanko Tserkovski (1869–1926), a bard of social progress, published *Pisma ot zatvora* (*Letters from Prison*) and *Iz gunkite na surtseto* (*In the Depths of My Heart*), both collections of verse. Todor Vlaikov (1865–1943) represented *narodnik* (populist) ideas, patriarchal tradition and milieu realism in *Sedyanka* (*Working Bee*).

The number of schools and *chitalishta* increased towards the turn of the century. Many town libraries and museums were built at that time. The cultural club *Slavyanska beseda* ('The Slav Reunion') was founded in 1880. The St Kliment Ohridski University of Sofia was inaugurated in 1888.

Fin de siècle and Symbolism

Reaction against the patriarchal and at times sentimental literary tradition from Ivan Vazov's times generated a later massive swing towards Symbolism, individualism and aestheticism. After the notable Russian influence on literature in the 19th century, aesthetic tastes were reoriented towards French authors. The views of the Bulgarian intelligentsia changed. The first literary salons in Bulgaria were set up by educated women – Soultana Racho Petrova, Maria Petrova-Chomakova and Mara Belcheva. Bulgarian literary celebrities gathered in the Tsar Osvoboditel café (demolished in the 1970s) on **Rakovski Street** in Sofia. Moderen Teater, the first movie theatre in Bulgaria was opened in 1908. Bulgarian drama also flourished around 1904–12. A Society of Bulgarian Publicists and Writers was set up in 1902, and it subsequently expanded into a National Writers' Union.

Cultural life was not concentrated only in the capital. In the town of **Toutrakan** the bookshop-owner Mavrodinov published Professor Krustev's *Misul* (*Thought*) magazine and the *Mladi i stari* (*Young and Old*) miscellany. Geo Milev's *Vezni* (*Scales*) magazine appeared in **Stara Zagora**. In **Yambol** a group of young people published the Futurist magazine *Crescendo* with the active participation of Marinetti himself (Marinetti was the guiding light behind the Futurist movement). The towns of **Stara Zagora** and **Sliven** were both provincial literary centres.

The era of individualism in Bulgarian literature commenced with the undisputed talent of Pencho Slaveikov ◊, poet, modernist, literary critic, universal spirit, and stoic. In poems such as *Kurvava pesen* (*Song of Blood*), *Ralitsa*, *Boiko* and the lyrical miniatures of *Sun za shtastie* (*Dream of Happiness*) he blended the best characteristics of the national

Ivan Vazov

literature with European achievements (Extract 3). For Pencho Slaveikov his art was Holy of Holies, combining German classical philosophy with Russian Humanism and English Romanticism (the myth of Prometheus). He was strongly influenced by the German philosopher Nietzsche. His anthology *Na ostrova na blazhenite* (*The Isle of the Blessed*), a literary mystification, ie a work of non-existing authors, rates among the most talented and curious books in literature.

The individualistic circle of *Misul* (1892–1907) united a Great Four: Dr Krustyu Krustev (1866–1919), patron and inspirer of the circle, Pencho Slaveikov, Peyu Yavorov (1878–1914) and Petko Todorov (1879–1916). Krustev, a professional literary critic, was the founder of Bulgarian aesthetics. The main objective of *Misul* was to cultivate aesthetic taste and to harmonize European and Bulgarian values. The circle attracted young authors like the poet Kiril Hristov, and prepared the ground for the adoption of modern conceptions which were forerunners of Symbolism; the aesthetization of suffering elevated the spiritual over the material. *Misul* played a leading part in moulding Bulgarian literary tastes at the turn of the century.

Peyu Yavorov ◊, a tormented soul and poet of dramatic split personality, tossed and turned between night, loneliness and unhappy love, far away from the madding crowd. Yavorov's verse is both modernistic and balanced – for example the collection *Bezsunitsi* (*Insomnia*). His contribution lies mainly in refining love lyrics and social verse. Geo Milev, another poet, called Yavorov 'the greatest master of poetic form'. Yavorov also wrote drama – *V polite na Vitosha* (*At the Foot of Vitosha*) and *Kogato grum udari, kak ehoto zagluhva* (*When Thunder Rolls, How the Echo Dies*). Yavorov's suicide in 1914 seemed in keeping with a mood of general disillusionment. Teodor Trayanov ◊ was perhaps the most consistent of the Symbolists, from *Regina Mortua*, 1909, to *Pantheon*, 1934. His themes include disintegration and death, spiritual creation, and the quest for freedom from material limitations. Trayanov employed a host of Symbolist images and expressive nuances. Many of his beloved images are associated with death, autumn and winter (Extract 10).

Petko Todorov (1879–1916) was the most gentle and least iconoclastic of the Great Four. He absorbed the strong influence of Ibsen on the one hand, and of Bulgarian folk poetry on the other, in *Idiliyi* (*Idylls*). He is the author of the plays *Zidari* (*Masons*) and *Strahil strashen haidutin* (*Strahil the Fearsome Haidut*). His themes were the individual will and freedom of man.

The early 20th century brought the acme of Bulgarian poetry. The verse of Dimcho Debelyanov ◊ is a must in Bulgarian literary anthologies. Debelyanov's verse is romantic, elegiac, psychological and confessional at the same time (Extract 6) – in collections such as *Spi gradut* (*The City Sleeps*), *Az iskam da te pomnya vse taka* (*I Want To Remember You Unchanged*) and *Da se zavurnesh v bashtinata kushta* (*When You Return To Your Father's Home*). The poet was killed in action in the first world war. Nikolai Liliev (1885–1960) wrote short poems on universal subjects, marked by unique harmony and melodiousness. His collections are *Ptitsi v noshtta* (*Birds at Night*), *Lunni petna* (*Moonspots*) and *Stihotvoreniya* (*Verse*). The poetic legacy of Kiril Hristov (1875–1944) lies in some of the finest nature descriptions in Bulgarian literature. In *Izbrani stihotvoreniya* (*Selected Verse*) Hristov explored personal and erotic subjects. The poet was known for his unstable temperament, swinging from egotism and nihilism to heights of patriotism. Dimitur Boyadzhiev (1889–1911) should also be named as a poet who expressed the horror of nothingness in verse in which death and love are interwined.

Symbolism to Communist ideals

A number of Bulgarian authors were attracted by Communist ideas which, for some, were just a temporary disease. Others, however, were permanently infected. Geo Milev (1895–1925) walked the path from Symbolism to Communism. He published his own magazines *Vezni* (*Scales*) and *Plamuk* (*Flame*) promoting both Modernist and Communist ideas. Milev based his most quoted epic poem *Septemvri* (*September*) on the 1923 uprising. He was closely linked to the European avant-garde, and Expressionism, in particular. Among his other works are 'Ad' ('Inferno') and 'Den na gneva' ('Day of Wrath'). He was also a translator, and compiled a number of landmark anthologies. Milev was killed in the wave of repression of 1925.

Hristo Yasenov (1889–1925) wrote serene youthful verse collected in *Ritsarski zamuk* (*Knight's Castle*). Like Milev, he embraced Communist ideas, and was killed in the 1925 purge. Anton Strashimirov (1872–1937), with prose works *Krustoput* (*Crossroads*) and *Horo* (*Reel Dance*), and plays *Vampir* (*Vampire*) and *Svekurva* (*Mother-in-Law*) was a pioneer in replacing old-fashioned realism with psychological penetration and mysticism. His characters are usually split personalities who act as if in a trance. In his choice of subjects, Strashimirov moved towards Communist ideology.

The early works of Lyudmil Stoyanov (1886–1973) were Symbolist, for example *Videniya na krustoput* (*Visions on Crossroads*). He had expert knowledge of European and Russian poetry, and translated many works. Communist influence is evident in his novels *Holera* (*Cholera*) and *Zhenski doushi* (*Womens' Souls*). The poet Emanouil Popdimitrov (1887–1943) in his later works also employed Communist motifs, while, like other Bulgarian poets, he began as a Symbolist. Many of his poems bear womens' names – Laura, Iren, Ema, etc. As the modern Bulgarian literary critic Svetlozar Igov put it, Emanuil Popdimitrov 'possessed the biggest poetic harem in Bulgarian literature'. His verse is more neo-Romantic than Symbolist; his brightest Romantic visions are love and nature.

Nikolai Rainov (1889–1954), writer of both prose and poetry, was also a scholar, philosopher, translator and art critic. His prose is stylized, melodic and exotic. Together with Sirak Skitnik (1883–1943), Rainov launched a new decorative style in Bulgarian art. Rainov expounded on the historical past of Bulgaria and ancient civilizations, for example in *Bogomilski legendi* (*Bogomil Legends*), *Videniya ot drevna Bulgaria* (*Visions of Ancient Bulgaria*), and *Ochite na Arabiya* (*The Eyes of Arabia*). Georgi Stamatov (1869–1942) wrote vitriolic satirical prose about the urban intelligentsia, often depicting careerist characters. His style combines Konstantinov's humour with Mihailovski's sarcasm.

More than twenty of the most prominent Bulgarian writers took part in the three wars – the Balkan War (1912–13), the Inter-Allied War (1913) and the first world war (1914–18). The wars altered poetic perceptions, and the shape of the literary scene changed dramatically. Almost all those who began as Symbolists eventually followed individual literary paths.

Zlatorog (*Golden Horn*) magazine, edited and published by the critic Vladimir Vasilev, and by Nikolai Liliev and Sirak Skitnik, appeared from 1920 until 1943. An eclectic and anti-ideological magazine, it was in a sense the heir to *Misul*. The Expressionist journal *Vezni* was published from 1919 until 1923, and the individualistic *Hyperion*, edited by Ivan Radoslavov, Teodor Trayanov ◊ and Lyudmil Stoyanov, the 'aces of Symbolism', was published from 1922 until 1931. *Razvigor*, a literary newspaper edited by Alexander Balabanov, was published from 1921 until 1927. These magazines served as cornerstones for the formation of literary circles.

Younger inter-war poetry

Two broad trends can be observed in the development of poetry between the world wars. One of them might be called 'intimate' or 'confessional' and the other 'social' or 'revolutionary'.

Asen Raztsvetnikov (1897–1957) was a vulnerable romantic with nihilistic and sceptical views. Darkness and grief were preferred subjects in the verse of Nikola Fournadzhiev (1903–1968). Nikolai Rakitin (1885–1934) wrote charming quiet verse. Author of more than twenty collections on idyllic and pastoral themes, and a passionate admirer of Bulgarian nature, he committed suicide to save his dignity. Atanas Dalchev (1904–77) expressed the drama of loneliness through innovative imagery preserving the moral tendencies of poets from the beginning of the century. *Fragmenti* (*Fragments*) is a famous collection of essays. He also translated verse from French, German, Russian, Spanish and Italian.

A number of women from that period devoted their perception and sensuality to poetry. Elisaveta Bagryana ◊ wrote rhapsodic, vitalist, intense, woman-centred poetry (Extracts 2 and 13). She was a

Elisaveta Bagryana

freedom-loving and unrestrained personality who made a cult of youth, the sea and travelling. Her collections include her most famous volume *Vechnata i svyatata* (*The Eternal and the Sacred*), 1927, *Zvezda na moryaka* (*Sailor's Star*), 1932 and the post-war *Ot bryag do bryag* (*From*

Shore to Shore), 1963. Dora Gabe (1888–1983) rates immediately next to Bagryana. She used subjects from everyday living and brought common household objects to poetic life. Her works include the collections *Pochakay, sluntse* (*Wait Sun*) and *Lunatichka* (*Sleepwalking Woman*).

Hristo Smirnenski (1898–1923) represented the social and revolutionary trend in poetry. He was a virtuoso at versification, and employed varied metrical and rhythmical patterns charged with high energy. He also wrote topical *feuilletons* and satirical works. Nikola Vaptsarov (1909–42) worked as a common labourer. He came from an Evangelist background. A born poet, he had the gift to 'feel' words almost palpably. Vaptsarov's poetry rests on two pillars – faith and romantic feeling. The world he dreamed of in his *Motorni pesni* (*Motor Songs*) made 'machines sing under a blue sky'. He headed a guerilla terrorist campaign in 1941–42, and was executed by firing squad. Nikolai Hrelkov (1894–1950) wrote proletarian verse with urban and international imagery. His most famous poem is 'Srednoshten kongres' ('Midnight Congress'). Another of the proletarian poets is Hristo Radevski (1903–) whose name became synonymous with the urge to sacrifice the individual self for the Communist cause.

The somewhat lonely figure of Nikolai Marangozov (1900–67) stands aside from general trends in poetic development. His verse has an archaic ring with its combination of folk narrative with exquisite modern imagery.

Inter-war fiction

Elin Pelin ◊ is a prominent prose writer from the period between the two wars. 'The land' might be said to be his obsession. His style is realistic, and his characters are the peasants from the region of **Shopsko** (Extract 11). He is a vital author who writes short stories and novels in a crystal-clear style and with humour about human dramas, sorrows and delights under an open sky – for example, *Geratsite* (*The Gerak Family*) and *Zemya* (*Earth*). He is also a classic children's writer.

Yordan Yovkov ◊ is the most celebrated psychological writer of Bulgarian prose. Yovkov's characters are people of flesh and blood, yet they are portrayed with spiritual perfection. He wrote several collections of short stories, including *Staroplaninski legendi* (*Legends from Stara Planina*) and *Vecheri v Antimovskiya han* (*Evenings at the Antimovo Inn*) (Extract 5). Another prose writer, Konstantin Konstantinov ◊, published *Den po den* (*Day by Day*), a collection of short stories (Extract 14), and *Kruv* (*Blood*), a novel. He is, however, appreciated particularly for his memoirs and travel sketches.

Trifon Kounev (1880–1954) wrote talented satirical pieces which provoked the anger of the Communist authorities after September 1944 and cost him his life. Dimitur Shishmanov (1889–1945), a highly sophisticated author, explored the relation between the ancient and the modern in his novel *Senki nad Akropola* (*Shadows on the Acropolis*). Shishmanov too was executed after the Communist takeover.

Three writers closely linked to folk tradition are Choudomir, Angel Karaliychev, and Georgi Karaslavov. Choudomir (1890–1967), from the town of **Kazanluk**, wrote exquisite short stories in a colloquial style, noted for their comic local characters. Karaliychev (1902–72) is a favourite Bulgarian author of children's prose, especially fairy tales. Karaslavov (1904–80) describes archetypal national characters in his novels *Tatoul* (*Thornapple*) and *Snaha* (*Daughter-in-Law*) and explores the manic and obsessive urge of dark energy in their souls, the impulses generated by the characters' vulgar and pragmatic psychology.

The satirical and modernistic prose of Svetoslav Minkov ♭ stands out from the literary mainstream. Minkov wrote about Bulgarian anti-utopias peopled with grotesque or exotic figures and crammed with fantastic and fearsome images of urban technology. Among his books are *Razkazi v taralezhova kozha* (*Stories in a Hedgehog's Hide*), *Drougata America* (*The Other America*) and *Imperiya na glada* (*Empire of Hunger*).

Dobri Nemirov (1882–1945) and Stiliyan Chilingirov (1889–1969) wrote historical fiction. Fani Popova Moutafova (1902–77), who also wrote widely read historical novels, was thrown into a Communist labour camp.

St. L. Kostov (1879–1939) is the most significant Bulgarian comedy playwright, with *Golemanov, Vrazhalets* (*Healer*) and *Zlatnata mina* (*The Gold Mine*).

Writers under Communism

After the Communist takeover in September 1944, Bulgarian literature for some time continued in its democratic momentum from the 1930s and 1940s when writers had gained European dimensions and cosmopolitan vision. Communism, however, affected literature and the lives of authors enormously. Printing and publishing were nationalized in 1948, liberal intellectuals retreated from art, or were compelled to retreat. Dimitur Talev, Mihail Arnaoudov, Trifon Kounev and Yosif Petrov became victims of physical repression, to mention but a few. Literature was forced to wear a Stalinist straitjacket. Some poets were given military ranks. Todor Zhivkov, the longest-serving Communist dictator, had some of his numerous writings published by Robert Maxwell (rumour has it that Zhivkov never even read all of his own works). Most notoriously, the Bulgarian writer Georgi Markov (1929–78) was murdered on Waterloo Bridge in London by Bulgarian Communist agents using a poisoned umbrella.

The new forms of packaged Socialist culture did not meet the moral criteria of a number of authors who emigrated to the West. Some wrote directly in English, German or French, and only now, years later, are their works being translated or rewritten into Bulgarian. George Paprikoff (1912–84) wrote a comprehensive *Works of Bulgarian Emigrants*, an annotated bibliography. Among these emigré authors are Stefan Popov (1906–89) with *Der Wille zum Gestalt* (*The Will to Form*), Hristo Ognyanov (1911–) with *Assisi Sonnets*, and Stefan Grouev, (1923–) with *Crown of Thorns*. Georgi Markov analysed the corrupt essence of the Communist regime in *Reports from Bulgaria from Abroad* and *The Truth that Killed*. Atanas Slavov (1930–) wrote *With the Precision of Bats*. Tsvetan Marangozov (1933–) published in Sofia in 1991 *Detsata na Ruso* (*Children of Rousseau*). *Homo Emigranticus* by Dimitur Bochev ◊ appeared in Bulgaria in 1993. Bulgarian intellectuals who settled permanently in Western countries and integrated with their cultural scene included Julia Kristeva, Tzvetan Todorov, Dora Vallier, and the Nobel-prize winner Elias Canetti. Others have returned after the start of democratic reforms and settled in Bulgaria.

Blinded by the promises of a bright Communist future, a number of authors for some time nourished utopian beliefs. The poet Penyo Penev (1930–59) wrote optimistic verse about enthusiastic builders of Communism – for example, in his collections *Dobro utro, hora* (*Good Morning, People*) and *Kogato se nalivaha osnovite* (*When Foundations Were Laid*). Gradually he lost his illusions and finally committed suicide. Veselin Andreev (1918–91), the author of *Partizanski pesni* (*Guerilla Resistance Songs*), whose name became synonymous with the iron will of the Communist through his poems, also committed suicide when he realized the collapse of Communist ideals.

Ideology was all-pervasive in Bulgarian society. Literary life was administered through plenums and directives, and also through frowning or patting on the back. After a string of quasi-reformist events which by coincidence happened in April, the poet Angel Todorov (1906–93) wrote that 'April is the party month'. Dimitur Metodiev (1922–), author of 'Pesen za generalnata liniya' ('Song About the General Party Line'), amended the Bulgarian national anthem accordingly. Bogomil Rainov (1919–) and Andrei Goulyashki (1914–) wrote novels about the will of Communists to sacrifice themselves, and also about the 'enemy inside' the system. Various new literary clichés arrived to serve Communist ideology – for example, 'antifascist resistance novel', 'Communist production novel', and 'positive hero in prose and poetry'. Kroum Velkov (1902–60) wrote 'September Prose'. Orlin Vasilev (1904–77), author of the play *Trevoga* (*Alarm*) was decorated as 'Hero of Socialist Labour'.

In the cat-and-mouse game between ideological censorship and gifted writers, some became susceptible to literary compromise. Others, however, stood their artistic ground and refused to turn into singers of an unsavoury political system. To express their individual self and remain unpunished, some authors developed elaborate codes of Aeso-pean imagery. Their painful romantic protest resembled that of Alexander Voutimski (1919–43) who had reacted against totalitarian shackles in his poem *Evropa-hishtnitsa* (*Europe the Predator*). Veselin Hanchev (1919–66) turned to philosophical and tragic themes in his verse. Ivan Peichev (1916–76) wrote poems in a personal and confes-sional vein. Andrei Germanov (1932–86) became famous with his intellectual quatrains. The suicide of Petya Doubarova (1962–79), a promising poet, was a reaction against a hostile and restrictive environment. The verse of Alexander Gerov (1919–) displays a hypersensitive reflex to the lack of individual freedom. Mihail Berberov (1934–) writes intellectual verse with complex imagery. The poetic associations of Binyo Ivanov (1939–) are surprising and powerful. The poetry of Valeri Petrov (1920–) uses subtle irony and abounds in word-games. The verse of Nikolai Kunchev (1937–) testifies to intense perception. Boris Hristov (1945–) writes dynamic and dramatic verse. Ivan Tsanev (1941–) is a fine psychological poet.

A number of authors had to pay a price for opposing the Communist mainstream. Yosif Petrov (1909–) was deprived of pen and paper in the labour camp, so he had to remember all his poems and reproduce them years later. The doors of publishing houses remained closed for Konstantin Pavlov (1933–) for ideological reasons. *Litse* (*Face*), a novel by Blaga Dimitrova ◊ and *Lyuti choushki* (*Hot Peppers*), a satirical collection by Radoi Ralin (1923–) were withdrawn from circulation for the same reasons. *Poetut i planinata* (*Poet and Mountain*), a play by Ivan Teofilov (1931–), was banned after the first night.

Younger poets show a general preference for a more or less discursive and philosophical manner of writing, a preoccupation with history and the ancient world, as well as a keen social reflex. This holds true for poets like Georgi Roupchev (1957–), Edvin Sougarev (1953–), Ani Ilkov (1957–), Roumen Leonidov (1953–), Irina Yordanova (1961–), Vladimir Levchev (1957–), Mirela Ivanova (1962–), Lyubomir Nikolov (1954–), Boiko Lambovski (1960–), and Boris Rokanov (1961–).

Prose under Communism

The prose of the earlier writers Dimitur Talev and Dimitur Dimov served as model for authors who began their writers' careers im-mediately after the Communist takeover in 1944. Talev (1898–1966) wrote an epic and serene historical tetralogy tracing the heroic past of Macedonia – *Zhelezniyat svetilnik* (*The Iron Candlestick*), *Prespanskite kambani* (*The Bells of Prespa*), *Ilinden* and *Glasovete vi chouvam* (*I Hear*

Your Voices). Dimov (1909–66), an outstanding novelist, portrayed conflicting and unusual characters and exposed the gap between the individual and the crowd from the early 1940s in *Tyutyun* (*Tobacco*), about Bulgaria, and in *Osudeni doushi* (*Damned Souls*), about the Spanish Civil War.

Many Bulgarian authors after 1944 resorted either to the country's historical past, or to the abstract future, sometimes as a way of avoiding the immediate and highly problematic present (also using science-fiction, folk motifs, exotic settings, or the grotesque) mainly because Socialist Realism did not allow a shade of suspicion to fall on bright perspectives. Emiliyan Stanev (1907–79) set some of his novels, for example *Antihrist* (*Anti-Christ*), in mediaeval Bulgaria. Stoyan Zagorchinov (1889–1969) wrote *Ivailo* about the leader of a peasant uprising from old Bulgarian history. Vera Moutafchieva (1929–) writes exclusively historical prose – *Poslednite Shishmanovtsi* (*The Last Descendants of the Shishman Family*) is one of her most popular novels. Stefan Dichev's (1920–) *Za svobodata* (*For Freedom*) and *Putyat kum Sofia* (*The Road to Sofia*) are both novels about the national liberation movement and were later televized. Anton Donchev (1930–) wrote *Vreme Razdelno* (*Time of Parting*) about historical forced conversions to Islam in parts of Bulgaria.

The quest for moral values is the driving force in the novels of many modern Bulgarian writers. Pavel Vezhinov (1914–83), among other things produced psychological science fiction with humanistic motivation – for example, *Barierata* (*The Barrier*) and *Beliyat goushter* (*The White Lizard*). Nikolai Haitov (1919–) sets *Divi razkazi* (*Wild Tales*) in his beloved **Rhodope Mountains**. Ivailo Petrov (1923–) presents a panoramic view of the Bulgarian village life in *Haika za vultsi* (*Wolf-Hunt*) with a critical eye for the changes in mentality. Dimitur Koroudzhiev (1941–) holds genuinely democratic views which he expresses in his novels *Domut na Alma* (*The Home of Alma*) and *Deset godini po-kusno* (*Ten Years After*). Viktor Paskov's ◊ novels include the successful, recently translated *Balada za Georg Henig* (*A Ballad for George Henig*), 1988 (Extract 12).

Contemporary Bulgarian playwrights include Yordan Radichkov ◊, who blends in a curious way national mythology and folklore in *Opit za letene* (*An Attempt to Fly*), 1979. He is also a prolific prose writer of parodic and grotesque evocations of village life and contemporary mores.

Literary life in Bulgaria is currently in a state of flux – from underfunded publishing and book distribution, to reassessment of literary and political values. No new magnificent palace of culture is likely to be erected in the near future, and the reading public shows little demand for hollow megalomaniac epics. The concern of many

Bulgarians, besides their own physical survival, is to keep Bulgarian art and literature of democratic dimensions going, often at the cost of personal deprivation.

CHITALISHTA

The following are *Chitalishta* in some of the larger Bulgarian towns. These are typically Bulgarian societies for literary, cultural and social activities, dating mainly from the period of national revival.

Dobrich: Yordan Yovkov, founded 1871. 200 000 volumes.

Kazanluk: Iskra. Life and works of the writer Choudomir.

Lom: Postoyanstvo, founded 1856. Collection of rare and valuable publications from 1806 to 1878.

Pleven: Suglasie, founded 1869.

Plovdiv: Georgi Turnev, founded 1900. Amateur arts education.

Shoumen: Dobri Voinikov, founded 1856. Old and rare books.

Sliven: Zora, founded 1859. Rich library, old books and manuscripts in foreign languages.

Sofia: Braille. For people with impaired vision.

Sofia: Tsar Boris III, founded 1928 under the auspices of Boris III.

Sofia: Slavyanska Beseda, founded 1880 by intellectuals from Slavonic countries.

Svishtov: Elenka i Kiril Avramovi, founded 1856.

Vidin: Tsviat, founded 1869.

BOOKLIST

The following selection includes the extracted titles in this chapter as well as those mentioned in the introduction which are available in English and other titles for further reading. In general, paperback editions are given when possible. The editions cited are not necessarily the only ones available. For most of the extracted works, the original publisher can be found in 'Acknowledgments and Citations' at the end of the volume, as can the exact location of the extracts and the editions from which they are taken. Extract numbers are highlighted in bold. Square brackets denote the date of publication of the work in its original language.

Anthology of Bulgarian Poetry, Peter Tempest, trans, Sofia Press, Sofia, 1980. **Extracts 3, 6 and 10.**

Bagryana, Elisaveta, *Elissaveta Bagryana, Introduced by Peter Dinekov . . . Ten Poems*, Kevin Ireland, trans, Sofia Press, Sofia, 1970. **Extract 2.**

Bagryana, Elisaveta, 'Fire Dancer's Destiny', in *The Devil's Dozen: Thirteen Bulgarian Women Poets*,

Forest Books, London, 1991. **Extract 13**.

Bagryana, Elisaveta, *Penelope of the Twentieth Century: Selected Poems*, Brenda Walker, Valentine Borissov and Belin Tonchev, trans, Forest Books, London, 1993.

Balkan Range, The: A Bulgarian Reader, John Robert Colombo and Nikola Roussanoff, ed, Hounslow Press, Toronto, 1976.

Bell, John D., *The Bulgarian Communist Party from Blagoev to Zhivkov*, Hoover Institution Press, Stanford, CA, 1986.

Boshkov, Atanasse, *The Splendour of Bulgaria*, David James Mossop, trans, George Neaf, Sofia, Geneva, Paris, 1993.

Botev (Botyov), Hristo, *Poems*, Kevin Ireland, trans, Theodora Atanasova, ed, Sofia Press, Sofia, 1955. **Extract 1**.

Brown, J. F., *Bulgaria under Communist Rule*, Pall Mall Press, London, 1970.

Bulgaria Past and Present, John D. Treadway, ed, Dept of Slavic Language and Literatures, Indiana University, Bloomington, IN, 1993.

Bulgarian Poets of Our Day: Literary Sketches, Sofia Press, Sofia, 1971.

Bulgarian Short Stories, P. Danchev, ed, Foreign Languages Press, Sofia, 1960.

Clay and Star: Contemporary Bulgarian Poets, Lisa Sapinkopf and Georgi Belev, ed, Milkweed Editions, Minneapolis, MN, 1992.

Crampton, Richard J., *A Short History of Modern Bulgaria*, Cambridge University Press, Cambridge, 1987.

Davidkov, Ivan, *Fires of the Sunflower*, Ewald Osers, trans, Forest Books, London and Boston, MA, 1988.

Debelyanov, Dimcho, 'Secret Sighs', in *Anthology of Bulgarian Poetry*, Peter Tempest, trans, Sofia

Press, Sofia, 1980. **Extract 6**.

Description of a Struggle: the Picador Book of Contemporary East European Prose, Michael March, ed, Picador, London, 1994. (Ivailo Dichev, Viktor Paskov, Ivan Kulekov, Stanislav Stratiev.)

Devil's Dozen, The: Thirteen Bulgarian Women Poets, Brenda Walker, Belin Tonchev, trans, Forest Books, London, 1991. **Extract 13**.

Dimitrova, Blaga, *The Last Rock Eagle: Selected Poems*, Brenda Walker, Belin Tonchev and Vladimir Levchev, trans, Forest Books, London, 1992.

Dimitrova, Blaga, *Journey to Oneself* [1965], Radost Pridham, trans, Cassell, London, 1969. **Extract 8**.

Documents and Materials on the History of Bulgarian People, M. Voinov, compiler, *et al*, Publishing House of the Bulgarian Academy of Sciences, Sofia, 1969.

Doubarova, Petya, *Here I Am, in Perfect Leaf Today*, Singular Speech Press, Canton, CN, 1992.

Elin Pelin, *Short Stories*, Marguerite Alexieva, trans, Mercia Macdermott, ed, Sofia Press, Sofia, 1990. **Extract 11**.

Elin Pelin, *Bag-Boys*, Elka Danova, trans, Sofia Press, Sofia, 1975.

Gabe, Dora, *Depths: Conversations with the Sea*, John Robert Colombo and Nikola Roussanoff, trans, Hounslow Press, Toronto, 1978.

Georgiev, Emil, *Bulgaria's Share in Human Culture*, Sofia Press, Sofia, 1968.

Georgiev, Emil, *Bulgaria's Contribution to Slavonic and European Cultural Life in the Middle Ages*, Sofia Press, Sofia, 1981.

Gladstone, William, *The Bulgarian Horrors and the Question of the East*, J. Murray, London, 1876.

Groueff, Stephane, *Crown of Thorns (The Reign of King Boris III of Bulgaria 1918–1943)*. Madison Books, Lanham, MD, 1987.

Gyllin, Roger, *The Genesis of the Modern Bulgarian Literary Language*, Uppsala University, Uppsala, 1991.

Hoddinott, R.F., *Bulgaria in Antiquity*, Benn, London, 1975.

Hristov, Boris, *The Wings of the Messenger*, Roland Flint, Betty Grinberg, Lyubomir Nikolov, trans, Petrikov Publishers, Sofia, 1991.

Hush, You Nightingales: Bulgarian Poetry, Andrei Filipov and Don D. Wilson, trans, Singular Speech Press, Canton, CN, 1993.

In the Fields: Bulgarian Short Stories, Marguerite Alexieva, Petco Drenkoff and Sider Florin, trans, Narodna Kultura, Sofia, 1957.

Introduction to Modern Bulgarian Literature: An Anthology of Short Stories, Nikolai Kirilov and Frank Kirk, eds, Twayne, New York, 1960.

Iovkov, Iordan, see Yovkov, Yordan.

Khristov, Boris, see Hristov, Boris.

Kiril and Methodius: Founders of Slavonic Writing, Spass Nikolov, trans, Ivan Duichev, ed, East European Monographs, Boulder, CO, 1985. **Extract 15**.

Konstantinov, Konstantin, *Day By Day*, Marjorie Hall Pojarlieva, trans, Sofia Press, Sofia, 1969. **Extract 14**.

Koroudzhiev, Dimitur (Korudzhiev, Dimitar), *The Garden with the Blackbirds* [1984], in *South-Eastern Magazine*, USA, 1993.

Kostov, Vladimir, *The Bulgarian Umbrella*, Harvester, Hemel Hempstead, 1988.

Lang, David Marshall, *The Bulgarians (From Pagan Times to the Ottoman Conquest)*, Thames and Hudson, London, 1976.

Levchev, Lyubomir, *The Left-Handed One*, John Robert Colombo and Nikola Roussanoff, trans, Hounslow Press, Toronto, 1977.

Levchev, Lyubomir, *The Mysterious Man*, Vladimir Filipov, trans, Ohio University Press, Chicago, IL, 1980.

Levchev, Lyubomir, *Stolen Fire*, Ewald Osers, trans, Forest Books, London and Boston, MA, 1986.

Manning, Clarence A. and Smal-Stocki, Roman, *The History of Modern Bulgarian Literature*, Greenwood, Westport, CN, 1974.

Markov, Georgi, *The Truth that Killed*, Liliana Brisby, trans, Weidenfeld and Nicolson, London, 1983.

Macdermott, Mercia, *A History of Bulgaria 1393–1885*, Allen and Unwin, London, 1962.

Milev, Geo, *The Road to Freedom: Poems and Prose Poems*, Ewald Osers, trans, Forest Books, London, 1988.

Modern Bulgarian Poetry, Roy Macgregor-Hastie, trans, Sofia Press, Sofia, 1976.

Moser, Charles A., *A History of Bulgarian Literature 865–1944*, Mouton, The Hague, 1972.

Paskov, Viktor, *A Ballad for Georg Henig* [1988], Robert Sturm, trans, Peter Owen, London, 1990. **Extract 12**.

The Peach Thief and Other Bulgarian Stories, R. Pridham and J. Norris, eds, Cassell, London, 1968.

Pinto, V., *Bulgarian Prose and Verse* [English introduction], Athlone, London, 1957.

Poets of Bulgaria, William Meredith, ed, John Updike and others, trans, Forest Books, London, 1988.

Slavov, Atanas, *The 'Thaw' in Bulgarian Literature*, East European Monographs (Columbia distr.), Boulder, CO, and New York, 1981.

Slaveikov, Pencho, 'There's not a Breeze or Breath in Motion', in

Anthology of Bulgarian Poetry, Peter Tempest, trans, Sofia Press, Sofia, 1980. **Extract 3**.

Stoyanov, Zahari (Stoianov, Zakhari), *Extracts from Notes on the Bulgarian Uprisings*, Maria Rankova, trans, Sofia Press, Sofia, 1976. **Extract 7**.

Thracian Treasures from Bulgaria, R. A. Higgins, ed, British Museum Publications, London, 1976.

Trayanov, Teodor, 'The Secret of the Strouma', in *Anthology of Bulgarian Poetry*, Peter Tempest, trans, Sofia Press, Sofia, 1980. **Extract 10**.

Under the Eaves of a Forgotten Village: Sixty Poems from Contemporary Bulgaria, Hounslow Press, Willowdale, Ontario, 1975.

Vaptsarov, Nikola, *Nineteen Poems*, Ewald Osers, trans, Journeyman, London and New York, 1984.

Vazov, Ivan, *Selected Stories*, Foreign Languages Press, Sofia, 1967.

Vazov, Ivan, *Under the Yoke*, Marguerite Alexieva and Theodora Atanasova, trans, Sofia Press, Sofia, 1976. **Extract 4**. Also, another version: Heinemann, London, 1894 / Twayne, New York, 1971.

Vazov, Ivan, *Selected Poems*, Peter Tempest, trans, Sofia Press, Sofia, 1976. **Extract 9**.

Window on the Black Sea: Bulgarian Poetry in Translation, Richard Harteis and William Meredith, trans, Carnegie Mellon University Press, Pittsburgh, PA, 1992.

Xristov, Boris, see Hristov, Boris.

Young Poets of a New Bulgaria, Belin Tonchev, ed, Forest Books, London, 1990.

Yovkov, Yordan (Iovkov, Iordan), *The White Swallow and Other Short Stories*, Ministry of Information and Arts, Sofia, 1947.

Yovkov, Yordan (Iovkov, Iordan), *Short Stories*, Foreign Languages Press, Sofia, 1965.

Yovkov, Yordan (Iovkov, Iordan). *The Inn at Antimovo and Legends of Stara Planina*, John Burnip, trans, Slavica Publishers, Columbus, OH, 1990. **Extract 5**.

Extracts

(1) THE BALKAN RANGE (STARA PLANINA)

Hristo Botyov (or Botev), *Hadzhi Dimitur*

The poetry of Botyov blends folk tradition, lyricism and revolutionary spirit. (This extract is not the complete poem.)

He lives, still he lives! In the mountain fast,
soaked in blood, he lies and groans,
a rebel, wounded in the chest,
a rebel, young and with a manly strength.

To one side he has thrown a gun,
to the other a sword in broken pieces,
his head rolls, his eyes are dulled,
his mouth describes the universe with curses.

The rebel lies, and in the sky
there burns a motionless and angry sun;
a harvester sings in fields near by,
and faster still his lifeblood runs.

It's harvest now. Slave girls – chant
your songs of grief. And you, sun, shine
upon this land of slaves. My heart
be hushed. One rebel more will die.

He who falls fighting to be free
can never die: for him the sky
and earth, the trees and beasts shall keen,
to him the minstrel's song shall rise . . .

By day he's shaded by an eagle,
a wolf licks gently at his wounds,
above, a falcon – bird of rebels –
tends to this rebel as a brother would.

The moon comes out and day grows dim,
on heaven's vault the stars now throng,
the forest rustles, quiet stirs the wind,
the mountains sing an outlaw song.

Wood-sprites, in their white-hued dress,
fair and beautiful, take up the tune,
hushed their footfall on the grass,
as all about him then sit down.

One sprinkles coolness over him,
another binds his wound with herbs
a third's quick kisses touch his lips
and softly smiles as he looks up at her.

(2) Bulgaria: Elemental Forces

Elisaveta Bagryana, *Elements*

This poem is evocative of the poet's persona, but also has a graphic elemental atmosphere of inherited way of life and topography.

Can you restrain the wind which comes down from the heights,
bursting through the gorges, tossing clouds above the threshers,
tugging at the eaves of houses, the covers of the carts,
tumbling children in the squares, knocking over gates and fences – in
 the town where I was born?

Can you restrain the Bistritsa, swirling in the spring,
shattering the icefloes, battering down the arches,
spilling from its watercourse, muddy and menacing,
and dragging off the cattle and people's homes and gardens – in the
 town where I was born?

Can you restrain the wine when its seething ferment rises,
with its heavy humid breath, stacked in giant casks
on which Cyrillic lettering records: the 'Black', the 'White',
in the chilly, stony cellars handed down from ages past – in the town
 where I was born?

Can you restrain me then – I'm self-willed, wandering, free –
true sister of the wind, of the water, of the wine,
lured on to boundless spaces, to what cannot yet be reached,
dreaming always of those pathways – ungained and still untried – can
 you restrain me now?

(3) Bulgaria: Summer

Pencho Slaveikov,
There's Not a Breeze or Breath in Motion

Slaveikov, a highly individual poet, enriched Bulgarian literature with new themes and forms. This poem is included in Anthology of Bulgarian Poetry – see Booklist.

There's not a breeze or breath in motion,
In field and treetop nothing stirs.
The dew has spread a jewel ocean
Where heaven her fair face observes.

Up early on the road I relish
The freshness of a summer dawn
And with invigorated spirits
To journey's end I'm lightly borne.

To journey's end, a quiet evening
Of cloudless skies and the caress
Of restful hearth and home to weave me
A thousand dreams of happiness.

(4) 'Byala Cherkva', Stara Planina

Ivan Vazov, *Under the Yoke*

*Fictional Byala Cherkva is described as a small town at the
northern foothill of Stara Planina. This scene takes place on the
eve of national liberation.*

On that cool May evening Chorbadji Marko, bareheaded and in his
dressing gown, was having his supper with his household in the garden.

The master's table had been laid as usual, under the vine, between
the clear cold jet of the brooklet that flowed through the garden and
twittered like a swallow day in and day out, and the tall spreading box
trees whose dark shapes stood out against the wall, always green,
summer and winter. The lantern was alight, hanging from the branch
of a friendly lilac tree which bent its scented sprays over the heads of
the household.

And it was a numerous one.

Beside Bai Marko, beside his mother and his wife, a swarm of
children sat around the table, big ones and little ones who, armed with
knives and forks, polished off the loaves and dishes in a trice. They full
justified the Turkish title of 'enemies of the loaf'.

From time to time the father beamed at these panting workers with
their sharp teeth and indomitable appetites, encouraging them with a
cheerful smile: 'Eat away, my children, eat and grow strong! Pena, fill
the dish again.'

The maid went to the spout where the wine was cooling, poured it
into a deep porcelain dish and brought it back. Bai Marko passed it
round to the children, saying benevolently:

'Drink, you rascals!'

And the dish made the round of the table. Eyes grew brighter, cheeks
flushed pinker, and lips were smacked in pleasure. Then Marko turned
to his wife who was frowning in disapproval, and said sternly:

'Let them drink in front of me, don't let them thirst for wine. I don't want them to be drunkards when they grow up.'

Marko had his own practical views on upbringing. Though an old-fashioned, uneducated man, he had a thorough grasp of human nature and knew that forbidden fruit is the sweetest. Because of this, to guard them against an inclination to pilfer, he was in the habit of giving the key of his money chest to his children.

'Gocho, go and open the sandalwood chest and bring me the bag with the coins!'

Then again he would tell another:

'There, my boy, go and count out twenty liras from the little basket and have them ready for me when I come back.' Then he would go out.

Although it was the custom of most fathers in those days to keep their children standing while they themselves had their meals, supposedly to teach them to respect their elders, Marko always sat his down at table. When he had visitors he also wanted his sons to be present.

'Let them get the habits of gentlemen', he would explain, 'and not be like wild animals and hide from people like Anko Razpopché.'

For Anko Razpopché writhed with embarrassment whenever he met a man dressed European fashion.

(5) Dobroudzha

Yordan Yovkov, *The Inn at Antímovo*

Yovkov, a subtle psychological writer, gives us a wealth of characters from Bulgaria's north-east.

Sarándovitsa's inn at Antímovo was not merely at a crossroads but at a place where many roads intersected. In autumn time, when caravan after caravan of carts from the whole Dobrudja travelled towards the wharf at Balchik and towards the watermills at Bátova, there was no other way for them to go except through Antímovo, past Sarándovitsa's inn. Then merry days began there. Outside there was always the sight of unharnessed carts, and while the famished horses dozed under their blankets, – in the inn pipes played, shouts were heard, and from time to time the wooden floor started to rumble as if it would collapse beneath the dancing of the young men. If a man went inside, he would see a blue cloud of cigarette smoke from floor to ceiling, and through it, caps, reversed fur-coats and moustachioed faces scorched by the sun and the wind. They all jabbered and, even though some were sitting down, most stood upright, with a glass of wine in one hand and a horse-whip in the other, – making as if they were all ready to be on their way.

Behind the counter, amid the smoke and the fog of the cooking sausages, stood Sarándovitsa, well-built, courageous and attractive even at her age, with her hair wound around her headscarf and her sleeves rolled up. She poured wine, prepared snacks, gave orders to the servants, and although overburdened with so much work, still managed to get in a reply to some jest thrown at her from afar, to smile when she needed to, to welcome and to despatch her guests with some kind word for each.

In the corner by the counter meanwhile, a stranger to all this hubbub, lying forward upon the table or with his head cast back so that his white beard jutted out into the air, slumbered Kalmúk . . .

Such was the memory I had of the Antímovo inn. Right up to late into the back end, as long as the weather was good and the roads dry, the inn filled up with people, and the jollifications continued without a break. The old wine had all been drunk, and the carts of the Préslav vintners began to arrive, bearing great tuns of wine which had not finished fermenting, with reeds for airholes and with cushions of dry rushes.

(6) Koprivshtitsa, Stara Planina

Dimcho Debelyanov, *Secret Sighs*

The poet strikes a nostalgic note in one of his famous elegies. Dimcho's father died when he was a young boy, and, in his adult years, the poet never again had an opportunity to return home.

To go back home again retracing
Your footsteps when the light is falling
And night is in soft arms embracing
Unfortunates their fate bewailing.
From weary shoulders to be shaking
The burden grievous times bequeath you,
To step into the courtyard, waking
The joy of her who longs to see you.

Then to be met in the old doorway,
To place on her frail breast your forehead
And bask in smiles as kind as always,
While softly saying 'Mother, mother . . .'
To view the room that's so familiar,
Your final resting place and haven

And in the silence there to whisper,
Upon the ancient icon gazing:
'I come to await the peaceful moment
Of sunset when my days are over . . .'

* * *

O secret sighs of a sad roamer
Who idly dreams of home and mother!

(7) PANAGYURISHTE, SREDNA GORA

Zahari Stoyanov, *Notes on the Bulgarian Uprisings*

*Stoyanov was a participant in and self-educated chronicler of the
heroic events in Bulgaria during the 1870s.*

'Rebellion! Uprising! Bobekov, quick, call the men together, ring the
church bells! Fire a few volleys to proclaim the uprising! To arms!
What are you waiting for? Our brothers are fighting already,' Benkovski
thundered at the top of his voice, everybody joining in.

'Let's wait a little! . . . Let's see how matters really stand . . . The
time is not ripe yet, we have not got anything ready,' the men of
Panagyurishté tried to protest.

Their feeble, though just protest had no effect. It remained a mere
voice crying in the wilderness amidst the fearful shots from a few rifles
in bai Ivan's yard, the bullets screeching hideously in the air. It is
curious that the first rifle I snatched up, a double barrelled hunting
piece, missed fire on both barrels. Volov came out after me with his
French rifle which he fired twice and whose roar broke the silence
which lay over the peaceful village at that hour.

The men of Panagyurishté resisted no longer; the die was cast; they
left bai Ivan's house quickly saying that they were going home to get
ready and to arm. When they left, they were no longer the timid and
shy men who had come a few minutes before. Evidently the rifle shots
and our fiery enthusiasm had lent them courage. With them left the
guards and the secretaries Belopitov and T. Georgev who also went
home to get ready, to throw away the hateful fez and don the national
sheepskin cap. Only we four apostles and the representative of
Peroushtitsa V. Sokolov remained in bai Ivan's house.

We, too, bustled around trying to attire ourselves in an apostle's
uniform but where were we to get it from, not having anything ready to
hand? We searched the room, we searched the whole of bai Ivan's

house to find some suitable articles of clothing. Benkovski was the only one of us who had a sheepskin cap, the rest of us only had our fezes, and you must admit that it just would not do to rush out into the streets rebelling against the Turks with the fez's tassle dangling on your head. Therefore we decided rather to go out bareheaded than wear a red fez. Fortunately, the Karlovo banner was in the house, though it had no staff yet. We managed to get a rough tree branch to which Ikonomov tied it any old how, as we could not even find nails to attach it with.

We rushed wildly from room to room in bai Ivan's house, shouting, even weeping that we had nothing ready, banging doors and cupboards as if the house was on fire.

It was not proper either for a rebel to go out into the streets wearing shoes. But where was one to find soft sandals at a moment's notice? Besides who would have the patience to put on puttees and tie up all the straps and bindings? Whoever managed to find sandals in bai Ivan's house of which we had taken full possession, put them on dry and stiff as they were, while some were forced to go out in slippers or woollen socks.

(8) The Rhodopes

Blaga Dimitrova, *Journey to Oneself*

Dimitrova gives a highly critical account of totalitarian times, in juxtaposition with the intransient beauty of the Rhodope Mountains.

Collective! The endless speeches, reports, articles, interviews have planted that word in my mind – a parasite which I am powerless to uproot. What was 'collective' about our life in that hut? We shared no common purpose, no common interest, no common rhythm. They tried to unify us through the medium of competitions: for the best kept room, the punchiest slogans, the brightest decorations. We were unimpressed. In other huts every square inch of wall flaunted the same portraits – drearily familiar already from the community centre, the canteen, the village square. The same slogans screamed at you: LABOUR HAS MADE THE MONKEY MAN! THROUGH SOCIALISM TO STRENGTH! At least we could breathe. The walls of our hut were bare, and the room had an illusory air of spaciousness.

[•   •   •]

I looked away from the cliff towards a rocky hillside where there nestled a group of huts that rejoiced in the name of Cherry–Chereshovo. High on a ridge above them stood, solitary, the house where Sadak was slowly losing his hold on life. I set off up the hill towards it, feeling Raffina's dry, bony hand drawing me. Through the rain I looked at the cottage with Vlad's eyes, and observed that he had embodied motifs from this poor peasant home in several of the new buildings he had designed down below.

It was indeed something of an architectural curiosity. The ground floor was a sort of courtyard, walled in on three sides but hospitably open on the fourth. Here in the summer the children would play, while Raffina's loom sang all day in the welcome shade. The upper storey was a single room with a veranda, its whole front wall composed of open lattice-work, beautifully carved. Sheltered on its windy side, the north-west, the house became a veritable swallow's nest, full of clean air and space and comfort.

(9) Rila Monastery

Ivan Vazov, *Near the Rila Monastery*

In these stanzas from the poem, Ivan Vazov touches upon the Rila Mountains' natural beauty.

Now am I truly home. All round me hills
And mountain ridges rear; tall virgin forests
Are rustling; clear as crystal, foaming torrents
Go roaring past. On every side life thrills.
Humming a song to soothe me, mother Nature
Enfolds me lovingly in her embraces.

Now am I truly home. Elenin Peak
Pricks azure heaven, beckoning, inviting;
From Britchebor there wafts a breath unique
And health-giving of firs and giant pinetrees;
While southward Tsarev Peak asserts its presence
With balding dome and sovereign remembrance.

Now am I truly home – a world it is
Which I adore and seek. Here I breathe freely
And lighter feel; a deep tranquillity
Now fills my breast and waves of new life, sweeping
Into my soul, thrill me with new sensations,
New strength, might and poetic revelations . . .

(10) River Strouma

Teodor Trayanov, *The Secret of the Strouma*

*Trayanov was one of Bulgaria's foremost Symbolists. The poem
from which these stanzas are taken is included in Anthology of
Bulgarian Poetry – see Booklist.*

Swiftly is the Strouma flowing,
Bosom chill with secret cares,
Mutely flowing, never slowing,
Nothing on the surface showing
But the golden leaves she bears.

On she flows through narrow valleys
Where sad echoes cannot soar.
Sombre summits cast stern glances,
Fleet-foot water nymphs and phantoms
Wander on the rocky shore.

(11) Shopsko

Elin Pelin, *The Windmill*

*Elin Pelin is a gifted story-teller who remained loyal to the
portrayal of rural characters from Shopsko (the region around
Sofia).*

Not even the unfinished and deserted skeleton of Lazar's windmill
spoils the beautiful view on all four sides of our village. For ten years it
has stood on the bare hill above it like a jagged monster, now become,
according to popular belief, the refuge of evil spirits, who hopelessly
shake its ragged wings extended in the shape of a devil's cross.

This deserted building, with its foundations overgrown with weeds, a
haunt of timid rodents, green lizards and poisonous vipers, this skeleton
bleached by rain and sun, with unplastered and gaping walls through
which the winds and the storms blow shrieking, although deserted and
neglected, is the only windmill from level Shopsko[1] to the endless
Philibe[2] Plain. It is also the only reminder of the year of drought left by
the skilful and masterly hand of Lazar Dubak famed for his jokes and his
various plans and ideas, begun with enthusiasm and abandoned with a
good-natured, deprecating smile.

Over the village and all the surrounding district, a terrible drought
had set in, burning everything, drying up the wells and the springs and
killing the cattle for lack of water.

The life-giving and babbling village brook which springs from the big rocks above the village itself, began to diminish and dry up day by day. It seemed as if a three-headed hala[3] were imbibing its clear waves which began to trickle helplessly from its source, only to be swallowed avidly by the burning earth. Along its bed, the rushes and grass withered and drooped as if struck down by hail. Its banks which were always damp, were now parched and cracked.

And one day the lively and merry clatter of the many water mills which filled the valley with a noisy and joyful echo, fell silent.

The peasants' hearts were saddened and full of care. They were frightened by the silence of the watermills whose heavy stones humming until now, could no longer grind the dry grain to flour.

Lazar Dubak's watermill, the tiled roof of which peeped welcomingly out from between the green branches of our walnut trees, fell silent, too. Desolation and silence reigned all around, and filled Dubak's heart, always so merry, with heavy thoughts.

[1]Popular name for the district surrounding Sofia.
[2]Turkish name of Philippopolis, today Plovdiv.
[3]A mythical monster resembling a serpent.

(12) SOFIA

Viktor Paskov, *A Ballad for Georg Henig*

Paskov's best-selling novel gives an impression of the capital at the turn of the century.

At the beginning of this century, when carriages travelled on the yellow cobble-stones of Sofia, and in the carriages sat ladies in crinolines and lords in tails; when in the parks brass bands played pot-pourris from *La Traviata*; when Ivan Vazov walked his dog before the National Assembly and when the Opera Union gave their first performance, Italian and Czech musicians arrived in Sofia to help a number of enthusiasts encourage Bulgarian musical culture. God knows what kind of pain, adversity and privations they encountered in their mission. I don't feel like speaking about that. I feel shame and anguish. Most of them returned to their homes in distress. The names of those who stayed are not known. They are preserved in institutions and encyclopedias, and it's good that we showed them at least that honour, we who trod on their backs, racing victorious towards the light-drenched world stage.

It seems that it was a warm autumn day in 1910. The train from Czechia arrived in the Sofia station, whistling and puffing. Master

Georg peered out of his carriage window with joyful wonder, a man about forty years old, tall and dignified, with red hair and blue eyes. The chest containing his strange tools travelled in the freight carriage. There were thin files, fine chisels, miniature planes, small saws, clamps, callipers, felt mallets and hooks, which I saw half a century later.

'We've arrived, Bozhenka!' he said to the young woman, blue-eyed like him. 'Come on, let's get off!'

Were they met at the Sofia station? It would seem so. Perhaps by the choirmasters Henrik Visner and Mazanek, at that time as young and enthusiastic as he.

Peace to their ashes!

(13) STRANDZHA

Elisaveta Bagryana, *Fire-Dancer's Destiny*

In the poem from which these verses are taken, Bagryana addresses her motherland and associates herself with the ancient custom of 'Nestinari'. The complete poem is included in the anthology The Devil's Dozen – see Booklist.

Then you taught your daughters,
deep in Strandzha's thicket,
to walk barefoot on glowing embers,
a match for their cruel lot . . .

And doesn't this dark atavistic gift,
even until recent summers,
explain our women's eternal fate –
to dance on glowing embers?

(14) STRANDZHA

Konstantin Konstantinov, *In Strandzha Mountain*

Konstantinov was a fine stylist, conveying a host of moods through landscape. 'Haidouks' were the guerrilla warriors in the struggle against the Ottoman Empire.

From Alan Kairak upwards the road wound along the flank of the mountain. Every two or three kilometers, we met either a charcoal-burner, or a peasant-woman, the latter mostly with a child in a slingbag on her back, hurrying towards the village. Then gradually the way became absolutely deserted. For a long time already the sea had been lost to our sight. There were a number of sloping hills rolling towards it, stretching away towards the distant horizon. A boundless expanse of waste forestland ran along both sides of the road, looking like black lichen on the yellowish surface of the mountain. Far and near, to right and left, charcoal-kilns were smouldering, and the smoke from them hung low, curling slowly over the disfigured earth. An ominous silence seemed to be hovering motionless in the sky, an ancient silence, primordial, such as surely weighed on the still unanimated world in the first day of its creation. And the autumn sun shone with a feeble brilliance that was like the reflection from another light, like a mirage sun over those desolate, dreary parts of the country.

For an hour or two now, we had been going up a bad, stony road, without meeting a living soul. We went deeper and deeper into the forest – a beautiful oak-forest which had surely been a paradise formerly for haidouks and which was already tinged with yellow. Through the trunks of the trees, we caught sight of glades covered with delicate, autumn grass, or dark ravines full of dead leaves. No bird, no sound, no rustling of leaves, no murmuring of springs, only the soft, lulling rise and fall of the horses' hoofs and the jogging of the village cart.

Half-lying on bags of hay and barley, we were shaken up and down with every movement of the cart – I and my driver, Dinyu Vulev, an awe-inspiring man, with shaggy eyebrows, unshaven, grey whiskers and gentle, brown eyes, who was from the Bourgas battalion in which he had re-enlisted when his term of service ran out. Now and then, we exchanged a word or two, then we would light a cigarette and remain silent for a long time. And a half-sleepy, half-awake thought kept coming into my mind. It seemed to me that I had been travelling like that for years. I couldn't remember when I had set off, I felt that it had always been like that and there would be no end to it. There was no other world and nothing else except that unfathomable forest and that road which led to the end of the world . . .

(15) Veliki Preslav

Chernorizets Hrabur, *On Letters*

Written in the ninth or tenth century, this is the first secular work in old Bulgarian literature. The author belonged to the literary school of Veliki Preslav, the ancient capital of Bulgaria.

And later God, Who loves man, Who arranges for everything and does not leave the Slavic human family barren of wisdom, but leads all men to wisdom and salvation, took mercy of the Slavic tribe and sent to them Saint Konstantin the Philosopher, called Kiril, a righteous man and true, and created for them thirty-eight letters, some after the Greek model, and others after Slavic speech. In the beginning he started in the Greek way. Thus they say 'alpha,' and he, 'az.' Both alphabets begin with 'a.' And just as the Greeks made their alphabet in the manner of Hebrew writing, so he took Greek letters for a model. The first letter of the Hebrew script is 'aleph' which means 'study,' as when you teach a beginning child and tell him, 'Study!' This is 'aleph.' And the Greeks, imitating this, said 'alpha.' And this Hebraic expression was adapted to the Greek language, so that now they tell the child, instead of 'seek learning,' just 'alpha,' which means 'seek.' In the same way, saint Kiril created the first letter 'az.' But being the first letter, given by God to the Slavic tribe to untie the mouth of those who by this alphabet learn wisdom, 'az' is pronounced with a wide opening of the mouth, while the rest of the letters are pronounced and said by a lesser opening of the mouth.

Biographies and important works

BAGRYANA, Elisaveta (1893–1991). Generally regarded as the leading Bulgarian woman poet of the century, Elisaveta Bagryana wrote rhapsodic, intense, archetypally woman-centred poetry (Extracts 2 and 13). She was a libertarian, unfettered personality who made a strong cult of youthfulness, elemental freedom, vitalist energy, using also themes of the sea and travel. She often writes of the **Black Sea coast**. Born in **Sofia**, she enrolled in Slavonic Studies at **Sofia University**, and her first poems appeared in 1915. She became a leading member of the inter-war Zlatorog circle. Her marriage was unhappy; she became close to her former teacher Boyan Penev, who died in 1927. Her pre-war volumes include her most famous collection Vechnata i svyatata (The Eternal and the Sacred), 1927, Zvezda na

moryaka (Sailor's Star), 1932, and Surtse choveshko (The Heart of Man), 1936. After 1944 she produced Pet zvezdi (Five Stars), 1953, dealing with themes such as the new Soviet-style woman, but the later collection Ot bryag do bryag (From Shore to Shore), 1963, returned to her more typical intense personal vein.

BOCHEV, Dimitur (1944–). Bochev shared the typical fate of Bulgarian émigré writers. He was born in the town of **Silistra**. While he was doing his compulsory military service, he was punished for his anti-militarist views. Bochev entered the **University of Sofia**, and was expelled twice for his political beliefs. He was arrested many times by the Communist secret police. In 1972 he emigrated to Cologne, where he contributed to the

Bulgarian programmes of Deutsche Welle and Radio Free Europe. He wrote for the anti-Communist magazine *Continent* published in Paris, which was associated with the names of Aleksandr Solzhenitsyn, Saul Bellow, Eugene Ionesco, Joseph Brodsky and Andrei Sakharov. Bochev's mother was beaten up by Bulgarian Communist agents who tried to make her testify against her own son. Public figures like François Mitterrand, Willy Brandt and Graham Greene were involved in the defence of Bochev's case against the system. He was a friend of Georgi Markov (1929–1978), the murdered Bulgarian émigré writer. He also kept in touch with Konstantin Pavlov (1933–), a poet who preferred to stay and suffer repressions *inside* the system. Bochev has written the novel *Mezhdinno katsane* (*Stopover*), and the collection of essays *Homo Emigranticus*. The main character in *Mezhdinno katsane*, a traveller in space, or a new biological 'homo emigranticus', is in an eternal existential quest which could also be called 'immigration to one's self'. He is both a mediator between and an observer of two worlds from which he feels equally alienated.

BOTYOV or BOTEV, Hristo (1848–1876). Hristo Botyov (the alternative modern pronunciation is 'Botev') was born in 1848 in **Kalofer**. His mother Ivanka was among the best singers of Bulgarian folk songs, and his father Botyo was a teacher, man of letters and orator. At the age of 15 Botyov went to **Odessa** where he studied only 13 months. Then after a short-term stay in **Bessarabia**, he returned to Kalofer to take over tutorial practice from his father. In 1867 Botyov emigrated to Braila, Romania where he earned a living through literature and translations. In Romania he met

Hristo Botyov

fighters for Bulgarian national liberation like Stefan Karadzha, Hadzhi Dimitur, Zhelyu Voivoda and Vasil Levski. He edited the newspapers *Duma na bulgarskite emigranti* (*Word of Bulgarian Emigrants*), *Boudilnik* (*Alarm-Clock*), and *Zname* (*Banner*) and contributed to other periodicals. In May 1876, following the start of the April uprising in Bulgaria, he crossed the Danube with his *cheta* to face the Turkish troops. The chetniks fought bravely but were defeated. Hristo Botyov, their *voivoda* (leader) was killed at **Vola Peak** in the Balkan Mountains near the town of **Vratsa**. Hristo Botyov is often named as Bulgaria's greatest poet. His verse is the perfect embodiment of his philosophical and social views and his life as a Bulgarian revolutionary. In about twenty poems he expressed the struggle for Bulgaria's liberation, and he portrayed the figures of Vasil Levski and Hadzhi Dimitur (Extract 1). Through the free and natural flow of his rhythms based on Bulgarian folklore and singing tradition Botyov conveyed his personal hopes and disappointments, at times bordering on nihilism. Hristo Botyov also wrote topical articles, *feuilletons* and epigrams on political subjects, displaying erudition surprising for his youthful age.

DEBELYANOV, Dimcho (1887–1916). **Koprivshtitsa**, the native town of Dimcho Debelyanov, keeps the memory of the poet fresh with a sculpture of his mother waiting for her son. It stands at the poet's tombstone. Dimcho Debelyanov was born into a patriarchal family and he preserved a longing for his native home until his death. The poet lost his father at the age of 9. The family moved to **Plovdiv** which marked a long period of privations. After finishing high school in **Sofia**, Debelyanov got a job as a clerk in a meteorological station. As he found the job dull and depressing, he quit in 1909, and started freelancing as a reporter, proofreader, shorthand writer and translator. He also worked as co-editor with Konstantin Konstantinov ◊ and Georgi Raichev for *Zveno* (*Link*) magazine. He volunteered to join the army during the first world war and was killed in action. Debelyanov was a melancholic daydreamer who wrote beautiful elegiac verse (Extract 6). His 'Cherna pessen' ('Black Song') is characteristic of his introvert nature. Debelyanov wrote some masterpieces of Bulgarian lyrical verse: 'Ti smutno se myarkash iz mornata pamet' ('You Flit Past in My Weary Memory'), 'Da se zavurnesh v bashtinata kushta' ('When You Return to Your Father's Home') and 'Pomnish li, pomnish li tihiya dvor' ('Do You Remember the Quiet Yard?'). Despite his knowledge of the cruelty and horror of war, Debelyanov's verse is quiet and resigned. His psychological and confessional poetry not only echoes the realities of the *fin de siècle*, but also represents the psychology of modern man.

Dimcho Debelyanov

DIMITROVA, Blaga (1922–). Dimitrova is the author of thirty poetry volumes, nine novels and biographies, some of them written in collaboration with her husband Yordan Vasilev, and three plays. Born in **Byala Slatina**, she read Slavonic Philology at **Sofia University**, was a postgraduate at the Gorky Institute in Moscow, and worked for various publishing houses. She became critical of the system, for example in her novel *Putouvane kum sebe si* (*Journey to Oneself*), 1965 – Extract 8. Another novel, *Otklonenie* (*Deviation*), was made into a prize-winning film. *Osudeni na lyubov* (*Condemned to Love*), 1967, contains anti-war verse about Vietnam. She has also translated from Polish, German, French, Swedish and Ancient Greek. Her later novel *Litse* (*Face*), 1981, full version 1991, was withdrawn from circulation, and many of her books were not published, although she did not become a banned writer. Her later verse includes the collection *Glas* (*Voice*), 1985. She became an MP in 1990 after the fall of the Zhivkov

Blaga Dimitrova

regime. She was elected as Vice-President of Bulgaria in January 1992, and resigned in 1994. Her work expresses her political questioning and her concern about the replacement of human values by ideology. Julia Kristeva writes of Dimitrova, 'Seldom has a woman's writing been at once more cerebral and more sensual.' Blaga Dimitrova has been awarded many prizes, among them the International PEN prize for translation, and the Herder prize in 1991.

ELIN PELIN (pen-name of Dimitur Stoyanov, 1878–1949). One of Bulgaria's pre-eminent writers of short fiction, Elin Pelin came from a peasant family in the village of **Bailovo**, near Sofia. From 1899 he lived in **Sofia**, writing for journals and editing, and spent a year in France. In 1914–18 he produced war pieces. In 1926–44 he was Director of the **Ivan Vazov Museum**, established in the author's Sofia home. He is best known for his short stories, focusing

realistically and with humour on rural life, hardships and characters, especially from the **Shopsko** district of his upbringing near Sofia. His first mature stories, such as 'Vetrenata melnitsa' ('The Windmill') – Extract 11, are collected in the two volumes of *Razkazi (Tales)*, 1904 and 1911. They are read for their evocative lyrical language and memorable characters. In 'Geratsite' ('The Gerak Family'), a longer story in the second volume, he portrays the decline of a patriarchal farmer Yordan Gerak and his family, divided by selfish indifference. In 'Zemya' ('Land'), 1922, the protagonist Enyo's land hunger destroys his brother, whom he almost murders, leaving him as a human vegetable; stricken with guilt Enyo sells up, goes off and dies a poor man, in the dead of winter. In 'Pod manaskirskata loza' ('Under the Monastery Vines'), 1936, he treats of the ties of religion and tensions of the flesh. He also wrote sketches, humoresques in Shopsko dialect, and children's books. In a speech of May 1949 to the Writers' Union he made some critical remarks about Socialist factory 'production novels' and the need to focus more deeply on the lives of individuals.

HRABUR (KHRABR), Chernorizets, ie The Monk (c900). The author's name is known only from the manuscript of his famous apologetical and polemical treatise *O pismeneh (On Letters)*, generally dated between the end of the 9th and the beginning of the 10th centuries (Extract 15). The name could be a pseudonym. In his short treatise, Hrabur, from the literary school of **Veliki Preslav**, sets out to defend the use of Slavonic by the church, established by the recent work of Cyril and Methodius, and to counter the view that God should be worshipped in only three tongues –

Hebrew, Greek and Latin. Hrabur observes that the Greek alphabet was created by many heathens, whereas the Slavs received a specially devised alphabet created by one saintly Christian man, Constantine-Cyril.

KONSTANTINOV, Konstantin (1890–1970). A native of **Sliven**, author of memoirs, travel sketches and short stories, Konstantin Konstantinov studied law and pursued a legal career. Settling in **Sofia** in 1908, he joined its circle of young writers, and contributed to journals. In 1920 his first volume of short stories appeared. His novel *Kruv* (*Blood*), 1933, depicted the violent events of 1925, and argued against social conflict. He reached maturity only in the 1930s with the collections *Treta klasa* (*Third Class*), 1936, *Den po den* (*Day by Day*), 1938, and *Sedem chasut zaranta* (*Seven O'Clock in the Morning*), 1940. In the story 'Prez stenata' ('Through the Wall'), the narrator becomes curious about an actress staying next door, when he hears singing followed by heart-rending sobs. After deciding there is really nothing he can do, he learns she has poisoned herself. The story 'Den po den' ('Day by Day' – Extract 14) tells of a small-town whore awaiting the return of a salesman for whom she feels affection. She learns that he has been killed in a bus accident, but still has to entertain some clients. Konstantinov addresses moments of personal crisis in banal settings, with intelligent, sceptical detachment. He is particularly valued for his travel essays, published in *Po zemyata* (*Over the World*), 1930, and *Nashata zemya houbava* (*Our Beautiful Land*), 1940, and also for his account of Bulgarian cultural life in the earlier years of the century, in *Put prez godinite* (*The Way through the Years*).

MINKOV, Svetoslav (1902–1966). Svetoslav Minkov was born in the town of **Radomir** into the family of a patriotic officer. Before finishing high school in **Sofia**, Minkov studied at the Military School in Hranice (Weisskirchen) in Moravia. Then he graduated in Slavonic Philology at the Sveti Kliment Ohridski **University of Sofia**, and studied at the Commercial Academy in Munich. After Minkov returned to Bulgaria, his first books had much in common with the aesthetics of diabolism. An ironic and rational distance could be observed at the bottom of his satirical prose. He showed keen interest in the industrial world and modern technologies. In a sense, his short stories and novels can be seen as anti-utopias with some elements of science-fiction. Minkov developed an original style abounding in the grotesque and sarcasm, eg *Damata s rentgenovite ochi* (*The Lady with X-ray Eyes*), 1934. He portrayed life in the modern city along grey everyday lines in *Razkazi v taralezhova kozha* (*Tales in a Hedgehog's Hide*). Minkov showed a taste for the exotic in his travel books *Drougata America* (*The Other America*) about Latin America, and *Imperiya na glada* (*Empire of Hunger*) about Japan. He was curious about the distant and the unknown, on the one hand, and sceptical about novelties and foreign models, on the other. He was also a prolific translator – Andersen's tales and the *Arabian Nights* are among his translations into Bulgarian.

PASKOV, Viktor (1949–). The prominent contemporary novelist Viktor Paskov studied music at the Conservatoire in Leipzig and employed himself as composer, opera singer and music critic in Germany. After 1987, he worked as text editor and screenplay writer at the Boyana

Motion Picture Studio in **Sofia**, and as an editor with Sofia Press Agency. During 1990–92, he lived in Paris. At present, he is Head of the Adriana Boudevska Theatre in **Bourgas**. He has published three novels, *Nevrustni oubiystva* (*Infantile Murders*), 1986, the best-selling *Balada za Georg Henig* (*Ballad for George Henig*), 1988, a retrospective account of Sofia, recently translated into English (Extract 12), and *L'Allemagne, conte cruel*, 1992, published in French. Another piece of his appears in the recent East European anthology *Description of a Struggle*. *Ballad for George Henig* won the French Grand Prix for literature. Paskov's subjects are artistic resistance and spiritual survival in the face of a brutal reality.

RADICHKOV, Yordan (1929–   ). Yordan Radichkov was born in the village of **Kalimanitsa**, in today's district of Montana. He worked as a correspondent for periodicals, as a literary consultant on film scripts for Bulgarian Cinematography, and was on the board of directors for *Literatouren front* (*Literary Front*) newspaper, renamed today *Literatouren foroum* (*Literary Forum*) to avoid the 'frontline' overtones. Radichkov, with his original talent, is one of the most prominent writers in modern Bulgarian literature. His prose is full of folklore motifs, comic effects, sublime Romanticism and ridiculously funny, even grotesque incidents. He is best known for his tales: 'Svirepo nastroenie' ('Violent Mood'), 1965, 'Barouten Bukvar' ('Gunpowder Primer'), 1969, 'Kozyata brada' ('Goaty Beard'), 1967, and 'Nie, vrabchetata' ('We the Sparrows'), 1968, which have been translated into several European languages. Radichkov's characters are usually village people who attract with their

Yordan Radichkov

frankness and naive backwardness. He amalgamated subjects from the Bible and painting in his prose, as well as unusual and archaic words. His plays *Soumatoha* (*Helter-Skelter*), 1967, *Lazaritsa*, 1979, *Opit za letene* (*An Attempt to Fly*), 1979, *Padaneto na Ikar* (*The Fall of Icarus*), etc, have been staged in theatres in Europe and the USA. He has also written numerous filmscripts some of which, due to political censorship, had difficulty reaching the cinemas.

SLAVEIKOV, Pencho (1866–1912). Born into the large family of the writer Petko Slaveikov, Pencho Slaveikov witnessed the tragic events of 1877–78, which he later described in his poem *Kurvava pesen* (*Song of Blood*), 1911–13. At the age of 22 he survived a serious accident which left him crippled for life. Having read philosophy at the University of Leipzig, Slaveikov was known for his erudition and varied intellectual interests. For a number of years he worked for the National Library in **Sofia** and for a year was Director of the National Theatre. At the same time he continued to write poetry as well as articles and critical reviews for a number of literary papers and magazines. Disgusted with the political situation and bureaucracy in Bulgaria, the poet left for Switzerland; he died soon after that near Lake Como.

Pencho Slaveikov, an individualist and ascetic intellectual, was the opposite of his father. He adopted a stoic attitude to life. In his writings he strove for universalism. As a modern critic he possessed a broad spectrum of interests comprising nearly the whole of European literature and philosophy. *Na ostrova na blazhenite* (*The Isle of the Blessed*), 1910, was one of the first modern literary mystifications,

which, unlike Macpherson's legends of Ossian, aimed not to conceal the author's self but to reveal his amazing ability to transform himself behind quite transparent masks. *Kurvava pesen* (*Song of Blood*), was a new Bulgarian national epic which contained a philosophy of Bulgarian history – suffering, stoicism, rebellion, song and blood. The exquisite lyrical miniatures in *Sun za shtastie* (*Dream of Happiness*), 1906–07, were in a rather different vein (Extract 3). The poem *Psalom na poeta* (*Psalm of a Poet*) expresses Slaveikov's acceptance and anticipation of death. Slaveikov's poetic talent was widely appreciated: he was nominated for the Nobel prize for *Kurvava pesen* and only his sudden death in 1912 prevented him from getting it.

STOYANOV, Zahari (1851–1889). A leading member of the nationalist school, journalist and self-educated chronicler, Zahari Stoyanov spent part of his youth as a shepherd in **Dobroudzha**. As a young man he was involved in the uprising in 1875, with Botyov and Stefan Stambolov, and also in the April rising of 1876. After the liberation, having attacked the policies of the ruler Alexander of Battenberg, he moved to **Plovdiv**, capital of then Eastern Roumelia, in 1882, where he supported unification with Bulgaria. He contributed to many periodicals. After about 1886 he became editor of the official newspaper *Svoboda* (*Freedom*) and chairman of the parliament. Stoyanov wrote numerous books, among them biographies of Levski, Botyov ◊, Filip Totyu, Hadzhi Dimitur and Stefan Karadzha. He is mainly remembered for his various intimately informed memoirs of the liberation years, especially for the three-volume monumental work *Zapiski po bulgars-*

Pencho Slaveikov

kite vustaniya (*Notes on the Bulgarian Uprisings*), 1884–92, describing in detail the uprisings of 1875 and 1876 (Extract 7). The work is popular, both for its lively and simple directness, and for its magnificently heroic sweep. It can hardly be defined as falling within a single genre as it employs epic, memoir, essay, travelogue, journalism. The style is polemic and emotional and the language sometimes borders on the outright offensive, but it is invariably talented.

TRAYANOV, Teodor (1882–1945). Regarded as one of Bulgaria's foremost Symbolist poets, Trayanov came from **Pazardzhik**, near Plovdiv. He studied mathematics and physics at **Sofia University**, and later at a polytechnic in Vienna. He was employed by the Foreign Ministry as a legation secretary, spending some time in Austria and Germany, and making contact with writers such as Rilke and Hofmannsthal. In 1921 he returned to Bulgaria and edited the Symbolist journal *Hiperion* (1922–31). He began publishing in 1899, at the age of seventeen, and his pre-first-world-war poetry was collected in two volumes, *Regina mortua*, 1909, and *Himni i baladi* (*Hymns and Ballads*), 1911. The prevailing tone in the first is melancholy, with frequent references to sorrow, night, pain, a black lake whose 'dead waters' reflect 'dead stars', tears, autumn, winter, death, taking leave of the beloved. Life is a phantasm; the poet faces the reality of night, loss and death. In the second volume the poet, 'pilgrim in black', seeks in death the liberation of the spirit from material limitation.

In *Bulgarski baladi* (*Bulgarian Ballads*), 1921, affected by the world war, he sounds a historical, national, martial note, to express the 'beauty and eternal forms of the Bulgarian spirit'.

In *Panteon* (*Pantheon*), 1934, he sets out in quest of a 'universal synthetic personality', combining the 'triumphant thought' of the sceptical Western mind with the 'elemental striving' and Messianism of Bulgarians. A whole series of verses is dedicated to poetic figures, such as Villon, Rimbaud, Rilke, Poe, Whitman, Shelley, and Bulgarian poets. After this volume he produced little more. Following the Communist takeover he was arrested and beaten to death by the police.

VAZOV, Ivan (1850–1921). Vazov is the most outstanding figure in the literary life of Bulgaria immediately after the liberation from Ottoman domination. Born in the picturesque Balkan town of **Sopot**, he was brought up in the best Bulgarian traditions. In his youthful years Vazov studied in Romania, then worked as a clerk in **Svishtov** and **Rouse**. After Bulgaria's liberation he emigrated to Odessa, because general political attitudes were hostile towards Russophiles like himself. Vazov returned to Bulgaria and settled in **Sofia**, where he died on 22 September 1921 and was buried near the church of **Sveta Sofia** (St Sophia). Much of Vazov's work is based on historical events: his best known novel *Pod Igoto* (*Under the Yoke*), 1889–90, is a reflection of traditional national life and the armed struggle against foreign domination (Extract 4). Ivan Vazov also wrote fine short stories, novellas and historical novels. His collected works fill over 100 volumes and much has been translated into foreign languages. In his poetry, especially in *Epopeya na zabravenite* (*Epic of the Forgotten*), 1881–84, can be found in the figures of the whole Bulgarian national Pantheon from Paisiy, the Miladinov brothers, Hristo Botyov

and Todor Kableshkov, to the unknown soldier. Vazov also created
poetic portraits of great men of letters, like Goethe, Hugo, Byron,
Schiller and Heine. He was likewise
successful as a playwright – eg the
plays *Borislav* and *Kum propast* (*Towards an Abyss*). The **Ivan Vazov
Museum** is established in the author's
Sofia home.

YAVOROV, Peyu (Peyu Totev
Kracholov, 1878–1914). Yavorov is
probably the most dramatic figure in
Bulgarian literary history. He grew up
in the southern town of **Chirpan**,
notorious for the fiery tempers of its
inhabitants. While still at high
school, Yavorov developed a passion
for poetry and was greatly influenced
in his own work by Vazov and
Karavelov as well as Lermontov,
Pushkin and Heine. After finishing
school he obtained a job with the post
office in **Pomorie** on the Black Sea

Peyu Yavorov

coast. His poetic talent was soon
appreciated by the critics and he was
offered an editorial position in **Sofia**
where he joined the *Misul* (*Thought*)
literary circle and acquired a new
social status. At the age of 30 he was
already working for the National
Theatre. He devoted his whole adult
life to the liberation of Macedonia,
and joined a *cheta* of fighters.

Yavorov's social verse was marked
by the literary tradition of the 1890s,
with epic narrative in the folk style.
His best more mature work is contained in a number of poetry collections. *Bezsunitsi* (*Insomnia*) manifests
an accumulation of psychic crises in
floods and ebbs of emotion. Yavorov
possessed something of Botyov's character with his perpetual striving for
heroic acts. He almost relished the
feeling of loneliness and detachment
from the crowd in a hostile world, and
he liked to express this in a theatrical
manner. His love lyrics, dedicated to
Mina and Lora, the two women in his
life, are among the most subtle, delicate and refined in Bulgarian literature – eg 'Dve houbavi ochi' ('Two
Beautiful Eyes'), 'Ela' ('Come'), and
'Shte budesh v byalo' ('You'll Wear
White'). His dramatic potential is
expressed in 'V polite na Vitosha'
('At the Foot of Vitosha Mountain')
and 'Kogato grum oudari . . .'
('When Thunder Strikes').

Yavorov's marriage to Lora
Karavelova, one of the most beautiful
and talented women of her time,
ended in tragedy. Lora's suicide was
blamed on Yavorov. He was tried for
murder and acquitted. But the poet
was too fragile and depressed to cope
with life. His second suicide attempt
was successful – when he died he was
merely 36.

YOVKOV, Yordan (1880–1937).
Yovkov's literary work is a reflection

Yordan Yovkov

of the people and life of his native **Zheravna**, as well as the vast expanses of the **Dobroudzha** region which he called 'my second birthplace'. After finishing high school in **Sofia**, Yovkov read law at **Sofia University**. His father's early death forced him to leave university and take up a teaching post in a village in Dobroud-

zha. He took part in the Balkan War, as well as the Inter-Allied War, in which he was wounded. His brief journalistic career was followed by an appointment with the Bulgarian Embassy in Bucharest, and he stayed with the Ministry of Foreign Affairs of Bulgaria till his death in 1937. Yovkov produced some of the most enjoyable masterpieces of Bulgarian prose. He was a romantic soul disguised as a realist. His literary talent is apparent in his collections of short stories *Staroplaninski legendi* (*Legends from Stara Planina*), 1927, *Vecheri v Antimovskiya han* (*Evenings at the Antimovo Inn*), 1928 (Extract 5), *Ako mozheha da govoryat* (*If They Could Speak*), as well as his dramas *Milionerut* (*The Millionaire*), 1932, *Boryana*, 1932, and *Albena*, 1930. The world of Yovkov is inhabited by neither saints nor diehard criminals, but by common and attractive sinners. That world strikes one with its symmetry and logic, and with the poetry of the whole. Yovkov's works have been collected in 15 volumes and some have been translated.

THE LANDS OF FORMER YUGOSLAVIA

BOSNIA-HERCEGOVINA; CROATIA; MACEDONIA; MONTENEGRO; SERBIA; SLOVENIA

Celia Hawkesworth

> 'For this is a town in which I was perhaps not the happiest, / but where even the rain is more than mere rain.'
>
> Izet Sarajlić, Sarajevo

'What country is this?' The question posed by Viola in the sixteenth century in Shakespeare's *Twelfth Night* is hardly easier to answer today, when the lands that were linked in two successive Yugoslav states between 1918 and 1991 are breaking up into their separate components and their final shape is far from clear. The historical and cultural developments of the individual areas were in any case distinct and so they are treated more or less separately in this survey.

Two of Yugoslavia's most striking characteristics were its multinational composition and its physical variety: from the mountains of **Slovenia**, bordering Austria and Italy in the north, the great plain of the **Danube basin** along the north-eastern border with Hungary and Romania, the wooded hills of **Bosnia** and **Hercegovina**, the rocky limestone landscape of the coast and islands, the rolling fertile hills of **Serbia** to the tobacco-growing warmth of **Macedonia** bordering on Bulgaria, Greece and Albania. There are lakes and rivers, ravines and fjords: the Yugoslav lands are a microcosm of continental Europe in both landscape and climate.

HISTORY

The Slav nations which came to make up the state of Yugoslavia share common origins and to a large extent language: in the course of the sixth century successive waves of nomadic Slav tribes arrived in the Balkan peninsula, where they settled. The general name 'Slav' has survived at the outer limits of these settlements, marking the meeting-point of Slav and non-Slav peoples: eg the Slovenes in the north-west and the region of Slavonia along the Danubian plain. Two of the tribes eventually gave their names to the people and territory around them, the Croats in the west and the Serbs in the south and east. From the earliest stage of this process, the Slav groups were subject to the rivalry of the increasingly divergent branches of the Christian Church: the Eastern Church with its focal point in Constantinople and the Church of Rome. The first mission of conversion of the Slavs in the Balkan peninsula was carried out by two brothers from Salonica, Saints Cyril and Methodius, in the ninth century. Their mission reached as far as Moravia. For the purpose of producing the first written texts in the vernacular Slav languages, Cyril and Methodius developed a script believed to be adapted from the Greek alphabet, called Glagolitic. This was soon modified in the eastern areas into the Cyrillic script used in the Orthodox Slav lands to the present day. In the western parts of the Balkans, Glagolitic continued to be used into the nineteenth century but in increasingly restricted areas: with the Schism between the Churches of Constantinople and Rome in 1154, the sphere of influence of each became gradually more clearly defined. Glagolitic vernacular texts were permitted only in predominantly rural areas in the western regions. With the arrival of the Hungarians in Central Europe, church organization in the Croatian state fell under the direct jurisdiction of Rome. At the same time, the towns of the Adriatic coast and islands, previously Byzantine possessions, fell gradually to Venice, coming also under the Church of Rome.

In the central Balkan region of Bosnia, there was an additional dimension: the prevalence of the dualist, Bogomil, heresy. The Bogomils, or Patarins, originated in Bulgaria (see chapter on Bulgaria) and spread into Bosnia at the end of the tenth century. Their thinking was closely related to that of the Manichaeans and Paulicians, and forms a link in the chain of heresies that spread in the course of the twelfth centuries through northern Italy and southern France (Boni homines, Cathars, Albigensians, Tisserands, etc).

Independent kingdoms became established in Croatia, Bosnia and Serbia between 925 and 1217. Reaching the height of its power in the late tenth century under King Tomislav, the Croatian kingdom then ran into dynastic difficulties and, under increasing pressure from

Venice, in 1102 joined the Hungarian kingdom under the Crown of St Stephen. The Croats remained in a more or less uneasy alliance with Hungary until the end of the Habsburg Empire. Bosnia too acknowledged Hungarian suzerainty from 1138, but attained considerable power under King Tvrtko (1353–91). Serbia grew into a strong state under the Nemanjić dynasty in the thirteenth century, and was poised to take over the remnants of the Byzantine Empire under Stefan Dušan in 1355. Following his sudden death, the kingdom rapidly declined under both internal and external pressure, leaving it vulnerable to the Ottoman forces in the fourteenth century.

In the mid-fourteenth century, the Ottoman Turks began to make their steady advance into Europe, overrunning the southern and central Balkan lands and Hungary, reaching as far as Vienna in 1529. The western borders of the Ottoman Empire were eventually established and administered by the Habsburg authorities as a military buffer zone, as were the southern and eastern borders of Hungary, once the Turks had been driven out in the seventeenth century. The division was then roughly between the Orthodox south and east of the South Slav lands, administered by the Ottomans, and the Catholic north and west, which formed part of the Habsburg Empire. The particular situation of the central region of Bosnia made for a further element in this jigsaw: for a variety of reasons, including successive waves of migrations in the wake of recurrent wars and smaller-scale disputes, there were large numbers of Slav converts to Islam concentrated in this region. There was thus a substantial Muslim but Slav population in the centre of the Balkans.

The Serbs were involved in an ultimately successful process of liberation from the Turks throughout the nineteenth century: the first armed uprising of 1804 was followed by a second in 1813 and then by lengthy diplomatic negotiations, leading to the recognition of an independent kingdom in 1882. By the first decade of the twentieth century, there were the beginnings of a parliamentary democracy on Western lines. The Croatian lands remained part of the Habsburg Empire, along with other areas – Styria, Carinthia and Carniola – inhabited by the Slovenes. Bosnia was administered by Austria from 1878 and formally annexed in 1908. With the end of the Habsburg Monarchy in 1918, all these areas joined the new entity of South Slav peoples, the Kingdom of the Serbs, Croats and Slovenes.

The new state was a mixture of peoples and traditions, agricultural, fiscal and legal systems which it would require exceptional skill to bind into a coherent unit. It took some time to draw up the borders, but in the end they corresponded roughly to ethnic distribution, although there were inevitably substantial minorities – particularly of Italians, Hungarians, Romanians and Albanians – in the new state, while there were significant groups of Slovenes, Serbs, Croats and Macedonians outside the new borders.

The most intractable problem, however, was the essential conflict between the Serbian and Croatian political traditions. The Croats looked to the new state to provide a more favourable form of partnership than that they had known in their problematic relations with the Hungarians. They anticipated that they would be granted an acceptable measure of autonomy. The Serbs, on the other hand, having waged an ultimately successful struggle against Ottoman occupation, become an independent kingdom in 1878, and enlarged their territory in the Balkan Wars of 1912, inevitably assumed that they would play a leading role in the new association. It was not long before friction developed into conflict and proceedings in parliament became increasingly unruly. In June 1928 during a debate, a member of the Radical Party shot five members of the Croat Peasant Party, including the leader, Stjepan Radić. Two of them were killed on the spot and Radić died some weeks later from his wounds. In January 1929 King Alexander dissolved parliament and instituted a period of personal dictatorship which had the effect of driving the Croat opposition underground or into exile. A secret organization, known as the Ustaše (rebels) was formed and in October 1934 one of their agents assassin-ated King Alexander in Marseilles where he had arrived on a state visit to France.

Alexander's son, Peter, was only eleven and a regency was estab-lished under Alexander's cousin Paul. It seems that Paul's aim was to liberalize the regime and endeavour to strengthen the unity of the country, but economic and political pressures proved overwhelming. In March 1941, Hitler presented the Yugoslav government with an ultimatum demanding its adherence to the Axis pact. Paul felt that he had no choice but to comply. There were immediate, vigorous demonstrations against the decision and during the night of 26–27 March, a group of army and air force officers carried out a coup in the name of King Peter. Paul, his co-regents and the young king left the country.

On 6 April, Hitler attacked Yugoslavia, with an air bombardment of **Belgrade** lasting 3 days and killing between ten and twenty thousand of the city's 250 000 inhabitants. In a matter of days the small, ill-equipped Yugoslav army was defeated, an enlarged independent Fascist state, including most of Bosnia and Hercegovina, was established in Croatia, under the Ustaša leader, Ante Pavelić. Serbia was occupied by the Germans, a puppet state under Italian control was set up in Montenegro and the remaining territories of Slovenia and Macedonia were handed over to their neighbours.

By the summer of 1941 two resistance movements had emerged: the

Royalist Četniks under General Draža Mihailović, and the Communist Partisans, commanded by Marshal Josip Broz (Tito). In a short time, Tito's Partisans proved to be the more effective force. The enemy launched seven major offensives against them, but all failed and in the winter of 1944–45 the defeated Germans withdrew. Tito established a provisional government in Belgrade, with considerable popular support. In 1945 the Federal People's Republic of Yugoslavia was proclaimed and a constitution modelled on that of Stalin adopted. Power resided in the League of Communists and its Secretary-General, Tito. Following the break with Stalin in 1948, Yugoslavia sought a new identity as the leader of the Non-Alligned Movement and instigator of the policy of workers' self-management.

More people were killed by their fellow countrymen in the civil war that took place in Yugoslavia during the second world war than died at the hands of the enemy. The war left indelible scars. Perhaps the single most important mistake of the Communist government was not to have allowed the population to come to terms with the appalling cruelty unleashed by the war: in the interests of national unity it was consistently underplayed. Fear and hatred were thus left to smoulder underground where they could be whipped up in the frenzy of nationalism that followed the collapse of Communism in the Yugoslav lands. Communism may have held the various peoples of Yugoslavia together in an artificial entity, but with wisdom and goodwill the chaotic, violent end of the state structure, instigated by self-interested politicians, could have been avoided.

LANGUAGES

Yugoslavia was a complex multilingual state, with some 27 recognized languages, 14 of which had more than 10 000 speakers. The three official South Slav languages are the ones that concern us here: Serbo–Croat (Serbian and Croatian, now also known as 'Bosnian'), spoken by the great majority of the population (16 400 000 speakers in the 1981 census), Slovene (1 760 000) and Macedonian (1 370 000). While closely related, the three languages are distinct.

Serbo–Croat

From a purely linguistic point of view, it is impossible to justify the proposition that Croatian is a separate language, although this has been an important part of forging a sense of Croatian nationhood. With the drive towards an independent Croatian state, there has been a deliberate endeavour to encourage the divergence of the Western, Croatian variant of the language from its Eastern or Serbian counterpart and this process will no doubt continue, possibly to the point where Croatian will have to be treated as a separate entity. Used in written form since the middle ages, the Serbian and Croatian variants of Serbo–Croat were not codified until the mid-nineteenth century. This involved first selecting a dialect as the standard language and refining the existing alphabets. It was agreed by the language reformers among both the Serbs and the Croats to base the standard on the most widespread dialect used throughout Serbo–Croat speaking territories. This was the dialect both of the rich oral tradition that had flourished through the centuries of foreign administration, and of the literature written in the republic of Ragusa (**Dubrovnik**) and other Dalmatian cities in the sixteenth and seventeenth centuries. The Serbian and Croatian reformers agreed on the use of the same dialect, but it proved impossible for either group to abandon the alphabet in which its cultural tradition was embodied: the predominantly Orthodox Serbs retained the Cyrillic script, while the Catholic Croats kept Latin. The compromise reached was that each letter of each alphabet should have its equivalent in the other, so that it is simple to transcribe from one to the other. It is therefore perfectly possible for either variant to be written in either script. Until the upsurge of Serbian nationalism in the late 1980s, it was common for publishers in Serbia to use the Latin script, thereby extending the potential market for their books. In the climate prevailing in the early 1990s, however, to print Serbian texts in the Latin script often denotes dissension from the dominant nationalist ideology. A further inevitable consequence of such a preoccupation with language as a symbol of national identity has been the tendency (official Bosnian government policy since December 1993) to identify in addition a further branch of Serbo–Croat: a distinct 'Bosnian language'.

Slovene

For several hundred years after their arrival the Slavs who settled in the Eastern Alps, speaking several South Slav dialects, felt no need of a special name: they used a version of the Slavonic word for Slav, *Sloveni*, to describe themselves. At the beginning of the nineteenth century, this designation was formalized: a scholarly society, Societas Slovenica was founded in **Graz** in 1810, in 1817 the first chair of *slovenisch* was established in **Ljubljana**, and in 1825 the first grammar, by Frančišek Metelko, appeared with the title *Lehrbuch der slovenischen Sprache*. Inevitably, in view of the mountainous terrain, the dialects of the Slovene language differ considerably from one another. There is consequently a discrepancy between the written and spoken forms of the language, to the extent that the standard form may be described as an artificial, 'book-language' which is not actually spoken anywhere, but is the only common language uniting the speakers of various

Slovene dialects, scattered through the regions of Styria, Carinthia, Carniola, Gorizia, Trieste and Istria.

Macedonian

When the first Slav missionaries, Cyril and Methodius, set out to convert the Slavs to Christianity the Slav dialect they spoke in their native Salonica, in present-day Greek Macedonia, was comprehensible as far afield as Moravia and Bohemia. Gradually, however, the various Slavonic vernaculars and church languages became increasingly divergent. Under the Ottoman occupation Slav cultural activity was reduced to hand-copying of church texts and only when Ottoman power began to wane in the nineteenth century did it become possible for the subject peoples to think about using their languages as the medium of education and culture. The Bulgarians and Macedonians spoke very similar dialects, but the larger Bulgarian community, with its history of ancient statehood, was bound to dominate in written language usage. The first outline of a modern Macedonian standard based on the 'Prilep-Bitola' dialects, is contained in Krste Misirkov's *Za makedonskite raboti* (*On Macedonian Matters*), 1903, most copies of which were destroyed. It was not until the Republic of Macedonia was established within Yugoslavia in 1944 that Macedonian was recognized as its official language. A commission was immediately set up to codify it and in 1951 a handbook of *Macedonian Orthography* was published. The Macedonian language may therefore be described as both the oldest and the youngest written Slav language.

It is easy to see that in these circumstances of linguistic fragmentation, political division and foreign occupation, language becomes an area fraught with emotion and tension, and literature is used often as a vehicle for extra-literary concerns, a surrogate for political expression.

CROATIAN LITERATURE

Medieval

The first vernacular Croatian texts can be dated from the ninth-century mission of Cyril and Methodius, who introduced the Glagolitic alphabet. The oldest surviving Glagolitic text is the Baška tablet from the island of **Krk** (c1100), commemorating the foundation of the Church of St Lucia. From the ninth century, when Croatia became an independent state, Glagolitic was used in all aspects of public life, which ensured continuity with other Slav cultures rooted in the Byzantine Slavonic tradition. The Croats constituted a linguistic oasis within the Catholic church and had to produce their own texts in order to educate the young clergy, who were mostly peasants with no knowledge of Latin. The earliest Glagolitic genres were those current in the Christian literature of early medieval Europe (eg homilies, apocrypha, hagiography). There were also secular stories translated from Greek, of which only one has been preserved: O premudrom Akiru (Akiros the Wise).

When the Slavs arrived in the Balkan peninsula, Latin culture was already established and the emerging Slav vernacular culture could not of course hope to rival it. On the contrary, Latin models provided a fruitful stimulus. The sphere of Glagolitic activity was soon drastically restricted: the Hungarians established a bishopric in Zagreb under Roman Church organization, using Latin throughout its sphere of influence, and as the Dalmatian towns and islands fell to Venetian control, they too adopted Latin as the language of the church.

The main areas of Glagolitic activity were, then, the islands of the **Kvarner Gulf, Istria** and the countryside and villages of the littoral. For all this limited geographical scope, however, it is nevertheless on the achievements of Glagolitic culture that Croatian vernacular literature was based, when it began to emerge.

As more secular texts appeared, the written language was increasingly influenced by the spoken language, particularly in the case of texts not for liturgical use: stories, songs, miracle plays. From the thirteenth century and increasingly in the fourteenth, vernacular texts began to appear in the towns, at first mainly for church use and notably for readers in convents who knew no Latin. Religious narrative poems, especially legends of saints, written in a pure Croatian popular language, were a particularly flourishing genre. In the late Middle Ages we find traces of translations, via Venice, of French legends. Adapted to an Italian milieu, these were immediately applicable to similar cultural conditions in the Croatian lands. The common occurrence of heroes' names in Dalmatian cities – **Orlandus, Oliverius, Tristanus** – is evidence of these legends' popularity. They were followed by The Book of Troy and the Alexander romance, and anthologies of wise sayings, notably the Distichs of Cato. During the fifteenth century the verse legends of the saints became increasingly elaborate. Particularly popular at this time were the miracle plays, Crkvena prikazanja, which form a transition from the medieval Glagolitic religious to the new secular artistic literature. The Croatian versions were imitations of the long-established Italian tradition. The first Croatian ones appeared in **Zadar** and its immediate environs, quickly spreading north and south and remaining popular well into the sixteenth century.

The important transformation of Croatian culture came at the transition from the 15th to the 16th century, when the rapid growth of commerce in the coastal towns provided the preconditions for Renaissance influence. The last of the Dalmatian towns and islands fell to Venetian control in 1480. The exception to this pattern was the

Republic of Ragusa (**Dubrovnik**) which was sufficiently prosperous and skilful in diplomacy to be able to buy its virtual autonomy as vassal to successive overlords. Now the Croatized core of town-dwellers formed a patrician class ready to respond to cultural stimuli from Italy. Young Croats began to visit Italy not as pilgrims, but as students and scholars, and teachers and scholars from Italy came to the Croatian cities.

Sixteenth to eighteenth centuries

The first poets of the 16th century made the final transition from devotional to secular writing, from medieval to Renaissance literature. This process is epitomized by the work of Marko Marulić (1450–1524), from **Split**, a poet, theologian and scholar. He symbolizes the three strands of Croatian culture, out of which its mature achievements have grown: the medieval Glagolitic/Church Slavonic tradition, Latin scholarship and Western, notably Italian, influences. Marulić's substantial Latin moralistic works were widely known and translated. He wrote also short moralistic and satirical works in the vernacular for the enlightenment of his fellow citizens. Such works were based on popular medieval genres. He was spurred to write his longer and artistically more serious Croatian works particularly by awareness that many women in convents, including his sister, had no knowledge of Latin and hence nothing to read. His most important Croatian work is the narrative poem *Judita* (*Judith*), 1521. Composed at a time when the vernacular was hardly established as a literary language and drawing on several dialects, at the same time as following an elaborate metrical scheme, the poem was too difficult to be popular, but Marulić was widely admired. There is undoubtedly an allegorical dimension to *Judita*: in the context of the proximity of the Ottomans to Split during Marulić's lifetime, the poem may be read as a call to the Christian powers to resist their advance. The frequency with which later Dalmatian writers refer to Marulić is evidence of his importance as a model and evidence also that they were writing with a conscious sense of developing and consolidating a literary tradition of their own.

The other main source of inspiration for early Croatian writers was the oral tradition, in which the vernacular as a vehicle for lyrical expression was most developed. The first lyric poets of sixteenth-century **Dubrovnik** both recorded oral poems and wrote in the style of the oral tradition. Through their work the diction of the tradition became established in artistic literature. Throughout the sixteenth and seventeenth centuries, therefore, while writers followed trends in Italy, producing numerous translations, there was a conscious sense of a Croatian tradition: lyric verse grew out of its language, combining this successfully with devices from the Petrarchan convention. In other genres, writers exploited social similarities to develop local versions of

Italian models. Examples are the works of the sixteenth-century dramatist from **Dubrovnik**, Marin Držić (c1508–67), who was one of the few non-nobles to achieve prominence in the literary life of the Republic. He studied in Siena in Italy, but was evidently more attracted to Renaissance comedy than to his studies: he spent much of his time watching the popular street theatre. On his return to Dubrovnik he was able to exploit his knowledge of this and its Classical models in a series of pastoral plays and plays modelled more or less closely on Plautus. His best-known work is *Dundo Maroje*, 1556, with its intricate plot of coincidence and intrigue, its vivid characters (some the stock figures of Plautine comedy) and imaginative exploitation of the Dubrovnik Croatian/Italian bilingualism. This play is regularly performed at the **Dubrovnik Summer Festival** and enjoyed even by spectators with no knowledge of Croatian.

Important figures in Croatian Renaissance literature who came from centres other than Dubrovnik are Petar Hektorović from **Hvar** and Petar Zoranić from **Zadar**. Hektorović (1487–1572) was born into a noble family, and lived through two peasant uprisings and two incursions of the Turks onto the island. As a result of this experience, he built a small fortified house in his native **Starigrad** which was a source of great pride to him. His intention was that it should be used in time of need as a refuge for all the people of the town regardless of social status. Hektorović's most important work takes the form of an epistle: *Ribanje i ribarsko prigovaranje* (*Fishing and Fishermen's Conversation*), 1568, is a narrative poem, describing a three-day fishing trip among the neighbouring islands which the poet made in the company of two fishermen from Starigrad. The route is precisely documented. At one level, the poem is loosely based on the eclogue convention, to the extent that the fishermen entertain the poet with witty conversation, riddles and song. Growing out of Hektorović's personal experience of civil strife, it is also a plea for his fellow nobles to recognize the worth of the common people both with the public purpose of urging all Christian peoples to unite against the Turks, and with the deeper personal, Christian, aim of asserting the value of each individual in the eyes of God regardless of birth.

Little is known about the life or early works of Zoranić (1508–before 1569), but his *Planine* (*The Mountains*), 1569, the first secular prose work in Croatian, has earned him an important place in literary history. Modelled on Sannazaro's *Arcadia*, it aims to celebrate the surroundings of Zoranić's native **Zadar** by giving places and landmarks a legendary history in the manner of Classical texts. Widely read in Classical and Italian literature, the writer's starting point is the neglect of his country and its language by his fellow countrymen.

The 17th century in Croatian literature is marked by a number of outstanding poets from **Dubrovnik**, one of the finest of whom is Ivan Gundulić (1589–1638), who wrote in a range of genres, from neo-Classical mythological and pastoral plays, to religious and epic verse. He is best known for three works: the devotional lament, *Suze sina razmetnoga* (*The Tears of the Prodigal Son*), 1622; the allegorical pastoral, *Dubravka*, 1628, and the epic *Osman* (the earliest extant copy dates from 1651). *Dubravka* contains elements of mythological drama, Classical pastoral and details from contemporary life. The title represents a complex of associations: the name Dubrovnik, the pagan connotations of an oak grove (*dubrava*) and the name 'Dubravka', a nymph who symbolizes freedom. It may be seen as typical of the patriotic tone which distinguishes Croatian literature composed in Dalmatia and Dubrovnik in the 16th and 17th centuries from its Italian models. *Osman* is a lengthy epic, in 20 canti, closely modelled on Tasso's *Gerusalemme Liberata*, which Gundulić had intended to translate. Following the battle of Chocim (1621) and the death of Osman (1622), however, he decided instead to write this complex work, celebrating the ultimate triumph of the Christian Slavs over the Turks.

In the second half of the seventeenth century the literature of Dubrovnik declined sharply, with the city's decreasing prosperity and the devastation caused by the earthquake of 1667. The main focus of Croatian literature now moved northwards.

Conditions for cultural activity in the Croatian lands other than Dubrovnik and Venetian Dalmatia were unfavourable. On the one hand the whole population, particularly of the northern region of Slavonia, was depleted by constant fighting and many old families died out. The Military Zone, established by the Habsburg Monarchy as a buffer against the Ottomans, was settled largely by refugees from Turkish rule, mainly Serbs, with no roots in the Croatian lands. The administrators in Inner Croatia tended also to be foreign, so that the middle class was predominantly German-speaking. In the prevailing conditions of constant fear of Turkish attack, the Renaissance and the Reformation found little echo. It was only with the Counter-Reformation and the activity of the Franciscans and the Jesuits that the situation began to change. With the growth of education that they stimulated, **Zagreb** was gradually able to emerge as a cultural centre.

The most important figures in Croatian literature of the eighteenth century were didactic writers, two of them Franciscans from the coast, Filip Grabovac (1697–1749) and Andrija Kačić-Miošić (1704–60), and the third a Slavonian, Matija Reljković (1732–98), whose education, like that of many of his countrymen, was gained in Western Europe in the Seven Years' War. Grabovac and Kačić-Miošić exploited the existence of the oral tradition in order to convey information to a wide public: Kačić's main work, *Razgovor ugodni naroda slovinskoga* (*A*

Pleasant Conversation of the Slav People), 1756, expanded 1759, is a chronicle largely in verse, containing some two hundred decasyllabic poems, aiming to give as full as possible an account of the history of the South Slavs from the earliest known records to Kačić's day. Aware that the traditional songs were not accurate, he took his material from whatever sources he could find: the Croatian 18th-century writer Pavao Ritter Vitezović (1652–1713), the Italian historian Mauro Orbini and the Venetian archives. The work enjoyed great popularity, both among the educated and the common people, who adopted some of the songs into their own tradition.

Nineteenth century

The main issue dominating Croatian culture in the first half of the nineteenth century was that of the language: resistance to both German and Hungarian domination, and the need to codify the vernacular for it to be used effectively as the standard literary language.

The most glaring immediate problem was the fragmentation of the Croatian lands: inner Croatia was limited to a restricted area around **Zagreb** (a small provincial town of some 8 000 inhabitants at the beginning of the century), in which the middle-class administrators were often foreigners from other parts of the Habsburg Monarchy; the northern region of Slavonia, with close cultural links with Hungary and administered directly by Vienna since the Turks were driven out in the late seventeenth century; the wide belt of the Military frontier along the eastern length of Croatian territory; and Dalmatia, also administered directly by Vienna since the downfall of Napoleon. All of these areas had to be given a sense of community in the first instance through a standardized common literary language.

The reform of the language was carried out by Ljudevit Gaj (1809–72). He was the motivating force behind the 'Illyrian Movement', working ultimately for the unification of the Croatian lands, through the revival of Croatian cultural life within a Pan-Slav framework. The 'Illyrian Movement' was successful for a time in linking people with a range of interests, aims and temperaments, and it achieved some important goals. It was doomed, however, because its ultimate aims were political and could not be tolerated by the Austrian authorities. In 1843 the use of the name 'Illyrian' was banned.

The most important writer associated with the Movement was the poet Ivan Mažuranić (1814–90), whose dramatic poem *Smrt Smail-age Čengića* (*The Death of Smail-Aga Čengić*), 1857, has become a classic of South Slav culture. The poem describes the downfall of a tyrannical local Ottoman administrator near the border with **Montenegro**. Drawing closely on the heritage of the oral tradition, and incorporating references to the Classical and Renaissance heritage of Croatian literature, it is a statement of belief in the liberation of South Slav culture from foreign dominance. Other writers connected with the Illyrian Movement were lyric poets whose work may be broadly described as 'Romantic'. The most important of these is Petar Preradović (1818–72), an officer in the Austrian Army who wrote his first poems in German but then committed himself fully to the aims of the Movement.

The novelist August Šenoa (1838–81) represents a transition from the Romantic to the 'Realist' era. He played a vital role in the mid-nineteenth century in creating a reading public through his popular, informative, historical novels, which brought to life many different eras of Croatian history. In several vigorous critical essays, he also emphasized the need for greater attention to aesthetic standards among his fellow writers. In the second half of the century prose emerged as the dominant genre, concerned with the main social issues of the time, such as the migration from the country to the town, with the attendant problems of neglect of the land and urban poverty. The most important prose writers were Ante Kovačić (1854–89), whose main work, U registraturi (In the Registry Office), 1888, traces the fortunes of a young peasant boy who is taken up by a benefactor and brought to Zagreb, where he eventually goes mad and burns down the registry office where he works; Ksaver Šandor Djalski (1854–1935), 'the Croatian Turgenev', who wrote nostalgic sketches about the decline of the Croatian nobility and their country houses in the hills of Zagorje, to the west of Zagreb; and Vjenceslav Novak (1859–1905), whose prolific works cover his native Senj, in the Croatian littoral, and the depths of poverty he encountered in Zagreb.

The end of the nineteenth century also saw the emergence of a strong, original poetic voice, that of Silvije Stratimirović Kranjčević (1865–1908). He introduced two new elements into Croatian poetry, personal meditative themes and the figure of 'the worker'. Passionately interested in the philosophy of a range of different cultures, Kranj-čević's most characteristic poems offer a panorama of human spiritual and intellectual experience from Ancient Egypt to the revolutionary movements of the late 19th and early 20th centuries. Most of Kranjčevic's best known poems, however, are a blend of Christianity and socialism, with Christianity reduced to the symbol of Christ Himself, as opposed to the corruption and distortions of the church.

Twentieth century

The beginning of the twentieth century saw a return to poetry, stimulated by the main protagonist of Croatian Modernism, Antun Gustav Matoš (1873–1914), a charismatic figure who earned the nickname 'rabbi', and was an important stimulus to others. This period in the cultural life of both Serbs and Croats, commonly referred to as 'Modernism' and characterized by a general sense of having definitively joined the mainstream of contemporary European culture, was a time when literary critics in both **Zagreb** and **Belgrade** had exceptional authority. Matoš's literary contribution was considerable: he produced a substantial collection of short stories, remarkable for their blend of realistic and fantastic elements, travel sketches, essays, and verse. The interwar period was dominated by avant garde writers, at first under the influence of Central European Expressionism, notably the poet A. B. Šimić (1898–1925) and the early Krleža ◊ (Extract 11), then by socially committed writing and work of Catholic orientation.

The outstanding poet of the period was Augustin, 'Tin', Ujević (1891–1955), a flamboyant figure, famous for his recitations in the café across the road from the National Theatre in **Zagreb**. The strongest poetic voice in Croatian literature between the wars, Ujević went through several phases of development. His contribution to the influential anthology, *Hrvatska mlada lirika* (*New Croatian Lyric Poetry*), 1914, introduced a new tone, breaking with the dominance of critics and calling for a new independence of expression. His first volume of poems, *Lelek sebra* (*The Lament of the Serf*), 1920, expresses defeat in the face of merciless fate, taking its essential tone from 'Svakidašnja jadikovka' ('Everyday Lament'), a poem included in all anthologies of Croatian verse. Ujević characterizes the language of his second volume, *Kolajna* (*Necklace*), 1926, as 'black with depth'; it expresses the end of all illusion, the muffled cry of a man 'crushed by the weight of the sky'. After these two volumes, Ujević broadens his range and adopts the free verse form, exploring the philosophical ideas of many cultures. His eclectic, erudite essays are characterized by an individual poetic style: *Skalpel kaosa* (*The Scalpel of Chaos*), 1938.

The dominant issue of the day was the so-called 'conflict on the literary left', between writers who believed that literature should be subordinated to political needs and those who considered that aesthetic considerations need not undermine political commitment. Krleža was active in the debate in the interwar period and in the first years after the second world war he was influential in ensuring that Socialist Realism did not take root in Croatian culture. After 1948 and the break with Stalin, this question was definitively solved. The writers around the journal *Krugovi* (*Circles*) established the freedom to exploit foreign models, notably the Soviet avant-garde and French Existentialism. The work of T. S. Eliot was particularly influential. The most important of these first post-war writers were predominantly poets, such as Ivan Slamnig (1930–), Slavko Mihalić (1928–) and Antun Šoljan (1932–93) who also wrote several novels, short stories and plays. Vladan Desnica (1905–67), belonging to a slightly older generation,

CROATIAN WRITERS BORN IN DALMATIA

Ivan Aralica, **Promina**, Northern Dalmatia, 10 September 1930 (novelist)

Rudjer Bošković, **Dubrovnik**, 18 May 1711–13 February 1787 (scientist, poet and philosopher)

Ivan Bunić, **Dubrovnik**, c1591–?1658 (poet)

Vladan Desnica, **Zadar**, 17 September 1905–4 March 1967 (poet and prose writer)

Markantun Dominis (Marko Antonije Gospodnetić), **Rab**, 1560–8 September 1964 (writer and scholar), imprisoned by the Inquisition, died in prison and his body was burned on the Campo di Fiore in Rome

Marin Držić, **Dubrovnik**, 1505–1567 (writer of comedies)

Ivan Gundulić, **Dubrovnik**, 8 January 1589–8 December 1638 (poet)

Petar Hektorović, **Hvar**, 1487–1572 (poet)

Jure Kaštelan, **Zakučac**, 18 December 1919–1994 (poet)

Silvje Strahimir Kranjčević, **Senj**, 17 February 1865–20 October 1908 (poet)

Vesna Krmpotić, **Dubrovnik**, 17 June 1932 (poet)

Ranko Marinković, **Vis**, 22 February 1913 (prose writer)

Marko Marulić, **Split**, 18 August 1450–5 January 1524

Ivan Mažuranić, **Novi Vinodolski**, 11 August 1814–4 August 1890

Vladimir Nazor, **Postire, Brač**, 30 May 1876–19 June 1949 (poet and prose writer)

Slobodan Novak, **Split**, 3 November 1924 (prose writer)

Vjenceslav Novak, **Senj**, 11 September 1859–30 September 1905

Luko Paljetak, **Dubrovnik**, 19 August 1943 (poet)

Vesna Parun, **Zlarin** (nr **Šibenik**), 10 April 1922 (poet)

Ivan Slamnig, **Metković**, 24 June 1930 (poet)

Augustin-Tin Ujević, **Vrgorac**, 5 July 1891 (poet)

Ana Vidović, **Šibenik**, 7 September 1800–12 September 1879 (poet)

Ivo Vojnović, **Dubrovnik**, 9 October 1857–30 August 1829 (playwright)

produced his best work at this time, notably the lyrical novel, *Proljeća Ivana Galeba* (*The Springs of Ivan Galeb*), 1957. The major prose writer to emerge in this generation was Ranko Marinković (1913–), whose novel *Kiklop* (*Cyclops*), 1965, is a burlesque account of the alienation of an intellectual on the eve of the second world war. Marinković has also written short stories and plays, of which the best known is *Glorija* (*Gloria*), 1955. Other important figures of this generation are the prose writer Slobodan Novak ◊ (Extract 12) and the poets Jure Kaštelan (1919–) and the somewhat older Dragutin Tadijanović (1905–).

The 1970s were characterized by 'young prose' writers, advocating post-modernist trends, introducing colloquial urban language into their works – Zvonimir Majdak (1938–   ) – and 'trivial' genres, such as the detective story – Pavao Pavličić (1948–   ). The dominant influence of this period was the work of the Argentinian Jorge Luis Borges. The 1980s saw a new interest in the historical novel, particularly in the work of Aralica ◊ and the emergence of consciously feminist prose, with a number of women writers establishing themselves: Irena Vrkljan (1930–   ), Slavenka Drakulić (1949–   ) and Dubravka Ugrešić (1949–   ) ◊ (Extract 20).

SERBIAN LITERATURE
Medieval

The beginnings of Serbian literature were closely dependent on the church and on the need to strengthen the foundations of the state. In both areas, cultural activity was modelled on Byzantine sources. The most popular literary genre was hagiography, with Serbian monks from the 13th to 17th centuries contributing lives of all the main Serbian rulers and church leaders. These remain a valuable historical source. At the time they played a vital role in preserving a literary culture through the centuries of Ottoman rule when there was virtually no possibility of education. In remote monasteries, hidden away in mountain valleys, laboriously and painstakingly copying manuscripts by hand, the monks kept the tradition alive. It was an unfortunate fact of Serbian cultural history that, just as the rest of Europe was beginning to take advantage of the spread of printing, the Serbs were forced back to reproducing texts by hand, and obliged by circumstance to do so until the late eighteenth century.

One of the central figures of Serbian medieval culture, who became the focal point of legends and continues to inspire writers to the present day, was the youngest son of Stefan Nemanja, the first ruler of the Serbian state. Opting for the life of a monk, rather than his father's court, he ran away to the centre of Orthodox monastic life, **Mount Athos**, where he took the name of Sava. He later proved himself an astute politician, playing an important role in preserving the integrity of the Serbian state. He reconciled his quarrelling brothers, and played the Roman and Greek authorities against one another, obtaining recognition from the Pope of Serbian political independence, by having his younger brother, Stefan the First Crowned, proclaimed king by a Papal legate. He then negotiated ecclesiastical independence from the Greek Patriarch. Serbia was granted an autocephalous Serbian church and Sava became its first Archbishop.

One of the enduring contributions of Serbian medieval culture to the

European heritage is the large number of monasteries and churches founded by successive Serbian rulers. These beautifully proportioned buildings, richly decorated with frescoes, have been a source of inspiration to writers through the ages.

The single most important event of Serbian history was the battle with the advancing Ottoman Turks which marked the downfall of the medieval state. The Battle of Kosovo Polje (the 'Field of Blackbirds') was fought on 28 June 1389. It has been described by R. Knolles in his *The Generall Historie of the Turkes*, 1603. Few details are known of the actual battle, but it became the focus of a complex myth which may be described as the central aesthetic of Serbian culture. The oral tradition has given the Serbs a means of coming to terms with the catastrophe by transforming it into a triumph. The crucial idea contained in the myth is that of choice: self-sacrifice in the name of a higher ideal. The story as it has been handed down contains all the essential elements of catharsis: the pure tragic hero, Miloš Obilić, slain after crossing enemy lines and killing the Turkish Sultan; the scapegoat, Vuk Branković, portrayed as the archetypal traitor; the ruler, Prince Lazar, asked on the eve of the battle to choose between the earthly kingdom and the kingdom of Heaven. If he chooses the former, the battle will be won, but if the latter his entire army will be eliminated. His choice is clear: in a magnificent poem describing the eve of the battle, he urges his fellow countrymen to go to the battlefield and build 'a church of silk', symbol of the abstract invulnerability of honour and sacrifice in the name of an enduring ideal.

Sixteenth to eighteenth centuries

Following the disaster of Kosovo, the remnants of the Serbian state moved north and endured for a further 70 years. Under the son of Prince Lazar, Stefan Lazarević, the Serbian court saw considerable cultural activity, the ruler being a poet himself and encouraging the arts and scholarship. On a small scale, the court resembled the new centres of Humanism in Western Europe. It was thus all the more poignant that this kind of activity should have come to an abrupt end when the independent Serbian state was finally extinguished in 1459: just as printing was beginning to spread throughout Europe, literacy in the Serbian lands was driven back to the Middle Ages, to the dedicated hand-copying of church texts. The question of access to a printing press remained one of the major obstacles to Serbian cultural development until the late eighteenth century. Presses were established for short periods of time in some centres (the first was in **Cetinje**, in **Montenegro**, 1493), but they were able to print only a very few volumes.

There was a major upheaval in Serbian cultural life in 1690: following the end of the war between Austria and Turkey, in order to avoid reprisals resulting from their collaboration with the Austrians, tens of thousands of Serbs – merchants, town-dwellers, the majority of those with any education or vested interests – left Serbia, led by the Patriarch Arsenije. They were granted land along the Hungarian border with Turkey, an area depopulated following the Turkish advance and vulnerable to attack. Following the Treaty of Karlowitz (1699), the Serbs were permitted to establish a Metropolitanate in the town of Karlowitz, or Karlovci, and granted various rights. The Serbian community in these lands grew rapidly into a prosperous, successful, commercial class, building richly endowed churches and elegant residential buildings in the towns where they settled. In time a vigorous cultural life developed, although it was hampered by the necessity of copying literary works by hand.

The other major obstacle was the literary language. On the one hand the language of the church, the language of education, had become increasingly divergent from the vernacular. In addition, this Serbian Church Slavonic had been heavily influenced both by Russian Church Slavonic and by the spoken Russian language, as young Serbs, both clerics and lay people, went increasingly to Russia for their education, at the same time as teachers and books were imported into the Serbian community from Russia. The result of these different processes was a hybrid literary language, with no rules of grammar or orthography, making a singularly inadequate vehicle of communication. The literary works produced in these circumstances could necessarily reach only a small group of people with a shared educational experience.

In the eighteenth century voices began to be heard calling for the use of the vernacular language at least for certain types of writing intended for a wider audience, notably sermons. It was not until the end of the century, and the work of Dositej Obradović (1739–1811), that significant progress was made. Unlike his more tentative predecessors, Obradović believed that the vernacular should be used for every kind of writing. In addition, through many contacts abroad he was able to secure access to printing presses in various centres. His contribution to Serbian culture is considerable. Although his original impulse was to become an Orthodox monk, he soon became disillusioned with the moral and educational standards of the church. Thereafter he travelled and studied in Europe, supporting himself by giving lessons. He spent some time in London around 1847. He absorbed the spirit of the Enlightenment and of the Habsburg monarch Joseph II's educational reforms and dedicated his life to raising the standard of education among his fellow countrymen. To this end he translated the key texts of many contemporary thinkers as well as some Classical works, such as Aesop's Fables. His most important work is a lengthy account of his own life, *Život i priklučenija* (*My Life and Adventures*), 1783, in which he derives intellectual and moral lessons from his own experience and encourages his readers to do the same. While Obradović's language is still heavily influenced by both the language of the Church and Russian, his work marked the beginning of a new era in Serbian culture, based on the spoken language.

Nineteenth century

Obradović belonged to the Serbian community in southern Hungary, the centre of Serbian education and culture in the seventeenth and eighteenth centuries. In the early nineteenth century, the circumstances of the Serbs underwent a transformation which shifted the focus of their national life back to Serbia and Belgrade.

In 1804 there was an uprising against the arbitrary rule of the local Ottoman administrators in **Belgrade**, led by Karadjordje (Black George). Although the rebellion was crushed in 1813, it marked the beginning of the end of Turkish rule in Serbia. It was followed by a second rising in 1815, under Miloš Obrenović, and a lengthy period of negotiation with Istanbul, resulting eventually in independence for Serbia. These two uprisings, led by local village headmen, were essentially popular.

Following the success of the first uprising, Obradović moved enthusiastically to Belgrade to contribute to the education of his countrymen. In cultural terms, the most pressing need was for a systematic literary language, comprehensible to the ordinary people. A remarkable conjunction of circumstances provided the answer to this need. Vuk Stefanović Karadžić (1787–1864) was the son of a peasant, who took advantage of the meagre educational opportunities available to him – the local monastery school and passing merchants whom he pestered to help him learn to read as he tended his father's sheep. As a result he was able to act as scribe to one of Karadjordje's units during the First Uprising but was then obliged to flee into Austria when the local Turks regained power. In Vienna he came into contact with a Slovene, Jernej Kopitar (1780–1844) who proposed a plan of action which would provide a basis for the cultural development of the Serbs. The key points of this programme were the systematization of the spoken language, its alphabet and orthography, and the compilation of a grammar and dictionary, on the basis of its usage in the oral tradition. Karadžić carried out this basic programme, and more besides, with exceptional zeal and dedication.

Karadžić's reforms met with vociferous opposition from the church and members of the Serbian community in southern Hungary who felt that, if they were implemented without modification, the Serbs would be cut off from a continuous literary tradition reaching back to their medieval kingdom. The times were against these reactions, however:

this was the age of Romanticism, of Revolution and faith in the Folk as the repository of the true spirit of the people. The historical moment combined with Karadžić's uncompromising personality to guarantee his success. In 1847 the first important literary works of nineteenth-century Serbia were published – in Karadžić's reformed alphabet.

One of these was the dramatic poem *Gorski vijenac* (*The Mountain Wreath*) – Extract 9 – by the Prince-Bishop of **Montenegro**, Petar Petrović Njegoš ◊. This is one of the central works of Serbian literature: it represents a concentrated statement of popular customs, beliefs, and language, drawing heavily on the forms and themes of the oral tradition. It is a plea for the survival of the intrinsic values of the vigorous Montenegrin culture. In a similar way to the Croatian work, *Smrt Smail-age Čengića*, it represents the end of the oral tradition as the central medium of expression of the Serbo–Croat vernacular.

The middle of the nineteenth century was dominated by lyric poetry, with echoes of Central European, particularly German, Romanticism. The first important lyric poet to write in the new reformed language was Branko Radičević (1824–53). Born into the Serbian community in southern Hungary, Radičević wrote eloquently of the hills of **Fruška gora**. He was followed by several other lyric poets, the most important of whom are Djura Jakšić (1832–78), who was also a painter of note, and Jovan Jovanović 'Zmaj' (1833–1904), whose work, particularly his satirical verse and verse for children, is still learned by heart to this day.

From the 1870s prose began increasingly to dominate. The short story was the commonest genre, developing naturally out of the tradition of oral story-telling. For the most part these stories centre on village life, describing the transition from the old patriarchal system to a modern, more urban social focus, often with deep nostalgia for the old ways. Many of these 'stories' are no more than anecdotes, recorded just as they would be related, with little attention to artistic form. Among such prose writers, one is outstanding for his craftsmanship: Laza Lazarević (1851–91), whose carefully constructed, economical tales with their convincing psychological portraits did a great deal to raise the general artistic standard of prose writing towards the end of the nineteenth century.

While the short story was the most popular form, there were also some interesting novels written in the course of the century: Jakov Ignjatović (1822–89), a contemporary of the Romantic lyric poets, wrote historical, social and picaresque novels, giving a frequently pessimistic account of the society of his day. At the end of the century a prose writer, Borisav Stanković (1876–1927), who excelled in evocative sketches of village life set out to write a 'social' novel on the lines of Russian and French Realism. His novel, *Nečista krv* (*Tainted Blood*) offers a detailed and informative picture of the orientalized society of his small native town of **Vranje** in southern Serbia at a period of transition, but the novel is chiefly remembered for its portraits, particularly that of the main character, Sofka, who dominates the whole work.

Twentieth century

The end of the nineteenth century and first years of the twentieth brought a radical change in Serbian literature: the emergence of a sophisticated, urban intelligentsia, educated in Europe, mainly in Paris. A group of influential literary critics and a number of outstanding poets, whose work echoed Parnassian and Symbolist modes, definitively reoriented Serbian literature towards Europe.

The most important poet of the period, who heralded what has been referred to as 'the golden age of Serbian poetry', was Jovan Dučić ◊. Dučić was born in **Hercegovina**, where he worked for a while as a teacher before studying in Geneva, from where he made frequent trips to Paris, and then joined the diplomatic corps in Belgrade. He served in Cairo and several European capitals before settling in the USA in 1941, where he died. Dučić's attention to form in both his prose and verse writings (Extract 3), reinforced by the voices of contemporary literary critics, guaranteed a 'European' standard of excellence and frame of reference for Serbian literature.

The end of the first world war introduced a completely new political context, when the Kingdom of the Serbs, Croats and Slovenes was created by joining South Slav areas of the former Habsburg lands to the Kingdom of Serbia in a new multinational state.

One of the oustanding writers of this period was Miloš Crnjanski ◊, whose first poems, *Lirika Itake* (*Poems from Ithaca*), 1920, and the prose work *Dnevnik o Čarnojeviću* (*Diary about Čarnojević*), 1921, express the prevailing mood of bitter disillusion with the devastation of the war. Crnjanski wrote a number of fine long poems, but is chiefly known today for his prose works: the moving panorama of the historical destiny of the Serbs, *Seobe* (*Migrations*), Part I 1929, Part II 1962, and *Roman o Londonu* (*Novel about London*), 1971, in which he gives a bitter account of the life of émigrés in London, where he himself lived from 1941 to 1965.

During the interwar years, several different literary orientations emerged, the most influential of which were the Expressionist, Surrealist and 'socially committed' groups. The whole period was dominated, as was the intellectual life of Croatia, by a struggle on the left in which the essential issue was the extent to which art should be subordinated to the immediate requirements of social transformation. It was a period of vigorous literary life, when a number of interesting writers were active. One of the most attractive of them was the poet and essayist

Stanislav Vinaver (1891–1955), immortalized by Rebecca West in her *Black Lamb and Grey Falcon* as the character of 'Constantine'.

The interwar period saw the appearance of the Bosnian poet and prose writer, Ivo Andrić ◊, who was to win the Nobel Prize for literature in 1961 (Extract 19).

This period was also the first in Serbian literary history when it was possible for women writers to establish themselves: the prose-writer and essayist Isidora Sekulić (1877–1958), a scholar of wide erudition in a number of fields, and the poet Desanka Maksimović (1898–   ) whose prolific lyric verse has on the whole followed traditional patterns, but whose *Tražim pomilovanje* (*I Seek Clemency*), 1964, is a remarkable work of great originality. Its starting point is the Law Code of the fifteenth-century Tsar Dušan, which Maksimović exploits to formulate a timeless plea for humanity and justice.

In the years immediately following the second world war, in the aftermath of the Communist revolution that took place in the course of the war, it was the older generation of socially committed writers, including several of the former Surrealists, who dominated, constituting a literary 'establishment' of radically minded poets. Their authority was short-lived, however: in the early 1950s a new generation of 'modern' writers, drawing their inspiration from more purely literary, European trends, confronted the 'establishment' which eventually conceded their demands for absolute freedom of creativity. In this process the names of two poets, Vasko Popa ◊ and Miodrag Pavlović (1928–   ) stand out. Their work, particularly that of Popa, who was at one time nominated for the Nobel prize for literature, has become known abroad, as has that of Ivan Lalić (1931–   ). Many other interesting poets have emerged since the 1950s, but it is nevertheless in prose that twentieth-century Serbian literature has excelled since the second world war.

The first theme to dominate prose writing was that of the war itself. There were several approaches, from early Socialist-Realist pieces to increasingly experimental and personal accounts. One writer who has considered the war from several angles is Mihajlo Lalić (1914–   ) from **Montenegro**. The novelist who set the process of critical examination of the war in literature in motion was Dobrica Ćosić ◊, whose later novels have offered a panoramic account of the most important currents of twentieth-century Serbian history (Extract 14). One of the most important novelists active between 1950 and 1970 was Meša Selimović ◊ from eastern Bosnia, best known for his works *Derviš i smrt* (*The Dervish and Death*), 1966 (Extract 2), and *Tvrdjava* (*The Fortress*), 1970, which examine fundamental questions of ideology and individual responsibility. Although set in the period of Ottoman occupation, both novels deal with contemporary preoccupations. The 1960s also saw the emergence of three Serbian prose writers who have contributed works of substance and originality and made considerable impact abroad: Borislav Pekić ◊ (Extract 1), Danilo Kiš ◊ (Extract 18), and Milorad Pavić ◊. Another leading contemporary novelist is Slobodan Selenić ◊ (Extract 15).

LITERATURE IN BOSNIA AND HERCEGOVINA

Apart from the expressly Islamic literature produced on the territory of Bosnia and Hercegovina, it was not possible before the disintegration of Yugoslavia to think in terms of a continuous tradition of Bosnian literature as an independent entity. With few exceptions, writers have tended to see themselves as belonging to either the Croatian or the Serbian traditions. This was the case from the Middle Ages to the end of Ottoman occupation, when the only education available was either within the framework of the Orthodox or the Catholic church, or Islamic. In this context, where Orthodox was synonymous with Serbian and Catholic with Croatian, it was natural that individuals should ally themselves with the cultural orbit into which they were born. Thus, for example, the outstanding writers Petar Kočić, from north-west Bosnia and Jovan Dučić ◊ from Hercegovina, identified themselves as belonging to the Serbian literary tradition. Ivo Andrić ◊, born into a Catholic family in western Bosnia, and a committed 'Yugoslav' also opted for close links with the Serbian literary tradition, acknowledging his roots in a Balkan rather than a Central European culture. A particularly interesting case is that of Meša Selimović ◊ (Extract 2), a Muslim from Bosnia, who saw himself explicitly as belonging to the mainstream Serbian rather than the regional Bosnian literary tradition. Nevertheless, elements of a specifically Bosnian cultural tradition in the literature of Bosnia and Hercegovina may be identified in the marked Islamic but European presence on the one hand and in a consciously multicultural orientation on the other. Two periods were particularly conducive to the development of specific identity: from the Austro–Hungarian occupation of Bosnia and Hercegovina in 1878 until the first world war it is possible to speak of the beginnings of a Bosnian (or 'Bošnjak') culture. But with the creation of the Kingdom of Serbs, Croats and Slovenes, writers tended again to gravitate to the main centres: respectively to Belgrade and Zagreb. Then again, from 1945, when the republic of Bosnia and Hercegovina was established, until its destruction in 1992, a flourishing cultural life created the context for the emergence of a number of gifted writers of Muslim origin who brought a particular flavour to their work.

Quite soon after the Ottoman occupation of Bosnia and Hercegovina, the Slav converts to Islam began to see themselves as a separate ethnic group, linked to the Arabic and Turkish cultural tradition. The educated people began to write in Turkish, Persian and less frequently Arabic. A tradition of oriental poetry written by Bosnian Muslims developed. There were in addition some prose works, written in Turkish, including the *Chronicle* by Mula Mustafa Bašeskija which contains a vivid picture of Sarajevo in the second half of the eighteenth century.

Apart from the limited activity of a private printing press in **Goražde**, 1519–23, there was very little opportunity for literary activity under the aegis of the Orthodox Church throughout the period of Ottoman occupation, and what there was must be seen as an integral part of Serbian literacy as a whole. On the other hand, the activity of the Franciscan order in Bosnia and Hercegovina produced works of a quite distinct nature. Appearing first in Bosnia at the end of the thirteenth century, the Franciscans paid great attention to education and culture. Secondary schooling in the monasteries was based on the Latin language and several young Bosnians later studied in Italy, Hungary, France or England where some of them settled and achieved prominent positions. One of the earliest known writers in this tradition is Juraj Dragić, a Humanist from **Srebrenica** who wrote in Latin, spent most of his life in Italy and died as Archbishop of Barletto near Naples in 1520. In the course of the seventeenth century, the Bosnian Franciscans began to write in their native language. The most popular genre was the chronicle. Important writers are Matija Divković (1563–1631), from a village outside **Vareš**, who used traditional oral tales in his published Sermons, and Lovro Sitović (died 1729) who wrote verse in the vernacular and a 'Latin–Illyrian Grammar'.

A process of 'national awakening' occurred in Bosnia and Hercegovina in the nineteenth century, under the influence of the successful risings in Serbia and the Illyrian movement in Croatia. Several Catholic and Orthodox writers engaged in the collection of songs and tales of the oral tradition. The most important of these were the Franciscans, Ivan Frano Jukić (1818–57) and Grgo Matić (1822–1905), who also wrote chronicles and invaluable accounts of the contemporary life of their country.

In the nineteenth and early twentieth centuries, the most important writers active in Bosnia and Hercegovina, but perceived as belonging to either the Croatian or the Serbian cultural orbit, are: Silvije Stratimirović Kranjčević (1865–1908), Antun Branko Šimić (1898–1925) [Croatian]; Petar Kočić (1877–1916), Aleksa Šantić (1868–1924), and Jovan Ducić ◊ [Serbian].

The unique feature of twentieth-century literature in Bosnia and Hercegovina is the emergence of several Muslim writers, working in the mainstream European literary genres. Of these the most important are

Safvet-beg Bašagić (1870–1934), Edhem Mulabdić (1862–1954), Skender Kulenović (1910–78), Mak Dizdar (1917–71), Izet Sarajlić ◊ (Extract 13) and Meša Selimović ◊ (Extract 2). Isak Samokovlija (1883–1955), who wrote about the poor Sephardic Jewish community of **Sarajevo** into which he was born, represents another specific aspect of the culture of Bosnia and Hercegovina. His admirable short stories share common features with those of the great Ivo Andrić. Together, this group of writers offers a rich account of the mixed cultural life of their native land.

MACEDONIAN LITERATURE

The whole question of Macedonian nationality, language and culture is fraught with tension and uncertainty. As we have seen, the ninth-century founders of the Glagolitic and Cyrillic alphabets, Saints Cyril and Methodius, were Slav speakers from the area in present-day Northern Greece traditionally known as Macedonia. But neither then nor through the following centuries, until the mid-twentieth century, was there any political entity to which the name 'Macedonia' was attached, and consequently no centre where a Macedonian culture could become established. There were efforts to use the Macedonian language for poetry, at **Ohrid** and **Struga** at the end of the nineteenth century. But after the first world war, when the territory was partitioned between Bulgaria, Greece and Serbia, a Macedonian literary language was prohibited. It is, therefore, difficult to speak about Macedonian literature until the formation of a Macedonian political entity and the codification of the standard language in 1944. The founder of the literary language in its present form was the philologist and poet, Blaže Koneski ◊ (Extract 10). The first post-war phase of Macedonian literature is marked by a similar tone to that of literatures in the other Yugoslav republics: the brief dominance of Socialist Realism. Some poets who were to become important published in this first phase, notably Slavko Janevski (1920–) and Aco Šopov (1923–1982), but more favourable conditions for their work came with the changes brought about in the early 1950s. As in the rest of Yugoslavia, the years following the break with Stalin led to the rapid introduction of modern themes and techniques and a conscious reorientation towards the West. The appearance of the first novel, *Selo zad sedumte jaseni* (*The Village Behind the Seven Ash Trees*), 1952, by Slavko Janevski, opened a new phase in the development of Macedonian literature. This process was continued and strengthened by the work of new generations of Macedonian prose writers who introduced a range of techniques from modern European fiction. Nevertheless, this prose continued to be marked by a strong strain of regional lyricism, with increasingly clear attention to modern expression. Two writers were particularly important in this process: Dimitar Solev (1930–   ), much of whose work centres on his unhappy childhood during the war; and Živko Čingo ◊ (Extract 6). It is chiefly in poetry that Macedonian literature in the mid-twentieth century has excelled. It is interesting to note that, whereas the work of T. S. Eliot influenced a whole generation of poets in Croatia and Serbia, in Macedonian poetry it is the voices of Esenin and Lorca which are chiefly felt. Following their fruitful influence, Macedonian poetry from the beginning of the 1960s acquired a new confidence and rapidly developed into a rich, vigorous, diverse and expressive medium. Aco Šopov continued to write accomplished verse, but of a more complex, modern orientation, while new voices such as those of Mateja Matevski ◊ (Extract 7), Radovan Pavlovski (1937–   ) and Bogumil Gjuzel (1939–   ) began to be heard.

SLOVENE LITERATURE

It could be said that the Slovene language was saved by the Reformation, because it was used in printed books as early as the 16th century, in order to foster Protestantism. With the Counter-Reformation, from the second half of the 17th century, devotional books in Slovene were printed by the Jesuits in order to undermine any remaining Protestant sympathies. In 1678 a printing press was established in **Ljubljana** to contribute to this process.

The first important Slovene secular work was first published in German. *Die Ehre dess Hertzegthums Crain*, (*The Glory of the Carniola Region, Slava vojvodine Kranjske*), 1689, by Ivan Vajkard Valvasor (1641–93), an historical and ethnographic study of the Slovene people. The introduction included the first known printed secular poem in the Slovene language, by an admirer of Valvasor, Jožef Zizenčeli. Valvasor was born in **Ljubljana**, the descendant of an old noble family from Bergamo. He fought in the war of 1663–64 against Turkey, travelled widely in Europe, studying the natural world, and collecting books and drawings. He began to publish in 1679, using all his wealth to spread knowledge of the Slovene lands, and selling his country manor, Bogenšperk, and his house in Ljubljana to finance his publications. For his widely praised, detailed study of the **Černičko lake** he was elected to the Royal Society in London.

In the second half of the 18th century, under the influence of the European Enlightenment, significant changes took place in Slovene culture. The first secular intellectual circles were formed, of which the most important was that of Baron Žiga Zois (1747–1819), a prosperous manufacturer who supported a group of writers in **Ljubljana**. Two names from this group have survived: that of the first Slovene playwright, Anton Linhart (1756–95) and the first poet of importance, Valentin Vodnik (1759–1819), whose work is based very much on the rhythms and metre of the oral tradition.

As in Croatia, the main obstacle to the development of literature at the beginning of the 19th century was the absence of a reading public: the Slovene population was scattered through several administrative provinces in Austria and the majority of the officials came from other parts of the Habsburg lands and spoke only German. The feudal, or semi-feudal landowners tended also to be German-speakers who cared little for literature and less for the Slovene language. The only people concerned with its survival were village priests and a few educated people of humble status. This dismal situation was changed by new ways of thinking gradually making their way into the consciousness of educated people, and given a spur by the four years of Napoleon's rule (1809–13), when several Slovene-speaking areas were joined together as the Illyrian Provinces and the use of the Slovene language was encouraged in schools.

After that experience, there was no stopping the momentum of national awareness. In the 1830s a group formed in Ljubljana, determined to make it a real cultural centre. The outstanding figure of the first half of 19th century in Slovene literature was Francè Prešeren ◊ who introduced a number of European, particularly Italian, forms and genres into Slovene poetry and enhanced its expressive power by his own remarkably accomplished verse (Extract 17). Just before Prešeren's death, in the revolutionary year of 1848, following the example of other national groups in the Habsburg lands, the Slovene people began to formulate and express new ideas. At first these took the form of a desire for the unification, within the Habsburg Monarchy, of Slovenes in one administrative unit. The generation of poets who appeared after Prešeren expressed a new confidence and energy in their verse. The most important figure of this generation was Fran Levstik (1831–87), poet, short-story writer, essayist, critic, philosopher. He was actively involved in the Young Slovene movement, campaigning for unification and national rights. Josip Stritar (1836–1923) is one of the pioneers of modern Slovene literature. A connoisseur of European literatures and the aesthetic trends of his day, he contributed greatly to enhancing the general artistic and literary level of Slovene writing in his lifetime.

After 1866, the Slovenes were granted a measure of autonomy and circumstances began to favour the emergence of a middle class which would show a new interest in Slovene culture. With this new reading public, from the 1870s onwards, there was a rapid growth in prose writing. One of the most original figures of this time was Ivan Tavčar (1851–1923), who wrote vividly about the history and contemporary state of his native **Poljane**. It is, nevertheless, with the names of two poets that the last decades of the 19th century are associated. Simon Gregorčič (1844–1906) and Anton Aškerc (1856–1912) were lyric poets of very different kinds, who both played a part in fostering an interest in Slovene literature and responding to the demands of the educated population for Slovene books, particularly in the new thriving commercial centre of Ljubljana.

The isolated figures who made their mark before the 20th century may be seen as pioneers: Slovene literature reached full maturity in the early 20th century with the work of four men born within two years of each other: Ivan Cankar ◊, Dragotin Kette (1876–1899), Josip Murn Aleksandrov (1878–1901) and Oton Župančič (1878–1949). Cankar turned his hand to several genres, but is chiefly known for his prose writings (Extract 5). The other three were poets, with Župančić being widely regarded, well into the 20th century, as the finest craftsman of the Slovene language. The decade before the first world war saw steady economic and cultural progress among the Slovenes. Increasingly, they began to demand the rights and status of a nation. The Slovene Préporod (Revival) movement emerged with the ultimate aim of creating a Yugoslav state.

With the formation of the new Kingdom of Serbs, Croats and Slovenes after the first world war, the context of Slovene culture changed completely: a university and Slovene Academy of Arts and Sciences were founded in Ljubljana, there was a rapid growth in numbers of periodicals, publishers and libraries throughout Slovene territories. A number of new writers appeared, anxious to assimilate European trends, notably Expressionism. It was at this time that Edvard Kocbek ◊ began to write. In politics, the period between the two world wars saw growing tension between centralist and federative tendencies which pushed the country from one crisis to the next until the outbreak of the second world war. Literature was marked by an increased preoccupation with social realism on the one hand and a tone of cynical detachment on the other. The devastation caused by the war – 20–25% of the Slovene population were deported, interned or killed – led to a new determination among all the peoples of Yugoslavia to forge a new, firm basis for the federation. Another highly regarded prose writer of this time is Ciril Kosmač ◊ (Extract 16).

Since the second world war, Slovene literature has produced a number of outstanding lyric poets, particularly Dane Zajc (1929–   ), Veno Taufer (1933–   ) and the younger generation including Tomaž Šalamun ◊ and Aleš Debeljak (1949–   ).

BOOKLIST

*The following selection includes the ex-
tracted titles in this chapter as well as
those mentioned in the introduction
which are available in English and other
titles for further reading. In general,
paperback editions are given when possible. The editions cited are not necessarily the only ones available. For most of
the extracted works, the original publisher can be found in 'Acknowledgments and Citations' at the end of the
volume, as can the exact location of the
extracts and the editions from which
they are taken. Extract numbers are
highlighted in bold. Square brackets denote the date of publication of the work
in its original language.*

Andrić, Ivo, *The Bridge on the Drina*,
[1945], Lovett F. Edwards, trans,
Collins Harvill, London, 1994.
Extract 19.

Andrić, Ivo, *The Days of the Consuls*
[1945], Celia Hawkesworth,
trans, Forest Books, London,
1992. Also translated as *Bosnian
Story*, Kenneth Johnstone, trans,
Lincoln–Praeger, London, 1958.

Andrić, Ivo, *The Damned Yard and
Other Stories* [1954], Celia Haw-
kesworth, trans, Forest Books,
London/Boston, MA, 1992.

Andrić, Ivo, *The Vizier's Elephant:
Three Novellas*, Regnery, Chicago, IL, 1970.

Andrić, Ivo, *The Pasha's Concubine,
and Other Tales*, Joseph Hitrec,
trans, Allen and Unwin, London, 1969.

Andrić, Ivo, *The Woman from
Sarajevo* [1945], Joseph Hitrec,
trans, Calder and Boyars, London, 1973.

Andrić, Ivo, *Conversations with
Goya: Bridges, Signs*, Menard
Press, with the School of Slavo-
nic and East European Studies,
London, 1992.

*Anthology of Modern Albanian Poetry:
An Elusive Eagle Soars*, Robert
Elsie, trans and ed, Forest Books,
London, 1993. (Contains works
by Albanians from Kosovo and
Macedonia.)

*Anthology of Modern Yugoslav Poetry
in English, An*, Janko Lavrin,
trans and ed, J. Calder, London,
1962.

*Anthology of Yugoslav Short Stories,
An*, A. Stipčević, ed, New Delhi, 1969.

Aškerc, Anton, translations in
*Anthology of Modern Slavonic
Literature in Prose and Verse*, Paul
Selver, trans, London and New
York, 1919; *Parnassus*, 1957; *The
Slav Anthology*, Portland, ME,
1931; *Slovene Poetry*, Cleveland,
OH, 1928.

*Big Horse and Other Stories of Modern
Macedonia, The*, Milne Holton,
ed, University of Missouri Press,
Columbia, MO, 1974. **Extract 6.**

*Black Lambs and Grey Falcons:
Women Travellers in the Balkans*,
John B. Allcock and Antonia
Young, eds, Bradford University
Press, Bradford, 1991.

Bloody Bosnia, Guardian and Channel 4 TV, London, 1993.

Cankar, Ivan, *The Bailiff Yerney and
His Rights* [1907], Sidone Yeras
and H. C. Sewell Grant, trans,
The Pushkin Press, London,
1968. **Extract 5.**

Cankar, Ivo, *Dream Visions and
Other Selected Stories* [1917 etc],
Slovenian Research Center of
America, Willoughby Hills, OH,
1982.

Cankar, Ivo, *The Ward of Our Lady
of Mercy* [1904], Državna založba
Slovenije, Ljubljana, 1976.

*Cimarron Review, Special Feature,
Yugoslav Poetry and Prose in
Translation*, No 96, July 1991.

Čingo, Živko, 'Argil's Decoration' [1962], in *The Big Horse and Other Stories of Modern Macedonia*, Milne Holton, ed, University of Missouri Press, Columbia, MO, 1974. **Extract 6**.

Contemporary Croatian Literature, A. Kadić, ed, Mouton, The Hague, 1960.

Contemporary Macedonian Poetry, Ewald Osers, trans, introduction by George MacBeth, Kultura/ Forest Books, London and Boston, MA, 1991.

Ćosić, Dobrica, *A Time of Death* [1972–75], Muriel Heppell, trans, Harcourt Brace Jovanovich, New York and London, 1978. **Extract 14**.

Ćosić, Dobrica, *South to Destiny*, Harcourt, Brace, Jovanovich, San Diego, CA, 1983.

Ćosić, Dobrica, *Into the Battle*, Harbourt, Brace, Jovanovich, San Diego, CA, 1983.

Crnjanski, Miloš (Tsernianski, Miloš), *Migrations*, Vol 1, Michael Henry Heim, trans, Harvill, London, 1994.

Day Tito Died, The: Contemporary Slovenian Short Stories, Forest Books, London, 1994.

Death of a Simple Giant and other Modern Yugoslav Stories, B. Levski, ed, Vanguard Press, New York, 1965.

Djalski, Ksaver Šandor, two short stories in *Great Short Novels of the World*, B. H. Clark, ed, New York, 1927.

Djilas, Milovan, *The Leper and Other Stories*, Lovett F. Edwards, trans, Methuen, London, 1965. **Extract 8**.

Drakulić, Slavenka, *Holograms of Fear* [1987], Ellen Elias-Bursać and the author, trans, The Women's Press, London, 1993.

Drakulić, Slavenka, *Marble Skin* [1989], Greg Mosse, trans [from the French], The Women's Press, London, 1994.

Drakulić, Slavenka, *How We Survived Communism and Even Laughed*, Verso, London, 1993.

Drakulić, Slavenka, *Balkan Express: Arguments from the Other Side of War*, Hutchinson, London, 1993.

Držić, Marin, *Uncle Maroje* [1556] (and *Grižula*), Summer Festival (Libertas), Dubrovnik, 1967.

Dučić, Jovan, *Plave legende – Blue Legends*, Kosovo Publishing Company, Columbus, OH, 1983.

Dučić, Jovan, in *Serbian Poetry from the Beginnings to the Present*, Vasa D. Mihailovich, trans, Yale Russian and East European Publications, No 11, New Haven, CT, 1988. **Extract 3**.

Gregorčič, Simon, *Alone*, Ljubljana, 1919; and poems in *Parnassus*, 1957, 1965, *The Slav Anthology*, Portland, ME, 1931, *Slovene Poetry*, Cleveland, OH, 1928.

Gundulić, Ivan, *Dubravka* [1628], in *BC Review*, Vol 9, 1976.

Gundulić, Ivan, *The Tears of the Prodigal Son* [1622], E. C. Hawkesworth, trans, London and Zagreb, 1990.

Gundulić, Ivan, *Osman* [1651], Zagreb, 1991.

Hawkesworth, E. C., *Ivo Andrić: Bridge between East and West*, Athlone Press, London, 1984.

Hektorović, Petar, *Fishing and Fishermen's Conversation* [1568], E. D. Goy, trans, in *BC Review*, Vol 15, 1979.

Introduction to Yugoslav Literature, B. Mikasinovich *et al*, eds, New York, 1973.

Ivo Andrić, E. C. Hawkesworth, ed, School of Slavonic and East European Studies, London, 1985.

Karadžić, Vuk Stefanović, see D. Wilson, *The Life and Times of Vuk Stefanović Karadžić, 1787– 1864*, Michigan Slavic Publications, 1986.

Kiš, Danilo, *Garden, Ashes* [1965], William J. Hannaher, trans, Faber and Faber, London, 1985/ Harcourt Brace, New York, 1975. **Extract 18**.

Kiš, Danilo, *A Tomb for Boris Davidovich* [1976], Penguin, London and New York, 1980.

Kiš, Danilo, *The Encyclopedia of the Dead*, Faber and Faber, London, 1990/Farrar, Straus and Giroux, New York, 1989.

Kiš, Danilo, *Hourglass* [1972], Ralph Mannheim, trans, Faber and Faber, London, 1992/Farrar, Straus, Giroux, New York, 1990.

Klaonica: Poems for Bosnia, Ken Smith and Judi Benson, eds, Bloodaxe Books, Newcastle upon Tyne, 1993.

Kocbek, Edvard, poems in *An Anthology of Modern Yugoslav Poetry in English* (see above).

Koneski, Blaže, *Poems*, Andrew Harvey, trans, André Deutsch, London, 1979.

Koneski, Blaže, *Poems, Zlaten venec*, Andrew Harvey and Anne Pennington, trans, Struga, Skopje, 1981. **Extract 10**.

Kosmač, Ciril, *A Day in Spring* [1953], Fanny S. Copeland, trans, Lincolns-Prager, London, 1959. **Extract 16**.

Kranjčević, Silvije Stratimirović, three poems in *An Anthology of Modern Yugoslav Poetry* (see above).

Krleža, Miroslav, *The Cricket Beneath the Waterfall and Other Stories*, Vanguard Press, New York, 1972.

Krleža, Miroslav, *On the Edge of Reason* [1938], Quartet, London and New York, 1986.

Krleža, Miroslav, *The Return of Philip Latinovicz* [1932], Zora G. Depolo, trans, Quartet, London and New York, 1989. **Extract 11**.

Lalić, Mihajlo, *The Wailing Mountain* [1957], Harcourt, Brace and World, New York, 1965.

Levstik, Fran, *Martin Krpan* [1858], Mladinska Knjiga, Ljubljana, 1960.

Maksimović, Desanka, *Greetings from the Old Country*, Yugo-Slavica Publishers, Toronto, 1976.

Maksimović, Desanka, *Poems from Norway* [1976], Idea, Belgrade, 1990.

Malcolm, Noel, *Bosnia: A Short History*, Macmillan, London, 1994.

Marinković, Ranko, *Gloria* [1955], in *Five Modern Yugoslav Plays*, B. Mikasinovich, ed, Cyrco Press, New York, 1977.

Marulić, Marko, extract from *Judita* [1521] in *Monumenta Serbocroatica*, T. Butler, ed, Michigan Slavic Publications, Ann Arbor, MI, 1980.

Matevski, Mateja, *Footprints of the Wind*, Ewald Osers, trans, Forest Books, London and Boston, MA, 1988. **Extract 7**.

Matoš, Antun Gustav, 'A Sonnet', in *An Anthology of Modern Yugoslav Poetry* (see above).

Matoš, Antun Gustav, 'The Neighbour' in *Great Short Stories of the World*, B. H. Clark and M. Lieber, eds, Halcyon House, Garden City, NY, 1925.

Matoš, Antun Gustav, 'At Saint Stjepan's', in *Contemporary Croatian Literature* (see above).

Mažuranić, Ivan, *The Death of Smail Aga* [1846], James Williams Wiles, trans, Allen and Unwin, London, 1925; also, *Smail-Aga Cengić's Death*, Društvo književnika hrvatske, Zagreb, 1969.

Mikasanovich, Branko, Dragan Milivojević, Vasa D. Mihailovich, *Introduction to Yugoslav Literature*, Twayne, New York, 1973.

Modern Poetry in Translation, No 8: Slovenia, T. Hughes and D. Weissbort, eds, London, Cape Goliard, 1970.

New Writing in Yugoslavia, B. Johnson, ed, Penguin, London, 1970.

Njegoš, Petar Petrović (Petar II, Prince Bishop of Montenegro), *The Ray of the Microcosm* [1845], Prvulovich, Zika Rad, trans, C. Schlacks, Salt Lake City, UT, 1992.

Njegoš, Petar Petrović, *The Ray of the Microcosm* [1845], Anica Savić Rebac and Darinka Zličić, trans, Vajat, Belgrade, 1989.

Njegoš, Petar Petrović, *The Mountain Wreath* [1847], Vasa D. Mihailovich, trans, Schlacks, Irvine, CA, 1986; also Vajat, Belgrade, 1986. **Extract 9**.

Norris, D. A., *The Novels of Miloš Crnjanski: An Approach through Time*, Astra Press, Nottingham, 1990.

North Dakota Quarterly, Out of Yugoslavia, Vol 61, No 1, Winter 1993.

Novak, Slobodan, 'Mother Antonia the Prioress', in *An Anthology of Yugoslav Short Stories* (see above).

Novak, Slobodan, *Twisted Space*, Zagreb, 1969.

Novak, Slobodan, *Gold, Frankincense and Myrrh* [1968], Celia Hawkesworth, trans, Most, Zagreb, Forest Books, London and Boston, MA, 1991. **Extract 12**.

Novak, Vjenceslav, extract from 'The Last of the Stipančići' in *Introduction to Yugoslav Literature*.

Obradović, Dositej, *The Life and Adventures of Dimitrije Obradović* [1788], University of California Press, Berkeley, CA, 1953.

Parnassus of a Small Nation, The, W. K. Matthews and A. Slodnjak, eds, J. Calder, London, 1957.

Parnassus of a Small Nation, The, 2nd enlarged edition, J. Lavrin and A. Slodnjak, eds, Državna založba Slovenije, Ljubljana, 1965. (Slovene poetry.)

Pavić, Milorad, *Landscape Painted with Tea* [1988], Christina Pribićević-Zorić, trans, Penguin, London, 1992/Knopf, New York, 1990.

Pavić, Milorad, *Dictionary of the Khazars* [1984], Christina Pribićević-Zorić, trans, Penguin, London and New York, 1990.

Pavić, Milorad, *The Inner Side of the Wind*, Knopf, New York, 1993.

Pavlović, Miodrag, *The Conqueror in Constantinople*, New Rivers Press, New York, 1976.

Pavlović, Miodrag, *Singing at the Whirlpool*, Exile Editions, Toronto, 1983.

Pavlović, Miodrag, *The Slavs Beneath Parnassus*, Angel Books, London, 1985/New Rivers Press, St Paul, MN, 1985.

Pekić, Borislav, *The Time of Miracles* [1965], Lovett F. Edwards, trans, New York, 1976; Northwestern University Press, Evanston, IL, 1994.

Pekić, Borislav, *The Houses of Belgrade* [1969], Bernard Johnson, trans, Northwestern University Press, Evanston, IL, 1978. **Extract 1**.

Pipa, Arshi, *Albanian Literature: Social Perspectives* (*Albanische Forschungen*, 19), Trofenik, Munich, 1978. **Extract 4**.

Popa, Vasko, *Selected Poems*, Anne Pennington, trans, introduction by Ted Hughes, Penguin, London, 1969.

Popa, Vasko, *The Little Box*, Charles Simic, trans, Charioteer Press, Washington, DC, 1970.

Popa, Vasko, *Earth Erect*, Anne Pennington, trans, Anvil, London, 1972.

Popa, Vasko, *Homage to the Lame Wolf: Selected Poems 1956–1975*, Charles Simic, trans, Oberlin College Press, OH, 1979.

Popa, Vasko, *Collected Poems 1943–1976*, Anne Pennington, trans, Carcanet, Manchester, 1978/Persea Books, New York, 1978.

Popa, Vasko, compiled, *The Golden Apple* [1966], Andrew Harvey and Anne Pennington, trans, Anvil, London, 1980.

Popa, Vasko, *The Cut*, Anne Pennington and Francis R. Jones, trans, Anvil, London, 1986.

Prešeren, Francè, *Selection of Poems by Francè Prešeren*, W. K. Matthews and A. Slodnjak, eds, John Calder, London, 1969. **Extract 7.**

Roads Lead Only One Way: A Survey of Modern Poetry from Kosova, John Hodgson, trans, Kosova Association of Literary Translators, Rilindja, Prishtinë, 1988.

The Sad Branch: Albanian poetry in Yugoslavia, Ali Podrimja and Sabri Hamiti, eds, Rilindja, Prishtinë, 1979.

Šalamun, Tomaž, *The Collected Poems*, Charles Simic, ed, Ecco Press, New York, 1988.

Sarajlić, Izet, 'Sarajevo', **Extract 13** (Celia Hawkesworth, trans).

Selenić, Slobodan, 'Two excerpts from *Fathers and Forefathers*', Ellen Elias-Bursać, trans, in *North Dakota Quarterly*, Vol 61, No 1, Winter 1993. **Extract 15.**

Selimović, Meša, *Death and the Dervish* [1966], **Extract 2** (Celia Hawkesworth, trans).

Selimović, Meša, *The Island* [1974], Serbian Heritage Academy, Toronto, 1983.

Šenoa, August, *The Peasant Rebellion* (abridged) [1877], Matica iseljenika hrvatske, Zagreb, 1973.

Serbian Poetry from the Beginnings to the Present, Vasa D. Milhailovich, trans, Yale Russian and East European Publications, New Haven, CT, 1988. **Extract 3.**

Shkreli, Azem, *The Call of the Owl* [1986], John Hodgson, trans, Kosova Association of Literary Translators, Prishtinë, 1989.

Shkreli, Azem, 'In Shkrel', in Arshi Pipa, *Albanian Literature: Social Perspectives*, see above.

Šimić, Antun Branko, poems in *Introduction to Yugoslav Literature* (see above).

Slovene Poets of Today, A. Mackin-non, trans, Slovene Writers' Association, Ljubljana, 1965.

Stanford Humanities Review, Vol 1, Nos 2 and 3, Fall/Winter 1990 (three women writers from Zagreb: Drakulić, Vrkljan, Ugrešić).

Stanković, Borisav, *Koštana* [1902], Novi Sad, 1984.

Stanković, Borisav, *Sophka* ['Tainted Blood', 1910], London, 1932.

Storm, No 6: Out of Yugoslavia, Joanna Labon, ed, distributed by Carcanet, London, 1994.

Tadijanović, Dragutin, *Selected Poems*, Croatian PEN, Zagreb, 1993.

Tišma, Alexander, *The Use of Man*, Faber and Faber, London, 1989.

Thompson, Mark, *A Paper House: The Ending of Yugoslavia*, Vintage, London, 1992.

Thompson, Mark, *Forging War: The Media in Serbia, Croatia and Bosnia-Hercegovina*, Article 19, London, 1994.

Ugrešić, Dubravka, *Fording the Stream of Consciousness* [1988], Michael Henry Heim, trans, Virago Press, London, 1991. **Extract 20.**

Ugrešić, Dubravka, *In the Jaws of Life*, Celia Hawkesworth and Michael Heim, trans, Virago, London, 1992.

Ugrešić, Dubravka, *Have a Nice Day: From the Balkans to the American Dream*, Celia Hawkesworth, trans, Cape, London, 1994.

Ujević, Augustin-Tin, poems in *An Anthology of Modern Yugoslav Poetry* and *Introduction to Yugoslav Literature* (see above).

West, Rebecca, *Black Lamb and Grey Falcon: A Journey through Yugoslavia*, Canongate, Edinburgh, 1993.

Župančič, Oton, *A Selection of Poems*, Državna založba Slovenije, Ljubljana, 1967; also in *An Anthology of Modern Yugoslav Poetry*, and *Introduction to Yugoslav Literature* (see above).

Extracts

(1) Belgrade

Borislav Pekić, *The Houses of Belgrade*

The novel, by one of Serbia's most prolific contemporary writers, describes a property dealer and recluse who shuts himself in his flat at the outbreak of the second world war to dream of the buildings he owned before the war, each of which he knew by a woman's name, recording every detail of their fate. In 1968 he eventually emerges only to be caught up in violent street demonstrations (a student protest this time) bewilderingly similar to his last experience of the outside world.

Even now, I probably can't explain why I never felt the need to give 17 Kosančićev Venac a name. Viewed from the street, the house had no special qualities. On a fine-grained brown plane, consisting of three vertical fields above a raised plinth which was pierced by three horizontal cellar windows, rose the ground floor and the second story, separated by two medallions in the shape of stone insignias in relief. On the third level a wooden door bound with forged iron opened onto a semicircular patio, while the whole building was topped by an almost flat roof, bordered by a balustrade with closely set railings in the form of stone skittles. It was natural that my own habitation should not inspire me in the same way as Simonida or the uninhibited, not to say lascivious, Theodora. Nevertheless, despite her lack of visual appeal, she possessed something unique. Since this was not visible from the outside, you had to go around and down onto the embankment, and look at her from the river, to see what it was that set her off: she possessed the finest orientation on the plateau of Kosančićev Venac, and her windows, facing west and overgrown with ivy, offered an unequaled view over the Srem plain.

From the window everything seemed new, *different*. But with the exception of the gas station, nothing on Srebrnička Street had actually changed. Not even the Turkish cobblestones had been replaced by macadam – something I had tried to get done before the war.

[. . .] I immediately told myself that my worry could not have been occasioned by the crowds I had encountered after stepping out of an empty street. Those people were quietly going about their business; indeed, most of them could have lived in my apartments without losing my self-respect. But I was no longer among them, among my own clientele, for suddenly I found myself in the midst of quite different people: again for the nth time and who knows at what cost, it was

March 27, 1941; once again I was hurrying to Stefan's auction and once again I came upon an unruly mob.

(2) BOSNIA

Meša Selimović, *Death and the Dervish*

This novel, concerned with personal morality and guilt in relation to a dominant ideology and power, has become one of the classics of twentieth-century Yugoslav literature. The extract is a speech made in a Sarajevo mosque by the main character, a dervish, who has learned that his brother has been killed by the authorities.

'Sons of Adam! I shall not give you a sermon, I could not even if I wanted to. But I believe that you would wish me now, at this time, harder than any I recall in my life, to speak to you about myself. Nothing has ever been more important to me than what I am going to say, but I do not seek to achieve anything. Nothing, other than to see sympathy in your eyes. I did not call you brothers, although I've never felt closer to you, but sons of Adam, appealing to what is common to all of us. We are people, and we think in the same way, especially when things are hard. You waited, you wanted us to be left alone, to look one another in the eye, saddened by the death of an innocent man, and disturbed by the crime. That crime affects you as well, because you know: when an innocent man is killed, it is as though we had all been killed. They've killed us numerous times, my murdered brothers, but we are appalled when it happens to those dearest to us.

Perhaps I ought to hate them, but I cannot. I do not have two hearts, one for hatred, the other for love. The one I have, now knows only sorrow. My prayer and my repentance, my life and my death, all that belongs to God, the creator of the earth. But my grief belongs to me. [. . .]

My brother Haroun is no more, and I can say only: My God, strengthen my strength through him who is dead.

Through him who is dead and not buried by the laws of God, not seen and not embraced by those closest to him before the great journey from which there is no return. [. . .]

I did not save him when he was alive, I did not see him when he was dead. Now I have no one but myself and you, my God, and my sorrow. Give me the strength not to shrink from grief for a brother and for mankind, and not to be poisoned by hate.

We live on earth for just one day, or less. Give us the strength to forgive. For he who forgives, is strongest. And I know that I cannot forget.

And I ask you, my brothers, not to be angry at these words of mine, not to resent them if they have hurt and saddened you. And if they have revealed my weakness. I am not ashamed at this weakness before you. I would have been ashamed not to have felt it.

And now go home and leave me alone with my sadness. It is easier now, I have shared it with you.'

(3) DUBROVNIK

Jovan Dučić, *Wine of Dubrovnik*

Dučić was born in Hercegovina, just inland from the Dalmatian coast, and he wrote many poems about the sea and particularly about the city of Dubrovnik in its Renaissance 'golden age'.

Quiet as silver, motionless, the sea
beyond the lawn – one hears the fountains dance,
the plash of spray; behind the laurel tree
peers marble Pan with wanton countenance.

Bright music sounds, for now there are guests here.
Out in the garden all the faces shine,
amused and happy, playful, free from care –
such a fine meal; insidious, that wine!

Gambolings, gentle turmoils now begin;
disorder grows – such doings in this crowd!
A friar (Dominican) twangs a mandolin;
a fervent captain says the Psalms out loud.

Then Ana de Doce, gray dame of note,
who stands for flawless virtue, perfect *ton*,
can be heard, 'midst her group of ladies, quote
a roaring tale from the *Decameron*.

(4) KOSOVO

Azem Shkreli, *In Shkrel*

This Albanian poet comes from the Rugovë upland district near Pejë (Peć), in Serbia's Kosovo province. The poem is an evocation of his home village. It comes from the section 'Archaic Songs' in his collection Angels on the Roads, 1963. The 'canons' are the old customary laws. (For Shkreli's biography, see p 422.)

Our ancestors, the elders say, looking for pastures,
settled on these rocks sheltering sheepfolds and graves.
They were not afraid of showers and freezing weather,
sharing joys like bread and shedding one tear for one dead.
And ever since they have had wolves and birds of prey for neighbors,
calling their children – and they've favored names – Wolf and Bird.

Creeks run down the slopes, on the cliffs clouds sport with thunder,
girls with fern-like eyes grow among pine-trees.
Old women remembering old times spin on their distaffs
lamenting new customs: 'O god, these daughters of ours,
they went astray, trampling the canons'! And mothers
still swear with a stone laid on their children's heads.

Bleating lambs rush and kneel by their mothers
and suckle them as they come down the slopes shining white
(does a small herd on a hill recognize its shepherd?).
In the rooms of men the lute hangs and sleeps,
no longer do heroes measure valor with bullets,
nor does the old plough scratch the tiny fields in the rocks.

The weathered cottage with sagging beams
will soon be a ruin on the slope.
And no one will remember – but who cares? –
that among these rocks where the devil lays eggs
and deer graze in moonlight a highland
mother once happened to bear a poet.

(5) LJUBLJANA

Ivan Cankar, *The Bailiff Yerney*

The novel tells the story of a bailiff's search for his 'rights' after his master dies and the farm is taken over by the son who dismisses Yerney. The bailiff has worked all his life on the farm, and made it the prosperous concern it now is. He is outraged but convinced that natural justice is on his side and 'the authorities' will endorse his claim to the land he sees as his own. He sets off on a journey, to Ljubljana and eventually to Vienna, to the court of the Emperor himself, in pursuit of his rights.

Ljubljana is a large town. Its houses are high; built in straight rows; so close one to another that no free space is left between them. The streets are always crowded, as if every day it were high mass and procession. There are so many priests that one might as well keep one's hat in one's hand. From morn till night bells ring and chime. It is like a fair; one is so bewildered one hardly knows what to look at, where to go, or to whom one dare speak. Yerney roamed through the streets for a long time, admiring the wonderful city. Then he went into a church, knelt before a side altar and prayed fervently. All was still and dark there in the church, so that Yerney could imagine he was speaking face to face with God. By the time his prayer was finished, faith had once again grown intense and profound.

'The road may still be very long,' he thought, 'the path may still be very hard and strewn with stones and thorns. But one day the road will come to an end; one day the door will open. God has hidden His justice as a miser hides his money. I may knock at a hundred doors in vain – the next one will fly open wide before me.'

He was once more in the streets, and asked of a city man who was passing by: 'Where are the judges, that I may make my charge and lay my case before them?'

At a loss, the gentleman looked at him, then smiled and said: 'Father, you had better look for a lawyer, who will speak for you and defend your cause.'

'Why should I need a lawyer, if my right is so evident that the blind might see it and the deaf hear it? I am not suing over a boundary, or a field-path; I do not want to deceive anybody. Why should I take a lawyer? I do not want a law-suit, it is justice I am seeking.'

'It will take you a long time to find it, my friend. Not a few have gone in search of it . . . they were many and they fell by the way – and the 'Pontius Pilates' washed their hands of it.'

With that he smiled and went his way.

'That man, too, has known injustice,' thought Yerney, 'for he laughed to keep himself from crying.'

(6) MACEDONIA

Živko Čingo, *Argil's Decoration*

*Čingo's two collections of short stories set in the village of
Paskvelija, describing the conflict of the old and the new, may be
read as a whole, and together they amount to a picture of the
world as a metaphor of the absurd.*

Paskelia is surely the loveliest spot in our valley, but, to be quite
honest, it's no setting for a story. It's so far away from the rest of the
world that you have to travel a good many miles, even from the nearest
road, before you hit the village. And now even the village has
vanished. 'Paskelia, my son, has gone to the devil,' said old Noer
Levkovski. 'Our Paskelia's dead, dear child. Poor Paskelia. Ah, and
what strapping young men were born there. Men and women such as
only the Good Lord Himself could have wished for. Those were people,
real people. Ah well, God rest their souls – our neighbours the Devievs,
uncle Nazer and Laster Tricheski – they were grand folk, indeed they
were. And old Daddy From – what about him? He was a musician if
ever I knew one. I swear you couldn't find such a fine piper even if you
travelled a long way from this valley of ours. A musician, you say –
that's nothing – even if he is a piper. Ah, but there was more to him
than that, you can take my word for it. Heaven help me if I lie. Old
Daddy From could wring the heart out of a stone with his playing. Ah
well, he's also gone.'

They've all gone, all gone from Paskelia. By now the woods have
surely grown up all around. Perhaps the birds have come down from the
hills and made their homes in the warm nests built by men. Perhaps the
vineyards of Paskelia have dried out, for vines are like people. They
soon wither if you leave them. And the vineyard cottages upon the hill
are surely deserted now. That was where the richest valley lay, right
below the cottages. In spring, of course, it was covered in green. That's
just what I wanted to tell you about. It was spring, and the whole valley
was green. Well, now, perhaps it wasn't really all green, but, believe
me, the leaves reached up till they brushed the sky and set it quivering
with green. Then everything round about was flushed with this golden
green of the sun and the leaves. Perhaps it wasn't all really like that,
you understand, but what the hell – that's how it seemed to me then. I
was in love. Yes, you see, even in those days one could fall in love.

(7) MACEDONIA

Mateja Matevski: *Roots*

The poet was born, in 1929, into an immigrant family in Istanbul, but soon after his birth the family moved to Macedonia, the landscape and spirit of which Matevski celebrates in his poetry.

We left our roots behind
by the far rivers
we left them behind under the stone
under the cloud under the dream
oh how we left them behind
under the corn under the flower under the oak
under the nightingale's plaint

We fled from them with the shallow words
of our age
we fled with empty day-dreams
with lies
with deceit
setting out secretly and hurriedly
we escaped through the sky of appearances
on wings of the wind with the colour of the bird
and the song of the snow

Bewitched we roamed through promised distances
we roamed through the rain over hilltop and rock
so we should come tired to our sleeplessness
that has lain locked behind the sun's grill

(8) MONTENEGRO

Milovan Djilas, *The Leper and Other Stories*

The prominent dissident, Djilas, best known perhaps for his The New Class and Conversations with Stalin, has written also several studies of his native Montenegro: Land Without Justice, Montenegro and Njegoš, an account of the life and work of the great nineteenth-century Montenegrin poet.

From my earliest youth my longing for the lake had been fostered by fearful tales in which it was so wonderful to lose oneself. It was scarcely an hour from my house, but it was deep in the forest on the far side of the Tara, and I saw it for the first time from the mountainside. With my elder brother, I had suddenly emerged from behind a knoll, and there below us, in the dizzy depths, stretched the dark, shadowy forest with the oblong lake, bluer and clearer than a piece of the sky itself. It was like a morning when one awakes from a dream. Everything seemed in vertiginous movement amid the mystery of the impassable, boundless forest.

I had dreamed of that first sight of the lake countless times, so that dream and reality perhaps were confused in memory.

However that may be, every time I burst out of the forest upon it, I still felt something of my first impression – of morning and of dream. Through long years, for all my life, that morning, that eye of the forest, glowed and shone in dream and in waking, in prison and in conflict with the realities of the everyday world.

Lake Biograd and the forests around it, huge trunks of every kind of tree close-packed against one another, were identified with my youth, with my first songs and my first disenchantments, and, forcing my way toward it through the freshness and dense greenery of the Jezerštica, I knew that I would not be able to resist my yearning to see its dark-blue eye shine once more upon me.

(9) MONTENEGRO

Petar Petrovic Njegoš, *The Mountain Wreath*

The Montenegrin Prince-Bishop Njegoš is one of the major figures of Serbian Romanticism. The dramatic poem from which these lines are taken, extolls the values of the Montenegrin way of life and is still known virtually by heart by many people in Serbia and Montenegro today.

Sirdar Radanja
Montenegrins, do you see this wonder?
Full fifty years I've spun of my life's yarn.
I've always spent my summers on Lovcen
and have clambered up to this high summit.
Hundreds of times have I gazed at the clouds
sailing in flocks from the sea down yonder
and covering this entire mountain range.
I've watched them float and rush now here, now there
with lightning bolts and with mighty rumble
and with the roar of terrible thunder.
A hundred times have I rested up here,
warming myself in the sun peacefully.
I've watched often the lightning beneath me,

listened to the thunder rending the sky,
as in the din of the frightening hail
the clouds below make everything barren –
but this wonder I have yet to witness!

Do you notice, upon your faith in God
how much there is of the sea and the coast,
of proud Bosnia and Hercegovina,
Albania way down there by the sea,
how much there is of our Montenegro?
The clouds cover all of these lands evenly!
The thunder's roar can be heard all around,
all beneath us the lightning keeps flashing,
but we alone are lying in the sun.
It has become rather hot up here now,
since the top of this mountain is always cool.

Obrad
Did you see this miracle and omen
when in the sky two flashes make a cross?
One flash came from Kom straight on to Lovcen;
the other flashed from Skadar to Ostrog.
They formed a cross made out of living fire.
How lovely it is just to look at it!
Never before in this wide world of ours
has anyone heard of or seen such a cross.
God help us Serbs in all our misfortune;
this, too, must be a good omen for us!

(10) OHRID

Blaže Koneski, *The Angel in St Sophia*

The poet is the central figure in the development of the Macedonian language and its literature since the second world war. This poem celebrates one of the Byzantine-style frescoes that abound in the medieval churches and monasteries of Macedonia, many of which have been expertly restored.

So many years you have lain
Under the plaster of the darkened wall
Now you are free in pure space again
Child of the deepest blue thought
Once again your eyes are blazing

And the wall is dawning like the sky.
But there's another hidden face
Beneath the plaster of my heart
The joy of my youth
Your sister in her beauty
No, there's no artist that can save her
With my life she'll fade forever.

(11) PANNONIA

Miroslav Krleža, *The Return of Philip Latinovicz*

Krleža is the most important Croatian writer of the twentieth century. This novel describes the return of a painter from self-imposed exile in Western Europe to his native Zagreb and the Pannonian countryside where his mother is now living.

At the end of the village, they met two nuns. [. . .]

Each of the sisters was carrying a basket of eggs and, meeting a gentleman driving in a carriage, they both greeted him piously, and with excessive humility, since he might possibly be an unknown representative of the authorities, and to the authorities it was a good thing to bow of one's own accord. For two thousand years now the church has carried baskets full of eggs, and during that time many authorities have changed both in towns and in provincial carriages. Such a policy of trifling courtesies could never do any harm.

The two sombre women in their Toledo costume with a gleam of sun on their starched head-dresses, quickened anew in Philip's mind images of the parallelism of events: those two nuns, with their skirts and rosaries and bizarre white head-dresses, like two strange, supernatural parrots, appeared there in front of him like two dark symbols of Kravoder mud. So the two centuries can persist parallel with each other for ages, like two alien races in a cage: monkeys and parrots! Those sombre women creep about the muddy hovels, steal baskets of eggs from cattle-breeders and coachmen, haul them along remote country roads to their ant-hills. Five thousand years old muddy Pannonia has lain there, with pigs grunting, horses neighing, and those sinister-looking parrots stealing eggs from the Pannonians like weasels, every one with her knight and saint in armour as her patron and celestial lover! Two worlds, next to each other at an unbridgeable distance. There was he, a godless, westernized, restless bird of passage, nervy and decadent, driving through Kravoder in Joe Podravec's carriage on a spring morning, with everything stirring, blooming, budding, everything moving like the wheel creaking under him and making a new rut in the road, rolling over so many tracks and footmarks on that road, down which numberless hordes had already disappeared into the mists. Yet all this was really a meaningless chaos!

Like the swish of a bare, shining axe, like the whirr of a steam-saw in the shining metallic revolutions of its keen circular blade, the higher overtones of our time cut like a razor through things and ideas, and vibrate with the clear note of a high-pitched exclamation, like the 'a' of a tuning-fork; so, impertinently, triumphantly, there sounded high above Philip's head the zoom of an airplane, echoing like the note of a celestial trumpet. Two worlds: London–Baghdad–Bombay in three days, and the inn at Kravoder with the nuns and their baskets of eggs! The Pannonian mire and civilization!

(12) The Island of Rab

Slobodan Novak, *Gold, Frankincense and Myrrh*

The novel offers an ironic account of the disillusion involved in living in a post-revolutionary society. The central character is the aged aristocrat, Madonna, who represents the former system stubbornly refusing to die out. Novak introduces a number of engaging, idiosyncratic characters and takes an infectious delight in mocking the sacred cows of his society, rejecting all cant in favour of the value of individual life.

I let the sun roll like a piglet in the hot milky dough of the golden day, scratch itself on the tops of the pine trees in the west, prick itself on the needles and cones. And when the wood grew darker, the sea was deserted, and the west grew grey, when the performance out there had come to an end, I was still drumming my fingers on my high balcony, on the 'balustrade', as though in the upper gallery, not knowing what to do with my freedom. I could have run round the whole town before darkness covered the sky, and before the boat from Rijeka carrying the day before yesterday's newspapers sounded its horn. I could have called in at Tariba's and settled there until closing time, or stood in that café watching the card-players led by Don Vikica. That was all I could have done. Or set off step by step on a patrol. Only, once the boat had come and gone, I would have somehow to move, because then the town looked like a church after vespers, the Potemkin lights along the shore went out, and the late Krok, the municipal policeman, would be able to find me by the arcade, frown at me with a watchful eye, and undertake swift steps in the sense of freeing public places of worthless elements.

(13) SARAJEVO

Izet Sarajlić, *Sarajevo*

Living in Sarajevo since 1949, much of Sarajlić's work is concerned with events from his own life and that of his whole generation who grew up in the second world war.

Now let all our dear and deathless ones find rest.
The swollen river flows under the 'Girls' Second' bridge.
Tomorrow is Sunday. Take the first train to Ilidža.
Assuming, of course, that it does not rain.
Tedious, ceaseless Sarajevo rain.
How did Cabrinović feel in gaol without it!
We curse it, swear at it, but still while it rains
We make assignations as in the most May-like May.
We curse it, swear at it, aware it will never turn
the Miljacka into the Guadalquivir or the Seine.
So what! Should I love you the less for that
and torment you the less through my pain?
Will that make my hunger for you
less and less my bitter right
not to sleep when the world is threatened by plague or war
and when the only words become 'don't forget' and 'farewell'?

But then, maybe this is not the town where I shall die,
it has certainly deserved one incomparably blither than I am.
This town in which I was perhaps not the happiest
but where everything is mine and where I can always
find at least one of you whom I love
and tell you that I am despairingly alone.
I could do that in Moscow too, but Esenin is dead,
and Yevtushenko surely somewhere in Georgia.
In Paris how could I call for an ambulance
when even Villon's calls for help were left unanswered?
Here, if I call the very poplars, my fellow citizens,
even they will know what it is that causes my pain.
For this is a town in which I was perhaps not the happiest,
but where even the rain is more than mere rain.

(14) SERBIA

Dobrica Ćosić, *A Time of Death*

Ćosić is the author of a series of novels depicting twentieth-century Serbian history. This work is the first part of a trilogy devoted to the first world war.

From Rudnik, General Mišić looked on an extraordinary scene: Podrinje, Mačva, and Pocerina had turned round and were streaming toward Šumadija and Pomoravlje, as though the Austro–Hungarian army had overturned that part of Serbia, with its villages and towns, and shaken it out – sky, river, and mud – to the accompaniment of the rumble of artillery. And now – from hills and valleys, amid mingled cloud and falling leaves – every living creature, everyone capable of flight, and everything that could be carried or dragged, were moving along the one road that led between fences and plum orchards, and fields of unharvested corn, to the center of Serbia. In this upheaval the road itself was fractured, disappearing into woods, villages, and empty fields. Down this glutinous, well-trodden defile – between blackened hedges and bare boundary stones, amid the mounting terror of both humans and animals – men and cattle, carts and dogs, poultry and domestic animals were all hurtling downward. All in the same direction. Opposite him.

For today he alone was travelling in the opposite direction; he alone was going toward the place from which everyone else was fleeing. Since leaving Kragujevac, he had not met or overtaken a living soul. It seemed that not even the crows were flying westward toward the battle front. Cold gusts of wind whipped up the rain; the mountain tops were already powdered with snow. Everywhere he encountered uneasiness in children and animals, and reproach and hatred in the glances of women and old men. He did not hide his face with his military cap, nor with the curtains of Prince Alexander's car. He met and endured every single look.

(15) SERBIA

Slobodan Selenić, *Fathers and Forefathers*

An important strand in this novel by one of the most prominent contemporary Serbian writers, describes the experiences of Elizabeth Blake, an Englishwoman who marries a Serb while he is studying in Britain and then moves to live with him in Belgrade. Her letters home to a Serbian friend reflect her gradual mastery of the Serbian language and her impressions of her new surroundings.

'Now, my dear Rachel, it is worst when I can't understand someone or something at all. Then I rage. Like a wild cat. Stevan says, Am I stupid? This began with that damned cousin Gordana. I come, maybe one or two weeks, and Stevan says to me that we have to go to a party at the Glishich family. Good, I think – I sit, I am silent, I survive. We get to the Glishich house, and there are a lot of people and they all know Stevan and they want to meet me. I was right off terrible muddled. All come to me and say, I am the godmother, I am the sister of an aunt, I am the cousin once removed, and I am saying left and right all I know: 'So please to meet you,' 'Delighted', but not enough. They are not horrible, to the contrary, kind, and all ask the same: how do I like Beograd, and I know that answer, Stevan taught me, so I say: Finest position in the world, the mouth of the River Danube into the River Sava, people so hospitable and all of them, they're pleased, but then they want, I don't know what for, they all want me right away to drink more *rakiya* and eat more meat and hot peppers, which I cannot, so I am even more muddled. And then, just when the commotion is largest, up comes that Gordana, sits down next and says: I am not a close relative with Stevan, but I love Stevan and Father Milutin very much, like my heart of hearts, because Father Milutin paid for school, money and everything, so I would have my crust of bread today and so this Gordana is asking me now if I want, the way she wants, for us to be *posestrima*. The slightest idea I haven't what *posestrima* is, but Stevan is far away, can't help me quick, and I see, someone else sits down next to me and says that he is the old uncle, and I, completely muddled, say all right, I think it would be best to be a *posestrima*. But that was a big mistake, because then Gordana starts to cry, she says, now we are together to death, she and I, and she kisses me, hugs, tears roll down her face, she says, never has such happiness been hers. You see, how furious I was, that I wasn't muddled any more, so I ask myself, oh my Lord, what is this, I am crazy or she is crazy, but nothing helps, because I can't hit that Gordana who does not let me go. Luckily Stevan comes, says we've had coffee, we can leave. I am glad, it is over.'

(16) SLOVENIA

Ciril Kosmač, *A Day in Spring*

The novel is set in Slovene territory fought over during the first world war by Austrians and Italians and in the second world war by Partisans, Italians and Germans. It describes the narrator's return after 15 years in exile to his beautiful native valley where the Alpine and Mediterranean worlds meet.

And yet I did not jump up at once. It was as if I were afraid that my landscape here, close behind my window, actual and alive, would not prove the same as the image of it I had borne with me in my memory in foreign parts. Because that is how it is: if you leave home while you're young you carry away only that which is dear to you. And what is dear is beautiful too, and grows more beautiful with the passing of the years, like oil paintings which mellow with time which softens the harsh contrasts and fills tiny crevices with microscopic light grey particles of dust. Similarly the faces that dwell in our mind are all fair and noble without harsh features or warts. All the landscapes are marvellous – the houses white, the roofs red, and the windows always bright. Some reflect the sun in the morning, others in the evening, but they are all aglow all the time because times and seasons do not change in a picture. No liquid manure flows down the cart tracks; there are no importunate midges, nor tiresome horseflies. All is quite beautiful. And that is why I did not jump up, but lay there blinking so as to see the picture of my valley once more in my mind's eye before it presented itself in all actuality to my sight.

Outside at this moment the sun was already a good fathom above the hilltops. The valley was divided lengthwise into two aspects. On the sunny side, a gentle, fertile slope still damp with dew; dreamy and blurred, it was screened by finely sifted strands of sunlight; while our steep and barren shady side was vivid and bathed in sunshine. The heath was already dry and so was that yellow, fluffy spring flower the name of which I forget. It quivers under the warm touch of the sunlight. Safe in its protection it fearlessly unfolds, opening its cups and with its perfume invites the fat, yellow, downy bumblebees, so like itself, buzzing on a low note as they seek for honey and at the same time lend their aid to the flowers in their loves. Such is a May morning on every clearing, along every cartroad, on every hill and grassy upland, and also at Obrekar Oaks. The laburnum is in flower among the young green of the beeches, the aspens are already so far in foliage that their leaves are almost aquiver; the cuckoo calls in Wolf's gully and over everything broods the endless expanse of a cloudless azure sky. And lo! – against the sky a circling eagle and his mate . . . They have left their safe secret shelter in the rocks below Vranyek and sailed forth, corsairs of the skies, upon their morning's predatory flight.

(17) SLOVENIA
Francè Prešeren, *The Master Theme*

This poem is the final sonnet of Prešeren's 'Garland' of fifteen sonnets, and represents a considerable tour-de-force, as it is composed of lines taken from the other fourteen sonnets, and yet reads as a fluent and moving poem in its own right. A great admirer of Petrarch, Prešeren was particularly drawn to the sonnet form, which he adapted to the Slovene language, thus establishing it as a popular form among his followers.

A Slovene wreath your poet has entwined;
A record of my pain and of your praise,
Since from my heart's deep roots have sprung these lays,
These tear-stained flowers of a poet's mind.

They come from where no man can sunshine find,
Unblest by soothing winds of warmer days;
Above them savage peaks the mountains raise,
Where tempests roar and nature is unkind.

They were all fed on many a plaint and tear;
Frail growth these blossoms had, so sad and few,
As over them malignant storm-clouds flew.

Behold how weak and faded they appear!
Send by your rays their glory to renew –
Fresh flowers will spread fragrance far and near.

(18) SUBOTICA
Danilo Kiš, *Garden, Ashes*

A haunting account of a boy's childhood in wartime, dominated by the figure of the boy's father, a Jew, who mysteriously disappears. The rich, lyrical texture of the work has won it wide international acclaim.

The branches of the wild chestnut trees on our street reached out to touch each other. Vaults overgrown with ivy-like leafage thrust in between these tall arcades. On ordinary windless days, this whole architectural structure would stand motionless, solid in its daring. From time to time the sun would hurtle its futile rays through the dense leafage. Once they had penetrated the slanting, interwined branches, these rays would quiver for a while before melting and dripping onto the Turkish cobblestones like liquid silver. We pass underneath these solemn arches, grave and deserted, and hurry down the arteries of the city. Silence is everywhere, the dignified solemnity of a holiday morning. The postmen and salesclerks are still asleep behind the closed, dusty shutters. As we move along past the low one-storey houses, we glance at each other and smile, filled with respect: the wheezings of the last sleepers are audible through the dark swaying curtains and accordion shutters. The great ships of sleep are sailing the dark Styx. At times it seems as though the engines will run down, that we are on the verge of a catastrophic failure. One engine starts to rattle, to lose its cadence, to falter, as if the ship has run aground on some underwater reef. But the damage has apparently been repaired, or possibly there had never been any damage at all. We are sailing downstream, at thirty knots. Alongside the panting sleepers stand large metal alarm clocks, propped up on their hind legs like roosters, pecking away at the fine seeds of the minutes, and then – charged to the point of an explosion, stuffed, enraged – they strain their legs against the marble surface of the night table just before beginning to crow triumphantly, to crow in swaying, bloody crests.

(19) Višegrad

Ivo Andrić, *The Bridge on the Drina*

Andrić, who won the Nobel prize for literature in 1961, set many of his works in his native Bosnia, exploiting it as a microcosm in which the potential for cultural, religious and national misunderstanding and conflict is concentrated because of the mixed Catholic, Orthodox, Muslim and Jewish population.

Here, where the Drina flows with the whole force of its green and foaming waters from the apparently closed mass of the dark steep mountains, stands a great clean-cut stone bridge with eleven wide sweeping arches. From this bridge spreads fanlike the whole rolling valley with the little oriental town of Višegrad and all its surroundings, with hamlets nestling in the folds of the hills, covered with meadows, pastures and plum-orchards, and criss-crossed with walls and fences and dotted with shaws and occasional clumps of evergreens. Looked at from a distance through the broad arches of the white bridge it seems as if one can see not only the green Drina, but all that fertile and cultivated countryside and the southern sky above.

On the right bank of the river, starting from the bridge itself, lay the centre of the town, with the market-place, partly on the level and partly on the hillside. On the other side of the bridge, along the left bank, stretched the Maluhino Polje, with a few scattered houses along the road which led to Sarajevo. Thus the bridge, uniting the two parts of the Sarajevo road, linked the town with its surrounding villages.

Actually, to say 'linked' was just as true as to say that the sun rises in the morning so that men may see around them and finish their daily tasks, and sets in the evening that they may be able to sleep and rest from the labours of the day. For this great stone bridge, a rare structure of unique beauty, such as many richer and busier towns do not possess ('There are only two others such as this in the whole Empire', they used to say in olden times) was the one real and permanent crossing in the whole middle and upper course of the Drina and an indispensable link on the road between Bosnia and Serbia and further, beyond Serbia, with other parts of the Turkish empire, all the way to Stambul. The town and its outskirts were only the settlements which always and inevitably grow up around an important centre of communications and on either side of great and important bridges.

Here also in time the houses crowded together and the settlements multiplied at both ends of the bridge. The town owed its existence to the bridge and grew out of it as if from an imperishable root.

(20) ZAGREB

Dubravka Ugrešić,
Fording the Stream of Consciousness

The author, born in 1949, is one of the liveliest writers of her generation. The setting of her novel is an international literary congress taking place at the Intercontinental Hotel in Zagreb.

Through the bus's tinted glass he watched long, boring streets of housing complexes until at last they came to the Old Town, the cathedral backed by a soft blue hill, a perfect backdrop for a film set in a small central European city.

'This view must be a favourite on postcards,' he said.

'How did you know?'

'Just guessing,' said Troshin with a smile. 'What do you think, Vitya?'

'Ah,' Sapozhnikov said noncomitally. He was still hugging his leather bag, still staring at her. She wore her hair short, with a long lock left purposefully hanging over her forehead, and sported flappy Chaplinlike slacks, blue-and-white striped stockings, and pink tennis shoes. The only ornament on her broad-shouldered man's jacket was a cheap pin in the form of a small oval mirror. At one point Troshin caught his own tired face in it and, when the girl turned, Vitya's open-mouthed stare. This was Vitya's second trip abroad. He had been in Bulgaria the year before. Things were finally going right for him. Things are finally going right for me, he'd said to Troshin in the plane.

When they piled out of the bus, the young woman proposed they take a taxi to the hotel, 'though it's only a ten-minute walk'. They walked. On the way Troshin kept his professional eye out for the telling first impression. Troshin found that all cities, or at least all cities in socialist countries, have one trait that stands out. In Moscow it is the incontestably enormous number of shops with signs like REMONT CHASOV or REMONT SUMOK, as if Muscovites spent all their time having their broken watches or torn handbags repaired. In Zagreb he was reminded of his favourite authors Ilf and Petrov: a FRIZERSKI SALON at every step as if the good people of Zagreb did nothing but have their hair done.

'You seem to have a lot of hairdressers here,' he said.

'Why not?' the young woman replied, blowing the lock out of her eyes.

Unlike Ilf and Petrov, Troshin noticed no undertakers.

When in ten minutes they actually did reach the Intercontinental, Troshin thought, 'Zagreb must be tiny.'

Biographies and important works

ANDRIĆ, Ivo (1892–1975). Serbian writer. Born in the small town of **Travnik**, in Bosnia, Andrić spent the first years of his life in **Višegrad**, the setting for many of his works and site of the famous bridge over the Drina (Extract 19). He attended secondary school in **Sarajevo** and university in **Zagreb**, Vienna and Kraków. He was involved in the Young Bosnia Movement, responsible for the assassination of Archduke Franz Ferdinand in Sarajevo in 1914. He spent the war years first in prison and then internment in Bosnia. After the end of the war he lived in Zagreb, participating in literary life there before moving to **Belgrade** and joining the Diplomatic Service. This career took him to numerous European cities, but also left him time for his writing: he published several volumes of short stories between the wars. His last post was that of Minister in Berlin, 1937–39.

Ivo Andrić

On the outbreak of war, he opted to return to Belgrade where he lived quietly, refusing to publish under the quisling government. This self-imposed embargo gave him the time to write longer works, and in 1945 he published three novels, *Na Drini ćuprija* (*The Bridge on the Drina*), *Travnička hronika* (*Travnik Chronicle*), and *Gospodjica* (*Miss*). In the years following the second world war, Andrić returned mainly to his favoured form, the short story, although he left an unfinished novel, *Omerpaša Latas* (*Omer Pasha Latas*), intended to complete a trilogy devoted to the three Bosnian towns of **Višegrad**, **Travnik** and **Sarajevo**.

Andrić's diplomatic career, his experience of several different European countries, and his wide reading in European literature guarantee his work a firm frame of cultural reference. Readers should not be misled by the fact that he chose to set the majority of his writings in the remote 'exotic' province of Bosnia: Andrić uses this setting as a microcosm of human society because of its concentration of cultures, Christian (Catholic and Orthodox), Muslim and Jewish, and consequent potential for con-

flict. Having lived through times of exceptional violence, Andrić does not shirk from depicting brutality and hatred in order to expose universal patterns of experience. But individual experience is counterbalanced always by other examples, so that the picture that emerges from his work is subtle and complex. It is characterized also by an unshakeable faith in the power of the imagination. A recurrent image for the varied constraints imposed on the individual by the circumstances of his birth and by society is the prison. In his most concentrated work, *Prokleta avlija* (*The Damned Yard*), 1954, the prison yard suggests that the only means of escape from such constraint is through the imagination, through the deep human need for stories and story telling, the capacity this gives us to formulate experience and to connect with other peoples and generations in order to begin to understand our lives.

ARALICA, Ivan (1930–). Croatian novelist. Aralica graduated in Slavonic studies in **Zadar**, where he worked as a teacher. He has become established as one of the leading figures in contemporary Croatian literature. His style is somewhat traditional compared to the emphasis on the Modernist and Postmodernist modes dominating the literary scene. His first works treated contemporary ethical and moral conflicts: *Ima netko siv i zelen* (*There is Someone Grey and Green*), 1977, but most of his works set such themes in historical contexts: *Psi u trgovištu* (*Dogs in the Market Place*), 1979, widely considered his best work; *Put bez sna* (*Journey Without Sleep*), 1982; *Duše robova* (*The Souls of Slaves*), 1984; *Okvir za mržnju* (*Framework for Hatred*), 1987. Aralica uses historical settings, filled with rich, informative detail, to treat both perennial and topical themes. His style combines features of the ancient chronicles, traditional oral literature, devotional works and the contemporary language. Aralica's novels focus attention on a section of Croatian society rarely treated in literature before him: the peasantry of the hinterland, the ancient 'Morlachs'. In his recent novels, Aralica has been turning increasingly to contemporary life.

CANKAR, Ivan (1876–1918). Slovene poet, prose writer and dramatist. The son of a village tailor, Cankar's childhood was spent in great poverty. He was born in **Vrhinka** (20 km south of Ljubljana), where there is a memorial museum. While at secondary school in **Ljubljana** he came into contact with contemporary writers, representatives of the Moderne, and began to publish verse. He founded a secret literary society of which he was president. He went to Vienna to study technology, but did not complete his studies, devoting himself increasingly to writing. He lived for ten years in the workers' suburb of Otakring, in the midst of poverty and misery. It was here that he wrote his finest works and became active in the Social Democratic Party. In 1909 he returned to Ljubljana. His appearance brought a new tone and fresh ideas to Slovene literature: his breadth of vision and radical outlook were quite new to the prevailing conservative cultural circles, as may be seen from the fact that the Bishop of Ljubljana bought up the entire edition of his first volume of poems (*Erotica*, 1899) and had it burned. Thereafter Cankar turned to prose (Extract 5), trying his hand at various genres with uncompromising energy. Well read, with a sound knowledge of several languages, hard-working and productive, he made a unique contribution to the

range and maturity of Slovene prose writing. There is a memorial room in **Roznik Hill**, above Ljubljana where Cankar lived in his Ljubljana days.

ČINGO, Živko (1935–   ). Macedonian prose writer and dramatist. Čingo was born in the village of Velgošta, near **Ohrid**, studied in **Skopje**, where he later worked at the Institute for Folklore and then as Director of Drama at the National Theatre. His original, suggestive prose is concerned with the conflict between the old and the new, and offers convincing portraits of peasant psychology, based on a deep understanding and knowledge of the rich traditional oral culture (Extract 6). While his language is close to the everyday language of the village, his world is a world of dream and hallucination.

CRNJANSKI, Miloš (1893–1977). Serbian poet and prose writer. Born into the large Serbian community in southern Hungary, which became part of Yugoslavia after the first world war, Crnjanski was educated in Timişoara, **Rijeka**, Vienna and **Belgrade**. He joined the Diplomatic Service and travelled widely in Europe. Posted to London in 1941, he remained there after the war until he returned to Belgrade in 1965. Crnjanski belonged to the first generation of Serbian Modernists to emerge after the first world war. His early poems are marked by angry protest at the dehumanization of the war. The same tone characterizes his short novel, *Dnevnik o Čarnojeviću* (*Diary about Čarnojević*), 1921, portraying a psyche undermined by the war. His most important work is *Seobe* (*Migrations*), published in two distinct parts in 1929 and 1962. The novel represents a concentrated statement of the historical experience of the Serbs, who moved from their heartland in 1690 and were permitted to settle in the Habsburg border region of southern Hungary in return for military service. They carry with them a sense of impermanence, of lives cut off from their historical roots and dominated by a sense that they must move on, in search of an ultimate home in the Orthodox motherland of Russia, a dream which proves illusory. The same sense of exile characterizes *Roman o Londonu* (*Novel about London*), 1971. Having started to write as a poet, Crnjanski cultivated in all his works an idiosyncratic, poetic style which reaches its height of expression in the concentrated form of the first part of *Seobe*.

ĆOSIĆ, Dobrica (1921–   ). Serbian novelist. Ćosić is concerned, in all his works, with twentieth-century Serbian history. His first novel *Daleko je sunce* (*Far Away is the Sun*), 1951, represented an important milestone in the depiction of the second world war in the literatures of Yugoslavia: it illustrates, without oversimplification, a typical moral dilemma faced by the Partisans. Several of Ćosić's novels are concerned with the history of one family from the last decade of the nineteenth century, focusing particularly on their destiny in the first world war to which Ćosić devotes a trilogy, *Vreme smrti* (*A Time of Death*), 1972–1975 (Extract 14). Ćosić's novels are concerned above all with the main political issues confronting the Serbs in the twentieth century, and in many ways they may be seen as a substitute for direct political activity. For many years he represented a kind of unofficial opposition, but later allied himself prominently to the nationalist cause of President Milošević, including a brief spell as President of Milošević's Yugoslavia.

DJILAS, Milovan (1911–1995). Prose writer (Extract 8). Born in the village of **Podbišće**, near Kolašin in Montenegro, he was active in the underground Communist movement before the war and spent some time in prison. He worked on a number of progressive literary journals before joining the Partisans and encouraging armed resistance in Montenegro at the outbreak of the second world war. Rising rapidly to high office, he was expelled from the Communist Party of Yugoslavia in 1954 for the several articles in *Savremene teme* (*Contemporary Themes*) because of their liberal position. He was one of the main instigators of the literary–philosophical journal *Nova misao* (*New Thought*), 1953, regarded as 'revisionist' by the regime. Later he was tried and spent many years in prison for publishing hostile propaganda in the West. He used his time in prison tirelessly, translating Milton's *Paradise Lost* and writing a series of lengthy works.

DUČIĆ, Jovan (1871–1943). Serbian poet. Dučić was born in **Trebinje**, Hercegovina. He studied in Geneva and Paris, joined the diplomatic service and, finding himself in Madrid when Yugoslavia was invaded by the German army, he went to the USA and died two years later in Indiana. The central figure of the 'Serbian Moderna' period in the first decades of the twentieth century, Dučić is seen as the main contributor to the 'golden age' of Serbian poetry in those years, paying painstaking attention to form and writing large numbers of sonnets, which often have a fluid quality contrasting with the strictness of the form. His poetry is a distinctive blend of Parnassian and Symbolist influences, varying in range from period piece evocations of **Dubrovnik** in the sixteenth and seventeenth centuries (Extract 3) to deeply personal, melancholy mood pictures and symbols of subtle power.

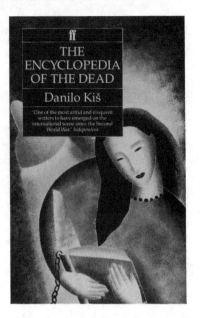

KIŠ, Danilo (1935–1989). Serbian novelist. Kiš is one of the best known contemporary Yugoslav writers in the West, particularly in France, where he lived for many years, before his untimely death. 'I write because I am dissatisfied with myself and the world. To express that dissatisfaction. And to survive!', so wrote Kiš in 1985. He belonged to a generation whose sensibilities were sharpened by first-hand experience of the violent realities of the twentieth century. He lived through the war as the child of a Jewish father who disappeared in what were to him mysterious circumstances: the search for this father colours much of his autobiographical novel *Bašta, pepeo* (*Garden, Ashes*) 1965 (Extract 18), and dominates some of his other works. His close observation of the oppression of Communist rule and particularly the Stalinist purges provides the material for his novel *Grobnica za Borisa Davidoviča* (*A Tomb for Boris Davidovich*), 1976. *Enciklopedija mrtvih* (*The Encyclopedia of the Dead*), 1983, is a collection of nine short stories, a meditation on the nature of love and death, where reality and fantasy, biblical stories, ancient legend and modern history combine in fresh and often startling textures. Some of the pieces are reminiscent of the work of Jorge Luis Borges in their quasi-scholarly reconstruction of largely fictitious texts and blurring of the boundaries between fact and fiction. But Kiš's tone is original and distinctive. A prevailing impression of sinister intrigue, terror and destruction is redeemed by occasional black humour and sheer poetry. At the same time, the lyrical quality of many of the stories is counterbalanced by Kiš's readiness to confront and depict violence and brutality. Ultimately, this complex material conveys a sense of the vitality and resilience of the human spirit, able to control and overcome essentially brutal experience by transforming it ironically into stories which shirk neither from violence nor from pure lyricism.

KOCBEK, Edvard (1904–1981). Slovene poet, philosopher, religious thinker, soldier, politician and short-story writer. Kocbek was born in the village of **Sv. Jurij kraj Ščavnice,** studied theology at **Maribor** and Romance languages in **Ljubljana,** Berlin, Lyon and Paris. Taught French in various Yugoslav cities. During the second world war Kocbek led the

Christian Socialist guerilla movement, of which he was leader, into action alongside the Communist Partisans. After the war he was vice-president of Slovenia for a short time, but soon broke with the Communists to spend the next fifteen years banned from publication. It was not until 1977 that two volumes of his *Selected Poems* appeared. In his life and work he strove for the right to express his Christian views and emerges as an uncompromising, courageous, and wise man, who had a profound influence on the following generation of Slovene intellectuals.

KONESKI, Blaže (1921–   ). Macedonian poet, short-story writer, essayist and linguist. Born in **Nebregovo**, educated at **Prilep** and **Kragujevac, Belgrade** and Sofia, Koneski taught at the **University of Skopje**, held numerous important offices in Macedonian cultural life, including the first Presidency of the Macedonian Academy of Sciences and Arts – he is an outstanding figure in both scholarship and creative writing. Koneski is the author of the first history of the Macedonian language and a comprehensive normative grammar, as well as other basic linguistic texts. He has an international reputation as a linguist, essayist, short-story writer and poet, and, as such, his contribution to establishing and enriching the Macedonian literary language is immeasurable. His poetry is both universal in its themes and deeply rooted in the legends and traditions of his native region (Extract 10): he uses figures from the traditional oral poetry to express timeless concerns.

KOSMAČ, Ciril (1910–1980). Slovene prose-writer. Born in the Slovene village of **Slap** which was then part of Italy, Kosmač was repeatedly convicted of hostile acts and eventually banned from all Italian schools because of his 'irredentist' activities. In 1931 he fled to **Ljubljana** and later lived for a time in France and in England. In 1944 he joined the Partisans in Slovenia. After the war he edited various literary journals and worked as director of 'Triglav-film' in Ljubljana, before settling in **Portorož** as a freelance writer. Widely regarded as one of the foremost Slovene prose writers of his time, Kosmač was concerned particularly with the life of villagers in the Slovene littoral under Italian rule, during the second world war and after the liberation (Extract 16). His concise, plastic prose is characterized by a lyrical, meditative quality, a blend of realism and fantasy.

KRLEŽA, Miroslav (1893–1981). Croatian playwright, novelist, essayist and poet. Krleža is the most important figure in Croatian literature in the twentieth century. Born in **Zagreb** where he attended elementary school, he was sent to the military academy in Budapest. During the first world war he fought in Galicia. Between the wars he spent some time in **Belgrade** in 1933 and 1934, when he founded the literary journal *Danas* with a group of Belgrade intellectuals. But he lived most of his life in Zagreb, where he edited a series of literary journals, often providing much of their contents himself. His writings were frequently censored or banned for their radical views, and always generated discussion and polemics. He refused to publish under the Ustasha government in the Independent State of Croatia during the second world war. After the liberation, he returned to intensive literary activity. From 1950 until his death he was director of the Yugoslav Lexicographical Institute in Zagreb and editor of the *Encyclopaedia of Yugoslavia*.

He began by writing poetry, and his most important verse work, considered by some his most important work altogether, is *Balade Petrice Kerempuha* (*The Ballads of Petrica Kerempuh*), 1936. Written in the 'kajkavian' dialect of **Zagreb** and its surroundings, enriched with archaisms, and characterized by gallows humour, the ballads express the history of the Croatian people through the voice of a peasant, victim through the centuries of poverty and persecution. This voice recurs in some of Krleža's stories about the first world war, where its authenticity makes a marked contrast with the caricatured portraits of officers in the Austro–Hungarian Army.

Krleža is chiefly known as a playwright. His first, Expressionist, plays deal with some of the basic myths of Western civilization. Krleža's 'classic' work is the cycle of plays relating to the Glembaj family, *Gospoda Glembajevi* (*The Glembays*), 1928, *U agoniji* (*Death-Throes*), 1928, and *Leda*, 1958. Krleža uses the family to express his vision of the rise and fall of the bourgeoisie in Central Europe, its origins in violence and exploitation, its hypocrisy and corruption. The plays, particularly the first, are strong statements, depending, like all Krleža's works, on the conflict of ideas. He wrote two other important plays: *Vučjak* and *Aretej* (*Aretheus*), 1959, in which he takes a broader view of the destructive effects of human stupidity through the ages.

Krleža published two volumes of stories, *Hrvatski bog Mars* (*The Croatian God Mars*), 1922, concerned with the first world war, and *Novele* (*Short Stories*), 1924, in which he explores some of the main themes of his novels: the fate of the intellectual in 20th-century European, particularly provincial, society. The best known of Krleža's four novels is *Povratak Filipa Latinovića* (*The Return of Philip Latinovicz*), 1932, his most developed account of the alienation of the artist (Extract 11). The others are *Na rubu pameti* (*On the Edge of Reason*), 1938, concerned with human stupidity and the individual's impotence to take a stand in the face of corruption and hypocrisy; *Banket u Blitvi* (*Banquet in Blitva*), 1938–39, a satirical picture of Central European society and *Zastave* (*Banners*), 1967, a vast panorama of modern Croatian history. One of the essential characteristics of Krleža's work is the dramatic clash of ideas and this drama is reflected in the numerous volumes of essays, diaries and polemical writings which represent an important contribution to the history of the cultural and political life of Croatia between the wars.

MARINKOVIĆ, Ranko (1913 –). Croatian novelist and playwright. Born on the island of **Vis**, Marinković studied in **Zagreb**, and worked at the Croatian National Theatre, and the Academy of Dramatic Art in Zagreb. His first short stories, published just before the second world war, are satirical observations on small town life, mostly in **Dalmatia**. His first play, *Albatros*, 1939, displays an intuitive understanding of the theatre as a medium. Since the war he has continued to write short stories, evoking the atmosphere of Dalmatian communities with black humour, collected in *Proze* (*Stories*), 1948, and *Ruke* (*Hands*), 1953, widely considered to be the best volume of short stories in Croatian literature. He has also written plays, of which the best known is *Glorija* (*Gloria*), 1955, an entertaining tragicomedy in which a

Mateja Matevski

circus dancer is asked by a monk to play the Virgin Mary in a tableau in the church in an effort to attract a larger congregation; and the novel, *Kiklop* (*The Cyclops*), 1965, which concerns the bewildered alienation of an intellectual in an urban setting on the eve of the second world war, and the fate of modern man, his uncertainties and fear in the face of encroaching totalitarianism. The novel's most striking quality is its burlesque style, a feature of all Marinković's work. The title of his most recent novel, *Zajednička kupka* (*Shared Dip*), 1980, described as an 'anti-novel', may be seen as a metaphor for the quagmire which human beings have made of the world.

MATEVSKI, Mateja (1929–). Macedonian poet. Born in Istanbul, Matevski studied in **Skopje** where he worked as a journalist and editor of several literary journals, and then as director of Radio-TV Skopje. His poetry (Extract 7) combines several of the main features of Balkan poetry: precise evocation of the natural world, vivid imagery and a sense of rootedness in the rich oral tradition, conveyed partly by a turn of phrase which tends to the epigram. At the same time these poems have a symbolic power which suddenly breaks through the careful description of their detailed material world.

NJEGOŠ, Petar Petrović (1813– 1851). Prince-Bishop of **Montenegro** from 1833 until his death. As head of state as well as of the church in Montenegro, Njegoš travelled extensively, particularly to Austria and Russia on political missions. Despite the demands of his public life, he was remarkably widely read in the Classics and European literature. His stature and breadth of reference made him one of the dominant figures of the Romantic period in Serbian literature. His best known work, *Gorski vijenac* (*The Mountain Wreath*), 1947, brings together the subject matter and to a large extent the style of the oral epic tradition in its many-layered account and celebration of the life and culture of Montenegro (Extract 9). His other great work is a long philosophical poem about the Fall, *Luča mikrokozma* (*The Ray of the Microcosm*), 1845, regarded by many as his finest achievement.

NOVAK, Slobodan (1924–). Croatian prose writer. Born in **Split**, Novak spent his childhood on the island of **Rab**, which plays a central part in his work. He was educated in **Split**, **Rijeka** and **Zagreb**, where he worked in the publishing house Zora until his retirement. Novak made his first impact with his short novel

Izgubljeni zavičaj (*Lost Homeland*), 1954, greeted as a lyrical evocation of childhood and of the restorative power of landscape. One of its central images is the identification of the Island of childhood with impotence and loss, and the Mainland of maturity with an inevitable set of obstacles. Novak's most important work is his novel, *Mirisi, zlato i tamjan* (*Gold, Frankincense and Myrrh*), 1968 (Extract 12), a first-person narrative of the experience of being trapped on the Island, caring for the aged, former landowner, Madonna. The narrator gradually comes to appreciate the true nature of the Old Order which Madonna represents – its intellectual freedom. The theme of the lost innocence of childhood is bound up here with the specific loss of illusion of the narrator's generation: the betrayal of expectations aroused by the rhetoric of revolution. The novel is characterized by an engaging generalized self-irony and the humorous treatment of a group of idiosyncratic islanders. Novak's central theme is developed also in his other major work, the trilogy of short stories, *Izvanbrodski dnevnik* (*Off-Ship Diary*), 1988.

PAVIĆ, Milorad (1929–   ). Serbian poet and prose writer. Pavić was born in **Belgrade**. Educated in **Belgrade** and **Zagreb**, he taught history of literature at **Novi Sad** university. Renowned at first for his scholarly studies and erudite, meditative poetry, in the mid-1970s Pavić turned also to prose: three volumes of short stories were published between 1973 and 1982. His reputation abroad rests on *Hazarski rečnik* (*The Dictionary of the Khazars*), 1982. This work offers scope for the exercise of Pavić's wit and erudition. The novel takes the form of an intricate scholarly mystery: to trace the history of the Khazars, a tribe known to have lived on the borders of what is now Russia in the late 9th century AD. All that was known of them was gathered in a single book of knowledge, *The Khazar Dictionary*, published in 1691 in an edition of 500 copies, all of which have been destroyed. The tribe itself disappeared at the precise moment when its ruler, the kaghan, had summoned a Christian, a Moslem and a Jewish scholar to interpret a dream and thereby decide which religion his people should adopt. The novel is arranged in three books, Red, Green and Yellow which contain respectively the Christian, Moslem and Jewish versions of all known information about the lost tribe. Readers are invited to 'use' the dictionary as they wish – following the different accounts of one event or character, reading each one through to the end, dipping in randomly or reading from the end to the beginning. There is a further dimension to the mystery: the novel is published in two versions – a male and a female one. Readers are warned that they are identical except for one paragraph which is 'crucially different. The choice is yours.' A second novel, *Pejzaž naslikan čajem* (*Landscape Painted with Tea*) was published in 1990.

PEKIĆ, Borislav (1930–1992). Born in **Titograd**, Montenegro, Pekić completed his secondary education in **Belgrade**. For much of his life, he lived in London, where he could write in peace, while maintaining close links with the literary life of Belgrade. A powerful intellect and prolific writer of novels, stories, plays, radio dramas and essays, Pekić has been a major, ironic presence in the literary life of Serbia since 1965 when his first novel, *Vreme čuda* (*A Time of Miracles*) was published. The novel exploits the Gospel accounts of Christ's miracles to explore the nature of dogma and its consequences for those affected by it, by focusing on the individuals on whom miracles were carried out in the name of a written 'Law'. The effects, unseen by Christ and his disciples who immediately move on, are always ultimately detrimental. Pekić continued to write short thematic novels (Extract 1) as 'light relief' while his main energy was concentrated on his vast eight-volume panorama of Balkan life from the late Middle Ages to the second world war, *Zlatno runo* (*The Golden Fleece*), 1977–82. His experimental work *Besnilo* (*Rabies*), 1983, set at Heathrow airport and describing the emergency following an outbreak of the disease, contains elements of the thriller and science fiction to give a bleak philosophical account of late twentieth-century European society. His novel *1999*, published in 1984, and described as 'an anthropological tale' is an Orwellian antiutopia.

POPA, Vasko (1922–1990). Serbian poet. Popa was born in a mixed Serbian and Romanian village in **Vojvodina**. He was educated in Vienna, **Belgrade** and Bucharest. Popa was instrumental in ensuring the right to absolute freedom of inspiration in the early 1950s. While individual poems contain the essential features of all his poetry – economy combined with rich resonance, deeply serious irony and playfulness – his work forms an unusually coherent whole. The starting point of Popa's endeavour is exploration. In order to establish what is enduringly true and valid, he starts by paring the universe down to its barest essentials, so as to rebuild it – gradually and systematically. Or the process may be seen as building an alternative universe, the meaning of which is

clear and controlled by the poet. This procedure entails a certain distance between the poet and his work which is reflected in the work's structure. Each of Popa's slim volumes is arranged in cycles, all of which are connected and which together form a complete statement. And each of the volumes is connected to the others in an intricate pattern. The poet begins by focusing on individual items from the real world – from a chair or a donkey to a sigh – and evoking its essential features. He then takes two of these items, bones and a pebble, and composes cycles around them which explore key aspects of human relations and in particular the pervasive presence of conflict. Popa applies this technique to a complete account of mythological and religious systems, and to the history and legend of his native Serbia. His language draws on the rich oral tradition of Serbia, riddles, children's games and colloquial speech, rearranging these features in a kaleidoscope of new, evocative combinations. His work may thus be seen to be deeply rooted in his native culture and traditions, but its taut texture communicates what Ted Hughes, in his introduction to the Penguin edition of Popa's poetry, has called 'the shock of recognition'. This may perhaps be defined as a painstaking distillation of a twentieth-century experience of an individual destiny in history.

PREŠEREN, Francè (1800–1849). Prešeren was the classic Slovene poet of the nineteenth century, whose work contributed much to the establishment of Slovene as a literary language. He was born in **Vrbas** in the **Gorenjska** region, near **Zirovnica** (there is a memorial room and small museum in his birthplace). Producing a remarkable corpus of poems by the time of his early death, Prešeren covered a range of different genres, using mostly Italian models of versification for his elegant, yet warm, above all accomplished verse. His opus shows a progression from tender, deeply personal love poems to tragic ballads and sharp satire, from youthful verve to a stoic resignation (Extract 17). Prešeren's tomb is in **Kranj** cemetery.

ŠALAMUN, Tomaž (1941–). Slovene poet. Born in **Zagreb**, Šalamun studied art history in **Ljubljana** and worked as assistant curator of the modern art gallery there. He has travelled widely, living in Italy, France, the USA and Mexico, and has a broad knowledge of twentieth-century poetry. He represents avant garde, post-modernist trends. Exuberant and individualistic, Šalamun belongs to a generation of East European writers who resent the politicization of all aspects of life and seek to give space to the personal. Like the work of many writers of this generation, his poems are iconoclastic, often funny, but fundamentally sceptical and often ultimately dark.

SARAJLIĆ, Izet (1930–). Bosnian poet. Born in **Doboj**, Sarajlić has lived in **Sarajevo** (Extract 13) since his student days. Much of his verse is concerned with the tragedy of the second world war: the death of his elder brother, a schoolboy shot by Italian forces in 1942, jolted him into a premature and painful adulthood. He has evolved a distinctive style in his verse, which has something of the public 'estrade' Soviet poetry of his day, and much of the self-irony of many contemporary poets throughout Eastern Europe.

SELENIĆ, Slobodan (1933–). Selenić was initially best known as a drama critic, but is now widely regarded as one of the finest Serbian novelists of his generation. His first novel *Memoari Pere Bogalja* (*The Memoirs of Pera the Cripple*), published in 1968, immediately won him a prestigious literary award. This was followed by several equally successful novels: *Prijatelji* (*Friends*), 1980, *Pismo glava* (*Heads or Tails*), 1982, *Očevi i oci* (*Fathers and Forefathers*), 1985, *Timor mortis*, 1989, and *Ubistvo s predumišljajem* (*Premeditated Murder*), 1993. *Prijatelji* was adapted for the stage in 1981 and a second play *Ruženje naroda u dva dela* (*Vilifying the Nation in Two Parts*) won the prestigious Sterija award for drama in 1988. Selenić is a sober, thoughtful, perceptive writer, concerned with exploring the intricacies of Serbian history and politics. His novel *Očevi i oci* (Extract 15) describes the experiences of Elizabeth Blake, an Englishwoman who marries a Serb studying in Britain and moves to live with him in **Belgrade**.

SELIMOVIĆ, Meša (1910–1982). Bosnian prose writer. Selimović lived in **Tuzla** and **Sarajevo**, before settling in **Belgrade**. As there was in his lifetime no specific Bosnian literary tradition, Selimović chose to regard himself as a Serbian writer, despite his Muslim background. Starting to write relatively late in life, he published three novels in quick succession, of which the most important was *Derviš i smrt* (*Death and the Dervish*), 1966 (Extract 15). These were followed by several other prose works, including another major novel, *Tvrdjava* (*The Fortress*), 1970. *Derviš i smrt* is a complex first-person narrative analysing relationships between ideology, power and integrity. The subtle texture of the narrative allows the author to suggest a certain capacity for self-deception which undermines the narrator's apparently earnest search to understand the truth of the events described in the novel. The work is a real *tour-de-force*.

SHKRELI, Azem. See under Albania.

TIŠMA, Aleksandar (1924–). Serbian poet and novelist. Tišma was born in **Horgoš**, Vojvodina, 1924, and was educated in **Novi Sad** and **Belgrade**. His prose is focused largely on the war and immediate post-war years and characterized by a documentary style. His most important novels are *Knjiga o Blamu* (*Book about Blam*), 1972, and *Upotreba čoveka* (*The Use of Man*), 1976. The latter novel explores a number of different ways of behaving and possible reactions to the war. The range of characters is broad and while their destinies are described in detail, they are more symbols of potential experience than developed individual psychologies. The horror of the war as it affects the small town of **Novi Sad** where they grew up is chillingly evoked. The novel offers a detailed account of the period, and is structurally interesting, with its focus shifting between individual characters, to general overviews, back and forth in time.

UGREŠIĆ, Dubravka (1949–). Ugrešić is a Croatian prose writer, engaged in research into Russian avant-garde literature. She has published four volumes of prose: a collection of sketches concerned with the

Dubravka Ugrešić

nature of writing, *Poza za prozu* (*A Pose for Prose*), 1978; a short novel, *Štefica Cvek u raljama života* (*Š.C. in the Jaws of Life*), 1981; a collection of parodies, *Život je bajka* (*Life is a Fairy-Tale*), 1983; the spoof detective novel *Forsiranje romana-reke* (*Forcing the Roman-Fleuve*), 1988 – published in English translation as *Fording the Stream of Consciousness*, 1991 (Extract 20); and a volume of ironic reflections on the war in Croatia seen from the USA where she was working at the time, *Američki fikcionar* (*American Fictionary*), 1993, published in English translation as *Have a Nice Day*, 1994. Ugrešić is one of the freshest voices in contemporary Croatian literature, the humour of whose works contains an underlying sorrow which has reached full expression in the tragic circumstances of the destruction of her native Yugoslavia.

ALBANIA

James Naughton

'. . . this day's march was fatiguing, but of all I ever saw the most stupendously beautiful; it is of no use describing precipices & forests, nor can language give an idea of them; but certainly even in Calabria, I never saw such magnificence.'
Edward Lear, letter of 1848

Situated on the Adriatic coast, its southern shores facing the Strait of Otranto and the heel of Italy, Albania is bordered to the north (north-west), north-east and east by Montenegro, the Kosovo province of Serbia, and Macedonia respectively. To the south and east Albania borders on Greece. In area (28 750 sq km) Albania is smaller than Belgium – but larger than Wales. Its population is estimated at around 3.4 million.

Travelling from north to south, Albania's main towns include **Shkodër**, or **Scutari** (population 82 000) on Lake Shkodër in the north, the port of **Durrës**, ancient Roman Dyrrachium (around 85 000), inland from Durrës the capital **Tirana**, or **Tiranë** (population approaching 250 000), further south, **Fier** (45 000) near the Classical site of **Apollonia**, and the port and naval base of **Vlorë** (74 000). Inland, south from Tiranë (Extract 8), are the Ottoman cities of **Elbasan** (83 000) (Extract 3), till recently polluted by a huge smoke-belching metallurgical plant, and **Berat** (44 000) with its fine old town and citadel. East of Elbasan, on the border with Macedonia, is **Lake Ohrid** (Extract 6), with **Korçë** (65 000) to its south in the eastern corner, towards Greece. Right in the south is **Gjirokastër** (25 000), famous for its citadel, mosques and well preserved Ottoman architecture. In Gjirokastër were born, curiously enough, both the Communist dictator Enver Hoxha (1908–85) and the novelist Ismail Kadare ◊, the contemporary writer best known to the outside world. Further south, over the Straits of Corfu, are the remains of the Illyrian, Greek, Roman and early Christian city of Buthrotum (modern **Butrint**). (Note that, confusingly, some books give place names with a definite suffix equivalent to 'the', eg Berati for Berat, Tirana for Tiranë, Shkodra for Shkodër, etc.)

Albania's mountains dominate much of its inland area, and are especially rugged in the north. Rivers flowing down to the coastal plain formed, before modern drainage, marshy flood areas, and the mountains still shelter some of the last European habitats for wolves, bears, lynx and jackals.

LANGUAGE

Among its birds of prey the eagle, *shqiponjë*, has become a national emblem. Albanians associate it symbolically and punningly with their language, which they call *shqip*, calling themselves *shqiptarë*, and their country *Shqipëri*: *shqiptoj* is to utter, to pronounce.

Apart from three million or so speakers in Albania itself, there are two or three million more, especially in adjoining Former Yugoslavia: in Kosovo (see Extract 4, chapter on Former Yugoslavia), with its capital Prishtinë (Prishtina), a region where they form the majority, and in Macedonia, where they make up perhaps a quarter of the population; there are fewer in Montenegro.

There is also an ancient community in southern Italy, in Calabria and Sicily, the Arbëresh, the first of whom were refugees from Turkish rule in the later 15th century; today they number about 90 000. Albanian can also be heard in some Greek villages; it was once more widespread, following influxes in the 14th–18th centuries.

Albanian is evidently descended from an Indo–European language of the Balkans spoken during classical antiquity. Usually the ancestor is plausibly claimed to be Illyrian. The Illyrians were a west Balkan tribal grouping whose lands were absorbed into the Roman Empire by the first century BC. However, Albanian is only recorded in texts from the fifteenth century, while the linguistic evidence for Illyrian is small (chiefly personal and place names). Modern Albanian is heavily overlaid by Latin, Greek, Slavonic and Turkish elements.

Albanian is divided into two dialect groups: Geg in the north, and Tosk in the south, with the **Shkumbin River** flowing past Elbasan to the Adriatic as roughly the demarcation line. Until recently both had regularly cultivated written forms. The present-day standard, as refined in 1972, is based more on Tosk than on Geg. In the past Albanian was also written in the Arabic and Greek scripts.

ANCIENT AND MEDIEVAL ALBANIA

Opinions vary about the origins and homogeneity of the Illyrians, but it seems that they were present at the latest by the 11th to 7th centuries

BC. The Greek geographer Ptolemy (cAD 127–148) mentions the tribe of the Albanoi, from whose name the modern words Albania and Albanians are evidently derived (and the related Italo–Albanian term Arbëresh; as we have already noted, the current native terms are different).

From the mid-7th century BC Greek colonies were founded on the coast: one at Dyrrachium, modern **Durrës**, a second, Apollonia, in 588 BC; another in the 6th century at Buthrotum, modern **Butrint**. From 146 BC central Albania became part of the Roman province of Macedonia. Soon afterwards the Romans built their famous Balkan west–east road, the Via Egnatia, starting from the coast and passing up the Shkumbin, past Lake Ohrid, and on to Thessalonica, and eventually Byzantium. With the division of the Empire in AD 395, Albania became part of the Byzantine Empire.

It seems that Christianity came relatively early, with bishoprics founded in the 2nd century. By the 5th century Albania was entered by Visigoths, Huns and Ostrogoths, followed by Slavs in the 6th century. However, by the mid-9th century most of present-day Albania again became a Byzantine province, subject to Bulgarian incursions. In 1081 the Normans, led by Bohemond, son of Robert Guiscard, landed, and were resisted by a force led personally by the Byzantine emperor Alexius Comnenus, an event vividly recorded by his historian-daughter Anna Comnena. The emperor was defeated outside **Durrës** (Dyrrachium, Durazzo) and forced to withdraw. The 11th and 12th centuries saw further Norman campaigns, the Venetians also vied for coastal power, while in 1269 Charles I of Anjou landed and founded a kingdom from the river Drin to Vlorë. Later the Serbs also invaded, under their powerful ruler Stefan Dushan (1331–55).

Now, however, the Ottoman Turks began to advance into Europe, defeating the Serbs and their allies at the legendary Battle of Kosovo Polje in 1389. Resistance to Turkish overlordship is symbolized to this day by the Albanian hero Skanderbeg (Gjergj Kastrioti Skënderbeg, 1405–68), whose stronghold was the citadel of **Krujë**, north-east of Durrës. A Turkish garrison having been installed, Gjergj was sent as a hostage to the Sultan at Istanbul. Converting to Islam, he began an army career, but turned rebel, seized his native Krujë in late 1443, and withstood all onslaughts. Despite costly victories, and Italian support, resistance crumbled after Skanderbeg's death by illness in 1468, and Krujë fell in 1478. Ever since, Skanderbeg has been a great theme for Albanian writers. Most recently, the siege of Krujë has provided material for Ismail Kadare's historical novel *Kështjella* (*The Castle*), 1974.

As a result of Ottoman rule, many Albanians sought refuge in southern Italy, but most of the population gradually accepted Islam.

Roman Catholics maintained a presence in **Shkodër**, in the north, while Orthodox remained mainly in the Greek-influenced south. Some Muslims became Bektashi, a tolerant sect which ignores conventional rules, such as abstinence from alcohol, and the veiling of women.

EARLIER LITERATURE

A first reference to Albanian writing, by the French Bishop of Antivari in 1332, tells us the Latin alphabet was used; the earliest existing fragment is a baptismal formula of 1462. The first Albanian-language book, in the Vatican Library, is the *Meshari* (*Missal*), 1555, of Gjon Buzuku, a priest from northern Albania. The earliest recorded poem, by the Sicilian cleric Lekë Matrënga (Luca Matranga) appears in a catechism, the second oldest monument in Albanian, entitled *E mbsueme e krështerë* (*Christian Doctrine*), 1592.

The first English translation of a work on Albania was printed in London in 1596: it is the *Historie of George Castriot, Surnamed Scanderbeg, King of Albinie; Containing his Famous Actes, his Noble Deedes of Armes and Memorable Victories against the Turkes for the Faith of Christ*, a translation (from the French) of *Historia de vita et gestis Scanderbegi, Epirotarum Princeps* (Rome, c1508–10). This 'History of Scanderbeg' was by Marin Barleti (c1450–c1512), the earliest known Albanian Humanist and historian, a cleric who settled in Padua after witnessing the Turkish occupation of Shkodër in 1478. His *De obsidione Scodrensi*, 1504, also mentions annals in the vernacular.

A number of the first authors were Roman Catholic priests from northern Albania. Frang Bardhi (1606–43) compiled the first dictionary, *Dictionarium latino-epiroticum*, with about five thousand entries, and a list of proverbs. The bishop–poet Pjetër Budi (1566–1623, drowned crossing the River Drin) composed over 3 000 lines of religious verse. Pjetër Bogdani (c1625–89), who became Bishop of Shkodër, then Archbishop of Skopje, produced the first original prose: his *Cuneus Prophetarum* (*Wedge of the Prophets*), Padua, 1685, is mainly theological and philosophical, in Albanian and Italian, but also includes poetry.

Among Italo–Albanian, or Arbëresh poets one of the freshest and most original was Jul Variboba (Giulio Varibova, 1724–c88), teacher and priest, born in Cosenza, and author of *Ghiella e Shën Mëriis Virghiër* (*Life of the Virgin Mary*), 1762, a narrative poem on the Nativity, set against a backcloth of Calabria, with reminiscences of folk song.

Islamic culture produced a substantial body of Albanian verse in Arabic script. Its authors include Nezim Frakulla (c1680–1760) whose *Divan* contains the first secular poetry, combining religious with natural themes and depiction of urban life; he also wrote love poetry. One of the more celebrated late 18th-century poets is Hasan Zyko Kamberi (18th–19th century), whose tomb in **Starje**, Kolonja district, southern Albania, became a shrine. Religious themes are important in his work, but also the life of the common people, in poems noted for strong satire. Another poet was Muhamet Kyçyku (1784–1844), from southern Albania, who studied in Cairo, and then returned to his native village. His verse is seen as marking a transition between older Muslim verse and the Revival poetry of the 19th century.

ROMANTICISM AND RILINDJA

By the later 18th century, under less immediate Ottoman authority, northern Albania was dominated by the Bushati chieftains, while southern territory was ruled by the notorious Ali Pasha, appointed governor of Ioannina, in northern Greece, in 1788. His remarkable court was described by Byron ◊, who visited him in 1809 at his stronghold of **Tepelenë**, and re-depicted his experiences in Canto 2 of *Childe Harold's Pilgrimage* (Extract 7). Ali Pasha extended his domain over southern Albania and much of northern Greece, but eventually, too independent, and besieged by the Ottomans, he was assassinated in 1822. A later English literary visitor, in 1848, was the artist and nonsense-poet Edward Lear ◊, who wrote about his travels in his *Journey of a Landscape Painter in Albania etc*, 1851, and in his personal correspondence (Extract 3).

The decades from the 1830s until the declaration of independence in 1912 are conventionally termed the period of *Rilindja* or National Awakening. Important impulses came from Arbëresh writers, especially Jeronim De Rada (Girolamo De Rada, 1814–1903), who collected local folklore and whose poetry and journalism were important in fostering national feeling. Among his Romantic verse, often in a metre reminiscent of Longfellow's *Hiawatha*, his first and best-known work is *Canti di Milosau, figlio del despota di Scutari*, 1836, which depicts the love of a noble young man from 15th-century **Shkodër** for Rina, a poor shepherd's daughter. In 1848 he founded a newspaper *L'Albanese d'Italia*, which included Albanian articles. Later he published a bilingual monthly *Fiamuri i Arbërit – La bandiera dell'Albania* (*The Albanian Flag*, 1883–88), which reached readers in Albania despite Ottoman censorship. It was many years in Albania itself before even primary schooling could be conducted in Albanian, and vernacular publications arrived from outside, from Italy, if Catholic, or, for example, in the late 19th century from Bucharest in Romania, with whose largely Orthodox Albanian community the Istanbul-based writers were in close contact.

Bible translation has often been important for establishing literary languages. A bilingual Greek–Albanian New Testament appeared in Corfu in 1827, translated by Vangjel Meksi, doctor of Ali Pasha; it was followed by versions in both Geg and Tosk varieties of Albanian, published by the British and Foreign Bible Society, 1872, 1879. These were translated by Konstandin Kristoforidhi (1827–95), son of a silversmith from **Elbasan**, who attended the Zosimea secondary school in Ioannina, where he taught Albanian to the Austrian vice-consul Johann Georg von Hahn, author of *Albanesische Studien*, 1853. He also produced a fine Albanian–Greek dictionary (published Athens 1904), and wrote works such as the tale *Gjahn i malësorëvet* (*The Hunt of the Mountaineers*), 1884, seen as one of the first works of modern literary prose. By now, several native Albanians had also published collections of folklore: Zef Jubani (1818–80) from **Shkodër** published the first book of Geg songs in Trieste in 1871, *Raccolta di canti popolari e rapsodie di poemi albanesi*, while Thimi Mitko (1820–90) from **Korçë**, who settled in Egypt, in 1878 published the first Tosk collection of folksongs, tales and proverbs, entitled in Greek *Alvaniki melissa* (*The Albanian Bee*).

A crucial moment in Albanian nationalism came in 1878 with the Berlin Congress, held after Russia's defeat of Turkey. A meeting in the Kosovar town of Prizren that year established an Albanian League, aimed at opposing annexations by Serbia, Montenegro, Bulgaria and Greece, all beneficiaries of Ottoman weakness. Armed conflict ensued with Montenegro, and fighting in Kosovo. The Turks turned against the League and crushed its forces, but the 'Albanian question' had been brought to European attention. The Young Turk Revolution of 1908 brought elections, but relations with the Young Turks also soured.

Leading figures in this national movement were the brothers Abdyl, Naim and Sami Frashëri. Naim Frashëri (1846–1900) is a father figure for modern Albanian literature. Born in the village of **Frashër**, in southern Albania, he was taught Turkish, Persian and Arabic as well as Islamic (Bektashi) theology, but was also educated in the Classics and influenced by modern European ideas. After some time in Istanbul, he became a civil servant in **Berat**, and a customs officer in **Sarandë**, but in 1881–82 he returned to Istanbul and became a censor at the Ottoman Ministry of Education, simultaneously involved in propagating Albanian letters. Naim Frashëri wrote 22 works, fifteen in Albanian, four in Turkish, two in Greek, one in Persian. His Albanian prose helped to set the language on an established course. He also helped set up the first Albanian school, in **Korçë**, in 1884. Among his verse, *Bagëti e bujqësi* (*Herds and Crops*), 1886, depicted the Albanian countryside in bucolic and Georgic style. His *Istoria e Skënderbeut* (*History of Scanderbeg*), 1898, an epic based on Barleti's account, is one of the more widely read Albanian classics. He also translated the first book of Homer's *Iliad*.

Like Naim, Sami Frashëri (1850–1904) attended secondary school in Ioannina, and spent most of his life in Istanbul. He wrote about fifty major works and articles, including school textbooks and the first school grammar. His manifesto *Shqipëria – Ç'ka genë, ç'është dhe ç'do të bëhetë* (*Albania – What She Was, What She Is, and What She Will Become*), 1899, became one of the most widely read and translated Albanian texts. He is also an important figure in Turkish culture: for his Turkish–French dictionaries in 1901 and his six-volume encyclopedia of Turkish history and geography (1889–99).

The work of Frashëri, De Rada, and others, was followed by writers such as the poet Andon Çajupi ◊ (Extract 4), who lived in Cairo, Ndre Mjeda (1866–1937), a Jesuit poet-scholar from **Shkodër**, and Gjergj Fishta (1871–1940), regarded as the leading national poet in his day. Fishta, a Franciscan, studied in Bosnia, and founded in **Shkodër** the first fully Albanian-language secondary school. In 1899 he co-founded the Bashkimi (Union) literary society, and in 1908 he participated in the Congress of Monastir, which approved his Roman-alphabet spelling proposals. He edited the periodical *Hylli i Dritës* (*The Day Star*), 1913–44, was a delegate to the Paris Peace Conference in 1919 and an MP in the first Albanian parliament. Fishta's major poetic work is *Lahuta e Malcis* (*Highland Lute*), 1905–06, a nationalistic epic depicting the Albanian–Montenegrin conflict. Another prominent poet, Asdreni (pen name of Aleks Stavri Drenova, 1872–1947) from near **Korçë**, was one of those who emigrated to Romania and lived in Bucharest. Drama and short fiction were practised, among others, by the Korçë-born populist Mihal Grameno (1872–1931). A prominent essayist living abroad was Faik Konica (1875–1942), who was born in northern Greece and studied in **Shkodër**, Istanbul, and Dijon; he founded the important journal *Albania*, published first in Brussels, from 1897, then in London, from 1902 to 1910; he also wrote a satirical novel *Dr Gjëlpëra* (*Dr Needle*), 1924.

INDEPENDENCE UNDER ZOG

The period 1912–44 is the first period of modern independence, during which the Albanians became the only inter-war European state with a Muslim majority (70%, with 20% Orthodox, and 10% Roman Catholics). Following more war in the Balkans, a declaration of independence was made in November 1912, which was endorsed by Austria–Hungary and Italy, neither of whom wished to see another state dominating the Strait of Otranto. A German ruler, Prince William of Wied, was briefly installed, but lasted only about six months, and during the first world war Albania was overrun by several foreign armies. Albanian independence was not established until 1920–21.

Many Albanians were left outside Albania, but internally the population was quite homogeneous, divided between the largely clan-based Geg mountaineers of the north, and the more agrarian Tosk villagers of the south. Albanians accounted for over 90% of the population, the rest being Greeks, Slavs, Turks and Vlachs (a Balkan grouping speaking dialects akin to Romanian). Such economic growth as occurred between the two world wars was largely subsidized by Italy.

The political élite split roughly into a camp of chieftains, former Ottoman beys and landlords, led by Ahmed Zogu, of the Muslim Mati clan, and a weaker, more Westernized bourgeoisie and intelligentsia led by the Harvard-educated Orthodox bishop and writer Fan S. Noli (1882–1965), notable as a translator of Shakespeare, Ibsen, Cervantes, Poe and others. Noli was Prime Minister for six months in 1924, following an insurrection against Zogu. Soon, however, after poor handling of government by Noli, Zogu re-invaded from Yugoslavia, and Noli retreated into exile, becoming Primate of the Albanian Orthodox Church in America. Zogu had himself crowned as King Zog in 1928, and under his astute, hybrid feudal and modestly Westernizing and secularizing rule Albania gradually made some headway, curbing the institutions of vendetta, blood-vengeance and brigandage.

A prolific writer, especially dramatist, in these years was Kristo Floqi (1873–194?), a Zogist Minister of Education. A leading writer, poet and author of stories depicting middle-class Scutarene life, was the strongly Italian-influenced Ernest Koliqi (1903–75), who became another Minister of Education, this time under the Italian occupation, and thus was dropped from Parnassus by the Communists. However, literature in the inter-war period was still dominated by poets, perhaps the most notable of whom are Migjeni and Lasgush Poradeci.

Migjeni (Millosh Gjergj Nikolla) ◊ poet, short-story writer, and village teacher, born in **Shkodër**, died of tuberculosis at the age of twenty-six. His poetry, in the slim volume *Vargjet e lira* (*Free Verse*), 1936, combines lyricism with an ambivalently progressivist ideological note (Extracts 1 and 2). His prose was posthumously published in the volume *Tregime nga qyteti i Veriut* (*Stories from the Town of the North*), 1954.

Lasgush Poradeci ◊ from **Pogradec** on Lake Ohrid is regarded as one of the finest Albanian poets. His poetry, published in Bucharest, was collected in two volumes, *Vallja e yjeve* (*The Dance of the Stars*), 1933, and *Ylli i zemrës* (*The Star of the Heart*), 1937. Influenced by folksong, but also by Romanian poetry, especially Eminescu (◊ Romania), he introduced a note of pantheistic mysticism (Extract 6). After the war he translated Burns, Pushkin, Lermontov, Mayakovsky, Goethe, Heine and Brecht.

FROM OCCUPATION TO COMMUNISM

In April 1939 Mussolini invaded and occupied Albania, and Zog was driven into exile. Between 1939 and 1943 Italy established a harsh dictatorship and made Albania a base for its invasion of Greece in 1940. When the Communist Party was founded in Albania at the end of 1941 it set up its own resistance group, alongside the National Front (Balli Kombëtar) and a pro-Zog royalist body. After a renewed occupation by Germany, and following civil war in 1943–44, the Communist partisans emerged victorious. Under Enver Hoxha (1908–85), they set up government in November 1944 and Hoxha remained Communist leader for over forty years.

The 1948 rift between Stalin and Tito enabled Hoxha to escape subordination to Yugoslavia, eliminate his pro-Tito opponents, and establish direct links with Moscow; Hoxha now became one of Stalin's most faithful disciples. However, after Stalin's death in 1953, tension grew with the Soviet Union, when the new Russian leader Khrushchev mended fences with Yugoslavia, and denounced Stalin in his secret speech of 1956. The final rift came in 1961, after Hoxha supported China against Moscow. China stepped in to provide economic help, though with difficulty, given the distance and its own economic situation. Encouraged by Mao's 'Cultural Revolution', Hoxha made religious practices illegal in 1967. This remarkable Sino–Albanian alliance only ended in 1978, after Chinese *rapprochement* with Yugoslavia.

Under Hoxha's rule Socialist Realism naturally became the official cultural doctrine, and many writers were unable to publish, or be mentioned. On the other hand, great efforts were made to spread education and mass literacy. Writings of the 1950s and 1960s were generally propagandistic. Prose writers in particular were meant to write endlessly about the partisans and the struggle for national liberation, and the building of socialism, even if a certain turning point came around 1961, after the appearance on the scene of new less conformist poets, such as Dritëro Agolli (1931–), a talented poet of the soil, later President of the Writers' Union from 1973–92, Fatos Arapi (1930–), and especially Ismail Kadare ◊. There was open disagreement on policy at a meeting of the Union of Writers and Artists held in **Tiranë** on 11 July 1961. Greater stylistic and thematic latitude was subsequently allowed, and literature became somewhat more exploratory, though still under tight restrictions.

English versions of propaganda 'Socialist Realist' works by Shevqet Musaraj (1914–86), Sterjo Spasse (1914–89) and Fatmir Gjata (1922–89) exist for the sociologically minded, nearly all printed in Tiranë. (There are also translations of the poet Agolli's Communist patriotic prose.) A more readily appealing fiction writer is Teodor Laço (1936–   ), from near **Korçë**, former head of the film studios, author of an inevitably awkward novel about 1948–49, *Përballimi* (*The Face-Up*), 1975, but also of some approachable, even atmospheric short stories portraying contemporary society.

The one author inside the country to make any reputation outside Albania during the Communist years was Ismail Kadare, who, with his first successful novel *Gjenerali i ushtrisë së vdekar* (*The General of the Dead Army*), 1963 (Extract 8), was hailed as an Albanian Yevtushenko, but in fact is much more non-conformist and heretical.

There was, however, no real 'thaw', even in the mild and temporary Soviet sense, and frozen cultural isolation pretty much continued, much more than elsewhere in the Communist Balkans; in 1973 there was a renewed campaign by Hoxha against liberalism and foreign influences.

Two crucial events occurred in 1985: Gorbachev came to power in Russia, and Hoxha died, succeeded by his deputy Ramiz Alia. This was to be the beginning of the end for the post-war Communist era, but it was not until the tumultuous events of 1989 in Eastern Europe, and especially the toppling of Ceauşescu in Romania, that any more radical policy changes were made. During 1990 rioting became widespread, there were attempts at mass emigration, and crowds occupied Western embassies. The following winter symbols of one-party rule such as the huge statue of Hoxha in the middle of Tiranë were removed, and in March 1991 elections were held, in which the somewhat reformed Party of Labour managed to hold on to power. A general strike in May, however, brought in a coalition which included non-Communists. Unrest continued, including a mass emigration in August when thousands of people boarded ships in **Durrës** and made them sail to Italy. A large programme of European Community (now European Union) food aid began, run by the Italian army. New elections were held in March 1992, and were won by the opposition Democratic Party.

Names of writers other than Kadare are not yet much in evidence to the eyes of the outside world, though a few publications exist. An effective lyrical psychological story about a pair of female eyes, by the woman writer Mimoza Ahmeti (1963–   ), from **Krujë**, appears, along with a story by Laço, in *Description of a Struggle*, a recent Picador anthology of East European prose.

In December 1990, before the first post-totalitarian elections, Albania's most famous contemporary writer, Ismail Kadare ◊, settled in exile in Paris. The notable poet and scholar Martin Camaj ◊ lived much of his life abroad: he studied in Belgrade, and worked in Italy, and in Germany (Extract 5). The critic and poet Arshi Pipa (1920–   )

composed poetry in jail, as a political prisoner for ten years until 1956; he escaped to Yugoslavia and went to the USA. And of course, there have been many active poets and writers in Kosovo, just over the border, among them the poet Azem Shkreli ◊.

Non-conformist writers and intellectuals in Albania suffered decades of physical and mental violence, which a few token words here cannot suffice to express. Now the numerous Albanians in Kosovo are faced with repressive policies from the government of Serbia, though for a time they were culturally freer than Albania itself, having achieved full cultural autonomy under the 1974 Yugoslav constitution. The Kosovo provincial assembly was dissolved in 1990, the one Albanian daily was banned, as was all Albanian-language radio and TV broadcasting, while courses taught in Albanian at the University of Prishtinë were suspended from 1991.

Albanian literature still retains its potent notes of exile and diaspora.

BOOKLIST

The following selection includes the extracted titles in this chapter as well as those mentioned in the introduction which are available in English and other titles for further reading. In general, paperback editions are given when possible. The editions cited are not necessarily the only ones available. For most of the extracted works, the original publisher can be found in 'Acknowledgments and Citations' at the end of the volume, as can the exact location of the extracts and the editions from which they are taken. Extract numbers are highlighted in bold. Square brackets denote the date of publication of the work in its original language.

Agolli, Dritëro, *The Bronze Bust* [1970], 8 Nëntori, Tiranë, 1975.

Agolli, Dritëro, *The Man with the Gun* [1975], 8 Nëntori, Tiranë, 1983.

Agolli, Dritëro, poems in *Anthology of Modern Albanian Poetry* (see below).

Albanian Contemporary Prose, Naim Frashëri, 1963.

Anthology of Modern Albanian Poetry: An Elusive Eagle Soars, Robert Elsie, trans and ed, Forest Books, London, 1993. **Extracts 1, 5 and 6.**

Bland, William B., *Albania* (World Bibliographical Series, Vol 94), Clio Press, Oxford, 1988.

Byron, Lord, *Byron* (*The Oxford Authors*), containing *Childe Harold's Pilgrimage* [1812–18], Jerome J. McGann, ed, Oxford University Press, Oxford and New York, 1986. **Extract 7.**

Çajupi, 'My Village', in Arshi Pipa, *Albanian Literature: Social Perspectives* (see below). **Extract 4.**

Camaj, Martin, *Palimpsest*, Leonard Fox, trans, Munich and New York, 1991.

Camaj, Martin, *Selected Poetry*, Leonard Fox, trans, New York University Press, New York, 1990.

Camaj, Martin, poems in *Albanica*, No 2, Spring 1991, issue devoted to Camaj.

Camaj, Martin, 'Mountain Feast', in

Anthology of Modern Albanian Poetry (see above). **Extract 5.**

Comnena, Anna, *The Alexiad of Anna Comnena* [c1148], E. R. A. Sewter, trans (from the original Greek), Penguin, London, 1969.

Contemporary Albanian Poems, Bardhyl Pogoni, trans and ed, Dragotti, Naples, 1985.

Description of a Struggle: the Picador Book of Contemporary East European Prose, Michael March, ed, Picador, London, 1994. Contains Ismail Kadare, extract from *The Concert*, Barbara Bray, trans (from the French); stories by Mimoza Ahmeti and Teodor Laço, Robert Elsie, trans.

Elsie, Robert, *Dictionary of Albanian Literature*, Greenwood, Westport, CT, and New York, 1986.

Elsie, Robert, *History of Albanian Literature*, East European Quarterly, New York, 1993.

Elsie, Robert, 'Albanian Literature in English Translation: a Short Survey', *Slavonic and East European Review*, Vol 70, 1992, pp 249–257.

Fenimore Cooper, Paul, *Tricks of Women and Other Albanian Tales* (translated from French and German), W. Morrow, New York, 1928.

Frashëri, Sami, *Pledge of Honor, an Albanian Tragedy* [late 19th century], S. F. Vanni Publishers, New York, 1945.

Frashëri, Naim, *Frashëri's Song of Albania* [1886], Ali Cungu, trans, Exposition Press, Smithtown, NY, 1981.

Frashëri, Naim, *Scanderbeg's Return and Other Poems*, Ali Cungu, trans, Tirana, 1970.

Gjata, Fatmir, *The Marsh* [1959], William Bland, trans, in the journal *Albanian Life*, London.

Kadare, Ismail, *The General of the Dead Army* [1963], Derek Coltman, trans (from the French), Quartet Books, London, 1986/

New Amsterdam Books, New York, 1990. **Extract 8.**

Kadare, Ismail, *The Wedding* [1968], Ali Cungu, trans, Naim Frashëri, Tirana, 1968/Gamma, New York, 1972.

Kadare, Ismail, *Chronicle in Stone* [1971], Arshi Pipa, trans, Serpent's Tail, London, 1987/ Meredith Press, New York, 1987.

Kadare, Ismail, *The Castle* [1974], Pavli Qesku, trans, 8 Nëntori, Tirana, 1974/Gamma, New York, 1980.

Kadare, Ismail, *Doruntine* [1980], Jon Rothschild, trans (from the French), Saqi, London, 1988/ New Amsterdam Books, New York, 1988.

Kadare, Ismail, *Broken April* [1980], John Hodgson, trans, Harvill, London, 1991/New Amsterdam Books, New York, 1990.

Kadare, Ismail, *The Concert* [1988], Barbara Bray, trans (from the French), Harvill, London, 1994/ W. Morrow, New York, 1994.

Kadare, Ismail, *The Palace of Dreams*, Barbara Bray, trans (from the French), Harvill, London, 1993.

Këndime Englisht-Shqip or Albanian-English Reader: Sixteen Albanian Folk-Stories, Margaret M. Hasluck, trans, Cambridge University Press, Cambridge, 1932.

Laço, Teodor, *The Face-Up: a Novel* [1975], 8 Nëntori, Tiranë, 1980.

Laço, Teodor, *A Lyrical Tale in Winter*, Ronald Taylor, trans, 8 Nëntori, Tiranë, 1988. (Short stories.)

Lear, Edward, *Journal of a Landscape Painter in Albania, &c* [1851], K. Bentley, London, 1851; as *Journal of a Landscape Painter in Greece and Albania*, Century, London, 1988; as *Edward Lear in the Levant*, J. Murray, London, 1988.

Lear, Edward, *Selected Letters*, Vivien Noakes, ed, Clarendon Press, Oxford, 1988. **Extract 3.**

Logoreci, Anton, The Albanians: Europe's Forgotten Survivors, Westview Press, Boulder, CO, 1978.

Mann, Stuart E., Albanian Literature: An Outline of Prose, Poetry and Drama, Quaritch, London, 1955.

Migjeni, Selected Albanian Songs and Sketches, Ali Cungu, trans, Naim Frashëri, Tirana, 1963.

Migjeni, 'Song of the Occident', in Arshi Pipa, Albanian Literature: Social Perspectives (see below), Extract 2.

Migjeni, Free Verse, Robert Elsie, trans, 8 Nëntori, Tiranë, 1991.

Migjeni, 'Blasphemy', in Anthology of Modern Albanian Poetry (see above), Extract 1.

Musaraj, Shevqet, Before the Dawn: a Novel [1965–66], 2 Vols, 8 Nëntori, Tiranë, 1981–82.

Norris, H. T., Islam in the Balkans, Hurst, London, 1993/University of South Carolina Press, Columbia, SC, 1993.

Perspectives on Albania, Tom Winnifrith, ed, Macmillan, London, 1992.

Pettifer, James, Blue Guide: Albania, A. & C. Black, London/W. W. Norton, New York, 1994.

Pipa, Arshi, Albanian Folk Verse: Structure and Genre (Albanische Forschungen, 17), Trofenik, Munich, 1978.

Pipa, Arshi, Hieronymus de Rada (Albanische Forschungen, 18), Trofenik, Munich, 1978.

Pipa, Arshi, Albanian Literature: Social Perspectives (Albanische Forschungen, 19), Trofenik, Munich, 1978. Extracts from Çajupi and Migjeni; also from Azem Shkreli (see Extract 4, chapter on Former Yugoslavia). Extracts 2 and 4.

Pipa, Arshi, Contemporary Albanian Literature, East European Monographs, Boulder, CO, distributed by Columbia University Press, New York, 1991.

Pitarka, Sulejman, The Fisherman's Family: a Play [1955], 8 Nëntori, Tiranë, 1980.

Poradeci, Lasgush, 'Pogradec', in Anthology of Modern Albanian Poetry (see above), Extract 6.

Prifti, Naum, Ciko and Benny: a Novelette [1988], Peter Prifti, trans, 8 Nëntori, Tiranë, 1988.

Prifti, Naum, The Wolf's Hide: Humorous Short Stories and Sketches, Peter Prifti, trans, 8 Nëntori, Tiranë, 1988.

Prifti, Peter, Socialist Albania Since 1944, MIT Press, Cambridge, MA, 1978.

Ressuli, Namik, Albanian Literature, Vatra, Boston, MA, 1987.

Roads Lead Only One Way: A Survey of Modern Poetry from Kosova, John Hodgson, trans, Kosova Association of Literary Translators, Rilindja, Prishtinë, 1988.

The Sad Branch: Albanian Poetry in Yugoslavia, Ali Podrimja and Sabri Hamiti, eds, Rilindja, Prishtinë, 1979.

Shkreli, Azem, The Call of the Owl [1986], John Hodgson, trans, Kosova Association of Literary Translators, Prishtinë, 1989.

Skendi, Stavro, The Albanian National Awakening 1878–1912, Princeton University Press, Princeton, NJ, 1967.

Spasse, Sterjo, The Awakening: a Novel [1974], 8 Nëntori, Tiranë, 1980.

Voices from Across the Water, Ewald Osers, trans, Johnston Green, Portree, 1985. (Includes poems by Martin Camaj and two others.)

Ward, Philip, Albania: a Travel Guide, The Oleander Press, Cambridge, 1983.

Wheeler, Post, Albanian Wonder Tales, Lovat Dickenson, London, 1936.

Zymberi, Isa, Colloquial Albanian, Routledge, London, 1991.

Extracts

(1) ALBANIA: CHRISTIANITY AND ISLAM

Migjeni, *Blasphemy*

This poem from the 1930s illustrates Migjeni's obvious social radical note, but also has topographical atmosphere and lyrical allure, full in the end of anxiety, ambivalence, and ambiguity about its themes.

The mosques and churches float through our memories,
Prayers devoid of sense or taste echo from their walls.
Never has the heart of god yet been touched by them
But still beats on amidst the sounds of drums and bells.

Majestic mosques and churches throughout our wretched land,
Spires and minarets towering over lowly homes,
The voice of hodja and of priest in one degenerate chant,
Oh, ideal vision, a thousand years old!

The mosques and churches float through memories of the pious,
The sounds of the bell mingle with the muezzin's call,
Sanctity shines from cowls and the beards of hodjas.
Oh, so many beauteous angels at the gates of hell!

On their ancient citadels perch the carrion crows
Their wings drooping dejectedly – the symbols of lost hopes,
They croak despairingly about an age gone by
When their ancient citadels once gleamed with hallowed joy.

(2) Albania: Looking West

Migjeni, *Song of the Occident*

Here, Migjeni illustrates the social–ideological note that will make him a Communist predecessor; but the text is profoundly ambivalent, an ideological drama: about progress, religion, the West. The West was just across the Adriatic, in Italy (where the poet died, of tuberculosis). There was King Zog's Westernism, but also Communism.

Song of the Occident, song of man drunk with faith in himself.
His song, another religion, with other temples, high masses,
where from morning until night human brains and feelings melt
in the apotheosis of iron, souls filter out of the smoke stacks,

their whistling mocks the old god and the sky,
their thick dirty smoke dulls the brightness of the sun.
Another religion, mad religion of the marvellous Occident.
Man walks exalted in an inconceivable delirium.

He listens to what his religion tells him, wounds the sky,
    pierces the earth,
tears the white horizons, lays nature bare, removes her clothing.
His cult, a naked cult, the enigma no longer gnaws at his brain.
He buries it and places on the tomb a token of contempt or homage.

Song of the Occident, song of man drunk with faith in himself.
His song a beautiful winged hope, wings of another life,
when the sun will change its course: it will rise in the Occident.
But, oh, the universe will lose its head with joy.

Its gay tango rhythm will enmesh the skeins of the old god,
will scandalize his faithful children on another planet.
Song of the Occident, song of man drunk with faith in himself.
Let us listen to the song wrapped in puffs of steam, drops of sweat!

(3) ELBASAN

Edward Lear, *A letter to his sister, 1848*

The artist, seasoned traveller and nonsense-poet made a visit to Albania in 1848, which he later described in his Journal of a Landscape Painter in Albania etc, 1851. This extract is taken from one of his letters to his eldest sister, Ann, dated 'Scutari, (ie Shkodër) 21 October 1848'. ('Han' refers to an inn.)

Sept 25th, – this day's march was fatiguing, but of all I ever saw the most stupendously beautiful; it is of no use describing precipices & forests, nor can language give an idea of them; but certainly even in Calabria, I never saw such magnificence. As for the wallnut & chestnut forests – & oak & beech woods – now beginning to be coloured by autumn – they are not to be imagined. Beyond all, the snowy peaks of the Bosniac mountains peeped up. Han from 12 to 2. Immense descent from 3 to 4, & then a long winding gorge by the river. Here some of the baggage came untied, & rolled off – had it been a few steps earlier, into the river it must have gone. Towards sunset, we had reached quite different scenery – a wide plain covered with olives, – & surrounded by low olive coloured hills – with high forms of mountains beyond – against which many a white minaret stood up like silver. This was Elbassan – where we were to pass the night. Alas!! – these places look so beautiful afar off – but are nought within. Elbassan particularly is a disgusting place, though very picturesque; the streets have the oddest look possible, being roofed over with old mats & sometimes vines – so that, except just over the shops or bazaars, they are quite dark. Of the 3 Hans we went into, only one was tolerable, & that had a clean room, but with no windows nor door; – the others, were as is all Elbassan – tumbled down & deserted.

I must tell you that, north of the river Scumbin, we entered a new tribe of Albanians – half Sclavonian by origin; their dress is more rich than even the southerns, as they wear a long crimson vest over the kilt of Fustianello – & over that again a spencer of scarlet trimmed with fur!! & such pistols & Boxes as project from their gilt leather belts!

Sept 26th – I tried to draw on the ruined ramparts of the town – but was surrounded by hundreds – & as I heard the Dervishes saying – shaitan! shaitan! [devil! devil!] – I was too glad to get to the Han with only a mob & hooting – After that I choose to have a kwass or man of the police – he costs a dollar a day – but it is not possible in the towns to draw without him. There were beautiful studies all round the walls of Elbassan – & I got a great many. From one of the towers, the high top of Mt Tomerit is seen plainly.

(4) Gjirokastër Region

Çajupi, *My Village*

*Compare this view of Albanian women with Byron's in a letter
to his mother: 'their women are sometimes handsome also, but
they are treated like slaves, beaten & in short complete beasts of
burden, they plough, dig & sow, I found them carrying wood &
actually repairing the highways [...] the women are the labour-
ers, which after all is no great hardship in so delightful a climate
...'*

Bare rocky mountains,
meadows full of grass,
fields of wheat, and beyond,
a flowing river.

A village in front of it
with a church and a graveyard
and a few tiny houses
scattered around.

Cold spring water
and excellent air,
the nightingale's song
and lovely women.

The men in the shadows
play and chat.
Fie! their women
work for them.

Women in the fields,
women in the vineyards,
women cut the grass,
women work at home.

Women do the harvesting,
women gather grapes;
they go out at dawn,
they come back at night.

The wife for her husband
in the heat of day
works and never rests,
not even on Sunday.

Poor Albanian woman,
who tills the soil with oxen,
and then comes home to
prepare lunch and dinner.

What's the point of having
a do-nothing husband
refreshing himself at the fountain
while you see to everything?

(5) NORTHERN ALBANIAN ALPS

Martin Camaj, *Mountain Feast*

The poet was born in the Dukagjin region of the northern Alps in 1925. A resonant lyrical poem gives literary form to violence, here the violence of the blood feud.

Blood was avenged today.
Two bullets felled a man.

Blood was avenged today.

Under the axe-head
The ox's skull bursts by the stream.
(Today there will be great feasting!)

Blood was avenged today.

The wailing of men gone wild
Mingles with the smell of meat on the fires.
And the autumn foliage falls
Scorched on the white caps
At the tables, outside.

Night. At the graves on the hill
Fresh earth, new moon.

The wolves have descended from the mountains
And drink blood at the stream.

(6) POGRADEC

Lasgush Poradeci, *Pogradec*

*Pogradec is a small town on the Albanian side of Lake Ohrid,
the source of the river Drin. Just across the border, in
Macedonia, the famous old church of St Naum's overlooks the
lake. Behind it rises the Mal i Thatë, 'Dry Mountain', dividing
Lake Ohrid from Lake Prespa.*

A shimmering sunset on the endless lake.
Ghostlike, a veil is slowly spread.
Over mountain and meadow the dark of night descends,
Settling from the heavens upon the town.

Over the vast land no more sound is to be heard:
In the village the creaking of a door,
On the lake the silence of an oar.
Over the Mal i Thatë an elusive eagle soars.
My youthful heart retreats into the depths of my soul.

The whole town, all life, retires to the realm of sleep.
Darkness rules the four quarters of the earth. And now,
Setting out on his journey through Albania,
Legendary Father Drin arises at St Naum's.

(7) TEPELENË

Lord Byron, *Childe Harold's Pilgrimage*

*Byron visited Tepelenë in 1809, from Ioannina in north-west
Greece, to meet Ali Pasha, whose native stronghold was here.
Tepelenë is depicted in the second canto of Childe Harold's
Pilgrimage, stanzas 55–59 (1813–14). 'Laos' is the river Vjosë;
'Tomerit' is Mount Tomorit, which rises above Berat.*

The sun had sunk behind vast Tomerit,
The Laos wide and fierce came roaring by;
The shades of wonted night were gathering yet,
When, down the steep banks winding warily,
Childe Harold saw, like meteors in the sky,
The glittering minarets of Tepalen,
Whose walls o'erlook the stream; and drawing nigh,
He heard the busy hum of warrior-men
Swelling the breeze that sigh'd along the lengthening glen.

He pass'd the sacred Haram's silent tower,
And underneath the wide o'erarching gate
Survey'd the dwelling of this chief of power,
Where all around proclaim'd his high estate.
Amidst no common pomp the despot sate,
While busy preparations shook the court,
Slaves, eununchs, soldiers, guests, and santons[1] wait;
Within, a palace, and without, a fort:
Here men of every clime appear to make resort.

Richly caparison'd, a ready row
Of armed horse, and many a warlike store
Circled the wide extending court below:
Above, strange groups adorn'd the corridore;
And oft-times through the Area's echoing door,
Some high-capp'd Tartar spurr'd his steed away:
The Turk, the Greek, the Albanian, and the Moor,
Here mingled in their many-hued array,
While the deep war-drum's sound announc'd the close of day.

The wild Albanian kirtled to his knee,
With shawl-girt head and ornamented gun,
And gold-embroider'd garments, fair to see;
The crimson-scarfed men of Macedon;
The Delhi[2] with his cap of terror on,
And crooked glaive; the lively, supple Greek;
And swarthy Nubia's mutilated son;[3]
The bearded Turk, that rarely deigns to speak,
Master of all around, too potent to be meek,

Are mix'd conspicuous: some recline in groups,
Scanning the motley scene that varies round;
There some grave Moslem to devotion stoops,
And some that smoke, and some that play, are found;
Here the Albanian proudly treads the ground:
Half whispering there the Greek is heard to prate;
Hark! from the mosque the nightly solemn sound,
The Muezzin's call doth shake the minaret,
'There is no god but God! – to prayer – lo! God is great.'

---

[1] 'santons': dervishes or holy men; [2] 'Delhi': a fierce warrior; [3] 'mutilated son': a eunuch.

(8) TIRANË

Ismail Kadare, *The General of the Dead Army*

This novel of the 1960s about an Italian general coming to repatriate the remains of soldiers from the second world war established Kadare's reputation abroad. The General of the title has passed the University, turns right past the Opera, and climbs up St Procopius Hill.

Having reached the summit they were able to look down the far slope to the artificial lake lying at its foot, surrounded by small hills and insinuating its variously shaped inlets among them. On the curving brow of the hill itself there stood a church, and beside it an open-air café. All around the café's dance-floor, tall cypresses quivered in the keen wind. In one corner, apparently abandoned, stood a big pile of crates with the words *Birra Korça* printed on them in black.

'It can't be very long since that lake was done up like that,' the priest said. 'And the café wasn't here before either.'

'It's a wonderful spot.'

'Indeed. You can see over almost the whole of Tirana from here.'

They turned their backs on the lake and gazed out across the city. The general's raincoat flapped loudly in the wind.

Their eyes came naturally to rest on the line of the main boulevard that bisected the city. A poplar swaying in the wind would conceal now the Presidency building from their view, now that of the Central Committee. When there was a particularly strong gust, a branch would move across in front of the tall clock tower apparently stuck to the minaret of the mosque, then conceal a portion of Skanderbeg Square, stretch across the façade of the Executive Committee building, and just manage to brush the State Bank.

'In my book on Albania it said that the buildings along the last section of the main boulevard, when viewed as a whole, form what looks like a giant fascist axe,' the general said, extending his arm in the direction of the buildings in question.

'Yes, that's quite true,' the priest said.

'Is it? I've been trying to see the resemblance for two or three minutes now with no success whatever.'

'Look more closely,' the priest said, stretching out an arm in his turn. 'The boulevard is the handle of the axe, that big building there, the Rectorate, is the head of the handle protruding beyond the blade itself, the opera house is the back of the axe, and the stadium' – and here the priest made a sweep of the hand to the right – 'represents the curved cutting edge.'

'It's odd,' the general said, 'but you know I still can't manage to make it out.'

'Perhaps because one needs to look at it from higher up than this hill,' the priest said. 'Or perhaps, more to the point, because after the war the Albanians did their best to eliminate the resemblance.'

Biographies and important works

BYRON, George Gordon, sixth baron (1788–1824). In 1809–11 the poet went to Spain, Malta, and Greece, swam the Hellespont, and was inspired with the idea of liberating Greece from the Turks, which eventually brought him to his death, of fever, in Missolonghi, helping the insurgent Greeks. In the autumn of 1809 he visited **Tepelenë**, travelling from Ioannina in northern Greece, in order to meet Ali Pasha, who was presently installed here at his native stronghold. In his long narrative poem *Childe Harold's Pilgrimage*, 1812–18 (Extract 7), the first two cantos of which gave him his first literary triumph in March 1812, Byron's Byronic hero, tired by a life of pleasure and sin, travels to, among other places, Albania. The exotic scene of Ali Pasha's court is depicted in the second canto. The journey and encounter were first described in Byron's correspondence, in a letter to his mother dated 12 November 1809, from Preveza in northern Greece. Of the Albanians, he said that they were 'brave, rigidly honest, and faithful; but they are cruel, though not treacherous, and have several vices but no meannesses. They are, perhaps, the most beautiful race, in point of countenance, in the world; their women are sometimes handsome also, but they are treated like slaves, *beaten*, and, in short, complete beasts of burden; they plough, dig, and sow. I found them carrying wood, and actually repairing the highways.'

ÇAJUPI, Andon Zako (1866–1930). Born Andon Zako Chako in the village of **Sheper**, in the Gjirokastër area, Çajupi's father had done well in the tobacco business. The son attended a French lycée in Egypt, studied law in Switzerland, and returned to Cairo, where he devoted himself to literature and involved himself in the national movement. A liberal-minded writer who wrote about the plight of the peasants, and spoke up against exploitation of women in Albanian rural society (Extract 4), Çajupi took his pen name from **Çajup mountain** in the Zagori district near his home village. His collection *Baba Tomorri* (*Father Tomorri*), 1902, named after Tomorr, the Albanian Parnassus, contains some realistic depictions of rural life, avoiding the typical nostalgia of writers in exile or diaspora. He also wrote successful plays, verse for children, and translated fables of La Fontaine.

CAMAJ, Martin (1925–1992). Originally from **Temali** in the northern Dukagjin region of the Albanian alps, Camaj became both an Albanologist and a prominent exile poet. He went to the Jesuit school in **Shkodër**, did Albanian studies in Belgrade, and graduate research in Italy, where he taught Albanian and studied linguistics in Rome. From 1970–1990 he was professor of Albanian studies at the University of Munich and lived in the village of Lenggries in Upper Bavaria until his death in March 1992. He published various volumes of poetry, his first in 1953–54, in Prishtinë; later also prose, including a lyrical novel interspersed with poems entitled *Djella*, Rome 1958, about a teacher's love for a young lowland girl, who eventually marries a driver. In his work, a sense of belonging to community and original values is shaped by exile and recreated by the sensibilities of the intellectual. As well as being represented in Robert Elsie's anthology (Extract 5), some of his poetry has been translated into English by Leonard Fox in *Selected Poetry*, New York, 1990. His poetry is discussed by Arshi Pipa in his *Contemporary Albanian Literature*, New York, 1991.

KADARE, Ismail (1936–). Born son of a post-office worker in **Gjirokastër**, Kadare studied at the Faculty of History and Philology, **University of Tiranë**, then at the Gorky Institute of World Literature in Moscow, till

Ismail Kadare
BROKEN APRIL

"*Broken April*, a haunting account of the paroxism of the vendetta in northern Albania between the wars, is one of the twin peaks of Kadare's career"
ROBIN SMYTH, OBSERVER

1960. He went into journalism, became a member of the People's Assembly, and travelled abroad under the Hoxha regime on a number of occasions, to China, France, and West Germany. He is the only Albanian author to have gained any wide international recognition, particularly in France, and has been translated into many languages. Not all the English versions are regarded by experts as adequate, whether translated directly from Albanian, or, as in some cases, taken from the French (for some comments, see Robert Elsie's article in *Slavonic and East European Review* on 'Albanian Literature in English Translation: a Short Survey'). Kadare began as a poet (he is represented in Elsie's *Anthology of Modern Albanian Poetry*), but abroad he has made his reputation as a novelist. On publication of his novel *Gjenerali i ushtrisë së vdekur* (*The General of the Dead Army*), 1963, he was hailed as an Albanian Yevtushenko, but in fact he was not only a rebel, but deeply heretical in his narrative and expressive subversions of Socialist Realist norms, in spite of managing to maintain his status as an official writer, permitted to travel abroad. His wife Elena (1943–), from **Fier**, is one of the first Albanian woman novelists.

The General of the Dead Army (Extract 8) has been seen as Albania's first great novel. In it Kadare alternates between fiction and authenticity, humour, quasi-documentary observation, and the macabre, presenting Albania through the fantasy narrative of an unlikely visit by an Italian general, accompanied by a priest, on a mission to dig up the remains of Italian soldiers killed twenty years ago in the war. He meets a German general sent for the very same purpose. Truth also merges with fiction in flashbacks to wartime events. In his second novel, *Dasma*

(*The Wedding*), 1968, he addressed the theme of women's liberation during two major Hoxha campaigns, on women's emancipation and the abolition of religion in a once predominantly Muslim country. In *Kështjella* (*The Castle*), 1970, Kadare is a parodic historical novelist, refashioning the image of the 15th-century Albanian hero Skanderbeg (who never appears) and the Ottoman siege of **Krujë**. In *Kronikë në gur* (*Chronicle in Stone*), 1971, Kadare makes his childhood home of old **Gjirokastër** (also birthplace of Enver Hoxha) the setting for grotesque and violent expressive narrative play. In *Kush e solli Doruntinën* (*Who Brought Back Doruntine*), 1980, translated as *Doruntine*, Kadare re-shapes an Albanian folk story of Constantine and his sister Doruntine into a fantastic, mythic detective story. *Prilli i thyer* (*Broken April*), 1980, re-exploits the theme of blood-feuding in northern Albania for expressive ends. Another recent work to be translated is *Nëpunësi i pallatit të ëndrrave* (*Palace of Dreams*), a fantasy allegory of an imperial Sultan's almighty oppressive institution to collect, classify and master the dreams and lay bare the minds of the populace.

LEAR, Edward (1812–1888). The famous nonsense poet and limerick writer was also an artist, valued particularly for his varied freshly conceived drawings, sketches and botanical, ornithological and topographical water-colours. He travelled extensively in Italy, the Mediterranean, Greece, Corsica, the Levant, Egypt, India and Ceylon and described his experiences in several fine travel books. His visit to Albania in 1848 is described in his *Journal of a Landscape Painter in Albania etc*, *1851*. Offending against Islamic custom by

drawing and painting living forms, he was pelted at **Ohrid** with sticks and stones, in **Tiranë** a Dervish cursed him, and he got into similar trouble in **Elbasan**. His travels are also described in his correspondence (Extract 3).

MIGJENI (1911–1938). One of the most prominent Albanian poets of the 1930s and a short-story writer, Millosh Gjergi Nikolla, pen name Migjeni, composed of his initials, was born in **Shkodër**, to a family of Slav background. He studied at the Serbian school in Shkodër, and at the Orthodox seminary in Monastir (modern Bitola, in Macedonia). On returning to Albania he became a village schoolmaster, but contracted tuberculosis and died at the age of twenty-six in Torre Pelice, after going for treatment to Turin, where his sister Olga was studying. His poetry, in the slim volume *Vargjet e lira* (*Free Verse*), 1936, confiscated, but reissued in 1944, combines personal

Migjeni

lyricism with a powerful, though also ambivalently progressivist ideological note of modern social strivings and aspirations (Extracts 1 and 2). His prose was posthumously published in *Tregime nga qyteti i Veriut* (*Stories from the Town of the North*), 1954. His work is represented in Robert Elsie's recent *Anthology of Modern Albanian Poetry*, and there are also samples of his poetry with commentary in Arshi Pipa's *Albanian Literature: Social Perspectives*.

PORADECI, Lasgush (1899–1987). Generally regarded as one of the finest Albanian poets, Lasgush Poradeci was born in **Pogradec** on the shore of Lake Ohrid. He studied at the Romanian school in Monastir (Bitola, in present-day Macedonia), the French college in Athens, the Academy of Fine Arts in Bucharest, and later at the University of Graz. His poetry, published in Bucharest, was collected in two volumes, *Vallja e yjve* (*The Dance of the Stars*), 1933, and *Ylli i zemrës* (*The Star of the Heart*), 1937. He was influenced by folksong, but also by Romanian poetry, especially Eminescu (◊ Romania). He is described as bringing a note of pantheistic mysticism into Albanian

poetry (Extract 6). From 1936 he lived in **Tiranë**, working as a schoolmaster. After the war he translated Burns, Pushkin, Lermontov, Mayakovsky, Goethe, Heine and Brecht. His work is represented in Robert Elsie's *Anthology of Modern Albanian Poetry*.

SHKRELI, Azem (1938–). Serbia's **Kosovo** province has a large Albanian population with its own literature (see the chapter on Albania). The contemporary Albanian poet Azem Shkreli was born in the **Rugova (Rugovë) Mountains** near **Peć (Pejë)**, and he later became head of the Kosovo film studios in **Priština (Prishtinë)**. He is the author of seven volumes of poetry, one novel, a collection of short stories, and drama. Shkreli's poetry draws strongly on his early experience and Rugovë traditional upland life (Extract 4, chapter on former Yugoslavia). His volume *Kënga e hutinit*, 1986, has been translated into English as *The Call of the Owl*, and some poems by Shkreli, along with work by other Kosovo and Macedonian born Albanians, also appear in Robert Elsie's *Anthology of Modern Albanian Poetry: An Elusive Eagle Soars*.

ACKNOWLEDGMENTS AND CITATIONS

The authors and publisher are very grateful to the many literary agents, publishers, translators, authors and other individuals who have given their permission for the use of extracts and photographs, supplied photographs, or helped in the location of copyright holders. Every effort has been made to identify and contact the appropriate copyright owners or their representatives. The publisher would welcome any further information.

EXTRACTS

POLAND: (1) Bruno Schulz, *The Street of Crocodiles*, G.M. Hyde, trans. (2) Günter Grass, *The Tin Drum*, Ralph Manheim, trans, Penguin, London, 1965, pp 39–40. © 1961, 1962 by Pantheon Books, Inc. Copyright renewed 1989, 1990 by Random House, Inc. By permission of Pantheon Books, a division of Random House, Inc, and Secker and Warburg Ltd, Reed Consumer Books Ltd. (3) Julian Przyboś, 'To Wawel', G. M. Hyde, trans. (4) Stanisław Wyspiański, 'Liberation', G.M. Hyde, trans. (5) Władysław Reymont, *The Promised Land*, G.M. Hyde, trans. (6) Julian Tuwim, 'Polish Flowers', G.M. Hyde, trans. (7) Jozef Czechowicz, 'The Joys of Winter', G.M. Hyde, trans. (8) Joseph Conrad, 'Prince Roman', in *The Informer and Other Stories*, Samuel Hynes, ed, William Pickering, London, 1992. (9) Cyprian Kamil Norwid, *Polish Jews*, Jerzy Strzetelski, trans, in Jerzy Strzetelski, *Outline of Polish Literature*, Jagiellonski Uniwersytet, Kraków, 1973. By permission of Barbara Strzyzewska. (10) Adam Mickiewicz, *Pan Tadeusz*, Jerzy Strzetelski, trans, in Jerzy Strzetelski, *Outline of Polish Literature*, Jagiellonski Uniwersytet, Kraków, 1973. By permission of Barbara Strzyzewska. (11) Władysław Reymont, *The Peasants*, Jerzy Strzetelski, trans, in Jerzy Strzetelski, *Outline of Polish Literature*, Jagiellonski Uniwersytet, Kraków, 1973. By permission of Barbara Strzyzewska. (12) Adam Bielecki, 'Morskie Oko', G.M. Hyde, trans. (13) Mieczysław Jastrun, 'In the Tatra', G.M. Hyde, trans. (14) Stanisław Ignacy Witkiewicz, *The Demonism of Zakopane*, G.M. Hyde, trans. (15) Thomas Keneally, *Schindler's List* (aka *Schindler's Ark*), Sceptre, London, 1994, p 83. First published in the UK by Hodder and Stoughton Ltd. First published in USA by Simon and Schuster Ltd. Copyright © 1982 by Hemisphere Publishers Ltd. By permission of Simon and Schuster Ltd. (16) Stanisław Grochowiak, 'The City', G.M. Hyde, trans. (17) Juliusz Słowacki, 'A Reassurance', G.M. Hyde, trans. **THE CZECH REPUBLIC:** (1) Karel Jaromír Erben, 'The Willow', in *An Anthology of Czechoslovak Literature*, Paul Selver, trans, Trench, Trubner and Co, London, 1929, pp 48–50. (2) Vladimír Páral, *Catapult*, William Harkins, trans, Catbird Press, NJ, 1993, pp 110–111. By permission of Catbird Press. (3) Ludvík Vaculík, *The Axe*, Marian Šling, trans, Harper and Row, New York, 1973, pp 91–92. Also published by André Deutsch. By permission of André Deutsch Ltd. (4) Karel Hynek Mácha, *May*, J. Naughton, trans. (5) Marie Majerová, *The Siren*, Iris Urwin, trans, Artia, Prague, 1953, pp 256–257. (6) Josef Škvorecký, *The Bass Saxophone*, Káča Poláčková-Henley, trans, Picador, London, 1980, pp 106–107. By permission of publishers Key Porter Books Limited, Toronto, Ontario, and Vintage/Chatto and Windus, Random House UK Ltd. Copyright © Josef Škvorecký 1977. (7) Bohumil Hrabal, *Cutting It Short*, in *Cutting It Short and The Little Town Where Time Stood Still*, James Naughton, trans, Abacus, London, 1993, pp 56–58. By permission of Little Brown and Company. (8) Milan Kundera, *The Joke*, new edition with Michael Henry Heim's translation revised by the author and Aaron Asher, Faber and Faber, London, 1992, pp

63–65. By permission of Vera Kundera on behalf of Milan Kundera. (9) Miroslav Holub, 'Five Minutes After the Air Raid', George Theiner, trans, in Miroslav Holub, *Poems Before and After*, Bloodaxe Books, Newcastle upon Tyne, 1990, p 37. By permission of Bloodaxe Books Ltd. (10) Karel Čapek, *War with the Newts*, Ewald Osers, trans, Picador, London, 1991, pp 204 and 207. © translation UNESCO 1985. By permission of UNESCO, Ewald Osers and Catbird Press. (11) František Halas, 'To Prague', J. Naughton, trans. (12) Tony Harrison, 'Prague Spring – on my birthday, 30 April', in *Selected Poems*, Penguin, London and New York, 1987. By permission of Tony Harrison. (13) Jaroslav Hašek, *The Good Soldier Švejk and His Fortunes in the World War*, Cecil Parrott, trans, Penguin, London, 1974, p 61. By permission of William Heinemann Ltd, Reed Consumer Books Ltd. (14) Franz Kafka, 'Description of a Struggle', in *The Collected Short Stories of Franz Kafka*, Nahum N. Glatzer, ed, Penguin, London, 1988, pp 19–20. Copyright © 1946, 1947, 1948, 1949, 1954, 1958, 1971 by Schocken Books Inc. By permission of Schocken Books, published by Pantheon Books, a division of Random House, Inc, and Secker and Warburg Ltd, Reed Consumer Books Ltd. (15) Franz Kafka, *The Trial*, Willa and Edwin Muir, trans, Penguin, London, 1953, pp 225–227. Copyright 1937, © 1956 by Alfred A. Knopf, Inc. Copyright renewed 1964, 1984 by Alfred A. Knopf, Inc. By permission of Schocken Books, published by Pantheon Books, a division of Random House, Inc, and Secker and Warburg Ltd, Reed Consumer Books Ltd. (16) Gustav Meyrink, *The Golem*, Mike Mitchell, trans, Dedalus, Sawtry, 1994, pp 91–92. Copyright © Dedalus 1995. By permission of Dedalus Ltd. (17) Jan Neruda, 'St Václav's Mass', in *Tales of the Little Quarter*, Edith Pargeter, trans, Heinemann, London, 1957, pp 176–177. By permission of Deborah Owen Ltd on behalf of Edith Pargeter. (18) Vítězslav Nezval, 'Moon Over Prague', Ewald Osers, trans, in *Three Czech Poets: Vítězslav Nezval, Antonín Bartušek, Josef Hanzlík*, Penguin, London, 1971, p 59. By permission of Ewald Osers. (19) Anthony Trollope, *Nina Balatka*, reprinted in the World's Classics series with the novel *Linda Tressel*, Oxford University Press, Oxford, 1991, pp 179–181. (20) Jaroslav Seifert, 'Prague', Ewald Osers, trans, in *The Selected Poetry of Jaroslav Seifert*, André Deutsch, London, 1986, p 36. By permission of André Deutsch Ltd and Dilia Theatrical and Literary Agency, Prague. (21) Božena Němcová, *Granny: Scenes from Country Life*, Edith Pargeter, trans, Artia, Prague, 1962, pp 192–194. By permission of Deborah Owen Ltd on behalf of Edith Pargeter.

(22) Ivan Klíma, *My First Loves*, Ewald Osers, trans, Penguin, London, 1989, pp 10–11. Copyright © 1985 by Ivan Klíma. English translation copyright © 1986 by Ewald Osers. By permission of HarperCollins Publishers, Inc, and Chatto and Windus, Random House UK Ltd. **SLOVAKIA:** (1) Janko Jesenský, *The Democrats*, Jean Rosemary Edwards, trans, Artia, Prague, 1961, pp 239–240. (2) Ladislav Mňačko, *The Taste of Power*, Paul Stevenson, trans, Weidenfeld and Nicolson, 1967, pp 148–149. By permission of Weidenfeld and Nicolson. (3) Jozef Cíger-Hronský, *Jozef Mak*, Andrew Cincura, trans, Slavica, Columbus, OH, 1984, p 95. (4) Martin Kukučín, 'At the Community Sheepfold', in *Seven Slovak Stories*, Norma Leigh Rudinsky, trans, Slovak Institute, Cleveland, OH, 1980, p 139. By permission of Norma L. Rudinsky. (5) Klára Jarunková, *Don't Cry for Me*, George Theiner, trans, Dent, London, 1971, p 65. By permission of J.M. Dent. (6) František Švantner, 'Malka', Andrew Cincura, trans, in *An Anthology of Slovak Literature*, compiled by Andrew Cincura, University Hardcovers, Riverside, CA, 1976, p 279. (7) Ivan Krasko, 'Vesper Dominicae', Jaroslav J. Vajda, trans, in *An Anthology of Slovak Literature*, compiled by Andrew Cincura, University Hardcovers, Riverside, CA, 1976, pp 21–22. (8) Pavel Vilikovský, 'Escalation of Feeling', J. Naughton, trans, in *Description of a Struggle: The Picador Book of East European Prose*, Michael March, ed, Picador, London, 1994, p 155. (9) Timrava (Božena Slančíková), 'Battle', in *That Alluring Land: Slovak Stories by Timrava*, Norma L. Rudinsky, trans, University of Pittsburgh Press, Pittsburgh and London, 1992, pp 79–80. © 1992 by the University of Pittsburgh Press. By permission of the University of Pittsburgh Press. (10) Janko Král', 'The Enchanted Maiden in the Váh and Strange Janko', J. Naughton, trans. **HUNGARY:** (1) Gyula Krúdy, *The Crimson Coach*, Paul Tabori, trans, Corvina, Budapest, 1967, pp 157–158. By permission of Corvina. (2) Attila József, 'Night in the Slums', published with the title 'Night in the Suburbs', Edwin Morgan, trans, in *The Penguin Book of Socialist Verse*, Alan Bold, ed, Penguin, London, 1970, pp 290–291. Originally published in Edwin Morgan, *Sweeping Out the Dark*, Carcanet Press. By permission of Carcanet Press Ltd. (3) Dezső Kosztolányi, *Anna Édes*, George Szirtes, trans, Quartet, London, 1991, pp 163–164. Translation copyright © 1991 Corvina, Budapest. By permission of Corvina and Quartet. (4) Ottó Orbán, 'Around My Stony Cradle', in *The Blood of the Walsungs, Selected Poems*, George Szirtes, ed, Corvina, Budapest, and Bloodaxe, Newcastle upon Tyne, 1993, p 70. By permission of

Corvina. (5) Maurus Jókai, *Timar's Two Worlds*, Mrs Hegan Kennard, trans, William Blackwood and Sons, Edinburgh and London, 1930, pp 1–2. (6) Sándor Petőfi, 'The Alföld', Watson Kirkconnell, trans, in *Hungarian Helicon*, Széchenyi Society Inc, Calgary, 1985, pp 401–402. (7) Zsigmond Móricz, 'Sullen Horse', in *Seven Pennies and Other Short Stories*, George F. Cushing, sel and trans, Corvina, Budapest, 1988, pp 158–159. By permission of Corvina. (8) György Konrád, *The Loser*, Ivan Sanders, trans, Harcourt Brace Jovanovich, New York, 1982, pp 236–237. English translation copyright © 1982 by Harcourt Brace and Company. By permission of Harcourt Brace and Company. (9) Péter Nádas, 'A Tale about Fire and Knowledge', Z. Kövecses, trans, *New Hungarian Quarterly*, Budapest, Winter 1989, p 40. (10) Sándor Weöres, 'Still So Many Things', William Jay Smith, trans, in *Ma – Today, An Anthology of Contemporary Hungarian Literature*, Corvina, Budapest, 1987, p 72. By permission of Corvina. (11) Miklós Mészöly, 'Lament for a Mother', in *The Kiss, 20th Century Hungarian Short Stories*, István Bart, ed, Corvina, Budapest, 1993, p 230. By permission of Corvina. (12) János Pilinszky, 'As I Was', in *Selected Poems*, Ted Hughes and János Csokits, trans, Carcanet, Manchester, 1976, p 55. Revised and enlarged as *The Desert of Love*, Anvil, London, 1989. By permission of Anvil Press Poetry Ltd. (13) András Fodor, 'A vízrenéző', G.F. Cushing, trans. By permission of András Fodor. (14) Gyula Illyés, *People of the Puszta*, 2nd ed, Corvina, Budapest, 1967, pp 25–26. By permission of Corvina. (15) Ferenc Juhász, 'Village Elegy', Watson Kirkconnell, trans, in *Hungarian Helicon*, Széchenyi Society Inc, Calgary, 1985, p 475. **ROMANIA:** (1) George Călinescu, *Poor Ioanide*, Dennis Deletant, trans. (2) Mircea Eliade, 'Twelve Thousand Head of Cattle', in *Fantastic Tales*, Eric Tappe, trans and ed, Dillon's, London, 1969, p 15. (3) Olivia Manning, *The Great Fortune*, Penguin, London, 1974, pp 16–17. First published by William Heinemann. By permission of William Heinemann Ltd, Reed Consumer Books Ltd. (4) Marin Sorescu, 'Village Museum', Dennis Deletant, trans. (5) Ion Pillat, 'Dusk in the Delta', Dennis Deletant, trans. (6) Lucian Blaga, *The Chronicle and Song of the Ages*, Dennis Deletant, trans. By permission of Editura Humanitas, Bucharest. (7) Alexandru Vlahuţă, *Picturesque Romania*, Dennis Deletant, trans. (8) Gabriel Liiceanu, *Păltiniş Diary*, Dennis Deletant, trans. By permission of Gabriel Liiceanu. (9) Mihail Sebastian, *The Accident*, Dennis Deletant, trans. (10) Daniela Crăsnaru, 'Transylvanian Town', in *Silent Voices: An Anthology of Contemporary Romanian Women Poets*, Andrea

Deletant and Brenda Walker, trans, Forest, London, 1986, p 94. By permission of Forest Books. (11) Grete Tartler, *Orient Express*, Fleur Adcock, trans, Oxford University Press, Oxford, 1989, p 5. © Fleur Adcock 1989. By permission of Oxford University Press. (12) Nicolae Iorga, *Romania As It Was Before 1918*, Dennis Deletant, trans. (13) Alexandru Vlahuţă, *Picturesque Romania*, Dennis Deletant, trans. (14) Richard Wagner, *Exit*, Quintin Hoare, trans, Verso, London, 1990, p 94. By permission of Verso. (15) Liviu Rebreanu, *Ion*, Dennis Deletant, trans. (16) Bram Stoker, *Dracula*, Puffin Books, London, 1988, pp 18–19. **BULGARIA:** (1) Hristo Botev, 'Hadzhi Dimitur', in *Poems*, Kevin Ireland, trans, Theodora Atanasova, trans, Sofia Press, Sofia, 1955, pp 61–62. (2) Elisaveta Bagryana, 'Elements', in *Ten Poems*, Kevin Ireland, trans, Sofia Press, Sofia, 1970, p 35. (3) Pencho Slaveikov, 'There's Not a Breeze or Breath in Motion', in *Anthology of Bulgarian Poetry*, Peter Tempest, trans, Sofia Press, Sofia, 1980, p 126. (4) Ivan Vazov, *Under the Yoke*, Marguerite Alexieva and Theodora Atanasova, trans, Sofia Press, Sofia, 1976, pp 19–20. (5) Yordan Yovkov, 'The Inn at Antimovo', in *The Inn at Antimovo and Legends of the Stara Planina*, John Burnip, trans, Slavica, Columbus, OH, 1990, p 11. By permission of Theresa Burnip. (6) Dimcho Debelyanov, 'Secret Sighs', in *Anthology of Bulgarian Poetry*, Peter Tempest, trans, Sofia Press, Sofia, 1980, p 168. (7) Zahari Stoyanov, *Notes on the Bulgarian Uprisings*, in *Extracts from 'Notes on the Bulgarian Uprisings'* (selected by Lyudmil Angelov), Maria Rankova, trans, Sofia Press, Sofia, 1976, pp 46–47. (8) Blaga Dimitrova, *Journey to Oneself*, Radost Pridam, trans, Cassell, London, 1969, pp 9 and 195–196. First published in Bulgaria by Narodna Kultura, 1965. Published in the USA by Simon and Schuster. By permission of Simon and Schuster, Inc. (9) Ivan Vazov, 'Near the Rila Monastery', in *Selected Poems*, Peter Tempest, trans, Sofia Press, Sofia, 1976, p 66. (10) Teodor Trayanov, 'The Secret of the Strouma', in *Anthology of Bulgarian Poetry*, Peter Tempest, trans, Sofia Press, Sofia, 1980, p 159. (11) Elin Pelin, 'The Windmill', in *Short Stories*, Marguerite Alexieva, trans, Mercia Macdermott, ed, Foreign Languages Press, Sofia, 1965, pp 15–16. (12) Viktor Paskov, *A Ballad for Georg Henig*, Peter Owen, London, 1990. By permission of Peter Owen Ltd. (13) Elisaveta Bagryana, 'Fire-Dancer's Destiny', in *The Devil's Dozen: Thirteen Bulgarian Women Poets*, Brenda Walker with Belin Tonchev, trans, Forest Books, London, and Svyat Publishers, Sofia, 1991, p 36. By permission of Forest Books. (14) Konstantin Konstantinov, 'In Strandzha Mountain', in *Day*

By *Day*, Marjorie Hall Pojarlieva, trans, Sofia Press, Sofia, 1969, pp 54–55. (15) Chernorizets Hrabur, *On Letters*, in *Kiril and Methodius: Founders of Slavonic Writing. A Collection of Sources and Critical Studies*, English translation by Spass Nikolov, edited by Ivan Duichev, East European Monographs, Boulder, CO, 1985, p 158. By permission of East European Monographs, Bradenton, FL. **THE LANDS OF FORMER YUGOSLAVIA:** (1) Borislav Pekić, *The Houses of Belgrade*, Bernard Johnson, trans, Harcourt Brace Jovanovich, New York and London, 1978. English translation © 1978 by Harcourt Brace and Company. By permission of Harcourt Brace and Company. (2) Meša Selimović, *Death and the Dervish*, Celia Hawkesworth, trans. (3) Jovan Dučić, 'Wine of Dubrovnik', *Serbian Poetry from the Beginnings to the Present*, Vasa D. Mihailovich, trans, Yale Russian and East European Publications, New Haven, CT, 1988, p 201. By permission of the Department of Slavic Languages and Literatures, Yale University. (4) Azem Shkreli, 'In Shkrel', in Arshi Pipa, *Albanian Literature: Social Perspectives*, Trofenik, Munich, 1978, p 189. (5) Ivan Cankar, *The Bailiff Yerney and His Rights*, Sidone Yeras and H.C. Sewell Grant, trans, The Pushkin Press, London, 1946, pp 55–56. (6) Živko Čingo, 'Argil's Decoration', in *The Big Horse and Other Stories of Modern Macedonia*, Milne Holton, ed, University of Missouri Press, Columbia, MO, 1974, pp 71–72. (7) Mateja Matevski, 'Roots', in *Footprints of the Wind*, Ewald Osers, trans, Forest Books, London and Boston, 1988, p 36. By permission of Forest Books. (8) Milovan Djilas, 'Woods and Water', in *The Leper and Other Stories*, Lovett F. Edwards, trans, Methuen, London, 1965, p 37. By permission of Reed Consumer Books Ltd. (9) Petar Petrovic Njegoš, *The Mountain Wreath*, Vasa D. Mihailovich, trans and ed, Schlacks, Irvine, CA, 1986, pp 9–10. (10) Blaže Koneski, 'The Angel in St Sophia', in *Poems, Zlaten venec*, Andrew Harvey and Anne Pennington, trans, Struga, Skopje, 1981, p 63. (11) Miroslav Krleža, *The Return of Philip Latinovicz*, Zora G. Depolo, Lincolns-Prager, London, 1959, pp 63–64. (12) Slobodan Novak, *Gold, Frankincense and Myrrh*, Celia Hawkesworth, trans, Most, Zagreb, and Forest Books, London and Boston, 1991, p 164. By permission of Forest Books. (13) Izet Sarajlić, 'Sarajevo', Celia Hawkesworth, trans. (14) Dobrica Ćosić, *A Time of Death*, Muriel Heppell, trans, Harcourt Brace Jovanovich, New York and London, 1978. English translation © 1978 by Harcourt Brace and Company. By permission of Harcourt Brace and Company. (15) Slobodan Selenić, *Fathers and Forefathers*, from 'Two Excerpts from *Fathers and Forefathers*', Ellen Elias-Bursać, trans, *North Dakota Quarterly*, Vol 61, No 1, Winter 1993, pp 157–170. By permission of *North Dakota Quarterly*. (16) Ciril Kosmač, *A Day in Spring*, Fanny S. Copeland, trans, Lincolns-Prager, London, 1959, pp 160–161. (17) Francè Prešeren, 'The Master Theme', in *Poems by Francè Prešeren*, W.K. Matthews and A. Slodnjak, eds, John Calder, London, 1969, p 65. By permission of the Calder Educational Trust. (18) Danilo Kiš, *Garden, Ashes*, William J. Hannaher, trans, Faber and Faber, London, 1985, pp 4–5. First published in the USA by Harcourt Brace Jovanovich, Inc. English translation copyright © 1975 by Harcourt Brace and Company. By permission of Harcourt Brace and Company and Faber and Faber Ltd. (19) Ivo Andrić, *The Bridge on the Drina*, Lovett F. Edwards, trans, George Allen and Unwin, London, 1959, pp 13–14. By permission of HarperCollins Publishers Ltd and Büchergilde Gutenberg Verlagsgesellschaft mbH. (20) Dubravka Ugrešić, *Fording the Stream of Consciousness*, Michael Henry Heim, trans, Virago, London, 1991, pp 42–43. By permission of Virago Press. **ALBANIA:** (1) Migjeni, 'Blasphemy', in *Anthology of Modern Albanian Poetry: An Elusive Eagle Soars*, Robert Elsie, trans and ed, Forest Books, London and Boston, 1993, p 14. By permission of Forest Books. (2) Migjeni, 'Song of the Occident', in Arshi Pipa, *Albanian Literature: Social Perspectives*, Trofenik, Munich, 1978, p 152. (3) Edward Lear, 'A letter to his sister, 1848', *Selected Letters*, Vivian Noakes, ed, Clarendon Press, Oxford, 1988, pp 92–93. (4) Çajupi, 'My Village', in Arshi Pipa, *Albanian Literature: Social Perspectives*, Trofenik, Munich, 1978, pp 122–123. (5) Martin Camaj, 'Mountain Feast', in *Anthology of Modern Albanian Poetry: An Elusive Eagle Soars*, Robert Elsie, trans and ed, Forest Books, London and Boston, 1993, p 35. By permission of Forest Books. (6) Lasgush Poradeci, 'Pogradec', in *Anthology of Modern Albanian Poetry: An Elusive Eagle Soars*, Robert Elsie, trans and ed, Forest Books, London and Boston, 1993, p 2. By permission of Forest Books. (7) Lord Byron, *Childe Harold's Pilgrimage*, in *Byron (The Oxford Authors)*, Jerome J. McGann, ed, Oxford University Press, Oxford and New York, 1986, pp 68–69. (8) Ismail Kadare, *The General of the Dead Army*, Derek Coltman, trans, Quartet, London, 1986, pp 147–148. By permission of Quartet.

PICTURES

p 3 – Adam Mickiewicz, courtesy of the Polish Cultural Institute, London; p 6 – Bruno Schulz, self-portrait from *The Book of Idolatry*; p 8 and p 43 – Tadeusz Kantor, courtesy of the Polish Cultural Institute, London; p 40 – Joseph Conrad, courtesy of Raffles Hotel, Singapore; p 41 – Witold Gombrowicz, from the portrait by Eliasz Kanarek; p 41 – Günter Grass, © Gerhard Steiol, courtesy of Martin Secker and Warburg; p 47 – Władysław Stanisław Reymont, courtesy of the Polish Cultural Institute, London; p 66 – Karel Čapek, courtesy of Catbird Press; p 71 – Ivan Klíma, courtesy of Penguin Books; p 117 – Tony Harrison, courtesy of Penguin Books; p 119 – Václav Havel, courtesy of the Press Office, Embassy of the Czech Republic, London; p 120 – Miroslav Holub, photograph by Mark Lumley, courtesy of Bloodaxe Books; p 123 – Franz Kafka, courtesy of Penguin Books; p 132 – Vladimír Páral, courtesy of Catbird Press; p 142 – L'udovít Štúr, from the portrait by J.B. Klemens; p 175 – Timrava, from Literárny archív Matice slovenskej; p 195 – János Pilinszky, photograph by Istvan Lugossy, courtesy of Anvil Press Poetry; p 217 – Gyula Illyés, photograph by Layle Silbert; p 218 – Ferenc Juhász, photograph by Demeter Balla; p 223 – Ottó Orbán, photograph by Lászlo Csigó, © Lászlo Csigó 1993, courtesy of Bloodaxe Books; p 238 – Mihail Eminescu, courtesy of Dennis Deletant; Mihail Sadoveanu, courtesy of Dennis Deletant; p 273 – George Călinescu, courtesy of Dennis Deletant; p 274 – Daniela Crăsnaru, courtesy of Forest Books; p 276 – Nicolae Iorga, courtesy of Dennis Deletant; p 279 – Liviu Rebreanu, courtesy of Dennis Deletant; p 291 – Cyril and Methodius, courtesy of Belin Tonchev; p 299 – Ivan Vazov, courtesy of Belin Tonchev; p 303 – Elisaveta Bagryana, courtesy of Forest Books; p 326 – Hristo Botyov, courtesy of Belin Tonchev; p 327 – Dimcho Debelyanov, courtesy of Belin Tonchev; p 328 – Blaga Dimitrova, courtesy of Belin Tonchev; p 330 – Yordan Radichkov, courtesy of Belin Tonchev; p 331 – Pencho Slaveikov, courtesy of Belin Tonchev; p 333 – Peyu Yavorov, courtesy of Belin Tonchev; p 334 – Yordan Yovkov, courtesy of Belin Tonchev; p 393 – Mateja Matevski, courtesy of Forest Books; p 397 – Dubravka Ugrešić, courtesy of Virago; p 421 – Migjeni, courtesy of Forest Books.

INDEX

This is an index of authors and other significant persons mentioned in the text. (A number of other authors are included in the booklists.) **(E)** = extract, **(B)** = biographical entry.